VOLUME TWO

Advances in Psychological Assessment

Dimensions of Psychological Research

VOLUME TWO

Advances in Psychological Assessment

PAUL McREYNOLDS
EDITOR

SCIENCE AND BEHAVIOR BOOKS, INC.
Palo Alto, California: 1971

Contributors

Jack D. Barchas, *Department of Psychiatry, School of Medicine, Stanford University, Stanford, California.*

Sidney W. Bijou, *Child Behavior Laboratory, Department of Psychology, and Institute for Research in Exceptional Children, University of Illinois, Champaign-Urbana, Illinois.*

Roland D. Ciaranello, *Department of Psychiatry, School of Medicine, Stanford University, Stanford, California.*

Kenneth H. Craik, *Department of Psychology and Institute of Personality Assessment and Research, University of California, Berkeley, California.*

Marvin D. Dunnette, *Departments of Psychology and Industrial Relations, University of Minnesota; and Personnel Decisions, Inc., Minneapolis, Minnesota.*

Lewis R. Goldberg, *Department of Psychology, University of Oregon, and Oregon Research Institute, Eugene, Oregon.*

David A. Hamburg, *Department of Psychiatry, School of Medicine, Stanford University, Stanford, California.*

Richard J. Harris, *Department of Psychology, University of New Mexico, Albuquerque, New Mexico.*

Douglas N. Jackson, *Department of Psychology, University of Western Ontario, London, Canada.*

C. James Klett, *Central Neuropsychiatric Research Laboratory, Veterans Administration Hospital, Perry Point, Maryland.*

Edward Lichtenstein, *Department of Psychology, University of Oregon, Eugene, Oregon.*

Maurice Lorr, *Department of Psychology, The Catholic University of America, Washington, D.C.*

Paul McReynolds, *Department of Psychology, University of Nevada, Reno, Nevada.*

Edwin I. Megargee, *Department of Psychology, Florida State University, Tallahassee, Florida.*

Elizabeth S. Menzies, *Department of Psychology, Florida State University, Tallahassee, Florida.*

Robert F. Peterson, *Department of Psychology, University of Illinois, Champaign-Urbana, Illinois.*

Donald K. Pumroy, *College of Education, University of Maryland, College Park, Maryland.*

Thomas F. Siess, *Department of Psychology, University of Western Ontario, London, Canada.*

Jon M. Stolk, *Department of Psychiatry, School of Medicine, Stanford University, Stanford, California.*

Duane L. Varble, *Department of Psychology, University of Nevada, Reno, Nevada.*

Contents

... *considering how short and limited the Wit of Man is to one thing and no more; I have been always of Opinion, that no Man could understand two Arts perfectly well, without proving defective in one of them: And that accordingly none might err in the Choice of that which was most agreeable to the Bent of his Natural Inclination, there should be* Triers *appointed by the State, Men of approved Sagacity and Knowledge, to search and sound the Abilities of Youth, and after due Search, to oblige them to the Study of that Science their Heads leaned most to, instead of abandoning them to their own Choice.*

Juan Huarte (1575)

Preface

This is the second in a continuing series of volumes on new developments in psychological assessment. As in Volume 1, all the papers in this work were solicited and prepared especially for this book, and have not appeared elsewhere. Further, and also as in that volume, the chapter topics were so selected and so arranged with respect to order as to lend an overall coherency and unity to the volume as a whole. This integration is reflected also in the fact that the references for all the chapters have been combined into one large bibliography at the end.

The primary purposes of this series are—as noted in the Preface to Volume 1—"first, to describe and evaluate selected new developments in assessment technology; second, to present innovative theoretical and methodological approaches to important issues in assessment; and third, to provide summaries of the current status of important areas in the field. In addition, occasional examinations of the historical backgrounds of important contemporary areas in assessment will be presented, in the belief that such perspectives are helpful in understanding the present scene."

It should be emphasized that *Advances in Psychological Assessment* is *not* modeled after the *Annual Review of Psychology* and other series which aim to bring the reader up to date on what has happened in an entire field since the previous volume. Rather, each volume in the *Advances* series is designed both to stand by itself and to complement the contents of previous volumes.

In planning and preparing this volume, I have been gratified and encouraged by the warm reception received by Volume 1. The positive response of the professional psychological community to that work has supported my conviction that there is a need in the area of assessment for a series of in-depth contributions examining new developments in the field.

The papers included in this volume represent a broad range of content, and their diversity speaks directly for the vitality of contemporary psychological assessment. The topics covered include a number of highly innovative areas, such as the uses of biochemical techniques and of experimental games in psychological assessment. Coverage is given to the rapidly increasing uses of automated procedures in evaluation, and to the new, but extremely important area of the assessment of environments. Other papers focus on problems of measurement in given subject groups, and still others on psychological tests in the more traditional sense. It is my hope that the book will be helpful, not only to the clinician, the counselor, and the serious student of assessment, but also—at least in some of its chapters—to research workers in a variety of other fields, including personality psychology, social psychology, and psychophysiology.

In preparing this and the previous volume, I have become increasingly aware of earlier works on the same subject. In this connection it may be of interest to the reader to note that we are approaching the four-hundredth anniversary of the first book on assessment. This book is *Examen de ingenios* (translated into English in 1698 as *The tryal of wits*); it was written by the Spanish physician Juan Huarte (1529-1588) and first published in 1575. The general themes of the book (a brief selection from which is presented immediately preceding this Preface) are that each individual possesses certain aptitudes; that each vocation requires for its best performance a certain combination of skills; and that therefore attempts should be made to discover individuals' aptitudes and to match their choices with their capacities. So old is aptitude assessment and vocational counseling!

A large number of authors have cooperated in producing this book. Each has maintained high standards of excellence in preparing his chapter, and what I believe to be the high quality of the book is, of course, due directly to the efforts of its contributors. In planning the book I depended heavily upon the counsel of Harrison Gough, Robert L. Weiss, and David P. Campbell, and I wish to indicate my gratitude to these persons for their suggestions. Mrs. Jacqueline Hutchins, Mrs. Frances Hitchcock, and Mrs. Susan Blaskovich were also of invaluable assistance in the preparation of the manuscript and in numerous other ways.

Paul McReynolds

CHAPTER I

Introduction

Paul McReynolds

The field of psychological assessment, like other special areas of psychology, is constantly undergoing change. New needs arise, new techniques are developed, old ways of doing things reach the end of their usefulness, and new theoretical conceptions alter the overall context in which assessment proceeds and has its meaning. This volume, in the succeeding chapters, presents a number of the newer directions in some detail. The purpose of this first chapter is to set the perspective in terms of which the material to follow will be most useful.

Specifically, the aims of this introductory chapter are, first, to survey briefly the current scene in psychological assessment; second, to undertake a limited conceptual analysis of the nature of psychological assessment; and third, to describe the plan and organization of the present book.

THE CURRENT SCENE

Psychological assessment, as currently practiced and as represented in this and the preceding volume of this series, includes a wide diversity of aims, tasks, techniques, and functions. Though often equated with the use and interpretation of psychological tests—in the narrow sense of pencil-paper, projective, and related performance tasks—psychological assessment is in fact much broader than this. It involves interview techniques, observational procedures, psychophysiological assays, unobtrusive measures, and a variety of other data-yielding procedures. Psychological assessment is concerned not only with measuring given attributes of individuals, but also with evaluations of groups of persons, such as families, clubs, and student bodies; with institutions, such as political parties, churches, and police forces; and with environments, such as homes, hospital wards, and physical locales.

We are, I suspect, in the beginning phases of what, in retrospect, will someday be seen to have been a revolution in psychological assessment. The characteristics of this revolution—or rapid evolution, if one prefers—are, first, a notable broadening of the functions and scope of assessment, such that assessment is no longer limited to making statements about postulated

I am indebted to Thomas J. Bouchard, Jr., Gerald P. Ginsburg, and H. Edward Tryk for their helpful comments on an earlier draft of portions of this chapter.

attributes of individuals; second, a drastic extension of the kind of techniques and instruments used in assessment, such that assessment psychology can no longer be identified, for all practical purposes, as the utilization of psychological tests; and third, an increased tendency to interpret assessment data in the context of the overall stimulus situation in which they were gathered, such that test data are no longer viewed as absolutes, or as approximations of "true" scores, but rather as relative indices which have their meaning in terms of other information.

Actually, the revolution, or evolution, of which I speak is already here. Psychologists already *are* engaged in assessing families, factories, and communities, as well as, of course, individuals, interpersonal interactions, and dyadic relationships. Further, they depend, in carrying out their assessment functions, on a wide variety of evaluation techniques including not only "psychological tests" but also a considerable diversity of observational, conversational, and physiological approaches.

The concept of a "psychological test" is an interesting one and has been both helpful and restrictive in the development of the field of psychological assessment. The general notion of a "psychological test" is that of a device, an instrument, a set of "things" that the psychologist carries around with him—e.g., the Stanford-Binet materials or the Rorschach cards—with which he gathers certain data that are then interpreted in terms of his special know-how. Another general conception of a "psychological test" is that of a set of rules of procedure, something like a recipe or a set of steps for chemical analysis, that the psychologist has in his head and which, when he applies it in the prescribed order and fashion, yields data which, again, he makes sense of on the basis of his special expertise.

Both of these general, everyday conceptions of psychological tests owe much—with respect to their popularity and general acceptance—to the notions of tests in chemistry and laboratory medicine. And the special mystique of "tests" in both medicine and psychology is related, at least in a genealogical sense, to the techniques of divination and fortune-telling practiced by medieval alchemists, and to the decisions by ordeal as sponsored by the medieval clergy (Mackay, 1932). There is much of interest that could be said about the psychological dynamics both of the person who, in "taking" a test, endows it—and by extension, the psychologist who "gives" it—with certain magical properties of insight, and also about the psychologist who, in employing the test, comes to use it as a crutch and to depend on it—because of his own needs—more than the facts warrant. There is also another hazard implied by the manner in which a "psychological test" is commonly interpreted. This is the danger of reifying the variable that the test measures. Thorndike's dictum that if something exists it can be measured is, in effect turned around, to read that if a measure is taken, something must exist. Since test-makers have a natural tendency to give names or labels to the variables on which their instruments yield scores, the result is a cluttering up of the theoretical literature with a plethora of psychological concepts afforded the mantle of reality. Even such well-accepted concepts as "intelligence," "anxiety," and "psychological adjustment" have been given, through the medium of psychological tests, a much stronger aura of fundamentality than they merit.

In my view it is a mistake to equate psychological assessment with test technology. The field of assessment is best conceived in terms of the functions it serves, rather than of the tools and methods it uses. I am not suggesting that psychological tests in the usual meaning of this term (see McReynolds, 1968) be de-emphasized, but I am recommending that other approaches— systematic observations, functional analyses, survey methods, physiological recordings, and so on—be accorded equal status and acceptance within the field of assessment. In view of the fact that psychologists already are carrying out the kinds of assessments I have indicated, this recommendation may seem gratuitous; that it is not is indicated by the fact that there are, as yet, no texts which systematically present the broadened conception of assessment that I have outlined.

A final word on psychological tests, in the traditional sense in which the Stanford-Binet, the Strong Vocational Interest Blank, and the Thematic Apperception Test can be taken as exemplars: tests *do* have much to commend them, and it would indeed be a tragedy if the current revolutionary mood in clinical assessment should result in the wholesale discarding of test techniques which have been developed with great care over long periods of time and which, when used in the right context, can be extremely useful. Thus, it is important that the present strong and highly welcome orientation toward new directions in psychological assessment build on the solid foundation in terms of the traditions of standardization, norms, reliability, stability, and validity that has been established by a half-century of concentrated efforts on test technology.

The Recent Literature

This section will call attention to a number of books on assessment published since Volume One of *Advances in psychological assessment* appeared, as well as a few worthwhile books inadvertently overlooked in the listing there (McReynolds, 1968, p. 5). The present listing does not purport to be complete, but it does include the major new works in the field that have come to my attention, and is intended to provide the reader with a picture of current developments in assessment.

Two standard texts have had new editions—Anastasi's (1968) *Psychological testing* and Cronbach's (1970) *Essentials of psychological testing.* Other broad, essentially standard texts include *Principles of educational and psychological testing* by Brown (1970), *Introduction to psychological measurement* by Nunnally (1970), and *Basic educational tests and measurements* by Stodola and Stordahl (1967). Payne and McMorris (1967) and Barnette (1968) have edited collections of readings. Buros' (1970) *Personality tests and reviews* provides a useful reference. Jackson and Messick (1967) have edited a broad work titled *Problems of human assessment.*

There have been a number of books published in specialized areas. Some of these are suitable for texts, depending on the purpose of given courses. The list includes: *The interpretation of psychological tests* by Allison, Blatt, and Zimet (1968); *The measurement and prediction of judgment and choice* by Bock and Jones (1968); *Human intelligence: its nature and assessment* by Butcher (1968); *Proceedings of the invitational conference on testing problems* (P. H. DuBois, Chairman, 1969); *A history of psychological testing* by DuBois (1970); two books on the content analysis of verbal behavior, one by Gottschalk and Gleser (1969) and the other by Gottschalk, Winget, and Gleser (1969). *Kompendium der psychodiagnosticschen tests* by Hildegard Hiltmann (1966); *The psychology of vocational choice* by Holland (1966); *Personality: measurement of dimensions* by Horst (1968); *Clinical information processing by computer* by Kleinmuntz (1969a); *Statistical theories of mental test scores* by Lord and Novick (1968); *New approaches to personality classification* by A. R. Mahrer (1969); *Personality and assessment* by Mischel (1968); *Measurement and evaluation in the classroom* by Nelson (1970); *Projective techniques in personality assessment* edited by Rabin (1968); *Scales for the measurement of attitudes* by Shaw and Wright (1967); *The semantic differential technique* by Snider and Osgood (1969); *People in context* by Stern (1970); *Family measurement techniques: abstracts of published instruments, 1935-1965* by Straus (1969); *The predictive validity of projective measures* by Suinn and Oskamp (1969); *Intelligence: some recurring issues* by Tyler (1969); and *Analysis of behavioral change* by Weiskrantz (1968).

The following books are also on specialized subjects, but are further characterized by the fact that they are primarily concerned with clinical assessment: *Assessment in clinical psychology* by Gathercole (1968); *Psychological testing: theory, interpretation, and practice* by Gekoski (1964); *Clinical psychological tests in psychiatric and medical practice* by Gilbert (1969); *The structural approach in psychological testing* by Kaplan, Colorelli, Gross, Leventhal, and Siegel (1970); *The psychological assessment of children* by Palmer (1970); *Psychological diagnosis in clinical practice* by Pope and Scott (1967); *Psychometric assessment of the individual child* by Savage (1968); *Neuropsychological testing in organic brain dysfunction* edited by Smith and Philippus (1969); *Psychodiagnosis in schizophrenia* by Weiner (1966); and *Mental testing in clinical practice* by Williams (1965).

It is beyond the purpose of this section to survey the journal and review literature appearing since the first volume of this series. There are, however, several papers to which, because of their general appeal, I would like to direct the reader's attention. These include contributions by Arthur (1969), Block (1968), Breger (1968), Fiske and Pearson (1970), Holt (1970), and Miller (1970).

TOWARD A BROADENED THEORETICAL BASE
FOR PSYCHOLOGICAL ASSESSMENT

The newer extensions and changing functions of psychological assessment have brought about the need for a reexamination of conventional ways of conceiving of the basic nature of assessment. The field of assessment, like any other area of technology, rests not only upon a varied assortment of learned skills, experiential expertise, and special procedures derived empirically in practice, but also upon various assumptions about the nature and functions of the field. This latter domain of understandings can be thought of as the philosophical basis of assessment. Such assumptions are of tremendous influence in determining developments and directions in the field, and yet they are rarely examined in detail. The purpose of this section is to undertake a limited and preliminary analysis of the underlying theoretical approaches to assessment. Obviously, the matter merits more detailed consideration than it can be given here, but I hope that this brief presentation may help to stimulate further discussion elsewhere.

Conceptual Models of Assessment

The theoretical structure underlying psychological assessment can be delineated in the form of a conceptual model that reflects the assumptions made regarding the nature of the data to be obtained and the uses to which they are to be put. Traditionally, psychological assessment has been conceptualized in terms of what I will refer to here as "the attribute model." Assessment theory typically has been developed and presented as if this were the only possible model, as if it necessarily reflects the fundamental nature of assessment. This, however, as Cronbach and Gleser (1965) have reminded us, is not the case; indeed, there are various possible assessment models that could be put forth, depending on the functions that assessment is conceived to serve. In this section I will briefly outline three such models. The first, the *attribute model,* is the classical and conventional approach to assessment; the second, the *decision model,* has been developed by a number of authors, in particular Cronbach and Gleser (1965); and the third, which I will designate the *analytic model,* is being proposed here for the first time as a formal assessment model, though the procedures central to it have all been used by others. As I conceive of them, these models are not mutually exclusive, and no one of them is presented as being more "right" than the others. Rather, each is most appropriate for a given kind of assessment problem. The situation is somewhat similar to the role of the corpuscular and wave models of light in physics—in which the model to be utilized depends on the phenomena to be dealt with.

The attribute model. As already noted, this is the classic approach to assessment; it grew out of the work of Galton (1883), Cattell (1890), Kelley (1923), Hull (1928), and others, and is represented today in all standard textbooks. Essentially, the aim of this approach is to measure given attributes—introversion, hostility, intelligence, anxiety, and the like—of given individuals; i.e., to place the individual at some point on the continuum represented by the attribute (for a fuller discussion of "attribute" see Horst, 1968). The dominance of the attribute model among assessment theorists is illustrated by Kelly's (1967) recent text, in which assessment is, in effect, defined as "... any procedure for making meaningful evaluations or differentiations among human beings with respect to any characteristic or attribute [p. 1]." This model can also be thought of as a *criterion model,* since—especially in its more conventional form—it focuses on prediction to a criterion of the attribute. While this characteristic of the model has been somewhat diluted by the relatively recent acceptance of the concept of construct validity, it is still implied in most theoretical discussions.

The major assumptions of the attribute model can be stated with respect to a given attribute of given individuals. First of all, it is assumed that all individuals in some sense "have," or can be characterized by the attribute (i.e., they can be placed at some point on the attribute continuum); second, it is assumed that the individuals differ among themselves with respect to the attribute (and also, possibly, that a given individual differs with respect to himself over time); and third, it is assumed that for each individual there is a "true" placement (score) on the attribute continuum, which is only approximated by assessment techniques.

The attribute model is primarily a trait orientation. It assumes that the individual "has" a given attribute (trait) to a certain degree, and that this degree can be measured. Now, it is in fact not at all obvious, from the philosophical point of view, what is meant by statements that an individual "has" certain attributes—e.g., anxiety, hostility, intelligence, and so on. My point here, however, is not to analyze these or other concepts, but simply to note that the attribute model encourages the reification of concepts, although admittedly it does not necessitate such reification. Thus one can conceive of attributes not as objective reflections of reality, but rather as convenient symbols for scientific analysis and professional discourse. In this connection, Tyler (1965) has distinguished between "trait" and "dimension," with the former implying differences in amounts and the latter differences in distances on a scale. The dimensional approach has been widely used for combining different measures in theoretical hyperspaces. Such dimensions, however, are typically given labels and tied to individuals, and thus are within the scope of the attribute model. Human habits of thought being what they are, the danger of reification of concepts, whether viewed as traits or as dimensions, is always present, and this tendency is clearly enhanced by the attribute model's assumption of "true" scores.[1]

The concepts of reliability and validity are part and parcel of the attribute model. Thus, reliability is related to the correlation between the obtained and the "true" scores, and validity to the correlation between the obtained score and some other estimate, whether obtained or inferred, of the attribute. These interpretations of reliability and validity, having been developed in the attribute model tradition, are not wholly applicable to other models. The highly sophisticated development of these concepts, which in a sense provides each instance of assessment with an independent criterion of the adequacy of that assessment, has done much to enhance the dominance of the attribute approach. There is, however, no a priori reason why analogous statistical criteria cannot be developed for other models.

Implicit in the attribute model, at least as usually carried out, is a theory of human behavior: namely, that behavior is essentially determined by

---

[1] This tendency is attenuated when the concept of "universe score" (Cronbach, 1970, p. 154)—i.e., a collection of possible measures—replaces the notion of "true score."

intraorganismic factors, i.e., by traits. The usual assumption is that if we understand the individual well enough, we will be able to predict his behavior, and that detailed knowledge of the behavioral setting—the stimulus situation— is unnecessary. It is essentially this characteristic of the attribute model that Mischel (1968) attacked so vigorously in his recent book. While in my opinion Mischel's criticisms are, as I will elaborate later, considerably overdrawn, there is clearly much truth in them.

In summation, we may say that the attribute model is limited by the narrowness of its underlying theory of behavior, by the fact that it encourages reification of posited attributes, and by the fact that it focuses solely on individuals. On the other hand, there is much to commend in the approach. After all, it *is* important to assess the characteristics of individuals, much of a person's behavior *is* determined by intraorganismic factors, and it is *not* inevitable that the use of attribute-constructs leads to their reification. Despite these positive features, however, it must be concluded that if we are adequately to conceptualize the assessment of groups and environments, and to take proper account of the influence of stimulus variables on behavior, additional assessment models must be developed and utilized.

The decision model. This approach to psychological assessment is quite new. While it has perhaps been developed most systematically by Cronbach and Gleser (1965; see especially pp. 133-149 for a brief summary), a number of other workers (Arthur, 1966; Cole & Magnussen, 1966; Darlington & Stauffer, 1966; Edwards, Lindman, & Phillips, 1965) have been involved. Historically it grew out of concepts of game theory and modern decision theory, and philosophically it can be traced to the utilitarian orientation of Bentham. The basic notion of the decision model is that the process of assessment can be conceptualized to include not only the *gathering* of certain kinds of data, but also the *using* of these data to arrive at decisions. This is in contrast to the traditional approach, in which the assessor conceives that his job is done when he has summarized his results and turned them over to someone else—say, a personnel officer—to use in arriving at a decision. The decision model, because of its greater comprehensiveness, is in a sense more realistic than the attribute model. It should be particularly useful in cases in which the questions asked can be phrased in terms of certain alternative *treatments*— whom to hire and whom to reject, whom to assign to this therapy and whom to assign to that therapy, and so on—and cases in which systematic account can be taken of the costs of making the decisions and of the gains and losses from correct and incorrect decisions. The decision model is concerned with strategies for making decisions, with plans for decision-making. Instead of focusing on the notion of validity, it emphasizes the concept of utility. Those decisions are best which maximize the overall utility. This model employs psychological tests, but their value is not simply a function of their validity; rather, it is related to "the specific type of decision problem, the strategy employed, the evaluation attached to the outcome, and the cost of testing [Cronbach & Gleser, 1965, p. 32]."

The decision model represents a different approach from the attribute model, but—at least in its present stage of development—it should be seen more as a supplement to than as a replacement for the latter. Unlike the attribute model, which tends to be a system of definite procedures and involves basically simple formulae, the decision model is more a general orientation, a problem-solving approach, and can become extremely complex mathematically.

The analytic model. There are a number of important trends in contemporary assessment practice that cannot adequately be conceptualized in terms of either the attribute model or the decision model. These trends include the assessment of groups, assessments of the environment, and various kinds of naturalistic studies. There is a need, therefore, for a broader and more complex assessment model. As a step toward meeting this need, I will now suggest the tentative outlines of what I will refer to as the *analytic model* of assessment. As we will see, this model represents not so much a wholly new departure as a bringing together and formalizing of an approach already widely employed in practice.

The purpose of the analytic model is to analyze a given psychologically meaningful area, a given behavioral domain, to provide a general picture of the behavior in context, i.e., an assay of the prevalence of, the conditions for, and the consequences of, the behavior. Any given assessment would hardly include all of these aspects, but they can all be conceptualized as part of an analytic orientation. One can say, somewhat loosely, that whereas the attribute model emphasizes prediction and the decision model emphasizes decision-making, the analytic model focuses on understanding.

The analytic approach as conceptualized here includes the following four aspects:

1. *The identification and description of behaviors and behavior settings.* This aspect involves the development and application of reliable techniques for delineating given behaviors—anxious behaviors, altruistic behaviors, hostile behaviors, delusional behaviors, and the like—and the environmental settings in which they occur.

2. *Assessment of the prevalence and distribution of the behavior.* This is the ecological aspect. It focuses on obtaining answers to questions such as: How widespread is the behavior? With which demographic variables—sex, age, marital status, and the like—is it associated? How is it related, in the frequency and distribution of its manifestation, to other behaviors?

3. *Assessment of the determinants of the behavior.* This aspect focuses on the classes of behavioral determinants. While in principle there are many ways in which such analyses could be designed, a particularly fruitful one uses analysis of variance techniques to determine the extent to which variability in given behaviors is a function of (*a*) individual differences, (*b*) situations, and (*c*) the interaction between these.

4. *Assessment of the consequences of the behavior.* A behavior is not adequately understood apart from its consequences. Assessment of this aspect involves not only the identification and description of the consequent behaviors, but also a specification of the degree to which the given behaviors are under the control of their consequences, and of the particular consequences that are reinforcing.

The analytic approach, as represented in the above four functions, involves a wide variety of assessment techniques. In the first two aspects listed above, observational procedures, particularly in naturalistic settings, unobtrusive measures, and rating scales play important roles. Psychological tests, however, also have a place; an example of this would be the use of the TAT (Veroff, Atkinson, Feld, & Gurin, 1960) in a normative study of motives. Barker (1968) and his colleagues have been leaders in developing methods for assessing naturally occurring behaviors and the settings in which they occur. A number of investigators (Barker, 1968; Craik, 1970b; Moos & Houts, 1968; Sells, 1969; Stern, 1970; Wohlwill, 1970; Wolf, 1966; see also Chapter III, this volume) have been active in developing procedures for environmental assessment.

One pioneering study with respect to the third aspect listed above is that by Endler, Hunt, and Rosenstein (1962). This investigation used an inventory technique and analysis of variance to investigate the relative contributions to anxiousness of intra-individual, situational, and interactional determinants. A similar procedure has been used by Endler and Hunt (1968) and Sidle, Moos, Adams, and Cady (1969). Assessment procedures concerning the relations between behaviors and their consequences can be divided into two quite different classes: first, analyses of relationships between given behaviors or behavior settings and their long-term consequences (e.g., the relation between early rearing conditions and later personality); and second, analyses of the control and modification of behaviors by programmed patterns of immediate consequences (reinforcers). The latter of these has been most developed by workers in the operant conditioning paradigm (see Chapter IV, this volume).

It is clear that the analytic model of assessment, as conceptualized above, is somewhat unstructured and very broad. Indeed, it may be objected that the model is so broad as to be more an outline of the scientific endeavor than of assessment as such. Yet the procedures encompassed within it are aspects of assessment as actually practiced. Further, it would be a mistake to attempt a rigid differentiation between scientific and assessment technologies.

An important characteristic of the analytic model, as viewed in its entirety, is the fact that it attempts to take into account *both* intraorganismic (personal) and situational (environmental) determinants of behavior. Traditionally, personality psychologists, employing the attribute model of assessment as their paradigm of investigation, have insisted that behavior is primarily determined by organismic variables. Social psychologists and stimulus-response theorists, on the other hand, have characteristically asserted that behavior is primarily determined by the existent stimulus situation. It is from this latter point of view that Mischel (1968), in the work referred to earlier, severely criticized assessment procedures based on what I am terming the attribute model. But in my judgment Mischel's apparent solution—to base assessment on contemporaneous stimuli—is too narrow. The view espoused here, that behavior is significantly determined by both organismic and situational factors, is essentially that espoused earlier by R. S. Woodworth, Kurt Lewin, Henry Murray, and others. Thus assessment procedures, in the context of the analytic model, include both instruments for assessing the individual and instruments for assessing the environment.

Because it is not concerned with prediction, the concept of validity—in the usual criterion sense—is less meaningful in the analytic than in the other two models; rather than validity, assessment techniques would be evaluated in terms of their *informativeness*—i.e., how much information they convey regarding a given behavioral-environmental domain. In order to know what a technique is informing one *about,* however, he must know what it is a measure of—i.e., what it is valid *for.* The analytic model is particularly appropriate for research, but it also has implications for the practical world. In a given situation, both the attribute and decision models presuppose that certain choices have already been made: what questions are pertinent, what decisions are to be made, and whether systematic, predictive assessment is indicated. These determinations, however, have to be made by some person or persons, and presumably the more adequate their overall knowledge about the behavioral-environmental domain concerned, the better able they will be to specify the kinds of attribute data needed and the particular questions to be decided. The analytic model is appropriate for this kind of situation. Further, the clinician may—and indeed typically does—use the analytic model when he seeks a broad, general understanding of a client in order to be in a position to deal with him on a rational and well-informed basis. As presently conceived, the analytic model represents more a particular orientation than a set of integrated, stepwise procedures. There appears to be no reason, however, why it cannot be more systematically developed, and it is hoped that the suggestions offered here will contribute toward that end.

Other Models

I have summarized above three different models for conceptualizing psychological assessment. These, however, are not the only possible assessment models. Thus, another alternative might be a discriminant function model (Cronbach & Gleser, 1965, p. 138). Arthur (1969) conceptualizes five different models, as follows: the diagnostic model, the experimental model, the behavioral model, the decision-making model, and the operations-research model. The last of these, which is "an extension of the decision-making model to optimize the total endeavor of the clinic rather than of single decisions [p. 190]," is especially interesting.

PLAN OF THIS BOOK

Each of the papers brought together in this book represents an important and interesting area in psychological assessment, and all of the papers together—taken as a group—afford a good picture of current directions in this field. I have arranged the chapters in what I believe to be a meaningful and helpful order; but each is intended to stand alone, and the contributions can profitably be read in any sequence.

The first of the substantive chapters—Chapter II, immediately following this Introduction—is on automated procedures in assessment and is by C. James Klett and Donald K. Pumroy. This challenging contribution is both fascinating to read and provocative in its implications. Its priority in ordering is reflective of the fact that automated procedures represent an innovation that is increasingly being applied over the whole range of assessment technology. The second substantive chapter (Chapter III)—on environmental assessment—also deserves priority in a book of this kind, as a way of pointing up the arrival and the importance of this broad area of assessment. Kenneth H. Craik's innovative chapter, on the assessment of places, is the first in a projected sequence, in the *Advances* series, on environmental assessment. In addition to providing very usable guidelines for behavioral scientists wishing to assess given places, this contribution also includes an important theoretical discussion of the rationale of environmental assessment.

The next two chapters are similar in that each is concerned with the assessment of a given class of persons—in Chapter IV by Sidney W. Bijou and Robert F. Peterson, with the assessment of children, and in Chapter V by Marvin D. Dunnette, with the assessment of executives. The Bijou-Peterson chapter will be of real use both to clinicians and to theoreticians of assessment. Like the Weiss chapter in Volume One, this contribution is in the behavioristic tradition. It proposes, in a way that is both original and convincing, the technique of functional analysis as an approach to assessment. I know of no paper that demonstrates more emphatically that assessment is in fact much broader than the use of conventional tests. Dunnette's interesting and authoritative chapter is unique in this series in two notable respects: first, in its focus on the assessment of managerial talents; and second, in its detailed delineation of the utilization of multiple assessment procedures. Both of these characteristics are important, not only in their own right, but also for their suggestive value in other assessment contexts.

Chapters V, by Dunnette, and VI, by Thomas F. Siess and Douglas N. Jackson, have in common the fact that they both are in the area of vocational psychology. The chapter by Siess and Jackson makes two major contributions. First, it presents an important new theoretical conception, along with supporting data, on the relationships between personality and vocational choices; and second, it provides helpful suggestions for vocational counselors on the use of personality data. In addition, this chapter is an important addition to the growing literature on the Personality Research Form and provides further evidence for the usefulness of that instrument.

The next two chapters each deal with the assessment of a class of personality variables; further, in both instances the variables concerned are motivational in nature. Chapter VII, by the present writer, is on the nature and measurement of intrinsic motivation. The topic of intrinsic motivation represents an exciting new direction in theoretical psychology, and this chapter provides a survey of techniques that can be used in the assessment of intrinsic motivational variables. Chapter VIII, by Edwin I. Megargee and Elizabeth S. Menzies, focuses on the assessment and prediction of aggressive behavior. As the authors point out, aggression is the major social problem of our time. The importance of developing adequate assessment procedures, for use in both research and clinical practice, is therefore very great. This timely chapter begins with a rigorous theoretical analysis and then provides a critical survey of the instruments available for the assessment of aggression.

This paper will, I believe, be influential in improving research on aggression.

The Megargee-Menzies chapter can also be seen as forming a group with the next two, in that all three are concerned, in one way or another, with the application of assessment procedures to clinical problems. Edward Lichtenstein's insightful chapter (IX) on techniques for assessing outcomes of psychotherapy not only surveys the available techniques for outcome evaluation but also sets forth important suggestions toward a new theoretical perspective in this research area. It is, I predict, a paper that will make a difference in how outcome research is henceforth conducted. Maurice Lorr in Chapter X carefully examines the problem of specifying the dimensions and categories used in assessing grossly deviant behaviors. Before reading this contribution, one would do well to remember that assessment consists not only of (*a*) instruments and procedures for measuring and categorizing, but also of (*b*) systems of dimensions and classes in terms of which the objects of assessment are to be ordered. Assessment, in a given domain, can be no better than these conceptual systems. Lorr's chapter brings together a vast amount of research and delineates an empirically derived system for conceptualizing the behavior of individuals considered to be psychotic. The research programs summarized in this chapter represent, in my judgment, one of the more significant developments in contemporary clinical psychological assessment.

Chapter XI by Duane L. Varble is concerned with assessment in a more classical sense. Following a precedent set in Volume One, this chapter examines the current status of a standard, widely used test, in this case the Thematic Apperception Test. It is interesting to note that this instrument is now thirty-five years old. Varble provides a rigorous, thoughtful, and judicious review of the literature, and offers some helpful conclusions as to the role the TAT can play in the changing assessment scene.

The following two chapters (XII and XIII) are both highly innovative, and neither is on a topic usually represented in books on assessment; but otherwise they have little in common. Richard J. Harris examines the role that "experimental games," a class of interaction situations now being widely studied in social psychology, can play in assessment. Readers will find this scholarly chapter—on a topic in which Harris has himself contributed widely—both informative and provocative; it is illustrative of the increasing breadth of the concept of assessment.

Chapter XIII by Jack D. Barchas, Jon M. Stolk, Roland D. Ciaranello, and David A. Hamburg is on biochemical procedures in psychological assessment. This chapter continues the precedent established in the previous volume, in the chapter by Averill and Opton, of giving appropriate attention to the place of physiological factors in behavioral assessment. As the reader will find, Barchas and his colleagues have succeeded in the difficult task of making technical material from one discipline (biochemistry) clear and meaningful to workers in another discipline (psychology), and they have done this without popularizing either the biochemical or the behavioral aspects. To the best of my knowledge, this is the first paper anywhere to review this important area of assessment, and it will, I hope, help to stimulate further work in the area.

I have placed Lewis R. Goldberg's chapter last, because it is different from all others in the book. It is an historical account of the development and elaboration of personality inventories. All serious students of assessment will find this paper essential, and all students, whether serious or casual, will find it delightful to read. It is scholarly, informative, and absorbing, and affords a perspective in terms of which the newer trends in the field can be better understood, and their purposes more fully realized.

CHAPTER II

Automated procedures
in psychological assessment

C. James Klett and Donald K. Pumroy

Psychological testing may soon evolve at the better equipped testing centers into a more or less completely automated procedure bearing only superficial resemblance to the traditional examination of today. The subject will be met at the assessment center by a receptionist or technician and led to a relatively small, soundproof room where he will be seated at a compact console consisting of a television screen, a modified typewriter keyboard, and several rows of buttons. The technician will provide some preliminary instructions, activate the console, and leave. The TV screen will brighten and a voice will say, "Hello. Today we are going to ask you to do some things that will help those working with you to know you better. If you have any trouble understanding what you are asked to do, please push the red button on your right and someone will provide assistance. Now, if you are ready to begin, press the green button directly in front of you marked *Start*." If the subject fails to depress the start button within a fixed time, a signal will be flashed to the technician that assistance is probably necessary. Similar signals throughout the testing procedure will allow the technician to monitor one or many testing cubicles. If the subject responds correctly by depressing the start button, he will be instructed to type his name using the keyboard in front of him. He will then be asked a series of questions about his background, to which he will respond by depressing the appropriate buttons on the console as directed. A series of psychological tests selected by the psychologist will be introduced in the same manner. When the testing is completed, he will be told to press the red button so that the technician will be summoned.

The responses of the subject will be sent by data phone to a central computing center and, in the interests of confidentiality, will be identified by a code number known only to the professionals working with the subject. The test data will be scored and entered into one or more computer programs designated by the psychologist. The subject's scores may be compared with appropriate normative groups in the central data bank, or they may be used in predictive equations which yield probabilities of suicide, responsiveness to

The assistance of Shirley L. Klett, Ph.D., at several critical stages in the preparation of this manuscript is gratefully acknowledged.

specific drugs or other treatments, or an estimate of length of stay for hospitalized patients. Finally, a concise statement of all these findings will be typed
on the output terminal in the psychologist's office for review. The report will
be incorporated in the subject's file together with additional comments of
the psychologist. The subject's data will remain on permanent file in the
central data bank where it can be recovered upon request. The results of
treatment and other outcome measures may be added at a later time. These
data will also become part of an ever growing normative pool with which to
compare future test protocols.

Although the system described does not yet exist, the current technology
of instrumentation, television recording, and computer science is adequate
for its construction, and in fact, a prototype of the system is available in the
Totally Automated Psychological Assessment Console (TAPAC) developed
by Allan E. Edwards at the Veterans Administration Hospital in Los Angeles
(1967). Other segments of this hypothetical testing procedure have also been
developed, and it takes only a little imagination to appreciate how they might
be incorporated into a single system.

THE TOTALLY AUTOMATED PSYCHOLOGICAL
ASSESSMENT CONSOLE (TAPAC)[1]

In appearance, the equipment consists of a console about two and one-
half feet wide, three feet deep, and four feet high. There is a one-foot-square
transilluminable projection screen flush with the face of the console, at eye
level for the seated subject. Below the screen are two rows of transilluminable
panels, each 3 x 1½ inches in size. To the left of these panels is a 1 x ¾ inch
illuminable button labelled *Ready,* and to the right is a grid concealing a
speaker. All of the transilluminable panels serve both as projection screens
and response buttons. Visual material is projected on the large screen and on
the smaller panels, and audio material is taped. The whole system is programmed by magnetically encoded information on the edge of film.

Edwards' description (1969) of the following tests that have been programmed for TAPAC illustrates the procedure:

Short-Term Memory Aural:
1. Ready button depressed.
2. Programmer commands audio tape for instruction and examples.
3. First aural pattern presented, followed one second later by second
pattern.
4. The screen illuminates, *Were the tunes the same or different?* Simultaneously, response panel 1 is illuminated *Same,* and response panel 2 is illuminated *Different.* Nonilluminated panels are inoperative.

---

[1] Since this section was written, TAPAC has been made commercially available by
Lehigh Valley Electronics of Fogessville, Pennsylvania. Although the physical appearance
of their equipment (see Figure 1) is different from Edwards' prototype and there have
been extensive changes in internal systems, the concept is essentially the same as that
described here.

Figure 1. The Totally Automated Psychological Assessment Consol (TAPAC).

5. Subject makes his response by depressing (touching) a panel.

6. Screen darkens and ready button illuminates inviting the next presentation. Aural patterns are composed of the Seashore Tonal Memory Task (Seashore, Lewis, & Saetveit, 1939), modified so that half the pairs are the same and half are different, and test length is doubled. Intervals between patterns are randomly varied between one second and ten seconds. A response recorder sums the number correct under each temporal condition. The test is in ascending order of difficulty, and if the subject misses any of the first four presentations, TAPAC alerts the technician monitoring in the next room.

Short-Term Memory Visual:

1. Ready button depressed.

2. Programmer commands audio for instructions and examples.

3. Visual pattern appears on screen for three seconds. At one or ten seconds later, the same pattern reappears on one of the panels together with a number of foils on other panels. The screen illuminates, *Which of the patterns below was just shown?*

4. Subject responds by depressing panel.

5. Screen and panels darken and ready button illuminates inviting next item presentation. Visual patterns are composed of the Moran Memory for Faces Test, modified for multiple choice presentation (Moran, Kimble, & Mefferd, 1960).

Paired Associates:
1. Ready button depressed.
2. Audio instructions and examples given.
3. A job title appears on the screen, and eight response panels illuminate, each with a common surname. If the subject touches a panel, the display immediately changes to a repeat of the job title, but only the correct surname is displayed on the panels. If the subject does not touch a panel within four seconds, the job title and correct surname are projected for two seconds.
4. Ready button illuminates, inviting next item presentation. There are five repetitions of eight job titles to which the subject must learn to associate the correct surname. Response recorded is the number correct on each repetition after the first series.

General Intelligence:
1. Ready button depressed.
2. Audio instructions and examples given.
3. First slide of Progressive Matrices (Raven, 1956) administered. This is a multiple choice, nonverbal intelligence test, which correlates .85 with the WAIS full scale IQ.
4. Response made by touching appropriate panel.
5. Screen and panels darken and ready button illuminates inviting next item presentation. Responses recorded are number correct for each subset.

Time Perception Aural:
1. Ready button depressed.
2. Audio instructions and examples given.
3. A pair of tones, equated for pitch and loudness, is presented with a .10 msec. separation. In half of the pairs, the duration of the two tones is also equated, but in the remaining pairs the two tones are of different duration.
4. The screen illuminates, *Were the two tones the same or different?* and simultaneously two panels illuminate *Same* and *Different.*
5. Subject responds, screen and panels darken, ready button illuminates. This is a modification of the Seashore Time Perception Test (Seashore et al., 1939). Responses recorded are number correct at different duration differences from which a detection threshold is derived.

Time Perception Visual:
1. Ready button depressed, audio instructions and examples given.
2. Medial eight panels begin flickering, each with same number of flashes per minute. However, one of the panels is flickering at a constant rate, the other seven with variable off-times.
3. Subject selects the constant panel.
4. Panels darken, ready button illuminates, new constant panel is armed, and next trial invited. This is a modification of the Weber (1965) Time Perception Task, which does not confound memory or set with time perception. Responses recorded are number correct with each variable off-time.

Picture Vocabulary:
  1. Ready button depressed, audio instructions and examples given.
  2. Screen illuminates with a figure, panels illuminate with words.
  3. Subject responds, screen and panels darken, and response buttons illuminate. This is a modification of the Full-Range Picture Vocabulary Test (Ammons & Ammons, 1954). Responses recorded are number correct for total test.

Reaction Time, Simple:
  1. Ready button depressed, audio instructions given.
  2. Central panel illuminates; screen illuminates, *Remove hand from panel as quickly as possible when its light goes off.*
  3. Subject touches panel until it darkens.
  4. Ready button illuminates. Response scored is time to remove hand from panel after it darkens. (25 trials)

Reaction Time, Disjunctive:
  1. Same as simple reaction time, but with both hands used; two panels are illuminated, and only one (randomly determined) is darkened.

Psychomotor Ability:
  1. Ready button depressed, audio instructions given.
  2. One of medial eight panels illuminates briefly, then another, then another, etc.
  3. Subject depresses illuminated panel as long as it is illuminated.
  4. After 20 jumps, ready button illuminates, and panels darken. Response scored is time-on-target per trial.

A variety of other tests have been programmed for TAPAC, but these examples should suffice to illustrate the concept and versatility of the equipment as well as some of its limitations. The particular tests described were selected primarily because the initial focus of attention was a group of older brain-damaged, aphasic patients, but there are a large number of tests directed at other areas which could as easily be programmed. Items from the MMPI or any other objective test could be presented on the screen, read from the tape, or both, and the subject could respond by depressing the appropriate illuminated panel. Projective test stimuli could be presented on the screen and some form of multiple-choice response obtained from the subject (e.g., McReynolds, 1966). The one limitation of the current version of TAPAC is that it does require a discrete response of the multiple-choice or true-false variety. While many tests could be modified for such a format, there would then be a need to establish new normative data and to establish the validity and reliability for significant changes as a result of the modifications. A later-generation machine incorporating a typewriter keyboard would provide for a wider range of responses by the subject to projective test stimuli. Tests requiring the physical manipulation of objects presents a greater challenge.

TAPAC was developed in response to a need for reliable psychological assessment that would eliminate inter-examiner, inter-geographic, and inter-epoch variance and reduce intrasubject variance by providing precise stimulus, response, and timing controls. TAPAC is completely self-paced, has good stimulus control, and is inherently impersonal. Patients report that they enjoy the procedure and typically give every evidence of good motivation and interest. Since the testing procedure can be interrupted at any time, fatigue is not a factor.

Little professional attention is required since TAPAC operates with a supervisory technician whose task is mainly scheduling, establishing rapport, data reduction, and file keeping. Typically, all instructions are handled by TAPAC, but on occasion, built-in alarms signal the technician that human intervention is desirable. In a situation where the number of professionals available is very limited in comparison with the number of patients who must be screened, TAPAC would seem to be particularly advantageous in systematically assessing all the patients capable of responding to this testing procedure.

An obvious improvement of TAPAC would be the establishment of a computer link. Output of the current version is digital in nature, responses being permanently recorded upon strip-charts and other digital print-out devices. Transcription of these data to a more convenient format is the responsibility of the technician. A computer link would facilitate compilation and manipulation of data as well as allowing for greater interaction of machine and subject.

Although TAPAC can be considered to be essentially a controlled-stimulus presenter or response recorder device, it seems more appropriate to think of it as a first step to a completely automated system as described earlier. Because of its comparatively enormous methodological versatility, it should stimulate and render feasible a good deal of research effort and can be expected to take its place in the clinical setting for routine testing.

OBJECTIVE TESTING

The earliest efforts in the automation of objective testing were the development of ways of recording responses so they could be easily transferred to punch card form (mark sense, optical scan answer sheets) and the preparation of computer programs for test scoring. Both of these features are now so commonplace that they hardly seem worth mentioning as examples of automation, but an older generation of psychologists will recall the time spent in scoring and will remember that these advances seemed remarkable when they first appeared. Nearly all objective tests given in any volume now use the optical scan answer sheets that can be read by computing equipment and recorded on punched card or magnetic tape for further processing. Many systems yield subtest scores directly from the answer sheets without intermediate handling of item data. Transformation of these scores to standard scores or T scores is an easy task for the computer, and although considerable ingenuity of programming may be involved, the display of these scores as a test profile is not a remarkable achievement. Actually, these applications and some others to be described are trivial for the computer but are important because of the savings in time and tedium.

Beyond the simple task of producing scores or score profiles was the goal of simulating the clinician's interpretation of the test data and even of producing a form of psychological report directly from the item responses. As might be expected, the greatest amount of energy in this direction has been devoted to the Minnesota Multiphasic Personality Inventory (MMPI, Hathaway & McKinley, 1951).

Five systems for scoring and interpreting the MMPI have been reported in sufficient detail to warrant discussion.[2] Of these, the Mayo Clinic program (Pearson & Swenson, 1967) is the earliest and, in some ways, the most extensive. This program was begun in 1959 and became operational on a trial basis in 1961. Since then, its use at the Mayo Clinic has been expanded so that the administration of the MMPI is a routine part of the admission procedure for most patients. In the five years prior to publication of the 1967 user's guide, the MMPI had been administered to over 150,000 patients.

The MMPI is usually presented to the patient after his intake physical examination and before more detailed laboratory examinations. Generally, this is a time during which the patient must normally wait for further medical attention. A professional instructs the patient in taking the test, presenting it as simply a routine aspect of the admission procedure. Twenty-three special cards have been developed for use by the patient in recording his responses, and he is given a special marking pencil. Once the patient understands the instructions, he is left to complete the test by himself and told to return the completed test in a special envelope when he is finished. Very little opposition to taking the test has been received from patients. In fact, many seem grateful for something to do while waiting for appointments. The preliminary trial in 1961 found that only 0.2 percent of the patients refused to take the test; 5.0 percent were physically, mentally, or educationally unable to take the test; and 5.6 percent of the tests were not returned or were returned unfinished. The latter figure includes those patients who did not have time to complete the test before other appointments.

The patient's answer cards are fed directly into the computer for scoring, analysis, and the preparation of a narrative report. Generally, the physician will obtain the report the day following administration. Since the physician receiving the report is likely to be an internist, the original development of the computer program for producing the narrative report was approached with the idea of providing a useful summary in nontechnical language. This feature has been retained through the years.

To develop the narrative summary, a series of statements were prepared for each of the MMPI scales which would fairly reflect an experienced clinical psychologist's description given in layman's terms. Five different statements are programmed for most of the scales to characterize low, normal, mild, moderate, and marked scores. The statements for the schizophrenia scale and the raw score ranges are as follows:

---

[2] A complete description of another system developed by Harold Gilberstadt at the MMPI Research Laboratory, VA Hospital, Minneapolis, has just been published by the Veterans Administration (1970).

1. Low (male, 20 or less; female, 22 or less). Shows strong interests in people and practical matters.

2. Normal (male, 19-26; female, 20-28). Has a combination of practical and theoretical interests.

3. Mild (male, 27-33; female, 29-36). Tends toward abstract interests such as science, philosophy, or religion.

4. Moderate (male, 34-40; female, 37-45). Probably is somewhat eccentric, seclusive, and withdrawn, and has many internal conflicts.

5. Marked (male, 41+; female, 46+). Probably has feelings of unreality, bizarre or confused thinking and conduct. May have strange attitudes and false beliefs. Consider psychiatric evaluation.

To expand the usefulness of the MMPI analysis, the computer program contains 11 branching operations, some of them designed to identify particular patterns of scores, some modifying the narrative description as a result of the age of the patient, and some dealing with unusual score (or scores) elevations. For example, if the F scale score is above 22, the profile is considered invalid, and only the high F description is printed. The patterns which are programmed include, for example, "involutional," "conversion," and "anxious psychopath." The computer subroutines make reference not only to scale scores in the configural routines, but also to sex and age. A computer search for the involutional pattern is conducted if the patient is 45 or more years old, whereas a search for the anxious psychopath is made if the patient is less than 45.

Many more branching operations could be added. The voluminous MMPI literature offers hundreds of suggestions. However, the authors of this system have attempted to restrict severely the amount of pattern analysis to provide as simple and useful a narrative account as possible.

In addition to the usual clinical scales, many other special MMPI scores have been proposed in the literature, based on different combinations of responses to the 566 statements. The Mayo program currently scores 13 of the more promising scales but does not include them in the report.

The developers of the Mayo Clinic MMPI program anticipated that the availability of MMPI results to physicians with little or no previous knowledge of the theory and practice of objective personality testing would lead to their learning more about the test, development of their own frame of reference in interpreting the results, and perhaps to more rigorous data collection or even the development of testable theories. These expectations have, in large measure, been fulfilled. Acceptance and use of the results have been very good. Also, many patients spontaneously verbalize emotional problems to their physician and request help after taking the test. Both the patient and the physician, then, become more aware of the existence of emotional problems embedded within a matrix of physical complaints.

The main purpose of the MMPI program developed by Kleinmuntz (1969b) was to identify college students experiencing emotional difficulties. His approach to analysis of the MMPI profiles began in 1963 and differs markedly from that of the Mayo Clinic. Where Pearson, Swenson, and their co-workers

(1967) took the standard interpretations of the scale elevation from the large body of MMPI literature, Kleinmuntz attempted to identify groups of "adjusted" and "maladjusted" college students by external criteria, and to devise a computer program which would separate the two groups on the basis of their MMPI profiles. Kleinmuntz obtained a total of 126 MMPI profiles from Carnegie-Mellon University students who represented a range of adjustment states from well-adjusted to maladjusted. Three methods were used to identify this group: (1) On the basis of two counselors' judgments, 65 students who presented themselves to the counseling center were classified as "adjusted" if their problems appeared to be primarily academic-vocational and maladjusted if their problems were emotional-personal. (2) All fraternities were asked to identify members of their house who were "most" and "least" adjusted; the study required 60 percent agreement among the members and resulted in the inclusion of 31 subjects—14 most and 17 least adjusted. (3) A random group of 30 profiles belonging to entering freshman was selected as a "normal" category on the basis that none had appeared at the counseling center or been mentioned in the second procedure above.

The 126 profiles selected to represent the range of adjustment-maladjustment were then presented to several psychologists experienced in MMPI interpretation. They were asked to sort the profiles, by means of the Q-sort technique, into 14 categories ranging from most to least adjusted. The psychologist who most closely agreed with the original criteria was then asked to "think aloud" while conducting his Q sort. In this way, sequential rules for conducting a pattern analysis were obtained for transfer to computer programming.

The initial trial of the program showed a high agreement between the computer and the expert, and attempts to improve upon the expert's classification (finally collapsed to three categories: adjusted, maladjusted, and unclassifiable) have continued.

A cross-validating study has been conducted using the MMPIs of four new samples, pitting the computer against experts. Kleinmuntz reports that the computer program has not achieved the same success rate as the experts, although the overall results "have been sufficiently encouraging" to continue.

While the external criteria and the Q-sort technique used by Kleinmuntz could be criticized, it may well be that the primary difficulty in transferring the rules for decision-making to validating groups lies in the MMPI. If one takes a pattern analysis approach to the MMPI, it is apparent that the number of significant patterns is not adequately sampled in Kleinmuntz's limited criterion group. Use of the single clinician in the original formulation of the rules could also lead to systematic error.

Two MMPI report systems have been devised for the convenience of users in the field. Both are similar in development to the Mayo Clinic program in that the interpretation of the scores and score configurations are drawn from the MMPI literature. Both provide a narrative summary which has been developed in much the same way as that of the Mayo system. Of the two, that developed by Fowler (1969) is perhaps closer in spirit to the Mayo form. This system has recently been offered by the Roche Psychiatric Service Institute of Nutley, New Jersey, as a diagnostic adjunct service for psychiatrists, practicing psychologists, and neurologists only. Qualified users who, for a nominal fee, subscribe to the service are sent a kit of instructions for administration of the MMPI. A charge is made for each completed MMPI returned for scoring and analysis, and the user receives a three-page report. The first page contains the narrative summary, and the second contains the score print-out and also, unlike the Mayo program, a print-out of any critical items to which the patient responded in the "undesirable" or "unusual" direction, e.g., a true response to "I am worried about sex matters." The third page of the report contains a computer print-out of the MMPI profile. Samples of the computer print-out have been included in several of Fowler's papers (e.g., Fowler & Miller, 1969).

The Roche service was undertaken with the idea that it might be particularly useful to professionals working in areas where the services of a psychologist trained in the interpretation of the MMPI were not available. Since the users of this service are professionals, it was thought that the inclusion of deviant items would bring special problem areas to the attention of the therapist. The elapsed time involved from completion of the test form in the user's office to the return of the report is primarily dependent on the mails, since turnaround time at the center is only one day. Computer time for the system as now in operation is only a few seconds. User response has been encouraging, and a few institutions have subscribed to the service.

A similar, but more extensive service is offered by the Institute of Clinical Analysis of Glendale, California (Dunlop, 1966). The scoring and analysis are accomplished in a manner analogous to the Mayo program. However, this service departs even more radically from the Mayo program in several important respects. Although the ICA service provides much material of particular interest to research workers, at the same time it directs most of its interpretation to the family physician as the major user. Indeed, ICA has produced an eye-catching brochure, a compendium of clinical interpretation, and an abstracted reference guide, all designed to facilitate interpretation of the report. It has also introduced the concept of emotional temperature based upon a new scale score called the Multiphasic Index (MI), which is an overall indication of psychopathology.

Again, the test is completed in the physician's office on modified optical scan answer forms provided to facilitate processing by the ICA program. The completed form is forwarded for scoring and report preparation. The user is provided with the interpretative material previously mentioned and a very comprehensive test report. Like the Roche program, a print-out of critical items is included in the report along with the scores and profile. Compared to the Roche program, however, the ICA narrative makes much greater use of psychiatric-psychologic terminology, e.g., "schizoid personality" and "ego defense." The ICA report also includes a list of major symptoms, emotional components, and problem areas deserving of special attention, and the scores for a number of special scales. The following ICA report for a 45-year-old male gives a clear idea of the amount and kind of information provided.

MULTIPHASIC INDEX EVALUATION

MI, EMOTIONAL DISTURBANCE INDEX 145 RANGE 65-150.
SCORES RISING ABOVE 89 REFLECT INCREASING DISTURBANCE.

PROBABILITY OF LOW DISTURBANCE	PROBABILITY OF MODERATE DISTURBANCE	PROBABILITY OF MARKED DISTURBANCE
1%	84%	15%

A SUMMARY MEASUREMENT OF THIS PATTERN REFLECTS A
MARKEDLY SEVERE DISTURBANCE IN EMOTIONAL ADJUST-
MENT. ENERGY IS CHANNELED INTO NUMEROUS DEFENSES,
AND THERE IS GREAT DIFFICULTY COPING WITH LIFE'S
CHANGES. REACTIONS TEND TO BE INAPPROPRIATE,
UNREALISTIC, AND SELF-DEFEATING. IN ANSWERING
TEST QUESTIONS, THE SUBJECT WAS MARKEDLY SELF-
CRITICAL WITH EXTREME UNDERAPPRAISAL OF POTENTIAL
ASSETS. THIS REFLECTS DEEP DISSATISFACTION AND
A POOR SELF-CONCEPT RELATIVE TO THE SUBJECT'S
EGO-IDEAL. OFTEN CALLED 'SENSITIZERS,' THESE
PERSONS ARE HIGHLY SENSITIVE TO CRITICISM OR
FEELINGS OF INADEQUACY.

NUMEROUS INTERNAL CONFLICTS APPEAR ALONG WITH FEELINGS
OF UNREALITY, STRANGE ATTITUDE, FALSE BELIEFS, ODD
OR CONFUSED THINKING, AND BIZARRE CONDUCT.
REPRESSIVE AND HYSTEROID DEFENSES ARE ATTEMPTING TO
ALLAY ANXIETY. INSTINCTUAL DRIVES ARE ALSO REPRE-
SENTED SYMBOLICALLY BY CONVERSION AND SOMATIZATION.
HYPOCHONDRIACAL PREOCCUPATION MAY BE PART OF A
DELUSIONAL SYSTEM.

SPECIAL CONSIDERATIONS

THERE IS EVIDENCE SUGGESTING A PARANOID TREND.
THERE IS BLOCKING OF DEEP OR POSITIVE EMOTIONAL
RESPONSE, HOSTILE REACTION TO REJECTION AND UN-
RESOLVED RESENTMENT TOWARD STRINGENT AUTHORITY
SURROGATES AND STRONG URGES TO ACT-OUT MAY RESULT
IN UNPREDICATABLE BEHAVIOR.
INVESTIGATE SUICIDAL OR SELF-DESTRUCTIVE THOUGHTS
OR PLANS.

A CONFIGURAL SEARCH FOR POSITIVE TRAITS AND STRENGTHS
SHOW CORRELATIONS FOR DESCRIBING THE SUBJECT AS
CONSCIENTIOUS, COMPLIANT, SENSITIVE, PERCEPTIVE,
PEACEABLE, METHODICAL, AND IMAGINATIVE.

PATTERN SEARCH FOR NEGATIVE TRAITS OR CHARACTERIS-
TICS UNDER STRESS SUGGESTS THE SUBJECT MAY BE
OPINIONATED, AUTOCRATIC, QUARRELSOME, SARCASTIC,
AND AGGRESSIVE.

FREQUENTLY DIAGNOSED--PATTERN RESEMBLANCE TO IDENTIFIED
CLINICAL CASES . . . SCHIZOID REACTION.

CRITICAL ITEMS. CHECK WITH SUBJECT FOR POSSIBLE MARKING
ERRORS.

INVESTIGATE SIGNIFICANCE OF RESPONSE

```
20. MY SEX LIFE IS SATISFACTORY ................... FALSE
27. EVIL SPIRITS POSSESS ME AT TIMES ............. TRUE
33. I HAVE HAD VERY PECULIAR AND STRANGE
    EXPERIENCES .................................. TRUE
44. MUCH OF THE TIME MY HEAD SEEMS TO HURT
    ALL OVER .................................... TRUE
48. WHEN I AM WITH PEOPLE I AM BOTHERED BY
    HEARING VERY QUEER THINGS ................... TRUE
66. I SEE THINGS OR ANIMALS OR PEOPLE AROUND
    ME THAT OTHERS DO NOT SEE ................... TRUE
114. OFTEN I FEEL AS IF THERE WERE A TIGHT
    BAND ABOUT MY HEAD .......................... TRUE
146. I HAVE THE WANDERLUST AND AM NEVER HAPPY
    UNLESS I AM ROAMING OR TRAVELING ABOUT ....... TRUE
156. I HAVE HAD PERIODS IN WHICH I CARRIED ON
    ACTIVITIES WITHOUT KNOWING LATER WHAT
    I HAD BEEN DOING ............................ TRUE
168. THERE IS SOMETHING WRONG WITH MY MIND ........ TRUE
179. I AM WORRIED ABOUT SEX MATTERS .............. TRUE
182. I AM AFRAID OF LOSING MY MIND ............... TRUE
184. I COMMONLY HEAR VOICES WITHOUT KNOWING
    WHERE THEY COME FROM ........................ TRUE
202. I BELIEVE I AM A CONDEMNED PERSON ........... TRUE
251. I HAVE HAD BLANK SPELLS IN WHICH MY
    ACTIVITIES WERE INTERRUPTED AND I DID NOT
    KNOW WHAT WAS GOING ON AROUND ME ............. TRUE
310. MY SEX LIFE IS SATISFACTORY ................. FALSE
323. I HAVE HAD VERY PECULIAR AND STRANGE
    EXPERIENCES ................................. TRUE
345. I OFTEN FEEL AS IF THINGS WERE NOT REAL ...... TRUE
349. I HAVE STRANGE AND PECULIAR THOUGHTS ......... TRUE
354. I AM AFRAID OF USING A KNIFE OR ANYTHING
    VERY SHARP OR POINTED ....................... TRUE
```

SALIENT CLINICAL FEATURES

PROFILE TYPE--HIGH RANGING PROFILE.

HISTORY, SYMPTOM REVIEW, OR OBSERVATION MAY REVEAL THE
FOLLOWING:

```
OVERT ANXIETY
 OVERT ANXIETY APPEARS MODERATE.
 AGITATED, TENSE, AND RESTLESS.
 SUBJECT ADMITS THE FOLLOWING:
  MARKED NERVOUSNESS OR TENSION.
  MARKED AUTONOMIC CONCOMITANTS.
DREAMS
 FREQUENT.
 RECURRENT.
EMOTIONAL CONTROL
 RIGID, COMPULSIVE DEFENSES.  DIFFICULT TO ADAPT
 NEW BEHAVIOR PATTERNS.
 NEUROTIC DEFENSES ARE ATTEMPTING TO CONTROL MORE
 DISABLING DYNAMICS.  LOSS OF CONTROL APPEARS
 THREATENING.
FAMILY OR MARITAL PROBLEMS
 STRONGLY INDICATED.
```

HOSTILITY
 HOSTILITY TENDS TO BE EXPRESSED DIRECTLY AND PERHAPS
 INTENSELY AT TIMES.
 THERE IS ADMISSION OF COMBATIVE OR ASSAULTIVE
 TENDENCIES WHICH MAY BE THREATENING.
 SOME COMBATIVE FEELINGS ARE ADMITTED.
HYPERACTIVITY
 CONSIDERABLY AGITATED OR RESTLESS.
 MOOD SWINGS.
 EUPHORIC EPISODES.
 DYSPHORIC EPISODES.
INTROPUNITIVE
 MARKEDLY INTROPUNITIVE AND SELF-DEROGATORY.
 THERE IS ADMISSION OF SOME FEELINGS OF GUILT, REGRET,
 OR UNWORTHINESS.
 INVESTIGATE SUICIDAL THOUGHTS OR TENDENCIES. SEE
 CRITICAL ITEM SECTION FOR SPECIFIC ITEMS.
SEXUAL DISTURBANCE
 THE RESPONSES SUGGEST FURTHER INQUIRY. SEE CRITICAL
 ITEM SECTION FOR SPECIFIC ITEMS.
 THE SUBJECT ADMITS BEING BOTHERED BY THOUGHTS OF SEX.
SOMATIC EXPRESSION
 SOMATIC CONCERN APPEARS MARKED.
 SUBJECT ADMITS THE FOLLOWING:
  HEADACHE.
  NECKACHE.
  PARAESTHESIA.
  PERCORDIAL DISTRESS.
  SLEEP DISTURBANCE.
  VASOMOTOR INSTABILITY.
DEFENSIVE MECHANISMS
 INTELLECTUALIZATION.
 OBSESSIVE-COMPULSIVE.
 PROJECTION.

                    STANDARD AND SPECIAL SCORES

THE SCORES PRINTED ON THIS PAGE ARE PRIMARILY USED FOR
RESEARCH. ALTHOUGH THE PRINTED REPORT INTERPRETS THEIR
NUMEROUS AND COMPLEX COMBINATIONS, THE CLINICIAN MAY
WISH TO STUDY THE NATURE OF EACH SCORE. FOR THIS
PURPOSE REFER TO THE MMPI-ICA REFERENCE GUIDE. THE
SCORES ARE LISTED IN RAW-SCORE FORM UNLESS SPECIFIED AS
T-SCORES.

INDEX OR SCALE   SCORE   NORM

AI ANXIETY INDEX 84 50
IR INTERNALIZATION RATIO .... 1.05 .... 1.00
A-R ANXIETY-REPRESSION RATIO
 A FACTOR--T SCORE .... 76 .... 45 TO 54
 R FACTOR--T SCORE .... 47 .... 45 TO 54
ES EGO STRENGTH--T SCORE .... 27 .... 60 OR MORE
TR CONTRADICTORY RESPONSE ...... 01 .... 3 OR LESS
F-K DISSIMULATION INDEX .... 17 .... -12 TO +8
DS DISSIMULATION SCALE .... 36 .... 35 OR LESS
MP POSITIVE MALINGERING .... 10 .... 19 OR LESS
CN CONTROL .... 30 .... 22 TO 30
ED EGO DEFENSIVENESS .... 25 .... 45 TO 65
FNF CRITIAL ITEMS .... 18 .... 3 OR LESS

```
AT   MANIFEST ANXIETY ............. 33 ........ 14 OR LESS
LB   LOW BACK .................... 13 ........ 10 OR LESS
RG   RIGIDITY DEFENSE ............. 07 ........ 3 TO 6
DY   MANIFEST DEPENDENCY .......... 32 ........ 19 OR LESS
DO   SOCIAL DOMINANCE ............. 14 ........ 19 OR MORE


RELATIVE ELEVATION OF CLINICAL SCALES . . . SEE GRAPH

HS-1 MARKED    D-2 MARKED     HY-3 MODERATE   PD-4 MARKED
MF-5 NORMAL    PA-6 MODERATE  PT-7 MODERATE   SC-8 MARKED
               MA-9 MODERATE  SI-0 MILD


OBVIOUS-SUBTLE RESPONSES OF CLINICAL SCALES . . . T-SCORES

     DO-106     HYO-102     PDO-94     PAO-89     MAO-80
     DS-41      HYS- 46     PDS-67     PAS-56     MAS-70


NOTE--NORMAL T-SCORE RANGE FOR OBVIOUS AND SUBTLE SCALES
IS USUALLY CONSIDERED BETWEEN 40 AND 60.  SCORES ABOVE
OR BELOW THIS RANGE INCREASE PROBABILITY OF ABNORMAL
TRAITS FOR THE SCALE IN QUESTION.

CAUTION--THIS REPORT IS STRICTLY CONFIDENTIAL.  IT IS
A DIAGNOSTIC AID AND SHOULD NOT BE SHOWN TO THE PATIENT.


R    3    0   21    4   25   33   33   33   21   17   34   43   27   38

RK   3    0   21    4   27   33   33   35   21   17   38   47   28   38

T   42   36   92   35   90   88   80   88   51   77   80   96   78   64

     Q    L    F    K  HS-1 D-2 HY-3 PD-4 MF-5 PA-6 PT-7 SC-8 MA-9 SI-0
```

[This last page of the report also includes a profile display of the usual clinical and validity scales.]

The emotional disturbance index at the beginning of the report is a unique feature of the ICA program (Dishman, Birds, & Dunlop, 1969). This is a single composite score derived as a weighted combination of many MMPI scales that has been found to discriminate between groups of normal and disturbed individuals. Also included is the associated probability that a person with a certain score would manifest low, moderate, or marked emotional disturbance.

In summary, then, both the Roche and ICA programs are directed to the user in the field. The Roche service is restricted to qualified psychiatrists, psychologists, and neurologists. The report it presents is designed to be as straightforward and useful as possible and is couched in relatively simple language. The ICA service, on the other hand, is directed to the family physician as well as the professional. Its report is much more extensive and technical; it presents results of a number of special scale scores and provides a teaching manual. In some ways the Roche report would appear to be more readily useful to the unsophisticated professional, such as a family physician, and the ICA more useful to the professionals.

For several years Finney (1967) has been working on a different aspect of automation, in which the MMPI and the California Psychological Inventory (CPI) constitute the raw data. Finney's interest has been in developing computer programming to such an extent that the narrative summary produced by the computer would be indistinguishable from that which might have been written by an expert. At the same time, Finney has made his problem more challenging by scoring the MMPI-CPI input on a total of 119 different scales, including 45 of which Finney himself has developed. The basic narrative data is developed from a pool of 952 descriptive statements, eight for each of the 119 scales. The statement chosen for each scale depends on the score for that scale.

Not only is there the problem of devising rules by which the computer can so order the statements as to create a logical flow, but there is the problem of providing appropriate transitional sentences and inserting such conjunctions as *but* and *and*. With the use of 119 scales, many of them overlapping the interpretive space, Finney has had more than usual problems with redundancy and, more seriously, with outright contradictions within the narrative summary. His approach to the elimination of contradiction has been to rewrite the statements attached to the scales contributing to the contradiction. For example, if a subject obtains both a high and a low score on scales which measure hostility, a closer examination may reveal that one scale reflects suppressed hostility whereas the other reflects expressed hostility. Such a redefinition of the scales dictates a rewriting of the descriptive statements attached to them so as to reflect the subtle differences. When the narrative summary is again written, the contradictory statements regarding hostility are now gone, and the report states that the subject is highly hostile but that this hostility is suppressed rather than expressed. Until the method has been used with a new sample of MMPI records, however, there is no way of determining if the scales have indeed been more carefully and accurately defined. It could be that, for some of the scales, the subtle distinctions which they appear to make are evanescent. Further work is planned to study this question. Finney has made a great deal of progress in his primary goal of producing a highly readable narrative report.

The MMPI is not the only objective test that has been automated. Eber (1964) has reported on the Sixteen Personality Factor Questionnaire (16 PF); Helm (1965) has programs for evaluating several inventories; and of course, Finney has worked with the California Psychological Inventory. It seems likely that as the present MMPI systems become better established and more widely known, psychologists will turn their attention to other tests as well.

PROJECTIVE TESTING

In addition to the considerable amount of progress already accomplished in the automation of objective tests such as the MMPI, there have also been some significant beginnings in the projective area. In some respects, this effort has been a greater challenge to the ingenuity of the psychologist because the very nature of these tests involves a free verbal response. Attempts to preserve the richness and diversity of response creates problems for the programmer, but probably even more critical are the problems introduced by the nature of language itself. The solution to the difficulties of dealing with thematic material has generally involved the development of some form of computer dictionary.

Inkblot Tests

There are several possible approaches to complete or partial automation of the two most common inkblot tests. As has been suggested, presentation of the stimulus cards could easily be incorporated as part of TAPAC if the multiple-choice form of the Rorschach is acceptable; or the cards could be presented by any similar device that would present the stimuli in some timed sequence, but provide for a free response. Automation of the inquiry itself could be accomplished by some variation of the method to be described in a later section on subject-computer interaction.

Work already reported has concentrated on three different facets of the total process. Moseley and Gorham have been concerned with computer scoring of the Holtzman Inkblot Technique (HIT); Piotrowski has developed a system for the interpretation of Rorschach scores; and Thomas has reported a storage and retrieval system which allows access to a large amount of Rorschach normative data.

Moseley's approach to computer scoring of the HIT is ingeniously simple in concept but subject to all the difficulties involved in language analysis. The method has been described in a series of publications by Gorham and others, culminating in a monograph containing considerable normative material (Gorham, Moseley, & Holtzman, 1968). The task was made somewhat easier because the HIT, in contrast to the Rorschach, demands a single response to each of the 45 stimulus cards. Moseley further simplified the programming task by restricting the subject's response to each blot to a maximum of six words. After accumulating an empirical list of words used by a large number of subjects in describing the inkblots, those words used at least twice were assembled in a dictionary and assigned scoring weights for each of 17 HIT scoring variables: Location, Rejection, Form Definiteness, Color, Shading, Movement, Integration, Human, Animal, Anatomy, Sex, Abstract, Anxiety, Hostility, Barrier, Penetration, and Popular. Other HIT variables were dropped because experience had shown they rarely occurred (Space, Balance), because they presented special problems in programming (Form Appropriateness, Pathognomic Verbalization), or because they were lost in the method of group administration to which they were committed (Reaction Time).

The success of the method depends upon the adequacy of the scoring key. Initial weights were assigned to each word by consensus of three investigators familiar with inkblot data, and later adjusted by comparison of computer scores and those obtained by expert hand scoring. As would be expected, the scoring key underwent a number of revisions in an attempt to approximate conventional hand scoring. Computer scoring was also improved by incorporating subroutines for pattern scoring of some variables that are interdependent, as well as by other statistical techniques. A reasonable degree of equivalence of the two methods of scoring was demonstrated in a series of reliability studies.

In a sense, the computer program which Piotrowski (1964) developed begins where Moseley's ends. His goal was to interpret inkblot data rather than to score it. He describes his program as consisting of "about 450 test components (parameters or variables) and nearly 600 rules in which the test components appear in varying combinations and proportions [page 1]." The input variables and the rules that govern their interpretation are derived from his own theory of the Rorschach. The output of his program consists of descriptive statements about the subject such as "Displays less than average emotional interest in others for a person of his intellectual level," "Uses strength defensively," and "Very little zeal. Practically no diligence." However, the program will also make diagnostic statements such as "Schizophrenic," "Obsessive-compulsive," or "Possibility of schizophrenia should be investigated."

The only test of the validity of the computer interpretation that was available for inclusion in his first report was a study of diagnostic agreement between machine and clinician on responses of 100 schizophrenics, neurotics, and some organic cerebral cases. There was 86 percent agreement between the computer diagnoses made from the earliest inkblot test records available for these patients and the clinical diagnoses made after neuropsychiatric follow-up.

Thomas, Ross, and Freed (1965) have used a program called KWIC (Key Word in Context) to index Rorschach responses for easy retrieval. Each key word in the response is listed alphabetically. A 60-character segment of the text associated with the key word and an index code indicating the card, area, position, and content of the response are available for recall, as well as other information such as word counts and biographical data on the subjects. The program is useful for studying the various types of content for different populations, the uniqueness of responses, the range of responses to certain blot areas, and other similar problems. The value of the program consists primarily in the flexibility in which information of different types can be extracted from a large file of data that would be difficult to deal with using conventional methods.

Sentence Completion

Veldman, Menaker, and Peck (1969) have developed a scoring system for sentence completion data using an approach similar to that of Moseley in scoring inkblot data. They have worked with a One Word Sentence Completion (OWSC), which was especially developed for automation and designed to obtain information relevant to the adjustment of college students. The problems encountered in developing their dictionary and scoring system are especially clearcut.

A 90-item OWSC, designed to sample more than twenty areas, such as motivation and attitudes, was administered to 1,000 female sophomore students in the College of Education at the University of Texas. The initial dictionary and scoring system was derived from the 90,000 responses (including blanks) obtained. The first step was to obtain a listing, by frequency of occurrence, of all responses to each of the 90 items individually. Counting the same word given to more than one item as a different response, there were a total of 16,829 words obtained from the 90-item scale. To keep the dictionary of responses to a reasonable length, only those words used by at least two different subjects for any one item were included. This restriction reduced the number of words to 7,142. There were, therefore, 9,687 unique responses, or about 10.5 percent of the total of 90,000. Attempts to deal with the problem of unique responses have occupied a good deal of effort in the later work of these investigators, although the problem was bypassed in this initial effort to generate a scoring system.

A list of 25 variables was derived to which the responses to the individual items could be assigned: e.g., positive vs. negative general self-perception; optimistic, cheerful vs. sad, depressed; independent, self-reliant vs. dependent, immature. The responses themselves could be rated as positive, negative, or neutral. Furthermore, an item could be considered as a "primary" or "secondary" item. For example, a response to an item such as, "My mother is ———" would be a primary response for scoring on the variable "attitude towards mother" whereas an item such as, "When I am in trouble, I go to ———" might elicit the response "mother" and would therefore be a secondary item which could be scored on the above variable only when the response happened to be "mother." It can readily be seen that the scoring of some variables might include several items—or only one. Unique responses were assigned a neutral weighting, although it was recognized that much valuable information might be lost in this way.

The dictionary and scoring system was applied to a separate sample of 79 female students, and the results obtained by the computer were compared with those obtained by two independent raters who were provided with a manual outlining the scoring method. Encouragingly enough, it was found that the results obtained by the computer correlated as well with the results obtained by the raters as the raters correlated with each other.

From this beginning, further work has been undertaken which has resulted in a more sophisticated approach. There have been three major changes. The 90-item form of the OWSC was reduced to 36 items, apparently by eliminating the empirically least useful items. The second major change was a quite successful effort to reduce the amount of data lost because of the response being unique, and finally, a new scoring system was introduced.

Veldman has distinguished four kinds of word equivalency. Besides reducing the number of responses through equating identical responses, the responses could also be reduced through syntactical equivalency. For example, the root word LOV could include all such words as love, loves, loved, loving, lovable, lover. Once the root word had been located, reference could then be made to a list of prefixes and suffixes for determination of the direction of the meaning. Finally, semantic equivalency (synonyms such as love-adore) and pragmatic equivalency (love-happy) further reduced the number of unique responses. Pragmatic equivalency raises new problems of agreement, however.

Using the 36-item OWSC and a new normative sample of 2,321 subjects yielded a total of 83,556 responses, of which 1,352 (1.6 percent) were blanks. Of the 82,204 words to be classified, 13,743 different response words were obtained using the procedure as outlined for ordering the words by frequency in the initial study. Of these words, 7,971 were unique responses (58 percent of the word pool or 9.5 percent of the gross total). This result was similar to that found in the initial study, but when the list had been further reduced by syntactical analysis, a total of 1,726 roots were retained which accounted for all but 2,397 (2.9 percent) of the original 83,556 responses. The number of unique responses was, therefore, effectively reduced by this approach. The 1,726 roots were collapsed into roughly 450 synonym groups.

Each synonym group was assigned an "affective weight" on a three-point scale of negative, neutral, positive. The affective weight constitutes the item score. The response itself is further classified into six general thematic categories:
   (1) Physical (body, quantity, nature, animals)
   (2) Roles (people, occupations, and institutions)
   (3) Emotional (affective states and attitudes)
   (4) Social (interpersonal behaviors)
   (5) Cognitive (ability, perception, academic)
   (6) Performance (success, ambition, control)
The items themselves are divided into four sets:
   (1) Self Description
   (2) Future Orientation and Goals
   (3) Stressors and Reactions
   (4) Social Attitudes and Interaction
The scoring structure therefore involves three dimensions: the three affect levels, the six response theme categories, and the four item-subset categories. Twenty-six scores were derived from these three aspects of scoring. The first six reflect characteristics of the individual protocol, such as number of blanks, number of populars (defined as given by more than 10 percent of the normative sample), and number of proper names given. The next four variables simply summarize the affect scoring in terms of number of negative, neutral, positive, and composite average, and the following four give the average affect level response to each of the four item-subsets. The last twelve variables describe the frequency and average affect level of each of the six thematic variables.

Veldman and associates have obtained over ten thousand protocols of various forms of the OWSC from high school and college students in Texas. In addition, about eight hundred Spanish language protocols have been obtained in Mexico, Venezuela, and Chile. Validating studies are underway, and some interesting results such as sex differences and score intercorrelations have already been reported. Efforts are also underway to achieve a more flexible scoring system capable of providing information in other specific areas.

The Thematic Apperception Test

Moseley's system of scoring the HIT was limited to six-word responses to each blot, and Veldman used a single-word sentence completion. More extensive content analysis of a wide variety of thematic materials has been accomplished through the use of the "General Inquirer" method, which was developed at the Harvard Laboratory of Social Studies (Stone, Dunphy, Smith, & Ogilvie, 1967). It consists of two basic parts: the dictionary or thesaurus of words, word roots, phrases, and combinations of words, which are grouped into categories called "tags"; and a set of computer programs containing the rules for carrying out a content analysis. For each application, it is necessary first to collect samples of verbal data of the type to be analyzed (TAT stories, suicide notes, autobiographical data) and to construct a dictionary by classifying the words and phrases into predetermined and theoretically relevant categories. For new material, the computer program assigns category labels (tags) to each word listed in the dictionary and summarizes the thematic material in a number of ways, e.g., frequency counts of tag occurrences.

Successful use of the General Inquirer with any sort of text depends upon acquiring an adequate sample of words for the dictionary and making an astute selection of appropriate tags. Application of this method to the TAT has been simplified by the existence of several scoring systems for n-Achievement, n-Affiliation, and n-Power, plus several collections of TAT stories scored by experts using such systems.

Smith (1968) has reviewed the application of the General Inquirer to the scoring of the three needs above. Three dictionaries were constructed to replicate the hand-scoring systems for the needs. Each of the dictionaries contained about twenty tags, with each tag containing from 5 to 150 words and phrases. The rules developed for the content analysis depend, with few exceptions, on the occurrence of two or more tags attributable to the need within the same sentence. The categories, of course, are those used in hand-scoring TAT stories, e.g., anticipation of successful attainment of a goal (GA+); anticipation of frustration or failure (GA−); activity instrumental toward attaining the goal (I+) or towards failure (I−); the blocking (B) of goal activity, either by external forces (BW) or personal deficiencies (BP); or the assistance or sympathy of someone in attaining the goal (Nup).

A set of published TAT stories was used in the development of the dictionary and content analysis program. After a number of adjustments of the dictionary and analysis program, several sets of TAT stories were scored on each of the three needs, and the results were compared with the scoring of the experts. Correlations between the computer scoring and the expert scoring ranged from .73 to .82 for several sets of TAT stories on the n-Achievement scoring program, .61 to .84 for n-Affiliation, and .41 to .73 for n-Power. In general, then, the success of this method parallels the relative agreement among experts on the definition of these needs and their scoring, and can be verified by referring to reliability studies on the hand scoring of these needs.

As has been discussed by others in the field, Smith points out that the degree of generalizability of any such dictionary and content analysis program to either novel pictures or to different subject populations is a prime restriction on the growth of automation of scoring systems for the TAT or for similar free verbalization material. Expert agreement in scoring TAT stories decreases with the use of novel pictures. Apparently, the computer is even more dramatically affected. Furthermore, since the computer is bound by the extent and the grouping of its dictionary of tags, the widely different vocabularies or vocabulary usages appearing in different population groups can be expected to exert an even more profound adverse effect on the use of computer program analysis.

THE INTERVIEW

In nearly every assessment situation, the psychologist is likely to want the kind of information traditionally obtained in a clinical interview. More and more, however, psychiatric histories are being obtained by having the patient complete a standard history form or, if a patient is interviewed, the responses are likely to be recorded on a form that can be read by a computer and made part of the data file. Programs have been written which translate the digital information stored in the computer to narrative reports that can be easily read and included in a clinical folder (Laska, Weinstein, Logemann, Bank, & Breuer, 1967). The primary criticism of these reports is that they tend to be somewhat stereotyped, but otherwise they seem to be acceptable.

A much more difficult task is to simulate an interview by computer which approximates an interaction between the subject and the machine. There have been a few promising and provocative attempts, but it does not seem likely for some time that these efforts will have the same impact on psychological assessment as the other applications that have been described.

Starkweather (1965) has developed a computer language called COMPUTEST for individual testing, instruction, and interviewing. The programming provides for presentation of information, interrogation of a subject, and variable reply to the subject's response using typewriter input-output. When this is used as a testing device, instructions and questions are typed by the computer, and the subject types his response. If the answer is clearly right or wrong, the computer may acknowledge before moving on to the next question, but if the reply is ambiguous or only partially correct, the computer may ask for clarification. Programming can also simulate either party in a clinical interview. When taking the part of the interviewer, the program scans replies to initial questions for diagnostic clues and sequentially modifies the balance of the interview by asking questions in these areas. It can also be programmed to simulate the part of a patient, responding to a variety of questions asked by the human interviewer. Starkweather points out that the program is not sufficiently developed for use with patients but sees the method as a valuable training exercise for the student. COMPUTEST is similar to another system called COURSEWRITER (Simmons, 1965), developed by International Business Machines (1964).

Cogswell and Estavan (1965; Cogswell, 1966) have worked on the problem of course planning with students. Initially the program evaluated the information in a student's scholastic folder prior to the interview and identified certain areas to be covered with the student. In the interview, the computer would present certain information to the student, e.g., the previous semester's courses and grades, and ask the student what courses gave him trouble. The computer would then ask the student to elaborate on any difficulties to which he admitted. The program also provided for the development of a tentative course plan for three years of high school. These plans were found to be generally less complete and satisfactory than those obtained by human counselors.

Weizenbaum (1966) has reported a program which he calls ELIZA that simulates a Rogerian-type nondirective interview. The program searches for key words in the input and responds with phrases stored in its memory. If key words are not found, the computer may respond with some innocuous neutral statement, return to a previous topic, or request additional input. Some phrases in the subject's input may also be stored for later use if appropriate. Colby, Watt, and Gilbert (1966) have extended this approach by increasing the number of key words and otherwise elaborated on the method.

Veldman (1967) has added a computer interview or inquiry to his sentence completion, using the COURSEWRITER program. The subject is instructed, as before, to respond with a single word to each of the incomplete sentences. If the response given by the subject is included in the dictionary of responses to that item, the computer asks a follow-up question to which the subject is instructed that he may reply in phrases or sentences if he so desires. For example, if the subject replies "hard, difficult, or challenging" to the sentence "My work has been ———," the follow-up question would be, "What do you find hardest about it?" If instead the response is "satisfactory," "successful," or "good," the computer would inquire, "To what do you attribute your success?" After the subject has replied to this question, the computer goes on to the next incomplete sentence.

If the subject replies with a response which is not in the dictionary, the computer will try to obtain an alternate response. The program is built so as to make three attempts to obtain a recognized response, using three approaches: "Can you think of a synonym for that?"; "Can you think of a similar word?"; "Give a different one-word response." These questions appear appropriately according to the subject's response, which can be the requested one word, a yes, or a no. If no recognized response can be obtained, the computer goes on to the next sentence.

The dictionary of responses to each item consists of all responses used by more than 1 percent of the normative sample described earlier. This approach to the OWSC was tried out on six male and six female students at the University of Texas, who first completed the paper-and-pencil version of the OWSC and were then provided with printed instructions for responding to the computer version. The results of this pilot study were then submitted to an experienced clinical psychologist, who compared the paper-and-pencil versions with the machine print-out. It was his opinion that an average of two-and-a-half responses per protocol would have been badly misinterpreted in any assessment of the paper-and-pencil version, and that valuable additional information was elicited by the machine for more than one-third of the sentences.

There are some obvious limitations on what can be achieved by all of these methods as they all rely on a typewriter terminal for input-output. To work effectively there must be direct access to the computer, but this is a hardware problem that can be expected to be overcome as methods of computer time-sharing and on-line capability become more advanced and available. More important, the program depends upon the ability and willingness of the subject to type his response to computer inquiry. Some subjects—the psychotic, illiterate, or retarded, to mention a few—are not likely to be suitable candidates. Despite these limitations, important applications of these highly creative efforts will certainly be found.

DATA BANKS AND CLINICAL DECISIONS

The methods that have been discussed facilitate the gathering of assessment data, provide for scoring, simulate the psychologist's interpretive function, and may even produce a narrative report for inclusion in the subject's folder. Usually, however, the psychologist is also called upon to predict various outcomes, formulate a diagnosis or other classification, or make certain administrative or therapeutic recommendations. To arrive at these kinds of decisions requires an integration of data from all phases of the assessment process. The most salient information relative to a particular decision must be identified and given proper weight in the decision process, or modified by consideration of other available information. Characteristically, the psychologist achieves these decisions intuitively and would be hard pressed to state explicitly what decision rules he uses. Probably, his rules change from one occasion to the next, and it seems very unlikely that any two psychologists use precisely the same rules. Because he is an imperfect data processor, he is likely to overlook important information at times or to make mistakes in the logic of his inferences. He can only consider a limited amount of data at any time. Finally, the validation of his operating rules is haphazard. Increasing the precision of the valid rules or rejecting those that are invalid is not likely to take place systematically. The assessment process can be considerably strengthened by the use of the computer as an aid in the decision process.

The mathematics and logic to accomplish this function of the psychologist have long been available, but the clinician of the past has not had the resources to approach his task in this manner. Even if the research efforts of others had generated equations for prediction or classification, the clinician would have been understandably reluctant to perform the required calculations. There was no easy way for his own experience to be entered into data banks for the creation of new decision rules or the refinement of old ones.

The increasing availability of computers should lead to some dramatic changes in this part of the assessment procedure. Methods for storage and retrieval of patient data have been developed (Schenthal, Sweeney, Nettleton, & Yoder, 1963), statistical programs of the required kind are readily available (Dixon, 1968), and some examples of the type of equations that will eventually be used for reaching clinical decisions have been reported (Klett & Moseley, 1965).

DISCUSSION

Traditionally, psychological assessment in a clinical setting has been a two-person interaction involving the use of certain standardized test materials or procedures and relying heavily on the skill, experience, and intuition of the clinical psychologist in eliciting pertinent information, observing a wide range of verbal and non-verbal behavior, modifying testing activity in response to the behavior of the subject, and integrating all of his observations into some sort of summary statement. Usually this is an extremely time-consuming process, and some aspects such as scoring of test material can be exceedingly tedious. It is not surprising that group-administered screening batteries using primarily paper-and-pencil tests that can be scored by clerks, and more recently by machine, have come into vogue. Except for individual testing of the occasional subject who is identified by the screening battery or specifically referred, the time of the psychologist is used in other pursuits. It is also quite natural that the impact of automation on other segments of our society should extend to the activity of the clinical psychologist.

Just as there was resistance by some clinical psychologists to group testing and paper-and-pencil tests, there are certain to be objections to automation of assessment activities if justified solely in terms of the reduction of tedium and time expenditure. Automation in industry has increased productivity at reduced cost and introduced greater precision in the execution of repetitive operations. Some of the more menial and dehumanizing tasks have been relegated to the machine. Still, there are some who claim that industrial automation is a mixed blessing and cite the loss of the skilled craftsman as one of its consequences. Since automation of psychological assessment might also have disadvantages, the important questions appear to be: What aspects of psychological assessment are most appropriately automated? and, In what ways can automation extend the limits of the psychologist or improve his methods? It would seem that it is by such criteria that the value of automation of psychological assessment should be judged.

For a substantial number of Americans, the modern trend towards automation in many areas of our daily life is viewed with distaste and even alarm. There was considerable resistance to digital dialing for long distance telephone calls, and the increased use of account numbers, billing numbers, or social security numbers has led some individuals to complain of loss of identity of the individual. Further, the prospect of huge personal data banks containing information from the cradle to the grave, to be used for nationwide establishment of credit or verification of income tax returns, or even for crime control or national security, raises grave issues. These are important issues for psychological assessment as well. Automated assessment is certainly a more impersonal experience than the traditional individual testing situation. For some subjects there may be loss of dignity or decreased feelings of self-worth involved in being so impersonally processed. From the clinician's point of view, there is the possibility that he is depriving himself of much important information by isolating himself from the subject. Obviously, some judgment has to be exercized depending upon the nature of the testing situation. The other question of confidentiality of information in large centralized data banks also has to be faced, but this is an ethical-legal issue that can be considered independently of the question of automation.

Another insidious aspect of automation to be guarded against is the tendency to concentrate on hardware and software rather than on the assessment procedures themselves. There is a halo-effect or aura of authenticity that surrounds any use of computers, and the user is in danger of being so awed or impressed by these aspects that he uncritically accepts the procedures themselves. The most sophisticated computer programming of some aspect (presentation, scoring, or interpretation) of an invalid or unreliable psychological test will not necessarily make it better, but somehow it may seem better if it is described as a "computer-based" method. Some may even neglect the often slow process of improving validity or reliability of a test in favor of the more challenging and fascinating process of adapting it for the computer. In all fairness to those engaged in this work, it must be said that the demands of computer programming have probably forced psychologists to think harder and in more concrete terms about what they were doing in an assessment procedure than they ever had before. The programming process has great heuristic value. Every rule must be objective and unambiguous, and the logic must be flawless. For example, as part of his effort to improve the sentence completion procedure, Veldman even enlisted the aid of a professional logician. There is no question that psychological assessment procedures will profit from this kind of attention as well as from the research made possible by the convenience of the automated methods.

SUMMARY

The purpose of this chapter has been to survey a range of isolated efforts to automate different segments of the psychological assessment process and to suggest by implication that these segments may, in the future, be integrated into a flexible, comprehensive, totally automated system. Some of the advantages, limitations, and arguments against these developments have been discussed. It seems certain that regardless of how today's psychologist views these beginnings, further development will continue along these lines. Already a considerable literature has developed and can be expected to grow. In addition to the key references selected to identify the individual efforts reviewed here, the reader is referred to the December 1968 issue of *Comprehensive Psychiatry*, the special supplement to the January 1969 issue of the *American Journal of Psychiatry*, the Spring 1968 issue of the *Journal of School Psychology*, and the March 1969 issue of the *American Psychologist*. All of these issues contain collections of papers on some phase of automation applied to problems of interest to psychologists. There have also been papers in this area presented at nearly every American Psychological Association meeting in recent years as well as symposia in 1964, 1968, and 1969.

In many people's minds, "automated" is a term virtually synonymous with "computerized," and in fact, nearly every application reviewed here does involve a computer as part of the system. The chapter might appropriately have been titled "Computer Applications in Psychology," but Veldman and Jennings have already used that title in a chapter for Wolman's *Handbook of Psychology* (in press). This reference will be a useful one for those interested in computer applications in the behavioral sciences, some of which are related to psychological assessment but are beyond the scope of the present chapter, e.g., computer simulation of personality. This reference also provides an introduction to computing and computing terminology that many will find valuable. In the present treatment no attempt was made to deal with the issues of computer hardware or the intricacies of programming, but rather the emphasis was on some of the more promising applications of this technology to the assessment process.

CHAPTER III

The assessment of places

Kenneth H. Craik

At long last, the assessment of environments is beginning to gain its proper share of scientific investigation. That the systematic description of environments has previously received disproportionately less attention than the description of persons has been consistently noted in critical reviews of psychological assessment (Anastasi, 1966; Sundberg & Tyler, 1962; McReynolds, 1968). Psychologists who have steadfastly studied environmental issues (e.g., Roger Barker, 1963, 1965, 1968; George Stern, 1962a, 1963, 1970) have earned deserved recognition and esteem. Architects, urban designers, transportation planners, natural resources managers, and other environmental decision makers who markedly influence the form and nature of the everyday environments of human behavior have increasingly sought behavioral guidelines for their applied endeavors (Burton & Kates, 1964; Taylor, Bailey, & Branch, 1967). Yet it is the current widespread sense of crisis concerning the quality of contemporary environments which is generating the sustained momentum for concerted research in the new field of environmental psychology (Craik, 1966b, 1970b; Proshansky, Ittleson, & Rivlin, 1970; Wohlwill, 1970).

This discussion will focus upon the systematic assessment of physical environmental settings, perhaps more simply termed *places.* Instances of places include streets, courtyards, meadows, and rooms. Places are similar to persons in being complex, multidimensional entities. Indeed, adaptation of concepts and techniques from the field of personality assessment offers a tremendous methodological resource for the assessment of environments.

In studies of the interplay between human behavior and the everyday physical environment, comprehensive, standard techniques must be available for assessing systematic variation in environments as well as in behaviors. Research on environmental description and evaluation seeks to identify not only what environments are preferred or not preferred by various observers, but also what descriptive responses of the observers mediate their preferences and, most pertinently, what specific environmental characteristics are associated with both descriptive and evaluative appraisals. Programmatic investigations of environmental impact, in which environmental characteristics serve as independent variables and behavioral responses as dependent variables, will require progress in understanding the dimensionality and taxonomy of environments. In order to study the behavioral antecedents of environmental transformations, in which the beliefs and values of participants, behavioral assumptions embedded in design decisions, etc., serve as independent variables, researchers must first have the capacity to differentiate systematically among the specific environmental outcomes of these complex socio-technological processes. Thus on many fronts, as these examples illustrate, the development of standard techniques for the comprehensive assessment of environmental settings is a prerequisite to the advance of environmental psychological research.

Five modes of analysis in the comprehensive assessment of places can be distinguished. Attention can be directed to: (1) the physical-spatial properties of places, (2) the organization of entities and components within places, (3) the traits of places, (4) the behavioral attributes of places, and (5) the institutional attributes of places. Each mode of analysis warrants brief review.

ASSESSING THE PHYSICAL AND SPATIAL
PROPERTIES OF PLACES

Geographers and natural resources managers have led the way in assessing environments along physical and spatial dimensions. In a coordinated research program, behavioral geographers have studied the ways in which inhabitants of flood plains and drought regions interpret natural hazards. Flood plains can be assessed along geomorphic dimensions (e.g., width of flood plain, slope of adjacent land) and hydrologic characteristics of floods (e.g., frequency, height of flood level, flood stage to flood peak interval, seasonality) (Kates, 1963; Burton & Kates, 1964; Burton, Kates, & White, 1968). Saarinen (1966) selected drought regions which varied in aridity-humidity on the basis of the Thornthwaite Moisture Index and employed the Palmer Drought Index to assess severity of drought, an idiographic concept referring to downward departures from the average rate of precipitation for each region. Frequency of floods and of droughts were related to interpretations of these natural hazards made by residents of sites which varied along these environmental dimensions.

A multidimensional physical assessment of campsites in the Adirondack State Park in New York employed the 40 descriptive variables listed in Table 1 (Shafer & Thompson, 1968). Ten randomly selected campsites were drawn from each of 24 campgrounds and systematically assessed. Factor analysis yielded nine descriptive dimensions (e.g., remoteness, white birch predominance, campground-lake expansiveness) that were employed in efforts to predict frequency of use over a five-year period. Thus, the design combined multivariate physical assessment with use of a behavioral criterion measure.

ASSESSING THE ORGANIZATION OF MATERIAL
ARTIFACTS IN PLACES

Places can be characterized by the assortment of material artifacts that are found within them. In a recent study, Laumann and House (1970) initiated

Table 1
Multidimensional Assessment of Adirondack Campgrounds

Criterion variables
1. Average annual total visitor days.
2. Average annual total visitor days per site; that is, criterion variable 1 divided by the total number of individual sites at that park.

Predictor variables
1. Area (acres) of the lake on which the campground is located.
2. Area (acres) of other lakes accessible by motorboat.
3. Area (acres) of other lakes accessible only by canoe portage.
4. Miles of shoreline for the lake on which the campground is located.
5. Miles of shoreline for other adjacent lakes accessible by motorboat.
6. Miles of shoreline for water accessible only by canoe portage.
7. Total acres of islands accessible by motorboat.
8. Distance (miles) to next nearest public camping area.
9. Total acres of islands accessible only by canoe portage.
10. Total population of permanent residents within a 25-mile radius of the park, divided by 1,000. Within the Adirondack recreation complex most public and private tourist attractions surround centers of population. Thus, this variable is an index of the density of tourist facilities.
11. Number of islands accessible by motorboat.
12. Number of islands accessible only by canoe portage.
13. Total number of designated campsites. The average number of campsites per year was used if a campground changed size over the five-year period.
14. Total number of campsites available for overflow use. Five-year averages also were used here if changes occurred over the five-year period.
15. Distance (0.1 mile) from campground office to nearest food supply.
16. Land area (square feet) of developed swimming beach.
17. Land area (square feet) of developed swimming beach covered with grass.
18. Land area (square feet) of developed swimming beach covered with sand.
19. Water area (square feet) of developed swimming beach.
20. Water area with sandy bottom (square feet) at developed swimming beach.
21. Average distance (feet) between campsites.
22. Average distance (feet) from campsites to nearest outlet for drinking water.
23. Average distance (feet) from campsites to nearest sanitation unit.
24. Average distance (feet) from campsites to nearest flush toilet.
25. Average distance (feet) from campsites to the edge of the nearest lake.
26. Average distance (feet) from campsites to the developed swimming beach.
27. Average slope (percentage) of the campground—measured with an Abney hand level.
28. Percentage of campsites with a lake front that occupants may use for swimming.
29. Percentage of campsites from which the lake is visible.
30. Percentage of campsites where highway traffic sound can be heard.
31. Average overstory density (percentage) of all tree species—measured with a densiometer (Strickler, 1959).
32. Average density (percentage) of tree boles—measured with a pantallometer (Nord & Magill, 1963).
33. Average density (percentage) of understory vegetation—measured with a pantallometer.
34. Average diameter breast height (0.1 inch) of dominant trees at campsite.
35. Average height (feet) of dominant trees at a campsite—measured with an Abney hand level.
36. Average number of white birch stems per campsite.
37. Average number of softwood stems per campsite.
38. Average number of hardwood stems per campsite.
39. Estimated average percentage of grass cover per campsite.
40. Distance (miles) to Whiteface Mountain—the high point of tourist attractions in the Adirondacks. Because of its uniqueness we felt Whiteface Mountain had a greater drawing power than the general type of tourist attractions included in predictor variable 10 (population density).

Source: Shafer and Thompson, 1969. Reprinted by permission of *Forest Science* and the authors.
Note.—Ten randomly selected campsites per campground were used to obtain average distances, percentages, vegetation densities, and slope measurements. An individual campsite was a circular plot 50 feet in diameter with the fireplace as its center.

study of the ecological distribution of objects and designed components in the urban environment. Social surveyors conducting home interviews with a sample of 897 native-born white adult males residing in the greater metropolitan area of Detroit employed the Living Room Check List (LRCL) to assess the contents and characteristics of their living rooms. While the respondent was completing a 10-minute questionnaire, the interviewer recorded the presence or absence of the 53 attributes contained on the LRCL (Table 2). Smallest space analysis (Lingoes, 1965a, 1965b, 1966a, 1966b) transformed the information in the 53x53 matrix of phi correlations for the living-room attributes into the graphic representation presented in Figure 1. The first axis appears to order living-room components along a social-class dimension, and indeed it is highly related to measures of income, occupational status, and educational attainment. Translucent curtains, bulky furniture, and a television set in the living room are related to lower social status, but plain curtains, large potted plants, and picture windows are associated with higher social status.

The emergence of this dimension is not surprising. Anthropologists have treated an inventory of household goods as an appropriate basis for analyzing standards and styles of living (LeBar, 1964; Lewis, 1969). Within our society, several well-known indices of social status have been based in part at least upon reports of household possessions, including observational recording procedures such as Chapin's Living Room Scale and Social Status Scale (1935), and self-report devices such as Gough's Home Index (Gough, 1949), the American Home Scale (Kerr & Remmers, 1942), and the Sims Score Cards (Sims, 1927).

A second dimension, identifying a traditional-versus-modern stylistic variation in decor, represents the methodological advance in Lauman and House's research. Traditional and French furniture, still-life paintings, candle holders, and piano are located at the "traditional" pole of the dimension while modern furniture, bare space, curtains with geometric designs, and solid carpets appear at the "modern" pole. Traditional decor in the living room is moderately related to high social status for its inhabitant; upward mobility tends to characterize the inhabitants of modern living rooms (Laumann & House, 1970).

As these investigators suggest, expansion of the Living Room Check List promises to afford more comprehensive assessments and perhaps a more differentiated taxonomy of living-room style. The living-room taxonomy can be employed in establishing systematically varied environmental settings for studying the impact of environment upon behavior (e.g., mood, social interaction) or for investigating direct responsiveness to places (e.g., descriptions, inferences, preferences). In addition, the extent to which the living room can be considered an indirect display of its inhabitants' social status, taste, or expressive behavior warrants further examination in its own right. Finally, the checklist inventory can be readily adapted to the assessment of other environmental settings of varying types and scales and is thus destined to become a basic method in environmental psychology.

Table 2
Living Room Check List

Floor
—— highly polished wood
—— unpolished wood
—— covered
—— other

Carpet
—— wall-to-wall carpeting
—— standard size rug
—— scatter rugs
—— other

Main carpet design
—— no carpet
—— solid color/tweed
—— floral
—— braided
—— oriental
—— other

Curtains and drapes
Translucent
—— lacy, ruffled
—— straight-hanging
—— other

Opaque
—— floral pattern
—— geometric design
—— light, neutral, solid color
—— dark, solid color
—— other

—— number of complete window
     casements

Furniture
—— modern functional
—— bulky old-fashioned, stuffed
—— traditional American
—— mixture, no consistent style
—— other

Walls
—— neutral or pastel paper or paint
—— bright color paper or paint
—— ornate paper
—— other

Books
—— many in shelves
—— a few around
—— none

General space factor (density, not size)
—— rather bare
—— below average
—— average
—— above average
—— densely furnished

General condition of living room and furniture
—— excellent
—— above average
—— average
—— below average
—— poor

General neatness
—— exceptionally orderly, nothing
     out of place
—— average neatness and order
—— things in disarray

Miscellaneous items
—— fireplace
—— piano
—— television
—— hi-fi set
—— candle holder of any type
—— religious objects
—— Bible
—— vases
—— enlarged photographs
—— knickknacks
—— artificial flowers
—— large potted plants on floor
—— antimacassars (doilies covering
     furniture)
—— encyclopedia set
—— clock (type:)
—— picture window over four feet wide
—— wall mirror(s)
—— outdoor nature scene painting
—— painting: people as subject
—— abstract painting
—— religious painting
—— still life painting
—— cut flowers
—— small potted plants on tables or sills
—— trophies, plaques, or similar objects

Note.—Reprinted by permission of E. O. Laumann.

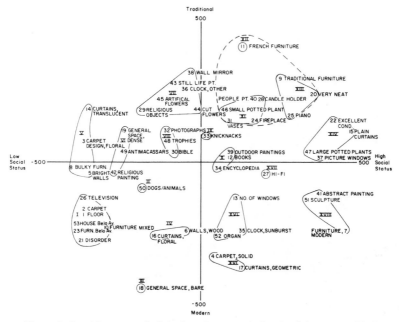

Figure 1. Graphic portrayal of the best 2-space solution for living-room objects.
Source: Laumann and House, 1970. Reprinted by permission of *Sociology and Social Research* and the authors.

ASSESSING THE TRAITS OF PLACES

The human observer is an essential and effective instrument in contemporary personality assessment. In living-in assessment programs professional assessment teams observe small groups of persons as they engage in situational tests, e.g., role improvisations, charades, and leaderless group discussions, as well as in interviews, projective tests, and informal social encounters during meals. Subsequently, the staff observers independently record their impressions of each person by means of character sketches, adjective checklists, trait ratings, and Q-sort descriptions (MacKinnon, 1967).

Observational assessment of persons provides a model for the sophisticated use of the human observer in environmental assessment. Tables 3 and 4 suggest that the basic components of observational assessment are much the same in these two contexts: the selection of observers, the media for presenting the persons or places to be assessed, the nature of response formats for recording observers' impressions, and criteria for evaluating the sensitivity and accuracy of the observational assessments rendered (Craik, 1968).

Person Perception versus Personality Assessment

It is immediately apparent that the structure of two fields of research is embodied in Table 3. In person-perception research the goal is an understanding of factors which influence the impressions formed by the observers.

Table 3
A Process Model for the Assessment of Persons

Observers	Presentation of Assessees	Nature and Format of Judgments (Attributions)	Validational Criteria

special competence groups:
  psychologists
  psychiatrists
  social workers
  admission officers
  personnel officers
  leaders
  diplomats
  clergymen
  counselors
 	
groups formed on the basis of relevant personality measures
 	
everyman, general public, etc.
	face-to-face interactions:
	  interviews
	  projective testing
	  situational tests
	  living-in assessments
	  field observations, etc.
	
	photographs:
	  faces
	  jumpings, etc.
	
	motion pictures, videotapes, unobserved or hidden observation of live behavior:
	  situational tests
	  interviews
	  projective test performance
	  cocktail parties, etc.
	
	personal productions:
	  handwriting specimens
	  drawings
	  poetry, stories, etc.
	
	test materials or scores:
	  CPI profile
	  projective test protocols, etc.
	
	stereotypic-demographic information:
	  age, sex, occupation, etc.
		free descriptions:
		  character sketches
		  biographies, etc.
		
		adjective checklists
		
		Q-sort descriptions
		
		ratings
		
		personological metaphors
		
		personological analogies
		
		empathic interpretations:
		  impersonations
		
		predictions of behavior:
		  test performance
		  social outcomes, etc.
			measures of objective characteristics of the person
			
			expert judgments
			
			self-reports
			
			any judgment-form in column 3 based upon more extensive acquaintance with the person (including peer ratings, etc.)

Thus, study of the interplay of elements in columns 1, 2, and 3 focuses upon the process of person perception (Tagiuri, 1969), while research on the relations between elements in columns 1 and 4 is directed to the accuracy of observers' interpersonal perceptions (Cline, 1964). In contrast, personality assessment seeks that combination of observers, media of presentation, and response formats which yields the most comprehensive and valid descriptions of persons. Although the search for the optimal combination has not been as thorough and precise as it might be, the use of multiple observers, multiple media, and multiple response formats has become standard practice in personality assessment (MacKinnon, 1967).

Environmental Perception versus Environmental Assessment

In the observational assessment of places, a comparable distinction can be drawn between environmental perception and environmental assessment. Study of the various ways observers comprehend environmental settings and of the influence exerted by media of presentation and response formats upon their descriptions is being carried out through research in environmental perception. In particular, the investigation of differences between environmental decision makers, e.g., architects, planners, decorators, resource managers, and their clients is receiving urgent attention (Craik, 1970c). In contrast, environmental assessment uses observers to obtain systematic descriptions of places. Thus, in both cases research on person perception and environmental perception analyzes the functioning of the human observational instrument while personality and environmental assessment employ that instrument to establish the attributes of persons and places.

Trait Attributions versus Trait Designations

The first and second components of Table 3 recognize that the social background and personality of observers and the context of observation may play a role in the outcome of observational assessments. Yet here again, another important distinction must be delineated between person perception and personality assessment. If one observer describes a person as generous, this act is a trait attribution, which can be studied within the paradigm of person perception research. However, if many observers consistently agree over many years of observation in describing a person as generous, these stable and consensual attributions form the basis for a trait designation, which can be considered a property of the person described. While the antecedents and consequences of trait designations and the ways in which they do or do not mirror the individual's behavior may be examined separately as worthwhile issues, the trait designations themselves are intrinsically significant and basic data for personality assessment, for which observational assessments are the unique source. Trait designations hold an analogous and equally fundamental place within environmental assessment.

Selection of Observers for Assessment Projects

Research on person perception and environmental perception investigates persons who differ in their comprehension of persons and environments in

Table 4
A Process Model for the Assessment of Places

Judges	Presentation of Environmental Displays	Nature and Format of Judgments	Validational Criteria
special competence groups:	direct experience:	free descriptions	measures of objective characteristics of places
architects	looking at		
planners	walking around and through	adjective checklists	
real estate appraisers	driving around and through		expert judges
stage designers	aerial views	activity and mood checklists	
space managers, i.e.,	living in		any judgment form in column 3 based upon more extensive acquaintance with the place
hotel, theatre, resort managers, building superintendents, etc.	simulative exploration	Q-sort descriptions	
	cinematic and photographic studies	ratings	
special user-client groups:	sketches and drawings	thematic potential analysis	
elderly persons		inferential judgments	
migrant workers	models and replicas		
college students		associative norms	
groups formed on the basis of relevant personality measures	tachistoscopic views	symbolic equivalents	
	laser beam presentations	multi-sensory equivalents	
everyman, general public, etc.	imaginal presentation	empathic interpretations: role enactments role improvisations	
		temporal characteristics: apparent duration sequential effects	
		motational descriptions	

Note.—Adapted from Craik (1968) by permission of the *Journal of the American Institute of Planners.*

ways which might shed light upon the basic processes involved. For the purpose of personality and environmental assessment, however, the task is to include any class of observers who may have access to or be sensitive to diverse attributes of the persons or places being assessed (column 1, Tables 3 and 4). If neighbors and work colleagues differ in certain aspects of their descriptions of a person but agree among themselves, then both descriptions must be considered in the final assessment. Similarly, if tourists and residents of a neighborhood disagree in certain facets of their descriptions of it but agree among themselves, then each portrait must find a place in the final assessment. Of course, observers viewing persons and places from various vantage points may display broad consensus in their descriptions, thus reducing the seeming complexity of the situation. However, the extent to which consensus does exist must be determined empirically.

Media of Presentation

A remarkable variety of media for presenting assessees to observers is available for personality assessments (column 2, Table 3). Although observational assessments based upon lifelong acquaintance have seldom received the systematic attention they warrant, they are often rendered by observers in the natural context of social life, for example, in the form of eulogies. But typically, observational assessments are made upon the basis of more fleeting glimpses of the persons described. Face-to-face interactions range from single modes (e.g., the interview, the projective test, situational tests) to more extensive media (e.g., living-in assessments which combine these modes with informal social encounters, and field observations under varied conditions). Observational media which do not entail face-to-face interaction between observers and assessees include simulations of such interactions by photographs, motion pictures, or videotapes, and one-way observations of live performances, as in clinical observations of family therapy sessions via one-way windows. Surrogate presentations of persons by means of their expressive productions (e.g., handwriting specimens, drawings, etc.) can also serve as a basis for observational assessments. Finally, personality inventory profiles offer a highly technical presentation of assessees, while demographic information offers factual but seemingly minimal presentations.

A wide variety of media for presenting places is also available (column 2, Table 4), varying in duration, immediacy, and completeness. In addition to direct presentations (e.g., looking at and walking or driving around and through them, aerial views, and long-term residence), the field of environmental design is currently experimenting with many traditional and new techniques of simulation ranging from drawings, sketches, models, and replicas to photographic, cinematic, and televisual presentations. A promising technique is the televisual exploration of models, in which a tiny camera is moved through the model while viewers observe the resulting image on a large television screen. Tachistoscopic presentations can be employed in studies of attention deployment while laser beam projections yielding three-dimensional images may be available for environmental assessments in the near future. Imaginal presentations of familiar places, in which only the name is presented, have been employed in studies of observers' enduring conceptions of them.

Nature and Format of Judgments

Once the persons or places have been presented, by whatever media, the observers must record their impressions. Free descriptions, such as character sketches of persons or analogous portraits of places, allow each observer to employ his favored terminology and concepts in evoking the attributes of the person or place being described. However, personality assessors have long acknowledged the limitations of character sketches for affording systematic and comparable descriptions, and consequently have developed supplementary techniques, such as adjective checklists (Gough & Heilbrun, 1965), trait-rating scales (Guilford, 1954), and Q-sort decks (Block, 1961), which provide comparable and quantifiable descriptions.

Predictions of the future behavior of persons hold an ambiguous place in observational assessment. On the one hand, research on individual differences in interpersonal accuracy employs observers' predictions of future behaviors and outcomes as an index of differential skill of the observers. While appropriate for identifying relatively good and poor judges of others, research on clinical predictions indicates that, on the average, predictions made by observers do not compete well with actuarial predictions. If the intent is to predict future behavior, actuarial combinations of observational impressions recorded by means of ratings, adjective checklists, and Q-sort descriptions are likely to be more effective than predictions made by observers themselves. If the intent is strictly descriptive, however, and if the predictions are consensual, observers' predictions sometimes still serve a meaningful role regardless of whether they are accurate. Thus, if all observers predict that a person will be successful as a physician or will commit suicide before he is 35, the predictions in their own right reflect significant descriptive information about the individual, whether ultimately valid or invalid.

Standard techniques for the observational assessment of places remain at an earlier stage of development than similar techniques for observing persons.

Adjectival Procedures

The Landscape Adjective Check List (LACL). As an initial step in developing this checklist, a diverse collection of 50 landscape scenes was presented by photographic slides to a class of 35 university students, who were requested to list 10 adjectives descriptive of each scene. They were asked to describe each scene independently of their descriptions of previous scenes, repeating adjectives whenever appropriate. An inclusive list of every adjective and descriptive phrase employed at least once by an observer in describing any scene was compiled. Although not every observer listed 10 terms per scene, a total of 1,196 distinct descriptive terms resulted. Examination of the frequency of usage of the terms revealed that a selection of all adjectives employed six or more times yielded a reasonably comprehensive array of adjectives. By eliminating certain redundant terms and adding terms which would contribute to the breadth of coverage, the current version of the

Landscape Adjective Check List (LACL) was constructed (Table 5; Craik, 1969a, 1970a).

The advantages of the Landscape Adjective Check List are its use of everyday language, the brevity and ease with which judgments are made and recorded, its breadth of coverage, and its wide and flexible applications and forms of analysis. The LACL can be used to gather descriptive impressions of landscapes quickly from large samples of observers in the field. Descriptions of the same landscapes by systematically selected samples of observers can be statistically compared. Descriptions of ideal and imaginary as well as actual landscapes can be recorded. The effects of changes in landscape conditions and features can be analyzed through observers' LACL descriptions. The influence of weather conditions and variations in natural lighting upon impressions of landscape can be investigated. Although further developmental effort employing a wider range of landscape scenes, observers, and media of presentation will contribute to its improvement, the LACL can be counted upon to yield useful findings in its present form.

Adjectival description of the built environment. Several efforts have been made to establish a comprehensive set of adjectives for assessing places within the built environment (Vielhauer, 1965; Craik, 1966a; Lowenthal, 1967; Canter, 1968, 1969; Collins, 1968, 1969; Hershberger, 1968; Winkel, Malek, & Thiel, 1968; Sanoff, 1969; Sonnenfeld, 1969). The items of the Environmental Description Scale (EDS) (Vielhauer, 1965; Kasmar & Vidulich, 1968) emerged from a systematic search of the literature of aesthetics, architecture, and interior decoration, and from university students who were asked to envision two rooms they liked and two they disliked and to list adjectives describing them. The initial larger list yielded by these procedures was reduced to the current set of 66 bipolar pairs on the basis of ratings of their appropriateness for describing six interior places presented to observers via photographic slides. The EDS afforded differential descriptions of three large university rooms (i.e., a dining hall, a library reading room, a lecture hall) and adequate test-retest reliability when the lecture hall was described twice at a three-week interval by a panel of 100 observers. Subsequent studies (Kasmar, Griffin, & Mauritzen, 1968; Moos, Harris, & Schonborn, 1969) have also demonstrated the capacity of descriptions made with the EDS to differentiate signficantly among rooms (i.e., different rooms are assessed differently).

In a comparable undertaking (Collins, 1968, 1969), a set of 142 bipolar pairs of adjectives were selected, guided by factor analysis, from an earlier listing which focused upon the physical and mood-atmospheric attributes of street scenes (Craik, 1966a) and from a large pool of 1,417 descriptive terms nominated by 102 university students who were asked to envision a room they knew well and to provide as many terms descriptive of it as possible. Collins' rating scales have been employed in a descriptive assessment of three libraries in Salt Lake City (Collins, 1969).

Adjectival descriptions of the built environment can be recorded on bipolar rating scales or on checklists. A worthy but laborious method, the use of rating scales requires a more precise understanding of the basic dimensions of environmental description in order to establish a reasonably brief, standard

Table 5
The Landscape Adjective Check List

___ active	___ eroded	___ majestic	___ serene
___ adventurous	___ eternal	___ marshy	___ shadowy
___ alive	___ exciting	___ massive	___ shady
___ arid	___ expansive	___ meadowy	___ shallow
___ autumnal	___ extensive	___ misty	___ sharp
___ awesome	___ falling	___ moist	___ sliding
___ bare	___ farmed	___ monotonous	___ slippery
___ barren	___ fast	___ motionless	___ sloping
___ beautiful	___ flat	___ mountainous	___ slow
___ big	___ flowery	___ moving	___ smooth
___ black	___ flowing	___ muddy	___ snowy
___ bleak	___ foamy	___ mysterious	___ soft
___ blue	___ forceful	___ narrow	___ spacious
___ boring	___ forested	___ natural	___ sparse
___ bright	___ free	___ nice	___ spring-like
___ brisk	___ fresh	___ nocturnal	___ stark
___ broad	___ friendly	___ noisy	___ steep
___ brown	___ gentle	___ old	___ still
___ burned	___ glacial	___ open	___ stoney
___ bushy	___ gloomy	___ orange	___ stormy
___ calm	___ golden	___ pastoral	___ straight
___ challenging	___ good	___ peaceful	___ strange
___ changing	___ grassy	___ placid	___ summery
___ clean	___ gray	___ plain	___ sunny
___ clear	___ green	___ pleasant	___ swampy
___ cloudy	___ happy	___ pointed	___ tall
___ cold	___ hard	___ powerful	___ thick
___ colorful	___ harsh	___ pretty	___ threatening
___ colorless	___ hazy	___ pure	___ towering
___ comfortable	___ high	___ quiet	___ tranquil
___ content	___ hilly	___ rainy	___ tree-studded
___ contrasting	___ hot	___ rapid	___ ugly
___ cool	___ humid	___ reaching	___ unfriendly
___ crashing	___ icy	___ reflecting	___ uninspiring
___ crisp	___ imposing	___ refreshing	___ uninteresting
___ cut	___ inspiring	___ relaxing	___ uninviting
___ dangerous	___ invigorating	___ remote	___ unusual
___ dark	___ inviting	___ restful	___ vast
___ dead	___ isolated	___ rich	___ vegetated
___ deep	___ jagged	___ rocky	___ violent
___ dense	___ large	___ rolling	___ warm
___ depressing	___ lazy	___ rough	___ watery
___ deserted	___ leafy	___ round	___ weedy
___ desolate	___ lifeless	___ rugged	___ wet
___ destroyed	___ light	___ running	___ white
___ dirty	___ living	___ rushing	___ wide
___ distant	___ lonely	___ rusty	___ wild
___ drab	___ lovely	___ sad	___ windy
___ dry	___ low	___ sandy	___ wintry
___ dull	___ lumpy	___ secluded	___ wooded
___ empty	___ lush	___ secure	___ yellow

Source: Craik, 1969a; 1970a.

procedure. Through factor analysis of bipolar ratings, researchers have sought to identify a minimal set of basic dimensions that are invariant across observers and places described. Factor analyses of room descriptions rendered on the EDS have identified four dimensions: aesthetic appeal (e.g., stylish, appealing), physical organization (e.g., orderly, well-organized), size (e.g., large, free space), and temperature-ventilation (e.g., comfortable temperature, good ventilation), plus a fifth, lighting (e.g., soft lighting, diffuse lighting) which emerged from the descriptions of only one room (Vielhauer, 1965; Kasmar & Vidulich, 1968). In the description of six rooms of a psychiatric ward (dayroom, dining room, lecture room, bedroom, bathroom, and meeting room) by 64 patients and 34 staff using the EDS, Moos et al. (1969) replicated the same four environmental description factors and also found that the fifth factor (lighting) appeared less consistently. Notably less agreement can be discerned among factor-analytic studies employing varying sets of bipolar adjectives (Kasmar & Vidulich, 1968; Canter, 1969; Collins, 1969; Hershberger, 1968; Sanoff, 1969) or between factor analyses of descriptions rendered by professional designers and lay observers (Canter, 1969; Hershberger, 1968). However these discrepancies are eventually resolved by further research; several findings (e.g., Canter, 1969; Collins, 1969) suggest that the basic dimensions of environmental meaning are not likely to be equivalent to the dimensions of semantic meaning identified by Osgood and his associates (Osgood, Suci, & Tannenbaum, 1957).

Complementing rating scales in the standardized recording of systematic adjectival descriptions, the checklist method requires a comprehensive, minimally redundant array of terms drawn from everyday usage in the general culture and pertinent subcultures. Among the method's advantages are the scope gained by the diversity of attributes encompassed in a 300-item checklist and the flexibility of application afforded by its nontechnical format (Gough & Heilbrun, 1965). The bipolar pairs of adjectives emerging from the nine studies of adjectival description already referred to have arisen from analysis of the environmental literature, professional vocabularies, and the spontaneous descriptive terminology of laymen. They offer a solid basis for deriving an environmental adjective checklist which would be appropriate for standard use in a wide range of research and applied contexts.

Rating Procedures

Landscape Rating Scales and the Graphic Landscape Typology. The objective assessment of landscapes along a standard set of visual dimensions will make important contributions to environmental psychological research (Craik, 1969a,b, 1970a) and to innovative practices in natural resources management (Litton & Twiss, 1966; Litton, 1968). A set of Landscape Rating Scales has been devised which embodies the main elements of Litton's system of visual landscape dimensions (Table 6; Craik, 1970a). Landscape Rating 1 refers to observer position, i.e., "the location of the observer as he looks upon a visual objective [Litton, 1968, p. 5]." Landscape Ratings 2 and 3 deal with the distance dimension. The distance designations in Rating 2 were based upon Litton's boundaries for the foreground, middleground, and background zones

Table 6
Landscape Rating Scales

I. The observer is—
1. looking down upon the scene.
2. looking straight on at the scene.
3. looking up toward the scene.
II. Extent of view: the distance to the most remote elements in the scene is—
4. less than ¼ mile.
5. ¼ mile to 3 miles.
6. greater than 3 miles.
III. Indicate the presence of—
7. foreground (*encircle "7" if present*).
8. middleground (*encircle "8" if present*).
9. background (*encircle "9" if present*).
IV. Is the observer afforded a panoramic view?
10. Yes, a sweeping expanse, with the scene falling away from the observer.
11. Yes, a horizontal expanse, with the wide view straight on from the observer.
12. No.
V. The scene is lighted by—
13. side light, with the sun low to either side of the observer.
14. back light, with the sun low and shining toward the observer.
15. front light, with the sun low behind the observer.
16. direction of light indeterminate.
VI. The scene presents a sense of vertical enclosure which blocks off the line of vision—
(*Encircle all items that apply*)
17. in all directions and entirely surrounds the observer.
18. directly ahead of the observer.
19. on the left side.
20. on the right side.
21. Does not apply—no sense of vertical enclosure.
VII. Does the scene contain an isolated form, composed of a single element or a group of elements, seen in profile or silhouette against the sky or against a distant background?
22. Definitely present.
23. Somewhat present.
24. Definitely absent.
VIII. Does the scene contain a surface shape, seen as an outline embedded in the landscape itself?
25. Definitely present.
26. Somewhat present.
27. Definitely absent.
IX. Focal view: are there elements in the scene which direct the line of vision along a prescribed pathway?
28. Definitely present.
29. Somewhat present.
30. Definitely absent.
X. The clouds in the scene have the appearance of—
31. delicate, feathery, sweeping fibers.
32. dense, billowing, white mounds, sharply outlined.
33. low, grey, thick, diffuse masses.
34. Does not apply—no clouds in the scene.

Source: Craik, 1970a.

(Litton, 1968). In some combinations of landscape configuration and relative observer position, the sense of foreground, middleground, or background can be absent from a landscape scene. Rating 3 taps this variable while Landscape Rating 4 distinguishes two principal variations in a compositional aspect of landscape form. Landscape Rating 5 treats the direction of lighting upon the scene. Indexing the extent and kind of enclosure, Landscape Rating 6 is directed to the spatial definition of landscape scenes. Landscape Ratings 7 and 8 bear upon landscape forms which can become salient features, and Landscape Rating 9 relates to compositional attributes which suggest a focal landscape. Of the many ephemeral landscape features, e.g. fog, hoarfrost, reflected images, sunset coloration, Landscape Rating 10 considers variations in cloud formation.

In addition, review of several thousand color photographic slides of landscape scenes led to the development of the Graphic Landscape Typology (Figure 2). In its use observers are instructed to nominate each landscape scene for membership in the most suitable landscape type.

Because this system of landscape dimensions and types employs the human observer as its measuring instrument in conjunction with the standard verbal and graphic materials, the extent to which it yields reproducible data which are not dependent upon a particular individual for their collection has been carefully appraised (Craik, 1970a). Substantial agreement has been demonstrated within and across diverse panels of observers, drawn from faculty and graduate students in forestry and conservation and in landscape architecture, from U.S. Forest Service personnel, and from general university students. Based upon photographic slide presentations of varied landscape scenes, these appraisals of the inter-observer objectivity of the dimensions and typology encoded in these standard procedures encourage further expansion and refinement of the techniques within the context of direct field application.

Additional rating procedures. The assessment of specific content of landscape scenes is also receiving attention. Techniques for conducting detailed analyses of the proportion of sky, vegetation, water, etc., within immediate, intermediate, and distant areas of landscape scenes has been developed (Shafer, Hamilton, & Schmidt, 1969). In an extensive study of landscapes within the watersheds of the Upper East Branch of the Brandywine in Chester County, and the North Branch of Neshaminy Creek in Bucks County, Pennsylvania, efforts are underway to develop a broad taxonomy of landscape dimensions for use in assessments conducted via photographic presentations and in the field (Coughlin & Goldstein, 1970; Rabinowitz & Coughlin, 1970).

In an important extrapolation from laboratory investigations, Wohlwill (1968) has shown that the rated complexity of landscape scenes displays a positive linear relationship to the amount of visual exploratory behavior directed toward them but a curvilinear relationship to evaluative ratings of them, with scenes of intermediate complexity tending to be most preferred. A panel of five judges assessed the complexity of the landscape scenes by rating each for the amount of variation along five attributes: color, shape, direction of dominant lines, texture, and natural versus artificial (i.e., mixed scenes received higher complexity ratings). In Exeter, England, Johns (1969)

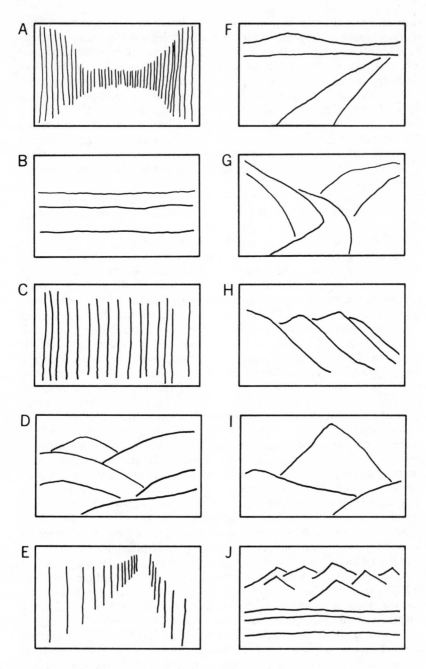

Figure 2. The Graphic Landscape Typology.
Source: Craik, 1970a.

has assessed the symmetry-asymmetry of landscaping in a sample of 96 of the simple, usually square or rectangular-shaped front gardens that are a standard feature of town houses there. Sketched ground plans of the gardens, including the most outstanding features only (e.g., trees, large bushes, prominent flower beds, ponds, garden-sculpture, etc.) were rated on the symmetry-asymmetry dimension. In the total sample, approximately half were asymmetrical (46 out of 96) but the percentage tended to be higher for detached houses (65 percent) than for attached houses (40 percent).

Unfortunately, the development of systematic rating scales for assessing attributes of the environment remains at an even less advanced stage for the urban environment than for landscapes. A notable study of Ciudad Guayana, an expanding industrial city in Venezuela, offers a guide to future research (Appleyard, 1969). A sample of 320 inhabitants were asked to identify the places they remembered best and to draw a map of the city. All buildings, establishments, and other landmarks which were noted or recalled by the sample were photographed and assessed along an array of building attributes. The sample of 188 buildings was rated on three classes of environmental characteristics by means of Form Intensity Scales (e.g., size, shape, presence of signs), Visibility Scales (e.g., extent of visibility, immediacy), and Significance Scales (e.g., use intensity, symbolism). These environmental dimensions were related to variations in the relative extent to which the structures were known to the region's inhabitants.

Other Promising Techniques

The development of techniques in environmental assessment need not be restricted to checklists and rating scales. Several novel possibilities remain frankly experimental or even untried (Table 4; Craik, 1968).

A modification of free descriptions, the procedure for establishing *environmental associative norms* requires observers to list as many free associations as possible, within standard time limits, for specific members of a class of environmental objects or components, such as lighting fixtures, door knobs, and carpets. Thus, for example, a sample of 50 entities drawn from the class *light fixtures* can be readily ordered along a continuum ranging from high to low associative value. By this procedure, places with systematically varied associative potential can be established by combining lighting fixtures, door knobs, carpets, etc., of known associative value.

As a complement to adjective checklists, *activity checklists* consist simply of a standard list of verbs useful for the comprehensive description of observed and potential activities in a place. In thematic potential analysis, brief stories by observers about what might happen in a place are analyzed by the methods developed in research on the Thematic Apperception Test.

Inferences as well as descriptive statements offer a basis for systematic environmental assessments. In addition to descriptive responses (e.g., "List five noteworthy features of the scene; identify as completely as you can the types of vegetation in the scene") and evaluative responses (e.g., "Suggest five ways in which this scene might be improved."), the Forest Landscape Response Booklet (Craik, 1969a) requires environmental inferences concerning

(1) the nature and origin of prominent features of the scene; (2) any human activities evident in the scene and their larger context; (3) the character of the surrounding countryside, e.g., within a five-mile radius; (4) the sorts of persons likely to be found in the location; (5) the kinds of wildlife likely to be found in the setting; (6) the consequences of certain specified hypothetical changes in the scenes; and (7) the likely appearance of the scene ten years hence. Analysis of the structured but open-ended protocols produced by such response booklets can provide the basis for the development of environmental *Q*-sort decks. The Gough Adjective Check List (Gough & Heilbrun, 1965) can be employed for more detailed study of inferences concerning the kinds of persons likely to be found in the places, while adaptations of the Guilford Consequences Test permits study of inferences about major environmental transformations, e.g., selecting a new highway route through an urban area (Craik, 1969c, 1970b). An environmental consequence can be appraised in terms of *spread,* the number of observers anticipating it; *range,* the number of valued features of the physical and social setting affected by it; and *magnitude,* its judged importance. The inferred consequences of proposed environmental transformations can also be compared to the actual consequences noted by observers during alterations and following completion of the project.

More exploratory efforts to record subtle impressions of places may include symbolic equivalents, in which observers record metaphors which express some aspect of their comprehension of a place, and multisensory equivalents, in which observers create a series of musical sequences, color images shown on a full-wall screen, and other visual, auditory, tactile, and olfactory projections which in some way represent their experience of a complex environmental setting.

Empathic interpretations of places can take the form of role enactments in which the observer is instructed to "be" the place and, being it, to describe himself; or it can take the form of role improvisations in which two persons are instructed to "be" different environmental settings (e.g., the Hudson River and the Mississippi River) and to improvise an interaction between themselves.

The temporal characteristics of places can be assessed in several ways. The apparent duration of a period of time spent in various places, or of journeys through different places at constant speeds, may differ to a reliable and stable degree. In addition, the accuracy of observers' recall of the sequence of elements in a journey (Carr & Schissler, 1969) may form the basis for assessing individual differences among places. Finally, systematic recordings of the observed, as opposed to recalled, sequence of elements in journeys through places can be recorded by means of notational systems which, akin to choreographic notational systems, permit trained observers to note the sequence of principal elements and features in a standard manner.

Experimentation in response formats is warranted not only in environmental assessment, but also in personality assessment. For example, recording of personological metaphors (e.g., animals, objects) and analogies (e.g., celebrities, literary characters) appropriate to each assessee in personality assessment is as feasible and potentially informative as the use of symbolic equivalents in environmental assessment.

ASSESSING THE BEHAVIORAL ATTRIBUTES OF PLACES

Although persons habitually present in a place (e.g., the regulars at an espresso cafe or neighborhood bar) can be considered as a special class of its entities and components, the behavioral capacities of the human organism warrant attention in their own right. Indeed, any stable activity patterns that tend to occur in a place contribute importantly to the overall character of that place.

Analysis of activity patterns can take several directions. The time allotted to various activities by individuals can be studied (Sorokin & Berger, 1939; Kranz, 1970). The spatial distribution of persons' ongoing activities can also be recorded, as in Chapin's studies of the locations of individuals' out-of-the-house activities such as socializing, relaxation, and recreation (Chapin, 1968; Chapin & Hightower, 1966; Chapin & Logan, 1969). However, environmental assessment aims to establish the behavioral properties of places and, focusing upon the place rather than the person, requires observation of the frequency of types of activities in places over time. The *behavioral density* of a place is indexed by the total frequency of all types of activities occurring within it during a standard period of observation. Put another way, a place's behavioral density is the likelihood that something is happening there at any given time. The range of different activities that occur in a place indicates the extent to which it possesses a *diffuse* or *focal* behavioral character. Finally, the relative frequency of specific kinds of activities occurring in a place identifies its activity profile, which can itself be either enduring or variable.

The taxonomic problem posed by the need to segment the ongoing stream of behavior is more difficult and complex than it may first appear to be. In his activity analysis of university students living in high-rise dormitories, Van der Ryn (1967) found it appropriate to differentiate among casual study, waiting-for-something-to-happen study, small-group study, and intense study out of the dormitory. In discussing a new methodological factor which promises to encourage and facilitate studies of activity patterns, Kranz (1970) has demonstrated the great utility of computer coding techniques in achieving detailed and refined classification of activities. Furthermore, through the use of factor and cluster analysis, empirically identified typologies of places can be generated to establish sets of places with relatively similar configurations of activities. These emergent typologies of places can be expected to bear some resemblance to behavior settings (Barker & Wright, 1955; Barker, 1968). Except for Barker's studies, the most frequent locale for research on the behavioral attributes of places has been the psychiatric ward (Ittelson, 1967; Srivastava & Good, 1968; Gump & James, 1970).

ASSESSING THE INSTITUTIONAL ATTRIBUTES OF PLACES

On April 6, 1970, while leading former President Lyndon B. Johnson on a tour of the newly refurbished press facilities in the White House, President Richard M. Nixon asserted that the briefing room looked much nicer than a Hilton hotel. "Hiltons are so sterile," said the President (New York *Times,*

April 7, 1970). This succinct presidential observation embodies the complex interrelationship between attributes of institutions and attributes of their physical environments. On the one hand, the physical environment of a specific hotel may evoke the trait attribution, "sterile." On the other hand, the possibility of generalizing to an entire chain of hotels suggests the existence of a management policy regarding physical design and planning that yields places which, although geographically dispersed, display a similar array of environmental traits. However, the issues thus raised concerning antecedent and concurrent institutional influences upon the form and use of the physical environment (Boutourline, 1967; Craik, 1970c) must be deemed beyond the scope of the present discussion.

The term *sterile* in such a descriptive assessment may encompass not only the physical elements of hotels but also their institutional climate or atmosphere (Lewin, Lippert, & White, 1939; Forehand & Gilmer, 1964; Tagiuri & Litwin, 1968), reflecting the organization's enduring norms, values, patterns of communication, expectations, rules, routines, and styles of personal relations. Considerable progress has been made in developing techniques for the systematic assessment of the institutional atmospheres of educational (Pace, 1968; Stern, 1970), psychiatric (Moos & Houts, 1968), neighborhood (Stern, 1970), and business and governmental (Tagiuri & Litwin, 1968) settings. For example, research by Stern (1970) on educational settings and by Moos and Houts (1968) on psychiatric wards has identified and assessed such dimensions of institutional atmosphere as Practicality, Change, Autonomy, Clarity, and Nurturance. Unlike other attributes of places, institutional characteristics also relate to a social system which may extend beyond the spatial-physical setting itself. Thus, an organization may move from one physical environment to another yet still retain its particular institutional character, or it may simultaneously occupy many scattered and varied physical settings but nonetheless achieve similar institutional atmospheres in each of them (Greiner, Leitch, & Barnes, 1968). In its own right, the institutional climate of a place must be considered an important level of analysis in comprehensive environmental assessments. In addition, the functional interplay between the physical attributes of places and their institutional climate, which has received little empirical study, is an obvious and significant topic on the agenda for environmental psychological research.

THE VALUE OF COMPREHENSIVE ENVIRONMENTAL ASSESSMENTS

The comprehensive assessment of places is clearly a complex, expensive, and in some respects curiously nonpsychological endeavor. At least five levels of analysis must be considered in assessing places, dealing with their physical-spatial properties, their organization of entities and components, their environmental traits, their behavioral attributes, and their institutional characteristics. While many useful procedures are already available for this purpose, considerable work remains to be done in developing an adequate standard technology for environmental assessments.

Without doubt, the most compelling justification for comprehensive environmental assessments is their appropriateness to the task of describing places systematically. As multidimensional entities, places, like persons, demand multivariate descriptive analysis (Craik, 1968, 1970b; Sells, 1968, 1969). In the long run, environmental psychology will be concerned only with those attributes of places which bear a functional relationship to human experience and behavior, i.e., which are present within a person's life space (Lewin, 1951; Barker, 1968). However, to avoid the circularity to which this orientation is prone, it is necessary to undertake the large task of systematically and empirically identifying such environment-behavior linkages. Research in environmental psychology is addressing itself to such issues as: How individuals differ in their interpretations of and dispositions toward various environmental settings? What aspects distinguish those environments that specific kinds of person do and do not prefer? What influence do environmental factors, taken as independent variables, have upon behavioral outcomes, taken as dependent variables? On every important issue, research in environmental psychology will be advanced by the use of comprehensive environmental assessments. On the basis of current concentrations of research effort (Craik, 1970b), it would appear that the classes of places holding the best chance of receiving comprehensive environmental assessments in the near future are psychiatric wards, residences, neighborhoods, and landscape settings.

In addition, important innovations may be achieved in the design and appraisal of the built and managed environment through the adaptation of techniques employed presently in personnel assessment and selection. In this instance, comprehensive descriptive assessments of samples of places drawn from a class of environmental settings (e.g., vest-pocket parks, housing projects, and psychiatric wards) will be related to extensive multidimensional analysis of criterion performances of each place in the sample. The development of systematic criterion variables will itself be a fruitful exploration of the specific behavioral and social meanings of the currently vague concept of environmental quality (Jarrett, 1966). The full application of the principles of selection to environmental design and management practice will require progress in a related area, the technology of simulation. If simulative techniques for presenting environmental settings can attain behavioral equivalence, i.e., if environmental trait assessments of simulated places match those based upon direct presentation, then the findings and guidelines accruing from the assessment and appraisal of built environmental settings can be applied, in new contexts and at the pre-construction stage, to selecting among alternate designs and plans for environmental settings (Craik, 1968, 1969a, 1969b, 1970c).

Although some facets of comprehensive environmental assessment are nonpsychological, such as the assessment of physical-spatial properties, they constitute essential prerequisites for basic and applied research in environmental psychology; they are unlikely to be undertaken by any other scientific or professional discipline, and they call for those forms of multivariate statistical analysis and design which have been pioneered by psychologists (e.g., Tryon, 1958a, 1958b, 1967).

Assessment of places will require the same degree of precision and care which psychologists readily devote to personological assessment. Environmental psychologists may initially experience difficulty in maintaining an equivalence in their standards for the two modes of assessment. For example, an observer requires about five minutes to describe a scene using the Landscape Adjective Check List (Craik, 1969a, 1970a). The present writer still discovers himself to be somewhat reluctant to make this allocation of research resources to the task of landscape description, although he considers altogether appropriate the five minutes which an observer requires to describe a person on the Gough Adjective Check List.

In the current period of environmental crisis, it may be tempting for psychological research to focus upon isolated and topical issues (e.g., pollution, conservation, population control) and to apply standard methods of attitude analysis and attitude change. If only this strategy is employed, however, an adequate understanding of the subtle and intricate ways in which persons respond to the everyday physical environment, influence it, and are influenced by it, will continue to elude us. Comprehensive environmental assessment is perhaps the most direct of several ongoing efforts (Craik, 1970b; Proshansky et al., 1970; Wohlwill, 1970) which grant full recognition to the significance of the everyday physical environment for human experience and behavior.

CHAPTER IV

Functional analysis
in the assessment of children

Sidney W. Bijou and Robert F. Peterson

This chapter is concerned with those assessment methodologies which have evolved from a functional analysis of behavior. While contrasting approaches to assessment will be found throughout this book, the reader may also wish to refer to a recent volume by Kelley (1969). His thorough but concise overview of the field suggests that assessment deals with the evaluation of human traits. A human trait is defined in Guilford's (1959) words as "any distinguishable, relatively enduring way in which one individual differs from another [p. 6]." Kelley indicates that psychologists work with a great variety of traits, including morphological traits (e.g., body types), physiological traits (e.g., differences in heart rates), aptitudes, skills, achievements, drives, interests, values, attitudes, temperaments, as well as with psychodiagnostic categories. He also points out that psychologists study traits (1) to learn how they are organized (e.g., Cattell's concept of crystalline and fluid forms of intelligence); (2) to delineate their determining conditions (e.g., sex, age, race); and (3) to solve practical problems that are found in counseling, therapy, and industrial management.

A few comments on Kelley's conception of assessment may help the reader to relate the psychometric approach to the functional approach presented here. First, Guilford's definition of a trait—the way in which one individual differs from another—is entirely compatible with a functional analysis of behavior. Second, the traits listed by Kelley, except for morphological and physiological traits, are all classes of behavior. To claim that a trait represents something else, like a hypothetical internal variable, is to give two names to the same class of behavior. For example, one might see one child striking another child. On the basis of this observation, he might conclude that the child doing the hitting is (1) aggressive and (2) has a "need" for aggression. Thus he characterizes the child as having both an aggressive trait and a need-for-aggression trait. Third, psychologists have used assessment procedures to predict the outcome of training or treatment, or to classify persons for statistical purposes. From a functional analysis point of view, the basic reason for

This analysis has generated in large measure from the research supported by the U.S. Office of Education, Division of Research, Bureau of Education for the Handicapped, Project No. 5-0961, Grant No. OEG32-23-6002.

assessing or diagnosing a person is to obtain information that can be used to plan a treatment program. (Throughout this chapter we shall use the term *treatment* to indicate a course of therapy, training, education, or rehabilitation.) Our focus, then, is the consideration of the kinds of data that help one develop and guide treatment programs.

Assessment as an aspect of the treatment of children may be viewed as consisting of four parts. The first involves an analysis of the difficulty that brings the youngster to the attention of some professional person. When the problem has been identified by the staff, they are in a position to determine whether they are equipped to deal with the problem. Assuming that the first phase of assessment leads to the decision to accept the child for treatment, the second part involves an evaluation of his behavioral repertoires. These two aspects of assessment have been termed *static* and *dynamic* (Ferster, 1965). The third part deals with evaluation of progress in the treatment program, and the fourth with assessment of behavior after the completion of treatment. The discussion of each of these four parts, in turn, will constitute the substance of this chapter.

INTAKE EVALUATION

Let us consider in detail the problems of assessing the nature of the disturbance which brings the youngster to the attention of a treatment agency. The presenting problem (designated as the "complaint factor" by Kanner, 1948) may be conceptualized as falling into one of three general categories. The first consists of *behavioral excesses*. This class usually includes the child who is labeled as a conduct problem or the youngster who is in continual conflict with his parents. It also includes the aggressive child, the hyperactive child, and those children who exhibit other behavioral problems which are often the basis for classifying them as predelinquent or delinquent.

The second category consists of problems relating to *behavioral deficits*. Here, we find the child who is not performing well in school; the very shy, withdrawn, or phobic youngster; the child who has few, if any, friends or does not know how to get along with his peers; and the youngster who does not or cannot talk. This category also includes children who are retarded in the development of skills.

The third group includes problems which involve behaviors under *inappropriate stimulus control*. The behavior displayed may be topographically satisfactory but occurs, from the point of view of society, in the wrong place or at the wrong time. Perhaps the largest number of childhood behavior problems falls into this group. Here we find the enuretic child who suffers from neither an excess nor a deficit of behavior; he simply makes a response at an inappropriate time and place. We also find in this group the child who is engaging in excessive self-stimulatory (sexual) behaviors. Most parents would not be overly concerned with this problem if their child did not display such behavior publicly. The problem, then, is not to reduce the frequent occurrence of behavior but to allow it to occur at a time and a place where it will not be observed. The weakening of such responses not only may be impossible, because of the powerful sensory feedback involved, but may, in fact, be undesirable. Problems of inappropriate stimulus control also include the child who does play with his peers but who does not know how to play in ways that maintain friendly peer relations. Certain cognitive and intellectual problems also belong here. Many children may have the academic behavior required in the classroom but are unable to display it when called upon by the teacher.

The reader can see that the classification of a child in these three categories raises the question: under what conditions does a psychologist place a particular label (phobic, retarded, hyperactive, schizophrenic, or even normal) on a particular child? In other words, what are the conditions controlling the behavior of the psychologist? Hence, assessment of the presenting problem may be viewed as an attempt to assess the conditions that have brought this child (through some adult, e.g., parent, teacher, judge) to the treatment agency. It may be that the child is behaving in a way that is highly aversive to the parents. Hence it would be of value to know the conditions that have made the problem serious enough to warrant bringing the child for treatment. It is possible, obviously, that the difficulty may lie not necessarily in the severity of the child's behavior, but simply in the effect this behavior has on the adults. Information or reassurance about the relative frequency (normality) of the occurrence of the problem among children is sometimes all that is needed to alleviate parental concern. Needless to say, the age of a child is a central variable in determining how a behavior will be labeled. A very young child with a certain behavior deficit might be considered normal; an older child, with the same deficit, grossly retarded.

Prior to a discussion with the child's parents, it may be helpful if the parents indicate areas of concern using a checklist of behavior problems (Peterson, 1961; Quay, 1966). Such a survey of complaints insures that they are questioned about a variety of problems (the therapist might otherwise overlook some difficulties), and at the same time helps the therapist to focus on main areas of concern.

While screening tests may help isolate the problem area, psychological tests in general provide only indirect information about the conditions which caused a child to be brought for treatment. Although one might test a child to survey his abilities and skills, such tests do not indicate behavioral contingencies that have actually caused his parents to seek professional assistance. Nor do current psychometric tests identify the conditions that may be responsible for the development and maintenance of deviant behavior.

The most frequently used procedure to obtain information about the child's history and present problem is, of course, the interview. When done skillfully, it is sometimes possible to get a certain "feel" for the conditions that control a child's behavior from the parent's description. The parent who reports his or her own interactions with a child may reveal important information about how a behavior problem evolved and how it is set off and maintained.

It is well-known that information obtained from an interview may be biased or nonfactual. This is especially true when the informant considers himself blameless for a child's behavior or when he is dissatisfied with previous treatment attempts. Furthermore, informants may select and provide data in response to certain cues from the interviewer or therapist, or on the basis of "demand characteristics" or reinforcement contingencies of the interview situation (Orne, 1962; Rosenthal, 1967; Krasner, 1958). The child who is being assessed may also respond to the same conditions. A study by Risley and Hart (1968) illustrates how certain environmental contingencies can cause a child to distort his verbal report when asked to describe his behavior.

As Bijou pointed out in an earlier paper (1969), the interview often reveals more about the informant than about the child. More often than not, the statements in a history from an interview are conceptualizations and interpretations of the child's behavior rather than objective descriptions of what he does and of the circumstances involved. Parents may say, "Toilet training was uneventful," or "He developed normally during the first year and a half." Such comments are of limited value because they are not accounts of the child's behavior in relation to objects, people, and situations.

Since information gleaned from interviews may provide an account of behavior without reference to their determining conditions, the data obtained might be best thought of as rough norms of development such as the age at which the child began to walk or talk. (It has been said that there is a relationship between the remoteness of the event recalled by the informant and its similarity to the Gesell norms.) For example, useful information about motor development would be the age at which the child lifted his head, turned over, sat upright, and crawled. It would also include a record of his weight and health status, his opportunities for moving about, and the basic practices (supportive, indifferent, or punative) of the members of the family to the child's movements.

Given the above problems, the professional worker may have to look beyond the information ordinarily available to him and make observations in the setting in which the child's problem occurs, i.e., the home, school, day-care center, etc. This procedure may be the only way to get information on behaviors which occur relatively infrequently yet are important to parents, teachers, and others. Aggressive behavior often falls into this category. A child may be described as extremely aggressive, yet systematic observation of his behaviors may reveal a relatively low frequency of aggressive behaviors. However, the intensity of this behavior often induces the parent to seek help.

Admittedly, the presence of an observer in a child's environment, particularly his home, alters the situation and may affect the behaviors of the child and those around him. Nevertheless, the chances are that the information obtained under these circumstances would be less biased than information obtained from tests and from retrospective accounts. An interesting alternative to using a live observer has been recently described by Sanders, Hopkins, and Walker (1969). These psychologists recorded a variety of classroom behaviors, using a time-lapse camera which operated every six minutes. Observations in natural settings will be discussed again in the next three sections of this chapter.

ASSESSMENT FOR PROGRAMMING TREATMENT

Once the presenting problem has been evaluated and the decision has been reached to treat the child, certain standard questions arise. Which problem should be selected as the initial target? Should treatment involve self-care, recreational, or academic skill, or should it be training in cognitive, social, or emotional behavior, or some combination of these? The decision is generally based upon the severity of the problem, i.e., its aversiveness to the parents, its debilitating effect on the child, or its possible causal relationships to the child's other problems.

Regardless of the problem selected, it is likely that treatment will involve instruction in some new behaviors. These behaviors will, of course, be broken down into a series of smaller responses so that the child will readily learn them. Planning treatment would obviously be facilitated if the therapist had available a detailed program which (1) placed the child's problem in relation to other behavioral skills; (2) divided the behavior to be learned into a series of steps; and (3) further divided each of these steps into units that formed the basic learning sequence. For example, Lent (1970) has analyzed the skills necessary for certain retarded children to achieve a satisfactory community adjustment. Figure 1 shows the first breakdown of these skills into vocational, academic, social, and personal areas. Figure 2 shows an additional breakdown of academic skills in graphic, reading, and quantitative behaviors. A specific subsection of quantitative behavior, time-telling, is detailed in Figure 3. The behaviors in Figure 3 are then further subdivided until only the most basic (i.e., where no further division can be achieved) units remain. The child proceeds through the sequence in the reverse direction starting with, of course, the behaviors in his repertoire. The other basic areas involving vocational, social, and personal skills are broken down in a similar fashion.

The second question to be answered in assessing for the purpose of constructing a treatment program pertains to where the treatment will take place. It is apparent that the structure of a treatment program will vary depending upon whether the problem is to be treated in its natural setting, such as the child's school or home, or in some special remedial setting (clinic, remedial class, hospital, etc.) where treatment procedures are designed so that behavior acquired will generalize to the original problem situation. It should be noted that the size of the problem—i.e., the number of specific skills that the child must learn in order to reach a particular set of terminal behaviors—may determine the most appropriate setting for treatment.

We shall consider separately the assessment procedure for planning a remedial program for social and emotional behaviors against those for remedial motor skills and cognitive abilities. Prior to doing so, however, we shall discuss the assessment of reinforcers since such an evaluation is a common component of all treatment categories.

One thing is sure, the best prepared treatment program will not produce change in the child unless he is motivated to respond as required. Hence, it is necessary to assess at the outset which objects, events, and conditions will

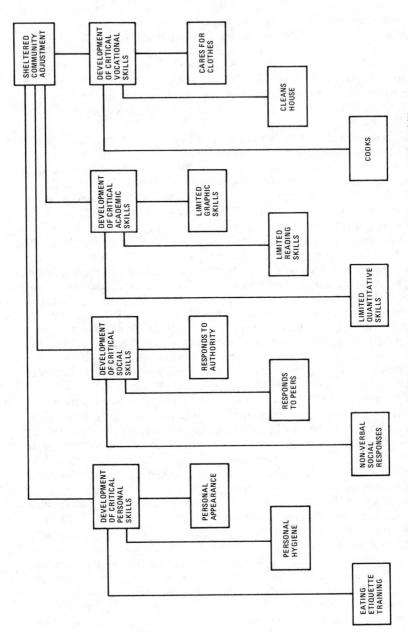

Figure 1. Analysis of sheltered-community adjustment into personal, social, and vocational skills.

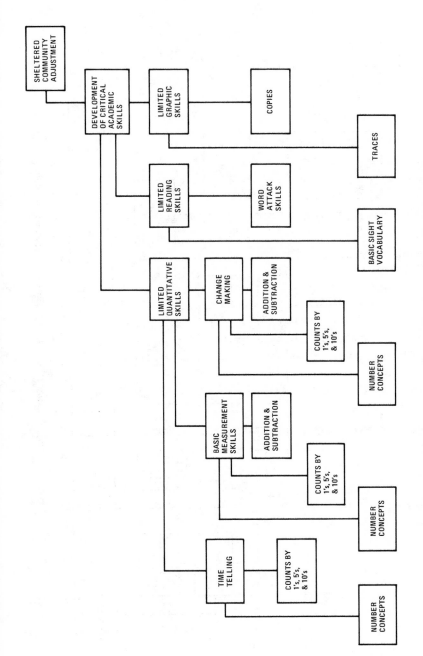

Figure 2. Analysis of academic skills into graphic, reading, and quantitative skills.

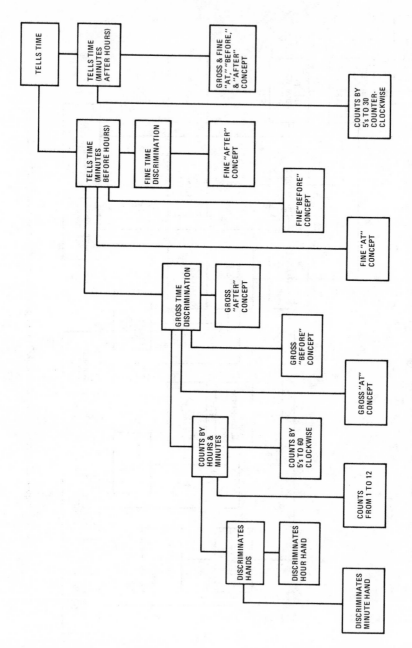

Figure 3. Analysis of time telling as one subdivision of quantitative skills.

serve as effective reinforcers for a particular child. To begin, the investigator can simply ask the child's mother and others who know him well about the kinds of things he likes to do, the way he responds to adults and peers, etc. Or one might obtain from the parents a list of tangible, social, edible, and situational events or conditions which might function as reinforcers. Such a survey would be similar to that used by Cautela and Kostenbaum (1967) for adults. Suggestions for potential reinforcers may also be obtained by presenting various stimuli and observing the amount of eye contact, emotional reactions, and approach behavior displayed. Since surveys and other informal approaches to motivational assessment do not measure those variables which might affect the strength of a reinforcer at a given time, they should be used with caution. These approaches are not substitutes for a functional test of a reinforcing stimulus. Such a test involves the presentation of a stimulus contingent upon a response followed by an increase in rate (or some other measure) of the response over operant level. Examples of assessing motivation in functional terms in the home, school, and clinic may be found in Hawkins, Peterson, Schweid, and Bijou (1966); O'Leary, O'Leary, and Becker (1967); Madsen, Becker, and Thomas (1968); and Brawley, Harris, Allen, Fleming, and Peterson (1969).

Assessment for the Preparation of Social and Emotional Programs

Basically, what is needed is information about the child's repertory of behaviors and the circumstances in which they occur, so that a program can be tailored for him. The assessment procedure would follow along these lines: First, the psychologist would obtain a report of the behaviors that are of concern to the parent, relating these examples to the child's earlier development, the parental rules and regulations, and a variety of other conditions. Next, he would attempt to assess the occurrence or non-occurrence of these behaviors and include in his assessment the specific environmental circumstances, both past and present, under which these behaviors had been or were likely to be observed by the parents. One of the underlying tenets of a functional approach, but obviously not new to the literature, is that behavior is always specific to specific situations. A particular behavior may not be completely absent from a youngster's repertory or occur in every possible environmental circumstance. The question is, then, under what specific circumstances does the behavior occur? The further assumption, of course, is that whatever behavioral difficulties are observed, they are lawfully produced from past (including genetic history) and present environmental circumstances.

Visiting the setting in which the problem behaviors take place, as we mentioned earlier, may entail certain difficulties (Peterson, 1967). The degree to which the observer wants to take specific records will depend upon the frequency of the behavior being observed and the clarity of its relationship to certain controlling variables. In some instances a brief period of observation may tell the psychologist all he needs to know about what circumstances produce the undesirable behaviors. For example, in the study by Hawkins et al. (1966), when the investigators went into a child's home and observed the interactions between mother and child, it soon became apparent how the mother's behavior was maintaining her child's undesirable behaviors. Such conclusions are not always so obvious, and the psychologist may have to resort to a more detailed procedure to record the behaviors of the parent, the child, and perhaps the siblings or peers. This recording may include the use of narrative records, that is, written descriptions of the behavioral events exhibited by parent and child, or the coding of specific categories of behavior from which the frequency of occurrence can be determined. The therapist may also ask the parent to record certain events in his absence. Methodology and techniques involved in a variety of recording methods have been discussed by Bijou et al. (1969).

The importance of situational assessment is illustrated by a number of recent studies. For example, Redd and Birnbrauer (1969) have demonstrated how two teachers had differential effects on the behavior (cooperative play) of a group of young children. When teacher A came into the room, the children evidenced considerable cooperative play; when teacher B was in the room, little cooperative play was displayed. Obviously, an observer listening to a verbal description from only teacher B would assume the children did not know how to play, yet extended observation of these teachers soon illustrated how differential reinforcement contingencies were producing and maintaining this behavior. An additional example of situational control of behavior has been produced by Wahler (1969). This study involved two youngsters who were considered deviant both in home and school settings. The initial treatment procedures which involved the modification of certain reinforcement contingencies were performed in the home. As a result, deviant behavior in the home decreased markedly; deviant behavior at school persisted. When the procedures were altered so that differential reinforcement was applied both at home and at school, behavior in school also improved.

As we indicated previously, normative data can play an important role in intake evaluation. It can also be of value in planning a treatment program. However, normative data, to be useful, should not only indicate the range and central tendency of a youngster's behavior, but also the range and mode for other individuals in the child's environment. In other words, we may need both subject norms and environmental norms. An example of the use of normative data to obtain a treatment frame of reference was recently provided by a youngster in a preschool class at the University of Illinois. According to the teacher's reports, this child was somewhat of a social isolate and did not interact verbally with other children. In fact, when measured, the youngster's overall level of verbal behavior was very low. After the situation was altered to increase the frequency of verbalizations, the question arose as to just how much this youngster should be expected to interact verbally with other children. Peer normative data provided one answer. A measure of the verbal interactions of other children in the nursery school setting provided data that could be used as a normative index. Environmental norms also provide information about the amount of environmental change that might be necessary to produce a given effect in a child. For example, an informal survey of some classroom practices carried out recently suggested that few teachers could markedly influence a youngster's desirable behavior, that is, on-task behavior, unless the teacher responded to him about 10 percent of the time. While these data should be considered tentative, they are illustrative of the kind of normative information that may be useful in providing for the functional analysis and treatment of a behavioral problem.

Assessment for Preparing Cognitive and Skill Programs

There are several subareas in this realm that need diagnostic investigation in order to produce an effective treatment program. First, it may be necessary to evaluate the child's home environment in terms of its role in stimulating, maintaining, or reducing intellectual performance. Information of this sort may contribute to a decision on the degree and kind of parental involvement in the treatment program. O'Leary (in press) cites R. Wolf who reports the development of a battery for rating such variables as opportunities for language practice, the quality of language models, and feedback for appropriate verbal usage. Wolf found correlations of .69 between intelligence test scores and environmental ratings, and .80 between achievement test scores and environmental ratings. While these findings need further substantiation, such ratings of a child's home environment could be extremely helpful.

The second area concerns the establishment of the entry point in the sequence of materials to be learned. The sequence may be specially prepared or it may be a commercially produced program. Assessment of the youngster's starting place (baseline) in the prescribed program may involve informal testing of the child's repertories, pre- and post-tests from published programs, or both. An example of some of the skills that might be evaluated is given in Figures 2 and 3.

As discussed earlier, motivational components of any treatment program are basic to the child's progress in that program. Some guidelines for the development of motivational systems applicable to academic and cognitive skills may be found in Bijou, Birnbrauer, Kidder, and Tague (1966); Skinner (1968); and Homme, Csanyi, Gonzales, and Rechs (1969).

ASSESSMENT OF PROGRESS IN TREATMENT

All too often, a treatment program is assessed by testimonials ("I think Jimmy is showing real improvement") or by the differences in psychological tests administered at the beginning and the end of treatment. Although both types of evaluation serve a purpose, neither provides reliable, continuous feedback on the child's progress. You may ask, Why is there a need for continuous feedback? The answer is simple. In behavioral analysis it is assumed that a child's progress in treatment is a function of the adequacy of the program prescribed for him. Hence, if there are indications that the child is not making reasonable advancement, the program should be scrutinized and modified accordingly. Program evaluation and modification are directly and continuously interrelated.

What is needed, then, are assessments in the form of running accounts of how the child is reacting to the contingencies which constitute his treatment program. Monitoring methods of this sort may be in the form of summary statements, rating scales, checklists, critical instances, and the like. The approach advocated here is that of scoring the frequencies of occurrence of a class or classes of behavior that are involved in the treatment program. This procedure has been used in monitoring rehabilitation programs (Meyerson, Kerr, & Michael, 1967), psychotherapy (Wolf, Risley, & Mees, 1964), academic achievement (Birnbrauer, Wolf, Kidder, & Tague, 1965), parent-child relationships (Hawkins et al., 1966), and classroom behaviors (Thomas, Becker, & Armstrong, 1968). The features of the approach are fivefold:

1. *Specification of the treatment situation.* The treatment situation is described in terms of its physical and social characteristics and the observable events that occur. The physical setting may be a part of the child's home, a hospital, residential institution, or a settlement house. It may be a nursery school, a classroom, or a room in a child guidance clinic.

2. *A code of stimulus and response categories.* The stimulus and response categories that make up a code are best derived from a survey of interactions in the treatment setting. Such a scrutiny also provides an estimate of just how frequently the target behaviors occur and often provides information on the feasibility of the situation for treatment.

The main problem in defining behaviors for inclusion in the code is preparing criteria so unequivocal that two or more observers will be in almost total agreement all the time. For example, if one wishes to record the number of times a child hits other children, he must define a hitting response so specifically that observers can easily discriminate hitting from patting, pinching, or shoving responses. Similarly, if one wants to count the number of times a child says "no," he must specify the criteria for "no" so that it is not confused with a grumble or other words, or with nonverbal forms of negative expression such as shaking his head or raising his arm as if to strike someone, etc. Definitions of responses can often be made more precise if they include criteria of loudness and duration.

Complex behaviors involving several categories of response are treated in the same way. For example, studies concerned with isolate behavior, aggressive behavior, and temper tantrums have established objective criteria for each class of responses subsumed in these categories.

3. *An objective recording procedure.* There are two main styles of recording: logging the incidences of behavior as they occur; and registering the frequencies of occurrences and nonoccurrences within a time interval. In recording frequencies, the observer makes only one mark in each time interval in which the response occurred. These tallies are sometimes referred to as Hansen scores (Altmann & Wagner, 1970). With this procedure, the maximum frequency of a response is determined by the size of the time unit selected. If a 5-second interval is used, the maximum frequency is 12 per minute; if a 10-second interval is employed, the maximal rate is 6 responses per minute, and so on. Therefore, in studies with a high frequency of behavioral episodes, small time intervals are used in order to obtain a high correspondence between the actual and recorded frequencies of occurrences.

4. *An estimation of the reliability of the recording.* The level of agreement by observers on the occurrence of a stimulus or response event, which is

ascertained prior to its use as a monitoring measure, depends on a number of factors: (a) the observational code; (b) the training of the observers; (c) the method of calculating reliability coefficients; and (d) the frequency of observations over sessions (time sampling).

5. *A method of presenting the data graphically.* The type of graphic representation used (bar chart, discrete curve, or cumulative curve) is a matter of preference and of appropriateness for the data. The goal is to provide a readily understandable account of the course of treatment.

The monitoring method described below was used to assess the treatment program for a 4½-year-old boy, Denny, who was referred to a remedial nursery school because of excessive aggressiveness, high output of aggressive fantasy play, and inadequate social skills (Sloane, Johnston, & Bijou, 1967). With this youngster, aggressive behavior was defined as an occurrence of the following:

(1) Physical assault: Hits with hands or object, kicks, bites or attempts to bite, scratches, pinches, grabs, or pulls at, jumps on or throws objects at other child or adult.
(2) Destructive behavior toward physical surroundings: Knocks material off shelves, overturns furniture, throws materials or equipment, kicks doors, walls, or furniture.
(3) Verbal assault: Verbally threatens physical assault (as defined above) or threatens violent action against child or adult. Example: "I'm going to kill you," or "I'll cut your scalp off." Verbally resents instructions, saying, "I don't like you," or "Go away" [pp. 218-219].

Fantasy play was defined as:

Explicit verbal statements referring to himself or others as imaginary characters or actions which carried out such roles once they had been verbalized. For example, if Denny made the statement that he was an Indian and carried around a drum and was beating it, the time intervals during which he was using the drum were scored for fantasy play [p. 220].

The child's social skills were not coded. Instead, a procedure was developed which specified how the youngster was expected to relate to the teachers and other children.

Fantasy and aggressive behaviors were recorded using a criterion of occurrence or nonoccurrence within each 10-second interval of observation. Reliability checks made on seven occasions showed observer agreement to average 93 percent. Details of the treatment procedure are too numerous to report here; suffice it to say that aggressive fantasy play and aggressive behaviors were reduced, and appropriate play and social skills were increased.

Further details and examples of this method of assessing progress in treatment will be found in Bijou, Peterson, and Ault (1968); Bijou et al. (1969); and Peterson, Cox, and Bijou (in press).

ASSESSMENT OF BEHAVIOR AFTER TREATMENT

The literature on the assessment of posttreatment behavior is considerable and varied. It includes research on the outcome of psychotherapy, on the relationships between training and performance on a job or in the armed services, and on the relationships between educational programs and tests of the effectiveness of school placement, occupation, or adjustment in society. We shall limit our discussion of the assessment of behavior after treatment to research on the outcome of therapy because this area has been mostly concerned with what happens to individuals. However, the reader is reminded that the term *treatment* refers throughout not only to therapy but also to training, education, and rehabilitation.

According to the most rigorous research attitude, the efficacy of a therapy program should be evaluated in terms of posttreatment behaviors that can be measured objectively, e.g., performance on the job or number of returns to the clinic (Luborsky & Strupp, 1962; Paul, 1967). This view, which has probably developed as a reaction to the unreliability of testimonials, has merit because it does insist on relating the effects of treatment to observable changes in the everyday life of the person, yet it does not actually exclude impressionistic data. However, it also has an inherent shortcoming because it tends to ignore the role of the environmental events that transpire between the termination of therapy and the time of the assessment. An assessment procedure which does not take into account environmental variables is defensible in treatment situations in which the environment is relatively constant. For example, medical treatment is performed within the context of a fairly stable organismic environment—the physiological functioning of anatomical structures. Even so, social and physical components of the environment must be taken into consideration, for it is obvious that they can produce conditions that further alter physiological functioning. Ulcer and heart patients are notable examples. This view may also be defensible in some phobic or other respondent-type behavior disorders since the recurrence of the environmental events which were at the basis of the problem (for example, a traumatic fall from a dock which led to a water phobia) is unlikely.

The rigorous research attitude is least defensible for evaluating the treatment of operant behaviors. The course of modified operant behavior after treatment is largely dependent upon the contingencies in operation during that interval, their relative dominances, and their characteristic schedules. Hence, the evaluation of therapy involving operant behavior requires a procedure that differs markedly from the medical model. It is this: the behavior of the individual should be monitored throughout the treatment program, and the data obtained at the end of treatment (terminal behavior compared to the operant level of that behavior) is the basic measure of the effectiveness of that program. Measures taken after the termination of treatment show the effect of conditions that have influenced the treated behavior. If these conditions did not maintain the terminal behavior, one might mistakenly conclude that the treatment was inadequate. On the other hand, if the behaviors were maintained, then the causal conditions are the interactions of the behavior from the treatment procedures and the posttreatment conditions. Does this imply that follow-up studies of treatment programs are unnecessary? No, it does not. They are needed to indicate whether the behaviors assessed at the end of treatment have been maintained, extended, or weakened by the contingencies in the natural environment. For example, in a study of an autistic child (Brawley et al., 1969), postchecks were taken over a period of eight sessions following a three-month interval. When the postchecks revealed that the child's behavior remained in approximately the same percentile range as that observed near the end of treatment, the youngster was discharged as a clinic case, and arrangements were made to enroll him in a special school. A briefer follow-up period was used in a study of objectionable behaviors of a four-year-old child (Hawkins et al., 1966). Here, after a 24-day interval, three observational sessions were conducted in the home to evaluate the status of the child's behavior. It was found that during these three sessions, the range of problem behaviors was as low as it had been during the terminal phase of treatment. Apparently, then, the mother was able to maintain the behavior she had acquired during the study.

Research on posttreatment operant behavior suggests that it is important to ascertain whether the effects of treatment have been maintained and, if they have not, to determine what action should be taken to reinstate them. The acceptance of this orientation would, among other things, lead to a critical review of the ways in which posttreatment environments are evaluated. Current assessment techniques include interviews, paper-and-pencil personality tests (e.g., MMPI), self-concept measures, thematic stories, patient checklists and self-ratings, therapist rating scales, factor-analytic batteries, mood scales, personal orientation inventories, self-regulation measures, peer rating scales, and so on. Hence some of the assessments are made by the patient himself, some by professional workers (e.g., therapist, social worker), and some by peers, members of family, and job supervisors. No matter which of the above techniques are used and no matter who does the assessing, these procedures do not yield a psychological definition of the person's environment. Or stated differently, none of the methods provides information about the person's environment *in functional terms,* and that information is what is needed. Defining the environment in functional terms is similar to, but not quite the same as, defining the environment on the basis of the individual's personal experience, or the way he "sees" things (e.g., Lewin, 1964). These concepts, however, are fraught with methodological difficulties and analytical dead ends. A functional definition describes *how the patient behaves in relation to the events in his life,* and the *how* is stated in objective terms. Information on the functional meaning of the environment is obtained only from observations of actual interactions of the person with people in his home, school, or job, and in his recreational and avocational activities. On the basis of such information, one can determine which situations are primarily supportive, neutral, and aversive for him.

The main criticism generally leveled at a functional analysis of the child's environment is that it is impractical. What is ordinarily meant by this comment is that it requires more time, effort, and money than the methods in current use. This is true, but an adequate psychological analysis of the environment cannot be made in any other way. As noted above, self-ratings and reports of feelings are not adequate substitutes for functional accounts. Although the method proposed is more costly than current methods, we do not know how much more, for we have not yet ascertained from actual experience how many environmental situations in a given case would require sampling and how extensive each sample should be. (It might be revealing to contemplate how the extensive use of a functional analysis in the medical sciences has led to an effective medical and health technology.)

An acceptance of the need for a functional analysis of the environment would also lead to a critical evaluation of the present practices employed in placing a patient, checking on his progress, assessing the environmental contingencies, and altering unfavorable situations. It is highly probable that radical changes would be indicated.

SUMMARY

Behavior analysis has been applied to the treatment of children's problem behavior with increased frequency during the last decade. One of the products of this effort has been the development of specialized assessment procedures. These procedures can be best understood if one keeps in mind that from a functional point of view the only reason for assessing a child is to obtain information that would be helpful in developing a treatment program for him. (Treatment is used here to mean therapy, training, education, and rehabilitation.) In fact, the adequacy of the treatment procedures and their successive revisions rests upon the comprehensiveness with which the observational measures are taken. The measures include an evaluation of the problem behaviors and the physical and social circumstances which maintain them. Techniques which monitor progress in treatment and which assess posttreatment behavior also play a significant role.

At the core of the behavioral approach is the assumption that assessment procedures are based on the *direct* measurement of the behavior and the circumstances that are involved in the treatment program. These direct measures may take many forms, but the one most often used is the frequency of occurrence of stimulus and response classes.

While a functional-behavioral approach emphasizes descriptive observational methods of assessing individual behavior, it may also utilize information from standardized psychological tests. For example, the results of an intelligence test, interpreted as a measure of school aptitude, may be used as indicators of the cognitive repertories of the average child in a given elementary school grade.

CHAPTER V

The assessment of managerial talent

Marvin D. Dunnette

Managers, administrators, and executives play an unusually important role in our society. Industry, in particular, seems to suffer a chronic need for more and better managers. A *Wall Street Journal* survey (Melloan, 1966) showed that more and more managerial jobs are going unfilled because of demands induced by rapid industrial growth, lowered birthrates during the 1930s, and relatively smaller numbers of college graduates choosing to enter the business world. In effect, personnel practice involving managerial talent has become a specialty in itself, one of particular importance to continued industrial growth and expansion.

A more intensive and more sophisticated survey of industrial and government practices related to managerial manpower (Campbell, Dunnette, Lawler, & Weick, 1970) showed them to be characterized by great diversity, poor planning, rather haphazard information gathering and decision making systems, and few systematic efforts to evaluate results. Problems of managerial manpower shortages were being attacked in many ways—ranging from strict selection strategies to elaborate (usually computerized) manpower inventory systems, specialized training and development programs, and the use of various incentives designed to lure and/or to retain the best managers. Survey respondents held sharply differing views about the major determiners and indicators of managerial and administrative effectiveness.

In an apparent effort to bring order to this manpower chaos, some industrial firms and government agencies have developed and implemented multiple assessment procedures for identifying and developing managerial talent. Happily, these instances of formal assessment programs are characterized by careful planning, precisely programmed procedures, and an impressive amount of evaluative research. Taking a look at their history, their current status, and the results of research on them should tell us a good deal about how useful such procedures may be when applied to other than managerial groups and to more general issues of behavior description, diagnosis, prediction, and modification.

This chapter includes: first, a conceptual and behavioral analysis of managerial effectiveness and a discussion of its implications for measurement and prediction; second, a description of the major features of multiple assessment procedures for pinpointing talent; and third, an overview of major research findings.

THE MANAGERIAL JOB AND MANAGERIAL EFFECTIVENESS

First, what are the features of a managerial job? Who is a manager? Most simply, a manager is any person with a job so broad that he needs help in getting it done. Usually, this help comes from other persons, but he might also receive help from other sources such as a computer system. A managerial job, therefore, requires that its incumbent utilize *his* resources primarily to identify, coordinate, and control *other* resources to get the job done properly. I have outlined this definition in greater detail elsewhere (Dunnette, 1967; Campbell et al., 1970). It is useful mostly because it points quite directly to the major parameters of effectiveness in managerial jobs: *ability, motivation,* and *opportunity* (Bray, 1966).

Ability refers to the usual individual differences characteristics such as aptitudes, skills, job proficiencies and specialized knowledges, and personality characteristics. *Motivation* refers to the interaction between a person's preferences for different job-related goals or rewards (e.g., money, autonomy, praise, recognition) and his expectancies about the likelihood of attaining them in any particular job. *Opportunity* refers to organizational practices or conditions that may either facilitate or hinder a person in utilizing his abilities efficiently to pursue his job-related goals. Examples of opportunity conditions in an organization include such factors as presence or absence of formal training programs, the reinforcement character of supervisory job behaviors, and any number of other organizational policies and practices.

In essence, then, a manager's effectiveness in utilizing others' resources depends upon his proficiencies (ability), his beliefs about contingencies between what he does on the job and what he may get out of it (motivation), and the organizational conditions surrounding him (opportunity). Moreover, no one of these factors exerts its influence independently of the others. As Bray has so forcefully argued (Bray, 1966), managerial behavior must be studied in the context of managerial-organizational interactions and *not* merely in relation to differences in ability among people.

Managerial-organizational interaction is complicated further by its dynamic qualities. Nothing stays the same for long. Changes in opportunity are likely to induce changes in motivation, in real or perceived ability levels, or in both simultaneously. It is certain that any single measure or "snapshot" description of a manager's level of effectiveness is bound to be the result of a unique combination of the three causal agents and their interactions at that particular point in time.

IMPLICATIONS FOR MEASUREMENT AND PREDICTION
OF MANAGERIAL EFFECTIVENESS

These considerations yield three important conclusions bearing on procedures used to identify and develop managerial talent:

1. First, assessments of managerial talent must not be restricted to measuring the usual individual differences variables. They must also include estimates of individual and organizational attributes relevant to motivational and opportunity factors.

2. Second, in assessment particular emphasis needs to be given to the behavioral demands of managerial jobs. Typical paper-and-pencil tests, requiring little more than self-descriptions of one's own behavior tendencies, offer far too narrow a range of stimuli for sampling adequately the diversity of behaviors relevant to managerial-organizational interactions. Techniques that simulate the basic ingredients of the manager-organization interaction should be used in order to estimate how a person may respond to the many information-processing requirements of a managerial job.

3. Recommendations based on assessment results (sizing up a person's so-called "managerial potential") should not stop with a mere portrayal of the assessee's present abilities and behavior dispositions. To give proper attention to the complexities of managerial-organizational interactions, recommendations must include estimates of how an individual may respond to various organizational reward contingencies. Moreover, they should include prescriptions outlining the job circumstances or organizational actions and practices most likely to create opportunity conditions so that personal abilities and preferences may be utilized in the best way possible. Finally, the recommendations should emphasize developmental steps that may be taken by both individual and organization to enhance the likelihood of his successfully performing a managerial job.

MULTIPLE ASSESSMENT PROCEDURES FOR MANAGERS

The above specifications for properly assessing managerial talent reflect the thinking that led Bray and his associates (Bray, 1966) to develop a multiple assessment procedure for use in the American Telephone and Telegraph (AT&T) Company's Management Progress Study.

First use of multiple assessment procedures on a large scale is credited to German military psychologists (Office of Strategic Services, 1948). The British adapted the German procedures for screening their officer candidates, and the U.S. Office of Strategic Services took over the approach from the British during World War II. Since that time, several studies of various applications of these procedures have been reported in the literature (Taft, 1959; Cronbach, 1960). By late 1969, multiple assessment programs were being utilized operationally for identifying management potential in several industrial firms and government agencies,[1] and an assessment program was being

---

[1] According to Byham (1969), the following firms and government agencies had implemented multiple assessment procedures: American Telephone and Telegraph Co.; Standard Oil Co. of Ohio (SOHIO); International Business Machines Corp.; Caterpillar Tractor Co.; General Electric Co.; Sears, Roebuck & Co.; Minnesota Mining & Manufacturing Co.; Olin-Mathieson Chemical Corp.; Wolverine Tube Co.; Wickes Corp.; J. C. Penney Co.; the Peace Corps; the Internal Revenue Service; and the Oak Ridge Atomic Energy Facility.

offered as a service to clients by at least one management consulting firm.[2]

The procedures employed by AT&T and most other programs have involved multiple methods for obtaining information about individuals and have used several staff observers whose judgments are pooled to develop trait or behavior ratings. Information is obtained by both clinical and statistical or mechanical means (Sawyer, 1966b). It is then combined mechanically to derive trait ratings and clinically to yield global predictions and recommendations, incorporating suggestions for organizational practices. The major innovation in the use of multiple assessment procedures has, of course, been the development of simulation techniques, which add to the scope of personal behavior tendencies that can be observed and evaluated.

Programs differ somewhat according to the specific nature of the instruments and simulations, but they are essentially similar in their use of many techniques, many staff observers, and simulations to elicit behavior episodes involving group process, information processing, and personal interaction variables. The description below of the approach used by Personnel Decisions, Inc., (PDI) will give the reader an overview of a typical multiple assessment procedure used for deriving development recommendations as well as estimates of managerial potential. The first step in designing the PDI program was to select and define the behavioral characteristics to be observed. To accomplish this, a thorough review of the literature was supplemented with opinions from experienced industrial managers about the critical behaviors they believed to be important to managerial success. The many suggestions revealed by these surveys were organized into a list of nine broad dimensions.[3] These dimensions then formed the basis for deciding upon the trait, motivational, and behavioral variables to be rated during and after application of the multiple assessment procedures. Those variables are listed below.

1. Verbal Intelligence
2. Quantitative Intelligence
3. Divergent Thinking
4. Breadth of Information
5. Practical Judgment
6. Oral Communications Skills
7. Written Communications Skills
8. Energy
9. Decisiveness
10. Personal Appearance

11. Personal Impact
12. Perception of Social Cues
13. Need for Social Approval
14. Interpersonal Competence
15. Forcefulness
16. Need Achievement
17. Need Advancement
18. Desire to Lead
19. Need Cognition
20. Inner Work Standards

---

[2] Personnel Decisions, Inc., of Minneapolis, Minnesota.
[3] These managerial behavioral dimensions included Technical Knowledge, Competence, and Proficiency; Planning and Direct Action; Organizing, Coordinating, and Integrating; Supervising Subordinates; Relations with Associates; Managerial Style; Acceptance of Organizational Responsibility; Acceptance of Personal Responsibility; and Communications Effectiveness. Each dimension was defined further according to actual critical behaviors discovered in studies by Flanagan (1951), Kay (1959), Williams (1956), Hemphill (1960), and Stewart (1967). The interested reader will find these investigations described in greater detail in Campbell et al. (1970).

21. Need Security	28. Resistance to Stress
22. Primacy of Work	29. Self-Esteem
23. Need Autonomy	30. Tolerance of Ambiguity
24. Behavioral Stability	31. Attention to Detail
25. Cognitive Complexity	32. Organization and Planning
26. Behavior Flexibility	33. Specialization Orientation
27. Ability to Delay Gratification	34. Social Awareness

Techniques were selected or invented to reveal the above variables. The techniques used and brief descriptions of them are listed below:

Interview. A two-hour interview is held with each participant. Information gathered is designed to reveal aspects of a participant's personal development, his work objectives, his attitudes toward his organization, his social values, scope of interests, nature of interpersonal relationships, idiosyncracies, etc.

In-Basket. This consists of a set of materials a manager might expect to find in his in-basket. The items range from telephone messages to detailed reports. Each participant is given two hours to review the materials and take appropriate action on them by writing letters, memos, and notes to himself. After completing the basket, he is interviewed about his approach to the task, his reasons for taking the actions indicated, and his opinions of his superiors, peers, and subordinates, as inferred from the materials. This interview is carried out in a role-playing format with one of the staff members playing the role of the man's new manager. Later, a different staff member plays the role of one of the participant's subordinates, a problem employee, in a corrective interview between the subordinate and the participant. [The In-Basket has been widely used and rather extensively researched. A good account of its use and the major results obtained is given by Lopez (1966).]

Stock Exchange Problem. This is a simulated business situation in which six participants are told that they are managers of an investment fund. Their job is to buy and sell stocks with the purpose, of course, of realizing profits for their investors. Stock quotations are changed each five minutes, and a wide variety of other information is presented at predetermined intervals. Participants' behavior is presumed to reflect their typical responses to situations placing a premium on organizing skills, working cooperatively with other people, handling a large amount of information, and other group process and cognitive variables.

Project Planning and Group Decision Problem. This is a second simulated business situation. Here, however, the six participants are asked to play roles as managerial trainees in a hypothetical firm, which annually gives an award to the trainee whose "project of the year" is judged to be best. Thus, each participant must plan his project and make a ten-minute oral presentation describing its merits and outlining a budget for implementing it. After all six have made their presentations, they engage in an hour's discussion about the relative merits of the various projects. At the end of the hour, they are required to rank the projects according to overall merit. Participants' behavior in this exercise is presumed to reflect such attributes as judgment, planning and organizing skills, oral communications proficiency, and effectiveness in working in situations where people are in competition with one another.

Paper-and-pencil tests. The following standardized tests and inventories are completed by the participants: (1) Wesman Personnel Classification Test; (2) Minnesota Scholastic Aptitude Test; (3) Employment Aptitude Series Tests of Verbal Comprehension, Spatial Visualization, Numerical Reasoning, and Verbal Reasoning; (4) Guilford tests of Ideational Fluency, Associational Fluency, and Expressive Fluency; (5) *Time* magazine's Current Affairs Test; (6) Ghiselli Self Description Inventory; (7) California Psychological Inventory; (8) Edwards Personal Preference Schedule; and (9) Strong Vocational Interest Blank.

Projective tests. In addition to a 100-item incomplete sentences inventory, each participant completes an autobiographical statement based on different life periods: (1) an account of important events during his high school years; (2) a projective account (mock autobiography) of his life during the ensuing five years; and, (3) a projective account (mock autobiography) of events during the year in which he reaches his fiftieth birthday. [Choice of this technique was based on successful results obtained with it in assessing Peace Corps trainees (Ezekial, 1968) wherein the trainees' autobiographies were scored on three dimensions—degree of differentiation, demand character of life experiences, and degree of self-determination over life decisions. These scores correlated well at .40 to .50 with ratings of success in the field two years later.]

Miscellaneous. An application-blank type personal history form, a brief managerial values questionnaire (England, 1967), and a questionnaire describing the current climate surrounding the participants' present job situation also are completed.

All the above techniques are administered according to standard instructions by the staff member or members responsible for each method. All interviews are conducted by individual staff members with individual participants. All tests, questionnaires, and situational exercises are administered to groups of participants. Two staff members observe each group problem, record their impressions of each participant, and independently describe the performance of each.

For each method, one or more of the staff prepare written reports. The interviewers write reports of their interviews. A report is prepared for actions taken on the In-Basket, including inferences drawn from the role-playing interviews. Similarly, observers for each of the group problems report on participants' performance, including ratings and rankings by both peers and observers. The paper-and-pencil tests are scored and summarized.

Personal characteristics selected for evaluation reflect the many and varied behavioral tendencies and descriptive characteristics believed to be important to managerial effectiveness. Some are directly related to things a manager is required to do in his job (e.g., organization and planning, decisiveness, attention to detail). Others refer to interpersonal behavior and influence (e.g., oral and written communications skills, personal impact, perception of social cues, interpersonal competence). Motives, attitudes, and values are also included (e.g., inner work standards, primacy of work, need for advancement, need for security). All, of course, are behavioral tendencies that presumably are related to the manager's ability to identify, allocate, and utilize optimally the financial, human, and material resources available to him.

Collecting the above information requires two and one half days. After a brief interlude for assimilation and summarizing of all information, the staff, six or eight members, meet to review the results and rate the participants on the 34 traits and motivational and behavioral variables. Each participant is reviewed separately; about 60 to 90 minutes is required for each man. A typical review session consists of reading all reports and test information available for a particular participant, followed by independent staff ratings on five-point scales for each of the 34 variables.

The behavioral data and ratings available for each participant are used to prepare a narrative report. This report emphasizes the participant's present abilities and behavioral tendencies in relation to present organizational circumstances and future opportunities. The report contains recommendations for training and job experiences likely to be beneficial to the participant. It forms a basis for continued career planning between the participant and organizational officials responsible for personnel decisions.

Programs now being used differ, of course, in a number of ways. Some of the major differences in conception and the nature of the actual operation are summarized below:

Techniques used. Obviously, many different written tests and inventories are utilized. The exercises and group discussions also differ in content. However, the programs, for the most part, are similar in using at least an In-Basket exercise, a group exercise emphasizing cooperative behavior, and a group exercise emphasizing competition.

Purpose. Programs differ in the degree of emphasis placed on *identification* as opposed to *development.* The PDI program described above places primary emphasis on using the assessment information for deriving training and development recommendations. Most earlier assessment programs (with the notable exception of the General Electric and SOHIO programs) placed heavier emphasis on assessing candidates either for specific jobs or for general management potential.

Staff members. Psychologists are always numbered among the staff members for the programs, but several also utilize line managers as staff members.

Use of reports. Programs differ widely in how the final reports are used and who sees them. Usually, a participant's immediate supervisor does *not* have access to the report. Obviously, decisions about how reports shall be used and who shall see them depend mostly on the organization's purpose for undertaking the program in the first place.

RESEARCH RESULTS

Research done on managerial multiple assessment programs has been extensive and generally excellent. Results of these investigations give evidence in a number of areas: (1) the nature of factors underlying assessment observations, and behavior and trait ratings made on assessment variables; (2) the relative contributions of different methods, tests, and staff members to behavior ratings and overall predictions; (3) relationships between staff predictions and behavior ratings and later organizational status of participants; and (4) relationships between organizational actions related to assessment results and the later organizational status of participants.

Factor Studies

Factor studies of assessment program ratings have been carried out on data gathered in four major multiple assessment programs: AT&T's Management Progress Study (MPS, Bray, 1964a, 1964b; Bray & Grant, 1966), SOHIO's Formal Analysis of Corporate Talent (FACT) program (Thomson, 1969; Donaldson, 1969), the Sears program (Bentz, 1967, 1969), and International Business Machines program (Hinrichs, 1969).

In the Management Progress Study, 355 men employed in six regional Bell System companies were assessed in summer programs during the years 1957 through 1960. Of the total, 207 held college degrees; 148 did not. The rating variables used to summarize the men's assessment performance are listed below:

1. Organization and Planning	14. Perception of Social Cues
2. Decision Making	15. Self-Objectivity
3. Creativity	16. Energy
4. Human Relations Skills	17. Realism of Expectations
5. Behavior Flexibility	18. Bell System Value Orientation
6. Personal Impact	19. Social Objectivity
7. Tolerance of Uncertainty	20. Need for Advancement
8. Resistance to Stress	21. Ability to Delay Gratification
9. Scholastic Aptitude	22. Need for Superior Approval
10. Range of Interests	23. Need for Peer Approval
11. Inner Work Standards	24. Goal Flexibility
12. Primacy of Work	25. Need for Security
13. Oral Communications Skills	26. Overall Staff Prediction[4]

Correlation matrices were computed separately for the college and non-college groups, and factored by Wherry's hierarchical method (Wherry, 1959). Though not identical, the factor structures were similar for the two samples. Each analysis yielded a higher-order general factor and several first-order factors. Factors common to both groups are named below, along with the rating dimensions loading most highly on each:

    I. *General Effectiveness:* Overall Staff Prediction, Decision Making, Organization and Planning, Creativity, Need for Advancement, Resistance to Stress, and Human Relations Skills.

---

[4]Overall Staff Prediction is a single staff rating of managerial potential denoted by the managerial level that an assessee is predicted to attain during his career with the company.

II. *Administrative Skills:* Organization and Planning, and Decision Making.

III. *Interpersonal Skills:* Human Relations Skills, Behavior Flexibility, and Personal Impact.

IV. *Control of Feelings:* Tolerance of Uncertainty and Resistance to Stress.

V. *Intellectual Ability:* Scholastic Aptitude and Range of Interests.

VI. *Work-Oriented Motivation:* Primacy of Work and Inner Work Standards.

VII. *Passivity:* Ability to Delay Gratification, Need for Security, and Need for Advancement (negatively loaded).

VIII. *Dependency:* Need for Superior Approval, Need for Peer Approval, and Goal Flexibility.

Thomson (1969) studied the factor structure of assessment ratings given to 119 managers who had participated in one of ten sessions of SOHIO's FACT program during a twenty-two-month period. The FACT ratings are made on thirteen dimensions: Amount of Participation, Oral Communication, Personal Acceptability, Impact, Quality of Participation, Personal Breadth, Orientation to Detail, Self-Direction, Relationship with Authority, Originality, Understanding of People, Drive, and Overall Potential. Correlation matrices were factored separately for ratings made by psychologist staff members and line manager staff members. Nearly identical factor structures of five factors each were obtained for the two sets of data. The factors are named below along with the rating dimensions defining them:

I. *Group-Task Effectiveness:* Impact, Amount of Participation, Oral Communication, Quality of Participation, Overall Potential, and Self-Direction.

II. *Need for Structure:* Orientation to Detail (likes detail), Originality (lacks originality), Self-Direction (is not self-directed), and Relationship with Authority (defers to authority).

III. *Interpersonal Effectiveness:* Personal Acceptability and Understanding of People.

IV. *Quality of Independent Thinking:* Personal Breadth, Overall Potential, Quality of Participation, Originality (is original), Self-Direction (is self-directed), Understanding of People, and Relationship with Authority (does not defer to authority).

V. *Work-Oriented Motivation:* Drive.

Hinrichs (1969) factored a correlation matrix based on ratings of 47 participants on 12 scales used in the IBM program. His results yielded the three factors shown below:

I. *Overall Activity and General Effectiveness:* Persuasiveness, Aggressiveness, Energy Level, Interpersonal Contact, Oral Communications, and Self-Confidence.

II. *Administrative Skills:* Decision Making, Planning and Organization, Written Communications, and Administrative Ability.

III. *Resistance to Stress:* Resistance to Stress and Risk Taking.

The Sears program uses an In-Basket exercise scorable on many dimensions, such as Planning, Compliance to Superiors, Social Sensitivity, Establishing Priorities, Taking Action, etc. Scores for participants who took the Sears In-Basket during 1968 and 1969 were correlated and factored (Bentz, 1969). Behaviors defining each of nine factors suggest titles such as the following:

I. *Overall Executive Orientation*
II. *Independent Administration and Control*
III. *Organizing and Planning*
IV. *Decisive Action Orientation*
V. *Courtesy and Understanding*
VI. *Information Acquisition and Transmission*
VII. *Profit and Cost Orientation*
VIII. *Human Relations Orientation*
IX. *Casual Informality*

These four analyses, along with yielding certain factors dependent on the particular variables rated in a given program, do show certain broad underlying dimensions such as Overall Activity and General Effectiveness, Organizing and Planning (Administering), Interpersonal Competence (Human Relations Ability and Understanding), Cognitive Competence (Intellectual and Quality of Thinking), Work Orientation (Work-Oriented Motivation), and Personal Control (Control of Feelings and Resistance to Stress). Other than these major areas of similarity, the results reflect the particular scales and dimensions chosen originally for each of the different programs. The results do, however, offer forceful testimony to the richness and wide range of behaviors sampled by these multiple assessment procedures.

Internal Analyses of Assessment Procedures

Internal analyses of data generated from multiple assessment programs show that staff members' ratings are of acceptable reliability and that each of the several procedures makes an important contribution to staff judgments on the various behavior dimensions. Evidence for these conclusions is presented below.

Reliability. Greenwood and McNamara (1967) utilized a team of four observers for twelve participants in the IBM program. Three observers were assigned to each situational exercise (simulation) involving six participants. Thus, over the two days of the program, six participants were evaluated by observers A, C, and D; in another exercise by A, B, and C; and in a third by B, C, and D. Each observer independently rated each of the participants on behavior dimensions (e.g., aggressiveness, persuasiveness) immediately after each exercise. Correlations between all possible pairs of raters were computed for data obtained in six IBM divisions for each of three exercises. The median of 432 reliability coefficients computed for ratings on a five point scale was .74, and the median of 432 coefficients for rankings of the six participants was .76. These values are slightly higher than the median values of .68 and .72 reported by Grant (1964) for ratings and rankings of 355 participants in the AT&T Management Progress Study.

Greenwood and McNamara (1967) examined separately the inter-rater reliabilities for various pair combinations of psychologist and line manager staff members. They found no consistent differences in degree of agreement between particular types of pairs (psychologist-psychologist, psychologist-manager, manager-manager), nor did differences in means or standard deviations between the two sets of ratings (psychologists and managers) show statistical significance.

Thomson (1969) found essentially the same result when he calculated correlations between psychologists' and managers' ratings on the SOHIO scales for 119 participants. His results are shown below:

Rating Scale	Correlation	Rating Scale	Correlation
Amount of Participation	.93	Self-Direction	.86
Oral Communication	.85	Relationship with Authority	.84
Personal Acceptability	.80	Originality	.85
Impact	.89	Understanding of People	.80
Quality of Participation	.81	Drive	.74
Personal Breadth	.82	Potential	.91
Orientation to Detail	.76		

Contribution of Methods to Staff Judgments. By far the most extensive analyses of internal relationships among various assessment methods and staff judgments have been done on the AT&T data (Bray & Grant, 1966; Grant, Katkovsky, & Bray, 1967; Grant & Bray, 1969). In addition to test information and ratings and rankings of participants' performance in the In-Basket and group exercises, two written reports based respectively on the personal interview and on responses to projective techniques[5] were prepared for each participant. In order to determine how information obtained from the interview and projective techniques affected staff judgments, the protocols were read by two psychologists and coded independently on a number of dimensions relevant to managerial behavior.

The dimensions were not the same for the two techniques. The following dimensions were rated from the projective protocols for 355 participants: Achievement Motivation, Self-Confidence, Work or Career Orientation, Dependence, Affiliation, Optimism-Pessimism, Willingness to Assume a Leadership Role, Willingness to Accept a Subordinate Role, and General Adjustment. Inter-rater reliabilities estimated from the two sets of independent ratings were gratifyingly high, ranging from .85 to .94 with a median of .91.

Dimensions rated from the interview protocols included Personal Impact-Forcefulness, Oral Communications Skills, Human Relations Skills, Personal Impact-Likability, Behavior Flexibility, Need for Approval from Superiors, Need for Approval from Peers, Tolerance of Uncertainty, Inner Work Standards, Primacy of Work, Energy, Goal Flexibility, Need for Advancement, Need for Security, Social Objectivity, Bell System Value Orientation, Ability to Delay Gratification, and Range of Interests. Here, the raters were directed to

---

[5]Three projective techniques were used: the Rotter Incomplete Sentences Blank; a specially developed 57-item Management Incomplete Sentences Blank; and six cards of the Thematic Apperception Test.

omit a rating if evidence in the report was insufficient to make the rating. Thus, of the 348 interview reports available for analysis, the number actually rated ranged from a low of 162 for Personal Impact—Likability to a high of 343 for Need Advancement. Inter-rater reliabilities estimated from the two sets of independent ratings ranged from .00 (Ability to Delay Gratification—Non-College Men) to .92 with a median of .80.

Ratings from the projective and interview reports, test scores, and ratings of performance in the simulation exercises were correlated with participants' scores on factors derived from the 25 rating dimensions (see page 86) and on overall staff prediction of potential for management. Results are summarized in Tables 1 and 2.

Clearly, staff judgments made important use of procedures unique to the multiple assessment approach. For example, performance in the group exercises and on the In-Basket strongly influenced staff judgments in the three critical areas of General Effectiveness, Administrative Skills, and Interpersonal Effectiveness. It is noteworthy that, with the exception of the mental ability test, the standardized paper-and-pencil tests had relatively little effect on staff judgments. Interestingly, the more clinical procedures (the interview and projective tests), usually believed to be most useful for deriving motivational and personality inferences, did indeed affect staff judgments most in such areas as Work-Oriented Motivation, Passivity, and Dependency. This series of analyses of the internal characteristics of AT&T assessment center techniques, staff procedures, and ratings tells us a great deal about the relative importance of various techniques and how they are used to derive judgments about the participants in multiple assessment procedures.

Though far more limited in scope than the AT&T studies, Hinrichs' (1969) evidence on 47 participants in the IBM program shows the following test and inventory scores to be correlated most highly with the various staff judgment factors:

    I. *Overall Activity and General Effectiveness:* personality test (Gordon Personality Profile), Ascendancy ($r = .56$); biographical inventory, Self-Confidence ($r = .43$).

    II. *Administrative Skills:* personality test, Self-Assurance ($r = .32$).

    III. *Resistance to Stress:* personality test (Ghiselli Self-Description Inventory), Occupational Level ($r = .44$), Initiative ($r = .36$); risk-taking test ($r = .36$).

    Overall Staff Judgment: personality test, Occupational Level ($r = .47$), Ascendancy ($r = .43$); risk-taking test ($r = .42$).

Unfortunately, Hinrichs gives no information about relationships between performance on group and simulation exercises and the staff judgments.

Predictive Validities of Assessment Judgments

Several investigators have correlated participants' assessment center results with various measures of later organizational status and/or job effectiveness. Studies have been examined according to the nature of criterion information: (1) those using overall estimates of organizational success, such as organizational level or salary progress, and (2) those which have attempted to validate

Table 1
Assessment Methods Showing High Correlations with Each of Eight
Behavior Rating Factors and Overall Staff Prediction for College
and Non-College Men in the AT&T Management Progress Study

Assessment method	College men	Non-college men
Factor I. General Effectiveness		
Performance in Cooperative Group Exercise		.60
Performance in Competitive Group Exercise	.67	
Performance on In-Basket	.60	.59
Interview: Personal Impact	.52	.48
Projective: Leadership Role	.48	.51
Personality Test: Dominance	.33	.22
Factor II. Administrative Skills		
Performance on In-Basket	.76	.68
Performance in Competitive Group Exercise	.48	.51
Mental Ability Test	.34	.72
Interview: Personal Impact	.42	.24
Oral Communications Skills	.33	.53
Projective: Leadership Role	.36	.36
Personality Test: Dominance	.30	.30
Factor III. Interpersonal Skills		
Performance in Cooperative Group Exercise	.39	.52
Performance in Competitive Group Exercise	.62	.45
Performance on In-Basket	.45	.49
Interview: Personal Impact	.44	.25
Human Relations Skills	.28	.46
Factor IV. Control of Feelings		
Performance in Competitive Group Exercise	.47	.36
Performance in Cooperative Group Exercise	.37	.35
Interview: Human Relations Skills	.23	.45
Tolerance of Uncertainty	.30	.40
Projective: Leadership Role	.29	.46
Dependence	−.28	−.42
Factor V. Intellectual Ability		
Mental Ability Test	.70	.62
Interview: Oral Communications Skills	.40	.47
Factor VI. Work Orientation Motivation		
Projective: Work or Career Orientation	.50	.56
Interview: Personal Impact	.36	.50
Inner Work Standards	.40	.43
Performance in Cooperative Exercise	.30	.39
Performance in Competitive Exercise	.45	.36
Performance on In-Basket	.44	.26
Factor VII. Passivity		
Interview: Need Advancement	−.57	−.67
Personal Impact	−.38	−.58
Need Security	.50	.37

Table 1 (Continued)

Assessment method	College men	Non-college men
Projective: Leadership Role	−.47	−.40
Achievement Motivation	−.41	−.50
Performance in Competitive Exercise	˙−.39	−.36
Performance in Cooperative Exercise	−.35	−.34
Personality Test: General Activity	−.43	
Factor VIII. Dependency		
Projective: Affiliation	.46	.41
Dependence	.49	.37
Overall Staff Prediction		
Performance in Competitive Exercise	.60	.38
Performance on In-Basket	.55	.51
Performance in Cooperative Exercise	.41	.42
Interview: Personal Impact	.49	.21
Oral Communications Skills	.41	.48
Projective: Achievement Motivation	.30	.40

assessment center behavior and trait ratings against company ratings of the same behaviors on the job.

Unfortunately, the AT&T Management Progress Study is the only one in which we can be certain no criterion contamination could have occurred. It is the only program in which assessment program results were collected for research only, with no one else in the AT&T organization having access to the results. Even so, most other investigators attempted to avoid spurious effects due to criterion contamination, or at least to estimate the magnitude of such effects; thus, their studies are useful for evaluating the relative validity of multiple assessment procedures for pinpointing managerial potential.

Overall Criteria of Success. In July 1965 five of the regional companies participating in the Management Progress Study submitted information on the current status of men who had taken part in the assessment procedures six to eight years previously. The data included management level achieved and current salary. Comparisons between staff predictions at the time of assessment and level achieved by mid-1965 are shown in Tables 3 and 4. The predictive validities of the assessment staff's global predictions are moderately high; for the college men, 31 (82 percent) of the 38 men who have made middle management were correctly identified by the assessment staffs; for the non-college men, 15 (75 percent) of 20 men who have made middle management were correctly identified. In contrast, of the 72 men (both college and non-college) who have not advanced beyond the first level of management, the assessment staffs correctly identified 68 (94 percent).

A second but rather coarse criterion of the men's organizational accomplishments since assessment is given by their salary progress over the ensuing years. The specific measure used was the difference between their salaries on

Table 2

Highest Correlation of Each Assessment Method with Staff Judgments

Assessment method	Overall staff prediction	I	II	III	IV	V	VI	VII	VIII
College sample									
Cooperative Exercise	41	44	31	39	37	18	30	-35	-18
Competitive Exercise	**60**	**67**	48	**62**	**47**	31	45	-39	-22
In-Basket	55	60	**76**	45	39	36	44	-18	-15
Mental Ability Test	36	47	37	22	23	**79**	17	-16	-24
Personality Test	29	33	30	27	28	-23	28	-43	-29
Projective Report	35	48	36	21	29	-33	**50**	-47	**49**
Interview	.49	.52	.42	.44	.30	.40	.40	**-.57**	.27
Non-college sample									
Cooperative Exercise	42	**60**	51	**52**	35	22	39	-43	-17
Competitive Exercise	47	57	44	47	36	17	36	-41	-33
In-Basket	**51**	59	68	49	24	27	26	-27	00
Mental Ability Test	44	51	**72**	28	32	**64**	22	-22	-20
Personality Test	24	22	30	-20	25	-19	18	-29	-34
Projective Report	40	51	41	35	**46**	25	**56**	-50	**41**
Interview	.48	.48	.53	.46	.45	.47	.50	**-.67**	.28

Note.—Boldface numerals indicate the highest correlation in each column for College and Non-college men. Factor Dimensions are:

    I General Effectiveness
    II Administrative Skills
    III Interpersonal Skills
    IV Control of Feelings
    V Intellectual Ability
    VI Work Oriented Motivation
    VII Passivity
    VIII Dependency

Table 3
Relationship between Assessment Staff Prediction and Level
Actually Achieved by July 1965 for 125 College Assessees

	STATUS IN JULY 1965		
STAFF ASSESSMENT PREDICTION	First-level management	Second-level management	Middle (third-level) management or above
Will make middle management in ten years	1	30	31
Will not make middle management in ten years	7	49	7

Source: Bray and Grant, 1966.
Note.—r (point biserial) = .44.

Table 4
Relationship between Assessment Staff Prediction and Level
Actually Achieved by July 1965 for 144 Non-college Assessees

	STATUS IN JULY 1965		
STAFF ASSESSMENT PREDICTION	First-level management	Second-level management	Middle (third-level) management or above
Will make middle management in ten years	3	23	15
Will not make middle management in ten years	61	37	5

Source: Bray and Grant, 1966.
Note.—r (point biserial) = .71.

June 30, 1965, and their salaries at the time of assessment. These data were available for 81 college men and 122 non-college men who had at least six years in management before being assessed. The higher and more significant correlations between assessment variables (both tests and ratings) and the salary progress criterion are shown in Table 5. Information in Table 5 shows clearly the superiority of staff judgments over paper-and-pencil tests. Since the staff judgments, in turn, depend so heavily on observations made during group and simulated exercises, these results give both direct and indirect evidence of the utility of the simulations techniques for estimating relative degrees of managerial potential in the Bell System. Moreover, the interview proves to be an important source of valid variance, appearing to be particularly useful for assessing such drive variables as Primacy of Work and Need for Advancement, and dependency or passivity variables such as Security and Approval needs.

These data constitute important support for comments made early in this chapter where it was argued that multiple assessment procedures had particular advantages over strictly individual difference measures for estimating motivational variables and for more directly observing and rating behaviors most like those important to fulfilling managerial job responsibilities.

Wollowick and McNamara (1969) correlated assessment results for 94 men who had gone through the IBM program with degree of increase in level of managerial responsibility during the three years after assessment. Level of management responsibility was based on a position code, taking account of such factors as number of persons supervised, job complexity, fiscal responsibility, skill and knowledge required, etc. Correlations significant at the .01 level were obtained for the following assessment measures:

Overall staff rating, .37.

Staff rating variables: Self-Confidence, .32; Written Communications, .29; Energy, .26; Decision Making, .29; and Resistance to Stress, .26.

Exercises: Cooperative Group Exercise, .28; Competitive Group Exercise, .25; and In-Basket, .32.

Tests: Ascendancy (Gordon Personal Profile), .39, and Vigor (Gordon Personal Profile), .32.

Unfortunately, there is strong likelihood in this study of criterion contamination. Decisions about assigning different levels of managerial responsibility to these men probably were based, in part, on assessment results. Wollowick and McNamara do not discuss this issue in their report of these results.

Since the Management Progress Study was undertaken, two-thirds of the operating companies in AT&T have established modified assessment centers, using no personality tests, to aid in selecting persons for promotion to first level supervision. By 1965, 12,000 craftsmen and 4,000 women had been assessed; in 1968, assessments were conducted for 3,000 men and 2,000 women.

A follow-up study (Personnel Research Staff, 1965) was done in 1965 to learn the effectiveness of the program. Since the results had been used for making personnel decisions, special precautions were taken to overcome problems of criterion contamination and problems of restriction in range.

Table 5
Correlations between Assessment Variables and Salary Progress
for College Men and Non-college Men in Four
Regional Companies of the Bell System

Assessment variables	College men Company A (N = 54)	College men Company C (N = 27)	Non-college men Company B (N = 83)	Non-college men Company C (N = 39)
Staff judgment (factors)				
I. General Effectiveness	.41	.51	.45	.52
II. Administrative Skills	.33	.33	.57	.45
III. Interpersonal Skills	.26	.36	.34	.33
IV. Control of Feelings	.34	.50	.17	.32
V. Intellectual Ability	.48	.30	.31	.07
VI. Work-Oriented Motivation	.16	.20	.29	.41
VII. Passivity	−.30	−.33	−.41	−.41
Performance exercises				
Cooperative Group Exercise	.15	.41	.37	.50
Competitive Group Exercise	.30	.50	.33	.28
In-Basket	.27	−.01	.44	.22
Psychological tests & inventories				
Scholastic Aptitude	.38	.32	.45	.28
Critical Thinking	.26	−.21	.46	.36
Contemporary Affairs	.35	.32	.26	−.09
Dominance (EPPS)	.26	.01	.40	−.05
Abasement (EPPS)	−.32	.13	−.25	.11
Change (EPPS)	.01	−.41	−.10	−.11
Endurance (EPPS)	.02	−.39	.07	.03
Aggression (EPPS)	.15	.49	.17	.01
Projective ratings[a]		(N = 81)	(N = 120)	
Dependence		−.35	−.20	
Achievement Motivation		.26	.30	
Interview ratings				
Oral Communication Skills		.22	.50	
Human Relations Skills		.20	.41	
Behavior Flexibility		.30	.04	
Need Approval-Superiors		−.36	−.27	
Need Approval-Peers		−.36	−.17	
Primacy of Work		.30	.25	
Energy		.35	.16	
Need Advancement		.49	.44	
Need Security		−.35	−.26	

Sources: Bray and Grant, 1966; Grant, Katkovsky, and Bray, 1967; Grant and Bray, 1969.
Note.—Only those variables with one or more r's greater than .30 are listed in this table.

[a] Men from the two companies were combined for the analyses of projective and interview variables. The salary progress measure for the projective and interview variables includes an additional year of company experience, up through June 30, 1966.

Five groups were identified for follow-up. The two most crucial groups included men rated "acceptable" in assessment who were actually promoted and a group of men promoted just prior to the start of the assessment program. If the acceptable group were found to be superior in performance and potential, it would be solid evidence that the assessment program had improved the accuracy of promotion decisions. The other three groups were (1) men rated "questionable" in assessment who were subsequently promoted anyway; (2) men rated "not acceptable" in assessment who were promoted anyway; and (3) men who were promoted after the assessment program was underway but who were never assessed.

Ratings and rankings of performance and estimates of potential were obtained in personal interviews with managers two levels above the men in the study. A combined rating and ranking was used to designate whether each man was an "above average" or "below average" performer on the job. In a similar way, immediate supervisors' ratings of potential were combined with district managers' rankings of potential to designate each man as having either "high potential" or "low potential."

Results of the two comparisons are shown in Tables 6 and 7. It is apparent that relatively more men with favorable assessment ratings are judged later to be effective and to have high potential. Nonetheless, the validity levels are very low, causing one to question whether the cost of such systematic assessments for promotion to first level is really warranted.

A number of factors may be causing these low validities, which are considerably lower than those obtained when multiple assessment procedures have been evaluated against managerial instead of supervisory job performance. Because these craftsmen programs have been used operationally, errors of leniency and rating distortions are perhaps introduced during assessment. This is particularly likely since no professional psychologists have been actually involved in the procedure. It is possible, therefore, that line managers asked to "run" these front line programs view such duty as an imposition and an intrusion on time better devoted to pursuing their day-to-day job responsibilities, and thereby give only half-hearted attention to the task of assessment. At any rate, any company intending to conduct multiple assessment procedures without the benefit of continued surveillance of professionals on their assessment staffs should examine the decision carefully in the context of the results reported above.

Behavior Rating Criteria. Earlier it was argued that a special advantage of multiple assessment procedures is that they reveal more explicitly how a person might respond to various organizational conditions and situational circumstances. Such information should then allow more informed recommendations for individualized or tailor-made training and development experiences, and for organizational actions to aid the maximal expression of each man's potential. We have already seen that assessment staff members are asked in most programs to express their observations in the form of a variety of trait, motivational, and behavior ratings. Presumably, these ratings should constitute the basic information for making individualized training and organizational action recommendations. Thus, it is crucial to learn something about the behavioral validity of such observations and ratings.

Table 6
Percentages of Men in Each Five Groups Who Were Designated
Above-Average Performers in Their Managerial Jobs
for All Companies Combined

	Total N	Number and percent "above average" N	%
Men assessed[a]			
Acceptable	136	93	68%
Questionable	61	40	65%
Not acceptable	26	12	46%
Men not assessed[b]			
Promoted since program	132	83	63%
Promoted before program	151	83	55%

Source: Personnel Research Staff, American Telephone and Telegraph, 1965.
[a] r (point biserial) = .13.
[b] r (phi) = .08.

Table 7
Percentages of Men in Each of the Five Groups Who Were
Designated as High Potential for Advancement
for All Companies Combined

	Total N	Number and percent with high potential N	%
Men assessed[a]			
Acceptable	136	68	50%
Questionable	61	24	40%
Not acceptable	26	8	31%
Men not assessed[b]			
Promoted since program	132	25	19%
Promoted before program	151	42	20%

Source: Personnel Research Staff, American Telephone and Telegraph, 1965.
[a] r (point biserial) = .14.
[b] r (phi) = .00.

Only a few investigators have correlated assessment trait and behavior ratings against coordinate trait and behavior ratings on the job, but their results do give support to the idea that assessment of staff members can diagnose behavior dimensions with a fair degree of convergent and discriminant validity (Campbell & Fiske, 1959).

Albrecht, Glaser, and Marks (1964) and Dicken and Black (1965) carried out follow-up studies of the later job effectiveness of managers who had gone through assessment programs earlier. Subjects in the Albrecht et al. study were 31 district marketing managers assessed by clinical procedures (personal history form, sentence completion test, human relations test, intelligence and critical thinking tests, and a two-hour interview) shortly after being promoted to managerial jobs. The assessment procedures were carried out in order to obtain ratings; they were not used in any way in the promotion process, and no reports of assessment results were given to anyone in the company. Thus, later ratings of job effectiveness should not have been contaminated in any way by knowledge of assessment results. Three psychologists ranked the 31 men according to predicted job effectiveness on four dimensions: Forecasting and Budgeting Effectiveness, Sales Performance, Interpersonal Relationships, and Overall Performance. After a year on the job, the 31 managers were ranked on each of the above dimensions by two managers above them and by their peers; the three sets of rankings were combined to form a composite index for each man on each dimension. Psychologists' clinical predictions and test scores were correlated with these composites. The assessment predictions yielded correlations of .43, .46, and .58, while test score correlations ranged from –.07 to .41 with a median of only .20. Thus, the psychologists revealed a good degree of diagnostic accuracy in their assessments; their ranking of the men on particular job dimensions was more highly related to effectiveness on corresponding dimensions than to effectiveness on other dimensions, as shown in Table 8.

This study is an effective demonstration of the feasibility of using assessment observations to predict particular aspects of managerial behavior rather than merely predicting an overall "go–no go" or success-failure criterion.

Dicken and Black (1965) obtained results generally similar to those just summarized, but their test battery was much more extensive, including the Strong Vocational Interest Blank, Minnesota Multiphasic Personality Inventory, Otis Quick Scoring Mental Ability Test, and other measures of clerical aptitude, spatial relations ability, supervisory knowledge, etc. Candidates for promotion to supervisory positions were tested for two firms, and narrative reports of about five hundred words were written for each candidate. Four psychologists independently read each report and rated the assessees on eight variables: Effective Intelligence, Personal Soundness, Drive and Ambition, Leadership and Dominance, Likeableness, Responsibility and Conscientiousness, Ability to Cooperate, and Overall Estimate of Potential.

Later (an average of three and one half years in one firm; seven years in the other), ratings were obtained on these same variables from company officials who had observed the assessees in their work settings. Table 9 shows correlations between assessment ratings and later company ratings for 31 men in one firm and 26 men in the other.

Table 8
Correlations between Assessment Predictions in Four Job
Areas and Composite Rankings of Effectiveness in the
Same Job Areas for 31 Marketing Managers

Assessment predictions	Composite effectiveness rankings			
	Forecasting and budgeting	Sales performance	Interpersonal relationships	Overall effectiveness
Forecasting and budgeting	.49	.15	.33	.34
Sales performance	.02	.58	.39	.39
Interpersonal relationships	.03	.24	.43	.27
Overall effectiveness	.35	.33	.40	.46

Source: Albrecht, Glaser, and Marks, 1964.

Results confirm the diagnostic capability of the assessment ratings. In nearly every instance, assessment ratings of specific variables show higher correlations with corresponding variables rated by company officials than with company ratings of non-corresponding variables. This is strong evidence that assessment staff members do discern behavioral tendencies among assessees that agree well with behaviors observed among them by other persons.

Thomson (1969) determined the current status of 119 managers who had participated in SOHIO's FACT program an average of a year and a half earlier. Ratings from each man's immediate supervisor and a higher level supervisor were pooled for the same thirteen behavior dimensions used by assessment staff members. The pooled ratings were correlated separately with psychologists' and line managers' assessment ratings. Table 10 shows the results.

Even though the validities are generally high, some of the behavior variables (Oral Communication, Orientation to Detail, Self-Direction, and Drive) do not meet the discriminant validity criterion. However, the majority of variables meet both convergent and discriminant criteria successfully, most notably Participation, Personal Breadth, Relationship with Authority, and Overall Potential.

In order to estimate possible effects of criterion contamination, Thomson carried out a separate analysis for the 18 subjects whose two supervisors both said they could not remember ever having seen or discussed the FACT report. For these men, the validities of psychologists' ratings for the 13 dimensions ranged from .12 to .78 with a median of .54; validities of the managers' ratings ranged between .09 and .73 with a median of .63. These values are substantially higher than those shown in Table 10 and are, of course, incompatible with any claim that validities for the larger group were spuriously elevated because of criterion contamination.

Manager-Organization Interactions

The foregoing validity evidence is impressive. Assessment program ratings show substantial validity for predicting not only global measures of managerial success but also for pinpointing accurately the major behavioral tendencies a

Table 9

Correlations between Assessment Ratings and Company Ratings of Assessees

	Firm 1 (N = 31)		Firm 2 (N = 26)		
	Correlation between corresponding variables	Mean correlation between non-corresponding variables	Correlation between corresponding variables	Test rating[a] (corresponding variable)	Mean correlation between non-corresponding variables
Intelligence	.40	.31	.65	.63	.06
Soundness	.37	.27	.29	.16	.17
Drive	.30	.16	.17	.43	-.10
Leadership	.41	.22	.19	.29	.07
Likableness	.30	.14	.40	.36	.16
Responsibility	.38	.09	.03	.19	-.04
Cooperativeness	.20	.24	.21	.40	.20
Potential	.51	.38	.31	.18	.19
Median values	.38	.23	.25	.33	.12

Source: Dicken and Black, 1965.

[a] For men in Firm 2, one set of psychologists' ratings was based on test results alone in addition to the ratings based on the 500-word assessment reports.

Table 10
Convergent Validities between Assessment Ratings and Pooled
Supervisory Ratings, and Median Correlations between
Non-corresponding Variables for 71[a] SOHIO Managers

	Psychologist Ratings		Manager Ratings	
Assessment Ratings	Validity	Median correlation between non-corresponding variables	Validity	Median correlation between non-corresponding variables
Participation	.58	.39	.65	.40
Oral communication	.44	.41	.37	.34
Personal acceptability	.33	.24	.37	.23
Impact	.50	.34	.47	.36
Quality of participation	.31	.34	.38	.27
Personal breadth	.55	.37	.52	.36
Orientation to detail	.19	.25	.14	.27
Self-direction	.42	.31	.35	.33
Relationship with authority	.35	.21	.37	.19
Originality	.45	.37	.45	.34
Understanding of people	.35	.25	.39	.27
Drive	.12	.20	.29	.23
Overall potential	.64	.40	.64	.36
Median	.42	.34	.38	.33

Source: Thomson, 1969.

[a]Of the 119 men who had been assessed, complete data were available for only 71.

man is likely to show in a job situation. A well-designed multiple assessment procedure can, therefore, be used with confidence to develop recommendations of the type suggested earlier in this chapter. However, recommendations for organizational actions and practices and for individually tailored training or development programs have not been studied systematically. In fact, most assessment programs have placed primary emphasis on the identification aspects of assessment and have, for the most part, ignored the organizational and developmental implications of the carefully derived diagnostic profiles developed during the multiple assessment procedure.

However, one careful investigation (Berlew, 1965; Berlew & Hall, 1966) of the effects of providing challenge in early job assignments does offer some intriguing leads. Subjects of the study were 44 college men assessed in 1956 as part of AT&T's Management Progress Study and an additional 18 college men assessed during 1957.

Degree of job challenge during each man's first year on the job was estimated from interviews conducted with company officials able to describe the job held by each man, the personalities and styles of his superiors, and organizational and physical contexts in which he worked. Berlew and Hall used the interview protocols to estimate the level of expectations the company had for each man in 18 specific behavioral areas ranging from "Opportunity to Exercise Imagination and Technical Competence" to "Demands made upon Personal Autonomy, Loyalty, and Initiative." The degree of expectation for each area for each man was rated from 1 (low) to 3 (high), and "job challenge" was defined simply as the sum of the rated expectations held by the company for each man. In other words, it was assumed that men would be more challenged in jobs where expectations were high and less challenged in jobs where expectations were low.

In 1962, global appraisals of each man's performance and potential were made. These were combined with an index of salary growth to form a Success Index. In addition, a number of measures of job performance, such as annual appraisals and interviewers' estimates of how well each man accomplished the above expectations, were summed to form a Performance Index. Correlations between first-year job challenges and status on the Success Index were .32 and .37 for the two groups; correlations between first-year job challenge and status on the Performance Index were .54 and .29 for the two groups. Thus, men judged to have more challenging first jobs were found to be performing better and accomplishing more after four or five years with the company than men judged to have less challenging first jobs.

However, ability level may have an indirect effect on the level of challenge experienced by a man in his first job. For example, Bray (1966) reported a correlation of .33 between overall staff assessment predictions and degree of job challenge for 98 men who had participated in the Management Progress Study.

Something occurs very early in a man's career to single him out for more or less taxing job assignments. It is likely that more effective men are able to demonstrate their effectiveness within a few months after being placed on their first jobs, and that they may then be assigned more challenging job activities. Elsewhere (Campbell, et al., 1970), I report results of correcting the job challenge correlations for possible effects of differential ability patterns. Those corrected coefficients (partial correlations between first-year job challenge and the Success and Performance indexes with assessment ratings held constant) still show moderate magnitudes of .24, .30, .48, and .21.

Thus, the evidence suggests that first-year job challenge is probably associated with later judgments of success and job performance, quite aside from the tendency for degree of job challenge to be associated with the overall effectiveness of men assigned to these jobs.

This finding is provocative because it clearly illustrates the kind of interaction between individual diagnoses derived from multiple assessment procedures and job and organizational conditions that have been emphasized in this chapter. Evidence from these studies shows that men doing better during assessment also do better in their management jobs; it also shows that men receiving especially challenging first job assignments do better in later managerial jobs. Most important, the evidence suggests the possibility of highly important multiplicative effects between early job challenge (opportunity) and assessment ratings (ability). Future research should tackle the difficult problem of tracing further the complex linkages between ability variables (broadly defined as those dimensions capable of assessment), motivation and opportunity variables (such as those studied by Berlew and Hall), and the emergence of different patterns of managerial job behavior.

INCREMENTAL VALIDITY OF MULTIPLE ASSESSMENT PROCEDURES

Because multiple assessment procedures are more costly than standardized paper-and-pencil tests and inventories, it is important to consider whether or not their special advantages are sufficient to offset their added cost. Glaser, Schwarz, and Flanagan (1958) seemed to show that situational and clinical procedures added little to what could be obtained from two short paper-and-pencil tests [basic ability ($r = .25$); supervisory practices ($r = .23$)] for predicting supervisory effectiveness. From 227 civilian supervisors working in two large military depots, Glaser et al. identified 40 individuals at each of two extremes in job proficiency who were equated for age, supervisory experience, and scores on the basic ability and supervisory practices test. Panel and individual interviews, a leaderless group discussion session, a role-playing situation, and a simulated management work situation were then applied to the subjects in order to identify behavioral differences between the high and low groups which were not related to test scores. Biserial correlation coefficients between these assessment procedures and status on the dichotomous supervisory effectiveness variable ranged from .08 for the management work simulation to .17 for the leaderless group discussion. Multiple correlations between various combinations of assessment procedures and tests were between .30 and .33. The level of predictive variance with the group discussion procedure was only 11 percent, but was still nearly twice the level of 6 percent shown for the basic ability test used alone. (The two tests in combination accounted for 7 percent valid variance.)

Other more recent studies at AT&T and IBM show results considerably more favorable for arguing significant incremental validities for multiple assessment procedures.

Bray and Grant (1966) determined the degree of significant variance which performance in group exercises added to overall staff predictions of assessees' career success. Using information shown in Table 5 of this chapter, they identified the judgment rating (based on either the group exercises or the In-Basket simulation) and the test or inventory score correlating highest with salary progress in each of the four groups shown in Table 5. For example, for college men in Company A, the judgment rating correlating highest with salary progress is derived from the competitive group exercise ($r = .30$), and the test correlating highest with salary progress is the Scholastic Aptitude Test ($r = .38$). Bray and Grant used these values to compute partial correlations between judgment ratings and salary progress with test or inventory scores held constant. Values they obtained are shown below:

	College Men		Non-College Men	
	Company A	Company C	Company B	Company C
	($N = 54$)	($N = 27$)	($N = 83$)	($N = 39$)
Partial correlation	.32	.39	.29	.42
Percent variance (r^2)	10%	15%	8%	18%

It is apparent that the special procedures unique to the Multiple Assessment Approach (simulations and group exercises) do yield ratings independently predictive of career progress in AT&T.

Wollowick and McNamara's (1969) analyses and results bear even more closely on the issue of incremental validity for multiple assessment procedures. Their subjects were 94 lower- and middle-level IBM managers who had gone through the IBM assessment program approximately three years previously (in 1964-1965). Correlations were computed between the subjects' degree of increase in managerial responsibility (between 1965 and 1968) and test scores, ratings of performance in assessment exercises, and staff ratings (behavior ratings) of assessees' characteristics. Multiple correlation coefficients were also computed for various predictor combinations.

The highest correlation for any test or inventory score was .39 for the Ascendancy scale on the Gordon Personal Profile; the highest correlation for any exercise was .32 for the performance rating on the In-Basket; the highest correlation for any characteristic was .32 for the behavior rating of Self-Confidence. Thus, each of these different sets of information contributed validity to variance in the criterion measure. Moreover, the best combinations of measures from each of the subsets yielded substantial and approximately equivalent multiple correlations. This is shown below:

Predictor Composite	R
Best test composite (Ascendancy and Vigor from Gordon Personal Inventory)	.45
Best performance composite (In-Basket and Cooperative Group Exercise)	.39
Best characteristics composite (behavior variable ratings of Self-Confidence, Written Communications Skills, and Administrative Ability)	.41

The most important and intriguing line of evidence showing how the various components contribute to overall prediction is the order in which they contribute significantly to a stepwise multiple regression equation. This is shown in Table 11.

The sequencing of the variables (first a test variable, then an exercise variable, then a characteristic variable, etc.) as they contribute to the multiple R is of particular interest. This sequence is convincing evidence that all three subsets of information contribute heavily to the predictive success of the multiple assessment program. The difference in magnitudes of multiple R's based on tests only and those utilizing, in addition, elements unique to multiple assessment procedures also constitutes impressive evidence for the

Table 11
Variables Contributing Significantly to Multiple Correlation
Coefficients in Stepwise Order

Variables and Source	R	R^2 (percent variance)
Ascendancy (test)	.39	15%
+ In-Basket (exercise)	.46	21%
+ Administrative Ability (behavior rating)	.51	26%
+ Vigor (test)	.56	31%
+ Cooperative Group Performance (exercise)	.59	35%
+ Interpersonal Contact (behavior rating)	.60	36%
+ Biographical Inventory Success Scale (test)	.62	38%

Source: Wollowick and McNamara, 1969.

incremental validities embedded in simulation, group exercises, and clinical ratings.

Hinrichs (1969) showed, however, that ratings of managerial potential based on information already available in the personnel records of 47 young IBM managers correlated moderately (r = .46) with assessment program ratings of their managerial potential. He argues from this finding that careful evaluation of personnel records "can perhaps provide much of the same information which evolves from the lengthy and expensive two-day assessment program [Hinrichs, 1969, p. 431]."

In my opinion, Hinrichs' argument, though reasonable, cannot be sustained on the basis of the single coefficient of .46 he reports in his investigation. Nearly 80 percent of the variance in the assessment program ratings remains unassociated with the ratings based on the personnel records; therefore, it seems highly probable (particularly in view of the AT&T and IBM studies discussed above) that the "lengthy and expensive" assessment program does contribute independent, valid, and usefully diagnostic information about men's abilities and behavioral tendencies that is not contributed by ratings based merely on file information.

SUMMARY

Managers, administrators, and executives are a critical natural resource in our knowledge-oriented, industrial society. Moreover, they are in short supply; more and more managers are needed to administer our constantly and rapidly expanding firms and institutions. Meeting these manpower demands requires procedures with increased precision for identifying persons with potential for effective managing and greater accuracy in planning and implementing educational programs and organizational practices to assure that persons with managerial potential may express it quickly and fully. This need for improved diagnosis of managerial capabilities has, during recent years, led a few firms and government units to undertake multiple assessment procedures for identifying and developing managerial talent.

In contrast to other more restricted and narrower methods of identifying human potential (such as paper-and-pencil tests and inventories), multiple assessment procedures have been characterized by careful planning, systematic and carefully programmed procedures, and an impressive amount of evaluative research. Research evidence suggests the following conclusions about multiple assessment procedures.

1. A variety of behavioral dimensions are observable during assessment. The nature of dimensions differs from program to program, but nearly all programs include such factors as Overall Activity, Organizing and Planning Skills, Interpersonal Competence, Cognitive Competence, Work Orientation, Personal Control, and General Effectiveness.

2. Behavior observations during multiple assessment procedures can be recorded and rated with high reliability. High levels of agreement are shown between pairs of psychologist staff-observers, between pairs of manager staff-observers, and between pairs of psychologist-manager staff-observers. When *both* professionals (psychologists) and nonprofessionals (managers) serve as staff members during the same program, they agree well with one another in diagnosing the attributes and behavior tendencies of participants.

3. All elements of multiple assessment procedures contribute important but differential aspects to overall judgments and behavior ratings developed during assessment. It is apparent, for example, that procedures unique to multiple assessment procedures (such as simulations and group exercises) strongly influence staff judgments in such areas as Interpersonal Competence, Organizing and Planning, and General Effectiveness. Moreover, ratings derived from protocols based on clinical procedures (such as interview and projective information) are most highly related to staff judgments of personality and motivational dimensions such as Work Orientation, Passivity, and Dependency.

4. Both overall judgments and specific behavior ratings have shown reasonably high validities for predicting, not only later organizational status (such as salary growth or level of managerial responsibility), but also the patterns of managerial behaviors shown by multiple assessment procedures participants in their later managerial jobs. This is an important finding, for it confirms the usefulness of multiple assessment procedures not only for estimating overall potential but for developing an accurate behavioral diagnosis or description of individual participants.

5. Limited evidence from AT&T suggests that multiple assessment procedures programs run solely by nonprofessionals may, for some undetermined reason, yield evaluations with validities considerably below those conducted either by all professionals or by teams of both professionals and nonprofessionals.

6. Finally, evidence is impressive that procedures unique to the multiple assessment approach do contribute incremental validities beyond those shown by paper-and-pencil tests and inventories alone.

We may conclude, then, that multiple assessment procedures for identifying managerial talent have been shown to possess the particular advantages suggested by their advocates. For example, multiple assessment procedures are not restricted to measuring only individual differences variables; they also provide information for estimating validly how individual attributes may relate to motivational and opportunity factors within particular organizational settings. Moreover, it is apparent that multiple assessment procedures do provide samples more directly relevant to the typical behavioral demands of managerial jobs. Finally, and most important, evidence showing moderately high relationships between trait and behavior ratings derived from assessment programs and coordinate trait and behavior ratings from job settings confirms that multiple assessment procedures program diagnoses may be used with confidence to make individualized training and organizational action recommendations. Such recommendations may form the basis for assuring greater accuracy in planning and implementing educational programs and organizational policies designed to help persons realize their top potential.

CHAPTER VI

The Personality Research Form and vocational interest research

Thomas F. Siess and Douglas N. Jackson

While personality theorists (Allport, 1961; Murphy, 1947) have traditionally viewed interests as emerging lawfully in the process of personality development, the major focus of much of contemporary research has been upon specific empirical predictions rather than upon testing basic theory. In a similar vein, a survey of current practices among vocational counselors would undoubtedly reveal that the interpretations and constructs that they typically employ are other than those of the personality theorist. In many instances, vocational interests are viewed as something apart from personality, requiring a different theory and different techniques of assessment.

Although the modal treatment of occupational interests has tended to minimize the role of personality, some investigators, particularly those concerned with the development of a theoretical framework for occupational behavior, have focused upon the possible link between vocational interests and personality. This relationship has been discussed in several ways. First, a common conceptual framework for vocational interests and personality is clearly assumed in a book by Darley and Hagenah (1955). Following their review of the vocational interest measurement literature, they say that "measured vocational interests reflect the needs and motivations of individuals [p. 191]." Second, the nature of the link between personality and occupational choice has been dealt with both conceptually and empirically. For example, Super's (1953) formulation concerning the process of occupational choice is built on the assumption that the choice of an occupation represents an effort by the individual to implement his self-concept. Stated operationally, this assumption would suggest that the choice of an occupation is at least in part predictable from the individual's self-description as reflected in a personality inventory. Suggestive, but not entirely conclusive, support for this hypothesis can be found in a variety of studies indicating that there appear to be distinct personality characteristics associated with different occupational groups (e.g., Roe, 1956; Segal, 1961; Siegelman & Peck, 1960).

PROBLEMS IN LINKING OCCUPATIONAL INTERESTS
TO PERSONALITY

Several difficulties arise in attempting to use these conceptual formulations and empirical relationships to advance understanding of the process of interest development or occupational choice. In the case of research regarding the development of vocational interests, one of the major difficulties arises from the fact that much of what is known about vocational interests is based on research using instruments intended primarily to meet the practical demands of the counselor rather than the demands of the interest theorist or research worker. This is best exemplified in the case of the interpretation of empirically-derived scales from the Strong Vocational Interest Blank (SVIB), one of the most widely used instruments in occupational psychology. Several problems become apparent when substantive or theoretical interpretations are sought for results from empirically-derived scales such as those in the SVIB (cf. Siess & Jackson, 1970).

First, there is the problem of placing a construct interpretation on scales which are complex and multidimensional in terms of their item content, and which lack a clear psychological definition apart from their manner of construction. This potential lack of isomorphism between the person's score on an empirically-derived scale and the level of a single attribute exacerbates the interpretive problem both for the client who wants to use these scores to arrive at a better understanding of himself, and for the research worker who is interested in generating testable hypotheses about the nature of vocational interests and personality.

The second problem has been termed the "reference group" problem. Not only does accurate interpretation depend upon knowledge or supposition regarding the precise nature of criterion groups (e.g., "successful men in the occupation" and "men-in-general" in the case of the SVIB), but also must take account of occupational and cultural changes. The role demands and behaviors appropriate for a variety of occupations have changed substantially for many occupations. For example, the occupation of aviator forty years ago probably attracted men challenged by risk and adventure to a greater extent than today; psychologists forming Strong's criterion group were largely academic experimental psychologists, rather than the more diverse group we comprise at present; and accountants were more like bookkeepers than the systems analysts and professional advisors that are often encountered now. These and other changes have necessitated revision of original SVIB scales. But such changes in occupational roles continue to evolve, often without clear understanding of their nature and extent. Thus, there is some risk in imputing a construct interpretation to an empirically-derived scale devised on the basis of particular administrative and psychometric procedures.

A third and equally serious objection to this approach is that it has diverted scientific inquiry away from the theoretically-based study of vocational interests and decision making, in relation to other processes relevant to personality. As Loevinger (1957) has aptly stated:

The argument against classical criterion-oriented psychometrics is two-fold: it contributes no more to the science of psychology than rules for boiling an egg contribute to the science of chemistry, and the number of genuine egg-boiling decisions which clinicians and psychotechnologists face is small compared with the number of situations where a deeper knowledge of psychological theory would be helpful [p. 82].

Recent efforts by David Campbell and his colleagues (e.g., Campbell, Borgen, Eastes, Johansson, & Peterson, 1968) to place greater emphasis upon substantive scales in the revision of the SVIB manifests an awareness of these problems.

The lack of emphasis upon theory in much vocational interest measurement and research, together with the unavailability of construct-oriented tests and proper analytical tools has, in our view, been largely responsible for the inconsistent empirical support received for the hypothesis that vocational interests and choice have foundations in personality. Cottle (1950), for example, factor-analyzed the MMPI, the Bell Adjustment Inventory, the Kuder Preference Record, and the SVIB. The results of this analysis showed that there was one set of factors common to the two personality inventories and a second set of factors common to the two interest inventories. There were, however, no factors which were common to both types of inventories. These apparently low relationships between personality and interests can be explained readily by pointing out that the personality inventories used in this and other studies have very similar and often identical items, have scales possessing item overlap, and use the same response format. Furthermore, the interest inventories used in the study are also similar in item and response format. These similarities within each type of measure, together with biases in the method of factor analysis used (cf. Jackson, 1969), may enhance the relationship between the personality scales on the one hand and the interest scales on the other, while obscuring the relationship between the two types of inventories, even though one may well exist (Siess & Jackson, 1970).

A further important problem in interpreting the data concerning personality correlates of occupational choice is that of imputing priority to personality variables based upon temporally post hoc data. In a large number of the published studies, the personality data were gathered after the choice of the occupation had been made. It is, therefore, difficult to know whether the choices were, in fact, a result of the individual's self-perception or if, on the other hand, the individual's self-perception changes as a consequence of having chosen some occupational role. He has become, as the sociologist Becker (1960) has termed it, increasingly committed to certain roles and role expectations. A second difficulty in the study of occupational choice has to do with the fact that the choice of an occupation is not a single event but rather a complex process spanning a number of years and encompassing a series of choices or decisions. These points have been underscored by Siess (1964).

There is a final consideration regarding the nature of occupational behavior relevant to the research on personality correlates of both occupational interests and occupational choice. In virtually all of the published research, subjects have been selected to represent certain occupations with the apparently implicit or explicit assumption that an occupation reflects a single role construct or a homogeneous set of role behaviors. It would appear more reasonable, however, to assume that a single occupation may well encompass a variety of role models, and that satisfaction within a single occupation could be achieved by individuals holding rather different role preferences. To clarify this point, the reader is asked to reflect on the apparent differences between psychologists who emphasize either a research, a teaching, or a service role. Studies treating occupations as single entities or role constructs undoubtedly tend to obscure similarities between sub-roles across different occupational groups, as well as obscuring differences between sub-roles within a single occupation.

RECENT EVIDENCE SUPPORTING A PERSONOLOGICAL INTERPRETATION OF OCCUPATIONAL BEHAVIOR

Two studies will be reported in this section. These were designed, first of all, to show the relevance of personological constructs in general and the Personality Research Form (PRF, Jackson, 1967) in particular for the study of occupational interests and occupational choice. Secondly, they are intended to avoid some of the difficulties in certain previous studies. The first of these studies represents an attempt to assess the relationship between personality and vocational interests using an analytic method focusing on correlations between, rather than within, methods of measurement. The second study attempts to look at the relationship between personality and choice behavior in a situation where the choice followed the administration of the personality inventory, and where greater control of relevant variables was possible than in naturalistic observation. Prior to describing and interpreting these studies, however, a brief summary of the conceptions underlying the construction of the PRF is in order, particularly because it is relatively new, and involved a unique combination of test construction strategies.

The Rationale and Development of the Personality Research Form

The Personality Research Form involved a number of innovations in the development of personality scales and used an elaborate sequential strategy for selecting items to optimize certain important properties in a personality scale. For readers who are interested in a detailed description of the sequential strategies used in test construction, the Manual (Jackson, 1967) or a more recent publication (Jackson, 1970) may be consulted. The following discussion represents a highlight of some of the salient features of scale construction and refers to a few of the recent studies bearing on the validity of the PRF.

One of the important guiding principles in the construction of the PRF was that the nature and the quality of the original item pool was a necessary precondition for deriving adequate scales. It was considered essential to develop carefully formulated theoretical definitions of the traits to be measured prior to preparing the item pool. Beginning with the variables of personality as originally defined by Henry Murray (1938) and his associates, careful definitions of each characteristic were formulated. These formed a basis for creating a grid of events and occasions, similar in certain respects to a facet design proposed by Guttman (1950) for factor-analytic studies, so that each trait might be represented and generalizable across the many different situations where it is assumed to occur. Thus, the variable of Achievement might be manifested in a variety of situations which called for an individual seeking to maintain a standard of excellence, and might be represented by different modes of expression in these various situations. This kind of analysis provided a basis for development of a large item pool—averaging over 100 items for each scale—which were carefully reviewed for clarity and conformity with the initial definition. An important aspect of this editorial process was the attempt to delineate the theoretically related constructs so that conceptual overlap and spurious correlation between scales was avoided. On this basis, a number of items were eliminated prior to their having been subjected to any empirical evaluation.

After editorial work on items had been completed, the preliminary item samples were administered to groups of college students under carefully supervised conditions. The reliabilities of the original scales in their long form proved to be quite substantial, with a median value of .92. The empirical evaluation of items proceeded sequentially, utilizing the high speed and flexibility of the digital computer to assist in decision making. First of all, biserial correlations were computed between every item and every total scale score in the set, as well as between each item and a specially constructed scale reflecting desirability bias. These biserial correlations are closely associated with the first unrotated principle component of an item set (Neill & Jackson, 1970). The decisional process regarding items involved, first, the elimination of items showing a higher correlation with the desirability scale than the scale for which they were constructed. Secondly, items with endorsement proportions in the keyed direction which were less than .05 or more than .95 were eliminated as providing only limited information and failing to differentiate subjects reliably. The next step involved the comparison of the item's biserial correlation with its own total score with that for every other score in the set of scales with which it was administered. Items correlating more highly with an irrelevant scale than their own scale were eliminated. This step was considered to be important if one wished to have scales sufficiently distinct so as to later be capable of demonstrating the properties of convergent and discriminant validity (Campbell & Fiske, 1959). If an item was able to pass these hurdles, it was retained with the other successful items, and a differential reliability index was computed. This index reflects the item's content saturation free from the effects of desirability bias. It has the effect of lowering a scale's correlation with desirability, while preserving the original definition of the content as much as possible. Items were next ranked on the basis of the Differential Reliability Index, and the best 40 items within each scale were retained. A computer program was prepared to maximize the similarity among two parallel forms in terms of content saturation, means, and standard deviations, and this program was applied to the items in order to provide forms which were substantively and statistically strictly parallel. A final editorial review sought to eliminate item redundancy within a form in order that the generalizability of the content measured by the scale might be enhanced. Final forms were constructed, and a variety of validational studies were undertaken.

The first validational study involved correlations between a number of measures, including a specially-constructed adjective checklist, and behavior ratings of the subject by persons who knew him well. These were incorporated into a multitrait-multimethod matrix, and the correlation between each scale and the relevant predicted criteria were computed. The median correlation between the PRF scale and a relevant adjective checklist was .56; the median correlation with an appropriate behavior rating measure of personality by a group of judges who resided with the subject was .52. In a further validational study, Jackson and Guthrie (1968) applied multimethod factor analysis (Jackson, 1969) to a set of PRF scale scores, together with self-ratings and peer behavior ratings, and found that the 20 PRF scales, in general, defined distinct multimethod factors. Eighteen factors were delineated among the 20 scales, with the three measures representing a trait generally being the highest on each factor. Dominance and Abasement defined opposite ends of a single dimension, while Impulsivity and Aggression loaded on the same factor in the same direction.

The Personality Research Form is available in standard forms (Form A and Form B, each comprised of 15 20-item scales of personality, making a total of 300 items). Longer forms (Form AA and Form BB) consist of the same 15 scales, contained in Forms A and B, together with 7 additional scales. Thus, there are 22 scales in each of the longer forms, each consisting of 20 items, making a total of 440 items. These comprise 20 content scales and 2 validity scales, Infrequency and Desirability.

The listing below, adapted from the PRF *Manual* (Jackson, 1967), organizes the scales into units on the basis of substantive areas. A line separates opposing poles of each domain. Scales included only on the standard forms (Forms A and B) are indicated by an asterisk.

A. Measures of Impulse Expression and Control
Impulsivity*
Change

Harmavoidance*
Order*
Cognitive Structure

B. Measures of Orientation toward Work and Play
Achievement*
Endurance*

Play*

C. Measures of Orientation toward Direction from Other People
Succorance

Autonomy*

D. Measures of Intellectual and Aesthetic Orientations
Understanding*
Sentience

E. Measures of Degree of Ascendancy
Dominance*

Abasement

F. Measures of Degree and Quality of Interpersonal Orientation
Affiliation*
Nurturance*
Exhibition*
Social Recognition*

Aggression*
Defendence

G. Measures of Test-Taking Attitudes and Validity
Desirability
Infrequency*

Interpretation typically involves first plotting the scores on a male or a female profile, each based on over one thousand college students selected from approximately thirty North American colleges, and then examining the profile for consistent patterns.

Vocational Interests and Personality: An Empirical Synthesis
In the first study to be reported (Siess & Jackson, 1970), both the SVIB and the PRF were administered to 212 male college students. The 22 scales of the PRF and 37 of the occupational scales from the SVIB were intercorrelated and factor-analyzed using a multimethod factor analysis (Jackson, 1969). In the present problem this method involved substituting an identity matrix (ones in the diagonal and zeros in the off-diagonal positions) for the original correlations between the SVIB scales. The same was done for the original correlations between the PRF scales. Doing this removed all of the variance unique to a single method of measurement, and only that variance common to the two types of inventory remains.

Discussion of Vocational Interest–Personality Factors
In the following paragraphs, we have listed the salient loadings (those

greater than ± .30) for each factor, followed by an interpretation of that factor. For the convenience of the reader, pairwise plots of Factors I and IV, II and III, and V and VII are presented in Figures 1 through 3, respectively.

Factor I

Endurance	.65
Engineer	.45
Achievement	.39
Chemist (Physicist)	.39
Production Manager	.34
Understanding	.32
Social Recognition	−.30
Succorance	−.30

The pattern of loadings for this factor suggest a preference for working with things, on one hand, or people on the other. The label, *Technically-oriented Achievement vs. Social Recognition,* is suggested by the salient factor loadings. Individuals scoring high on the positive pole of this dimension would probably be those who are willing to work diligently towards distant and perhaps abstract goals and to respond positively to the challenge of a very difficult task. On the other hand, people at the negative pole would tend to be dependent upon rewards which are social in nature. They could be expected to respond most favorably to visible symbols of prestige and social status, and to rewards such as praise and advancement. Seeking to achieve a standard of excellence would probably be characteristic of those people at the positive end of this dimension. Alternatively, for those at the negative pole working in a social context with opportunities for satisfying social dependency needs would be more important.

Factor II

Dominance	.69
Nurturance	.50
Desirability	.49
Public Administrator	.49
Exhibition	.45
Affiliation	.44
Personnel Manager	.44
YMCA Secretary	.43
Social Science High School Teacher	.35
YMCA Physical Director	.35
Guidance Counselor	.34
Minister	.31
Experimental Psychologist	−.36

This factor is clearly a social service dimension, reflecting the desire to

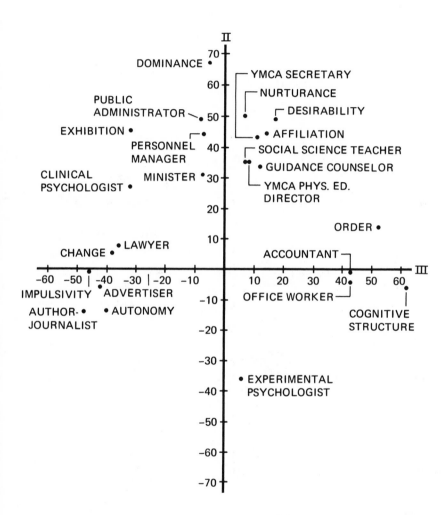

Figure 1. Factor plot of dimensions derived from multimethod factor analysis: Factor I–
      Technically-oriented Achievement vs. Social Recognition; and Factor IV–
      Practical.

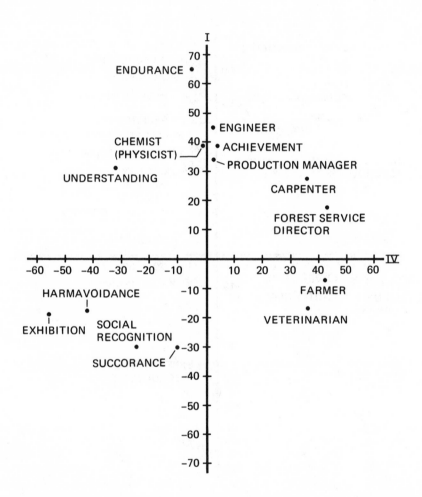

Figure 2. Factor plot of dimensions derived from multimethod factor analysis: Factor II–
Human Relations Management; and Factor III–Impulse Control vs. Expression.

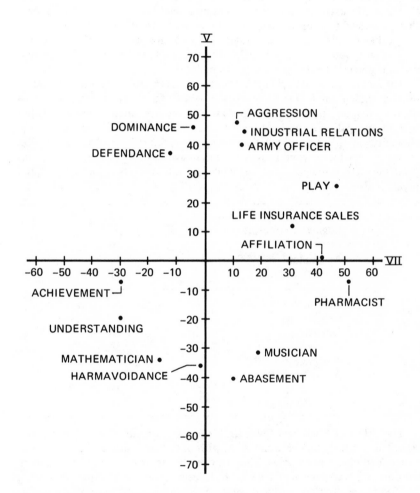

Figure 3. Factor plot of dimensions derived from multimethod factor analysis: Factor V–
Aggressive Leadership; and Factor VII–Social Contact.

help others. The fact that the highest positive loading is that for the Dominance scale would suggest, however, that this desire does not involve becoming subservient to others. Since the general pattern of loadings on this dimension suggests an individual who achieves satisfaction from directing the activities of others, it has been named *Social Control and Service* or *Human Relations Management,* rather than simply *Social Service.* One would expect that an individual scoring high on this dimension would be at ease in dealing with other people and would enjoy being an active participant in structuring a social situation. The desire to help others may also involve a need to do that which is perceived as being socially desirable.

The fact that the Clinical Psychologist scale has a moderate positive loading on this dimension (.27), while the Experimental Psychologist scale has a negative loading, provides some support for the hypothesis suggested earlier that an occupation should not be viewed as a single role construct. While psychologists in different specialties may have a number of characteristics in common, this factor would suggest that clinical psychologists find situations involving social influence satisfying while this role is reversed for experimental psychologists.

Factor III		
	Cognitive Structure	.62
	Order	.50
	Accountant	.41
	Office Worker	.41
	Clinical Psychologist	−.32
	Exhibition	−.32
	Lawyer	−.36
	Change	−.38
	Autonomy	−.40
	Advertising Man	−.42
	Impulsivity	−.46
	Author-Journalist	−.48

The title which has been given to this factor is *Impulse Control vs. Expression.* This is a truly bipolar dimension, with both personality and occupational scales loading on both poles. The positive and negative poles of this dimension are arbitrary and could easily have been reversed. The person scoring high on the positive end of the dimension would be expected to have a preference for a closely structured and well-regulated environment governed by clearly formulated rules. By contrast, an individual scoring high at the negative pole would prefer to have a loosely controlled and unstructured environment. Furthermore, this individual might be expected to rebel against restraints and regulations or at least would be rather impatient and uncomfortable with them.

It is interesting to note that the scales representing the Verbal-Linguistic group of the SVIB have loadings on the same end of the dimension as the PRF scales implying impulse expression (e.g., Exhibition and Impulsivity). It is possible that this convergence between interests in Verbal-Linguistic occupations and Impulsivity reflects a history of successful and reinforced practice in manipulating verbal symbols in novel ways. This being the case, one would expect that these individuals would also demonstrate above average verbal fluency. This in turn would lead to the hypothesis that this factor might represent a convergence of vocational interests, personality, and ability variables.

Factor IV

Forest Service Director	.47
Farmer	.42
Veterinarian	.36
Carpenter	.36
Understanding	−.32
Harmavoidance	−.42
Exhibition	−.56

This factor is probably best characterized as a *Practical* dimension. Individuals obtaining a high score on the positive end of this dimension would probably prefer activities involving mastery over concrete and practical aspects of his environment such as those associated with the skilled trades. They would not be overly concerned about physical risk, nor would outdoor activities be unpleasant. The negative loadings for the three personality scales on this dimension suggest still another appropriate interpretation. One would predict that individuals who are high on this dimension would find situations in which they are the focus of attention quite distasteful. One might further predict that they would enjoy activities which required a degree of manual skill in preference to those involving general intellectual curiosity.

Factor V

Aggression	.48
Dominance	.46
Industrial Relations	.45
Army Officer	.40
Defendence	.37
Musician	−.31
Mathematician	−.34
Harmavoidance	−.36
Abasement	−.40

This is an *Aggressive Leadership* or a control dimension. It appears to involve a different kind of control than was reflected by Factor II. Where the social control implied in Factor II would appear to be motivated by humanitarian concerns, this factor seems to involve a preference for aggressive leadership, oriented primarily toward management and authority. The two factors also vary in the style of social control employed. Factor II would involve persuasion and the adroit use of subtle forms of social influence and advising. Factor V describes a form of direct influence, involving the direction and command of others. The occupations with negative loadings on this scale would appear to be those particularly marked by an absence of the opportunity to fulfill aggressive and dominance needs. It can be noted, parenthetically, that the Industrial Relations scale of the SVIB used here was based on a criterion sample of industrial psychologists. This points again to the fact that sub-groups within an occupation can be characterized by rather distinct sets of personality characteristics.

Factor VI

Sentience	.66
Understanding	.57
Doctor	.38
Architect	.34
Change	.33
YMCA Physical Director	.30
Musician	.30
Harmavoidance	−.36
Banker	−.47

This factor might best be labeled *Esthetic and Intellectual Interests.* The common bond between these scales would seem to be a sensitivity to a variety of experiences and interest in interpreting those experiences in the framework of a consistent world view. Those scoring high on the positive pole would be expected to take particular interest in man's relationship to his environment, and especially ways of improving and enriching man's experience. This interest in human welfare is probably intellectual and impersonal in nature, rather than reflective of a desire for direct social contact and influence such as that suggested in Factor II.

Factor VII

Pharmacist	.51
Play	.47
Affiliation	.41
Life Insurance Sales	.31
Achievement	−.30
Understanding	−.30

This factor might best be called *Social Contact.* It seems to reflect a desire for casual and pleasant social participation which remains uncomplicated and perhaps superficial. Persons scoring high on this factor probably find social contacts pleasant and enjoyable for their own sake. They probably readily accept other people and have a light-hearted and easy-going orientation toward others.

Implications for the Interpretation of Interest Constructs

For the counselor, these data suggest that SVIB scales can be interpreted in terms of personological constructs. For example, it would appear reasonable to interpret an SVIB profile with high scores on Group X (Lawyer, Author-Journalist, and Advertising Man) and low scores in the Business Detail occupations as indicative of a preference for an occupational environment which is free of close restraints, routine, and demands for conformity. Similarly, high scores in the Social Service group suggest a need to help other individuals while, at the same time, exerting some degree of control over their activities.

In a similar fashion, these findings provide a basis for interpreting personality scales in occupational terms. It is reasonable to assume that most counselees would have some difficulty determining the occupational significance of terms such as *Nurturance, Cognitive Structure,* and *Sentience.* On the other hand, while occupational titles or occupational stereotypes are not completely unambiguous, they will probably make a significant contribution to the counselee's understanding of his PRF scores. Thus, it would probably be helpful to tell a client who has high scores on Dominance, Nutrurance, and Exhibition that he has characteristics which are similar to individuals who are interested in occupations such as Public Administration and Personnel Management. Likewise, the finding that the PRF scales for Order and Cognitive Structure define a factor with positive loadings for the Accountant and Office Worker scales contributes, first of all, to the construct validation of the PRF scales and secondly, to the "surplus meaning" of these scales in occupational terms.

For the research worker, these dimensions would appear to explicate interest constructs in a way suggestive of a number of hypotheses which could be tested experimentally. This is, perhaps, particularly valuable in light of the fact that the SVIB has generated a vast array of correlational research but almost no experimental research. As a consequence, little is known about factors influencing the development of vocational interests, or about the reasons why particular interests are related to satisfaction in certain occupational roles. One of the hypotheses suggested by the present data would involve the interpretation of the scales in the Verbal-Linguistic group on the SVIB in terms of a desire to be free from restraints. If this is the case, it is reasonable to predict that individuals with high scores in this area would be those who would persist for a longer period of time and find satisfaction in a situation which is rather unstructured. On the other hand, people with low scores in this area would be expected to be dissatisfied with this kind of environment and would persist for a relatively short period of time if given free opportunity to leave the environment. A second experimental hypothesis involves the scores on the Social Service group of the SVIB. The data presented here suggest that experimental settings which vary in the degree to which an individual can direct the activities of others would be differentially satisfying for high and low scorers in the Social Service group. One might further predict that there would be an interaction between measured interests and the type of leadership situation which was involved. If the situation were one which had some prominent humanitarian goal, one would predict that those scoring high in the Social Service area would find this most satisfying.

If, on the other hand, the leadership role was a more traditional, authoritarian one, the greatest degree of satisfaction and tenure would be expected for those individuals with high scores on SVIB scales such as Army Officer and Industrial Relations.

In general, these data suggest ways in which a scale designed to measure personological constructs can be used to explicate measurement of behavioral domains that are not yet adequately mapped in terms of some theoretical framework. The interpretation of these data suggests a small and manageable number of meaningful motivational constructs that provide a basis for the development of a parsimonious theoretical framework regarding the nature and origin of vocational interests. These data also suggest new directions for the interpretation of interests in the context of counseling practice, and they bring to the fore a number of interesting, experimentally testable hypotheses. Indeed, they suggest that it may soon be possible to formulate new sets of superordinate constructs encompassing personality and vocational interests meaningfully and comprehensively.

TOWARD AN EXPERIMENTAL PSYCHOLOGY OF
OCCUPATIONAL CHOICE

As we have noted, the study of occupational choice has been largely, if not wholly, dependent upon naturalistic observation. It has seemed appropriate to study occupational decision making in the natural world, as this is where it takes place. But just as it would be difficult, if not impossible, to derive the laws of physics from observing taxicabs in a large city, so are there difficulties in studying occupational choice *in vivo*. The real world is complex, and the scientist rarely has a sufficient opportunity to study simultaneously, much less control, all of the influences directing the course of an event such as an occupational decision. While these arguments are quite familiar ones advanced in support of the experimental method, they have not, to our knowledge, been sufficiently appreciated in the study of work and vocational choice. We would therefore like to advance, as illustrative of an experimental approach, a study in which a variety of opportunities for different experiences were presented to subjects, from which they could indicate choices. On the basis of this information, certain lawful relationships are educed between personality and decision making. We by no means wish to imply that this study is exhaustive of the possibilities for experimental studies, but only that interesting and useful inferences may be drawn on the basis of experimental results.

The study was designed to assess the relationship between personality and choice behavior in a context which made it possible to circumvent some of the difficulties of investigating occupational choice in a more naturalistic setting. About a month prior to the experiment, the PRF had been administered in a large introductory psychology course in which the students were also required to serve as subjects in the research conducted by the staff and graduate students in the Department of Psychology. It was common practice in this course for students to be given a brief description of a study for which subjects were needed and then to be invited to volunteer. Since this choice of experimental task seemed to provide a reasonable analogue for some aspects of the process of occupational choice, it was decided to use this situation to carry out the study.

An experiment preference questionnaire was constructed, using the definitions of the traits measured by the PRF as a basis for writing descriptions of a number of experiments. On a preliminary form there were eighteen hypothetical experiments representing eight personality traits. For example, one experiment emphasized the fact that subjects would be working in groups and was designed to appeal to individuals scoring high on Affiliation. In another experiment intended to be related to Dominance, emphasis was placed on the fact that subjects would direct the activities of others. There were two experiments described, based on each of the definitions of the Achievement, Affiliation, Endurance, Exhibition, Nurturance, and Order scales, and three for the Harmavoidance and Dominance scales. The Harmavoidance scales were worded in the reverse direction of the trait description so as to emphasize the fact that risk would be involved. This preliminary form of the preference questionnaire was administered to a group of 58 introductory psychology students who were told that the experiments were being conducted in the department, and that the experimenters wanted to allow volunteers to take part in research in which they were particularly interested. They were asked to read the experiments and then rank them in order of preference. The preference rankings were intercorrelated, and the resulting correlation matrix was inspected to see if the experiments representing each trait were positively correlated. This initial analysis showed that four of the preliminary experimental descriptions did not reflect the dimensions intended and they were discarded. In all other cases, the pairs of experiments were significantly positively correlated and therefore were retained. The distribution of ranks suggested, however, that some of these were either highly desirable and popular, or highly undesirable and unpopular. Therefore, the descriptions were slightly modified in the final form to make them less desirable or undesirable. The final form of the questionnaire contained fourteen experiment descriptions. It was administered in the same sections of the introductory psychology course in which the PRF had been administered. Subjects were given a questionnaire entitled *Student Participation in Psychological Research* and received the following instructions:

The following is a list of some research projects in psychology for which volunteer participants are needed. In order to allow student volunteers to take part in areas of research in which they are particularly interested we would like some indication of your preferences. Please read carefully the following descriptions of experiments. After reading all of the descriptions we would like you to indicate your preferences.

The subjects were then instructed to rate each experiment on a seven-point scale ranging from "strongly interested" in participating to "strongly opposed" to participating.

The fourteen descriptions used in this form are given below, followed by the bracketed personality construct each was designed to represent. This latter information was not, of course, made availabe to subjects.

1. *Social Psychology.* Volunteers will be asked to fill out a questionnaire and participate in group activities with their friends. We shall observe how interpersonal associations in friendship groups and social systems in general are formed and maintained. [Affiliation]

2. *Visual Tracking.* This is a study with implications for industrial psychology which tests subjects' vigilance over a period of time in certain tracking tasks. The experiment requires a certain degree of concentration and perseverance. [Endurance]

3. *Aeronautics Simulation.* This study requires volunteers to undergo certain physiological changes commonly experienced by space pilots, in order to test their ability to withstand changes in gravitational pressure, anoxia in an oxygen chamber, the loss of visual cues, rapid temperature changes, and other controlled conditions. [Negative Harmavoidance]

4. *Role Playing.* In this study, students will be asked to act as stooges for the experimenter and to assume various roles before small groups of other students. Conditions will be varied to determine how readily the students will accept the authenticity of the stooges' role playing. [Exhibition]

5. *Inter-Nation Simulation.* Participants will be asked to act in the role of leaders of hypothetical nations and will make decisions about the development of troops and military supplies, and will carry on international trade negotiations. [Dominance]

6. *Preschool Training.* As part of a study investigating the effects of a new, specially designed nursery school on the adjustment and improvement of children when they begin their formal schooling, a number of volunteers are needed who will put in a few hours supervising the activities of these children. [Nurturance]

7. *Group Dynamics.* Students will be randomly assigned to various work groups to participate in performing certain tasks. Groups of various sizes and interactional patterns will be formed with a view to ascertaining which ones are most effective and most satisfying to the members. [Affiliation]

8. *Filing Codes.* This project requires volunteers to work on a variety of filing systems based on newly developed coding devices. Our aim is to discover more efficient methods of organizing scientific information in order to minimize any clutter or confusion. [Order]

9. *Perceptual-Motor Efficiency.* This experiment is designed to investigate the effects of fatigue and distraction on the long-term performance of subjects on an array of perceptual-motor tasks. [Endurance]

10. *Audience Preferences.* Volunteers will be asked to read short prepared scripts to small groups composed of different types of students. We shall observe the reactions of these various "audiences" to short plays which differ in style and content. [Exhibition]

11. *Long-Term Hospitalization.* Volunteers are needed who will spend one or two sessions playing cards with, reading to, etc., long-term hospitalized patients in a local hospital. We wish to investigate the effects of such activities on the psychological well-being of these patients, as measured by certain tests. [Nurturance]

12. *Decision Hierarchies.* Students will organize and direct the activities of small work groups which will be put under their control and asked to adhere to their decisions. We shall investigate the dynamics of effective leadership, the most effective types of power hierarchies, and the optimal communication networks used by authorities. [Dominance]

13. *Office Planning.* In this industrial psychology experiment, students will be asked to study office layouts that have been shown to be inefficient, and will attempt to reorganize them so as to reduce confusion and increase efficiency. [Order]

14. *Drug Study.* This experiment will investigate how certain drugs influence autonomic arousal and subsequent ability to perform on various tasks, when subjects are under various conditions of sensory deprivation. [Negative Harmavoidance]

A total of 379 subjects, 178 males and 201 females, completed both the PRF and the experiment choice questionnaire. The seven relevant PRF scales and the fourteen experiment choice ratings were correlated separately for the males and the females.

The correlations between PRF scale scores and the preference ratings of experiments were first examined for convergent and discriminant validity. For the male data, 11 of the 14 predicted correlations were significant at the .05 level, a percentage of 79. In contrast, only 18 of the 84 non-predicted correlations were significant, a percentage of 21. In no case did a non-predicted correlation exceed the median value of the predicted correlations. The female data showed generally similar evidence, although there was a suggestion that patterns of personality may be revealed in experimental choices in a somewhat more crystallized form in males.

A multimethod factor analysis (Jackson, 1969) with analytic varimax rotation was performed on the matrix of correlations between experimental choices and PRF scores for the males and separately for the females. These are presented in Tables 1 and 2, respectively. This analysis focuses only upon common variance between the experiment choice situation and the PRF in appraising convergent and discriminant validity.

An examination of Table 1 reveals that in every instance the predicted scales load the appropriate factor, indicating that indeed the choice of an experiment does relate to personality, and that this relation is predictable from knowledge of a person's scores on a personality questionnaire and an analysis of the task descriptions upon which the choice is based. For the females, there is also evidence for convergent and discriminant separation. For four of the seven factors extracted, predicted measures have the highest loadings on their own factor, while for the others, there is some inconsistency. Although delineation of factors could undoubtedly have been improved had we chosen to employ a Procrustes-type rotation, or even graphical adjustment, the evidence seems satisfactory even with varimax positioning of axes. It is not surprising that the two dimensions on which females showed the least crystallized behavior—those characterized by PRF scales for Dominance and Endurance—are among those which might reflect the greatest role conflict, and hence inconsistency, for females.

While the present results are most encouraging from the vantage point of those seeking experimental approaches to the study of vocational choice, it would be premature to over-generalize these particular findings. Volunteering a few hours of one's time for an experiment is not the same as choosing a lifelong occupation. But, given the economy of techniques such as the procedure described in this study, it becomes relevant to seek to explicate the degree of similarity between such volunteering behavior and naturally-occurring occupational choice. Furthermore, this kind of approach makes it possible for an experimenter to investigate the effects of assigning people to non-preferred tasks or to personality-dissonant work tasks. Hopefully, further studies such as the one reported here may provide an empirical foundation for theory development in this important area.

The data in the two studies reported above provide additional support for the widely held notion that vocational interests and vocational choice emerge lawfully in the process of personality development. Perhaps more significantly, a number of hypotheses which can be pursued experimentally have been suggested, and the research has pointed to some promising approaches from the standpoint of research design and data analysis. Finally, the data have a number of immediate implications for the practicing counselor. To underscore the use of these findings in counseling, two case reports which illustrate several points made in the earlier discussion are presented below. The first of these illustrates the importance of personality data in understanding the role conflicts which arise as a job evolves over a period of years. The second illustrates the problems associated with the single-role conception of occupations.

Case 1: A problem of conflicting role pressures. Consider first the case of Mr. Roland Conlan. He had worked for ten years as a regional manager in the sales department of a national firm selling electronics supplies. For the first eight years he had worked very effectively, and had risen rapidly in the

Table 1
Multimethod Factor Analysis of PRF and Experiment Choices for Males
(Only the four highest loadings on each factor are given)

Factor I	
Exhibition: Role Playing	.70
Exhibition: Audience Preferences	.66
Exhibition: PRF	.51
Harmavoidance: Drug Study	.20
Factor II	
Endurance: Visual Tracking	.66
Endurance: Perceptual-Motor Efficiency	.64
Endurance: PRF	.33
Order: Filing Codes	.21
Factor III	
Nurturance: Long-Term Hospitalization	.71
Nurturance: Preschool Training	.70
Nurturance: PRF	.52
Affiliation: Group Dynamics	.20
Factor IV	
Dominance: Decision Hierarchies	.72
Dominance: Internation Simulation	.62
Dominance: PRF	.56
Order: Office Planning	.23
Factor V	
Affiliation: Social Psychology	.62
Affiliation: Group Dynamics	.52
Affiliation: PRF	.27
Harmavoidance: Drug Study	.21
Factor VI	
Harmavoidance: Aeronautics Simulation	−.66
Harmavoidance: Drug Study	−.49
Harmavoidance: PRF	.42
Affiliation: PRF	−.23
Factor VII	
Order: Filing Codes	.59
Order: Office Planning	.48
Order: PRF	.28
Dominance: Internation Simulation	.21

company hierarchy. During the next two years, his work began to fall off. He did not get along with his co-workers, he seemed to resent the newer managerial staff of the company, and he became increasingly depressed. He seriously considered leaving the company but hated to give up the seniority he had achieved.

Table 2
Multimethod Factor Analysis of PRF and Experiment Choices for Females
(Only the four highest loadings on each factor are given)

Factor I
Nurturance: Long-Term Hospitalization .... .73
Nurturance: Preschool Training .... .69
Nurturance: PRF .... .50
Affiliation: Social Psychology .... .22

Factor II
Harmavoidance: Drug Study .... −.70
Harmavoidance: Aeronautics Simulation .... −.64
Harmavoidance: PRF .... .53
Endurance: Perceptual-Motor Efficiency .... −.27

Factor III
Exhibition: Role Playing .... .69
Exhibition: Audience Preferences .... .69
Exhibition: PRF .... .37
Dominance: PRF .... .19

Factor IV
Order: Filing Codes .... .64
Order: Office Planning .... .56
Affiliation: Group Dynamics .... .26
Endurance: Visual Tracking .... .23

Factor V
Affiliation: Social Psychology .... .57
Affiliation: PRF .... .51
Affiliation: Group Dynamics .... .46
Nurturance: Long-Term Hospitalization .... .22

Factor VI
Dominance: Decision Hierarchies .... .63
Dominance: PRF .... .54
Affiliation: Social Psychology .... .29
Dominance: Internation Simulation .... .27

Factor VII
Endurance: Perceptual-Motor Efficiency .... .51
Dominance: Internation Simulation .... −.37
Harmavoidance: Aeronautics Simulation .... .25
Nuturance: Preschool Training .... −.25

The head of the sales department became aware of Mr. Conlan's dissatisfaction, and referred him to a counseling psychologist for assessment and recommendations. In the initial interview he expressed concern that his responsibility and authority had become increasingly diluted. He was especially troubled by the fact that he could no longer make decisions on his own, but had to do everything through committee. He also complained that his co-workers did not understand his decisive, straightforward manner, and had, on occasion, suggested that he was blunt and insensitive to other people.

After his interview, Mr. Conlan completed a battery of tests, which included the SVIB and the PRF. On the SVIB, his high scores were mostly on the managerial scales. Highest among the scores were Sales Manager, Senior CPA, President of Manufacturing Concern, and Production Manager. He had generally low scores on the Social Service scales. These scores were consistent with his present occupational role, and provided little support for any of the alternative careers he had proposed in the initial interview.

These scores, when considered in relation to those from his PRF, did begin to provide some insight into the conflict Mr. Conlan was facing. The highest scores on the PRF were on the Dominance, Autonomy, and Aggression scales, and the lowest scores were on the Affiliation, Nurturance, and Exhibition scales. It can be recalled from the results of the first study reported above that these high scores were those associated with the dimension labeled *Aggressive Leadership,* and that the scales on which he scored low defined the factor called *Human Relations Management.*

In discussing these scores in a second interview with Mr. Conlan, it was found that when he began his career in the sales department, the regional office in which he was located was very small, and he was allowed to act on his own. Over the years, as the region grew, new men joined the office. Two of them were graduates of a business school which emphasized the "human relations" approach to management. All of the men in this department preferred to distribute authority, to be consulted regarding important decisions, and to make them democratically through committee.

The nature of Mr. Conlan's conflict thus became clear. He preferred an authoritarian managerial role and, indeed, was allowed to work in that fashion for a number of years. In time there was a shift to a "human relations" emphasis which he could not understand or accept, even though his interests were still most like those of a cross-section of successful managers surveyed as a criterion group a number of years before.

It was recommended that Mr. Conlan be transferred to a small office where he could work independently and make many of his own decisions. This has been done, and reports are that Mr. Conlan's performance has improved and he is much happier in his work.

Case 2: A problem of mistaken role perception. Paul Michaels had been an engineer for a number of years, but grew tired of the routine of his work and decided to return to school. Because he had enjoyed the experience of working with people, he applied and was accepted for graduate work in psychology.

To make up for deficiencies in his undergraduate program, he was required to take several courses in experimental psychology and quantitative methods. He started out the year very enthusiastically, and was doing very well in his courses. After the end of the first term, however, he grew increasingly dissatisfied and found it hard to keep up with his work. At this point he made an appointment at the counseling center. He expressed concern about whether or not he really belonged in psychology. The counselor administered both the SVIB and the PRF.

On the SVIB, his high scores were on the Psychologist, Psychiatrist, and Rehabilitation Counselor scales. He had reasonably high scores on all the Social Service scales, and on the Business Contact group. By themselves, these scores seemed consistent with his choice of psychology as a career. On the PRF, his highest scores were on the Nurturance, Affiliation, and Dominance. These scales were prominently represented on the dimension referred to earlier as *Social Control and Service* or *Human Relations Management*.

In discussing these results with Mr. Michaels, it became evident that the reason for his dissatisfaction was that he had assumed his graduate work would train him for a service role. Instead, he found that most of his courses were theoretical and methodological. While his interests were consistent with the former role, they were not with the latter.

Mr. Michaels and his counselor considered two possibilities. One was to apply for a graduate program in psychology with a stronger professional or applied emphasis. Mr. Michaels was concerned that even there, the theoretical and quantitative emphasis might be too great.

The second alternative considered was that of switching to a graduate program in social work. This seemed to be well suited to his needs, although he hesitated because he saw social workers in a stereotyped "do-gooder" role. He finally decided to pursue this course, and now appears to be doing very well.

SUMMARY

This chapter had two major objectives. First, it demonstrated the general relevance of personality theory and the particular relevance of the Personality Research Form (PRF) to the psychology of vocational behavior. Second, it provided guidelines to the counselor for using these principles to help individuals make vocational decisions. Data from a multimethod factor analysis of PRF and Strong Vocational Interest Blank scores were presented to illustrate that personality and vocational interest measures tap common dimensions, and that personological interpretations of these obtained vocational interest factors are useful both for understanding the nature of vocational behavior, and in counseling practice. Additional data illustrated the use of experimental tasks in studying personality correlates of vocational choice, and for understanding underlying processes involved with vocational decision making and satisfaction.

CHAPTER VII

The assessment and dynamics
of aggression

Edwin I. Megargee and Elizabeth S. Menzies

It is rare for psychologists to agree with one another. It is rarer still for them to agree with laymen. Yet if someone were to propose that aggression is the major behavior problem of our time, a surprising consensus would probably be found. This trend is demonstrated not only by a steadily increasing rate of violent crimes, which is far outstripping the growth in population, but also by the social alienation that threatens to polarize liberal against conservative, young against old, and black against white. The inability of people to resolve their differences amicably is evident not only on the battlefields of Vietnam and in the halls of Congress, but also in campus disruptions, spiraling divorce rates, and bitter labor disputes.

Unlike other national problems such as economic inflation or environmental pollution, aggression is of particular concern to the clinical psychologist because he is supposed to be an expert in interpersonal relations. Homicide is as fundamental a disruption of interpersonal relations as one is likely to encounter, so psychologists as scientist-professionals concerned with human behavior should be able to make a unique contribution to the assessment, understanding, and management of violence and aggression.

The present chapter is concerned with but one of these roles, namely the assessment or prediction of aggressive behavior. This activity is intimately related to the total problem, however, for prediction must be based on understanding of the phenomenon, and understanding in turn depends upon sound research. To complete the circle, research depends on measurement or assessment. For this reason, before reviewing some of the instruments that have been devised to assess or predict aggression, we shall present a brief overview of some of the problems involved in doing research on aggression and in coming to an adequate understanding of this phenomenon.

Buss [1961, p. 1] has defined aggression as "a response that delivers noxious stimuli to another organism." This definition is as good as any and better than

Preparation of this report was supported in part by NIMH Grant No. MH15623-01 to the senior author. The writers wish to thank Jim Meyer and Ronald Nuerhing for their assistance in the library research and Lynn Bowers for her work in preparing the manuscript. Parts of this chapter are based on a paper on "The assessment of violence with psychological tests" prepared by E. I. Megargee for the National Commission on the Causes and Prevention of Violence.

most. The major drawback is that it excludes behavior that is aimed at injuring other organisms but fails to do so. Thus, the guerilla who plants land mines along a jungle trail would not, according to Buss's definition, be engaging in aggressive behavior if no one came along the trail to receive the "noxious stimulation" that results when one steps on a "bouncing Betty." However, Buss's definition does avoid the tricky question of intentionality which plagues many others.

Buss also proposes that there are two fundamental kinds of aggression, *angry* and *instrumental.* Angry aggression is reinforced by injury to the victim, whereas instrumental aggression is a means to some other end. The senior author once had a schizophrenic patient who shot a cow belonging to a farmer against whom he had a grudge. This patient was engaging in angry aggression, in contrast to a matador who plunges a sword into a bull's heart, not out of malice, but instead as a means of gaining prestige and money. For the cattle involved, the distinction is academic, but the difference is crucial for the clinician and the researcher, for quite different dynamics and drives operate in the two instances. Aggression studied in the laboratory is often of the instrumental variety, with the subject delivering noxious stimuli in order to please the experimenter; such data may not apply to angry aggression, particularly the extremely angry aggression known as violence.

If one surveys the theoretical and research literature it quickly becomes evident that the term *aggression* has been applied to many diverse sorts of behavior. Some of the major parameters which differentiate investigations in this area include:

The nature of the subject population. Psychologists such as Neal Miller (1948), as well as ethologists such as Konrad Lorenz (1966) and Niko Tinbergen (1953, 1968), test their hypotheses regarding aggressive behavior through experiments and observations on animals, while many other psychologists use only human subjects. Among those studies which are limited to the human species, important differences can be found as a function of the age, social class, or cultural background of the subjects (cf., Rosenquist & Megargee, 1969). Moreover, the dynamics of aggressive behavior are apt to differ as we move from the individual case to small groups or nation-states (Megargee & Hokanson, 1970).

Victim of the attack. The nature of the victim is another important variable. As Hartmann, Kris, and Loewenstein (1949) have pointed out, aggressive behavior is rarely unmixed; typically the aggressor has ambivalent feelings toward his victim. This conflict can shape the nature of the aggressive response. Moreover, different degrees of aggressive drive strength and different inhibitions or taboos against aggressive behavior will be found for different potential victims (Miller, 1948). The interaction of drive and inhibitions helps determine whether or not the aggressor's attack is delivered to the primary target or displaced onto another target.

Mode of aggressive response. Different societies have different rules about aggressive behavior, but it is safe to say that in all societies some modes of attack are more permissible than others. There are important differences between verbal and physical aggression. Verbal and physical attacks may be direct—that is aimed at the victim himself—or indirect as in physical attacks on his property or verbal slander against his reputation. There are also important differences associated with the intensity of the attack. Many college sophomores who willingly deliver mildly painful shocks to fellow experimental subjects would not be willing to throw the switch to execute a condemned man in the electric chair. While such distinctions may seem quite obvious, nevertheless hypotheses regarding violence are often tested with much milder forms of aggression, and questions regarding physical aggression are all too often answered by reference to experiments using verbal aggression.

The aggressive attack can also vary as a function of its overtness or obviousness. Any clinician who has worked with passive-aggressive or hysterical patients is well aware of the many devious ways in which hostility can be expressed. Similarly, the distance between the attacker and his victim can be an important consideration. Killing a Vietnamese child is permissible (although regretable) when done by means of bombs from high altitudes; it is of questionable propriety when done with a machine gun from a helicopter; it is an atrocity when done face to face on the ground with a knife or pistol.

Legitimacy of the attack. A dimension underlying many of the above considerations is whether or not society condones a particular form of aggression. In most societies homicide is permissible under certain circumstances, such as war or self-defense, but not under others. Aggressive acts that are performed with the experimenter's implicit approval in the laboratory may or may not be related to illicit aggression in the streets. Since the individual's particular value system is a major determinant of the legitimacy of aggressive behavior, it too must be considered and evaluated in conducting research and in making clinical predictions. One of the present writers, for example, found a positive relationship between a psychological test measure and socially acceptable aggression, but a negative relationship between that same measure and antisocial aggression (Megargee, 1965b).

It can be seen therefore that literally and figuratively the term *aggression* covers a multitude of sins. There are many kinds of aggressive behavior, and most individuals will engage in some types but not in others. Research findings based on one type of aggression may not apply to the dynamics of another, even though both sets of behavior are called aggression. The clinician, in both his research and professional roles, must be continually aware of the many and varied parameters that influence whether or not an individual will engage in aggressive behavior and, if he does, the form the aggressive response is likely to take.

Given the diversity of findings in aggression research, psychologists, like other scientists, attempt to organize the data by forming theories. As might be expected, there are many different explanations of the origins and dynamics of aggressive behavior. Some theorists such as Lorenz (1966) and Freud (1929) maintain that man's aggression stems primarily from his physiology and that aggressive drive is an innate characteristic of the organism. Others such as Dollard, Doob, Miller, Mowrer, and Sears (1939) and Bandura and Walters (1963) hold that the primary sources of aggressive behavior are to be found in an individual's life history and environment. A psychologist's

136EDWIN I. MEGARGEE & ELIZABETH S. MENZIES

approach to the study of aggression in his laboratory and to the prediction of aggression in the clinic will, of course, vary as a function of the theoretical position he adopts.

However, while there is considerable diversity in theories of aggression (Megargee, 1969b; Megargee & Hokanson, 1970), there is nonetheless general agreement that the strength of an aggressive response is determined by the interaction of three major classes of variables. The first is *instigation to aggression,* that is, aggressive drive or motivation. Instigation is composed primarily of *hostility,* a relatively enduring, predisposition to injure some victim, and *anger,* a temporary aggressive drive. To predict instrumental aggression, however, one must also consider the degree to which other drives may be satisfied through aggressive behavior. The second major class of variables are *taboos* or *inhibitions* against aggressive behavior that act to block the overt expression of aggressive instigation. Whether these taboos are learned, as most theorists suggest, or are innate, as Lorenz (1966) has hypothesized, it is clear that the relative strength of an individual's instigation and inhibitions helps determine whether an aggressive act takes place. The third major class of variables are stimulus or *situational factors* that may act either to facilitate or impede the overt expression of aggression. Even though instigation exceeds inhibition, an aggressive act may not occur if a repressive authority such as a policeman or a parent is standing by; similarly, an individual who finds himself part of a football team or a lynch mob might find his overt expression of aggression facilitated by his fellows or by onlookers.

To summarize, we can state that the response strength (P) of an aggressive act (J) directed at a particular target (T-1) can be expressed as:

$$P_{J \cdot T-1} = (A_{T-1} + S_a) - (1_{J \cdot T-1} + S_i)$$

in which A_{T-1} represents the total instigation to aggression from various sources directed at target T-1; S_a represents situational factors facilitating aggressive behavior; $1_{J \cdot T-1}$ represents the net sum of inhibitions or taboos against directing act J at victim T-1; and S_i represents situational factors inhibiting the overt expression of aggression.[1]

For the aggressive act to occur, $P_{J \cdot T-1}$ must exceed zero; that is, the sum of instigation and facilitating factors must outweigh the inhibitions and impediments:

$$A_{T-1} + S_a > 1_{J \cdot T-1} + S_i$$

The psychologist who would predict aggressive behavior should therefore assess both motivating and inhibiting forces and estimate the degree to which the individual's milieu will support or interfere with the performance of particular aggressive acts. In practice, as we shall see, most of the psychological

---

[1]See Megargee (1969b) for a fuller discussion of these factors.

tests designed to help the clinician predict aggressive behavior focus on instigation and neglect inhibitions and situational factors.

As is the case with any sort of behavior, the fact that instigation outweighs
inhibition only means that the response is possible. Before a particular response can emerge in overt behavior it must compete with the other possible
responses. In most situations a range of responses, both aggressive and nonaggressive, are possible, and they may be directed at a variety of targets. A
police officer who is called a "pig" by an unruly demonstrator may ignore
the insult, laugh at the demonstrator, counter by calling him a "freak," take
him aside for a lecture, arrest him gently, or arrest him using considerable
force. (Except in rare circumstances, such as the contagion of aggression
exemplified at Jackson State College and Kent State University, he would
not shoot the demonstrator because inhibitions would block such an extreme
response.) By the same token, the officer could express his hostility directly
to the demonstrator, or to the ringleader who incited him, the university
which presumably infected him with such ideas, or even the police sergeant
who gave the officer such a difficult assignment. Some responses, such as
ignoring the insult, might not satisfy the aggressive instigation aroused but
could satisfy other needs such as a desire to spend his day off fishing instead
of giving testimony at the youth's arraignment.

For aggressive act J directed at target T-1 to occur, its response strength
must exceed that of all alternative responses:

$$P_{J \cdot T\text{-}1} > \begin{cases} P_{J \cdot T\text{-}2,\,3 \ldots N} \\ \text{or} \\ P_{K,L \ldots N \cdot T\text{-}1} \\ \text{or} \\ P_{K,L \ldots N \cdot T\text{-}2,\,3 \ldots N} \end{cases}$$

Where $P_{J \cdot T\text{-}2,\,3 \ldots N}$ represents the same aggressive response directed at another target, $P_{K,L \ldots N \cdot T\text{-}1}$ represents alternative responses at the original target,
and $P_{K,L \ldots N \cdot T\text{-}2,\,3 \ldots N}$ represents all other possible responses directed at all
other targets. While consideration of this *response competition* complicates
matters tremendously, overlooking it can lead to error.

Thus it can be seen that psychologists who attempt to devise tests to assist
in the prediction of aggression have posed themselves an extremely difficult
task. An individual's potential for aggressive behavior is not fixed or absolute.
The clinician who attempts to assess an individual's potential for aggressive
behavior must obtain a sample of behavior under the highly artificial conditions that typically prevail in his office and use these data to predict responses in quite different circumstances. The problem is compounded by the
limitations that ethics place on the behavior he can sample. For example, one
of the most valid ways of assessing an individual's inhibitions might be for the
clinician to slap his face or spit in his eye. If the patient refrained from hitting
the clinician in the mouth, the clinician could infer with some confidence that

the patient has unusually strong inhibitions against aggression. However, professional ethics (as well as a healthy regard for his own well being) prevents the clinician from obtaining such a direct sample of behavior. Instead he resorts to more indirect methods and asks the patient what he would do if someone spit in his eye, or shows him a picture of one person slapping another in the face and has him make up a story about it. It is questionable whether these less immediate behavior samples are as useful in predicting aggression. Unfortunately, the question is not one that is amenable to empirical investigation, for the same ethical restraints apply in the laboratory as in the clinic.

Despite these difficulties, the importance of the problem has prompted a number of psychologists to construct tests for the purpose of predicting aggressive behavior. In the balance of this chapter these tests will be surveyed. The list of measures reviewed, while extensive, is not exhaustive; the writers have omitted those for which little if any data are available. Space limitations have also prevented us from reviewing the literature on these instruments in any detail.

The instruments are presented in order of their directness. The most direct measures are the situational tests. These are followed by very obvious self-report measures, self-report inventories, projective techniques, and finally by physiological measures. The most direct measures provide a behavior sample which is closely related to the criterion the clinician wishes to provide. Unfortunately, in order to achieve directness it is usually necessary to sacrifice subtlety, so that responses to direct measures are more subject to distortion or dissimulation. On the less direct measures, such as the Rorschach, the unstructured nature of the task often conceals the purpose of the test from the patient and makes it more difficult for him to dissemble. However, because the behavior sampled is further removed from the criterion, there is often a lower correlation between indirect measures and the overt aggression that the clinician hopes to predict.

SITUATIONAL METHODS

The practical and ethical problems associated with eliciting aggression in the laboratory have already been noted. Some investigators, however, have devised ingenious equipment, laboratory situations, and research designs through which mild overt aggression can be studied. Santostefano and Wilson (1968) constructed a series of nine pairs of alternative situations to assess aggressive response modes by choice of action rather than by fantasy or language. The Miniature Situation Test (MST) invites a subject to choose between two tasks such as tying up the experimenter's wrists as opposed to helping the experimenter put on a glove.

To establish the construct validity of the MST, Santostefano and Wilson compared the performance of two groups of institutionalized delinquents, matched for background and current offense, but differing in the amount of aggressiveness displayed within the institution. In six out of the nine of the MST situations, the aggressive Cell House subjects were discriminated from the less aggressive Honor Dormitory subjects. Moreover, both delinquent groups differed significantly from a control group of high school students.

Buss (1961) designed an apparatus to measure the intensity of sanctioned aggressive responses in the laboratory, the Buss Aggression Machine (BAM). Two subjects, one of whom is really an accomplice, interact by means of various buttons and lights on wooden panels. The subject is told that he is to assume the role of an experimenter who is to train the accomplice in a conceptual task by shocking him after each incorrect response. The subject is instructed in the delivery of electric shock, the intensity of which is indicated by buttons numbered from one to ten. Since the subject must know what intensities are represented by the ten buttons, he is administered a shock from buttons one, two, three, and five. He discovers that the shock level at one is just above touch threshold while that at five is extremely painful.

The subject then instructs the accomplice, whom he continues to believe is another subject, in the task and attaches electrodes to him. While the subject must administer some shock to comply with the experimenter, he is free to select the intensity. Buss argues that the selection of intensities above the pain threshold is evidence of angry as well as instrumental aggression. Studies conducted by Buss (1961) indicate that the more aggressive subjects do use higher levels of shock, and that men's shock levels greatly exceed those of women.

Leibowitz (1968) studied the relationship of three measures of aggression—the BAM, role-playing (RP), and the Buss-Durkee Hostility (BD) measures. Although there were significant relationships between RP and BD, Leibowitz feels that his results indicate that verbal and physical aggression are two orthogonal dimensions. Shemberg, Levanthal, and Allman (1968) explored the relations between the BAM and indices of aggression as measured by a behavioral rating scale. Among their four groups, males and females rated either high or low on an aggression scale, the authors found significant differences in BAM scores. In contrast to results from Buss's pilot studies, Shemberg et al. found no differences between males and females and no interaction between sex and ratings of aggression.

Paradigms similar to the BAM have been used in other laboratory investigations. Berkowitz (1968) has used a somewhat similar paradigm, but instead of having the subject vary the intensity of the shock, he signals his evaluation of a fellow student's work by varying the number of shocks from one to ten. This variation probably has a greater instrumental aggression component than Buss's. Hokanson in a series of studies has monitored blood pressure levels in subjects who, after receiving a shock from a "fellow subject," have the choice of responding by countershocking the fellow subject, by rewarding him, or in a recent series of studies, by shocking themselves (Hokanson, 1970).

Other experiments, particularly with children, have used less artificial situations than those described above. A typical experimental design requires that nursery school children observe either aggressive or passive adult models. The amount of aggression that occurs in subsequent behavior is then rated by teams of observers (Bandura, Ross, & Ross, 1961; Bandura & Huston, 1961). Another approach is to show children films in which adult models sat on an inflated Bobo doll and abused it in a number of novel, aggressive ways. The subjects then entered a room that contained the same play material they had seen in the film, and experimenters rated the amount of this distinctive aggressive behavior displayed (Bandura, Ross, & Ross, 1963). Still other investigators have been interested in the effects of aggressive cartoons on children's behavior (Lövaas, 1961; Mussen & Rutherford, 1961; A. Siegel, 1956), while Feshbach (1961a) studied film-induced fantasy aggression in adults.

Other laboratory studies have investigated the dynamics of aggression by giving the subject various sorts of tests and then measuring his verbal aggression. Typical of these studies is an investigation by Thibaut and Coules (1952) in which subjects were required to write personality evaluations about ostensible fellow subjects. Negative evaluations were taken as evidence of verbal aggression. A similar paradigm is to expose the subject to various sorts of harassment and then to measure his attitude toward the experimenter or have him in some way evaluate the experimenter's competence. For an example of this type of investigation see Feshbach (1955).

ADJECTIVE CHECKLISTS

An adjective checklist (ACL) procedure requires the subject to check or rate the adjectives in a list which he feels are descriptive of himself or, in some situations, of others. Nowlis (1953; Nowlis & Nowlis, 1956) is generally credited with having initiated the use of this kind of instrument. His list, the Mood Adjective Check List (MACL), the Multiple Affect Adjective Check List (MAACL, Zuckerman & Lubin, 1965), and a checklist developed by Lorr and his colleagues (Lorr & McNair, 1966; Lorr, Daston, & Smith, 1967) have been most widely used in recent research on aggression. The Gough-Heilbrun Adjective Check List (Gough & Heilbrun, 1965) and Clarke's Activity Vector Analysis (Clarke, 1956) also have aggression scales, but thus far have not been used extensively in aggression research.

Lorr et al. (1967) reported that three factor analyses of their scale yielded five replicated factors, one of which was Anger-Hostility. These authors collected evidence of construct validity for their mood scale by administering it to college students, first in an ordinary class session and later just prior to their final examination. Their hypothesis that scores on the Tense-Anxious and Angry factors would increase significantly in the latter condition was supported at the .001 level. This study replicated the findings of an earlier investigation with a neurotic sample (McNair & Lorr, 1964).

Heimstra, Ellingstad, and DeKock (1967) found that subjects who scored high on aggression on the Nowlis MACL did significantly poorer on a simulated automobile-driving task than did low-scoring subjects. Okel and Mosher (1968) examined changes in mood as a function of guilt over aggressive behavior. There was a significantly greater increase in guilt following aggressive behavior among subjects who scored high on the MACL measure of hostility-guilt. This is one of the few measures that attempts to measure inhibition as well as instigation to aggression.

The Zuckerman and Lubin (1965) MAACL may be administered in either of two forms; on the "Today" form subjects check the adjectives that describe their current feelings, while on the "General" form, adjectives that characterize them over time are checked. Thus it attempts to differentiate the relatively enduring personality trait of hostility from the temporary emotional state of anger. This trait-state distinction has proved to be quite useful in anxiety research (Spielberger, Lushene, & McAdoo, in press). If the MAACL can be shown to differentiate the two constructs validly, it could have considerable importance.

Zuckerman, Persky, Eckman, and Hopkins (1967) tested the convergent and discriminant validities of a number of psychological techniques in a multi-trait-multimethod study of anxiety, depression, and hostility. The checklist was the poorest discriminator of all the measures with the psychiatric sample, although admitted hostility (MAACL) showed some convergence with fantasy hostility elicited through projective techniques among normal subjects. Bloom and Brady (1968), on the other hand, found no significant relationship between psychiatrists' ratings of hostility in their patients and hostility as reflected on the MAACL.

The MAACL has fared somewhat better in other studies. Knapp, Zimmerman, Roscoe, and Michael (1967) were able to measure increases in anxiety, depression, and hostility in 300 college students at the end of a long testing session. Bourne, Coli, and Datel (1968) identified hostility as the dominant affect on the MAACL protocols of soldiers in South Vietnam during periods of anticipated enemy attack.

The Activity Vector Analysis (AVA) is a checklist designed to measure aggressiveness, sociability, emotional control, and social adaptability in industrial settings (Clarke, 1956; Merenda & Clark, 1968). Merenda and Clark (1968) administered the AVA and the Gough and Heilbrun (1965) Adjective Check List (ACL) simultaneously to college students to determine the amount of convergence and divergence between the two instruments. They concluded that both scales measure substantially the same behavioral and personality variables, although the AVA was said to accomplish this result more efficiently and parsimoniously.

It seems clear from the brief survey above that much research remains to be done on adjective checklists as valid and reliable measures of aggression and hostility. McReynolds (1968) has noted the utility of the technique for assessing anxiety, but he acknowledges the basic limitation imposed by its restriction to adjectival forms. It seems likely, however, that checklists will remain in the psychologist's armamentarium, for few instruments generate such rich sources of data combined with brevity and ease of administration.

INVENTORIES

Inventories, sometimes called "questionnaires" or "opinionnaires," present the testee with a series of statements; although there are some variations, generally his task is to indicate whether he agrees or disagrees with the statements, or whether they are true or false descriptions of himself. The items are grouped into scales that are designed to measure various personality attributes. The items for some scales are chosen rationally on the basis of the expert opinion of the test author or a group of judges. Other scales are based on empirical item analyses in which the responses selected are those which discriminate groups possessing the attribute in question from groups lacking this trait. Still other tests are based on factor-analytic item selection in which the correlation of each item with the underlying factor is used as the criterion for inclusion.

Rationally Derived Scales

Several hostility scales have been constructed through rational selection of items from the Minnesota Multiphasic Personality Inventory (MMPI) item pools. Among them are:

Iowa Hostility Inventory. Moldawsky (1953) submitted 100 MMPI items that appeared to measure aggressiveness to a group of judges. The 25 items that they agreed assessed hostility comprise the present inventory. Validity data on this scale are mixed. Dinwiddie (1954) and Buss, Durkee, and Baer (1956) have reported positive findings, but Charen (1955) and Shipman (1965) obtained generally negative results. The data available in the literature generally suggest that while the Iowa Hostility Inventory does have some relation to aggression, the correlations are most often too small and unreliable to be useful in the individual case.

Cook and Medley Hostility Scale (Ho). MMPI items that discriminated successful from unsuccessful teachers were presented to judges who selected 50 as assessing hostility (Cook & Medley, 1954). The *Ho* scale correlates positively with a number of measures on the Buss-Durkee Hostility Inventory (Jurjevich, 1963b). Subjects high on the *Ho* scale have been found to be more likely to miss appointments to participate in experiments (Snoke, 1955); to be more likely to attribute hostility to photographs (McGee, 1954); and to deliver stronger shocks to subjects making errors on a verbal learning task (Loussef, 1968). However, Megargee and Mendelsohn (1962) found no significant differences between extremely assaultive, moderately assaultive, and nonviolent criminals and normals; Jurjevich (1963a) found delinquent girls did not differ from normals; and Shipman (1965) found no relationship between *Ho* scale scores and ratings of verbal and physical hostility in a sample of psychiatric patients.

Inhibition of Aggression (Hy-5). Hy-5 is one of the subscales selected by Harris and Lingoes (1955) from the MMPI Hysteria scale. It is one of the few scales that significantly differentiated violent from nonviolent criminals in Megargee and Mendelsohn's (1962) study. However, it did so in the *reverse* direction, the assaultive criminals being assessed as having more inhibition of aggression than the nonviolent criminals.

Siegel Manifest Hostility Scale (MHS or Jh). This scale consists of 47 MMPI items which four out of five judges agreed reflected manifest hostility (S. Siegel, 1956). Mixed results have been obtained with this scale. Positive correlations were found between MHS scores and scores on the California *F* scale, the Buss-Durkee Inventory, and the Rosenzweig Picture-Frustration study;

however, no significant relationship was found with Elizur's Rorschach Hostility Scale or with ratings of verbal hostility or hostile attitudes in psychiatric patients (Shipman & Marquette, 1963; S. Siegel, 1956; Siegel, Spilka, & Miller, 1957). In the laboratory, MHS scores have been found to relate to the intensity of electric shock delivered to a subject for making errors in a learning task (Loussef, 1968) and to hostility on the TAT when anger has been aroused (Rosenbaum & Stanners, 1961). Studies using clinical samples have found no differences in the MHS scores of assaultive and nonassaultive criminals and normals (Megargee & Mendelsohn, 1962) or between the scores of delinquent and nondelinquent girls (Jurjevich, 1963a). Shipman and Marquette (1963) did find that MHS scores correlated significantly with ratings of physical hostility on one sample of neuropsychiatric patients, but Shipman (1965) was unable to repeat this finding on a subsequent sample.

Not all hostility scales have been made up of MMPI items. A number of other instruments have scales for the assessment of aggression and hostility as well.

Waterhouse and Child Psychological Insight Test. This instrument, designed for use in research on the effects of frustration, consists of 150 statements. The subject is asked to rate on a six-point scale the degree to which each statement characterizes himself (Waterhouse & Child, 1953). The 15 statements that list extrapunitive responses to frustration make up the Aggression scale. With the exception of the correlation with the Sarason scale reported below, the only validational data that the present writers have been able to locate is the content validity of the items themselves.

Bell Adjustment Inventory. First published in 1934, the Adjustment Inventory was revised in 1962, at which time a scale for the assessment of hostility was added. Data presented in the manual (Bell, 1962) show that this scale significantly differentiated between groups judged to be high and low in hostility. Aside from this there are few, if any, validity data available on this new scale.

Autobiographical Survey. Sarason's (1958) Autobiographical Survey includes a hostility scale composed of 23 items, many drawn from the MMPI, which describe various kinds of hostile behavior. The subject is to answer "true" or "false" to indicate whether he has ever engaged in such acts. A sample item, similar to those on the scale, might read, "I have often had quarrels with my father." Sarason (1958) found that the hostility scale was not related to psychotherapists' ratings of their patients' hostility; however, in a subsequent study Sarason (1961) found that the scale had significant positive correlations with scales on the Buss-Durkee Inventory and the Waterhouse-Child Aggression Scale. This instrument has been used primarily in research on the verbal conditioning of hostile words (Ganzer & Sarason, 1964; Sarason & Minard, 1963).

The Edwards Personal Preference Schedule (EPPS). Like the other tests that have been devised to assess Murray's system of manifest needs, Edwards' Personal Preference Schedule has a need aggression (*n Agg*) scale. In an effort to control for the effects of social desirability, Edwards adopted a forced-choice format in which the respondent selects the more applicable of two statements equated for social desirability. This procedure makes the EPPS scales ipsative and complicates their interpretation and statistical analysis (Radcliffe, 1965; Stricker, 1965).

Validational research on the EPPS *n Agg* scale has included several studies in which it has been correlated with other test measures of hostility. These investigations have shown significant positive correlations with the Buss-Durkee Hostility Inventory total score and the Siegel MHS (Ford & Sempert, 1962), and with the Gough-Heilbrun Adjective Check List *n Agg* scale for women but not for men (Megargee & Parker, 1968). Edwards (1959) reported a significant negative correlation with the Guilford-Martin Agreeableness scale, and Gough (1964) found a significant negative correlation between the EPPS *n Agg* scale and the CPI Sociability scale; however, the correlations with the CPI scales relating more closely to aggressive acting out fell short of significance. Megargee and Parker (1968) found no relation between the EPPS and TAT *n Agg* measures, and Van de Castle (1960) found the EPPS unrelated to perception of aggression on the Rorschach.

The few studies that have been carried out using non-test criteria of hostility or aggression have generally reported insignificant results. Bernberg (1960) found no significant difference on *n Agg* between large samples of prison inmates and normals, and Zuckerman (1958) found rebellious student nurses did not differ from submissive, conforming, or dependent ones. McKee and Turner (1961) found no relations between adult *n Agg* scores and ratings of aggressive drives made in adolescence, and Van de Castle (1960) found the *n Agg* scale unrelated to the perception of aggressive words in a binocular rivalry situation.

Impulse Control Categorization Instrument (ICCI). This is a straightforward, obvious instrument that resembles the Waterhouse-Child scale in certain respects. Designed for use with latency age boys, the ICCI consists of 24 descriptions of situations and possible responses. The subject indicates whether he would be likely to respond in the indicated fashion. One item, for example, states, "If a boy spit in my face, I would hit him right away"; another reads, "If a boy smashes my models, I complain but do nothing [Matsushima, 1964]." Preliminary reliability and validity data are promising, but much more research must be done before any definite conclusions about its usefulness can be drawn.

Personality Research Form (PRF). The most recent of the tests designed to measure Murrayan constructs, Douglas Jackson's PRF, also contains a need aggression scale. A great deal of sophisticated work has gone into the construction of this instrument, with unusually great emphasis being placed on its discriminant validity even at the item level. In the manual, Jackson (1967) reports significant positive correlations ranging from .36 to .66 between *n Agg* and behavior ratings of aggression, from .21 to .73 for trait ratings, and .38 for self-ratings.

S-R Inventory of Hostility. This new test, like the Rosenzweig P-F study which helped inspire it, has its roots in the notion that instigation to aggression stems from frustration (Dollard et al., 1939). In this instrument, Endler and Hunt (1968) present descriptions of 14 frustrating situations, and the respondent indicates on a five-point scale the degree to which he would react with each of ten modes of responses. The possible response modes include physiological, extrapunitive, and intropunitive reactions. Like the MAACL, the S-R Inventory seems designed to assess the temporary emotional state of anger as opposed to hostility. However, rather than focusing on the immediate arousal level, it attempts instead to secure a retrospective evaluation of typical anger level in various situations, thus blurring somewhat the trait-state distinction.

Empirically Derived Instruments

Minnesota Multiphasic Personality Inventory (MMPI). Because the present chapter must focus on instruments specifically constructed to predict aggression, little space can be devoted to the discussion of tests, such as the MMPI, that were built to measure other dimensions. However, despite the fact that the MMPI was designed to assist in differential psychiatric diagnosis, the instrument has often been used to assess aggression as well. Therefore, we shall give a brief overview of these investigations.

The vast literature on the MMPI has shown that the test, while fallible, is nonetheless a useful aid to differential diagnosis. (See Butcher, 1969; Dahlstrom & Welsh, 1960; Megargee, 1966a.) A number of studies have demonstrated that it is possible to discriminate antisocial populations, such as juvenile delinquents or adult criminals, from normally socialized groups using the regular MMPI scales (e.g., Hathaway & Monachesi, 1953; Wirt & Briggs, 1959). Similarly, other studies have shown that the MMPI can differentiate schizophrenic and paranoid patients from normals (Dahlstrom & Welsh, 1960; Megargee, 1966a). Insofar as there is a higher incidence of acting out and violence among criminals and psychotics than is to be found in the general population, the MMPI scales can be regarded as having some utility in the assessment of aggressive proclivities, since it can help categorize an individual as belonging to a group in which there is a high base rate of violence.

The clinician, however, usually is faced with the task of making finer discriminations. In a probation setting for example, he deals exclusively with criminals and must help determine which of these criminals are potentially dangerous and which can safely be placed on probation. Similar assessment decisions are found in neuropsychiatric settings. By and large the studies that have compared assaultive and nonassaultive criminals or contrasted violent and nonviolent patients have found that the regular MMPI scales are not capable of differentiating aggressive from nonaggressive people within deviant populations (Erikson & Roberts, 1966; Megargee & Mendelsohn, 1962; Shipman & Marquette, 1963). It is for this reason that a number of psychologists have attempted to derive new MMPI scales for this purpose. Some of these scales were constructed using rational methods and have already been examined; others were based on empirical analyses and will be reviewed below.

Overt Hostility (Hv) and Hostility Control (Hc). These two MMPI scales (both empirically derived by Schultz, 1954) used therapists' ratings of Veterans Administration patients as criteria. Megargee and Mendelsohn (1962) found that neither scale differentiated assaultive criminals from nonassaultive criminals or normals. Similarly, Shipman (1965) found no relationship between either scale and ratings of verbal or physical hostility and hostile attitudes in a sample of psychiatric patients. Jurjevich (1963a) found that delinquent girls did not differ from normals on the *Hv* scale but there was a significant difference on *Hc*. Butcher (1965) found that his groups of eighth graders rated as most aggressive and as least aggressive were both significantly higher on the *Hc* scale than the groups rated as average in aggressiveness. The data thus cast serious doubts on the validity of these scales.

Adjustment to Prison (AP). Although this scale was empirically derived by contrasting unruly and assaultive prisoners with nonviolent ones (Panton, 1958), Megargee and Mendelsohn (1962) did not find that it differentiated the violent from the nonviolent criminals in their study.

Overcontrolled Hostility (O-H). Megargee (1965a, 1965b, 1969b, 1971, in press) has suggested that one of the major reasons that psychological tests have not been better at differentiating assaultive from nonassaultive individuals is that aggressiveness is not a unitary phenomenon. He has proposed that there are at least two principal kinds of assaultive offenders, the undercontrolled and the overcontrolled. The former is characterized by minimal inhibitions against aggressive behavior, while the latter has rigid, excessive inhibitions against any form of aggressive acting out. In some cases aggressive instigation can accumulate to the point where it overwhelms the inhibitions of the overcontrolled type. When this occurs it can, according to Megargee, result in extreme violence. Support for this formulation has come not only from Megargee's laboratory (Megargee, 1966b) but also from studies carried out by independent investigators in this country (Molof, 1967) and abroad (Blackburn, 1968a, 1968b, 1969b).

Megargee, Cook, and Mendelsohn (1967) recently reported the derivation of an MMPI scale, *O-H*, that appears to assess the overcontrolled hostility that, in some individuals, can lead to overt violence. While it is clearly not a global instrument for the assessment of aggression, the validational data reported suggest that the *O-H* scale might be usefully included in a test battery with other instruments to detect a particular type of potentially assaultive individual who might otherwise be overlooked (Megargee, 1969a; Megargee, Cook, & Mendelsohn, 1967; Blackburn, 1969a).

California Psychological Inventory (CPI). Like the MMPI, the CPI is a multiphasic inventory with scales that reflect a number of behavioral dimensions. None of these scales is an aggression scale per se. However, several scales, particularly the Socialization Scale (*So*), have been shown to be quite sensitive predictors of antisocial delinquent behavior (Gough, 1965). Few studies have been carried out comparing the CPI patterns of assaultive and nonassaultive criminals. The data thus far obtained have not as yet demonstrated any reliable patterns differentiating these groups, but there are indications that the CPI might be capable of making such discriminations if a program of research, preferably using multivariate profile comparison methods, were to be undertaken (Megargee, 1966b, 1971; Mizushima & DeVos, 1967).

Buss-Durkee Inventory. While most test authors, as we have seen, attempt to build global tests of hostility or aggression, Buss and Durkee (1957) constructed scales designed to measure several different kinds of hostile and aggressive behavior: assaultiveness, indirect aggression, irritability, negativism, resentment, suspicion, and verbal aggression. They also provided a scale to assess guilt over expression of hostility, so that inhibitions are appraised as well as instigation. The Buss-Durkee Inventory is thus built on a conceptually sounder basis than most of the other instruments surveyed (Buss, 1961; Buss & Durkee, 1957). Factor analyses of the tests have indicated there are two principal factors which Buss identifies as aggressiveness and hostility (Buss, 1961), although others prefer to interpret them as reflecting overt and covert hostility (Bendig, 1962).

Despite the promise of the scale and the rising interest in aggression over the past decade, relatively few investigators have explored the validity of the Buss-Durkee Inventory. Some correlational studies have been carried out to demonstrate its relationship to the MMPI hostility scales (Jurjevich, 1963b), the Rotter *I-E* scale (Williams & Vantrees, 1969), and projective tests such as the Rorschach and the Iowa Picture Interpretation Test (Buss, Fisher, & Simmons, 1962). However, there have been few studies that relate the instrument to non-test behavioral criteria, perhaps because the studies that have been conducted have been disappointing. Miller, Spilka, and Pratt (1960) found no differences on the Buss-Durkee total score between homicidal and non-homicidal paranoid schizophrenics, and Leibowitz (1968) found the inventory unrelated to physical aggression as measured by the Buss Aggression Machine. Buss et al. (1962) related the Buss-Durkee scores of psychiatric patients to a variety of criterion measures with mixed results, finding significant correlations with some criteria but not with others.

Zaks and Walters Aggression Scale. Zaks and Walters (1959; Walters & Zaks, 1959) have reported the derivation and preliminary validation of a scale for the measurement of aggression. Although the initial results appeared quite promising, the present writers have not been able to locate reports of any subsequent validational research.

Proverbs Personality Test. A unique approach to the assessment of aggressiveness was taken by Bass (1956), who based a personality inventory on agree-disagree responses to various proverbs selected as representing Murray's needs list. A factor analysis of the scale scores yielded four factors, one of which Bass identified as hostility, comprised primarily of the need-Aggression, need-Autonomy, and need-Rejection scores. On the basis of this factor-analytic data, he constructed a 30-item hostility scale and obtained norms in a subsequent study (Bass, 1957). The present writers are not aware of any further research using this instrument.

Factor-Analytic Instruments

Factor-analytic personality researchers feel that selection of the personality traits to be measured should be carried out empirically rather than by relying on theory, informal observations, or introspection. The major thrust of the personality research of investigators such as Cattell, Eysenck, and Guilford is to identify these basic personality traits with the statistical tool of factor analysis. Once these basic traits or factors have been identified, they typically devise inventory scales to measure them so as to simplify further research. The Sixteen Personality Factor Questionnaire, the Guilford-Zimmerman Temperament Schedule, and the Maudsley Personality Inventory are examples of such instruments.

Aggression is, of course, a concept that has been formulated on an intuitive basis to group together a set of behaviors having in common the delivery of noxious stimulation; *instigation, hostility, anger,* and *inhibition* are also hypothetical constructs and theoretically-based intervening variables. As one might suppose, none of the factor-analytic instruments have equivalent constructs. However, the description of some of the factors suggests that they might relate to aggressive behavior.

As yet researchers have not applied factor-analytic instruments to the assessment or prediction of aggressive behavior with anything approaching the vigor that has been displayed with such tests as the MMPI or TAT. It would seem that most investigators who study aggression prefer to use concepts and instruments that originated in the clinic rather than in the laboratory, while the factor-analytic test authors have been more interested in the prediction of positive attributes such as achievement or leadership.

PROJECTIVE TECHNIQUES

Like the multiphasic inventories, projective tests are typically wide-band instruments designed to assess a broad range of personality functioning and behavior, overt and covert, conscious and unconscious. Instigation toward and inhibition against aggression are but two of the many personality characteristics reflected in projective tests.

While the more structured inventories have the advantage of fairly standardized administration, scoring, and interpretation, the projective techniques do not. It is rare, for example, to find two clinicians who administer the TAT in exactly the same fashion or for that matter, choose the same cards for presentation. For many of the projective techniques there are no commonly agreed-upon scoring procedures, so a number of different scales, all purporting to assess hostility, have been devised for such instruments. Moreover, for some tests there is even disagreement about the direction of the relationship that should be found between test signs and overt behavior. Some psychologists maintain that the relation should be inverse because projective techniques tap the preconscious or unconscious; others hold that the relationship should be direct, while still others maintain that the relationship will vary, being direct in some circumstances but indirect in others. Hence it is difficult to evaluate the proper role of projective techniques in the assessment of aggressive behavior. Evidence that one worker might regard as supporting the usefulness of projective tests, another worker might take as indicating a lack of validity.

The literature on most of these techniques is so vast that it is far beyond the scope of this chapter to review it. Therefore, the major techniques will simply be described and the writers' global appraisal presented. The reader can then consult the primary literature to assess for himself the adequacy of those tests in which he has a particular interest.

Completion Techniques

Sentence completion. Several studies have shown sentence completion methods to be useful in such diverse areas as the assessment of aggression in OSS personnel (Murray & MacKinnon, 1946) and elementary school children (Rohde, 1946), and in evaluating aggressive responses to discrimination among Negro and white college students (Touchstone, 1957). These studies were hindered by the use of rather vague, impressionistic criteria of aggressive behavior. Other investigators, using better defined criteria, as well as more objective scoring methods, have also reported positive results. Several found it possible to differentiate aggressive from nonaggressive delinquents (Jenkins & Blodgett, 1960; Mosher, Mortimer, & Grebel, 1968; Kingsley, 1961); others found it possible to differentiate levels of hostility and aggression within normal populations (Kinzie & Zimmer, 1968; Beach & Graham, 1967). The scanty data available thus far indicate that sentence completion techniques would be useful ones on which to concentrate future research.

Rosenzweig Picture-Frustration Study. The Rosenzweig P-F Study is one of the few projective techniques specifically designed to measure constructs relevant to aggression. Strongly rooted in frustration-aggression theory, the P-F Study presents the respondent with cartoons that depict frustrating situations. The test-taker indicates the cartoon figure's probable response to the frustration, and his response is classified according to whether aggression is directed outward against the environment (extrapunitive), inwardly against the self (intropunitive), or whether the situation is somehow neutralized so that the frustrating or aggressive components are removed (impunitive). The instrument is a relatively obvious one, which makes it particularly subject to dissembling (Bjerstedt, 1965; Megargee, 1964). Because it is an easily administered, reliably scored instrument that assesses important variables in both psychological theory and clinical practice, a considerable literature has accumulated. Much of the literature consists of personality research studies in which the instrument has been used to evaluate differential responses to frustration. Studies of its clinical usefulness have generally focused on the relation of the extrapunitiveness score to overt aggressive behavior, but results have been equivocal. Clinically aggressive samples have often been found not to differ from nonaggressive samples; in fact they often score somewhat lower (Megargee, 1971).

It is difficult to determine the implications of such findings for the test's validity. Rosenzweig (1950) has stated that there are three different levels of response to projective techniques; the subjective, the objective, and the projective; and the nature of the relationship between test and overt behavior will vary from level to level. By examining the total picture we can reconstruct the level of response, but as Bjerstedt (1965) has pointed out, such after-the-fact analyses can be used to rationalize any set of data, and their use casts doubt on the test's clinical usefulness in a test battery.

Construction Methods

Apperceptive techniques. Since the original publication of the Thematic Apperception Test, a whole family of storytelling tests has been developed, all based on the assumption that the story elicited reveals facets of the storyteller's personality (Neuringer, 1968). The literature on these tests is difficult to evaluate because the methods vary from study to study: (*a*) different examiners structure the task differently for their subjects; (*b*) different sets of cards are used, with some investigators creating unique cards for use in their particular studies; (*c*) different scoring systems are used—some look at the total incidence of themes dealing with aggression, others focus only on aggressive behavior initiated by the "hero" of the story, while still others look not at the story content but at the behavior of the storyteller as he works on the task; (*d*) the criteria of overt aggressive behavior against which the test data are validated also vary widely, including both verbal and physical, overt and covert, social and antisocial aggression; and (*e*) a variety of subject populations have been used—including both children and adults, middle class and lower class, men and women, clinical and normal populations—and insufficient attention is paid to the question of whether the findings can be generalized beyond the specific group of subjects being sampled.

By and large, the primary conclusion that can be drawn from the welter of studies that have been performed is that the relation between test aggression and overt aggression is extremely complex and dependent on many of the factors mentioned above. This can be illustrated by a few representative findings:

(*a*) "Card pull," or the extent to which the scene depicted suggests aggressive themes, has been found to be of major importance. Many authorities suggest that the less the card suggests aggression, the more an aggressive theme indicates instigation to aggression; by the same token, inhibitions against aggression are revealed by a reluctance to tell aggressive stories when the cards strongly suggest such themes. Data have been reported that support these hypotheses (Kagan, 1956; Megargee, 1967; Murstein, 1963, 1965c; Saltz & Epstein, 1963).

(*b*) Lesser (1957) found a positive correlation between fantasy and overt aggression in children whose mothers approved of aggressive behavior, but a negative correlation for those whose mothers disapproved.

(*c*) While most studies of middle-class children failed to find a significant correlation between overt and fantasy aggression, Mussen and Naylor (1954) found a significant positive correlation in a sample of presumably less inhibited lower-class delinquents. Megargee and Cook (1967), however, failed to replicate this finding using a more aggressive delinquent sample.

While the variety of findings and studies, many of which appear to contradict one another, makes it impossible to arrive at simple conclusions regarding the efficiency of the TAT and its cousins in assessing aggression, it is possible that the very complexity of these tests may eventually prove to be their most valuable asset. One of the problems noted in conjunction with the structured tests was an oversimplified notion of the dynamics of aggression. Aggression, as we have seen, results only after a conflict between instigation and inhibition and after competition among the possible responses. Only a complex instrument can hope to assess such a complex interplay of variables. Whether the TAT is such an instrument, can be determined only if the present series of one-shot studies is replaced with broad programmatic research. An integrated series of studies should be conducted to determine the relation between various aspects of test performance and various types of aggressive behavior as a function of systematic changes in test administration, test stimuli, and subject populations.

The Hand Test. The Hand Test, a relatively new projective technique, seems to have considerable potential for the assessment of aggression. The test consists of nine drawings of hands in various positions, and the subject is asked to report what he thinks the hands are doing. The creators of the test (Bricklin, Piotrowski, & Wagner, 1962) have devised an objective scoring system which is said to measure aggression and acting-out tendencies. Prison inmates, juvenile delinquents, and neuropsychiatric patients characterized by assaultive and aggressive tendencies have been found to score higher on the Hand Test Acting Out Score than their nonviolent fellows or normals in a number of studies (Bricklin et al., 1962; Wagner & Medredeff, 1963; Wetsel, Shapiro, & Wagner, 1967; Wagner & Hawkins, 1964; Brodsky & Brodsky, 1967), and only one investigator has reported a failure to obtain such differences (Drummond, 1966). In addition, Hodge, Wagner, and Schreiner (1966) found the test to be sensitive to hypnotically induced hostility.

A recent variation of the Hand Test is the Paired Hands Test (Zucker & Jordan, 1968), composed of photographs of pairs of hands which are of different races as well as of both sexes. As yet no studies have explored the validity of this instrument for the assessment of aggression.

Association Techniques

Inkblot techniques. The literature on the relationship between aggressive behavior and inkblot techniques such as the Rorschach Test and the Holtzman Inkblot Technique (HIT) is somewhat more orderly than that on the apperceptive methods. Researchers have been reluctant to create new inkblots or scoring conventions, and there has been less debate about the direction of the relationship to be expected between overt behavior and test variables.

Using more ambiguous stimuli than the apperceptive methods, the inkblot examination gives a sample of perceptual-associative behavior in which the subject reports, often after a certain amount of self-censorship, what he thinks the inkblot resembles. The verbal report can be scored not only for its manifest content but also for the perceptual determinants of the response.

Like the multiphasic inventories, the Rorschach is a wide-band technique that has been used to assess a variety of personality disorders. As a perceptual-associative task, it is probably most sensitive to the psychoses in which disturbances in perception and association are the fundamental symptoms. Its usefulness in the assessment of the schizophrenias and allied disorders makes it helpful in the prediction of aggression insofar as there is a higher base rate of aggressive behavior associated with these conditions. However, the major question is how sensitive the inkblot techniques are to differences in aggressiveness within homogeneous populations of normals, neuropsychiatric patients, or criminals.

A number of investigations have focused on the relationship between overt behavior and measures of hostile content on the Rorschach and Holtzman Inkblot Techniques. Several scales have been devised by workers such as Hafner and Kaplan (1960); Holtzman, Thorpe, Swartz, and Herron (1961); Murstein (1956); and Finney (1955). Most of these systems are closely related and based on the original inkblot hostility scale devised by Elizur (1949). A recent study (Megargee & Cook, 1967) has shown that these scales are so closely related that they are virtually interchangeable.

The relationships between inkblot content scores and various criteria of overt aggressive behavior in samples of normals, neuropsychiatric patients, and delinquents have been reviewed by Buss (1961) and Megargee (1971). A consistent trend in the literature has been for more significant positive correlations to be reported in studies that used neuropsychiatric patients as subjects than in studies focusing on delinquent or criminal populations. Megargee (1971) has suggested that this trend may be the result of the relative lack of subtlety of content scores and greater motivation to distort responses among correctional samples.

As with the apperceptive methods, the criterion problem is a major factor in establishing the validity of inkblot hostility scales. Megargee and Cook (1967) related the scores on five inkblot content scales to eleven different criteria of overt aggressive behavior in a sample of juvenile delinquents. The criterion measures used included self-reports and observations of direct and indirect verbal and physical aggressiveness. Many of the correlations were insignificant; of the significant correlations that were obtained, moreover, some were positive and others negative. This study, which also investigated the relationship of several TAT aggressive content scales to the same 11 criteria, demonstrated the complexity of the criterion problem and highlighted one reason that different studies using different operational definitions of aggression have often obtained contradictory results.

Fewer studies have investigated the relationship between aggressive behavior and the determinant scores. While these scores have the advantage of greater subtlety, they are generally more difficult to score reliably. Moreover, in the case of the Rorschach, determinant scores have been plagued by psychometric inadequacies that make them difficult to manipulate statistically, although these drawbacks have been largely overcome in the HIT. Partly because of the problems of scoring and analysis, the literature on the relationship of determinant scores to aggressive behavior has been less rigorous than that on the content scales. The data that have been collected suggest that differences in aggressiveness may be reflected in the use of color and movement on the Rorschach or HIT (Megargee, 1971).

In practice, of course, the clinician makes use of both content and determinant scores. Few studies have looked at both together, but those that have indicate that this approach is the most promising (Sommer & Sommer, 1958; Piotrowski & Abrahamsen, 1952). More integrated research of this kind needs to be performed. An obvious first step would be to determine whether skilled clinicians, responding to whatever aspects of the protocol they choose, can predict aggressive behavior validly on the basis of a Rorschach or HIT examination.

Expressive Techniques

Projective drawings. The use of projective drawings of the human figure is second in popularity only to the Rorschach in current clinical testing (Sunberg, 1961). While many clinicians interpret them intuitively, Machover (1949) has formulated a number of explicit hypotheses with regard to the "meaning" of various elements within such drawings. She has postulated that certain aspects of drawings—talon-like fingers, heavy slash lines for a mouth, teeth featured in the mouth, and the like—indicate tendencies to aggression.

Many research studies have attempted to test Machover's formulations, but most of the evidence reported has failed to provide unequivocal empirical support for her hypotheses (Swensen, 1957, 1968; Jones & Thomas, 1961). In regard to aggression, for example, Naar (1964) was unable to differentiate delinquents from nondelinquents on the basis of their projective drawings, and Koppitz (1966) found that only one sign out of 30 tested supported Machover's hypotheses with regard to aggression, although four signs appeared to be characteristic of hostile attitudes and impulsivity.

Interpretation of the results noted above, however, needs to be tempered with a critical appraisal of the research designs that have been used and with an application of the problems basic to the validation of the projective drawing technique. Hammer (1968) and Swensen (1957, 1968) have noted many defects of design in the research reported in the literature, such as the use of psychiatric diagnoses as criteria, the use of inadequate samples of drawings, differences of interpretive set among clinicians, misinterpretation of hypotheses, the use of signs without regard to context, and the comparison of group means rather than deviation scores. A major difficulty of the technique itself lies in the fact that a method to control for the quality of drawings (i.e., varying degrees of artistic skill) has not yet been devised (Swensen, 1968).

Generally speaking, studies that have met Hammer's (1968) and Swensen's (1957) suggestions for research have obtained more encouraging results, but as yet few sophisticated investigations, using a combination of signs, have focused on the validity of the DAP as a measure of aggression. One exception is Griffith and Lemley's (1967) study in which the joint presence of two signs predicted verbal, but not physical, aggression.

Doll play. Projective doll play has been one of the most popular methods of assessing aggression in children in both the clinic and the laboratory (Haworth, 1962). The child is typically presented with a group of dolls representing the family constellation and with a doll house; he is encouraged to play with them while verbalizing what is happening. Some investigators use a completely unstructured situation; others set the stage by announcing, for example, that the "mother doll" has just brought home a new "baby doll" and asking the child to show how the "brother doll" reacts.

As with other techniques, research on doll play has suffered from a lack of standardization, which makes it impossible to compare the results of different studies. The stimulus materials and their administration vary from one study to the next, and reviews of the literature show that the experimenter and the way he presents the task strongly influence the aggressiveness of the child's doll play (Cohn, 1962; Levin & Wardwell, 1962; Isch, 1952). Moreover, there are no standardized or agreed-upon methods for measuring the aggressiveness of the child's doll-playing behavior.

Doll play has a high degree of content or face validity; consequently, the literature on empirical validation of the method is scanty in comparison to the number of investigations that have made use of the technique. The studies that have sought to validate the method against ratings of aggressiveness by teachers or patients have been contradictory and discouraging. Some construct validity has been provided, however, by research showing aggressive doll play to increase as a function of maternal aggression and rejection (Isch, 1952), sibling rivalry (Henry & Henry, 1944; Miller & Baruch, 1950), and separation from the parents (Ryder, 1954; Sears & Pintler, 1947; Sears, 1951); and to vary as a function of parental disciplinary practices (Hollenberg & Sperry, 1951; Sears, 1947).

PHYSIOLOGICAL MEASURES

At several points we have noted that instigation to aggression can be thought of as being composed in part of hostility, an enduring personality trait; and in part of anger, a temporary state of emotional arousal. Most of the measures that have been reviewed measure hostility, because clinicians are most interested in assessing enduring personality characteristics and therefore attempt to put the client at ease so that the influence of temporary emotional states such as anxiety, anger, and fear are minimized. However, we should not neglect anger, for while hostility often leads to chronic mildly aggressive behavior, it is anger that is more often responsible for impulsive acts of extreme aggression or violence. Indeed the very title of Truman Capote's book *In Cold Blood* points up the rarity of the dispassionate killer.

The study of emotional states has a long history in psychology, going back to William James and beyond. As we all know, emotional states are accompanied by visceral correlates, and every adult has learned to distinguish between the inner feelings associated with joy, fear, and anger. The controversial question has been whether these states of arousal are in fact physiologically different, or whether we simply learn to interpret a generalized pattern of arousal so that it conforms with our cognitive definition of the situation.

During the last decade, work by a number of investigators (Ax, 1953; Schachter, 1957; Sternbach, 1966; Funkenstein, King, & Drolette, 1957; Wolf, Cardon, Shephard, & Wolff, 1955) has demonstrated that it is possible to distinguish among these emotional states using autonomic measures. Experimenters who have induced anxiety or anger in experimental subjects through various manipulations have noticed distinctive differences in the autonomic reactions associated with these emotions. The pattern associated with anger directed outward has been described in general as a noradrenaline-like reaction with increased dyastolic blood pressure, muscle potentials, and skin conductance, and a decreased heart rate.

On the basis of these findings, some investigators have gone on to infer that different physiological mechanisms are responsible for mediating the different emotional states. At present these suggestions are simply speculation that must be verified through further research. Whether or not this hypothesis is confirmed, the fact that investigators in different laboratories have been able to reliably differentiate the "anger-out" pattern from other emotional states means that autonomic nervous system measures can be added to the psychologist's armamentarium of assessment devices. Thus far, such measures have been used almost exclusively in the laboratory to determine the effects of various stimuli or behavior patterns on anger level (Hokanson, 1970). However, Hokanson is presently moving toward research designed to determine whether differences in autonomic response patterns are useful in the clinical assessment of aggression as well.

MISCELLANEOUS TECHNIQUES

In addition to the techniques reviewed above, many other measures that purport to assess aggression have been devised. For the most part, little evidence for their reliability and validity is to be found in the literature. A few of the more common techniques will be noted here.

A number of investigators have employed a "scrambled sentence" task to differentiate hostile and aggressive subjects (Caine, 1960). Scrambled sentence items are typically composed of a subject, object, and two verbs, one of which is neutral and the other hostile. The testee's choice of verb determines whether his sentence solutions will be deemed hostile or neutral. Other investigators have compared the rate of learning hostile and neutral words. According to Buss [1961, p. 107], ". . . the aggressiveness or hostility of the learner should affect learning of hostile stimuli." Of course, in such studies adequate matching for word frequency and the like is essential.

Another family of methods focuses on differences in the readiness to perceive violence or hostility. Shelby and Toch (1962) used a binocular rivalry task in which an aggressive scene was administered to one eye and a neutral scene to the other and the subject was required to report what he perceived. They found this measure was related to tendencies to behavioral violence among institutionalized offenders. Similar results were obtained by Allport (1955) with tachistoscopic presentations of hostile and neutral material to determine the differences in threshold, if any. Such measures, if valid, would appear to be assessing inhibitions more than instigation.

A number of investigations have compared the intensity of responses in children who had undergone a frustration trial (failure or non-reward) with the intensity of responses following a nonfrustration or reward trial (Longstreth, 1960; Olds, 1953, 1956; Haner & Brown, 1955; Screven, 1954). In these studies, increases in the amount of pressure the child exerts on a plunger after he has been frustrated are interpreted as indicating increased aggressive instigation. Mussen and Rutherford (1961) used the verbalized desire to destroy a balloon as their measure of aggression in comparing frustrated and nonfrustrated groups of children.

More recently, Gottschalk and Gleser (1969) have reported a content analysis technique for measuring various psychological states. Of the five scales these authors have developed, three are said to measure hostility (the Hostility Directed Outward, Hostility Directed Inward, and Ambivalent Hostility scales). A systematic method for coding samples of verbal behavior, which may have been obtained in any of a variety of settings, has been devised. The Gottschalk-Gleser Content Analysis Scales have evolved from an extensive series of studies (Gottschalk & Gleser, 1963), and impressive reliability, validity, and normative data are reported for them.

SOME CONCLUDING REMARKS

It is clear that many diverse techniques have been used for the assessment and prediction of aggressive behavior. This variety presents both a strength and a weakness. The eagerness of psychologists to invent new techniques has prevented premature fixation on a particular approach, but too many workers are content with face validity for their new instruments and have too little regard for empirically establishing their reliability, validity, and generality. New tests of hostility and aggressiveness should not be published until the basic data called for in the *Technical Recommendations for Psychological Tests* have been gathered. This yardstick should be applied not only to tests published for clinical assessment, but to tests designed for use in personality research as well. Too many investigations, involving thousands of man hours and dollars, have been crippled by the use of an unvalidated, hastily constructed "test" as the independent or dependent measure of aggression.

More studies are needed to determine the interrelationships and redundancy of existing tests and to make recommendations as to those that should be used in future research (Megargee & Cook, 1967). The next logical step is to find how these measures relate to different criteria of aggression in various populations.

Our review of the literature also showed that most tests are based on an oversimplified concept of aggression. The need is for a new generation of sophisticated instruments that will assess inhibitions and instigation as a function of situational events and stimuli, along with studies of how these factors interact to produce overt aggression, displacement, response substitution, and the like. The comparison of existing measures recommended above should provide valuable clues as to the kinds of instruments that will be most useful in this second phase. The research conducted on the assessment of aggression thus far is sufficiently promising to indicate that such efforts would be rewarded and would result in more accurate prediction.

CHAPTER VIII

The nature and assessment
of intrinsic motivation

Paul McReynolds

One of the most important and exciting developments in contemporary theoretical psychology has been the progress made toward understanding a class of motivation that, though its boundaries are somewhat ill-defined, has come generally to be referred to as *intrinsic motivation.* It would be a gross error to suppose that we are yet close to a satisfactory comprehension of this important category of human behavior, but a great deal of empirical information has been obtained, and a number of heuristic theories have been proposed.

An important aspect of this emerging area of motivational psychology has been the appearance of a new family of assessment techniques, concerned with the measurement of intrinsic motivational variables. While most of these instruments are still in the early stage of development and, in addition, are limited by the fact that there are important aspects of intrinsic motivation that they fail to cover, they nevertheless clearly constitute an important new direction and new resource in assessment technology. The purposes of this chapter are, first, to examine the concept of intrinsic motivation; second, to describe and review the instruments available for its assessment; and third, to set forth several suggestions for further development in this area of psychological measurement.

THE CONCEPT OF INTRINSIC MOTIVATION

Preliminary Analysis

In order to come to grips with the manifold problems of motivation, it is necessary to examine carefully the instances in which behavior appears to be motivated, and if possible to divide these behaviors into meaningful classes. Analyses of this sort have suggested to a number of theorists that one plausible division is in terms of those behaviors that are *intrinsically* motivated and those that are *extrinsically* motivated. Intrinsically motivated behaviors are those which appear to be carried out because of an appeal inherent in, or intrinsic to, the activity itself, or conversely, which appear to be avoided or terminated because of an aversiveness inherent in the activity. Extrinsically motivated behaviors, on the other hand, are those which are carried out in order to attain or avoid a given end state or goal. Intrinsic behaviors are sought or avoided for their own sake; extrinsic behaviors are *means to ends*.

Examples of behavior reflecting *positive intrinsic* motivation would be a person's playing bridge, listening to music, or writing a novel—all performed as a function of the motivational attractiveness of these activities; an example of a behavior reflecting *negative intrinsic* motivation would be an individual's declining to play another game of chess because the activity has become boring to him. Examples of behavior indicative of *positive extrinsic* motivation would be a rat's running a maze in order to obtain food, or a man's painting his house so that it will be attractive; an example of a behavior implying *negative extrinsic* motivation would be a student's studying in order to avoid failure in a course.

The concept of extrinsic motivation is closely related to that of *instrumental behavior,* in that acts which are considered to be extrinsically motivated are "instrumental" to the attainment of given ends. Most of modern motivation theory has been concerned with extrinsic motives; thus, hunger, sex, pain-avoidance, anxiety-reduction, achievement, power, and affiliation motives appear to be mainly of this class. Intrinsically motivated behavior, on the other hand, is that which is often described—somewhat metaphorically—as being sought "for its own sake." There is no standard term for referring to the class of behavior that is intrinsically motivated, but I wish to suggest the term *autonomous behavior* for that function, and will so use it in this chapter.

The distinction between instrumental and autonomous behaviors is not always easy. A given behavior could be either or both. For example, conceive a man trimming his hedges: if he finds this task appealing in itself, then it is autonomous behavior; but if he is doing it only in order that his yard will look neat, then it is instrumental. Clearly, the same behavior can be autonomous for one person and instrumental for another. Further, the categorization of a given activity might change over time; for example, a boy might begin practicing on a musical instrument because of an interest in doing so (intrinsic motivation) but presently the practice might become boring, so that external incentives (extrinsic motivation) would be required to maintain the behavior. Or conversely, an opposite change might occur; for example, a man might take up tennis in order to lose weight (extrinsic), and come eventually to play tennis for the sheer fun of it (intrinsic). The change from intrinsic to extrinsic has not been given a particular name, but the reverse appears to be the same as that referred to by Woodworth (1918) as "a mechanism becoming a drive," and later designated by Allport (1937) as "functional autonomy."

The following four features are particularly characteristic of autonomous behaviors: (1) The behaviors constitute a sequence; they have an ongoing quality; they are better described as process than as end. Thus, typical intrinsic behaviors are read*ing* a story, play*ing* tennis, and listen*ing* to a symphony. All of these occur over time, and would be meaningless in any other sense. Thus, one does not read a novel in order to reach the last page; rather, it is the whole, ongoing process of reading the story that is motivationally important. (2) The ongoing nature of the behaviors involved, however, is not completely fixed; rather, it is in some degree unpredictable, variable, changeable, not only in an internal sequential sense, but also with respect to prior, similar experiences; i.e., it has an innovative, novelty-seeking quality.[1] (3) The volitional aspect of the ongoing behavior is one of involvement in the activity, so that the performance of the activity as such—aside from its goal—assumes an impelling quality to which the individual may become strongly and personally committed. (4) The affective aspect of the ongoing behavior is, when positive, one of zest, excitement, and challenge, and when negative, one of blandness, boredom, and apathy.

All of the above characteristics contrast markedly with the nature of instrumental behavior. Thus, in the latter the focus is strictly on the end result, rather than on the behavioral process as such; the aim is the efficient, predictable, non-varying performance of the task; the volitional aspect is one of inner obligation or external coercion; and the affective aspect is, when positive, one of satisfaction and relief, and when negative, one of frustration and anxiety.[2]

Historical Background

The current interest in intrinsic motivation is more a renaissance than a new discovery, and references to certain features of this class of motivation can be traced back to the ancient Greek philosophers. Some aspects—particularly those concerned with novelty-seeking behaviors—were discussed extensively in the eighteenth and nineteenth centuries. We will begin the present review, however, with R. S. Woodworth, who can be considered the leading pioneer in the scientific approach to intrinsic motivation. In his 1918 *Dynamic psychology*, Woodworth took the position that the motivation for the bulk of human activities is not derived from "instincts" such as hunger and thirst, but rather is inherent in the process of carrying out the activities. "As a general proposition," he wrote, "we may say that the drive that carries forward any activity, when it is running freely and effectively, is inherent in that activity. It is only when an activity is running by its own drive that it can run thus freely and effectively; for as long as it is being driven by some extrinsic motive, it is subject to the distraction of that motive [p. 70]"; and elsewhere he noted that a child, given free choice, will pursue an activity only when it is "intrinsically interesting [p. 67]" to him.

Another important precursor of the present scene was L. T. Troland's 1928 book—the first text on motivation as such—which in its discussion of human novelty-seeking behavior reached a level of sophistication that has scarcely yet been surpassed. After this book, however, the growing dominance of tension-reduction models was such that interest in novelty-seeking motivation went into a drastic and prolonged eclipse. Throughout most of the thirties and forties, the restrictive influence of the Hullian and Freudian models, both of which asserted that all behaviors can be explained in drive-minimization

---

[1]Novel input may also be involved in instrumental behavior. For a discussion of the kinds of novelty-oriented behavior see McReynolds (1962).

[2]It should be emphasized, however, that the posited distinction between intrinsic and extrinsic motivation is principally one of theoretical convenience and utility, and that actual behavior can in most instances be assumed to be influenced by both classes of determinants.

principles, was so great as to depress almost completely any interest in intrinsic motivation. Though Allport, in 1937, argued that certain human activities may exist autonomously, i.e., independently of the physiological drives, his proposal was generally not well received.

Allport was a personality theorist, and personality theorists, it is fair to say, were quicker than the laboratory-based motivation psychologists to see the need for concepts of intrinsic motivation. Thus Murray and Kluckhohn (1953), in one of the classic papers in this area, suggested a category termed "modal activity," in which the satisfaction "is normally concurrent with the activity [p. 14]," rather than being dependent upon its ultimate effect. And Maslow (1954, 1955) described what he termed "growth motivation" in explaining behavior that appears to enhance, rather than to reduce, tension. Koch, though not a personality theorist in the usual sense, presented a paper from this orientation at the Nebraska Symposium on Motivation in 1956; in it he conceptualized a motivational state in which behavior is intrinsically determined. It is important to note that Murray and Kluckhohn's (1953) "directional" and "modal" behaviors, Maslow's (1955) "deficiency" and "growth" motives, and Koch's "states A and B" are all the same family as the present "extrinsic" and "intrinsic" motivations.

But while the personality theorists were delineating the distinction between two kinds of motivation, a number of laboratory-based experimental psychologists were approaching the same problem from a different perspective. This impetus took the form of a renewal of interest in novelty-associated behavior, something essentially dormant since Troland. Woodworth, in 1947, posited an inherent motive to perceive, and Hebb, in 1949, emphasized the role of variable stimulus input in maintaining efficient performance. Harlow and his colleagues (Harlow, 1950, 1953; Harlow, Harlow, & Meyer, 1950) were able to show that monkeys will perform for the "intrinsic" motivation of manipulation and puzzle solving; and Montgomery (1951), about the same time, undertook a series of experiments on exploratory behavior in rats. It was also in this period that Berlyne (1950, 1954) began his still continuing work on curiosity. I myself became interested in this area as a graduate student, when I attended a colloquium given by Hebb, and in subsequent papers (McReynolds 1954, 1956, 1960) posited that individuals have innate tendencies to obtain and assimilate novel percepts, and distinguished between "incongruency motives" and "perceptualization motives"—a pairing theoretically akin to the present extrinsic and intrinsic distinction. Leuba, in 1955, proposed that organisms seek such inputs as will maintain an optimal level of stimulation. Two other highly important early papers on the role of novelty in stimulus input were those by Dember and Earl (1957) and Glanzer (1958); and, Woodworth, in 1958, set forth the final version of his capacity-oriented theory of intrinsic motivation. Berlyne's (1960) important book *Conflict, arousal, and curiosity* brought much of the previous work together and posited a relationship between arousal variables and curiosity. Two other key contributions of this period were the book *Functions of varied experience,* edited by Fiske and Maddi (1961), and a paper by Hunt (1963) which systematically developed the concept of intrinsic motivation.

In addition to its roots in personality and experimental psychology, the concept of intrinsic motivation is imbedded in educational and personnel theory. Thus, in the former, Hilgard and Russell in 1950 distinguished between intrinsic and extrinsic relations between tasks and goals; and in the latter, Herzberg, Mausner, and Snyderman in 1959 developed the notions of "motivator" (intrinsic) and "hygiene" (extrinsic) factors in occupational adjustment.

The concept of intrinsic motivation, then, has important roots in several different psychological fields. From being considered in the 1940s as a tenuous and peripheral determinant of behavior, it has come now to be generally accepted (Murray, 1964; Berlyne, 1965) as a pervasive and important category of behavior. The concept, however, is not a simple one, and it must be remembered that to label a category is not to explain it. In my view it is most plausible, on the basis of evidence now available, to posit two different kinds of intrinsic motivation (McReynolds, 1970a), one concerned with what I will call "innovative behavior" and the other with what I will tentatively term "commitment behavior" (both being instances of autonomous behavior).

Innovative Behavior

By innovative behavior I will refer to those activities of a person, both overt and covert, that can plausibly be conceived to lead to relatively immediate alterations in the person's internal representation of his overall stimulus environment. In other words, *innovative behavior* will be used as a class name to include the behaviors sometimes referred to in the technical literature as "novelty-seeking," "variation-seeking," "stimulus-seeking," and "sensation-seeking," as well as the areas of curiosity and exploratory behavior. The term *innovative behavior* appears to fill a certain void in the literature:[3] none of the other terms just noted are sufficiently broad to encompass the class of behavior under consideration, and the most widely used one, "novelty-seeking," has a certain aura of superficiality—as implied by the use of the word *novelty* to refer to knickknacks and trivia. In actuality, some degree of innovativeness pervades most of those aspects of human life that we consider most interesting, most significant, and most civilized (see, e.g., Barnett, 1953).

The theoretical analysis of innovative behavior has taken two directions. The first has focused on the characteristics of stimuli that induce investigatory behavior. This approach has studied the influence on innovative behavior of a group of stimulus characteristics—including novelty, complexity, change, and uncertainty—that Berlyne (1960) has referred to as "collative variables." This approach is particularly congenial to the stimulus-response tradition, which holds that behavior is determined primarily by associative factors and is essentially under the control of the stimulus situation. The second approach

---

[3]For our present purposes *innovative behavior* is defined in the way indicated above. In terms of previous connotations the term has the limitation that it has sometimes been used more or less synonymously with *creative behavior*. It should be noted, however, that creativeness and innovativeness are not the same, i.e., that one can be innovative without being creative (though the converse, presumably, is not possible). All dictionaries emphasize both *change* and *newness* in delineating the word "innovate."

emphasizes the internal characteristics of the organism and studies innovative behavior as a function of the contemporary state of the individual. This orientation is particularly congenial to personality theorists, who hold that behavior is significantly determined by subject variables. Both of these approaches are essential in a complete psychology, but our interest in the present chapter will be primarily on the second approach, i.e., on individual differences variables.

There is now solid evidence to confirm the everyday observation that some individuals have strong, and others comparatively weak, tendencies to engage in innovative behavior, and further that the same persons differ in this respect from time to time. How are these differences to be explained? How is such motivation to be accounted for? Traditionally, the explanation has been that innovative behavior is "natural." Such an explanation, however, even if true, is not very helpful, since it does not specify the conditions under which innovative behavior will occur. Through efforts toward more adequate understanding, two different, though related kinds of models have been developed. Both posit that as a function of certain conditions—often I am afraid, unspecified—there is an optimum of some variable x, such that too much innovative behavior raises x above the optimum, and too little such behavior permits x to decline too low (the former state is generally characterized as exciting, the latter as boring); hence the organism is motivated toward an optimal level of innovative behavior.

These two theoretical approaches differ in that one focuses upon physiological arousal, whereas the other implicates cognitive factors. Both approaches have several different versions. Thus Berlyne (1960, 1967), who has developed the former approach most intensively, posits that organisms tend to maintain an optimal input of *arousal potential* (the characteristics of stimuli which induce arousal); and Fiske and Maddi (1961) propose that organisms seek optimal *levels of activation* for given tasks. Within the cognitive camp, I myself (McReynolds, 1956, 1960, 1970a) have theorized that individuals tend to engage in such innovative behavior as will maintain an optimal *rate of alteration in cognitive structure;* Glanzer (1958) views the organism as an information processing system and proposes that the organism seeks an optimal *amount of information* per unit time; Hunt (1963), though he notes that an optimal arousal hypothesis cannot be dismissed, appears to favor an optimal incongruity principle; and Walker (1964) posits that organisms attempt to maintain an optimal *input of stimulus complexity.*

I will not undertake here a critical comparison of all these different conceptions; it is sufficient for present purposes to note that all of them postulate some kind of optimum function that is served by the input of novel, variable, and/or complex stimuli.

Commitment Behavior

There is good reason to believe that much of the behavior that appears to be intrinsically motivated is, in principle at least, explainable in terms of the optimal innovation paradigm outlined above. It seems doubtful, however, that it all is. That is, behavior of the type that "carries its own motivation"—

to speak metaphorically—appears to encompass more than the novelty-complexity-uncertainty aspect of behavior, even when these are considered very broadly. One of the more conspicuous features of much intrinsic behavior is the degree of personal involvement and dedication that the individual invests in the activity. I have suggested elsewhere (McReynolds, 1970a) that, pending a more complete understanding of this class of motivation, we refer to it as *commitment motivation*. Examples of behavior of this type would be not only the commitments that some people make to causes—such as peace movements, defenses of academic freedom, or crusades against a disease—but also the commitment that, say, a boy very interested in baseball or in model rocketry makes to these activities. These commitments, it should be noted, appear to be different in kind from extrinsic goals.

Other theorists have discussed what I am calling commitment motivation—sometimes in almost the same words—though they have not, I believe, made the distinction that I am proposing between innovative and commitment behaviors. Thus Koch, in discussing State B (intrinsic) motivation, observed that "you do not merely 'work at' or 'on' the task; you have *committed yourself* to the task . . . [1956, p. 67]." DeCharms (1968) also has provided a stimulating discussion of the psychology of commitment; in his conception a state of free personal commitment is identified with intrinsic motivation. At present the study of commitment motivation is in its infancy, and the only statement that can be made with much certainty is that there is an urgent need for further investigation of this important aspect of human life.

APPROACHES TO ASSESSMENT

In order to apply or develop a given set of theoretical constructs, it is necessary to have at hand a variety of appropriate techniques for measuring the postulated variables; such mensuration can, in turn, help to advance theory. In other words, theory and technology necessarily advance together, and neither can get too far in front of the other. In the area of intrinsic motivation, efforts toward assessment have been concerned almost exclusively with innovative behavior—with novelty-seeking, change-seeking, and related behaviors—and very little, as yet, with commitment motivation.

A number of important theoretical ideas have been influential in determining the kinds of tests constructed. Perhaps the most significant of these has been the view that individuals differ in their optimal (preferred) levels of innovative input. A number of instruments, including the Sensation-Seeking Scale (Zuckerman, Kolin, Price, & Zoob, 1964), the Change Seeker Index (Garlington & Shimota, 1964), the Stimulus-Variation Seeking Scale (Penney & Reinehr, 1966), and the Obscure Figures Test (Acker & McReynolds, 1965) have been focused on the assessment of this theoretically important variable. Though it has not been explicitly stated, these—and all other tests in the area— have been concerned with individuals' characteristic (trait) levels of innovative behavior, rather than with their equally important current (state) levels.

Another theoretical conception that has played an important role in the development of measures of intrinsic motivation is the distinction proposed by Maddi and his colleagues (Maddi & Berne, 1964; Maddi, Propst, & Feldinger, 1965; Pearson & Maddi, 1966) among (1) the desire for an input of novelty; (2) the production of novelty through internal (fantasy) events; and (3) the active production of novelty via a focus on external events (curiosity). Thematic techniques (Maddi & Berne, 1964; Maddi et al., 1965) have been designed for the assessment of each of these, and the Simile Preferences Inventory (Pearson & Maddi, 1966) for the second one. Pearson (1970) has extended this analysis—and developed a Novelty Experiencing Scale—to suggest four different forms (*External Sensation, Internal Sensation, External Cognition, Internal Cognition*) of novelty experiencing. In a somewhat related approach, McReynolds (1964) has proposed a distinction between ideational and motoric modes of innovative behavior.

Berlyne in 1960 differentiated between specific and diversive exploration: the former is directed toward the resolution of a given question, the latter toward increasing the input of novelty and change. Most assessment techniques in this area have been concerned with the latter class, which bears on optimal level constructs, but more recently Day (1969) has constructed an instrument, the Ontario Test of Intrinsic Motivation, that focuses on specific curiosity.

The separation made by Herzberg et al. (1959) between motivator and hygiene factors, referred to earlier, has been instrumental in the development of two important assessment devices. Herzberg and Hamlin (1961) applied the distinction to the concept of mental health, and Hamlin and Nemo (1962) designed the Choice-Motivation Scale to assess relevant individual differences; this has been followed by the Picture Motivation Scale (Kunca & Haywood, 1969). The Herzberg et al. orientation differs from most others in that its conception of intrinsic motivation is not limited to innovative behavior. Thus Kahoe (1966), working in this tradition, suggests that five intrinsic motivational factors (esthetics, achievement, creativity, responsibility, and psychological stimulation) are involved in vocational adjustment.

TECHNIQUES FOR ASSESSMENT

We turn now to an examination of the various instruments that have been devised for the assessment of intrinsic motivation. These procedures represent for the most part a fairly early stage of technological development; nevertheless, in the relatively short history of this area of assessment, a considerable variety of tests has come into use.

It will be convenient to group the instruments into the following categories: (1) self-description techniques, (2) thematic approaches, (3) stimulus preference techniques, and (4) performance measures. We will first review the tests used with adults and then, in a final section, will review the special approaches available for use with children. It may be noted that this listing does not include interview or observational techniques, since neither has yet been systematically developed as a tool for the assessment of intrinsic motivation. It is clear, however, from the beginning work of Biemiller (1962), that reliable assessments of intrinsic motivation can be made on interview data. With respect to observational methods, the most pertinent work is that of Barker (1968) and his associates. Thus, one of the variables on which they have rated children's motivation is "direct interest" (Wright & Barker, 1950, p. 263), a category that appears to be at least roughly analogous to the present "intrinsic motivation."

Self-Description Techniques

The most widely used approach for the assessment of intrinsic motivation is the inventory model, in which inferences about a person's motivation are made on the basis of his responses to questions about his characteristic activities and attitudes. The adjective checklist technique has been used much less, though the Gough-Heilbrun Adjective Check List (see below) does include a "Change" scale, which can be used as a measure of intrinsic motivation.

The inventories can be divided into two groups: first, those which attempt the global assessment of the innovative aspect of intrinsic motivation, variously referred to as need for change, stimulus-seeking, or sensation-seeking; and second, those scales designed to provide a pattern of scores, based on a dimensional analysis of intrinsic motivation. The first class can be further broken down into two groups: first, special scales (Sensation-Seeking Scale, Change Seeker Index, and Stimulus-Variation-Seeking Scale) designed to assay given aspects of innovative motivation; and second, scales on standard, wide-range personality inventories (Personal Preference Schedule, Personality Research Form, California Psychological Inventory, Omnibus Personality Inventory) which appear to measure variables related to innovation.

Currently, there are two major tests in the second, broader class referred to above: the Novelty Experiencing Scale and the Ontario Test of Intrinsic Motivation.

The Sensation Seeking Scale (SSS). This scale (Zuckerman et al., 1964) is intended to provide a measure of an individual's "optimal stimulation level." It consists of 34 two-statement items, for each of which the subject must make a choice. (Sample: A. "I enjoy the thrills of watching car races." B. "I find car races unpleasant.") The test includes separate, but largely overlapping scales for men and women. It has been quite widely used and only a selection of studies can be noted here (for a recent review see Masterson, 1970a). Split-half reliabilities (Zuckerman et al., 1964) are reported as .68 and .74 for men and women, respectively. Farley and Farley (1967) obtained a correlation of .47 between the SSS and the extroversion scale of the Eysenck Personality Inventory. Other work (Zuckerman, Persky, Hopkins, Murtaugh, Basu, & Schilling, 1966) has indicated the scale to be positively related to the Psychopathic Deviate and Hypomanic scales of the MMPI; to the Dominance, Adventurousness, and Bohemian Unconcernedness scales on the 16 PF test (Gorman, 1970) to a measure of category breadth (Taylor & Levitt, 1967), to the Change Scale on Edwards' Personal Preference Schedule, and also to the Gough-Heilbrun Adjective Check List (Zuckerman & Link, 1968), and to the scientific and social-service interest patterns on the Kuder (Kish & Donnenwerth, 1969a). Kish and Busse (1968) have reported a low negative correlation between the SSS and age, and low positive correlations between the SSS and intellectual variables.

The Change Seeker Index (CSI). This instrument, devised by Garlington and Shimota (1964), consists of 95 True-False items (Sample: "I like to wear clothes that will attract attention"). Purpose of the scale is to assess "the need for variety in one's stimulus input [p. 919]." The test was developed from an original list of 211 items, primarily on the basis of internal consistency criteria. Corrected split-half reliabilities of .89 and .92 and a test-retest (about one-week interval) reliability of .91 are reported. Normative data indicate that college students score higher than psychiatric patients on the CSI. Scores are not significantly related to intelligence (Shipley-Hartford) but are correlated on the order of $-.2$ with age. Acker and McReynolds (1967) found the CSI to correlate .59 with the Originality scale of the OPI, .45 with the Change scale of the PRF, and .62 with the SSS. Stock and Looft (1969) reported insignificant correlations between the CSI and a number of demographic variables; there was a significant relationship (.35), however, between change-seeking and political liberality. The present writer (McReynolds, in press), in a use of the CSI that can be conceived as contributing to its construct validity, found it to predict significantly whether subjects would choose to participate in an unknown task.

The Stimulus-Variation Seeking Scale (SVSS). This scale was developed by Penney and Reinehr (1966) and consists of 100 True-False statements (Sample: "I dislike trying new restaurants"). The scale is designed "to determine the amount of exteroceptive stimulus-variation seeking customarily engaged in by an individual [p. 631]." Test-retest reliabilities (one-month interval) of .84 and .87, for college men and women respectively, are reported. With respect to discriminant validity, the SVSS is not significantly related to the Taylor Manifest Anxiety Scale or the California *F* Scale; with respect to convergent validity, high SVSS scorers were shown to perceive more autokinetic movement and to show more originality on the Unusual Uses Test (Guilford, 1956) than low scorers. McReynolds (unpublished data) found the SVSS not to correlate significantly with a measure of preference for complexity in schizophrenics; the subjects scored significantly lower than the normal sample reported by Penney and Reinehr (1966).

Innovation scales on standard personality tests. Several of the major personality tests include scales to assess the need or desire for change. While not as widely used in intrinsic motivation research as the instruments described above, these scales nevertheless have much to recommend them, especially in instances in which one is using the longer tests for other purposes. The Edwards (1959) Personal Preference Schedule (EPPS) measures 15 needs, including the need for change. This scale has a corrected split-half reliability of .79, and a test-retest (one-week interval) coefficient of .83. The more recent Edwards (1966) Personality Inventory (EPI) also includes a change score; this variable in Pearson's 1970 study correlated .49 ($p < .01$) with the SSS and .37 ($p < .01$) with NES total (see page 168). Stern's (1958) Activities Index (AI) yields a Change-Sameness score, with a reported reliability (KR-20) of .67; in Pearson's paper this scale correlated .48 ($p < .01$) with SSS.

The recent Omnibus Personality Inventory (Heist & Yonge, 1968) includes a 32-item Complexity scale; high scorers are described as "tolerant of ambiguities and uncertainties; they are fond of novel situations and ideas [p. 4]." The variable correlates .40 ($p < .01$) with the Aesthetic scale on the Allport-Vernon-Lindzey Scale of Values (Allport, Vernon, & Lindzey, 1960) and .32 ($p < .01$) with a preference measure of complexity; it has a corrected split-half reliability of .76 and a test-retest (three- to four-week interval) reliability of .91. The OPI also includes several other scales relevant to intrinsic motivation in college students (McReynolds, in press). The OPI Test Manual is outstanding.

Jackson's (1967) Personality Research Form (PRF) (see Chapter VI, this volume) includes a Change scale. A high scorer is described, in part, as one who "Likes new and different experiences; dislikes routine and avoids it [p. 6]." An advantage of this test—and thus of the Change scale—is that it is available in two forms. Reliabilities (odd-even) of the two are .68 and .51. Validity studies yielded correlations varying from .22 to .38 between Change and behavior and trait ratings. The scale correlates .40 (women) and .45 (men) with the Impulsivity scale on the same test. Acker and McReynolds (1967) obtained a correlation of .45 ($p < .01$), and Pearson (1970) a value of .57 ($p < .01$) between the PPF Change score and the SSS.

Another widely known personality test that includes a Change scale is the Gough-Heilbrun (1965) Adjective Check List (ACL). This scale, which because of its adjectival approach can be a useful alternative or supplement to the inventory format, has test-retest (ten-week interval) reliabilities of .69 (men) and .78 (women).

Intercorrelational data. We have now reviewed those scales which measure innovative motivation as a single dimension. A variety of data on the intercorrelations among the scales are available. Penney and Reinehr (1966) obtained a correlation of .33 ($p < .05$) between a version of the SSS and the SVSS. Acker and McReynolds (1967) reported a coefficient of .62 between the SSS and the CSI, and McReynolds (in press) later obtained a value of .68 between these two scales. McCarroll, Mitchell, Carpenter, and Anderson (1967) intercorrelated the SSS, CSI, and SVSS on 97 college students, with the following results: SSS-SVSS, .60; SSS-CSI, .70; and SVSS-CSI, .77 (all values significant at $p < .01$). And Stock and Looft (1969), in the study referred to earlier, obtained these coefficients: SSS-SVSS, .65; SSS-CSI, .82; and SVSS-CSI, .82.

The ACL and EPPS Change scores are interrelated .19 (Heilbrun, 1958). ACL Change is reported by Zuckerman and Link (1968) to correlate .43 with the SSS and .34 with the EPPS Change score; in the same study the SSS and EPPS Change intercorrelated .46 (for all values, $p < .01$). The Complexity scale on the OPI was found to correlate .46 ($p < .01$) with the Change-Sameness scale of the AI (Heist & Yonge, 1968). Pearson (1970) has recently reported a number of pertinent coefficients: SSS-EPI Change, .49; SSS-AI Change, .48; SSS-PRF Change, .57; EPI Change-AI Change, .57; EPI Change-PRF Change, .63; and AI Change-PRF Change, .71 (for all values, $p < .01$).

The various values above, with only a few exceptions, have a striking consistency about them, and many approach the reliabilities of the instruments involved. It seems clear, then, that despite the different names given to the scales, they are all getting at the same motivational variable.

Novelty Experiencing Scale (NES). This new instrument (Pearson, 1970) is one of the two devices referred to above as being designed to provide a relatively broad assay of innovative motivation. The NES was designed to provide measures of four postulated forms of novelty-seeking motivation. These four forms are derived from the assumption that the source of novelty can be either internal or external, and the quality of novelty experiencing can be via either sensation or cognition. The test consists of 80 activities (Sample: "Scuba diving in the Bahamas") to which the subject responds by circling "Like" or "Dislike." The test also includes a ten-item Desire for Novelty scale, based on the work by Maddi, Charlens, Maddi, and Smith (1962), to be described later. Reliability (KR-20) coefficients for the scales range from .76 to .87. Except for the correlation between the External-Cognitive and the Internal-Cognitive (.50) variables, intercorrelations among the scales are low. Correlations with global scales (SSS, EPI Change, AI Change, PRF Change) are low except for the External-Sensation dimension. This fact suggests that it is essentially this dimension that the global scales are tapping. The NES is too new for much information to be available on it, but it appears to be a highly promising instrument. The theory on which it is based is plausible, though not compelling, and the test has the advantage of taking some account of the intricacy of intrinsic motivation.

Ontario Test of Intrinsic Motivation (OTIM). This instrument, developed by Day (1969, 1970), is the newest of the intrinsic motivation tests. It may also be one of the best. It represents a careful attempt to assess "specific curiosity" in the context of Berlyne's system. The main part of the test consists of 90 True-False items (Sample: "I like meeting people who give me new ideas") selected in order to yield scores concerning three different aspects of specific curiosity. The first aspect concerns interest areas and is patterned after the ten categories of the Kuder Preference Record (Kuder, 1953)—literary, scientific, outdoor, mechanical, computational, clerical, musical, persuasive, artistic, and social service. The second aspect concerns stimulus input and is divided into three categories—novelty, ambiguity, and complexity. The third aspect refers to the manner of response, which can take any of three forms—consultation, observation, or thinking. This three-dimensional model yields 90 cells (10 x 3 x 3), with each cell represented by one item. In addition to the 16 scores already noted, plus a total score, the OTIM includes ten-item scales of Diversive Curiosity and Social Desirability. Reliabilities (KR-20) of the total score from .80 to .95 are reported; sub-scale reliabilities are considerably lower, as would be expected from the lesser number of items. Intercorrelations among the scales support the hypothesis of the independence of specific and diversive exploration. Adequate validity data are not yet available, but the test development procedures used have been highly sophisticated and closely related to theory, so it is possible that the instrument will prove quite useful.

Thematic Approaches

The Thematic Apperception Test (TAT) has been widely used in the assessment of different human motives (Atkinson, 1958; Chap. XI, this volume), including achievement, affiliation, and power. There have been two major investigative efforts that involve the use of thematic techniques in assessing components of intrinsic motivation.

Thematic assessment of the need for variety. As already noted, Maddi and his colleagues theorize that the need for variety can be broken down into at least three separate dimensions: (1) the desire for novelty, (2) the fantasy production of novelty, and (3) curiosity. In a series of studies these investigators (Maddi & Berne, 1964; Maddi et al., 1962, 1965) have developed thematic apperceptive measurement techniques for each of these variables.

The Maddi et al. procedure is modeled after that of Atkinson (1958). Four pictures are projected on a screen for twenty seconds each, and the subjects are allowed four minutes for writing each story. The *Desire for Novelty* measure reflects the extent to which characters in a story express a wish for novel experiences; the *Novelty of Productions* score, on the other hand, is indicative of the level of unusual content in the story as such. The third variable, *Curiosity,* is scored on the basis of fantasy attempts to obtain answers to perplexing problems.

Inter-scorer reliabilities (Maddi et al., 1965) are satisfactory, being .87 for desire for novelty, .92 for novelty of productions, and .90 for curiosity. Split-half scale reliabilities, however, are not outstanding, being .41, .63, and .68 (corrected) for the three variables, respectively. Desire for novelty and novelty of productions intercorrelated $-.28$ ($p < .05$), and this value has been interpreted to indicate the conceptual separateness of the "passive" (desire for novelty) and "active" (novelty of productions) forms of the "need for variety." Novelty of productions correlated $-.09$, and desire for novelty $-.27$ ($p < .05$) with curiosity. None of the three were significantly correlated with WAIS vocabulary. Novelty of productions, but not the other two variables, was significantly related to a measure of the complexity of figures completed by the subjects. The curiosity variable was significantly related to two behavioral measures of exploratory behavior.

The Maddi et al. TAT techniques just described have proved of considerable use in helping to elucidate the nature of intrinsic motivation. Further, they can be expected to find use by other investigators who, for other reasons, are employing the TAT. The Maddi measures, however, have relatively low reliability, and supporting validity data are still rather sparse. Many investigators of intrinsic motivation, therefore, will generally prefer other kinds of measurement devices.

Beswick's assessment of curiosity. Beswick (1964) has developed a theory which conceptualizes curiosity as a particular cognitive strategy. In carrying out research on the theory, he has developed a system for scoring curiosity imagery in TAT stories (Beswick, 1961, 1968, 1970). This system includes five major categories for scoring TAT content: (1) indications of wonder and interest, (2) perceptual investigatory behavior, (3) problem solving behavior,

(4) exploratory role behavior, and (5) cue-response sequences directed toward resolution of uncertainty. Inter-rater reliability is reported as .91; test-retest data are apparently not available. Junior high school children for whom an attempt had been made to arouse curiosity scored higher than controls, and subjects with high curiosity scores were found to have checked out more library books than low-curiosity students. Biemiller (1962), however, failed to find a relationship between the Beswick score and measures of breadth of interest. In sum, Beswick's TAT curiosity measure appears to have promise, but insufficient data are available to permit a clear understanding of the nature of the variable it assays.

Stimulus Preference Techniques

This section will summarize a variety of procedures that have been developed for assessing different aspects of intrinsic motivation by use of the following paradigm: The subject is presented with two (or more) stimuli, and asked to indicate which one he prefers; the stimuli differ on some dimension such as complexity or novelness. It is assumed that (1) the predominance of the subject's choices reflects his motivational tendency, and (2) this result can be generalized to other, non-test situations. The preference technique has been widely used in experimental work, but there have been only a few attempts to develop standardized test-like procedures of this kind.

Experimental applications. I will note briefly several experimental usages of the preference paradigm, as a way of illustrating—the listing is far from exhaustive—the range of techniques that can be adapted to given studies. McReynolds and Bryan (1956), in what I believe to have been the first individual differences study of innovative motivation, presented subjects with a tray containing 78 small cardboard pieces. Half of these (jigsaw pieces) were odd shaped and had unusual words printed on the bottom sides; the other half were all triangular and had common words printed on the bottom sides. The subject's task was to pick up approximately half of the pieces, one at a time, for use in a categorizing game; novelty-seeking motivation was estimated from the relative number of novel pieces selected. In a later study, McReynolds (1963) presented schizophrenics with projections of novel and familiar 35mm slides; the subject could look at each picture as long as he wished, and it was assumed that preferences for novel and familiar stimuli were reflected in looking times. Berlyne (1958a) projected pictures of animals in pairs—one novel and one familiar—in order to determine which figure would be more likely to attract orienting movements; another, analogous experiment (Berlyne, 1958b) utilized pairs of stimuli varying in complexity. Haywood (1962) presented subjects with stimulus pairs consisting of one novel and one commonplace visual stimulus, and inferred novelty-seeking motivations from the subject's choices.

Preference for complexity. Stimulus complexity has been considered one of the major collative variables, and a number of studies have used the motivational appeal of complex stimuli as an individual differences variable. Two inventories, the OPI and the OTIM, include scales for complexity motivation, and Maddi et al. (1965) devised a performance measure of need for complexity.

By far the greater amount of work in this area, however, has utilized the preference technique.

Current research on complexity-simplicity as a motivational variable has two main roots: first, the construction by Welsh (1949) of a Figure Preference Test and the subsequent development by Barron and Welsh (1952) of the Barron-Welsh Art Scale; and second, the analysis by Berlyne (1960) of the role of complexity as an important collative variable. The number of experiments in which complexity is an independent variable is now legion (see, e.g., Berlyne, 1958a, 1963; Berlyne & Lewis, 1963), but a relatively small number of techniques have been used for individual difference studies. Except for the Barron-Welsh Art Scale, none of these have attained a status— in terms of standardization, reliability data, and the like—that would entitle them to be referred to as "tests." The major techniques used have been: (1) an adaptation by Skrzypek (1969) of a figure complexity preference procedure developed by Munsinger and Kessen (1964); (2) the systematization by Eisenman (1967a; Eisenman & Rappaport, 1967) of a preference procedure utilizing geometric figures constructed by Vanderplas and Garvin (1959); (3) the development by Day (1965, 1967) of a set of twenty random-shaped geometric figures varying in numbers of sides from 4 to 160; and (4) the adaptation by McReynolds (1970b) of random shapes constructed by Vitz (1966) to an individual differences assessment paradigm.

The Barron-Welsh figures are non-representational line drawings, divided into two classes—simple and symmetrical, and irregular and asymmetrical. The subject indicates which ones he likes, and from this a Preference-for-Complexity score can be derived. The test has been widely used in studying creativity (Tryk, 1968) and has been reported to correlate significantly (.30) with the CSI (Garlington and Shimota, 1964), and with a performance measure of preference for irregular patterns (.32) (Berlyne & Lewis, 1963). The other three sets of stimuli referred to above all derive genealogically from Attneave and Arnoult's (1956) methodology for generating random shapes. Skrzypek's (1969) procedure utilized two different sets of stimuli (in test terminology, two "forms"), each comprised of 28 pairs (one "complex" and one "simple") of shapes. The subject indicates the one he prefers, and from his responses an overall score is determined. Skrzypek found the preference for complex stimuli to increase after perceptual isolation. Moore (1970; see especially p. 118), using one form of Skrzypek's procedure, found complexity preference to correlate .29 ($p < .05$) with a measure of intelligence, and $-.30$ ($p < .025$) with a measure of field dependence. In her study, chronic process paranoids obtained higher complexity preference scores than did chronic process nonparanoids. In Eisenman's technique there are nine polygons which the subject either rank-orders in terms of preference, or from which he chooses the three most, and the three least, preferred. This procedure has been used in studying the relation of personality variables to complexity preference (Eisenman 1967a, 1967b, 1967c, 1968; Eisenman and Rappaport, 1967). Day's (1967, 1968, 1970) work has focused mostly on establishing the independence of the dimensions of complexity, pleasingness, and interestingness. The Vitz (1966) stimuli consist of eight "random walk" and six "random line" figures varying in complexity. McReynolds (unpublished research) found subjects' overall level of preference for these figures to correlate .46 and .47 ($p < .01$) respectively with the SSS and the CSI. At present the techniques used by Skrzypek and by Eisenman are most readily adaptable to specific research usage. None of the complexity-preference assessment techniques, however, are as yet highly developed in terms of the usual test criteria (reliability and stability data, concurrent validity data, etc.).

The Choice Motivator Scale (CMS). This instrument, which has gone through several forms, is designed to measure two theoretically independent motivational orientations: "motivator" or intrinsic motivation (IM) factors and "hygiene" or extrinsic motivation (EM) factors. The test, developed in the context of the Herzberg et al. (1959; Herzberg & Hamlin, 1961) motivation theory, presents the subject with twenty pairs of occupations (e.g., house painter vs. bus driver); the subject chooses the one he would rather be and then indicates the reasons for his choice. The test is scored in terms of these reasons, which can be classified in terms of whether they represent IM (e.g., concern with the challenge of the job) or EM (e.g., concern with salary). The first form of this scale, developed in 1962 by Hamlin and Nemo, yielded differences between recovered and unimproved schizophrenics (the former were more intrinsically motivated). Haywood and Dobbs (1964) produced evidence that high IM scorers are more likely than high EM scorers to approach tension-inducing situations, and Haywood and Weaver (1967) found that IM students performed most efficiently under task-intrinsic incentives, whereas EM students performed best under task-extrinsic incentives.

As noted, there have been several forms of the CMS. Carl Haywood altered the procedure in 1966 (unpublished) to a multiple-choice format. The scale was further revised in 1967 (Form NP) and in 1968 (Revised Form NP) by Nancy Haywood; also in 1968 the latter investigator (personal communication) devised a format titled Occupational Preference Inventory (to avoid the puzzlement that subjects sometimes feel with the term "Choice Motivator Scale").

Though not yet a well-developed psychometric instrument, the CMS appears to have considerable promise. Parallel form reliabilities of the original version were reported (Hamlin & Nemo, 1962) as .67 (IM) and .65 (EM); Haywood and Weaver (1967) obtained a split-half reliability of .68 for the IM-EM difference; and the test-retest reliability of Revised Form NP (Miezitis, reported in Kunca and Haywood, 1969) averages between .74 and .79. A number of studies have now been done utilizing the CMS; they have been summarized by Kunca and Haywood (1969) and Haywood (1970).

The Similes Preference Inventory (SPI). This instrument, developed by Pearson and Maddi (1966), consists of 54 items, each being in the form of a simile with five choices. Item 1, e.g., is "Limp as: (*a*) a desk, (*b*) a lump, (*c*) a busted blimp, (*d*) a towel, and (*e*) a rag." The various alternatives have been keyed in terms of novelty, and the subject's overall score is taken to reflect his preference for novelty. The test was formulated in the context of the Maddi et al. theory described earlier and is intended as a structured measure of the active internal form of the need for variety.

The SPI is one of the more carefully developed of the tests described in this chapter. Further, it has a good theoretical basis and has the advantage of being restricted in its aim to the measurement of a single, limited, meaningful aspect of intrinsic motivation. Reliability (KR-20) values of .93 to .95 are reported, along with a test-retest (two-month interval) coefficient of .61. The test is not significantly related to measures of verbal intelligence or social desirability set. It correlates .45 ($p < .005$), .03, and $-.07$ respectively with the Maddi et al. measures of Novelty of Production, Curiosity, and Desire for Novelty described earlier. The .45 value is noteworthy, since the SPI is intended to measure the same variable as the TAT novelty of productions score, and *not* the same as the two other TAT scores. Uribe and McReynolds (1967) found the SPI to correlate .44 with a special measure of creative production, .54 with self-ratings of creativity, and .52 with the Obscure Figures Test (OFT), to be discussed below (for all r's, $p < .01$). Kish and Donnenwerth (1969b), however, found the SPI and OFT to intercorrelate only .06; in this study the SPI and SSS were intercorrelated .03. The latter of these is understandable in that the SPI and SSS are intended to measure different variables; the former value, however, is less easily rationalized, since the SPI and OFT appear theoretically to have much in common. It is perhaps significant that Uribe and McReynolds tested college students, whereas Kish utilized psychiatric patients as subjects.

Performance Measures

A direct method for estimating a person's innovative motivation would be to present him with the opportunity to perform innovatively, and then to assay the extent to which he does so. This is analogous to free-choice exploration in the animal literature. There are a number of techniques within the creativity assessment literature (cf. Tryk, 1968) that employ this paradigm. We will not examine these here but instead will focus on several procedures more directly concerned with intrinsic motivation.

Measures of performance variety. The paradigm here is to require that the subject complete a task which can be performed with varying degrees of stereotypy or variability. It has a direct parallel in animal work on alternation behavior and maze stereotypy (e.g., in the Dashiell "Checkerboard" Maze). A good example of this work at the human level is provided by Zlotowski (1965; see also Zlotowski & Bakan, 1963). This investigator presented process and reactive schizophrenics with a set of eight levers which they were to pull in any order over a series of trials. Reactive patients were significantly more variable than process subjects.

The Howard Maze Test. This instrument has been widely used for the measurement of individual differences in performance stereotypy. Developed by Howard in 1961 in three forms, the test was designed to assess "stimulus-seeking behavior." Each form consists of a simple pencil-paper maze in which there are several alternate paths from beginning to end; the subject completes five copies of the maze, and his score is the amount of change in paths. Forms A and B are highly intercorrelated (Howard & Diesenhaus, 1965), but Form A (pyramid) has been much the more used; Domino (1965) reported a corrected split-half reliability of .91 for this form. Sidle, Acker, and McReynolds (1963) found schizophrenics to show less maze (Form A) variability than nonschizophrenics. Domino's study yielded evidence that college students scoring high on Form A participate in a greater variety of extracurricular activities than do low-scoring students. Acker and McReynolds (1967) reported correlations of .16, .05, and .09 between Maze A and the SSS, CSI, and PRF change respectively.

The Obscure Figures Test (OFT). This test, developed by Acker and McReynolds (1965; McReynolds & Acker, 1968), is intended to measure an individual's capacity for cognitive innovation. This latter term, in the present writer's (McReynolds, 1964, 1970a) theory of motivation, refers to the process whereby newness and alteration is introduced into cognitive structure; as noted earlier, it is posited that this tends to occur at a certain optimal rate. The OFT consists of 40 ambiguous line drawings; the subject is instructed to indicate what each figure might be and to be as clever and original as possible in his answers. Scoring is done on the basis of detailed, written criteria, and norms are available. Inter-scorer reliability is reported as .90, and test-retest reliability as .93. The OFT correlates .33 ($p < .05$) with the Shipley-Hartford (Shipley, 1940) intelligence scale. Acker and McReynolds (1967) reported the OFT to correlate .25 with the SSS and .26 with the CSI (for both, $p < .05$); Kish (1970) reported a correlation of .43 ($p < .01$), and Masterson (1970b) a value of .23 ($p < .05$) between the OFT and the SSS. From relationships between the OFT and the MMPI scales, Kish (1970) concludes that "the cognitive innovator tends to be extroverted" and "somewhat emotionally labile and impulsive [p. 99]." It would appear that the OFT, like the SPI, is a measure of an individual's tendency to produce novelty internally. Uribe and McReynolds (1967) obtained a correlation of .52 between the two scales; while Kish (1970) failed to find a significant relationship, it seems likely that his finding may be due to an extremely limited range (Kish & Donnenwerth, 1969a). Kish (1970) concludes that the OFT reflects both the *capacity* and the *motivation* to perform innovatively.

Assessment in Children

Though the various procedures that have been employed for the assessment of intrinsic motivation in children are not fundamentally different from the techniques already described for adults, it is convenient to bring them together for review. It is probable, of course, that some of the techniques already considered, though not specifically developed for use with children, could successfully be used with that age range. For example, Masterson (1970c) has produced evidence that the OFT can be meaningfully employed with fifth-grade children.

First of all, we should note—though our main interest here is in systematized test techniques—that a rather wide variety of special experimental procedures has been utilized in the area under discussion. Three illustrative studies will make this clear. McReynolds, Acker, and Pietla (1961) devised an observational method for assessing curiosity; the technique involved presenting children with a situation in which they might freely explore a variety of objects and a system for rating the curiosity they displayed. Smock and Holt (1962) adapted materials from Berlyne (1958a) in order to determine children's preferences for novel versus non-novel stimuli. May (described in Cantor, 1963) offered children choices of cards varying in complexity as a means for assessing individual differences in complexity preferences.

The children's Reactive Curiosity Scale (RCS). This test, developed by Penney and McCann (1964), consists of 100 True-False items, 90 in the curiosity scale (sample item: "I like to visit zoos") and 10 in a lie scale. The inventory is intended for use with fourth, fifth, and sixth grade children and is intended to measure the tendency to seek new, varied, and complex stimuli. Test-retest (two-week interval) reliabilities range from .65 to .78. Scale scores are not significantly related to a measure of intelligence, and—for sixth but not fourth grade children—are significantly correlated with measures of originality based on Guilford's (1956) Unusual Uses Test. Penney (1965) obtained significant negative correlations between the RCS and the Children's Manifest Anxiety Scale (CMAS) (Castaneda, McCandless, & Palermo, 1956); this result is in accord with the conclusion of the McReynolds et al. (1961) study, referred to above, that high anxiety tends to depress novelty-seeking behavior. A study by Peters and Penney (1966) provides some evidence of construct validity for the RCS. Subjects were divided into high-curious and low-curious groups on the basis of the scale and then given the task of marking 20 T-mazes; as predicted, the former group showed more variation in the task than the latter group.

Maw and Maw's assessments of children's curiosity. In this section I will summarize briefly certain assessment aspects of an extensive and ingenious program of research that has been carried on by Wallace H. and Ethel W. Maw (1964, 1965; W. H. Maw, 1967, 1970) on curiosity in elementary school children. In the course of this investigation a number of devices for the assessment of curiosity have been developed. One of the major approaches employed by the Maws has been a system of ratings of curiosity by the subjects themselves, their teachers, and their peers (Maw & Maw, 1961, 1963, 1964, 1965; Maw, 1967). The teacher's rating amounts to a ranking of children (in a class) on curiosity and has a test-retest reliability of around .77. The peer judgments involve students matching other members of the class with standard descriptions of children of varying levels of curiosity; it was found to correlate .54 with teacher ratings. The self-rating procedure is a scale entitled "About Myself"; its odd-even reliability has been reported as .91, and its correlations with the teacher ratings and peer ratings as .11 and .15, respectively. Another instrument developed by Maw and Maw (1961, 1962) termed the "Which to Discuss" test, is intended to measure a child's acceptance of unbalanced and unfamiliar stimuli. This test consists of 20 pairs of geometric figures; in each instance one of the pair is more unbalanced than the other, and the child indicates which he would choose if he were to hear a story about one of the two figures. Split-half reliability of the scale is reported as .91. Subjects rated high in curiosity scored significantly higher on this test than children rated low in curiosity. In addition to these test devices, Maw and Maw (1964, Appendices B, C, & D) have developed, in a more preliminary fashion, a considerable variety of extremely interesting approaches to the assessment of curiosity in children. These techniques deserve to be given more attention than they have received.

Picture Motivation Test (PMT). This instrument, the last to be described in this chapter, is one of the most innovative and potentially important scales that has come forth in recent years. The test was developed by Kunca and N. Haywood (1969) in the context of Herzberg's conception of human motives, as outlined earlier in this chapter; it was designed in part to make the intrinsic-extrinsic idea of the CMS applicable to children. The PMT includes 20 items with each item consisting of two cartoons. Each cartoon depicts a boy engaging in some activity, and each has a brief subheading. (A sample item is presented in Fig. 1.) The subject indicates which activity he would like best, and his score is based on the number of "intrinsic cartoons" that he chooses. The purpose of the scale is thus to obtain a measure of intrinsic motivation. Though still an experimental test, the PMT is actually based on considerable preliminary work and has now been administered to a large number of nursery through second grade children, including mentally retarded and non-English-speaking subjects (Haywood, 1970). For the 20-item scale the test-retest reliabilities (two-week interval) range from the .60s to the low .80s and are somewhat higher for a shorter scale of 13 selected items. Because of its recentness, validity data are not yet available on the PMT, but the idea of the test is highly credible, and it is possible that the procedure will prove of wide utility.

SUMMARY

We have considered in this chapter a wide variety of instruments designed for the assessment of intrinsic motivation. It would be easy to criticize most of these devices and to note the generally immature level of test technology that they represent. I believe, however, that there would be little point in doing this, since the experimental nature of most of the devices has been plainly stated by their authors. For myself, while I am aware of the limitations of the techniques, I am much more impressed by the ingenuity that they display and the great potential that they hold for important research on motivation.

There are several rather obvious conceptual problems with which future test developments in this area must be concerned. I have already alluded to the need for making a systematic measurement distinction between current (state) and characteristic (trait) levels of innovative behavior. Another important need is for a more stringent analysis of the concept of optimal rate, or level of stimulus variability. The term *optimal* level is generally only vaguely defined and tends to be equated with *preferred* level, or with an individual's characteristic performance; this approach is at best preliminary and tentative. A further and highly important need is for a definitive conceptual and empirical analysis of the different aspects of innovative behavior and the interrelationships among them. Maddi and his colleagues, and Day—working in Berlyne's system—have made important contributions on this problem. A

EXPLORE A CAVE   PLAY WHERE IT IS SAFE

Figure 1. Sample item from the Picture Motivation Test. The subject chooses which of the two activities he would like best. The one on the left represents intrinsic motivation.

useful distinction, I suspect, can be made between ideational and motoric modes of obtaining variety, and probably a number of additional stylistic patternings could be identified. An especially urgent aspect of this problem is the question of whether the motivations to seek variety and to seek complexity are independent (Maddi et al., 1965; Stock & Looft, 1969; Moore, 1970). Next, it may be observed that the great bulk of available devices for the assessment of intrinsic motivation are concerned with the aspect of that motivation that I have referred to as innovative behavior; there is, therefore, a strong and obvious need for the development of techniques for the measurement of other aspects of intrinsic motivation. And finally, I wish to emphasize the need for the future development of interview and observational techniques, particularly those useable in naturalistic settings, for the assessment of intrinsic motivation.

CHAPTER IX

Techniques for assessing outcomes of psychotherapy

Edward Lichtenstein

Sparked primarily by the behavior modification movement and also given impetus by the client-centered movement's persistent empirical emphasis, outcome research in psychotherapy is enjoying a renaissance. In terms of research design, control groups, and the questions posed, outcome studies are becoming increasingly sophisticated. There is general agreement that simple, global questions, such as "does therapy work?" are not appropriate, and also that the outcome-process dichotomy is not a meaningful one (Paul, 1969a; Sargent, 1961). Both Kiesler (1966), representing psychotherapy research, and Paul (1967, 1969a), representing a behavior modification view, are in essential agreement on the importance of methodological paradigms that seek to answer more specific questions including both process and outcome components. As Paul (1967) puts it, the appropriate research question is: *"What* treatment, by *whom,* is most effective for *this* individual with *that* specific problem and under *which* set of circumstances [p. 111, italics his]." The assessment of effectiveness is fundamental for investigating this question and requires adequate measures of personality and/or behavior change.

In addition to the researcher, still another group is vitally concerned with assessing treatment outcome: practicing clinicians, particularly those concerned with operating public or private clinics. Hard pressed for resources to devote to outcome research, service clinicians nevertheless would like to be able to evaluate treatment in order to justify their efforts and to improve their procedures. They may be discouraged by writings that stress the inadequacy of current measures and/or the futility of outcome research at our current state of knowledge (e.g., Strupp, 1963; Hyman & Berger, 1965). Perhaps as a result of this pessimism, as well as of other factors, there is generally inadequate record keeping and discouragingly little research produced by psychiatric and psychological clinics (Ladd, 1967).

This paper takes the more positive view that controlled outcome research can and should be done. It is also the writer's conviction that systematic

The influence of my colleagues in the University of Oregon Clinical Training Program, all of whom are engaged in behavior change research, can be seen throughout this paper. In particular, Robert L. Weiss and Stephen M. Johnson contributed helpful suggestions. Sarah Lichtenstein provided editorial assistance.

collection of outcome data in applied settings—where no control groups are available—can have an important impact on the accumulation of knowledge about treatment effectiveness. While most current outcome measures are flawed, they may still provide useful information. The aim of this chapter is to consider the relative merits of current techniques for both research and applied settings. The usual criteria for assessment devices—reliability, validity, utility—will be employed, but special attention will be given to the somewhat unique problems of psychotherapy research (e.g., the hello-goodbye effect, Hathaway, 1948). Attention will also be given to the differing needs of the clinician working in an applied setting and the researcher who has greater resources and more control of his environment. The cost of obtaining a given measure will, therefore, be considered.

The main focus will be on individual psychotherapy with outpatient adults although other material will be presented when appropriate. Issues concerning strategies of psychotherapy research (e.g., Paul, 1967; Bordin, 1965) and research design (e.g., Goldstein, Heller, & Sechrest, 1966; Paul, 1969a) will be considered only when relevant to the major concern of evaluating outcome measures. A bibliography of research in individual psychotherapy through 1967 counted nearly 700 outcome studies (Strupp & Bergin, undated). Obviously, no single chapter can do justice to such a large body of literature, and considerable selectivity in reading and reporting has been exercised, with emphasis given to the more recent literature. The earlier literature has been reviewed by Lorr (1954) and Zax and Klein (1960). Strupp and Bergin (1969), Muench (1968), and Farnsworth (1966) have reviewed many of the more recent measures as well as some of the important conceptual issues.

Behavioral versus Personality Assessment

The choice of outcome criteria depends on the theoretical convictions and interests of the investigator. The major conceptual issue is whether to emphasize personality or behavioral measures. This issue arises from the behavior modification challenge to the psychodynamic approaches (e.g., Ullman & Krasner, 1965), and is the most important controversy on the current clinical scene. With its emphasis on changing overt behavior and its rejection of personality change as the primary goal of therapy, the behavioral approach leads to markedly different ways of assessing outcome. Overt behavior has been used as an outcome measure in numerous studies of children, inpatients, outpatients, and subjects. These studies generally support the effectiveness of behavior modification therapies and encourage more extensive use of behavioral criteria (Franks, 1969; Bandura, 1969).

The psychodynamic approach also legitimizes behavioral measures, but these are interpreted as signs or indicators of personality change. For the behaviorist, the behavior speaks for itself; it is viewed primarily as a sample, and the major issue is the representativeness of the behavior sample for the goals of psychotherapy. While previous reviews of outcome criteria have focused on personality measurement, this paper will consider behavioral measures as well. Both personality and behavioral measures are equally accountable to sound measurement principles.

Choice of Informant or Point of View

In addition to the issue of what variables to measure, yet interacting with this issue, is the question of *who* is to provide the outcome data. There are three major sources of data: the client, the therapist, or some third party which would include members of the client's family, peers, or a neutral observer (rater). All three sources can, in principal, supply either behavioral data or personality data. For example, a therapist or a judge can rate personality traits or observe the client's behavior in therapy as he engages in some performance task. The client may provide reports of his behavior, e.g., sexual performance, or take a personality test. The point of view utilized imposes certain constraints on many measures which no amount of scaling or psychometric sophistication can overcome. Unfortunately, this is true of the data from those informants who are most accessible and economical, the client and the therapist.

The client's data are influenced by: (1) his degree of self-awareness and memory distortion, determining whether he can report his behavior or feelings accurately; (2) his idiosyncratic verbal habits; (3) his desire to please or displease the therapist (or experimenter); and (4) his tendency to justify first, his need for treatment, and later, the appropriateness of his termination. Hathaway (1948) has discussed these latter two issues under the label of the hello-goodbye effect. Put another way, the client's behavior is sensitive to the demand characteristics (Orne, 1962) of the situation, which are likely to lead to impression management. Impression management factors are generally thought to affect only the more obvious self-report measures such as the MMPI or self-rating scales. However, it should be recognized that they can affect any measure where the client knows he is being observed with respect to his progress in treatment. There is now overwhelming evidence that projective tests are sensitive to impression management (Masling, 1960), and even performance measures dear to a behaviorist, such as the snake avoidance procedure, are susceptible to demand characteristics.

The therapist is biased by: (1) his particular theories and assumptions concerning behavior disorder and behavior or personality change; (2) his involvement with the client and with therapy (his own hello-goodbye effect); and (3) his limited sample of client behaviors—the one or several hours of verbal report he obtains each week.

Both client and therapist measures can be said to suffer from reactivity, whereby the measurement process itself produces unintended sources of influence on the data (Webb, Campbell, Schwartz, & Sechrest, 1966; Campbell & Stanley, 1963). The subject's (client or therapist) knowledge that he is being studied and that change is expected may affect his performance, particularly when he is retested with the same procedures. For both client and therapist, the more global or inferential the measure used, the greater the opportunity for reactivity factors to operate. Experimental procedures or instructions can be used to equate or minimize the effects of reactivity on internal validity. For example, if two different therapies are compared, impression management factors may be assumed to be equal in both groups. However, reactivity may still influence the external validity or generalizability of the obtained results (Webb et al., 1966).

Third parties are too numerous and varied for their limitations to be easily listed here. Their data are usually more expensive but more objective than those of client or therapist. Much depends on the information they are given and the responses required of them. If, for example, the data are the client's verbal behaviors in a post-therapy interview (Spitzer, Endicott, & Cohen, 1967), then it must be recognized that many of the constraints on client self-report—e.g., impression management—also will affect the third party measure. Similarly, if measures are derived from case files (e.g., Pascal & Zax, 1956) or from judgments of therapy process notes (Robbins & Wallerstein, 1959), they are also influenced by the above-noted constraints on therapists. There is the advantage, however, that the data generators—e.g., therapists—may be unaware that they are in an experiment. In spite of these possible limitations, third party measures are much preferred in research because of their relative freedom from the distortions of client and therapist reports, and because they can provide information about client behavior in natural settings.

Convergence among Points of View

Aside from the specific question of the correlation between any two measures of outcome, there is the important issue of the convergence of measures of the same variable obtained from two or more classes of informants. Therapist ratings "seem to measure an independent factor in change, or perhaps it is simply point of view that is being measured [Strupp & Bergin, 1969, p. 62]." In the Cartwright, Kirtner, and Fiske (1963) study, a therapist's perception of change emerged as a separate factor even when client, therapist, and judges (using TAT data) used the same rating scales measuring the same conceptual variables. Another example comes from Rogers, Gendlin, Kiesler, and Truax (1967). "In general, our unbiased raters and our schizophrenic patients tended to make similar evaluations of the therapeutic relationship; therapists, on the other hand, evaluated the relationship in ways so discrepant from the other two groups as to be negatively associated [p. 77]." Although this conclusion refers to what is essentially a process rather than outcome measure, the implications for therapist data are still profound.

Obviously, such data have implications for client report measures as well. Indeed, as Strupp and Bergin (1969) note, client self-evaluation usually falls out as a separate factor in factor analytic studies (Cartwright et al., 1963; Forsyth & Fairweather, 1961). Clearly, neither client nor therapist has an exclusive patent on reality. Indeed, both are suspect in relation to data from third parties or objective performance measures. The lack of convergence apparently arises from the fact that clients and therapists may be holding different conceptions of improvement (Carr & Whittenbaugh, 1969), are using different sets of data, and are often making judgments requiring considerable inference. While divergence between client and therapist may reflect the multi-dimensionality of psychotherapeutic change (Strupp & Bergin, 1969), the "method-variance" (Campbell & Fiske, 1959) interpretation has yet to be ruled out.

The behaviorist is less beset with such difficulties since he is more likely to be concerned with inter-rater or client-informant agreement on the frequency of overt behavior and this is usually quite high (Paul, 1966; Ober, 1968). But behaviorists must deal with evidence showing lack of convergence among measures of the same construct when verbal self-report, behavioral, and physiological indices of fear show low intercorrelations (e.g., Lang, 1968). Lang interprets such data to mean that the three response systems—verbal, motor, psychophysiological—are relatively independent. In other words, fear is assumed to be a multidimensional construct. Social learning theory posits that low or zero-order correlations among indicants of the three response systems may be attributable to their having had different reinforcement histories (Bandura, 1969).

The writer has argued above that the two major issues concerning outcome measures are: (1) who is to provide the measures—the client, the therapist, or a third party? and (2) what kind of data are to be used—personality indicators or behavioral events? The discussion of specific techniques is, therefore, primarily categorized around the first of these, termed *point of view*. Within viewpoint, measures are organized according to the nature of the task (personality tests, self-ratings, performance tests) and the setting in which the data are obtained (within therapy sessions, in the clinic, or in the natural environment). The behavior versus personality change issue will be touched upon throughout as appropriate.

THE CLIENT TAKES A TEST

Test taking by the client is still the major source of outcome measures. Tests may be broad- or narrow-band instruments and may measure traits, symptoms, aspects of self-concept, or responses to specific stimuli. Standardization and economy of administration and scoring make tests attractive to both the research and the applied clinician. They are generally subject to the biases of the client's point of view although validity scales, subtle items, and empirical keyings may offer some protection, depending on the particular measure used.

Broad-Band Tests

These instruments provide scores on several traits and/or symptom syndromes:

MMPI. The MMPI continues to be the most widely used broad-band measure of outcome. Dynamic personality theorists consider it to be superficial, and behaviorists are distrustful of self-report and trait concepts. Yet a wide range of researchers employ the MMPI as an outcome measure (Truax, Schuldt, & Wargo, 1968; Levis & Carrera, 1967). Its psychopathological orientation, familiarity to most clinicians, and the large mass of data already accumulated about its strengths and weaknesses contribute to the MMPI's popularity. While some of its competitors may have sounder psychometric properties, they are not as well validated as measures of psychotherapeutic change. Changes in pre-post MMPI profiles have been related to independent ratings of client improvement in a variety of studies (Dahlstrom & Welsh, 1960; Schofield, 1966), and the test-retest reliabilities of the clinical scales are generally quite adequate (Dahlstrom & Welsh, 1960). However, there is a regression-toward-the-mean tendency upon retesting which implies the need for control groups when evaluating change. Of interest to settings where control groups are not available, is Rosen's (1966) procedure for estimating the significance of the change in a given scale score.

The MMPI and similarly constructed inventories have been sharply criticized on the grounds that they are greatly influenced by response sets or styles, notably acquiscience and social desirability (e.g., Jackson & Messick, 1962; Messick & Jackson, 1961). Most of these criticisms have been answered empirically (Rorer & Goldberg, 1965; Lichtenstein & Bryan, 1965; Block, 1965) and conceptually (Rorer, 1965; Heilbrun, 1964). However, a related issue does have important implications for outcome assessment: the MMPI's internal structure or dimensionality. Numerous studies (e.g., Block, 1965; Messick & Jackson, 1961) attest to high correlations among MMPI scales and indicate that only two factors are needed to account for the interscale correlations—partly a function of items appearing on two or more scales. The most pervasive factor is easily seen as an overall adjustment or adequacy-of-functioning dimension. Most of the clinical scales load heavily on this factor; as Block (1965) notes, it is redundantly measured by the MMPI. Yet researchers sometimes report pre- and post-therapy changes in MMPI scores as though the scales were orthogonal and each significant difference was an independent corroboration of a treatment effect (e.g., Levis & Carrera, 1967). Strupp and Bergin (1969) noted that scales *D, Pt,* and *Sc* are especially useful as change indices. However, *Pt* and *Sc* were found to correlate between .64 and .87 in eight different samples (Dahlstrom & Welsh, 1960), and factor analyses usually show all three scales loading on the same factor (Block, 1965). One should either acknowledge the intercorrelation of the clinical scales or use factorially derived scales that are relatively independent (e.g., Block, 1965). Further, it is clear that factorially derived scales could permit a much more economical assessment of the two main factors.

The dimensionality issue is especially crucial when mean differences pre- and post-therapy are used. Contemporary diagnostic use of the MMPI (e.g., Marks & Seeman, 1963) focuses heavily on configural properties or profile shape. These configural properties are often difficult to identify and use in a pre-post design. Having MMPI experts judge improvement using pre- and post-treatment profiles is one method of doing this (Schofield, 1966). While some gain in clinical representativeness may be achieved, there is considerable loss in practical economy. There is also considerable evidence to cast doubt on the ability of clinical judges to use MMPI information in a configural manner (Goldberg, 1968). Useful reviews of the MMPI as an outcome measure are found in Dahlstrom and Welsh (1960) and Schofield (1966).

Other objective tests. Several well constructed broad-band inventories focus on "normal" personality traits. The Sixteen Personality Factor Questionnaire (16PF, Cattell & Eber, 1964) offers a factor-analytically-derived inventory with homogeneous scales, lower inter-scale correlations (no item overlap), and adequate reliability if Forms A and B are combined. The unfamiliarity of the trait language of the Sixteen Personality Factor Questionnaire perhaps accounts for its infrequent use among clinicians, although several of the factors have clear psychopathological significance. The California Psychological Inventory (Gough, 1957) and the newer Personality Research Form (Jackson, 1967) may provide relevant scales, particularly for counseling contexts.

Projective tests. This is another class of broad-band personality measures. Inspection of recent research indicates that projectives are now infrequently employed in outcome research, a trend consistent with a more general decline in their usage (Thelen, Varble, & Johnson, 1968). The great cost of administration and scoring; complex problems of reliability (Holzberg, 1960), which are particularly important in pre- and post-treatment designs; the generally unimpressive results of validity studies; and the realization that projectives are not so immune to situational variables and impression management as was formerly believed (Masling, 1960)—all contributed to this decline. The Menninger Clinic Psychotherapy Research Project is the major exception to the trend away from projectives (Siegel & Rosen, 1962). In this study, judgments based on a battery of tests including the Rorschach and TAT constitute one important set of variables. The TAT has been used with some success by the client-centered group (Dymond, 1954b; Rogers et al., 1967). Although in one carefully done study (Cartwright et al., 1963) it appeared to be contributing primarily method variance, the TAT remains the most promising of the projectives for outcome assessment.

Narrow-Band Measures

Narrow-band tests are designed to measure specific variables of relevance to psychotherapy. Anxiety has been the variable of by far the greatest interest to therapy researchers, and numerous measures have been developed (see McReynolds, 1968, for a comprehensive review of anxiety measures). Several of these, including the much used Taylor Manifest Anxiety Scale, are composed of MMPI items and measure "reports of feelings and behaviors assumed to be symptomatic of anxiety [McReynolds, 1968, p. 292]." The TMAS has been used in several studies of treatment outcome (McNair, Callahan, & Lorr, 1962) but is probably interchangeable with other measures of the MMPI's primary factor. Volsky, Magoon, Norman, and Hoyt (1965) carefully validated their own MMPI anxiety scale, but then found no differences between their counseled and non-counseled subjects.

The IPAT anxiety scale (Cattell & Scheier, 1963) is a 40-item test intended to measure both covert and overt anxiety. Test-retest and internal consistency reliabilities are high (McReynolds, 1968), and the scale has shown sensitivity to treatment effects (Paul, 1966; Cattell, Rickles, Weise, Gray, & Yee, 1966).

Investigators working in the behavior modification tradition tend to be skeptical about broad dispositional traits and focus instead on person-situation interactions (Mischel, 1968). Such a focus is not necessarily incompatible with self-report tests but leads to an interest in what McReynolds (1968) has termed stimulus-oriented and specific anxiety-proneness measures. Much of behavior therapy research focuses on stimulus-specific anxiety and fear, particularly snake (or other small animal or insect) phobias and test anxiety.

Special fears. The Fear Survey Schedule (FSS) simply asks the respondent to indicate the intensity of his current fear reaction to a variety of stimuli. The version developed by Geer (1965) yielded a consistency reliability of .94 and showed moderate (.39-.57) correlations with trait measures of anxiety. Geer also demonstrated validity for several of the items by relating FSS scores to behavioral avoidance of the feared stimulus. Factor analysis indicated four major areas of fear: interpersonal events, death and illness, water, and discrete objects (Rubin, Katkin, & Weiss, 1968). The FSS is used as a screening device in the selection of subjects with specific phobias and also has provided outcome data in several studies (Paul, 1969b, c).

The Fear Thermometer (FT, Walk, 1956) is more clearly situational in that the subject is asked to approach the feared stimulus, e.g., a snake, and then to rate his fear at the point when he can approach no closer, using a 10-point scale. Several studies (Davison, 1968; Cooke, 1966) report low correlations between FT scores and approach behavior; subjects frequently get near to or handle the stimulus but report being quite fearful.

Test anxiety. Test-taking anxiety research has utilized what McReynolds (1968) terms specific anxiety-proneness measures, and he has summarized the pertinent data on the Test Anxiety Questionnaire (TAQ, Mandler & Sarason, 1952), the Test Anxiety Scale (TAS, I. G. Sarason, 1958), and the Achievement Anxiety Test (AAT, Alpert & Haber, 1960). The split-half reliability of the TAS has been found to be as low as .57 (Suinn, 1969); otherwise, these three tests have satisfactory test-retest reliability and are easy to administer. Suinn (1969) found that both FSS and TAS scores tended to decrease after a five-week retest interval as did his own 50-item Test Anxiety Behavior Scale (Suinn, 1969). There seems to be no obvious basis for choosing among the several measures of test anxiety. The AAT has the possible advantage of attempting to measure both the facilitating and debilitating effects of anxiety. While the TAQ, TAS, and AAT have all been used (Paul, 1969b, c; Garlington & Cotler, 1968), they are subject to the usual criticisms of obvious self-report tests and should be interpreted cautiously.

Various psychophysiological indices of fear have been used, including GSR, heartrate, respiration, and palmar sweat (Lang, 1968; Paul, 1966). The hardware and technology involved makes these measures useful for the researcher rather than the applied clinician. Such psychophysiological data are free from most of the biases affecting the client's verbal reports. However, they present the investigator with a host of new technical problems if he is to rule out artifacts and obtain good data. The reader is referred to Lacey (1959) and Stern and Plapp (1969) for technical discussions and to Lang (1968, 1969) for problems of interpretation.

Self-Concept Measures

Originally popularized by the client-centered group (Rogers & Dymond, 1954), the Q sort continues to enjoy wide use as a measure of self-concept. The 100-item Q sort devised by Butler and Haigh (1954) is the most frequently employed. The client is asked to provide self- and ideal-self-descriptions. Clients typically show much greater self-ideal discrepancies than do normal subjects; correlations were all close to zero in five client samples summarized by Butler (1968). Data from several studies (Butler & Haigh, 1954; Shlien, Mosak, & Dreikurs, 1962; Truax et al., 1969) indicate that lowered self-ideal discrepancies as a function of changes in the self-concept occur in successful therapy. Many of these data have been nicely summarized by Butler (1968).

The Q sort also offers convenience of statistical treatment and potential for being adapted to individual clients. That is, one can construct a deck with items appropriate to a given client and then calculate self-ideal discrepancies. In this vein, Kelly's (1955) REP test may be construed as an idiosyncratic self-concept measure; Cartwright and Lerner's (1963) study illustrates its use. Shlien (1962) has argued that the discrepancy between self and ideal is an abstract, generalized variable that transcends any particular measurement device. He has proposed several novel measurement devices including having the subject generate his own items or asking him to overlap circles or squares that represent his real and ideal selves. The client's self-sort can also be scored for overall adjustments in the manner described by Dymond (1954a).

On the negative side, Block and Thomas (1955) have shown that normal subjects' adjustment may not be linearly related to self-ideal discrepancy; defensive adjustments may also produce high self-ideal correlations. Block (1962), replying to Shlien's abstraction hypothesis, has argued that Levy's (1956) data suggest that self-ideal discrepancies may simply represent generalized response styles without any personality meaning. Phillips, Raiford, and El-Batrawi (1965) found no significant changes in self-ideal discrepancies and were led to question the validity of the Q sort. Butler (1968), however, has argued that a more appropriate interpretation of these data "is that no systematic changes of any kind resulted from the therapy [p. 13]."

It seems clear that the preponderance of evidence supports the validity of the Q sort as an index of self-satisfaction that is sensitive to change in treatment. However, Q sort scores correlate highly with certain other self-report measures such as the MMPI (Strupp & Bergin, 1969). Nevertheless, the economy of the Q sort, its intimate relationship to client-centered theory, and its demonstrated validity in outcome studies make it the most useful of all self-concept measures. It also would be useful as a means of exploring possible self-concept changes resulting from behavior therapy.

Personal Orientation Inventory (POI). The POI (Shostrom, 1964) is unique in its emphasis on positive mental health rather than psychopathology. "It is based on the assumption that a mentally healthy individual is self-actualized and this self-actualization expresses itself in his system of values [Fox, Knapp, & Michael, 1968, p. 565]." Test-retest reliabilities have been in the .90s, and several studies have demonstrated concurrent validity by the "known group" method (Fox et al., 1968; Knapp, 1965). Moreover, its relatively modest correlation with MMPI scales (Shostrom & Knapp, 1966) supports the assumption that the POI is tapping something other than the usual neuroticism or health-sickness dimension. The POI also seems fairly resistant to faking or impression management (Braun, 1969). Its nature would seem, however, to make it applicable primarily to verbal, well-educated clients. Although the relations between POI scores and overt behavior are still unclear (Culbert, Clark, & Bobele, 1968), it is likely to be used often in contexts such as sensitivity training where enhancement of the functioning of already well-adjusted persons is a major goal.

THE CLIENT RATES HIMSELF

There is no clear distinction between standardized tests and self-ratings; both are subject to the same sources of error and distortion. As Strupp and Bergin (1969) note, "Patient self-ratings of outcome are too numerous and unstandardized to list here . . . there is little evidence that they add significantly to what is measured by standardized self-report instruments [p. 61]." The "homemade" nature of many of these measures inhibits comparison across studies. Two major exceptions to these generalizations are self-ratings to measure mood and client recordings of the frequency of specific behaviors.

Mood

Interest in mood stems from drug research and a related concern with depression, for which mood variation is one of the major defining attributes. Moreover, since the concept of mood refers to a subjective state, it can be argued that the client is the most appropriate informant. The Psychiatric Outpatient Mood Scales (POMS) were developed by Lorr and McNair (1966; McNair & Lorr, 1964) to study effects of drug treatments. The patient is asked, "How much have you felt the way described during the past week including today," and he rates each adjective on a four-point intensity scale. Since mood is known to fluctuate, it is important to specify the time referent. Factor analyses have identified tension-anxiety, anger-hostility, depression, vigor-activity, and fatigue-inertia factors. The POMs have been shown to be fairly sensitive measure of mood changes due to drug use and psychotherapy. The Clyde Mood Scale (Clyde, 1963) contains six factors which are fairly similar to the POMS and has also been used primarily in drug research. The items can be rated by professional or nonprofessional staff as well as by the client.

Depression, which shows up as a factor in the mood scales noted, has been the subject of particular attention (e.g., Lubin, 1965; Zuckerman & Lubin, 1965; Endicott & Jortner, 1966; Beck, Ward, Mendelson, & Mock, 1961), mostly with inpatient populations. Except for the Endicott and Jortner measures, which require administering and scoring of the Holtzman Ink Blots, these scales are short self-administered tests which can be adapted for outpatient use. Lewinsohn and his colleagues (Martin, Weinstein, & Lewinsohn, 1968; Lewinsohn & Atwood, 1969) have used Lubin's (1965) Depression Adjective Check List in case reports. Lubin's measure, which has several alternate forms to facilitate repeated testing, has been incorporated into the Multiple Affect Adjective Check List (MAACL; Zuckerman & Lubin, 1965). A problem in discriminant validity arises in the measurement of affect states; the depression, anxiety, and hostility scales of the MAACL all show very high intercorrelations.

Client Record Keeping

Client self-monitoring of the frequency of occurrence of specific behaviors has been used often by behavior modifiers. Base-line data are obtained before treatment procedures are instituted, and the target behavior is monitored during and perhaps after the course of therapy. The often implicit assumption is that the relatively discrete, salient nature of certain events makes them more easily countable and less vulnerable to the usual pitfalls of client self-reports. The methodological limitations of self-monitoring have been discussed by Kanfer (in press). He notes that where observable behaviors are at issue— e.g., smoking or eating—observer reliability can be established; but where the client is monitoring private events—e.g., sexual fantasies—direct corroboration is not possible. Attempts to confirm the client's reports, however, have been all too infrequent. One exception is with smoking behavior where several investigators have used informants (Ober, 1968; Powell & Azrin, 1968; Azrin & Powell, 1968; Schmahl, Lichtenstein, & Harris, in press) and have found client reports to be highly reliable. Reactivity is also a major problem for self-monitoring, because the instruction to monitor can easily communicate the desirability of change, particularly in treatment contexts. Self-monitoring has been shown to affect the rate of cigarette smoking outside of a treatment setting (McFall, in press). Reactivity can, however, be controlled by proper design. Behaviors that have been monitored by clients include dating (Rehm & Marston, 1968), sexual intercourse and conversation time (Stuart, 1969), deviant sexual arousal (Barlow, Lietenberg, & Agras, 1969), study time (Keutzer, 1967), and sleeping (Kahn, Baker, & Weiss, 1968). Where behaviors relevant to treatment goals can be specified, self-monitoring, especially when aided by wrist counters or record forms checked by informants, can be a very useful source of data. Such data are economical and can be obtained easily in applied settings. One must not forget, however, that client self-report is subject to memory, impression management, and reactivity distortions, and that informants are likely to observe only a small percentage of the target behavior.

THE CLIENT PERFORMS

Most desirable are direct measures of the client's problem behavior. Third parties may participate as raters, but usually minimal inference is required of them. The client's performance may be observed directly in the laboratory, or his behavior in natural settings may be inferred from records.

Laboratory Performance

Behavioral research on systematic desensitization treatment of phobias (Rachman, 1967; Paul, 1969c) has made extensive use of laboratory performance data. The basic paradigm is one in which the subject is asked to approach and handle the phobic object, usually a snake, rat, or spider. The distance between the subject and the phobic object yields a score. The test is best administered by persons with no knowledge of treatment conditions or results in order to minimize experimenter bias. However, there is obvious potential for demand characteristics or the hello-goodbye effect to operate, although these may be minimized by de-emphasizing the treatment aspects

(Davison, 1968) or by instructing the subject not to push himself (LoPiccolo, 1969). The data from the subject's approach to the feared stimulus may be analyzed as simple difference scores or may be converted to a ratio score based on pretreatment level; the two scores intercorrelate highly. Investigators differ in their methods of calibrating the subject's approach behavior, ranging from a three-point scale (Cooke, 1968) to a 15-point scale (LoPiccolo, 1969). Since both the stimulus—e.g., size and type of snake—and the manner of arranging and calibrating the approach behavior vary widely, there is no way of comparing the absolute scores of subjects from different studies (as one could do with MMPI scores, for example). It would be desirable for snake phobia researchers to standardize their procedures.

Levis (1969) described an apparatus to overcome some of these difficulties wherein the subject presses a button that moves the feared stimulus a given unit closer to him. Such a procedure affords the possibility of standardization across laboratories and also provides response latency data and ease of psychophysiological measurement. Avoidance behavior may also be measured outside the clinic or laboratory. Ritter (1969) used a 44-item Height Avoidance Test which took place on the roof of a seven-story building, and Lazarus (1961) also gave in vivo performance tests to his phobic subjects.

Paul's research on speech anxiety (1966) nicely illustrates another performance measure. Speech phobic subjects were requested to give a test speech before an unfamiliar audience of at least 10 persons. Trained observers coded 20 "observable mainfestations of anxiety," e.g., knees tremble during the speech. The obtained scores were reliable and showed difference among the experimental and various control groups.

Standard social situations involving parent and child have proved valuable in identifying and modifying the deviant behavior of children (Wahler, Winkel, Peterson, & Morrison, 1965; Johnson & Brown, 1969). Such situations are more difficult to contrive for adults but do offer the potential advantages of direct observation of behavior, control, and economy. A study by Rehm and Marston (1968) is an example of this approach. Working with male subjects who reported social anxiety when interacting with females, they presented taped, simulated situations and measured the adequacy of response.

Inferred Performance Measures

It is sometimes possible to obtain nonreactive performance measures from institutional records (Webb et al., 1966). Grade point average provides the most appropriate and stringent measure of the effects of treatment procedures for test anxiety (e.g., Johnson & Sechrest, 1968) or underachievement (Kipnes & Resnick, in press), and has been widely used in studies of counseling effectiveness. Frequency of legal offenses provides an excellent measure of the effectiveness of treatment programs for delinquent adolescents (Schwitzgebel & Kolb, 1964; Teuber & Powers, 1953). Income level could be a useful measure of outcome in that dynamic therapies purport to improve a client's productivity, and incidence of divorce could index the effectiveness of marital counseling. The stimulating volume by Webb et al. (1966) may suggest more useful indicators of this sort.

The questionnaire can be used to obtain follow-up information on the reasonably objective achievements of clients subsequent to treatment. Campbell (1965) obtained data on income level, occupation, honors, etc., on counseled and non-counseled subjects twenty-five years later. These data were used to derive a "contribution to society" scale which differentiated between counseled and non-counseled subjects.

These are measures of inherent meaningfulness. If they reflect positive results in a properly designed study, they provide strong evidence of treatment effectiveness (Johnson & Sechrest, 1968; Schwitzgebel & Kolb, 1964). Negative results (e.g., Teuber & Powers, 1953), however, are more difficult to interpret. The vulnerability of these public record measures to situational factors outside the research context—e.g., illness, fluctuations in the national economy—are such that they may fail to reflect a moderate but true treatment effect. Moreover, as Webb et al. (1966) note in their evaluation of archival records, "although the investigator may not himself contaminate the material, he may learn that the producer or repository already has [p. 111]."

The work of Krumboltz and his associates (Krumboltz & Thoresen, 1964; Thoresen & Krumboltz, 1968, 1967) illustrates the ingenious measurement of a target behavior occurring in natural settings. The focus was on the Information Seeking Behavior (ISB) of high school students counseled regarding their educational and vocational plans. Three weeks after counseling, the subjects underwent an assessment interview to determine the frequency of ISB. The accuracy of subjects' reports in these interviews was checked by interviewing a sample of persons from whom information was sought. Out of 85 ISBs, 79 were verified, six were unconfirmable, and there were no false reports (Krumboltz & Thoresen, 1964).

THERAPIST RATING SCALES

While therapist rating scales have much the same advantages and disadvantages as patient self-ratings, the therapist does have an additional practical virtue—his accessibility. He is probably the data source whose cooperation is easiest to secure, and this point alone would urge that therapist judgments be quantified. Therapists can also acknowledge and attempt to compensate for their biases (Lazarus, 1963). Knight's (1941) criteria, developed from a psychoanalytic perspective, have influenced raters of varying orientations (e.g., Wolpe, 1958; Lazarus, 1963). Knight's criteria were: symptomatic improvement, increased productiveness, improved adjustment and pleasure in sex, improved interpersonal relations, and improved ability to handle ordinary conflicts and stresses.

Global rating scales are the simplest approach and require the least therapist time. For the most part, such global rating scales are homemade, and ask about only a few gross dimensions, e.g., severity of illness (McNair et al., 1962) or freedom from symptoms (Lazarus, 1963), and have been used in but one study or by one research group. A 9-point rating scale originally used in Rogers and Dymond (1954) and continued in other client-centered studies (e.g., Van der Veen & Stoler, 1965) "correlates so highly with other more complex and sophisticated ratings (Cartwright, Robertson, Fiske, & Kirtner, 1961) that it may well be the measure of choice [Strupp & Bergin, 1969; p. 62]."

The therapist can also be asked to rate the client on specified variables, usually traits or symptom syndromes. Cartwright et al. (1963) represent probably the most ambitious effort of this sort. Fourteen 10-point Behavioral Adequacy Scales, "designed to give maximum coverage of variables investigated in previous research [p. 166]," were developed. Variables included contentedness with self, relationship to others, quantity and range of emotional response, and the like. Each scale had five anchor positions consisting of detailed descriptions of behavior appropriate to a given scale level. The median stability coefficient for the 14 scales was .68, and there also seemed to be adequate internal consistency. However, the therapist's ratings on these scales were not highly related to the client's or to diagnosticians' ratings on the same scales.

The development and salient characteristics of the Interpersonal Behavior Inventory (IBI) have been summarized by Lorr and McNair (1966). "The IBI presently consists of 140 statements of manifest interpersonal behaviors that yield 15 category scores [p. 581]." The correspondence of obtained factor structure with theoretical expectation has been the major source of validity thus far. Little is yet known about the relation between IBI scores and other indices of behavior change. The Lorr group has also utilized a variety of other therapist and patient measures in addition to the ones described (McNair et al., 1962; Lorr, McNair, Michaux, & Raskin, 1962).

THIRD-PARTY MEASURES

Observation or ratings of the client by someone other than his therapist are a valuable data source, relatively free from many of the problems that beset client and therapist measures. Third-party measures can be obtained from verbal behavior in the therapeutic sessions, from assessment interviews outside of therapy, and from the client's behavior in the community.

Within-Therapy Measures

Since the client's behavior in therapy is usually the most accessible, much attention has been given to deriving outcome indices from it and from related data such as case notes. Zax and Klein (1960) provide a good review of earlier within-therapy outcome measures, including early client-centered measures (Snyder, 1945; Raimy, 1948), and the Discomfort Relief Quotient (Dollard & Mowrer, 1947). These measures currently appear to be little used or, in the case of the client-centered group, to have been retired by later theoretical developments (e.g., Rogers, 1959). This paper, therefore, will be concerned with more recent measures.

The major within-therapy measurement thrust of the client-centered school has been directed toward operationalizing the process conception of psychotherapy stated by Rogers (1959). The Experiencing Scale is the most important of the process measures. Experiencing refers to "the degree to which the client manifests inward reference in his verbalizations . . . when searching for the meaning of the personal events, feelings, and ideas he is reporting [Rogers et al., 1967, p. 589]." It is rated from the client's verbalization in therapy, using a 7-point scale. Starting with the initial effort of Rogers (1959) a great deal of effort has gone into refining the measurement operations (e.g., Walker et al., 1960; Tomlinson & Hart, 1962; Kiesler, Mathieu, & Klein, 1964; Rogers et al., 1967). Currently, naive undergraduate raters are presented with a batch of four-minute transcribed segments sampled from the cases under scrutiny. Inter-judge reliabilities have varied with the amount of data (e.g., transcript and/or tape) and the experience of the judges, but are usually satisfactory. Several validity studies (Walker, Rablem, & Rogers, 1960; Tomlinson & Hart, 1962; Truax, Carkhuff, & Kodman, 1965) indicate that the Experiencing Scale (and its close cousin, Self-Exploration) usually behaves the way client-centered theory says it should, though the results with schizophrenic clients were not confirmatory (Rogers et al., 1967).

The Experiencing Scale deserves attention because it represents a painstaking and moderately successful attempt to measure a theoretically derived construct related to outcome. It further deserves attention because it illustrates the limitations of the personality or inner-experience approach to outcome: one is still left with the question of the relation between changes in Experiencing and behavior outside of therapy and the clinic. Aware of this issue, client-centered researchers have usually sought relationships between Experiencing scores and such traditional instruments as the MMPI, Q sort, or therapist ratings (Rogers et al., 1967). Even when significant relationships are found (e.g., Tomlinson & Hart, 1962), such data are only partially satisfying because of the previously discussed difficulties in interpreting these other outcome measures. Zax and Klein's (1960) comment about a previous decade of research still holds: "Unless phenomenological changes and changes in verbal behavior in therapy can be related to concomitant behavioral changes in the family and the community, their significance remains unclear [p. 444]."

Much the same analysis could be made of the Menninger Clinic Psychotherapy Research Project's efforts to measure intrapsychic change (Robbins & Wallerstein, 1959; Sargent, 1961). Again, there is the application of sophisticated measurement techniques—e.g., paired comparison judgments—and emphasis on remaining faithful to theory. Here, however, third parties must be highly trained clinicians, and the raw data are the therapist's process notes rather than therapy interactions. The rationale is the desire not to intrude on the neutral therapy process and the conviction that therapist impressions are a legitimate way of indexing ego functions (Sargent, 1961). The Menninger studies provide general guidelines for the measurement of change in psychoanalytic therapy, but the data are still not available that would indicate whether the effort is worthwhile. Many researchers and most practitioners will not possess the commitment to theory needed to justify the cost of measuring Experiencing or intrapsychic change.

Assessment Interviews

Moving outside of the therapy session itself, third parties may be used to generate and/or judge data from assessment interviews. The use of third party interviews may reduce—though certainly not eliminate—those factors confounding therapist and client ratings. Clearly, these are expensive data to come by, requiring a skilled interviewer and trained raters.

Social Ineffectiveness Scale. The SIS was the major outcome measure used by Frank and his colleagues in their influential therapy research project (Imber, Frank, Nash, Stone, & Gliedman, 1957; Frank, Gliedman, Imber, Stone, & Nash, 1959; Frank, 1959). These data have recently been utilized by the client-centered group (Truax, Wargo, Frank, Imber, Battle, Hoehn-Saric, Nash, & Stone, 1966). The patient is interviewed by an experienced clinician other than his therapist, and both the interviewer and an observer independently rate the patient on 15 categories focused on interpersonal relationships. A similar interview and procedure is carried out with a relative. The separate ratings are discussed, and the final score thus combines the judgments of four trained clinicians using information from both the patient and a close relative. Although it has shown some validity (Imber et al., 1957), the complexity and cost of the measure has undoubtedly inhibited use by other research groups (see Lyerly & Abbott, 1966, for a concise description of the scale's properties).

Psychiatric Status Schedule (PSS). The PSS (Spitzer, 1966; Spitzer et al., 1967) can be administered by a single, clinically inexperienced but trained interviewer. Most of the items are brief, nontechnical descriptions of small units of behavior, and little inference is required. Thus, it offers greater convenience than the Social Ineffectiveness Scale (computerized scoring is also possible). The PSS yields scores on factor-analyzed dimensions of psychopathology at two levels of specificity, as well as data on role functioning, interpersonal relations, and drug and alcohol use. Internal consistency estimates are high—.80 to .89 for the four summary symptom scales—and interjudge reliabilities are even higher. Preliminary validity studies seem promising though primarily based on inpatients. The PSS combines a high degree of both psychometric and clinical sophistication and will likely be used frequently in the future.

The tradition of the psychiatric mental status examination has yielded numerous rating scales, primarily used with inpatients and based on either interview data or ward behavior. However, such rating scales may be adapted for use with outpatients. For example, Lewinsohn and his colleagues (Lewinsohn & Atwood, 1969; Martin et al., 1968) have used depression scales developed by Grinker, Miller, Sabshin, Nunn, & Nunnally (1961). Useful summaries of such scales can be found in Lyerly and Abbot (1966) and Klett (1968).

Still within the clinic, one may use therapist notes or case file data to derive outcome measures. Pascal and Zax (1956) describe an interesting and simple "target behavior" approach: Was the client's major presenting problem improved or not? While their method is admittedly subjective, it is inexpensive and would seem applicable to many service-oriented clinical settings.

Outside the Clinic

Data may be obtained from informants who are able to observe the client in the community or from raters who follow the client into his home or work setting.

Informants. If one is interested in the overt, social behavior of the client, it would seem appropriate to seek data from friends or relatives who have an opportunity to observe the client in natural settings. This method has been used sporadically with outpatient populations (e.g., the Social Ineffectiveness Scale). When the focus is on more inferential variables, there may be puzzling discrepancies between the client's and the informant's data, as was the case in Rogers' (1954) attempt to assess Emotional Maturity. Rogers found more agreement between therapist and informants than between client and informants. Behavior therapists have made occasional use of informants to report on more specific symptoms and behaviors. This procedure has been employed in clinical reports on the effectiveness of Systematic Desensitization (e.g., Lazarus, 1963; Paul, 1969b) and in research with smoking subjects (Ober, 1968; Azrin & Powell, 1968), where there has been consistent subject-informant agreement. Research on the treatment of alcoholism—another discrete, easily observable behavior—has also used informants (Hill & Blane, 1967). Finally, informants have been helpful in evaluating the community adjustment of ex-hospital patients (Ellsworth, Foster, Childers, Arthur, & Krocker, 1968).

The use of informants requires consideration of certain methodological issues. In the smoking studies, the subjects nominated their informants, thus creating possible sampling bias (Ober, 1968; Azrin & Powell, 1968). Further, informants may vary in their relationship to different subjects and thus, in their opportunity to observe the relevant behavior. The informants also may be influenced by their knowledge that the subject has been given treatment or is being studied. Finally, there are the practical problems of securing cooperation from informants who may have little at stake in the outcome of the therapy or the research and who are contacted only by mail (Rogers, 1954). Most community informants will tend to be untrained, and care must be taken to make their task as explicit and non-inferential as possible (Powell & Azrin, 1968). These problems notwithstanding, the data to be obtained are sufficiently valuable to warrant greater application of this approach to psychotherapy research.

Direct observation. The observation of problem behaviors in natural settings has been championed by behavior modifiers. It is most easily done with children, in homes or in schools (e.g., Patterson, Ray, & Shaw, 1969) or with hospitalized patients (Ayllon & Azrin, 1968). Direct observation has proved to be such a powerful tool in these contexts that wider use seems desirable.

Observational procedures have their own methodological problems. These problems include "the question of observer reliability and generalizability of observation data, . . . observer bias, . . . reliability of data sampling, . . . and the problem of the effect of the observer upon the interaction which he observes [Patterson & Harris, 1968, p. 1]." Observer reliability is a function of the complexity of the rating task and the experience of the raters. The reliability of data sampling is in large part an economic matter: how often or for how long a period can an experimenter afford to observe? For example, Patterson and Harris observed each member of their families for 100 minutes over 10 days. The frequency of events during the first 50 minutes was compared to the frequency during the last 50 minutes. The median correlation across different events was .50, and there was considerable variation among different behaviors. Unlike the community informant, observers are employed by the experimenter, who can take steps to minimize observer bias "by careful training, ... by permitting practice effects to take place before the critical data are collected, and by 'blinding' the observer to the hypotheses [Webb et al., 1966, pp. 175-176]."

Effects of being observed have been demonstrated by several investigators. These effects appear to be greater when observers are present (Patterson & Harris, 1968) than when electronic equipment is used (Moos, 1968; Purcell & Brady, 1966). Encouragingly, habituation over time seems to occur, although few researchers may be able to afford the ten sessions obtained by Patterson and Harris (1968).

Much of the behavior modification work with children requires observation of one or two criterion behaviors. However, investigators may also be interested in capturing all the interactions that occur between given persons during a specified time period. This requires a coding system with its attendant scoring and reliability problems. That these can be resolved, with effort, is attested to by the work of Patterson et al. (1969) with children, and Lewinsohn's adaptation and extension of the Patterson system for use with depressed adults (Lewinsohn, 1968). Both approaches look at interactions from a social learning orientation, and while both systems are too complex to be summarized here, they are basically concerned with reinforcement exchanges among family members. The client's family is asked to stay within a designated area of the house, usually the kitchen-dining area and living room, and to ignore the presence of the observers. Lewinsohn has used two or three days (about one hour per day) of observation pre- and post-therapy so that reactivity (i.e., "guinea pig") effects are undoubtedly present. However, such observational data have been useful in several carefully described case reports (Lewinsohn & Atwood, 1969; Lewinsohn & Shaffer, in press).

Observational data are very expensive to collect, but their inherent meaningfulness and their demonstrated utility in behavior-change research often make the effort worthwhile for research purposes. The practitioner can also use home observations—these take no longer than the time required to give and score projective tests—but he will not likely apply any standardized coding or scoring system. The possibility of wireless radio transmitter recording of behavior deserves further investigation and may reduce reactions to being observed. Clients can also be given tape-recorders and asked to record interactions during specified time periods. Finally, parents can be trained to observe their own children and families (Patterson, in press).

Placing observers or recording apparatus in homes to measure behavior may seem intrusive, especially to those who view tape-recorded therapy sessions with suspicion. But it is likely that more data of this sort will be collected in the future. Such data have value for the increasingly influential social learning model, and technologies are now developing that make its collection feasible. If it is possible to televise events on the moon 239,000 miles away, surely it will be possible to televise events in a home three miles away. Assessment devices have long been used to provide signs that would predict how subjects would behave in their natural environments (many tests are intended to provide indicators of internal processes, but these internal processes are assumed to mediate or predict overt behavior). Such predictions have generally been unsatisfactory (Mischel, 1968). Both researchers and clinicians should now be less inhibited about demanding the opportunity for direct observation of relevant behavior.

CONCLUDING REMARKS

The investigator of psychotherapy outcomes must choose between client-specific, tailor-made criteria or general criteria that can be applied to all clients, such as trait anxiety. It is impressive that investigators representing very different psychotherapeutic approaches are converging on the research utility of tailoring change criteria to the individual client (Strupp & Bergin, 1969; Shlien, 1966; Krumboltz, 1966; Volsky et al., 1965; Rickard, 1965). Shlien's solution to the uniqueness problem "is to translate individual performances or meanings at the highest level of abstraction [1966, p. 128]." Operationally, this translation indicates the use of the Q sort with its attendant limitations.

For most investigators the solution to the problem of client uniqueness is to use more concrete, behavioral measures (Krumboltz, 1966) and to pay more attention to each client's presenting complaint (Volsky et al., 1965). Several ways of doing this are available. At the case report level, the procedures described by Pascal and Zax (1956) or Rickard (1965) are suitable. The therapist sets a specific goal(s) based on the client's complaint and determines if it is reached. The operant conditioning model—where base-line observations are made, reinforcement contingencies manipulated, and base-line conditions then reinstated—is a powerful version of single case study.

Battle, Imber, Hoehn-Saric, Stone, Nash, & Frank (1966) described a target-complaint approach amenable to group studies. Clients were asked to state their complaints and then rated their own improvement on these problems using a standard scale. Behavioral research with groups of clients or subjects who have very similar problems—phobias, test anxiety, smoking, obesity—represents another means of capitalizing on client-specific criteria. Finally, Volsky et al. (1965) describe a study by Jewell in which clinicians made specific judgments as to what the counselor's goal for a client should be, and a second team of judges determined whether the specific goals had been met. This procedure can be seen as a controlled, objective implementation of the paradigm described by Pascal and Zax (1956).

The use of tailor-made criteria avoids the assumptions that all clients should change along some given dimension and enables the investigator to manage the criterion problem at the time rather than depend on future advances in personality theory and measurement. The usefulness of this approach in behavior modification research urges that it be employed more extensively.

It would be inappropriate to expect that a survey such as this would lead to definitive guidelines for choice and action. A variety of approaches to measurement of outcome have been described to emphasize the many alternatives open to researcher and clinician. One conclusion with which the writer hopes the reader will emerge is that treatment outcome can be meaningfully evaluated even though any one measure is imperfect. "If no single measurement class is perfect, neither is any scientifically useless [Webb et al., 1966, p. 174]."

Outcome measures have examined against two major considerations: Does the measure yield signs or indicators of some inferred personality trait, or provide frequency information about some observable behavior? Is the measure produced by a psychotherapy participant or by a third party? The writer's preference is for behavioral and/or third party measures, and he does not entirely share Farnsworth's (1966) faith that the application of psychophysical scaling techniques can produce more valid rating scales for use by client, therapist, and informant. But this is not to say that personality measures ought to be discarded. Rather, it would be desirable to include personality measures in behavior modification studies and behavioral measures in psychodynamic research. Such data would eventually permit a more realistic confrontation and eventual integration between the behavioral and psychodynamic approaches. This point is similar to Strupp and Bergin's (1969) plea that studies include measures of both internal and external criteria.

There is also a great need for outcome evaluation to become routine in clinics, counseling centers, and even in private practice. An informative paper by Ladd (1967) documents the infrequent collection of quantitative data in clinics and counseling centers. Economic considerations such as convenience and amount of staff time involved will heavily influence the instrument choices of service-oriented clinicians. It does seem feasible to obtain at least one set of data from the client; for example, the MMPI or the Q sort. Further, the therapist can provide inexpensive outcome data, perhaps by means of the client-centered nine-point rating scale or by means of Lazarus' (1963) five-point scale. Clients can be trained to become better record keepers, and counting problem behaviors will sometimes have a therapeutic effect. The data that would thereby be accumulated would have limited, but real value, particularly if client-specific criteria are used. Carefully described case reports or series of case reports can still play an important role in the accumulation of knowledge (Ford & Urban, 1967). The development of systematic desensitization as a therapeutic procedure is an excellent illustration of the interplay between clinical reports and laboratory research (Paul, 1969b, c). The selection and collection of proper outcome data by both clinician and researcher can facilitate this process.

CHAPTER X

Dimensions and categories for assessment of psychotics

Maurice Lorr

In this chapter an effort will be made (1) to describe the basic minor syndromes and major disorders to be found in psychotics; (2) to describe a set of computer-derived categories or types; (3) to relate the statistically determined categories to standard diagnostic classes, to stereotypes established by consensual validation, and to drug-response types; and (4) to evaluate the newer conceptual schemes in terms of their value for research and clinical practice.

PSYCHIATRIC NOMENCLATURE

The standard psychiatric nomenclature has long been judged unsatisfactory by many in the field, and investigators have been working to formulate more objective alternatives to the present system. A major basis for complaint is rater unreliability due to lack of objectivity in the criteria for class membership (Lorr, Klett, & McNair, 1963). Another weakness is the absence of clear-cut decision rules for combining multiple indicators into a diagnostic decision. A third and more important complaint is that the categories are of little use for prognosis or treatment selection. Finally, there is the possibility, even more fundamental, that some of the categories are too broad or too narrow, overlap too much, or are incorrectly defined.

These dissatisfactions with the system have produced a wide variety of strategies for solving its various ills. Many investigators have sought to objectify and quantify the vague and ill-defined terms of the categories by applying rating schedules, behavior inventories, and a structured interview. The problem of decision rules has been approached by the use of several decision models available in the literature. Other workers have sought to establish the existing categories more firmly by means of consensual validation. In this procedure experts are asked to describe each class in terms of objectively defined scales or symptoms.

Still other investigators have endeavored to approach the problem freshly, unencumbered by the present psychiatric scheme. Their view is not that the clinically derived categories as a whole are, in any sense, invalid. Such a perspective would indeed be absurd. However, they see merit in deriving a quantitative system of classification on the basis of modern multivariate techniques. Their expectation would be that most clinical categories would be verified, others would require some correction, and still other new classes would emerge.

The process involves several distinct phases. First, it is necessary to choose and measure a set of characteristics on the basis of which individuals can be evaluated and compared. It is essential, of course, that all major sources of behavior variation be represented. Out of the analysis of these descriptors, a set of dimensions can be established. The second phase applies typological procedures for identifying any homogeneous subgroups to be found in the population. Once the subgroups are identified and established, decision functions can be specified for assigning new individuals to the subgroups represented.

The next section will be concerned with the dimensions of assessment that have emerged out of the first phase of investigation.

DIMENSIONS OF ASSESSMENT

The Minor Syndromes

A snydrome is ordinarily defined as a group of signs and symptoms that occur together with high frequency and, at the same time, are independent of other symptom complexes. Since the syndrome represents a correlated set of variables observable within a specified sample, it is basically a statistical concept. In a clinical setting it is the clinician who notes the covariation of signs and symptoms within a patient sample and gives the complex a name. In a research setting the investigator correlates the symptoms and behaviors recorded for all members of a specified sample, and then extracts any functional unities to be found within the symptom relationships by the method of factor analysis. Thus, the clinician's syndromes and the researcher's factors are fundamentally the same.

The first factor-analytic study of psychotic behavior was reported by T. V. Moore in 1933. Moore constructed his own rating schedule and obtained ratings on social history, ward events, behaviors, and interview behaviors, of a substantial sample of functional psychotics. A cluster analysis of the intercorrelations uncovered some seven syndromes. Subsequently, Degan (1952) refactored the Moore data and found four additional higher order syndromes, referred to here as major disorders.

Following development of the Psychiatric Rating Scale (PRS), Wittenborn and his colleagues (1951) conducted a series of factor analyses designed for "the development of a quantified method for multiple psychiatric diagnoses [p. 290]." The seven dimensions derived from interview and ward ratings were Paranoid Schizophrenia, Excitement, Manic State vs. Depressive State, Anxiety, Hysteria, Paranoid Condition, and Phobic-Compulsive Reaction. About the same time, Guertin (1952) conducted a factor analysis of schizophrenic symptoms and identified the six syndromes of Excitement-Hostility, Retardation and Withdrawal, Guilt Conflict, Confused-Withdrawal, Persecuting-Suspicious, and Personality Disorganization.

In 1955, Lorr, Jenkins, and O'Connor reported a factor analysis of interview and ward behavior of a large patient sample rated on the Multidimensional Scale for Rating Psychiatric Patients (MSRPP). The nine dimensions
isolated were labeled Excitement, Resistiveness, Paranoid Projection, Grandiosity, Anxious Depression, Perceptual Distortion, Motor Disturbances, Activity Level, and Conceptual Disorganization. A second analysis (Lorr,
O'Connor, & Stafford, 1957) yielded nine syndromes.

A subsequent revision of MSRPP (Lorr, Klett, McNair, & Lasky, 1962)
resulted in the 75-item Inpatient Multidimensional Psychiatric Scale (IMPS),
a rating schedule based entirely on interview behavior. Analysis of a large
block of data collected on the IMPS (Lorr, McNair, Klett, & Lasky, 1962)
gave evidence for ten syndromes subsequently confirmed in another sample
(Lorr, Klett, & McNair, 1963). They were named Excitement, Hostile Belligerence, Paranoid Projection, Grandiosity, Perceptual Distortion, Anxious
Depression, Retardation, Disorientation, Motor Disturbances, and Conceptual
Disorganization.

The equivalent of the ten psychotic syndromes established in the United
States with IMPS was next sought in data obtained from six other countries
(Lorr & Klett, 1969b). In addition to the ten listed above, measures of two
other syndromes were included: Functional Impairment and Phobic-Obsessive
(Overall, 1963b; Lorr, Sonn, & Katz, 1967). Samples of drug-free, newly-
hospitalized psychotic men and women in England, France, Germany, Italy,
Japan, and Sweden were interviewed and rated on the IMPS. The pooled
ratings of 100 men and 100 women in each country's sample were correlated
and factored. With only a few exceptions, each of the syndromes previously
isolated was confirmed. The data were not separated by sex since the psychotic syndromes had been shown to be structurally the same for men and
for women (Lorr & Klett, 1965).

Spitzer and his colleagues (1967) have developed the Mental Status Schedule (MSS), a form which incorporates structured interview questions used in
conjunction with a standardized rating schedule. The factor scales derived
correspond closely to those measured by IMPS. These dimensions, listed in
the same order as given for IMPS, are as follows: Agitation-Excitement,
Belligerence-Negativism, Suspicion-Persecution-Hallucinations, Grandiosity,
Depression-Anxiety, Retardation-Emotional Withdrawal, Disorientation-Mem-
ory, Inappropriate/Bizarre Appearance or Behavior, and Speech Disorganization. Other factors assessed, not measured by IMPS, are Suicide-Self Mutila-
tion, Somatic Concern, and Denial of Illness. Except for absence of a separate
perceptual distortion factor in the MSS, the two systems correspond closely.

What, then, are the better established syndromes? The twelve to be described below are referred to as "minor," or elementary, in contradistinction
to the more inclusive "major" disorders. The minor syndromes are isolated
from the correlations among the symptoms. The major disorders, on the other
hand, emerge from analysis of the correlations among the elementary syndromes. Each syndrome is conceptualized as a polar variable present to some
degree in all persons observed. It is assumed that the more severe the disturbance, the greater the probability that deviant behaviors will be manifested.

Thus, a low score on a syndrome implies a mild disturbance while a high score implies a severe disturbance. The syndromes are functional unities without implication regarding antecedents or possible causal factors.

The descriptions that follow are, of course, abbreviated. For precise definitions of the various scales, the reader is referred to the manual for the IMPS.

Excitement (EXC). The patient's speech is hurried, loud, and difficult to stop. His mood level and self-esteem are elevated, and his emotional expression tends to be unrestrained or histrionic. He is also likely to exhibit controlling or dominant behavior.

Hostile Belligerence (HOS). The patient's attitude toward others is one of disdain and moroseness. He is likely to manifest much hostility, resentment, and a complaining bitterness. His difficulties and failures tend to be blamed on others.

Paranoid Projection (PAR). The patient gives evidence of unfounded fixed beliefs that attribute a hostile, persecuting, or controlling intent to others around him.

Grandiose Expansiveness (GRN). The patient's attitude toward others is one of superiority. He exhibits unwarranted fixed beliefs that he possesses unusual powers. He may report a divine mission or may identify himself with well-known or historical personalities.

Perceptual Distortions (PCP). The patient reports false perceptions, such as voices and visions that threaten, accuse, or demand.

Obsessional-Phobic (OBS). The patient reports uncontrollable compulsive acts and rituals, recurrent obsessional thoughts, specific phobias, and ideas of depersonalization and change.

Anxious Depression (ANX). The patient reports vague apprehension as well as specific anxieties. His attitudes toward himself are disparaging. He is also likely to report feelings of guilt and remorse for real and imagined faults. The underlying mood is dysphoric.

Impaired Functioning (IMP). The patient complains of inability to make decisions, to concentrate, or to work. He may also report a loss of interest in people, sex, and social activity.

Retardation and Apathy (RTD). The patient's speech, ideation, and motor activity are delayed, slowed, or blocked. In addition, he is likely to manifest apathy and disinterest in the future.

Disorientation (DIS). The patient's orientation with respect to time, place, and season is defective. He may show failure to recognize others around him.

Motor Disturbances (MTR). The patient assumes and maintains bizarre postures, and makes repetitive facial and body movements.

Conceptual Disorganization (CNP). Disturbances in the patient's stream of thought are manifested by irrelevant, incoherent, and rambling speech. Repetition of stereotyped phrases and coining of new words are also common.

The dimensions described thus far have been established principally on the basis of observations recorded in the interview. Because psychiatric aides and nurses have frequent opportunities to observe and interact with patients, ward rating schedules have long represented a source of information. The question then arises as to what extent the descriptive dimensions identifiable in ward and hospital observations agree with those found in interview. Since the patient can interact with other patients, aides, nurses, doctors, and visitors in the milieu of the hospital, a greater range of interpersonal behaviors is available than in the interview. The section that follows will review dimensions established in ward observations.

Ward Behavior Dimensions

The syndromes to be described are those measured by the Psychotic Inpatient Profile (PIP), a nurse's observation scale (Lorr & Vestre, 1969). It was deliberately designed to measure behavioral dimensions identified in the interview as well as patterns to be found only in ward ratings. The 12 syndromes measured by PIP, established through factor analysis, are as follows: Excitement, Hostile Belligerence, Paranoid Projection, Grandiosity, Perceptual Distortion, Anxious Depression, Impaired Functioning, Retardation, Seclusiveness, Care Needed vs. Competence, Disorientation, and Psychotic Disorganization. Only Seclusiveness and Care Needed are unique to ward behavior. Psychotic Disorganization combines the symptoms to be found in Motor Disturbances and Conceptual Disorganization in interview data.

The first effort to test the equivalence of the syndromes across the two media (Lorr & Cave, 1966) was based on ratings of 814 newly admitted schizophrenics. The data consisted of interview ratings and ward ratings made within three days of the interview. A special hypothesis-testing procedure applied to 80 marker variables yielded ten factors, eight of which were common to the ward and interview measures. The second study (Lorr & Hamlin, 1970) was based on ratings obtained on a sample of 125 psychotics that included paranoid and nonparanoid schizophrenics, depressives, and manics. A multimethod factor analysis procedure developed by Jackson (1969) was applied to the correlations among the ten IMPS scores and the twelve PIP scores. The procedure applied removes the masking effects of method or instrument variance, which is confounded with trait variance in a conventional factor analysis. The results indicated clear convergence of similarly labeled interview and ward syndromes for eight of the factors identified. The remaining two factors that emerged were equally plausible. Conceptual Disorganization (interview) and Psychotic Disorganization (ward) defined one syndrome, while Motor Disturbances (interview) and Care Needed (ward) defined the second. It may be concluded that the elementary syndromes are demonstrable both in interview and in ward behavior. The main difference is that elicitation of inner states, beliefs, and perceptual experiences call for special skill and activity on the part of the observer.

The elementary syndromes, as clinicians know, are by no means independent. They combine in meaningful ways into more inclusive hierarchical structures. For example, paranoid projection may combine with perceptual distortion or grandiosity. Depression is correlated with functional impairment and to some extent with retardation. In schizophrenia, bizarre and manneristic behaviors are often associated with disorientation and psychomotor retardation. Thus, as in studies of intelligence, investigators have attempted to identify broader and more general dimensions of behavior disturbance. The next section will be concerned with these major disorders.

The Major Disorders

The major functional psychoses listed in the *Diagnostic and Statistical Manual* (Committee on Nomenclature, 1968) include schizophrenia, the affective disorders, and the paranoid states. These groupings are, of course, not defined solely in terms of current symptoms and behaviors. Equally important are differentia such as duration of the disturbance, recurrence, type of onset, and premorbid personality. However, presently discernible symptoms do play a central role in the definition of these more general groupings.

Fairly recently, efforts to define the major psychotic disorders entirely in terms of current disturbances of thinking, mood, and behavior have shown significant convergence. When the correlations among the scores that define the minor syndromes are examined by multivariate techniques, five more inclusive behavioral dimensions can be demonstrated.

Analyses aimed at higher-level, or major, disorders have been reported since the time of Moore (1933), who identified four. A summary of early findings based on the IMPS and on other scales such as the PRS is reported elsewhere (Lorr, Klett, & McNair, 1963). In a definitive study Lorr, Klett, and Cave (1967) correlated and factored the ten IMPS syndrome scores of 2,303 functional psychotics rated while on a minimum of drugs. The analyses disclosed five dimensions, which were named Disorganized Hyperactivity, Schizophrenic Disorganization, Paranoid Process, Psychotic Depression, and Hostile Paranoia.

Confirmation of these dimensions may be found in studies by Overall, Hollister, and Pichot (1967) with the Brief Psychiatric Rating Scale (BPRS) and by Cohen, Gurel, and Stumpf (1966) with the Symptom Rating Scale. Cohen et al. factored correlations among ratings of a large sample of chronic schizophrenics made on the Symptom Rating Scale. Of the five factors found, three, Deteriorated Thinking, Depression-Anxiety, and Paranoid Hostility, correspond to the IMPS' Schizophrenic Disorganization, Psychotic Depression, and Hostile Paranoia.

Overall et al. (1967) employed the BPRS in five studies, each involving large groups of psychiatrically ill subjects rated by psychiatrists, by psychologists, and by nurses. The data revealed four major disorders, labeled Withdrawal-Retardation, Thinking Disturbances, Anxious Depression, and Paranoid Hostile-Suspiciousness. Examination of the 16 defining scales of the BPRS indicates that these factors correspond remarkably to the IMPS major disorders called Schizophrenic Disorganization, Paranoid Process, Psychotic Depression, and Hostile Paranoia. The missing dimension, Disorganized Hyperactivity, can be accounted for by the absence of scales descriptive of excitement or agitation in the BPRS.

The most recent test of the major disorders of current behavior was based on the cross-cultural sample described earlier (Lorr & Klett, 1968). Approximately 1,100 men and women newly hospitalized in England, France, Germany, Italy, Japan, and Sweden were interviewed and rated on the IMPS by two observers. The correlation among the scores on the minor syndromes was factored to identify common behavior patterns present. The analyses were conducted separately by sex on the data of each country. Except for Hostile Paranoia, each of the other four dimensions appeared in each of the countries. Sex differences were negligible, a finding consistent with prior reports that men and women differ little with respect to the types of minor syndromes manifested (Lorr & Klett, 1965).

Table 1 indicates how each of the major disorders is defined in terms of the minor syndromes. The first, *Disorganized Hyperactivity,* is primarily characterized by excitement, conceptual disorganization, and motor disturbances. Less frequently present are grandiosity or hostile belligerence. It should be noted that this dimension, while reflecting a manic excitement, is more general in character since schizophrenic-like behaviors are included.

The second disorder, called *Schizophrenic Disorganization,* is characterized by psychomotor retardation, functional disorientation, and motor disturbances. Conceptual disorganization is also associated, but less frequently than the other symptoms. The conventional schizophrenic subtypes that appear to be best described by this behavioral class are the simple, the hebephrenic, and the withdrawn catatonic.

The third major disorder has been labeled *Paranoid Process.* It is characterized by paranoid projection, perceptual distortion (hallucinations), grandiosity, and obsessive thinking. The conventional diagnostic category corresponding most closely to Paranoid Process is, of course, the paranoid subtype listed under schizophrenia.

A fourth disorder, called *Psychotic Depression,* is primarily characterized by anxious depression, functional impairment, and obsessional and phobic symptoms. The syndrome represents the affective disorders on the depression side. Since the disorder reflects current mood and behavior, it most likely reflects the symptom pattern common to involutional melancholia, manic-depressive illness (depressed type), and psychotic depressive reaction.

The fifth disorder, somewhat narrower than the previous four, is called *Hostile Paranoia.* The disorder is defined by a hostile belligerence and paranoid projection. Only the paranoid subtype of schizophrenia has any resemblance to this disorder. Hostile Paranoia is most closely associated with Disorganized Hyperactivity, suggesting a common element in hostility.

CATEGORIES OF ASSESSMENT

The standard psychiatric nomenclature for functional psychosis presents a collection of descriptions of patient subtypes or categories. For example, schizophrenia includes a simple type, a hebephrenic type, a catatonic type, and so on. Thus, the system is conceptually typological rather than dimensional. It has been said that the scheme is unsatisfactory and in need either of modification or of replacement. What are some possible typological solutions to the problems of the present system? Three types of solutions have been tried. One approach is to establish a stereotype of each of the classes through consensus, on the assumption that the diagnostic classes are adequate, but the problem lies in lack of objective quantitative definitions. A second

Table 1
Syndromes Defining the Major Psychotic Disorders

Minor Syndromes	Disorganized Hyperactivity	Schizophrenic Disorganization	Paranoid Process	Psychotic Depression	Hostile Paranoia
Excitement	**				
Hostile Belligerence	*				**
Paranoid Projection			**		**
Grandiosity	**		**		
Perceptual Distortion			**		
Obsessional-Phobic			**	**	
Anxious Depression				**	
Functional Impairment				**	
Retardation		**		*	
Disorientation		**			
Motor Disturbances	**	**			
Conceptual Disorganization	**	*			

*Correlations of .25 to .39.
**Correlations of .40 and higher.

more pragmatic approach is to classify patients on the basis of their response to drugs. The third approach is to apply statistical procedures to objective measures of symptomotology in order to recover any subgroups to be found in the data. The assumption and the findings of each approach will be considered in turn.

Psychiatric Stereotypes

This approach assumes that the diagnostic classes are valid. What is needed are (a) objective symptom definitions, (b) clearly specified weights for combining symptoms, and (c) a quantitative procedure for deciding how cases are to be allocated to one and only one class.

An objective quantitative definition of the conventional diagnostic types in terms of the Brief Psychiatric Rating Scale (BPRS) was the approach used by Overall and Hollister (1964) and Overall (1963a). A total of 38 experts were asked to conceive of a typical patient belonging to each of 13 standard psychotic subtypes. The task was to produce a rating profile for each subtype representing the levels of severity on the 16 scales of the BPRS. The mean rating profiles obtained were, for the most part, in close accordance with clinical expectations, but some were distinctly different. Further, grouping of subtypes to reduce overlap resulted in four major classes characterized as paranoid, schizophrenic, depressive, and manic. Next, four different decision models were applied to test out their efficiency for assigning rating profiles to the 13 diagnostic stereotypes. These decision procedures included a distance measure, a Bayesian probability procedure, a profile correlation, and a normalized cross-product index. The results obtained supported the consensual validity of the conventional U.S. nomenclature as of 1952. In yet another analysis (Overall, Bailly, & Pichot, 1968), 125 experts in French psychiatry provided BPRS rating profiles for 12 different hypothetical hospital patients representing the 12 French diagnostic classes. Agreement among judges in their definition of the types was again high.

Smith (1966) also was concerned with a strategy for refining the present classification scheme by providing a more precise set of terms and a decision function. He viewed diagnosis as a process of matching clusters of observable symptoms with clusters of symptoms found by other clinicians over a long period of time. Smith selected 41 symptoms, each carefully defined, to represent 38 psychotic, neurotic, and character disorders. Fourteen trained diagnosticians sorted all 41 symptoms into four categories according to the degree to which they thought the symptom characterized each disorder. From the pool of these ratings the conditional probabilities of each symptom for each disorder were derived.

The conditional probability model used applies differential weights to each symptom for each syndrome so that the most likely diagnosis will be assigned to any particular pattern of symptoms found. The model revealed an 86 percent rate of conceptual agreement among diagnosticians over the 38 miscellaneous psychiatric disorders. It also achieved 87 percent agreement with clinical evaluations on a sample of 30 psychiatric patients.

These three studies indicate that if the conventional diagnostic classes are objectified and suitable decision procedures are applied, it is possible to achieve comparatively high agreement rates. However, consensual validation of the nomenclature must not be confused with empirical validation by clinical observation or statistical procedure. The stereotypes derived are basically learned and conventionalized concepts, and not necessarily modal profiles of actual subtypes. Accordingly, attention will now be turned to objective typological procedures for recovering any existing subgroups within a sample.

Statistically Derived Behavioral Types

The approach of ignoring standard clinical nomenclature entirely starts with the question, What homogeneous subgroups of patients with common score profiles may be found within the measured descriptors? This approach has been applied with varying degrees of success by Lorr, Klett, and McNair (1963), by Overall and Hollister (1964), and by Katz, Lowery, and Cole (1966). Katz has applied the Katz Adjustment Scale (KAS), which reflects relative ratings of patient symptoms and social behavior. Overall's descriptors consisted of the BPRS scales. Lorr and his colleagues have employed the IMPS, a measure of current interview behavior referred to previously. The categories isolated on the IMPS will be described first.

The subgroups or types to be described emerged out of typological analyses of four large independent samples (Lorr, 1966). Two of the samples represented acute psychotics, mainly first admissions. The remaining two samples consisted of newly admitted chronic cases and a group of long-term cases whose drug treatment had been discontinued. In all instances patients were on a minimum of drugs before and during the interview. The procedure consisted of a 30- to 60-minute semi-structured interview. Following the interview the interviewer and his observer independently rated the patient on the 75 items in the IMPS. The two ratings were then combined and converted into 10 standardized minor syndrome scores.

The typological analysis (Lorr & Radhakrishman, 1967) consists of feeding blocks of 150 profiles into a computer. The profiles are grouped into homogeneous and mutually exclusive sets on the basis of several indices of similarity. Finally, subgroups isolated in various blocks are matched and combined. No subgroup is retained unless it appears in at least two blocks.

IMPS Psychotic Types

The average syndrome standard score profiles of each subgroup are presented in Table 2. The reference population for the standard scores is a large sample of newly admitted psychotics. The names given the subgroups are intended to be descriptive of their manifest behaviors only. The syndromes that characterize a subgroup are those on which all members score some specified distance above the mean of the reference group. Syndromes on which members of a subgroup score as frequently above as below the mean are undifferentiating and may be ignored. Likewise, if all members of a type score below the population mean on a particular syndrome, then that specific form of behavior deviation does not characterize the subgroup. This is because a low score represents the absence of deviant behavior. The nine male patient types found may be described briefly as follows.

Excited. Members of this group are characterized mainly by elevated scores on Excitement. Most also have high scores on Conceptual Disorganization. In addition, some members of the subgroup manifest above-average scores on Grandiosity. Scores on all other syndromes are well below the scale mean. A large fraction of those diagnosed as manics may be found in this subgroup.

Excited-Hostile. The score of all subgroup members are above the scale mean on Excitement and Hostile-Belligerence. Elevated scores on Paranoid Projection are also common. Although many of the group show elevated scores on Conceptual Disorganization, others exhibit below average scores, as may be seen from Table 2. Members of the subgroup are diagnosed either as manics or as paranoids.

Hostile Paranoid. Most members of this subgroup are characterized by scores elevated on both Hostile Belligerence and Paranoid Projection. Excitement scores, in contrast to the Excited-Hostile type, are all below the scale mean. Approximately two-thirds of the subgroup are diagnosed paranoids.

Hallucinated-Paranoid. The third distinctive paranoid subgroup consists of patients scoring high on the syndromes that measure paranoid beliefs and tendencies to hallucinate. Members thus misinterpret the action of others as persecutory and hear voices that accuse, threaten, or order. Of this group 70 percent are diagnosed as paranoid types.

Grandiose Paranoid. All members of this subgroup attain very high scores on Grandiosity. In addition most members, but not all, manifest high scores on Paranoid Projection and Perceptual Distortion. Approximately 78 percent are diagnosed paranoids.

Anxious-Depressed. The members of this class are all distinguished by elevated Anxious Depression scores. A majority of the subgroups are

Table 2
Mean Syndrome Standard Scores of Nine Psychotic Types among Male Patients

Psychotic Type	SYNDROME									
	EXC	HOS	PAR	GRN	PCP	INP	RTD	DIS	MTR	CNP
Excited	1.29	-.65	-.80	-.32	-.53	-.68	-.48	-.28	-.03	.47
Excited-Hostile	1.42	1.39	.33	.05	-.51	-.75	-.74	-.46	-.29	.34
Hostile Paranoid	-.52	.80	.17	-.42	-.55	-.43	-.55	-.24	-.40	-.61
Hallucinated-Paranoid	-.53	.04	1.24	-.23	1.32	-.05	-.24	.22	-.52	-.12
Grandiose Paranoid	.12	-.41	.20	2.02	.51	-.46	-.45	-.14	-.61	-.13
Anxious-Depressed	-.46	-.63	-.80	-.54	-.43	1.15	-.45	-.45	-.44	-.62
Retarded-Motor Disturbed	-.70	-.83	-.68	-.56	-.55	-.30	1.43	.06	.52	-.26
Disoriented	-.43	-.84	-.93	-.60	-.38	-.88	.87	3.29	.39	.18
Anxious-Disorganized	-.50	.10	1.28	-.44	2.20	1.19	1.61	.62	1.18	.48

diagnosed as depressives (psychotic or involutional), the remainder as schizo-affective or acute undifferentiated.

Retarded-Motor Disturbed. Members of this class are distinguished by retardation and by disturbances in motor behavior (bizarre or manneristic movements and postures). While the diagnoses vary (acute undifferentiated and catatonic), most are within the schizophrenic disorder.

Disoriented. All members of this type are not only retarded and motor disturbed but also extremely disoriented. The most frequent psychiatric diagnosis is schizophrenia, simple type.

Anxious-Disorganized. The most striking characteristic of this subgroup is the presence of anxious depression in conjunction with behavior disorganization typically labeled "schizophrenic." Members are diagnosed about equally often as paranoid and as acute undifferentiated. It seems likely that the type represents the acutely disturbed schizophrenic in an early stage.

IMPS Cross-Cultural Types

The cross-cultural study previously referred to (Lorr & Klett, 1969a) provides further evidence for the patient types identified with the use of the IMPS. The equivalence of the psychotic types established in U.S. data was sought in data obtained from each of the six countries (England, France, Germany, Italy, Japan, and Sweden). The analysis was based on data representing approximately 100 men and 100 women in the age range between 18 and 56.

In order to establish a metric comparable to that used in U.S. studies, each of the syndrome measures was converted into standard score form on the basis of U.S. means and standard deviations. For the typological analysis, unlike factor analysis, cases were first separated by sex and then searched for types country by country. Subgroups determined to be equivalent in the various samples were combined. In all, six male types and seven female types were isolated in at least two samples. The mean standard score profiles of five of the larger subgroups recovered are presented in Table 3. As may be seen from the table, the extent of correspondence between the profiles of

Table 3
Mean Syndrome Standard Scores of Five Psychotic Types
for Cross-Cultural and U.S. Samples

Psychotic Type	SYNDROME									
	EXC	HOS	PAR	GRN	PCP	ANX	RTD	DIS	MTR	CNP
Excited										
CC-Male	1.75	−.51	−.76	.53	−.54	−.92	−1.01	−.27	−.74	−.04
CC-Female	1.41	−.21	−.84	−.16	−.55	−.97	−.95	−.46	−.81	−.04
U.S.-Male	1.29	−.65	−.80	−.32	−.53	−.68	−.48	−.28	−.03	.47
Anxious-Depressed										
CC-Male	−.66	−.79	−.91	−57	−.61	1.26	−.39	−.43	−.67	−.74
CC-Female	−.61	−.94	−.98	−.53	−.58	1.50	−.28	−.48	−.65	−.78
U.S.-Male	−.46	−.63	−.80	−.54	−.43	1.15	−.45	−.45	−.44	−.62
Grandiose Paranoid										
CC-Male	−.61	−.69	.05	1.81	.24	−.76	−.47	−.40	−.56	−.19
CC-Female	.10	−.33	.75	2.77	.96	−.89	−.73	−.45	−.58	−.29
U.S.-Male	.12	−.41	.20	2.02	.51	−.46	−.45	−.14	−.61	−.13
Hallucinated-Paranoid										
CC-Male	−.62	−.46	.98	−.38	1.27	−.58	−.62	−.30	−.72	−.56
CC-Female	−.63	−.33	1.20	−.31	1.10	−.82	−.58	−.39	−.66	−.46
U.S.-Male	−.53	.04	1.24	−.23	1.32	−.05	−.24	.22	−.52	−.12
Retarded-Motor Disturbed										
CC-Male	−.82	−.84	−.72	−.52	−.52	−.83	1.16	.37	.35	−.40
CC-Female	−.87	−.91	−.97	−.50	−.60	−.72	1.38	.11	.24	−.26
U.S.-Male	−.70	−.83	−.68	−.56	−.55	−.30	1.43	.06	.52	−.26

men and women, and of both with the U.S. male profiles, is rather striking. These findings indicate that much the same subgroups will be found in several Western cultures. Since they appear in a variety of cultural settings and possess the requisite objectivity and reliability, these types could provide a sound basis for research on psychopathology.

Correspondence with Standard Diagnosis

The extent of correspondence between American Psychiatric Association diagnostic subtypes and computer-derived subtypes is illustrated by the data in Table 4 taken from a study of acute psychotics. The computer subtypes are listed on the left side of the table. At the top of the table are listed the independently determined standard diagnoses. The Depression category represents all cases diagnosed depressed regardless of subtype. It may be seen that manics are categorized either as Excited or as Excited-Hostile. Those diagnosed depressed are categorized mainly as Anxious-Depressed. The standard paranoid subtype members, however, subdivide into five subgroups: Excited-Hostile, Hostile, Grandiose, Hallucinated, and Anxious-Disorganized. Since the schizophrenic paranoid type is widely acknowledged to be too broad, this differentiation should be helpful.

Table 4
Distribution of Initial Diagnoses of the Nine Patient Male Types

				INITIAL DIAGNOSIS				
Psychotic Type	Manic	Paranoid	Schizo-Affective	Acute Undif-ferentiated	Depression	Simple	Catatonic	Chronic Undif-ferentiated
Excited	4	5	3	2	1	1	0	2
Excited-Hostile	5	26	3	2	1	1	0	1
Hostile Paranoid	0	18	1	1	4	2	0	1
Grandiose Paranoid	1	15	0	1	1	0	1	2
Hallucinated Paranoid	0	7	0	0	0	0	2	0
Anxious-Disorganized	0	8	0	7	1	0	1	2
Anxious-Depressed	1	2	7	6	28	3	1	3
Retarded-Motor Disturbed	0	3	2	11	4	1	4	5
Disoriented	0	1	0	1	0	4	2	2
N	11	85	16	31	40	12	11	18

The remaining schizophrenic subtypes correspond much less closely to the computer subgroups. However, the data indicate clearly that the Schizo-Affective and the Acute Undifferentiated each include two opposed profiles. Both include excited and depressed or retarded cases that might well be separated. The simple schizophrenic tends to be diagnosed as Disoriented or as Anxious-Depressed. The catatonic is typically classed as Retarded-Motor Disturbed. Those classified as Chronic Undifferentiated—a diagnostic waste basket—are distributed almost randomly to the various computer subtypes.

A Typology of Schizophrenia

A typology based on community behavior and assessed by patient relatives has been developed by Katz (Katz et al., 1966; Katz, 1968). Ratings were obtained on the KAS, a schedule that measures 12 scales such as Belligerence, Verbal Expansiveness, Negativism, Helplessness, and Suspiciousness. The sample consisted of 24 acute schizophrenics, selected from a larger number. Each patient was rated prior to his entrance into the hospital by significant relatives. When the correlations among the rating profiles of the 24 cases were factored, six type-factors were identified. The three paranoid subtypes found were: Type I: agitated, hyperactive, belligerent, and well integrated; Type IV: withdrawn, helpless, and suspicious; Type VI: verbally expansive, hyperactive, and bizarre. Other subtypes were: Type II: withdrawn, retarded, and periodically agitated; Type III: helpless, anxious, and nervous; and Type V: hyperactive and helpless. Comparison with available IMPS rating profiles indicated that four of the KAS subtypes received highly similar descriptions on the IMPS. Two of the paranoid subtypes (I and VI) appear to correspond to the IMPS Excited-Hostile and Grandiose Paranoid types. The KAS Type II appears to correspond to the Retarded-Motor Disturbed while KAS Type III is paralleled by IMPS Anxious-Depressed.

The findings suggest that, despite differences in observers (lay people vs. professionals) and differences in statistical procedures (factor analysis vs. typological analysis), there is much the two typologies have in common. For example, it is significant that in both schemes the conventional paranoid category has been subdivided into several subtypes. The results suggest that eventually there will be convergence onto a single set of behavioral types. Interview, ward, and community behavior yield roughly equivalent subgroups.

Treatment Response Types

A third approach to patient classification is to use treatment response as the criterion. The idea is to group patients differentially on the basis of their response to each treatment. For example, patient subgroups that respond differentially to particular drugs may be considered as fundamentally different in kind. Such special-purpose subgroups are particularly useful in decision making.

One should be aware, however, of the limitations of this approach. Each new treatment calls for the collection of more data, for identification of new treatment-response subgroups, and for the further cross-validation of any findings. As one wit has said, this approach implies that it would be important to classify together headaches, rheumatism, and bruises because they all respond to aspirin. In the same way syphilis and meningococcal meningitis would be classed together as responsive to penicillin. An adequate system for classification of the behavior disorders cannot be based solely on patient response to current therapeutic techniques. In general, an adequate system of classification must take into account etiology, processes leading to the disorder, and prognosis. These requirements are of especial importance in any taxonomy for the behavior disorders in which, unlike physical medicine, causal agents have not been established for particular diagnoses. For these reasons a general-purpose typology is far more likely to provide a sound basis for advancing the understanding of abnormal behavior.

The studies to be described were concerned with finding the treatment of choice for a particular patient type. Investigations that sought to identify treatment-response types will be mentioned only incidentally. Overall and Hollister (1966, 1968) have applied several procedures to the problem. One approach involved use of the prototypic stereotypes based on existing diagnostic classes which were described earlier. These investigators found that three major syndrome clusters could account for the differences among the 13 stereotypes of conventional classes; those were paranoid, schizophrenic, and depressive. Overall used data from seven drug groups to evaluate the potential usefulness of the three groups. Patients were assigned on the basis of pretreatment rating profiles to one of the three classes as determined by a similarity index. Significant overall differences between drugs were found. But more importantly, significant interactions between drugs and patient-type were observed for certain pairs of drugs. This means that a specific drug was most effective with a specific type of patient.

Another approach taken by Overall consisted in generating subgroups by application of factor analysis to patient BPRS score profile correlations. Experience in controlled double-blind studies of the anti-depressive drugs had proved disappointing. One explanation was that the patients represented a heterogeneous sample with diverse therapeutic needs. Factor analysis of four sets of correlations among 40 depressed patients resulted in three depressive subtypes (Overall & Hollister, 1966). The three subtypes were characterized as anxious, hostile, and retarded depressives. To study the relative influence of thioridazine hydrochloride and imipramine hydrochloride in 77 depressed cases, each drug was allocated to one of the three depressive subgroups. Significant interactions between patient-type and drug treatment were found. Thioridazine was superior for anxious-tense patients while imipramine was the drug of choice for retarded depression.

Katz (1968) has compared five of his schizophrenic subtypes to determine whether they respond differentially to drugs. In the initial analysis no significant interaction between patient-type and drug was obtained, although the groups did respond differently to the drugs in general. The acute panic state responded best, and the withdrawn, periodically agitated group responded least. In a subsequent cross-check of findings on a new sample, the acute panic type and the expansive paranoid again turned out to be most responsive. In a third comparison Katz compared Type II (withdrawn and periodically agitated) with Type IV (withdrawn, helpless, and suspicious) on changes in the IMPS major disorder syndrome score called Schizophrenic Disorganization. When the two subtypes were compared for response to fluphenazine and thoridazine, a significant interaction between drug and patient-type was obtained. Thus there is evidence that one can predict which kind of patient responds best to which drug.

Inasmuch as our concern here is with psychotic subtypes and not with antipsychotic drugs or treatment response groups, important related studies can only be mentioned. Klett and Moseley (1965), for example, obtained multiple correlations between pretreatment symptoms and outcome as measured by scores on three IMPS major disorders. The regression equations generated in a study of three phenothiazines suggested that the pattern of predictors differed among the drugs. Using regression weights from one sample, they predicted outcome in another sample of patients. They found that for all three outcome measures, the patients who received the drug of choice had better outcomes than patients who did not. Goldberg (1968), using other measures of outcome, also successfully predicted outcome. Improvers on four phenothiozines had different pretreatment patterns.

AN EVALUATION OF APPROACHES

The Psychiatric Conception

The reader who has come this far has probably begun to consider the relative merits of the two approaches to classification of the behavior disorders, one clinical and the other clinical-statistical. The present nomenclature is derived mainly from observations of skilled clinicians in clinical settings and in a sense it has never been rigorously or systematically tested. Although the system has a long history, the diagnostic categories are by no means established. Anyone who will take the trouble to examine successive editions of the official diagnostic manual will note that substantial changes have been made over the years. As one noted scientist has commented, there are really fifty or so psychiatric nomenclatures—one for each nation. No single set of definitions has ever been adopted internationally. To quote Norman Cameron, former American Psychiatric Association president:

It is important for persons working in the abnormal field to realize that the current official psychiatric classifications are not based on final and convincing scientific evidence. They are children of practical necessities. Decisions as to the group in which a given behavior disorder can fall depends upon schemata that actually were adopted both in this country and in Great Britain, by a majority vote of the practicing members of large associations.

Most of the limitations of the conventional diagnostic scheme have already been noted: lack of objectivity in defining terms, absence of procedure for combining signs into a classification decision, and low rater reliability. Also noted were the relative lack of validity for use in such matters as selecting patient treatment or for assessing outcome. To these defects two other difficulties should be added. The first is that the psychiatric categories represent mixtures of social history and current behavior. As a consequence it is difficult to evaluate the separate contributions of each symptom, sign, or life history event to the prediction of some desired outcome. The entire syndrome must be evaluated on an all-or-none basis. If the diagnostic category does represent a disease entity then there is no issue. However, many clinicians and investigators cannot accept this unproved assumption. Treatment of the psychiatric category as an Aristotelian entity or class also prevents the investigator from separating the symptom profile from the social history. Members of two classes quite similar symptomatically may differ in their life history antecedents. For example, involutional melancholia and manic-depression (depressed type) may have identical symptom patterns and yet differ in age and number of illnesses experienced.

There is much evidence that most of the critical variables defining the psychotic categories are not qualitative and discrete, but in fact are continuous in character. Therefore, to assess change resulting from natural causes or treatment, outcome measurement variables ought to be quantitative and continuous. If, for example, anxious depression were a disease entity like pneumonia, it would be either present or absent. But if it is a psychological function, it should vary in degree. Undoubtedly, a major reason why investigators have resorted to rating scales is that they better reflect the continuous variation of the psychotic syndromes.

The Clinical-Statistical Conception

The modern model of the behavior disorders is both dimensional and typological. Since it derives from the application of both clinical observation and multivariate statistics, it may be called a clinical-statistical model. The object is to build a structure that will usefully represent psychopathology. The dimensional schemata will be examined first. An important characteristic of the model is that all patients are systematically assessed on all syndromes. Conventional procedures are unsystematic in that each patient is processed in a slightly different way and with respect to differing sets of variables. Some areas are examined in detail while others, possible of importance, are neglected or overlooked. The dimensional approach offers an objectively defined minimal set of descriptors that represent most of the measurement space. The

MAURICE LORR

various syndromes included are relatively independent and non-overlapping. Furthermore, since life history events are excluded from the framework, there is no confounding of data sources. By separating life history variables such as type of onset, number of prior illnesses, and premorbid characteristics from current behavior and symptomotology, it is possible to evaluate the independent contribution of each variable to any outcome to be predicted.

Let us now examine the typological conceptions proposed. It has been argued that typologies are unnecessary when measurement data are available. When persons are grouped into subsets, information is lost, and therefore direct measurements lead to more efficient predictions and decisions. If this argument is sound, then it is first necessary to indicate what purposes typologies serve before contrasting the new and the old typologies.

A type may be defined as a subgroup of persons who are distinguished by possession of a common set of characteristics that set members apart from other classes. As everyone knows, types facilitate communication. The unique pattern of attributes defining a type facilitate their recognition and their differentiation from nonmembers in a given domain. To label a person a depressive, for example, is to suggest immediately a broad pattern of traits and expected behaviors. The expectation is that the depressive will be dejected in mood, self-reproachful in attitude, and will be a good candidate for certain tranquilizers.

Knowledge that types or subgroups exist is important in and of itself and reflects an increased understanding of a domain. The presence of naturally occurring subgroups within a larger sample implies that there are multiple modes in the data even when the data appear to be essentially continuous. Knowledge of types can facilitate the discovery of laws unobservable or obscured within mixed samples. The study of antecedents, structure, and processes is advanced once subgroups have been identified. As reported earlier, the effects of drug treatment can be determined more meaningfully by relating them to patient type.

Information relative to type membership may increase the accuracy of prediction to external criteria. Improvement in predictive accuracy takes place through the operation of interactions and higher order dependencies among predictor variables. Interactive joint effects are ordinarily ignored in multiple linear regression. Another basis for enhanced ability to predict is that members of a type are more homogeneous in score profile than people in general. Thus there is the likelihood that type members will also be more homogeneous as to criterion-relevant behavior than a mixed sample.

What then are the advantages of some of the proposed typological schemes over those provided in the standard nomenclature? For one, they now have a more objective and systematic basis in computerized typological procedure. Typology has long been in disrepute among scientists; types were usually generated by novelists, clinicians, and philosophers. The main reason for this status was that in the absence of a methodology for searching data and finding types, those generated lacked an empirical basis. During the past fifteen years a wide variety of typological techniques have been proposed and developed. The nature and role of similarity indices is now better understood.

Finally, modern computers make it feasible to search large blocks of data for homogeneous subgroups. For these reasons it is now possible to explore data systematically and to replicate findings in known samples of patients using objective typological procedures. To support the multivariate approach to typology does not mean that conventional psychotic typology is or should be discarded. The newer procedures merely make it feasible to test out the clinically derived classes. It seems likely that many will be confirmed, others will be split into smaller subgroups, and still others combined.

CHAPTER XI

Current status of the Thematic Apperception Test

Duane L. Varble

Introduced in 1935 by Christina D. Morgan and Henry A. Murray, the Thematic Apperception Test (TAT) is one of the earliest projective tests still being used today. Like most of the projective instruments, the TAT began as a clinical instrument (Murray, 1938). Unlike most other projectives, however, the TAT also has an important separate history as a nonclinical research instrument (e.g., McClelland, Atkinson, Clark, & Lowell, 1953; Atkinson, 1958; Atkinson & Feather, 1966; Heckhausen, 1967). The work of McClelland and associates on achievement and related motives has provided a great deal of information about the empirical parameters of the TAT. Interestingly, however, this work has had virtually no impact on the clinical use of the TAT.

While perhaps not as popular as formerly, the TAT remains a major instrument in the clinical armamentarium. In a recent survey, McCully (1965) found that 71 percent of the directors of American Psychological Association—approved internship centers who responded to his questionnaire felt the thematic techniques to be very important to the practicing clinician. This percentage dropped to 46 percent when clinical faculty members of psychology departments with APA-approved clinical psychology programs were sampled (Thelen, Varble, & Johnson, 1968). However, less than 10 percent of these faculty members felt the thematic techniques were of little or no importance, and more specifically, 71 percent expressed the attitude that the TAT should be required in the curriculum of doctoral candidates in clinical psychology. While this latter point speaks well for the TAT, it should be noted that a conclusion of the survey by Thelen et al. was that many academic clinicians, particularly the younger faculty members, see projective techniques in general as declining in importance and not firmly supported by research.

The purpose of the present chapter is to assess the current status of the TAT. This will be accomplished by reviewing the literature deemed most appropriate for determining the status of the TAT with the *current* aspect of the title emphasized. Most of the studies covered in this chapter were published after 1962. There are several reviews of the TAT literature up to 1962, of which two—those by Murstein (1963) and Harrison (1965)—are outstanding. Even the literature of the TAT since 1962 is too extensive for this chapter to include a comprehensive review. Again, the concentration of effort has been on studies which would help in determining the current status of the test.

An assumption in writing this chapter has been that the reader will already have some familiarity with the theory behind the TAT and will have some knowledge of its properties and interpretation. These aspects of the test will be covered in only a limited fashion in the chapter. The reader who does not have this familiarity with the TAT would be well advised to read Murstein (1965a) or Megargee (1966).

The chapter will review some of the more recent books and viewpoints briefly. It will then consider the current status of the reliability and validity of the TAT, including a selective review of the major areas of current research. These areas are hostility or aggression, achievement, affiliation and power, and those factors which affect the use of the TAT to measure drive states. The chapter will end with an evaluation of the TAT as a clinical instrument and as a research tool.

IMPORTANT THEORETICAL AND EMPIRICAL WORKS

Perhaps the most important book on the TAT in the past decade is that by Murstein (1963). This is a thoroughly readable and quite comprehensive look at the theoretical and research aspects of the TAT, with important ramifications for other projective techniques. Murstein covers in synopsis form the most widely accepted theories of projective techniques. He also summarizes each of the more comprehensive methods of interpretation or analysis for the TAT, dividing them into quantitative and nonquantitative groups. Murstein places the systems of Dana (1959), Eron (1950), McClelland et al. (1953), and Pine (1960) in the quantitative category in that each has a specified method for deriving numerical scores. The nonquantitative category consists of the systems of Bellak (1954), Henry (1956), and Piotrowski (1950). Murstein's work does not cover all of the TAT interpretative systems. Perhaps the most serious omission is that of Arnold (1962). The heart of this system is sequence analysis of content, but there is a method for obtaining a numerical "motivation index" which would place the system within the quantitative category in Murstein's classification.

In his book Murstein also has an easy-to-understand chapter on reliability. He starts by noting the peculiar problems involved in assessing the reliability of projective techniques, covers some of the TAT empirical studies of reliability, and finishes by suggesting remedies for the problems raised. The section of the book on validity is equally good, with the material being covered in a scholarly yet easy-to-follow fashion.

Another book which has undoubtedly had, and will continue to have, an important impact—at least on researchers using the TAT—is the volume by Zubin, Eron, and Schumer (1965) entitled *An experimental approach to projective techniques*. This book, while not restricted to the TAT, has several chapters devoted to it as a framework for discussing other projective techniques. The authors state frankly in the preface that the purpose of the book is to return projective techniques to the scientific fold. Some clinicians may see in this statement the implication that projectives used in a non-research fashion are unrespectable. However, this is not the intention of the authors. Rather, their intention is to discuss and evaluate the theory, research, and problems of projectives in a critical objective manner so that clinicians and researchers alike may evaluate the ways in which they use the different projective techniques. The book carries out this intention admirably well. The section on the TAT is recommended reading for anyone intending to use this instrument in either a clinical or research setting.

There are a number of additional edited books, or books with chapters in which theoretical and research aspects of the TAT are covered more or less comprehensively. Perhaps the most directly relevant is an edited book by Kagan and Lesser (1961), which is actually the report of a symposium dealing exclusively with various aspects of the TAT. All sixteen psychologists involved have made substantial contributions to the TAT literature, and their contributions to the symposium have frequently been quoted individually in later research literature.

Another edited book, Murstein's (1965a) *Handbook of projective techniques,* is also relevant. The section on the TAT consists of the republication of articles considered by the editor as being of primary importance for understanding this instrument. In this situation, of course, another editor might well have chosen a different set of studies for inclusion in the book. In fact, Megargee (1966) did elect to present a somewhat different emphasis and therefore selected different articles for inclusion in his *Research in clinical assessment.* However, in terms of providing an individual unacquainted with the TAT with an overview of the technique, either Murstein's or Megargee's choices have much to commend them.

From the standpoint of overall coverage of the TAT, the most comprehensive chapter is that by Harrison (1965) in the *Handbook of clinical psychology.* Harrison covers not only the theory, research, and problems of the TAT, but also discusses applications of the technique in both applied and research settings. Though he strives to remain objective in his coverage of the TAT, he is unable to suppress his positive bias toward the technique. His chapter presents one of the most complete surveys of the research literature on the TAT up to and including 1962.

In a recent book, Suinn and Oskomp (1969) have reviewed a large number of research studies using projective techniques. There is a relatively short section in which the TAT is the focus. The authors' approach is to present and evaluate relevant research studies under such headings as "the relation of thematic material to personality" and "the relation of thematic material to psychotherapy." The idea of summarizing in review form some of the better research studies is a good one. Unfortunately, in the section on the TAT, the studies reviewed are not very current and the coverage is not very complete.

Almost all of the books on psychological assessment or personality measurement have at least one chapter devoted to the TAT. An example is the explanation of the TAT in rather simplified terms presented by Kleinmuntz (1967) in his book on personality measurement.

There are a number of books and chapters which are less concerned with the theory and research of the TAT and more concerned with its clinical uses. Some of these were mentioned earlier (Henry, 1956; Arnold, 1962; Pine, 1960). Each of these authors has his own approach to using the TAT.

A good description of the clinical use of the TAT as a broadband instrument is presented by Rosenwald (1968). The TAT is seen as being especially useful as a clinical technique, and Rosenwald sets forth case material to demonstrate the utility of the instrument. This approach is informative, but Rosenwald's interpretation of the use of the TAT seems unduly restrictive.

Harrower (1968) is another clinician who has used the TAT extensively. Her approach is a structured one in which the TAT is usually seen as being a part of an overall system of psychological evaluation.

The TAT is used widely for both research and clinical purposes in all the English-speaking countries as well as in Japan, India, and Sweden—to name but a few of the other countries where the TAT is being utilized. Lindzey (1961) has summarized the use of projectives in cross-cultural research. He feels that projectives have a combination of advantages and problems, but that the former are more important than the latter in cross-cultural usage of such instruments as the TAT.

A good example of cross-cultural research using the TAT is the study reported by DeRidder (1961). DeRidder used the TAT to check hypotheses concerning the personality of the urban Africans in South Africa. The study has several methodological weaknesses, with the major question involving inadequate control groups. But the study is rather complete and certainly has some useful information about the personality of the urban South African.

A NOTE ON SCORING SYSTEMS

None of the scoring systems will be discussed individually in this chapter. However, they are too important to ignore completely and a general comment is appropriate. Unlike the Rorschach, the TAT is still a very individualized technique. To quote Murstein (1963), "there would seem to be as many thematic scoring systems as there were hairs in the beard of Rasputin [p. 23]." Murstein suggests several reasons for this multitude of interpretive methods. These include Murray's lack of detailed scoring instructions and the nontechnical nature of the TAT. However, for most clinicians who find themselves with a surplus of patients, the major deterrent for utilizing any of the formal interpretive systems is simply that these require too much time. In addition, many who use the TAT, particularly in research, are interested in specific needs, presses, and other aspects of the personality. The content orientation of the TAT makes the construction of special systems to assess these appear easy, e.g., systems to assess amount and kinds of aggression, achievement, and affiliation.

In earlier years there were several attempts to formulate comprehensive scoring systems for the TAT. None of these systems has received any long-lasting support, and there have been no recent approaches to comprehensive scoring.

RELIABILITY

Some three and a half decades after the TAT's introduction, reliability is still largely an unsolved problem. For some clinicians the concept of reliability is meaningless when applied to projective techniques. For them the TAT is a technique and not a test. As a technique the TAT may have value for the individual clinician and the individual subject, but only with difficulty, if at all, can it be assessed objectively (Murstein, 1968a).

Projective tests, including the TAT, have special reliability problems. Reliability estimates for objective personality inventories, such as the Minnesota Multiphasic Personality Inventory (MMPI), are primarily concerned with random error. Such tests may use any of the conventional methods of obtaining reliability estimates, e.g., split-half, parallel forms, or test-retest. However, none of these conventional methods is especially appropriate for estimating the reliability of the TAT. Since each of the TAT cards is more or less unique in terms of central and peripheral figures and backgrounds, neither the split-half nor parallel forms approaches is adequate. Test-retest reliability estimates are also of questionable worth. If the retest is done after a considerable time interval, the psychological state of the subject is likely to have changed, and what comes out in the form of stories should reflect these changes without being considered unreliable (Harrison, 1965). However, Kleinmuntz (1967) has made the reasonable suggestion that there should be less divergence in scores made by one individual in successive protocols collected over a period of time than in scores of different individuals. The problem is one of requiring a test to be sensitive to changes over time and yet reflect stable and enduring characteristics. Further, Murstein (1968a) has pointed out that test-retest reliability may suffer because the subject looking at a card may focus on one aspect of the stimulus at one time and another part of the same card on another occasion without the change in focus being necessarily due to a clearly understood aspect of his personality e.g., creative challenge, novelty seeking, and the like.

Murstein (1963) has suggested that a standardized procedure for administering, scoring, and interpreting the TAT would improve the test's reliability and validity considerably. With a few exceptions this suggestion has not been carried out to date, and in view of the TAT's appeal as an individualized instrument, it seems highly unlikely that any standardized approach will be generally adopted. Thus, in addition to the problems of reliability outlined above, the TAT has the added problems of different cards being used in different studies, with different instructions and different scoring systems.

The major exception to the unstandardized orientation to the TAT is McClelland and Atkinson's highly structured use of the TAT to study motives. This approach, which will be discussed in more detail in the next section, is the only system which has attained a consistently high level of one form of reliability—in this case, interscorer reliability. By providing a detailed manual of scoring instructions, this approach has enabled coders to obtain reliability coefficients which approach or surpass .90 (McClelland, Clark, Roby, &

Atkinson, 1949; Kagan & Moss, 1959). It should be noted, however, that this is interscorer reliability or agreement between scorers (which in a true-false type inventory would be 1.00) and not test reliability as such.

VALIDITY

The first question is, validity for what? A review of the literature indicates that the question of the TAT's validity has received very little direct attention during the last decade. At the same time the TAT has been used to study a wide diversity of topics. In a very real sense, each of these studies could be considered as having a bearing on the test's validity. To review all this material in the limited time and space available would be impossible. However, a sampling of typical validity studies will be presented. This will be followed by a summary of some of the current major areas of research involving the TAT.

Typical Validity Studies

When the question of TAT validity comes up, the authors of various texts and chapters frequently go back to the very early studies (e.g., Harrison, 1940a, 1940b; and Eron, 1950) to support or refute the test's value. There are a number of more recent reports that can be used, however. Since there are studies available which support the validity of the TAT and studies which question the test's validity, it would be easy to defend either position by selective review of the research. A more appropriate approach is to examine some studies supporting each view.

Supportive Studies

The TAT is not generally considered very well-suited or useful for differential diagnosis. In recent years there has been much questioning of the value of the traditional psychiatric diagnostic classification system itself. In spite of these facts, the TAT is frequently used in the clinician's battery of tests for the psychologist's contribution to differential diagnosis. One of the few recent reports supporting the TAT's power to successfully distinguish between normal and abnormal groups are two studies reported by Lindzey (1965). In these studies TAT protocols from homosexual and normal college subjects and from homosexual and normal prisoners were analyzed using clinical vs. actuarial methods. In both of these studies the clinicians were more successful in predicting criterion than the objective indexes were. In one study (college students) a psychologist using the method of blind analysis of TAT protocols was able to distinguish between homosexuals and heterosexuals with 95 percent accuracy.

The prediction of personality variables is another area in which the TAT is heavily relied upon. A supportive study in this area is reported by Henry and Farley (1959). Blind interpretations of TAT protocols of 36 normal adolescents were systematically compared, by an elaborate triad matching technique, with similarly blindly-derived summaries of selected criterion data (objective test scores, summaries of observations and interviews, and Rorschach interpretations). An analysis of variance showed that the nine experienced psychologists who acted as judges had little individual item agreement among themselves, but that each judge made enough correct matches to criterion to yield highly significant results at all levels. The authors conclude that the TAT, when handled properly, is a valid predictor of personality variables, at least in an adolescent population.

Nonsupportive Studies

Unfortunately, each of the above two studies which support the validity of the TAT can be matched by studies whose results shed grave doubts on the TAT as a valid instrument.

In the area of differential diagnoses a study by Little and Shneidman (1959) is particularly damaging to the reputation of the TAT. The subjects in this investigation consisted of three normals, three neurotics, three individuals with psychosomatic disorders, and three hospitalized psychotics. The design was somewhat complicated, but essentially consisted of an attempt by twelve specialists for each of four tests (TAT, Make a Picture Story, Rorschach, MMPI) to match the judgments of a group of criterion judges who had interviewed the subjects extensively. There was little agreement between the test judges and the criterion judges. The normal subjects, in particular, were often misclassified by the test judges. Worst of all, those judges using the TAT consistently misclassified the normal subjects as seriously disturbed. Of all the tests used, the TAT had the lowest reliability, the poorest predictive ability, and fared the worst in general.

In the area of personality variable prediction the TAT, as well as other tests, had a poor showing in a study by Horowitz (1962). In this study experienced clinicians and naive introductory psychology students predicted personality dimensions of individuals in psychotherapy. The predictions were made as various kinds of information were systematically increased in steps, i.e., various test results and such specific items of biographical information as age, sex, marital status, occupation, and education. The TAT contributed little to the accuracy of the predictions. The correlations between the predictions and the therapists' criterion descriptions were low. As a matter of fact, the clinicians would have fared better if they had not consulted the test results at all but simply made their predictions on what they believed to be an average patient in that clinic (e.g., base rate description).

It hardly needs to be pointed out that none of the above studies is flawless in design, and supporters and critics alike have plausible explanations for the results of each study. For example, Murstein (1963) suggests that the positive results obtained by Henry and Farley (1959) are most likely due to the fact that the TAT judges and criterion judges were familiar with each other and shared a common theoretical orientation. Certainly, this is a valid point. Judges predicting behavior rather than predicting the judgments of other judges would be much more impressive.

If nothing else, the four studies reviewed illustrate the truth of that old saying concerning statistics, which roughly paraphrased states: tell me what you want to believe and I'll find evidence to support it! This must explain how Jensen (1959) could review the TAT research and conclude that "the validity of the TAT is practically nil [p. 313]," while Harrison (1965) summarized TAT validity by saying, "There is impressive evidence that the technique possesses intrinsic validity [p. 597]." Murstein's (1963) contention that increasing reliability is the first step toward increasing validity is difficult to dispute. The same may be said for his (Murstein, 1968a) idea that as a test the TAT must establish better statistical validity, while as a technique it must meet the difficult criterion of efficient usefulness. The researches which are reviewed in the section to follow are indirect reflections of the TAT's validity primarily as a test and secondarily as a technique.

MAJOR AREAS OF RESEARCH

Hostility

The area of hostility and aggression has been a popular one in terms of researchers' utilizing the TAT. In addition to the intrinsic interest in aggression as a human phenomenon, the TAT has been viewed as being a natural method for assessing the important relationship between aggression in fantasy, or stories, and aggression in reality. This in turn has been a sub-issue in the whole problem of predicting overt behavior from fantasies. With regard to hostility, a large number of studies, based upon varying assumptions, using different cards and predicting different outcomes, have been conducted. Most of these studies have been reviewed by Buss (1961), Murstein (1963), and Zubin et al. (1965). As might be expected, the results of these studies are inconsistent. Even the conclusions of the reviewers are somewhat in disagreement. For example, on the relationship between overt aggression and thematic aggression to cards of varying degrees of stimulus relevance, Murstein (1963) concluded that "cards with low or medium stimulus pull for hostility tend to differentiate persons high and low on overt aggression more readily than highly hostile cards [p. 319]," whereas Buss (1961) concluded in his review that "unambiguous pictures are the best stimuli for yielding indicants of behavioral aggression [p. 154]." These examples afford a good illustration of the complexity of measurement problems in this area. In this particular controversy, James and Mosher (1967) have pointed out that in Kagan's (1956, 1959) research, used by Buss (1961) to reach his conclusion, the unambiguous cards tended toward the medium ambiguous range of Murstein's standards. Thus, a major difference between the studies was in differences of definitions of ambiguity of the cards used. (The problem of card ambiguity will be discussed later.)

There have been a number of attempts to clarify the relationship between fantasy and overt aggression. Murstein (1965b) tried with limited success to differentiate the effects of card stimulus, background factors, and personality variables on projection of hostility in the TAT. Megargee and Cook (1967) compared TAT and Holtzman inkblot scales with varied criteria of overt aggression in a juvenile delinquent population. They found quite different patterns depending on the criteria and scales used. James and Mosher (1967), using only thematic stimuli, found thematic aggression in response to high-pull cards to be related significantly to physically aggressive behavior, but that thematic aggression in response to low-pull cards was not related to fighting behavior in a boy scout population.

Coleman (1967) used the TAT, the Rosenweig Picture-Frustration test, and the Rorschach to predict overt aggression in a normal population of 10-year-old and 13-year-old English school boys and found that only the Rorschach and card 18BM of the TAT had a direct relation to overt aggressive behavior. He interpreted his results to support the assumption that the nature of the stimuli affect the relation between fantasy and behavior. However, the fact that the Rorschach is very unstructured and card 18BM very structured toward aggression makes his results appear contradictory. He handles this contradiction by assuming that the unstructured nature of the Rorschach allows freedom to respond aggressively, and the aggressive stimulus pull of card 18BM inhibits behaviorally nonaggressive children from responding with aggressive fantasy. This is a plausible but complicated explanation, and it leaves unexplained the lack of power of differentiation of the less structured TAT cards.

Another interesting relationship between overt hostility and fantasy hostility concerns the cathartic effect of expression of aggression in fantasy in the reduction of overt aggressive drive. Pytkowicz, Wagner, and Sarason (1967) found that for some male subjects (daydreamers), TAT stories served to reduce hostility toward the examiner. Reversing this idea somewhat, Shalit (1970) investigated the question of whether the hostile content in fantasy is reduced by vicarious participation in overt hostility in a field study. New national service recruits in Israel were tested first in 1966, a year before the Arab-Israel Six-Day War, then in 1967 immediately following the war, and finally in 1968, a year after the war. All indexes of fantasy hostility were significantly lower in 1967 than in either the previous or following year. Shalit concludes the reduction of hostile content of fantasy may have occurred as a result of vicarious participation in the hostility. However, this conclusion must be regarded as tenuous because of the large number of uncontrolled variables involved.

Perhaps the most fitting way to end this section on hostility and aggression is by discussing one of the best-designed and most complete studies for determining the causes of the manifestation of hostility in TAT stories. Murstein (1968b) used a field-interaction method involving the independent variables of the stimulus (three levels of scaled pictorial hostility), background ("impersonal" or "look your best" instructions), and personality (peer and self-concept evaluation as hostile or friendly). Nine different scoring systems of hostility were examined by use of an analysis of variance design. When the results were analyzed, the stimulus proved to be the most powerful determinant of TAT hostility. That is, the difference between cards of high aggressive pull and cards of low aggressive pull accounted for the major portion of variance among the variables. Additionally, the self-concept was found to be considerably more important than the objective possession of hostility. Finally, little difference in importance was found for seven of the nine scoring systems used. Murstein's method and statistical design is a distinct improvement over most other research studies in this area and should be considered a model.

Achievement, Affiliation, and Power

The assessment of motives is one of the tasks for which the TAT has been used most extensively. The pioneering work of McClelland, Atkinson, and their associates has been particularly important in this area and has involved the development of a general theory of motivation. McClelland et al. (1953) assume that TAT pictures arouse motives in much the same manner as do the cues in real life situations and that these motives are based on the subject's past experiences. The critical aspect of the assumption is that if achievement, for example, is present in the thematic story, then one may safely conclude that the subject is actually motivated to achieve, rather than simply to engage in wish-fulfilling fantasy.

The achievement motive (n Ach) is by far the most studied of the needs in the McClelland-Atkinson system, although there are also scoring systems for affiliation (n Aff) and power (n $Power$). A sampling of some of the more recent research in these areas will now be presented.

Veroff, Atkinson, Feld, and Gurin (1960), in a nationwide survey of 1,619 adults using thematic apperception methods to assess motivation, found n Ach to increase as a function of education for both men and women. Moss and Kagan (1961) examined the behavior ratings and TAT protocols of adult men and women who had participated in a longitudinal research program; they found significant correlations between adult thematic n Ach and ratings of achievement from interviews. On the negative side, Cole, Jacobs, Zubok, Fagot, and Hunter (1962) compared honor students, assumed to represent high n Ach, and a control group; the four-card McClelland test indicated no significant differences with the women but a significant difference for men, with the control group showing higher n Ach—a result contrary to the prediction. Broverman, Jordan, and Phillips (1960) studied 37 members of a church who filled out a questionnaire supposedly tapping achievement motivation through striving for job level advancement; they found a clear relationship between striving and imagery, but it was the opposite of the expected direction, with the most active strivers showing the least achievement imagery.

Atkinson (1958, 1964; Atkinson & Feather, 1966) has elaborated on McClelland's theory by including the subject's expectation of success and/or failure as a factor influencing his disposition to act. A number of experiments (e.g., Atkinson, Bastian, Earl, & Litwin, 1960; Meyer, Walker, & Litwin, 1961) tend to support Atkinson's theory. Thus, when the motive to achieve success is stronger than the motive to avoid failure, the individual tends to seek out tasks in which the probability of success more closely approximates .50 than is the case for a less achievement-oriented group. When the motive to avoid failure is stronger, the individual avoids tasks of intermediate difficulty in which the arousal of anxiety concerning failure is greatest.

In contrast to these supportive studies, a number of explicit tests of Atkinson's assumptions have failed to support his theory (Murstein & Collier, 1962; Easter & Murstein, 1964; Murstein, 1963). Heckhausen (1967) surveys much of the research on achievement conducted both in this country and in Europe. The interested reader should consult his book, especially for cross-cultural studies.

The McClelland-Atkinson approach to the study of achievement has been criticized by several workers, including Murstein (1963b) and Harrison (1965). The most frequent criticism is that the McClelland et al. version of n Ach is over-simplified. For example, Feshback (1961) criticized the McClelland approach for failing to distinguish between the intensity of the drive and characteristic ways of coping with the drive. Similarly, Lazarus (1961) has questioned the assumption that achievement motivation expressed in TAT stories will also show up in overt behavior; instead of this direct relationship between fantasy and behavior, he has postulated that fantasy frequently functions as a substitute for behavior.

Skolnick (1966) investigated the question of a direct vs. a substitutive relation between fantasy and behavior in a longitudinal study of 44 men and 47 women with data collected over a period of 20 years. She correlated adolescent and adult TAT scores on Achievement, Affiliation, Power, and Aggression with behavioral measures made at corresponding times. The result was an impressive matrix of correlations, which, however, was inconclusive as far as definitive relationships were concerned. Skolnick suggested that the direct relationship between fantasy and behavior received more support than the inverse or substitutive relationship. However, there were enough shortcomings in the method and results of this study to make it possible for both McClelland (1966) and Lazarus (1966) to draw their own conclusions about the meaning of Skolnick's work.

Current research on achievement-related motives is becoming more sophisticated and complex. Raynor (1969, 1970) has elaborated on Atkinson's model of the effects of immediately expected success and failure on achievement by including also the effects of expected future outcomes on the strength of motivation. Raynor (1970) predicted and found in two studies that students high in n Ach and low in anxiety received higher grades when they conceived a good grade in a particular college course to be related to their own future career than when they did not see the course as important. Also, the difference in grades between those high in perceived importance of the course and those low in this respect was larger for the high n Ach-low test anxiety group than for the low n Ach-high test anxiety group. Although this study has the usual problems of self-report measures and a restricted population, it is certainly a step in the direction of more meaningful research on achievement.

Finally, there are a large number of individual difference variables which appear to influence the results of studies of motives, e.g., differences between men and women (Lesser, Krawitz, & Packard, 1963). Some of these variables are discussed later in this chapter in the section on subject condition as related to TAT performance. However, one problem which should be mentioned here is the criticism of the usual McClelland-Atkinson method of scoring. This method derives a motive score for, say, achievement, by summing all motive cues across all stories written by a subject, i.e., by the use of the frequency approach. Zubin et al. (1965) and Murstein (1963), among others, have criticized this method because it does not differentiate between negative and positive scores in arriving at a motive score for that person. Until recently no one had derived a better method. However, Terhune (1969) found that the standard scoring methods for assessing n Ach, n Aff, and n Power produced skewed and bimodal score distributions. He made an analysis of the relationships of scores for individual stories to the total motive score. The results suggested that scores on individual stories reflect motive intensity for n Ach; but for n Aff and n Power, high and low scores seem to indicate merely presence or absence of the motives. Terhune concluded that TAT-derived motive scores are best obtained by simply counting stories exhibiting a given motive, rather than by summing the number of motive cues across all stories written by a subject. It will be interesting to see if this simplified scoring method will be as useful as the standard method used by McClelland and Atkinson.

Unusual Uses and Approaches
Of the hundreds of published research studies available, only a limited number can be specifically discussed in the present chapter. The studies now to be noted will illustrate several of the varied ways in which the TAT has recently been employed.

Wohlford and Herrera (1970) were interested in extensions of personal time variables including retrotension (past) and protension (future) using Cuban and American children as subjects. Four independent variables were tested simultaneously: stimulus cue, nationality, sex, and grade in school. Using a scoring system developed by Wohlford (1968) the TAT stories were rated for specific instances of extensions of personal time. The stimulus cue, which was a male or a female figure, had the most powerful main effect on one extension variable—cognitive protension. That is, the variation of the card cues had the most effect on determining future orientation in the stories. The other variables had mixed effects, however. One of the interesting findings was that the Cuban children had significantly shorter personal time extensions of all types than the American children.

Another interesting use of the TAT involves the use of conjoint or family stories, i.e., stories made up by both marriage partners, or all the members of a family. This approach has been used most frequently by Winter and his associates (Winter, Ferreira, & Olson, 1965, 1966; Winter & Ferreira, 1969, 1970). In their most recent study, 22 families with normal children and 33 with abnormal children were asked to make up conjoint TAT stories and were also tested by the technique of "unrevealed differences" (Ferreira & Winter, 1965). A factor analysis of the material resulted in the emergence of seven factors described by the investigators as: (1) middle-class good adjustment, (2) fast performance, (3) sullen silence, (4) lack of task orientation, (5) inefficient communication, (6) hostile interaction, and (7) dependency. If these results hold up after cross-validation, the authors plan to use these seven factors to form the basis for a more meaningful system for classifying families. Their intention is to avoid such gross classification as normal and abnormal, and to develop a system less determined by psychiatric diagnostic considerations.

Winget, Gleser, and Clements (1969), using a similar approach, found that the TAT could differentiate between poorly-adjusted married couples and well-adjusted couples when conjoint TAT stories were used for data.

Brender and Kramer (1967) were interested in combining an old idea, the relationship between TAT stories and dreams, with some newer technology, a sleep lab. In this study the TAT stories of 13 subjects were compared with the dreams of the same subjects. The TAT stories were collected first, and then the subjects participated in a sleep study. When it was established that they were dreaming, they were awakened and asked to report their dreams. Both the dreams and the TAT responses were scored by a form of Murray's need-press system. Data analysis indicated that the dreams and the TAT stories tended to show some of the same needs for each subject, but that other needs were expressed only on one of the two forms. Affiliation and play were both significantly positively correlated in their appearance in both dreams and TAT stories. Dominance showed a significant negative correlation.

These studies are only a few examples of the many atypical ways in which the TAT is used. The flexibility of the TAT is one of the reasons it has been so popular. This same flexibility is also one of the reasons that there are problems in establishing standards of reliability and validity for the test.

FACTORS AFFECTING PERFORMANCE ON THE TAT

Card Cue Values

When the TAT is used in research, it is desirable to know the cue value of a particular picture across a number of subject populations. This information makes it possible to separate the general effects of the card from the specific scorable content obtained in the stories. Information on card cue value is an essential requirement for measuring the strengths of various needs (Dana, 1968).

There is no standardized method for determining the cue value of any given card across needs or populations. This lack of standardization is primarily the result of the custom-made nature of many studies utilizing the TAT. In studies of hostility or aggression, for example, most researchers decide for themselves which cards will be differentiating in terms of measuring hostility (Breger, 1963; Nelson & Epstein, 1962; Pytkowicz et al., 1967; Saltz & Epstein, 1963; Schaefer & Norman, 1967). Murstein is one of the few to consistently employ cards systematically scaled for hostility (Murstein, David, Fisher, & Furth, 1961; Murstein, 1965c; Murstein, 1968b). Even here, the known cue value of the cards is restricted by Murstein's use of a college population.

The situation is similar for studies of achievement, except that for males there are agreed-upon criteria for achievement cards of high and low cue value (Haber & Alpert, 1958). Recent research has indicated that cue content for achievement also interacts with extraneous variables such as occupation (Veroff, Feld, & Crockett, 1966) and race (Cowan & Goldberg, 1967).

One of the most researched topics relative to card cue or stimulus value concerns the question of TAT card ambiguity. Level of ambiguity of the TAT cards has been considered of importance for some time. Frank (1939) contended that the greater the ambiguity the more significant the personality material elicited by the projective instruments. This was also a common assumption of early workers who used the TAT. This assumption has recently been questioned (cf. Murstein, 1965b; Kaplan, 1967), and there is now even the suggestion that the lack of ambiguity may often be a prerequisite for personality assessment (Epstein, 1966).

There are two different approaches to the measurement of ambiguity in the TAT. The first method consists of having subjects make value judgments about the stimulus value of the pictures (Jacobs, 1958), and the second involves examining the actual responses of some reference group (Murstein, 1964). In line with this second method of measurement, Murstein (1963) has provided a workable definition of ambiguity as referring to uncertainity of meaning attributed to a given card. Thus, measurement of the degree of uncertainty is most appropriate in terms of alternative responses to the stimulus rather than in terms of judgment of the stimulus properties of the picture.

However, even though there is now general agreement that the uncertainty of responses is the critical factor in ambiguity, there is still controversy over how this uncertainty should be measured. Murstein (1964) asked subjects to respond to the TAT by means of a structured story sheet on which they reported who was in the picture, what was going on, why this was happening, and how the story would end. He then categorized the responses within the four variables of "who," "what," "why," and "end," and computed ambiguity values by means of a formula developed by Kenny (1961). By means of this method Murstein was able to develop norms for the ambiguity of different TAT cards.

Kaplan (1969a, 1970) questioned Murstein's (1964) use of only one response per subject to each stimulus, feeling that intrasubject variability was neglected and reliability of the ambiguity estimate restricted. To overcome these problems Kaplan had subjects respond with a number of stories to each of 10 TAT cards. These responses were then scored for themes according to Eron's (1950) Checklist. For each subject a list of themes emitted in response to a given card, in the ordinal position in which it was emitted, was used. Indices of the relative strength of occurrence of a given theme for a given card were obtained by use of a special formula (Kaplan, 1969a, p. 26). Kaplan found little agreement between his estimates of ambiguity and those of Murstein. The controversy has continued as Murstein (1969) answers Kaplan, and Kaplan (1969b) retorts. However, the essential point both authors make is that ambiguity of the TAT is an important consideration in its future use, and Murstein (1969) has promised to publish full normative listings in the near future.

Subject Variables

Two major classes of subject variables or conditions which affect performance on the TAT have been identified by Dana (1968). The first class contains those continuous, relatively permanent variables such as race, religion, social class, education, intelligence, and values. The second class, which is made up of more transitory states, influences the expressed needs in stories by inhibition or suppression. Included in this class are anxiety, conflicts, defensiveness, feelings of guilt, and self-esteem needs. These variables are also considered as a separate class from those deliberately aroused states that are manipulated in order to show the existence of a need (e.g., Lesser et al., 1963, deliberately aroused achievement motivation in adolescent girls).

Among the first class of variables, Veroff et al. (1960), in a nationwide sample of both sexes, demonstrated the contributions of age, education, father's income, occupation, and race to scores on *n Ach, n Aff,* and *n Power.* Rosen (1961) has also shown the effects of social class, family size, birth order, and age on *n Ach.* Other variables of this type which affect *n Ach* are geographic region and neighborhood experience (Nuttall, 1964) and religion (Veroff, Feld, & Gurin, 1962). Much of the research concerning the second class of subject conditions has been performed in the context of Atkinson's conception of the effect of the fear of failure on *n Ach* (Atkinson & Litwin, 1960; Alpert & Haber, 1960). Sampson (1963) has presented rather impressive evidence suggesting that anxiety or conflict over fears of failure inhibit and/or distort obtained achievement scores. Byrne (1961) found similar results when relating anxiety to *n Aff.* Affiliation motives are also affected by approach and avoidance tendencies (Byrne, McDonald, & Mikawa, 1963).

A number of investigators have attempted to delineate the particular subjective conditions that affect the expression of hostility or aggression. These conditions include conflict (Nelson & Epstein, 1962), guilt (Saltz & Epstein, 1963; Shore, Massimo, & Mack, 1964), and self-concept (as an aggressive or nonaggressive person; Murstein, 1965c, 1968b).

Subject conditions of both classes—the more enduring population characteristics and the more transitory, situational type—are important in TAT research. It is necessary for the examiner to know who (demographic variables) took the test and under what conditions (situational variables) before any valid interpretations or meaningful results can be obtained. For example, a middle-aged, middle-class male subject is likely to be affected by the cultural values concerning open expressions of hostility and sexuality. This influence is especially likely if the examiner is an attractive young female trying to be her naturally seductive self. This brings us to two other important variables influencing the expression of needs on the TAT, i.e., examiner effects and arousal conditions.

Administration and Examiner Effects

The most obvious examiner effect would appear to concern the personality of the examiner. Bernstein (1956) has shown that both the presence of an examiner and individual differences among examiners influence the expression of needs on the TAT. Turner and Coleman (1962), on the other hand, concluded that there were only slight effects produced by examiners with different personal characteristics, different amounts of test experience, and different attitudes toward the test. Veroff (1961) and Veroff, Feld, and Gurin (1960) found some examiner effects on certain variables in their nationwide survey. In the latter study *n Ach* scores for women and *n Power* scores for both men and women were significantly affected. Martin (1964) and Strivzer (1961) have found sexual imagery to be affected by examiners and/or social setting.

It is the present writer's opinion, based on a review of the available research, that there may well be an interaction between examiner effects, subject conditions, and arousal conditions. This interaction is undoubtedly complex, but our use of the TAT would be greatly enhanced if it were better understood. Murstein (1968b) has made a beginning attempt in this direction.

The question of group vs. individual administration has received some attention because of the obvious advantage of group administration for research purposes. Murstein (1963) summarized much of the research on the question of group administration. He concluded that there are differences in the results of group vs. individual administration but that these differences are sufficiently small that for research studies concerned with studying limited numbers of characteristics the group method can be used. In a clinical setting, however, such factors as facial expressions, response time, and inquiries, which are unique to an individual administration, may be important.

Other examiner characteristics such as age and sex have not received much recent attention except in the context of arousal conditions (Barclay, 1969, 1970). The effects of other variations in administration, such as multiple choice responses, different number and sequence of cards used, and the like, are summarized in Murstein (1963). He concludes that the content, and to some extent the formal properties of the stories, are extremely sensitive to variation in administration. However, he sees the large number of variations used in test administration as being indicative of the TAT's flexibility and usefulness.

Arousal Conditions

The deliberate manipulation of conditions for arousing given motives has been used primarily to investigate the adequacy of particular scoring systems and the validity of an approach for measuring a particular need (i.e., if a subject is tested under neutral conditions and then tested again under aroused conditions, the difference in scores between these two administrations is said to demonstrate the existence of the need in that subject as well as the ability of the scoring system to measure it). A good example is *n Ach*. For males, the arousal conditions frequently involve instructions designed to create pressure for demonstration of intelligence and leadership ability. In most females, instructions creating a desire for social acceptance have been successful (Dana, 1968). There are exceptions: women who have a predominantly male value orientation are successfully aroused by the male arousal instructions (French & Lesser, 1964). Orso (1969) found an interesting relationship between achievement arousal and affiliation arousal for a college co-ed population. Female *n Ach* scores increased significantly after affiliation arousal and decreased significantly after the standard achievement arousal. For this sample, achievement in the form of acceptance was seen as desirable while the standard form of male achievement was not.

For *n Aff* the usual arousal conditions emphasize fear of rejection (cf. Carrigan and Julian, 1966). The manipulation of approach and avoidance affiliation motives have also been successful in increasing and decreasing *n Aff* scores (Byrne et al., 1963; Rosenfeld & Franklin, 1966). The manipulation of sexual arousal, in order to test the expectation that sexual themes would appear in the TAT stories of aroused subjects, received considerable attention during the decade of the 1950s but has not been as popular during the past ten years. For males the most common arousal technique has been to show slides of nude women before the subjects give their stories (Martin, 1964; Strivzer, 1961).

A somewhat unusual arousal approach is that utilized by Barclay (1970). In a study utilizing both males and females, Barclay used two male dominant cards and two female dominant cards to measure the effect of an anger-arousing female examiner. He found that, in contrast to the control group, aroused groups responded to aggressive arousal with increases in sexual motivation. This study was a replication of an earlier study using a male examiner (Barclay, 1969).

Arousal conditions for hostility or aggression are difficult to carry through adequately because of such undesirable side effects as anxiety and defensiveness. There is always the possibility, as Barclay's (1969, 1970) experiments demonstrate, that arousal of anger or hostility may lead to increases in conceptually unrelated imagery. Several successful attempts at hostility arousal have been made, however. An impersonal examiner and a frustrating task were successful for Breger (1963), while instructions to respond "impersonally" were successful for Murstein (1965c, 1968b).

In summary, research involving arousal conditions has been shown to be of value by demonstrating the existence of a need or motive, and by demonstrating the capability of various scoring systems to measure such needs. At the same time, the use of arousal conditions presents many difficult problems from a methodological viewpoint. The test-retest (neutral condition then aroused conditions) paradigm has ample opportunity for error. There is also the problem of matching arousal conditions to the subject and situation. Arousal conditions that are too weak may have no effect, while arousal conditions that are too strong may have a multitude of side effects. Finally, there is the obvious problem of interactions with examiner effects. One of the conclusions reached by Barclay (1970) was that imagery on various TAT pictures may be explained, at least in part, by examiner cues. Rosenthal's (1966) work on *Experimenter effects in research* makes the importance of this contaminating influence painfully clear.

In closing this section on the various factors influencing TAT results it may be worthwhile to examine the relevance of these factors to the clinical situation. Many clinicians using the TAT feel as Harrison (1965) did when he stated: "Most of the administrative and stimulus variations demonstrated in the laboratory are mainly of academic interest and are not of primary importance in the usual testing situation. Ordinarily an examinee is not presented with a 0.2 second exposure of pictures in color while standing in semidarkness listening to an alluring female administrator who is deliberately creating a hostile atmosphere by making sharply critical remarks [p. 568]." The important point which may be missed by those who have this attitude, however, is that in less extreme form, card stimulus factors, subject conditions, examiner effects, and arousal conditions do exist, whether the clinician takes cognizance of them or not. Furthermore, these factors, either in combination or separately, can have a powerful influence on TAT stories; e.g., Murstein (1968b), in his study of hostility, found the stimulus to be the prime determinant of the stories told by the subjects. The import of this influence is left undetermined if such factors are ignored by the clinician or researcher.

CONCLUSION

Evaluating the status of an instrument like the TAT is a subjective matter, and one always has to choose the perspectus from which the judgments are to be made. In a rather curious way, the position of reviewer or evaluator is very similar to that of the subject in a clinical or research setting who is required to write stories to the various TAT cards. Indeed, reviews of this sort probably say as much about the reviewer as they do about the test being evaluated. With these limitations in mind, the present author will venture the conclusion, from a rather restricted prospectus of past, present, and near future, that the TAT has a great deal to offer as a projective instrument. There are blemishes on the record of the TAT, but there are still a large number of clinicians who feel that at least a part of the TAT is useful, and also a sizable number of researchers who have modified the test to serve purposes of their own. Because of this popularity the TAT will not soon disappear as an entity (although it might disappear as a "test").

From a wider perspective and a longer range viewpoint, the picture is not as bright for the TAT. This perspective requires that the TAT as it presently exists be examined against the hard criterion of usefulness in the competitive, changing world. It should be noted that the TAT is not alone in this regard. All psychological assessment instruments undergo constant reexamination, but perhaps the projective techniques are currently receiving the closest scrutiny. The remainder of this chapter will be devoted to viewing the TAT from this wider perspective.

Clinical Uses

At the beginning of the chapter, a general conclusion of a recent survey of attitudes toward projective techniques (Thelen et al., 1968) was noted: namely, that many academic clinicians see projective techniques as declining in importance. An even more recent survey of all universities granting the doctorate in clinical psychology (Shemberg & Keeley, 1970) substantiates this conclusion. Shemberg and Keeley were interested in comparing the diagnostic training practices of today with those of five years ago. They found shifts away from training in projectives with a corresponding increase in emphasis on objective approaches. Further, many newer programs are de-emphasizing training in diagnostics in general. While these authors feel there is still a significant overall emphasis on diagnostic training in current doctoral programs, there is little doubt that the trends just noted will have a significant impact on projectives, including the TAT, in the future.

Murstein (1963, 1968a), in discussing the current status of projectives, distinguishes between projective "tests" and projective "techniques." He feels a test implies a standard situation with an emphasis on measurable responses, while the same material used in an unstandardized manner can be termed a technique. As a technique the TAT may have value for the individual clinician and the individual subject, but be of little value to the profession as a whole. The technique approach was satisfactory in the days when psychodiagnosis was the major function of the clinician and he was given a good deal of time to accomplish his task. Those days, however, are rapidly disappearing. The clinician's time is increasing in value, and quick methods of assessment are becoming a necessity. The TAT as it is presently constructed and utilized requires too much time and effort to remain a viable instrument for the majority of clinicians in the future.

Research concerning the TAT's usefulness and reliability is becoming substantially more sophisticated. But in the present author's opinion, this research is still too inadequate and incomplete to justify the continued use of the TAT as a test. To overcome these shortcomings and to recognize the necessity for shortening the time required for administration, scoring, and interpretation, it appears that the TAT will need redevelopment. This redevelopment will have to be along the lines of a more highly structured and standardized version of the test, which would then be suitable for self-administration and computerized scoring, or administration and interpretation by a nonprofessional worker. The price for such efficiency will be forfeiting some of the charm and flexibility many current clinicians now see in the TAT. However, some writers (Murstein, 1963; Zubin et al., 1965; Dana, 1968) have already suggested ways of improving the TAT psychometrically to keep it in good standing in the future.

Research Uses

As a research tool the TAT has been generally acknowledged to be a few years ahead of other projective tests (Dana, 1968). This lead in research sophistication has been primarily the result of the early work of McClelland, Atkinson, and their colleagues. Murstein (1968a) feels that the TAT is solidly entrenched as a research instrument, primarily as a measure of aroused need states. Some recent surveys (Mills, 1965; Crenshaw, Bohn, Hoffman, Mathews, & Offenback, 1968) on research use of projective techniques tend to support this conclusion.

Mills surveyed the *Journal of Projective Techniques* from 1947 to 1965 and found that for research use the TAT consistently ranked second behind the Rorschach. In a more extensive survey of ten widely read psychological and psychiatric journals, Crenshaw et al. (1968) also found the TAT to be second to the Rorschach in research usage except for the period of 1960-1964, when the TAT ranked first and the Rorschach second. Their data show an increase in use of projectives in research from 1947, peaking in 1955 and declining to a moderately high stable level through 1965. They interpret this trend as representing primarily validational studies early in the period surveyed, to both validation and applied studies at the peak, and primarily applied studies during the latter part of the period surveyed. It is the present author's impression that Crenshaw et al. are correct in their interpretation of the research history of the TAT, except to note that the early 1960s were a period of intensive study of the TAT itself. Further, when compared with psychological research in general, research using the TAT has shown a definite decline. In the past five years (1965-1970), while psychological research in general is increasing tremendously, the use of the TAT (and other projective techniques) has remained stable or declined. It appears that the heyday of projective techniques, including the TAT, is past.

Nevertheless, the promise of the TAT that excited so many people after its introduction in 1938 remains, even if somewhat elusive. The recent research on the TAT has improved considerably over that of the past, and hopefully this and continuing research will help to keep the early promise alive.

CHAPTER XII

Experimental games
as tools for personality research

Richard J. Harris

Recent years have seen an enormous increase of interest in reports of empirical investigations of a class of highly structured interaction situations known as experimental games. While game research has not yet progressed to the point of providing standardized techniques for diagnostic use in the individual case, it holds great promise for such applications. Further, it has already proved valuable in assessing the motives of groups of individuals and in providing interesting answers to such general issues of personality research as the degree of cross-situational consistency in individual's behavior. Accordingly, a general review and an attempt to relate this growing field to assessment psychology seem appropriate at this time.

Specifically, this chapter will (1) outline the growth of this area of empirical research from what was initially a purely mathematical examination of the logic of decision making; (2) point up the relevance of research on experimental games to the problem of assessing intra- and interpersonal motives; (3) provide a representative review of the attempts made so far to relate individual differences to behavior in experimental games; and (4) advance some suggestions for making research in this area even more relevant to the study of intraindividual consistencies. The restricted nature of these goals precludes a comprehensive review of the literature on experimental games. For such a review, the reader is referred to Apfelbaum (1966) or Krivohlavy (1967a, b). An excellent introduction to the normative theory of games is provided by Anatol Rapoport (1966).

ORIGINS IN GAME THEORY

For over two centuries mathematics has been used to aid in making decisions in situations where (as at the gaming table or in the weather forecasting center) the outcome of the decision can be foreseen only probabilistically, but where "nature" or "chance" determines the outcome completely impartially. About a quarter of a century ago, Von Neumann and Morgenstern (1944) first extended the use of mathematics to decisions in which the outcome of each of the decision maker's possible choices depends not on the impartial workings of chance, but on the choices made by another decision maker who has preferences of his own and whose outcomes are in turn dependent upon what the first person chooses to do.

Von Neumann and Morgenstern saw this mutual interdependence of the two or more decision makers as the crucial defining characteristic of social decisions. They therefore incorporated all other aspects of social interaction (e.g., communication between players, cooperative or competitive motives, the possibility of binding agreements, etc.) either into the "rules of the game," which define the precise nature of the interdependence among the players, or into the "utility functions," which define—for each player and for each possible outcome of the interaction—that player's degree of satisfaction with that particular outcome. The empirical situations in which this condensation of operative variables seems to require least abstraction from "real life" are the parlor games like tic-tac-toe, chess, checkers, etc.—whence the theory expounded by Von Neumann and Morgenstern was labeled as the "mathematical theory of games." This theory consists essentially of a number of mathematically stated basic assumptions about the goals of the persons involved in a social interaction together with a number of principles which, if followed, guarantee that the subject will come as close to these goals as possible.

The unfortunate success of game theory. The mathematical theory of games per se has inspired a huge volume of further mathematical analyses, but relatively little empirical research. Schloss (1959), for instance, listed 1,228 references on game theory, only 30 of which were empirical investigations. From the point of view of the social scientist, game theory has been both too successful and too unsuccessful to provide the sort of theoretical framework that, say, dissonance theory (Festinger, 1957; Brehm & Cohen, 1962; Festinger, Allen, Braden, Canon, Davidson, Jecker, Kiesler, & Walster, 1964) and social exchange theory (Homans, 1961; Thibaut & Kelley, 1959) do for empirical studies within their respective areas. Game theory's prescriptions as to how to select a response strategy when involved in a purely competitive situation (a "zero-sum" game, in which the sum of the payoffs to the players is exactly zero for all possible outcomes of the game), are quite compelling. Only a few empirical studies (e.g., Kilgard, 1966; Kaufmann & Becker, 1961) were necessary to demonstrate that the prescribed strategies are indeed discovered and used by naive subjects, provided that they are not too complex. (For the most complex situations, mathematical learning theory—cf. Suppes and Atkinson, 1960—or theories of problem-solving behavior—e.g., Newell, Shaw, and Simon, 1958—provide more adequate predictions of behavior than does game theory.)

The fortunate failure of game theory. The same principles that proved so successful in generating solutions to zero-sum games are glaringly unsuccessful when applied to situations in which the possibility of mutual cooperative gain exists (i.e., "non-zero-sum" games). One class of non-zero-sum game in particular, the Prisoner's Dilemma (PD) game, makes this failure quite obvious.

The Prisoner's Dilemma takes its name from an anecdote, attributed by Luce and Raiffa (1957) to A. W. Tucker, in which two cohorts in crime are grilled separately by the police. The police carefully explain to each prisoner (who must choose in isolation from his partner) that if neither confesses, they will both receive a one-year sentence for a minor crime in which they were both caught red-handed. If both confess, they will each get the standard sentence for the major crime of which they are suspected, five years in prison. If, however, one of them "turns State's evidence" while the other holds out, the person who confesses will get off with a reprimand from the judge and will in addition have a crisp $100 bill slipped into his wallet, while the hold-out will be given the maximum sentence for the crime, twenty years in prison.

Application of the most intuitively acceptable axiom of game theory—the "sure thing" principle—reveals that from either prisoner's point of view, his best choice, irrespective of what he believes his partner will do, is to confess. If he is convinced that his partner will not confess, then he himself should confess, since he will thereby avoid any prison sentence and earn $100 as well. If he is convinced that his partner will confess, then again his only rational alternative is to confess in order to hold his sentence to five years. Paradoxically, two "rational" prisoners faced with this situation fare worse (five years in prison for each) than do two persons who are so "irrational" as to refuse to confess (thereby receiving only one-year sentences).

This conflict between individual rationality and group rationality suggests several personal characteristics which may be important in determining whether a particular person or pair of individuals will respond cooperatively in situations having the same outcome structure as the PD. We might suspect, for instance, that persons who indicate through their evaluations of a number of hypothetical situations that they prefer situations in which both they and others achieve moderate rewards to situations in which they achieve high rewards at the expense of others (Sawyer, 1966a; Apfelbaum, 1969) would respond cooperatively in the PD, as would individuals who have a particularly broad definition of *ingroup* as revealed by high scores on a scale of Internationalism (Lutzker, 1960). On the other hand, we would expect very competitive responses from subjects who approve of manipulating others for personal advantage (Christie, Gergen, & Marlowe, in press) or whose fathers are entrepreneurs rather than bureaucrats (Crowne, 1966). Even a person who is generally inclined to seek cooperative solutions must, when faced with a PD game or a similar situation, be able to trust the other person. Similarly, he himself has a strong motive to violate any implicit or explicit agreement to cooperate since this would give him his most desirable outcome, and we might expect truthworthiness to play a role in such situations. From yet another point of view, a person with an extremely high fear of failure might be unwilling to take the risk of not confessing. Conversely, a person with a high need for achievement might be unwilling to settle for his second-best outcome.

Altruism, competitiveness, internationalism, Machiavellianism, trust, suspicion, achievement motivation, modeling of one's parents' role in our nominally capitalistic economy, fear of failure—all of these are encompassed within the narrow confines of a situation involving only two persons having two objectively observable responses each. No wonder that the PD has been so much more inspiring to empirically oriented social scientists than zero-sum games. Game researchers have wisely retained Von Neumann and Morgenstern's emphasis on the importance of the "outcome structure" of a social situation and have concentrated their efforts on studies in which the interdependence between the participants' outcomes is defined precisely and explicitly, and is known to both players. These highly structured interaction situations are referred to as experimental games.

A Representative Game Study

An observer who looked in while a session of Harris's (1970a) study (which was conducted in a psychiatric hospital) was underway would have seen two patients seated at small tables on which partitions had been mounted in such a way as to preclude their seeing each other, while permitting full view of the experimenter (E) and of the blackboard behind him (Figure 1). The material written on this blackboard appears in Figure 2.

E asks, "Would each of you please pick a card for trial 4?" After a few seconds of deliberation, the patient in the right-hand booth picks up an orange index card lying in front of him and holds it up. The left-hand patient has in the meantime selected and held up to view a white index card, leaving his orange card flat on the table. E announces that "Mr. Smith chose orange and Mr. Jones chose white. Mr. Jones therefore receives 6 cents and Mr. Smith gives back 4 cents." E takes 6 cents in canteen coupons (which can be used at the hospital canteen just like cash) from a box sitting on a portable table to his right and, walking forward, hands it to Mr. Jones. He then retrieves 4 cents in coupons from Mr. Smith's coupon box, walks back to the blackboard, and asks, "Would each of you please pick a card for trial 5?"

After 7 trials are completed, E says, "OK. That's the last trial in this particular situation. Now I'm going to write a description of the next interaction situation on the board."

"In this situation, if both of you hold up an orange card, you both receive 4 cents. If each of you holds up a white card, you each give back 2 cents. If one of you holds up an orange card and the other, a white card, the person holding up the white cards receives 16 cents and the person holding up the orange card gives back 14 cents. Any questions?"

"OK. Let me ask *you* a few questions, just to make sure we're clear on what happens for each combination of choices. Mr. Jones, if on a particular trial, you hold up a white card and Mr. Smith holds up an orange card, what happens?"

The questions continue until each of the patients has answered four or more questions correctly. E then asks for the patients' choices for the first trial, and the patients interact for 7 trials in this new game. At E's request, the patients do not talk to each other while each interaction sequence is in progress. Upon completion of the fourth game, the patients are asked to come out of their booths and sit next to each other while they discuss the experiment with E. Special care is taken to talk over any hostility generated by the interaction, pointing out how the nature of the situation tends to force a competitive response in any group.

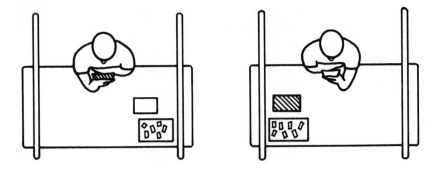

Figure 1. Physical arrangement of subjects and experimenter during paranoid–non-paranoid (PNP) study.

This study is typical of game research in a number of ways, and atypical in others. As the formal definitions provided in the next section show, the game described in Figure 2 is a Prisoner's Dilemma game where holding up an orange card is the cooperative response (corresponding to "holding out" in Tucker's anecdote) and the white card represents noncooperation ("turning State's evidence" in the anecdote). A majority of experimental game studies employ PD, and a sizable percentage of the remaining studies employ other games but mistakenly label them as PD or misleadingly label them as variations of the PD.

On the other hand, the method of presenting the outcome structure to the subjects of this study is atypical, the most common method being to present subjects with a payoff matrix like that shown in Figure 3. It is explained to the subjects that player A chooses between the rows of the matrix and player B chooses between the columns, with the payoff to player A being the left-hand number in the resulting cell and the payoff to B being the right-hand number in that cell. The reader should be certain that he understands the relationship between the matrix format of Figure 3 and the description of the outcome structure provided by Figure 2, since almost all studies report the nature of the game employed in this matrix format (which is a legacy of the mathematical theory of games), even if a more elaborate format were used in describing the outcome structure to the subjects. A number of studies

Choices		Outcomes		
Yours	His	Yours	His	
▨	▨	5¢	5¢	If you choose orange and he chooses orange, you receive 5c and he receives 5c.
▨	☐	−4¢	6¢	If you choose orange and he chooses white, you give back 4c and he receives 6c.
☐	▨	6¢	−4¢	If you choose white and he chooses orange, you receive 6c and he gives back 4c.
☐	☐	−2¢	−2¢	If you choose white and he chooses white, you give back 2c and he gives back 2c.

Figure 2. Information written on blackboard behind experimenter during PNP study.

have investigated the effects of presentation format on the subjects' game-playing behavior (e.g., Pruitt, 1967; Evans & Crumbaugh, 1966a; Gallo, Funk, & Levine, 1969).

Almost all studies forbid communication between the subjects (except implicit communication through their choices) unless the effects of adding communication to the situation are to be studied explicitly (e.g., Loomis, 1959). Most studies employ more elaborate apparatus than did the study described here, with the outcome of each trial being indicated to each subject by the lighting up of one cell of a display like that of Figure 3. Often several subject pairs are run simultaneously, with electronic apparatus automatically recording the outcome of each trial for each pair.

TYPES OF EXPERIMENTAL GAMES

There are a large number of experimental games, each having distinctive structural features and each therefore providing somewhat unique opportunities for the identification of individual differences.

In the following paragraphs the most commonly studied games will be defined and their properties discussed. The emphasis in the discussion of each game will be on the kinds of individual-difference dimensions which might be expected to relate to behavior in that game, and the conditions under which various response strategies are optimal. Any investigation of the correlates of game behavior should consider the possibility that what is being observed is simply differences in the rationality of subjects' responses to the structure of the situation in which they find themselves. This should be the basic "null hypothesis" to which hypotheses involving more exotic personality variables are contrasted.

$$\begin{array}{c c} & \quad 1 \quad\ \ ^{\mathbf{B}}\ \ \quad 2 \end{array}$$

$$\mathbf{A}\ \begin{array}{c} 1 \\ 2 \end{array}\ \begin{array}{|c|c|} \hline 5¢,\ 5¢ & -4¢,\ 6¢ \\ \hline 6¢,-4¢ & -2¢,-2¢ \\ \hline \end{array}$$

Figure 3. Outcome matrix representing same game as extended description in Figure 2.

Note.—Player A (row-player) determines the row from which the outcomes are selected; player B (column-player) determines the column. The first (left-hand) entry in each cell is row-player's payoff; the second (right-hand) entry, column-player's payoff.

Commonly Studied Games

Each of the games discussed in the present section has the property that it looks the same to both players. In other words, the game can be described to both players at the same time in phrases such as, "if you choose response 1 and he chooses response 2, then you receive 3 points and he receives 2 points," with each player taking "you" as a reference to himself. Any such game will have a payoff matrix which takes one of the four forms outlined in Figure 4. Usually $T_1 = T_2$, $S_1 = S_2$, $R_1 = R_2$, and $P_1 = P_2$; but so long as the two sets of payoffs are related by some interval transformation ($T_2 = aT_1 + b$; $S_2 = aS_1 + b$; etc.), the game may be considered interval-symmetric; and if the two sets of payoffs have the same rank order they may be considered ordinally symmetric. Because of the predominance of studies in which the payoff sets are identical, the subscripts on T, R, P, and S will be dropped in the following discussions. Moreover, that response which makes it possible for S to receive T and impossible for him to receive S will be labeled as his D response, with his other response being referred to as the C response. T is defined as the particular player's largest available payoff in an unequal-outcome cell.

Prisoner's Dilemma. This game was discussed extensively in the introductory section of this paper. A game is a Prisoner's Dilemma (PD) if and only if its outcome matrix takes the same form as one of the matrices in Figure 4, and $T > R > P > S$ for both players.[1] Many authors add the further, interval-scale restriction that $R > (T + S)/2 > P$, and the present chapter will refer to PDs meeting this additional restriction as Restricted PDs. In PDs for which $(T + S)/2 > R$, alternation between the (T,S) and the (S,T) cells yields higher average payoff than does consistent mutual choice of the cooperative response. Lave (1965) has found that players do in fact arrive at alternation strategies when playing nonrestricted PDs.

---

[1]This mathematical expression translates into English as "T is greater than R, which is in turn greater than P, which is in turn greater than S." In other words, if both players choose C, each receives his second highest payoff; if both choose D, each receives his second lowest payoff; if one chooses C, and the other chooses D, the person choosing C receives his lowest payoff while the person choosing D receives his highest payoff.

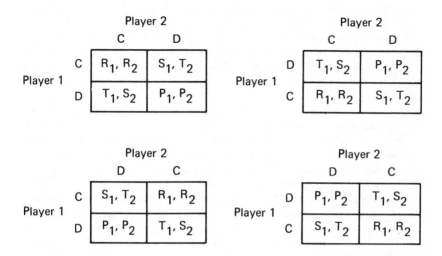

Figure 4. The four possible forms of the outcome matrix of the Interval-Symmetric Game.

Note.—In each of the four cells of each of these matrices, the payoff to player 1 (the row-player) appears to the left and receives a subscript "1," while the right-hand payoff (identified by the subscript "2") is the payoff to player 2 (the column-player). The particular letters chosen to represent the responses and the outcomes are those introduced by Rapoport and Chammah (1965) because of their relevance to the Prisoner's Dilemma game. "C" stands for the cooperative response; "D," for the defecting (noncooperative, competitive) response. R_1 and R_2 are the "rewards" for mutual cooperation; P_1 and P_2, the "punishments" for mutual defection; T_1 and T_2, the "temptations" to defect; and S_1 and S_2, the "sucker's payoffs" for allowing yourself to be double-crossed. These labels are less appropriate for games other than PD. However, for any interval-symmetric game, T for a particular player can be defined as the largest payoff to that player in an unequal-outcome cell (i.e., a cell that is not ranked identically by the two players); S is defined as the payoff diagonal to T; P is the payoff that results if both players try to get T; and R is the payoff that results if each player selects the response (C) that precludes his receiving T. The characteristic of these four matrices that distinguishes them from other experimental games is the existence of two diagonally placed equal-outcome cells (the CC and DD cells) and of two diagonally placed unequal-outcome cells (CD and DC).

As pointed out in the introductory section, the only individually rational choice for either player in a one-trial PD (a PD which is to be played only once) is the noncooperative response, D. So compelling is the feeling that mutual noncooperation in the PD is stupid, no matter what game theory might say, that almost all researchers in this area devote their theoretical effort to explaining why subjects defect (fail to cooperate) so often when, from the game theorist's point of view, they should try to explain why any cooperative responses are observed. (For a debate on whether Howard's theory of meta-games provides a "hard-nosed" basis for recommending mutual cooperation in the one-trial PD, cf. Howard, 1966, 1969, 1970; Harris, 1969a, c, 1970c; and Anatol Rapoport, 1967a, 1969a, b.)

A large part of this feeling comes from observing subject pairs in iterated PD games (where the game is played several times by the same pair) who lock in on long sequences of mutual D's (DD's), thereby consistently losing points, when both could be winning points "if only . . . ." This dismay is somewhat better founded in the iterated PD, since 100 percent noncooperation is not a dominant strategy in the iterated game though it is an equilibrium strategy, one in which neither player can increase his payoffs by switching to another strategy if the other player continues to play his equilibrium strategy. Amnon Rapoport (1967) points out that unconditional noncooperative responding is still optimal against any noncontingent strategy (e.g., random choice of C on 0, 10, 20, 80, or 100 percent of the trials) on the other player's part,[2] and has given examples of contingent other-person strategies for which 100 percent cooperative responding is optimal. Harris (1969d) provides an algebraic method of computing these optimal response strategies, and proves that unconditional cooperation is optimal against the increasingly popular "tit-for-tat" strategy (matching subject's response on the previous trial) for any Restricted PD.

Chicken. The second most frequently studied experimental game is Chicken, which gets its name from its close analogy to the once-popular teenage past-time of driving two carloads of humans directly toward each other to determine which is so "chicken" as to swerve away. Formally, $T > R > S > P$ for any Chicken.

It is clear from the anecdote and from the definition that the risky response in this game is the noncooperative one (D), while the opposite is true in PD. Further, and perhaps most importantly, the noncooperative response is no longer dominant. Moreover, non-matching choices are much more stable in Chicken than in PD in that the rational reaction for a person who finds himself in the cell in which he receives S and his partner receives T is to continue to choose C on subsequent trials rather than risk decreasing his outcome from S to P.

It can be argued that the structure of Chicken is more similar to that of international power politics than is PD, and that Internationalism might therefore be a better predictor of behavior in Chicken than in PD. This might help explain why Lutzker (1960) found a significant relationship between Internationalism and behavior in a Chicken game, while neither Pilisuk, Potter, Rapoport, and Winter (1965) nor Pilisuk, Skolnick, and Overstreet (1968) found such a relationship in a 21-alternative version of PD, despite the inclusion by Pilisuk et al. (1965) of a condition in which the context and the descriptions of the choices available to the subject were designed to maximally simulate an arms race.

In any one-trial Chicken game both CD and DC are equilibrium outcomes in that either player reduces his own payoff by a unilateral switch in his

---

[2] More generally, a noncontingent strategy is any strategy in which the choices of the player employing the strategy are unaffected by the other player's responses on previous trials.

response selection. If he is willing to resort to a random selection of his response (i.e., to a mixed strategy), the mixture defined by a probability of cooperating equal to $(S - P) / (T + S - R - P)$ gives an outcome intermediate between P and R. For the iterated Chicken game, alternation is an attractive strategy when $T + S > 2R$. There are other-person strategies against which 100 percent cooperative responding is optimal, including tit-for-tat when the game is a Restricted Chicken (as was true for Restricted PD) and also, in sharp contrast to PD, against any noncontingent strategy in which the other player chooses the cooperative response with a probability lower than that dictated by the mixed-strategy equilibrium defined above.

Battle of Sexes and Apology. Luce and Raiffa (1957) discuss extensively a game defined by the relations $T > S > R = P$. The anecdote from which this game gets its name involves a husband and wife, one of whom prefers going to the opera and one of whom prefers going to the wrestling matches, but each of whom prefers going to his or her nonpreferred activity together with the spouse to attending the preferred activity without this companionship. This game is labeled by Harris (1969b) as "Luce & Raiffa Battle of Sexes" (L&R BS) and has been empirically studied by Willis and Joseph (1959) and by Klein and Solomon (1966).

Before discussing the logical structure of L&R BS, two additional games, whose empirical study by Wyer (1969) and by Flint and Harris (1970a, b) was inspired by Anatol Rapoport's (1967b) singling them out as potentially valuable but relatively ignored games, will be defined. Rapoport and Guyer (1966) illustrate the game they label as Battle of Sexes (BS) with the same anecdote as L&R BS but with the additional assumption that the worst possible outcome for each player is to stick obstinately to his preferred activity and have the bluff called $(T > S > R > P)$.

The game of Apology is based on an anecdote in which two persons who insulted each other the previous night while dead drunk now encounter each other on the street. Best for either would be for the other to apologize while remaining silent himself; next preferred would be if he apologized while the other remained silent; next preferred would be if neither apologized; and worst of all would be if both blurted out their apologies. Thus for Apology $T > S > P > R$. (It seems that, on the basis of the suggested anecdotes, the labels for Battle of Sexes and Apology should be reversed. The Rapoport-Guyer labels will, however, be retained in the present chapter.)

All three of these games have in common the fact that both players prefer either of the two cells in which they obtain unequal outcomes to either of the two cells in which the two receive equal outcomes. They also share with Chicken the property that either unequal-outcome cell is an equilibrium cell. Unlike Chicken, an alternation strategy provides the only way in which ordinally equal and moderately satisfactory per-trial payoffs can be attained when any of these three games is played several times.

The differences among BS, L&R BS, and Apology reside in the consequences of shifting from what Rapoport and Guyer (1966) define as the "natural outcome" cell, i.e., in the present context, the equal-outcome cell providing the larger payoff. (Since $R = P$ in L&R BS, the natural outcome cell in that game will be assumed to be DD, the outcome which results if both players try for their largest payoff.)

If we assume that the payoff sets for the two players are identical, then it can be seen that a player who unilaterally shifts from the natural outcome in any of these three games thereby increases both his own payoff and that of his partner. However, in BS the unilaterally shifting player helps himself more than his partner (and is thus labeled by Rapoport as a "Leader"), while in Apology and in L&R BS he helps his partner more than himself (and is thus labeled as a "Hero"). On the assumption that players differ in submissiveness and/or in willingness to tolerate inequitable outcomes, we would expect a negative correlation between heroism and leadership and thus a negative correlation between being the unilateral shifter in BS and the same tendency in Apology. Flint and Harris (1970a) found a correlation of $-.792$ ($p < .01$) between these two types of game with respect to an index (number of CDs–number of DCs) of this behavior.

Maximizing Differences Game. A game which has received considerable attention from McClintock and his associates (e.g., McClintock & McNeel, 1966a, b, 1967) is the Maximizing Differences Game, defined by $R > T > P = S$. The MD game is a "no conflict" game since two players faced with a situation where a single combination of choices provides each with his most satisfying outcome would certainly have no reason for selecting any other response. As Marwell and Schmitt (1968) have argued, however, logically trivial games may be psychologically quite interesting, and this has certainly been the case with the MD game. The repeated finding that subjects playing the MD game (or at least a game in which the experimenter-defined payoffs fit the definition of the MD game) select the competitive response a high proportion of the time (e.g., McClintock & McNeel, 1966a, b, 1967) has provided compelling evidence that a subject's satisfaction with an outcome is not necessarily even monotonically related to the payoffs, and may instead be more closely related to a weighted average of his own and the other player's experimenter-defined payoffs. The importance of this dimension of interpersonal motivation—concern for the other player—will be considered in more detail in the final section of this chapter.

Other 2x2 Games

Any 2x2 game (a game involving two players, each of whom has two alternatives) which does not fit the definition of a "commonly studied" game will be referred to in the present paper as a "nonsymmetric" game. If a more detailed classification is desired, the ordinal classification system of Rapoport and Guyer (1966) or the interval-scale classification system developed by Harris (1970b) may be consulted. These systems will not be described in the present chapter.

More Complex Two-Person Games

Given the premium put by social scientists on originality over systematic research, it is inevitable that the austere 2x2 game would be embellished in a number of ways. A few of these more complex games have received sufficient empirical attention to warrant specific mention here.

Graduated games. Several authors (e.g., Sawyer & Friedell, 1965; Messé & Sawyer, 1966; Gallo et al., 1969) have suggested that cooperative resolutions of conflict in two-person situations may be facilitated by providing a more finely graduated range of choices to each player than that available in a 2x2 game. This is accomplished by employing an *nxn* game in which the corner cells meet the definition of some 2x2 game (usually PD), while the payoffs for other cells are directly proportionate to the number of steps by which each selected response is removed from the extreme of the response continuum. Hamburger (1969) has proved that the 2x2 submatrices of graduated, *n*-alternative versions of all but a few 2x2 games—the same few games which can be presented in Pruitt's (1967) "decomposed" format—have different properties than the parent matrices from which they were derived.

No-play option. Miller (1967) compared three standard PDs with the same games when a third, no-play option is added such that selection of this option by either player leads to a payoff of zero to both players on that trial. Miller provides a number of explanations for his finding that the addition of the no-play option significantly increases the probability of mutually cooperative responses. He omits, however, the obvious explanation that the logical structure of the 3x3 game which results from the addition of a no-play option is drastically different from the logical structure of the 2x2 PD game in a way which makes selection of the noncooperative response less compellingly rational.

Trucking game. In this oft studied game, devised by Deutsch and Krauss (1960), each player assumes the role of a trucking company operator. Each player's payoff is inversely proportional to the time it takes him to move his truck from a starting point to a delivery point. Two routes exist for this: a long, twisting route which guarantees a loss on the trial, and a much shorter route which, however, contains a narrow, one-way stretch which intersects with the other player's short route and through which both trucks, traveling in opposite directions, cannot pass at the same time. A typical pair of subjects playing this game for imaginary amounts of money will lose large amounts of this imaginary money on each trial by each obstinately insisting on being first through the one-way lane rather than developing an alternation strategy of taking turns at being first through. This is reminiscent of the long strings of mutually noncooperative and mutually punishing responses often seen when subject-pairs play the PD. However, as the optimality of alternation strategies suggests, the trucking game is much more closely related to L&R BS than to PD.

EVIDENCE ON INDIVIDUAL DIFFERENCES IN BEHAVIOR IN EXPERIMENTAL GAMES

Thus far we have seen some of the reasons for expecting experimental games to provide a fruitful tool for personality research. Now it is time to see how successful researchers have been in applying this tool. First some empirical evidence will be presented which suggests that there are indeed large individual differences in game-playing behavior which cannot be accounted for by situational factors. Then evidence that the constellations of organismic variables associated with gross differences such as sex, age, and presence of psychosis affect game-playing behavior will be examined. Next the frustration of researchers who have attempted to specify the particular personality dimensions responsible for these differences will be reviewed. Finally a single study which used game behavior as a diagnostic tool in the individual case (more accurately, for individual subject pairs) will be mentioned.

Scale-free Tests of the Importance of Individual Differences

Studies which correlate each subject's scores on a number of personality measures with his behavior in a single type of game establish only a lower bound on the importance of individual differences in this area. It is always possible that some untried or even undiscovered measure (test, scale) would have yielded much higher correlations with game behavior. A scale-free approach to setting an upper bound on the importance of individual differences as a determinant of game behavior would be to have each subject interact in two or more types of games. The squared coefficient of correlation between the subjects' behavior in the two games represents the percentage of variance which must be attributed to individual differences. Few game studies have utilized within-subject designs, and most of these fail to report relevant correlations, using the design principally to reduce the variability of estimates of between-subject effects. The exceptions are described below.

L&R BS games. Willis and Joseph (1959) had 20 subject pairs play 50 trials of a L&R BS game and then 50 trials of a three-alternative version of this game; another 20 subject pairs played the three-alternative game and then a four-alternative version. The same subject was the winner of both games in 29 of the 40 subject pairs; each player won one game in seven cases; and there was a tie for total number of points won in one or both games for four of the subject pairs.

"Psychologically interesting" interval-symmetric games. Flint and Harris (1970a) had each of 35 subject pairs play seven different experimental games. These included all of the four types of games classified by Anatol Rapoport (1967b) as "psychologically interesting." The between-game correlations for this study based on the measure CD-DC (the number of trials on which the row-player received a lower payoff than the column-player, minus the number of trials on which he received a higher payoff) ranged from .035 to .792 with a median of .500. Fifteen of these 18 correlations exceeded the .33 value needed for significance at the .05 level.

The partner as a situational variable. Although the results of the Flint and Harris (1970a) study seem to provide compelling evidence of the existence of individual differences, an alternative explanation of these results is possible. Since each subject played all seven games with the same partner, which member of each pair would be "dominant" (receive more points than his partner) may have been determined in the first game played by the pair by purely chance factors with both players accepting this verdict throughout all seven games. To test this explanation, a second study was conducted in which each of 160 subjects played 100 trials of each of 4 games. Half of the subjects (the

Fixed group) played all 4 games with the same partner while the other half (the Mixed group) played each game with a different partner. The games employed were a PD, a Chicken, an Apology, and a BS. The overall magnitude of the CD-DC intercorrelations is statistically significant for the Fixed group but not under Mixed conditions; and the difference between the two groups in overall magnitude of intercorrelations is statistically significant. Failure of the between-game correlations to reach statistical significance under Mixed conditions leaves the hypothesis of purely random determination of dominance in the first game played by a pair still tenable.

Gross Differences

As Knapp and Podell (1968) have pointed out, failure to find significant differences in the behavior of widely different populations in experimental game behavior would cast considerable doubt on the value of attempts to ferret out specific individual differences. Fortunately, there is considerable evidence that broadly different populations do indeed differ in their reactions to various experimental games, though there is also controversy over just how to describe those differences.

Sex of subjects. Of 26 studies which were reviewed for the present chapter because they tested for differences between males and females, nine (Lutzker, 1961; Marlowe, 1959; Bixenstine, Potash, & Wilson, 1963; Komorita & Mechling, 1967; Miller, 1967; Wilson & Kayatani, 1968; Minas, Scodel, Marlowe, & Rawson, 1960; and Evans & Crumbaugh, 1966b) reported no statistically significant differences. The following discussion will concentrate on those studies which did find differences. It must be emphasized that all of the sex differences to be discussed in this section were observed in studies of American college students and cannot be interpreted as evidence for innate differences between the sexes.

Bixenstine, Chambers, and Wilson (1964) found that females playing a nonsymmetric game against a program of 80 percent matching of a subject's response on that trial were more cooperative than were males. Moreover, males were more cooperative in the column-player's role than in the row-player's role while the reverse was true for females. The expected payoff of the cooperative response is greater than for the competitive response for column-player against the strategy the experimenter employed while there is no difference in the expected payoffs available to row-player against this matching strategy.

Halpin and Pilisuk (1967), in a study involving a Restricted PD in which the subject had the additional task of predicting what response his partner would make on the next trial (with an additional 1 cent gain or loss for a correct or incorrect prediction), found that males were "more liable to realize that the optimal strategy was to predict C on all trials . . . [and] more liable to play the game as though Other was always going to choose C [p. 270]." A later, more detailed report of this study (Halpin & Pilisuk, 1970) indicates that the subjects played against a preprogrammed, noncontingent strategy of 70 percent cooperative choices and that males showed a more rapid decline than did females in futile attempts to communicate with the partner through cooperative response on trials on which the subject predicted non-cooperation from the partner and a more rapid increase in exploitative choices of D on trials where a C was expected from the partner. This tendency of males to respond more competitively than females when playing PD against a noncontingent strategy (under which circumstances the optimal strategy is 100 percent D) has also been found by Pilisuk, Skolnick, and Overstreet (1968) in a 5-alternative version of a Restricted PD; by Tedeschi, Lesnick, and Gahagan (1968) for the first 2, 5, or 10 trials but not all 100 trials of a Restricted PD; and by Tedeschi, Bonoma, and Lindskold (1970), also in a Restricted PD. These latter authors also found that females were less likely than males to take advantage of possession of a threat option by competing on trials on which they threatened the partner with a large loss of points should he fail to choose C.

Benton, Gelber, Kelley, and Liebling (1969) in a study of behavior in a complex "doubting game," in which—for the particular false-feedback conditions used by the author—it is rational never to doubt the message sent by one's partner, found no overall difference in doubting rates for males as compared with females. They did, however, find that females in the 75 percent deception condition showed an increase in (self-defeating) doubting behavior over trial blocks while all other groups showed either a steady or a decreasing trend, and that female subjects in the 75 percent deception condition who indicated suspicion of the trustworthiness of their partner before the interaction began showed more doubting behavior during the interaction than any other group. Grant and Sermat (1969) found in a study involving a Restricted Chicken game that males were more likely than females to cooperate on a trial on which they predicted that their partner would compete and less likely to cooperate when they expected cooperation from their partner.

The present author has found only one exception to this general rule of more rational behavior on the part of males than females. Marwell, Ratcliff, and Schmitt (1969) had subjects play a game which either forced equal outcomes or forced unequal outcomes, then switched to a Maximizing Differences game. In the equity condition female dyads were much less competitive than were male dyads. Since the cooperative response is dominant in the MD game, the males' behavior certainly seems less rational than the females. However, under conditions of inequity, males were slightly less competitive than under equity conditions while females were much more competitive. The females were thus less rational than the males in allowing a manipulation which is logically irrelevant to selection of a response strategy in the game (relative resources before beginning the game) to influence their game behavior rather drastically. The results of Marwell et al. (1969) and those discussed in preceding paragraphs of this section are consistent with the assumption that males assign a slightly negative weight (on the order of $-.2$) to their partner's outcomes and are quite responsive to structural factors which alter the optimality of various strategies for maximizing this weighted average, while females seem relatively unresponsive to structural factors.

The latter part of this hypothesis is consistent with the considerable evidence that females respond more emotionally than males to experimental game situations. We have already discussed their decision to doubt their partner (at the cost of a reduction in their own expected payoffs) when the partner lied to them more than 50 percent of the time (Benton et al., 1969). With the help of additional questionnaire data, Marwell et al. (1969) explained the female subjects' greater competitiveness under conditions of inequity as follows: the subject with the lower total accumulated points at the beginning of the MD game feels entitled to earn more points than her "ahead" partner and so selects the competitive response; the partner, in turn, resists this attempted reduction of her outcomes. Borah (1963) found that female subjects playing a game-board version of the trucking game in which shocks were available, used shocks less often than did males. In a Restricted PD game in which the outcomes were shocks of different intensities, Bixenstine and O'Reilly (1966) found that females reacted in a much more retaliatory way than males to being shocked by their partner. Rapoport and Chammah (1965a, b), Bixenstine et al. (1964), and Rapoport and Dale (1966) all report data indicating that women react more punitively than do men to being double-crossed in the PD.

However, an incidental finding by Dolbear, Lave, Bowman, Lieberman, Prescott, Rueter, and Sherman (1969) suggests that the greater responsiveness of males to the logical structure of interaction situations may not be a sex difference at all. These authors studied differences in behavior in a 30-alternation version of the PD versus the usual 2-alternative PD and incidentally discovered that major field of study (technical vs. nontechnical) was a more important determinant of cooperative behavior than was sex of subject. The correlation between sex and major field was .85, so it is entirely possible that the sex differences discussed above may actually be differences in the major fields of the experimental subjects, with females tending to come from nontechnical majors. Keeping in mind Miller's (1967) comment about the mental block many of his subjects had against "any sort of arithmetic game," the suggestion by Dolbear et al. (1969) will strike a responsive chord in anyone who has attempted to teach introductory statistics to psychology majors.

Finally, two studies reveal statistically significant sex effects that are not easily interpreted in terms of rationality. Steele and Tedeschi (1967), in a study involving 42 interval-symmetric games of widely different types, each played by a different like-sexed subject pair, found that the probability of a "cooperative" response following a trial on which the subject had "competed" and his partner had "cooperated" was higher for males than for females. The wide and incompletely specified range of games employed makes this finding difficult to interpret. Grant and Sermat (1969) found that males competed equally often against male and female partners, while females competed more against males than against females. (Each subject was actually competing against a preprogrammed strategy but was led to believe that his partner was either a male or a female.)

College students vs. mental patients. The obvious expectation that patients, especially paranoid patients, would be less cooperative than students because of their lower willingness to trust others, has in general not been supported by the data. Harford and Solomon (1967, 1969) found no differences among college students, paranoid patients, and nonparanoid schizophrenics in their probability of cooperating on the first trial of a Restricted PD. Over all 30 trials, the students were significantly less cooperative than the patients. The difference in the effects of two initial treatments was smaller for the paranoids than for the other two groups, with students being more trusting (i.e., more often both predicting and themselves selecting the cooperative response) against an initially competitive than against an initially cooperative program. Harford and Hill (1967) found that alcoholic patients resembled the college students more than the schizophrenic sample in their differential reactions to these two programs.

Knapp and Podell (1968) provide partial support for these findings. These authors found statistically significant differences between students at a California state college and a random sample of patients in a California state mental hospital in percentage of cooperative responses on the first trial of a Restricted PD, with the students being more cooperative than the patients. This difference was no longer statistically significant after 100 trials. There was, however, a significant interaction between the population difference and a difference in the preprogrammed strategies against which the subjects played, the patients being significantly less affected by the difference in programs. A third population, inmates at a California state correctional institution, was nearly identical to the students in first-trial cooperation, did not differ from the other two populations in percent cooperation across the full 100 trials, and was not significantly affected by the difference in program.

Klein and Solomon (1966) found that paranoid patients as compared to nonparanoid patients were less responsive to the other player's change from a 100 percent competitive to an unconditional alternation strategy across two sessions of a L&R BS game. (Alternation is the only cooperative strategy available in this game.)

The present author's comparison of paranoid vs. nonparanoid patients playing four different PD games was mentioned earlier in this chapter. In this study the paranoid-nonparanoid difference did not reach statistical significance. Further, in recruiting volunteers for the study, the author found that the patients were much more responsive to appeals based on the possible value of the research in generating ideas for future treatment programs than they were to appeals based on the amount of money they might receive through participating. The common experience of adjustment to hospital life may produce strong group identity capable of overriding the obvious prediction of more distrust and thus more competitive behavior from mental patients than from "normals." This suggestion receives some support from a study by Wallace and Rothaus (1969) involving a Restricted PD in which they obtained 88 percent cooperative responses from subject pairs composed of schizophrenic patients from the same ward of the Houston VA Hospital and 39 percent cooperation from different-ward pairs.

Ethnic background. Uejio and Wrightsman (1967) report that Wong (1964) and Wilson and Wong (1965) found that groups of students of Japanese ancestry were significantly more cooperative in an ingroup-outgroup PD than were students of Caucasian ancestry. All four subjects in each group were of the same race. (In ingroup-outgroup PD two subject pairs play a PD to determine how much money each pair will receive, and the two members of each pair play a similar PD to determine how that pair's "winnings" for the trial are to be distributed among the two Ss and E.) Wilson and Kayatani (1968), however, failed to replicate this finding and in addition found that between-group cooperative choices were not decreased by pitting Caucasian subject pairs against Japanese pairs. Uejio and Wrightsman (1967) informed Ss of Caucasian or Japanese background that they were playing a Restricted PD against a person of the same or of a different ethnic background. Each S in fact played against a preprogrammed strategy of 76 percent noncontingent cooperation. The differences among these four groups were statistically nonsignificant.

Harford and Cutter (1966) found no greater decrease in the amount of cooperation shown by Caucasian boys (ages 6-12) when their partner was switched from a Caucasian boy to a Negro peer than when the change was to a second Caucasian. Wrightsman, Davis, Lucker, Bruininks, Evans, Wilde, Paulson, and Clark (1967), in a "PD" in which the subject chose first on each trial, found no effect of the perceived race (Negro vs. white) of their partner on the extent to which Caucasian female undergraduates cooperated.

A grab bag. McClintock and McNeel (1966a) found that Belgian students are more competitive in a Maximizing Differences game than are American students, especially under conditions in which both Ss' cumulative score is displayed. Acceptance of McClintock and McNeel's conclusion must, however, be tempered by the fact that there are wide differences among college populations in this country. Bussey, Marks, and Escover (1968) found that the percentage of cooperative responses in a PD-Chicken hybrid was a decreasing function of age for their samples of pairs of age 8, 12, 16, and 20 years. Sampson and Kardush (1965) obtained a number of complex interactions between age (7 to 8-year olds vs. 9 to 11-year olds), sex, reported social class, and race. Crowne (1966) reported that sons of entrepreneurs were significantly more competitive than sons of bureaucrats in a Restricted PD, though this difference did not hold for daughters or for sons with "unrealistic" Rotter's (1942) Level of Aspiration patterns. Marlowe and Kalin (1968) found that males reported by their fraternity brothers as heavy drinkers were more competitive in a PD game played against 80 percent noncontingent cooperative feedback than were light drinkers. Klein and Solomon (1966) found that married patients were more submissive than unmarried ones against a strategy of unconditional noncooperative responses in a Luce & Raiffa Battle of Sexes game. (Submissiveness is in fact the rational response to this strategy in this game.) Klein and Solomon failed to find any significant effects, however, of the patients' age, age at first hospitalization, privileged vs. nonprivileged hospital status, or IQ. Finally, Watts (1970) found no differences in game behavior between athletes and non-athletes when they played like partners. When, however, each pair consisted of an athlete playing a non-athlete, the team athletes (football and track) cooperated less often than did their non-athlete partners, while the reverse was true of the participants in individual sports (track and gymnastics).

Specific Personality Dimensions

As we move to attempts to specify dimensions of personality differences relevant to game behavior, the results become somewhat discouraging. Studies which include a large number of correlations between personality variables and game behavior do not find very many more statistically significant correlations than would be expected by chance; studies which use only a few, theoretically relevant personality variables often find significant correlations between some combination of these variables and some aspect of behavior in the game situation, but these relationships do not hold up when replicated in successive studies or even (often) in the second phase of the same study; and the magnitude of the correlations that do reach statistical significance is seldom impressive.

Massive surveys of personality measures. Several studies have employed a large number of personality measures, thus providing the possibility of testing the overall null hypothesis.

Wallace and Rothaus (1969) studied the behavior of mental patients in a Restricted PD played for 10 trials. These authors correlated scores on the Army General Classification Test, four subscales (Good Impression, Achievement via Conformance, Femininity, Sociability) of the California Personality Inventory (Gough, 1957), an overall cooperation predictor based on a linear combination of these four subscales, and the Fundamental Interpersonal Relations Orientation-Behavior scale (FIRO-B, Schutz, 1958) with "17 behavioral and attitudinal measures taken for both individuals and dyads during the actual play of the game." The authors noted the fact that 6 percent and 1 percent of the 1,700 correlations were significant at the .05 and .01 levels, indicated that analysis of the higher (around .30) correlations revealed "no clustering around any single predictor [p. 379]," and refrained from further discussion of the personality variables.

Such Spartan refusal to capitalize on chance is rare. For instance, Klein and Solomon (1966) found 4 of 66 correlations statistically significant at the .05 level; Pilisuk et al. (1965) analyzed the relationship between 5 personality variables and game behavior in at least three different ways and found one statistically significant correlation; McKeown, Gahagan, and Tedeschi (1967) obtained five results which were statistically significant at the .09 level or better out of 56 correlations; and Pilisuk et al. (1968) obtained one statistically significant relationship (for females, but not for males) after correlating five individual difference measures with five different dependent measures. None of these authors hesitated to identify and to discuss those correlations which did reach statistical significance; nor is it necessarily desirable that Wallace and Rothaus' procedure be adopted in such cases. There is always the hope that either the authors or their readers will be able to discern the crucial concept which unites the findings and explains why these particular correlations reached significance while the others did not, or at least that the correlations will be replicated in future studies.

The Flint and Harris (1970a, b) studies which were cited earlier as evidence for individual differences included attempts to specify the nature of the differences. The median absolute magnitude of the 56 correlations calculated by

Flint and Harris (1970a) between row-player's or column-player's CD-DC score and his scores on McReynolds and Guevara's (1967) Success-Failure Inventory, Christie and Merton's (1958) Machiavellianism scale, and two of the subscales of Wrightsman's (1964) Philosophies of Human Nature scale, was only .057. Flint and Harris (1970b) computed the multiple correlation between the 16 subscales of Edwards' Personal Preference Schedule and each of eight dependent measures for each of the four games and each of the four experimental groups. Only four of these 128 regression analyses yielded statistically significant ($p < .05$) multiple correlations.

Self-Esteem. One of the few personality measures that has been used by enough different investigators in a wide enough range of experimental situations to permit successive refinement of hypotheses about its relationship to game behavior is the dimension of self-esteem (*SE*). A trio of studies (Pepitone, 1964; Faucheux & Moscovici, 1968; Pepitone, Faucheux, Moscovici, Cesa-Branchi, Magistretti, Iaconoa, Asprea, & Villoni, 1967) employed the same PD-Chicken hybrid game, with *S* playing against a preprogrammed, non-contingent strategy of 62 percent random cooperative choice. This strategy can be exploited by choosing the noncooperative response on every trial. As he had predicted on the basis of extensive theoretical and empirical considerations, Pepitone (1964) found that subjects given a success experience (high *SE* subjects) competed significantly more often than did low *SE* subjects, presumably because the former felt that they deserved more points. Faucheux and Moscovici (1968) found even larger differences between high *SE* and low *SE* subjects when the fact that they were interacting with a preprogrammed (and thus exploitable) sequence was made clearer. More importantly, when "chronic" self-esteem was used as the variable (i.e., subjects were assigned to high and low *SE* groups on the basis of a premeasure), Pepitone's finding of greater competitiveness by high *SE* subjects was reversed significantly.

Pepitone et al. (1967) reviewed these findings together with the results of a study involving Italian subjects which found greater competitiveness by low *SE* subjects even when self-esteem was manipulated. The authors suggest that this result may have been due to an overrepresentation of chronically low self-esteem subjects, relative to the French (Faucheux & Moscovici, 1968) and American (Pepitone et al., 1967) samples.

Pilisuk et al. (1965) have subsequently found no significant relationship between self-acceptance as measured by the Rogers and Dymond Q-sort technique and behavior of truly interacting subject pairs in a 21-alternative version of a Restricted PD.

Other specific personality variables. Turning to other specific variables which have been employed in more than one study, we note first Deutsch's (1960) classic finding of a positive relationship between authoritarianism, as measured by the California *F* scale, and competitiveness in a 2-trial Restricted PD. Subsequently Gahagan, Horai, Berger, and Tedeschi (1967, as cited in Tedeschi et al., 1968) found no difference between high and low authoritarians in a 100-trial PD game, but McKeown et al. (1967), using a Restricted PD in which one player's payoffs were all positive while only T and R were positive for the other ("weak") player, found that two of the five significant

(.09 level or better) correlations involved authoritarianism. Both of these relationships were significant at beyond the .01 level and, despite the fact that only 5 of 56 significance tests run in the study yielded significance at the .09 level or better, all five results withstood a cross-validation performed by comparing results for subjects run early in the semester with late-semester results. Friedell (1968) found in an Attack-Retaliation game closely related to Chicken that authoritarianism increased the propensity to retaliate, reducing the other's payoff from $1.50 to $0.15 but also cutting one's own payoff from $0.15 to $0.10. On the other hand, neither Fry (1965), using a 3x3 coordination game, nor Wrightsman (1966), using a turn-taking version of the PD, found any significant relationship of behavior to authoritarianism. Finally, the only significant relationship of a personality variable to behavior in the Pilisuk et al. (1965) study of a 21-alternative PD was a tendency for pairs of subjects who were both high in Tolerance for Ambiguity to become "doves" (which requires meeting several criteria indicative of a cooperative approach to the game) more often than did subject pairs in which one or both members of the pair had lower ambiguity-tolerance scores. Half of the 18 items on the Tolerance for Ambiguity scale devised by these authors were known to have high correlations (presumably negative, though this is not stated) with the F-scale.

Another popular personality variable is the Internationalism scale, which Lutzker (1960) found to correlate positively with cooperation in a Chicken game. McClintock, Gallo, and Harrison (1965), in a study involving a game in which one player has no influence on the other's payoff while the second player has virtually complete control over his partner's outcome, found that Internationalists in the high-power role responded more punitively than did Isolationists to their simulated partner's having, in a previous session, forced them to lose points. This presents a less noble image of the Internationalist than did Lutzker's results. Pilisuk et al. (1965) found no difference between Internationalists and Isolationists in behavior in a 21-alternative version of the PD, even under conditions designed to simulate an arms race as closely as possible. Pilisuk et al. (1968) again found no relationship of behavior to Internationalism in this game.

Bixenstine et al. (1963) devised a measure of ethicality, none of whose subscales correlated significantly with behavior in a PD game played against one of two noncontingent strategies. However, they found that the difference between two of the subscales, N (a measure of moderate, conventional endorsement of ethical principles) minus F (a measure of extreme, moralistic ethics) did correlate significantly positively with cooperation in the situation. This new measure of flexible ethicality was unrelated to cooperative behavior in a nonsymmetric game (Bixenstine et al., 1964).

The Friendliness scale of the Guilford-Zimmerman Temperament Survey correlated significantly with percent cooperative choices for females in the Pilisuk et al. (1968) study but was unrelated to behavior in the Bixenstine et al. (1964) study.

Christie et al. (in press) found that subjects scoring high on the Machiavellianism scale (Christie & Merton, 1958) became increasingly more exploitative (as compared with Low-Mach Ss) over trials in a Restricted Chicken game played against a program of 80 percent noncontingent cooperation, though the main effect of Machiavellianism was nonsignificant. Subsequent studies by Daniels (1966), using a 7-alternative, turn-taking version of the PD; Wrightsman (1966), using a nonrestricted PD; and Condry (1967), using a 10x10 coordination game, have failed to detect any significant correlations of game behavior with Machiavellianism.

Murdoch (1968) found that, under conditions of high salience of the social responsibility norm, Berkowitz and Daniels' (1964) revision of Harris' (1957) Social Responsibility Scale correlated with the amount of help rendered to the low-power subject by the high-power subject in Thibaut's "bargaining as payoff" game. Scores on this scale were, however, unrelated to behavior in the Wrightsman (1966) and Condry (1967) studies.

Four of the subscales of Wrightsman's (1964) Philosophies of Human Nature scale were found by Wrightsman (1966) to distinguish between trusting and distrusting subjects in the first of two experiments involving a turn-taking version of the PD. Two of these subscales (Favorability and Trustworthiness) also were related to the classifications in the second experiment involving the same game, though now the only difference of any magnitude was between subjects classified in the "garbage" category of "Others" and the other two classifications. Uejio and Wrightsman (1967) found that the Altruism, Trustworthiness, and Strength of Will scores correlated positively and significantly with level of cooperation in a Restricted PD when the subject knew his partner was Caucasian (whether he himself was Caucasian or Japanese) but correlated negatively and nonsignificantly with cooperation when the partner was known to be Japanese. Wrightsman, Davis, Lucker, Bruininks, Evans, Wilde, Paulson, and Clark (1967) found a significant relationship between scores on Altruism and behavior in the 90 percent competitive feedback condition of an experiment in which the subject always chose first in what was otherwise a Restricted PD, but found no significant relationship for this same scale in the other three strategy conditions, nor for the other subscales in any of the four conditions.

There are three measures which, to the present author's knowledge, have been used only once, with favorable results. Crowne's (1966) finding of greater competitiveness in a Restricted PD by sons of entrepreneurs did not hold for entrepreneurs' sons who displayed "maladjusted" patterns on Rotter's (1942) Level of Aspiration Board. Fry (1965) found that pairs of subjects whose scores on the Allport and Allport Ascendance-Submission scale were not in adjacent quartiles performed better in a 3x3 coordination game. And Murdoch (1968), in a study using the "bargaining as payoff" game, found that subjects who were assigned the higher-power role during the interaction (and who thus decided how the available points were to be distributed when both players chose to bargain) later answered Vinacke and Ragusa's (1964) Exploitative-Accommodative Strategy Scale in a more exploitative manner than did the low-power subjects.

Personality measures which have been used without success in predicting game play thus far include Absolutism-Pragmatism with respect to politico-military strategy and a measure of Attitudes toward Nuclear War (Friedell, 1968); Agreement Response Tendency (Klein & Solomon, 1966); monetary risk preference (Pilisuk et al., 1968; Pilisuk et al., 1965); Kogan and Wallach's (1964) Social Risk Taking measure (Pilisuk et al., 1965); Gough's (1957) California Personality Inventory, the Army General Classification Test, and Schutz's (1958) FIRO-B scale (Wallace & Rothaus, 1969); and the Buss-Durkee Hostility Inventory (Buss, 1962), the Rehfisch Rigidity Scale (Rehfisch, 1958), Chein's Personal Optimism and Anti-Police Attitudes Scale (cited as personal communication to Wrightsman, 1966), Crowne and Marlowe's (1960) Social Desirability scale, and Edwards' (1957) Social Desirability scale (Wrightsman, 1966).

The logical symmetry of the Pearson product-moment correlation coefficient suggests that any game behavior which correlates highly with some measure of an individual-difference dimension could be used to predict (assess) an individual subject's position on that dimension. However, the only published reports of such an application known to the present author are those of Ravich's use of marriage partners' behavior in the trucking game (Ravich, 1966; Ravich, Deutsch, & Brown, 1966) or the Ravich Interpersonal Game/ Test developed from it (Ravich, 1967, 1969; Game is set, 1968; Model-railroad, 1967) as an indicator of their typical modes of interaction. Ravich (personal communication) emphasizes that the RIG/T is used to assess the characteristics of the dyad, rather than of either individual member thereof. The partners' experiences in the game are reported to be of therapeutic value.

One aspect of the Ravich et al. report which deserves comment is that the authors made no attempt to use underlying personality dimensions as intervening variables but instead took the game-playing behavior of their clients as a relatively direct measure of their typical approaches to interpersonal interaction. This, in the present author's opinion, is apt to be the most fruitful application of experimental games to personality research in general and to assessment in particular. The ultimate goal of assessment is, after all, to be able to predict cross-situational consistencies in an individual's behavior. Paper-and-pencil measures have been used for this purpose in the past because of their convenience and because of the unavailability or impracticality of methods for collecting meaningful samples of behavior under standardized conditions. Experimental games provide just such samples of behavior. It would therefore seem appropriate to concentrate less on the relationship between game behavior and paper-and-pencil measures, and more on the direct assessment through within-subjects designs of the magnitude and the qualitative nature of intraindividual consistencies in game-playing behavior and, ultimately, in social interaction in general.

A promising dimension of behavioral consistency. One dimension along which individuals will almost certainly be found to vary is that of the degree of concern shown for the outcomes of the other person(s) involved in an interaction situation. A great deal of evidence has accumulated that the objective payoffs provided to a subject in a game study correlate rather poorly with the individual's subjective satisfaction with (the utility of) those outcomes (cf. especially Messick & Thorngate, 1967; McClintock & McNeel,

1966b). Several authors (Anatol Rapoport, 1956; Hoggatt, 1967; Sawyer, 1966; Harris, 1969b) have suggested that subjects may in general seek to maximize a weighted average of their own and others' objectively defined payoffs, though much research and theory (e.g., McClintock & McNeel, 1966a; Messick & McClintock, 1968) seems to assume that subjects must either be completely individualistic, completely competitive, or completely cooperative. Apfelbaum (1969) suggests that the criteria actually employed by subjects (e.g., earn as much for myself as possible so long as this is not over x percent more than my partner receives) may be too complex to summarize as a single dimension.

Most research on the altruism-sadism dimension has had the goal of assessing the general level of competitiveness in whole populations rather than identifying any individual's position on this dimension, though Sawyer and Friedell (1965), Wyer (1969), and Apfelbaum (1969) have each shown that an individual's responses (on a paper-and-pencil questionnaire) to various hypothetical situations varying principally in their allocation of available rewards between himself and the others involved are predictive of that person's behavior in experimental games. The recourse to paper-and-pencil measures in these studies is, in the present author's view, unfortunate and could be avoided by the use of within-subjects designs in conjunction with games whose structures vary in ways likely to elicit different responses from persons assigning different weights to the others' payoffs.

SUMMARY

The great promise of experimental games as tools for personality research and assessment has not yet been fulfilled, in large part because of failure to exploit their greatest strength, namely their status as samples of behavior in well-defined, tightly controlled, and yet meaningful interaction situations. It is earnestly hoped that the present chapter will help encourage psychologists who wrestle with problems of assessment to exploit the enormous potential usefulness of experimental games in the assessment of consistent individual differences in approaches to social interaction.

CHAPTER XIII

Neuroregulatory agents and psychological assessment

Jack D. Barchas, Jon M. Stolk,
Roland D. Ciaranello, and David A. Hamburg

Hormones and compounds that act as transmitters or regulators in the central nervous system (CNS) only recently have been studied as they relate to psychological assessment. To date, these studies have been primarily at a basic research level and concerned with the investigation of the relation of such compounds to behavior. Eventually, the goal of research in this area is to provide an additional set of techniques to aid in the overall issue of assessing human functioning. This type of biochemical data may provide additional information to help in diagnosis, predict the outcome of a particular treatment, choose the treatment procedures to be utilized, or, at the minimum, give further information about the "status" of the patient. Eventually, the question of the interrelationship between *psychological factors* and *biochemical factors* in etiology and maintenance of certain forms of illness becomes a major one. The potential use of information concerning neuroregulators in treatment of some disorders is of the greatest potential importance.

This review will focus on the catecholamines (CA) and the indoleamine (IA), serotonin (5-hydroxytryptamine, 5-HT). CA and IA are formed from amino acids. There are a number of derivatives of each of these two classes that take their names from the parent ring structure and the presence of an amino group (Figure 1). These chemicals belong to a class of compounds referred to as biogenic amines. The original compounds in this class are the adrenal catecholamines—epinephrine (adrenaline, E) and norepinephrine (noradrenaline, NE). These two compounds are viewed as hormones of the adrenal medulla and have been extensively studied biochemically and pharmacologically. Only small amounts of the compounds can enter the brain due to their inability to pass the blood-brain barrier (BBB). More recently, CA have been found to be formed in the brain, where they are thought to

Work of the authors' laboratory presented in this paper was supported by MH 13,259, MH 16,632, NASA NGR 05-020-168, and ONR N00014-67-A-0112-0027. J. B. holds NIMH Research Career Development Award MH 24,161. We should like to thank several persons for critically reading the manuscript, including Drs. H. Keith H. Brodie, Jefferson DoAmaral, and Rudolf Moos, of Stanford University, and Dr. Gerald P. Ginsburg, of the University of Nevada. We should also like to thank Mrs. Rosemary Schmele and Mrs. Judy Lookabill for their secretarial assistance and Miss Jill Leland for preparing the figures.

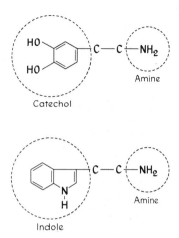

Figure 1. Diagram of catecholamine and indoleamine structure.

function as synaptic transmitters or neuromodulators. The principally occurring CA in brain are NE and dopamine (DA). The IA are also present in high amounts in brain. 5-HT is the most extensively studied member of this group. The IA, like the CA, may function as synaptic transmitters in the CNS or as modulators of neuronal function.

Because of the lack of proof as to their mode of function in the brain, CA and IA are classed here as "neuroregulators"; however, we will usually be describing their alleged neurotransmitter role. The brain neuroregulatory agents (sometimes called neurohormones) share common characteristics of neurotransmitters elsewhere: enzyme systems are necessary for the production and destruction of the chemical messengers; storage mechanisms must be present; the transmitter must be released in the vicinity of a sensitive receptor, and be in an active form; specific target cells must be able to receive and act upon the message of the transmitter to effect an appropriate action; and finally, mechanisms must exist for terminating the effects or the activity of the neurohumor.

Both the CA and the IA are found in very discrete areas of the brain thought to be involved in emotional behaviors, and are affected by many drugs known to alter the behavioral state of the organism. These findings led to the implication of the importance of these in behavior. This approach has received further support from investigation of changes in the concentration or utilization of these compounds in the brain as a consequence of behavioral states.

This chapter will examine the importance in behavior of: (1) adrenal gland CA as hormones, (2) brain CA as neuroregulators, and (3) brain 5-HT as a neuroregulator.[1] Various aspects of processes involving neuroregulators have been subject to major reviews including the following: neuroregulators and

---

[1]A list of commonly used abbreviations may be found in Table 1.

Table 1
Commonly Used Abbreviations

ACTH	Adrenocorticotropic Hormone
αMT	Alpha-Methyltyrosine (AMPT, αMPT)
BBB	Blood-brain barrier
CA	Catecholamine(s)
CNS	Central Nervous System
COMT	Catechol O-Methyl Transferase
DA	Dopamine
DOPA	3, 4-Dihydroxyphenylalanine
E	Epinephrine, Adrenaline
5-HT	Serotonin (5-Hydroxytryptamine)
5-HTP	5-Hydroxytryptophan
HVA	Homovanillic Acid
IA	Indoleamine(s)
MAO	Monoamine Oxidase
MHPG	Methoxyhydroxyphenylglycol
NE	Norepinephrine, Noradrenaline
PCPA	Para-Chlorophenylalanine
PNMT	Phenylethanolamine N-Methyl Transferase
TH	Tyrosine Hydroxylase
TPH	Tryptophan Hydroxylase
VMA	Vanillylmandelic Acid

emotional illness (Eiduson, Geller, Yuwiler, & Eiduson, 1964; Schildkraut & Kety, 1967; Mandell & Spooner, 1968; Mandell & Mandell, 1969; Schildkraut, 1970; Hamburg, 1970; Williams, 1970; Himwich, 1971), CA (Axelrod, 1959; Rothballer, 1959; Acheson, 1966; Wurtman, 1966; Euler, 1967; Mason, 1968; Melmon, 1968; Geffen & Livett, 1971), 5-HT (Garattini & Valzelli, 1965; Erspamer, 1966; Garattini & Shore, 1968; Page, 1968; Sjoerdsma, 1970), and psychopharmacology (Kety & Sampson, 1967; Bloom & Giarman, 1968a; Efron, 1968; Hollister, 1968; Klein & Davis, 1969; Clark & Giudice, 1970; Cooper, Bloom, & Roth, 1970; Smythies, 1970; Rech & Moore, 1971).

CATECHOLAMINE PHYSIOLOGY AND BIOCHEMISTRY

Synthesis of the Catecholamines

CA are synthesized and exert their actions in a number of tissues. Of primary concern for this review are those CA produced in the adrenal medulla and secreted from it as hormones influencing other areas of the body, as well as those CA synthesized by nerve cells and probably used as transmitters across synapses in the brain, in which case CA are viewed not as hormones, but instead as neuroregulatory agents locally made and utilized. Like the adrenal medulla, the brain has the metabolic machinery to form CA through the metabolic steps described below. Although formed in great quantities in the adrenal medulla, only a very small amount of the adrenal CA reaches the brain from the blood, because of the BBB that impedes the passage of all but extremely minute amounts of these compounds. Because of the BBB, both adrenal and brain must be viewed as separate, extremely active, CA-synthesizing compartments with little or no cross-supply between the two.

A schematic representation of the synthetic pathway of CA is shown in Figure 2. The initial enzyme in CA biosynthesis is tyrosine hydroxylase (TH). Enzyme activity in the brain is greatest in those areas known to have high concentrations of CA-containing nerve endings. As will be discussed in detail below, TH appears to be the rate-limiting step in CA formation and, thus, assumes an important role in regulating the levels and activity of CA in various tissues (Spector, Gordon, Sjoerdsma, & Udenfriend, 1967).

The product of tyrosine hydroxylation, dihydroxyphenylalanine (DOPA), is rapidly decarboxylated to DA by the enzyme aromatic L-amino acid decarboxylase. Normally, DA is found in high concentrations primarily in the basal ganglia of the brain. DA has important roles in motor function and may also have a role in emotional behaviors and endocrine function.

Conversion of DA to NE is accomplished by the enzyme dopamine-β-oxidase (DβO). NE is generally thought to be the predominant transmitter in the peripheral adrenergic nervous system. This is the system that contributes the bulk of the CA that appears in the urine. Changes in urinary CA or CA metabolite content as a response to stress or other forms of behavior reflect alterations in peripheral rather than CNS CA concentration. These alterations are brought about as a consequence of changes in impulse flow to adrenergically innervated organs, and to secretion into the blood of the CA stored in the adrenal medulla. The brain also contains enzymatic machinery for forming NE where it may serve as a transmitter in certain areas of the brain (Vogt, 1954).

The final synthetic enzyme, phenylethanolamine N-methyl transferase (PNMT), converts NE to E. Enzyme activity is high only in the adrenal medulla, although low levels of PNMT activity and, thus, E formation have been found in mammalian brain (Barchas, Ciaranello, & Steinman, 1969).

Storage of Catecholamines after Formation
The physiologically active CA are stored in submicroscopic granules within the adrenal medulla or in nerve cells. The medulla of most adult mammals contains two types of granule-containing chromaffin cells—one storing E, the other NE.

Disposition and Metabolism of Catecholamines
After their synthesis, CA may be disposed of in various ways. The bulk of the CA within the cell is stored within granular structures in close proximity to the site of release as shown for nerve cells in Figure 3. In the brain, the CA that is released may be handled in different ways: (1) it may react with an appropriate receptor, thereby resulting in the propagation of a nerve impulse; (2) it may be actively transported back into a CA-containing cell by a mechanism called "reuptake," which may be of particular importance in the brain since some theories of emotional illness have involved this mechanism, and certain drugs used in treatment alter reuptake; (3) the compound may be metabolized outside the neuron; or (4) it or its further metabolites may be excreted in the urine.

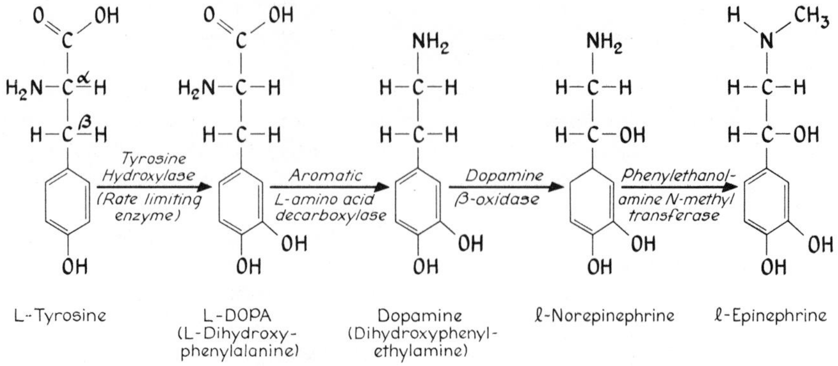

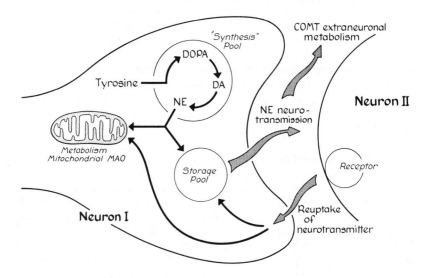

Figure 2. Metabolic pathway of catecholamine synthesis.

The metabolic pathways for each CA are shown in Figures 4 (NE), 5 (E), and 6 (DA). The most important intracellular enzyme involved in the degradation of CA is monoamine oxidase (MAO). The MAO pathway results in the removal of the terminal amino group; this causes a marked loss of activity in the compound.

The second major enzyme catabolizing CA, catechol O-methyl transferase (COMT), is believed to be located extraneuronally. Reaction with COMT

Figure 3. Schematic model of a catecholamine neuron. (Because many of the findings were made at the National Institutes of Health and the National Institute for Mental Health, this model is sometimes referred to as the "NIH Neuron.")

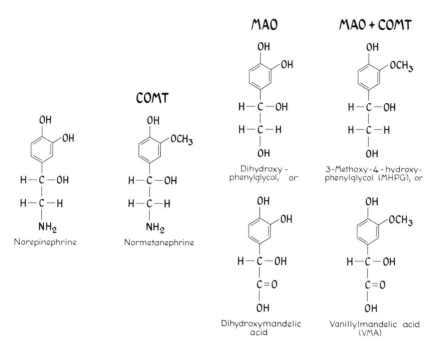

Figure 4. Metabolic pathway of norepinephrine.

results in the addition of a methyl group to one of the hydroxyl (−OH) groups of the CA. Again, this metabolic step decreases the biological activity. The CA can be inactivated by one or the other, or both, of the two enzymes resulting in the formation of a number of metabolites. After removal of the amino group, the metabolites of NE and E are the same (Figures 4 and 5). The enzymes for metabolism of CA are all present in the CNS. CA released from the adrenal gland or the sympathetic (adrenergic) nervous system circulate through the body and are taken up by several tissues where they are metabolized by MAO or COMT or by both enzymes. These processes occur very actively in the liver. Many of these metabolites can be measured in the urine after the release of CA from the adrenal either normally or in times of stress. The most generally used indicators of CA secretion from the adrenal are the levels of E, NE, or vanillylmandelic acid (VMA) in the urine. As will become evident from further discussion, a great deal of important information has been inferred from the pattern of CA catabolism in the brain, i.e., whether MAO or COMT activity is altered.

Regulation of Catecholamine Formation

The factors regulating CA biosynthesis have been under intensive investigation during the past few years. It has become clear from the work of several investigators (Euler, 1962; Gordon, Reid, Sjoerdsma, & Udenfriend, 1966; Alousi & Weiner, 1966; Roth, Stjärne, & Euler, 1966; Sedvall & Kopin, 1967)

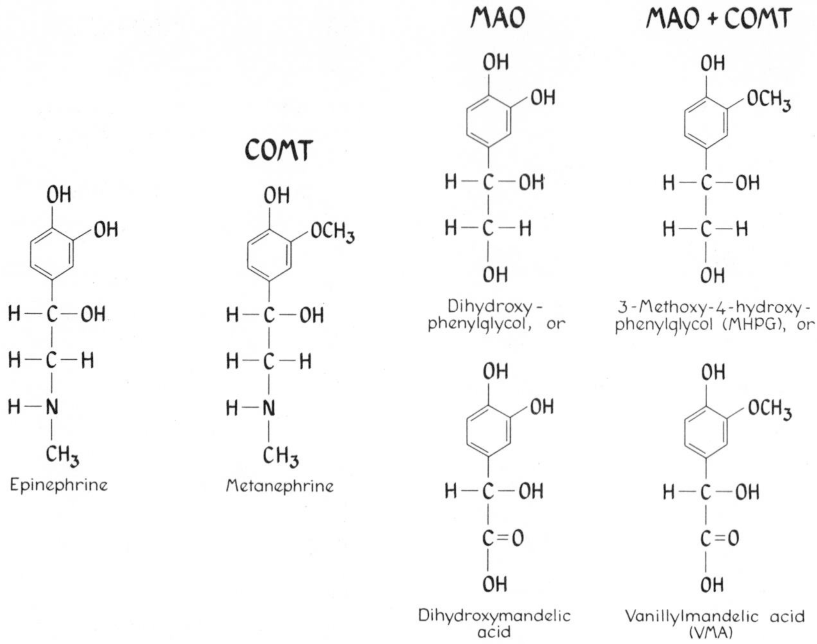

MAO   MAO + COMT

OH   OH

⟋OH   ⟋OCH₃

COMT

OH   OH   H—C—OH   H—C—OH

⟋OH   ⟋OCH₃   H—C—H   H—C—H

                                  OH   OH

H—C—OH   H—C—OH   Dihydroxy-   3-Methoxy-4-hydroxy-
                               phenylglycol, or phenylglycol (MHPG), or
H—C—H   H—C—H

H—N   H—N   OH   OH

CH₃   CH₃   ⟋OH   ⟋OCH₃

Epinephrine   Metanephrine

                               H—C—OH   H—C—OH

                               C=O   C=O

                               OH   OH

                               Dihydroxymandelic Vanillylmandelic acid
                               acid   (VMA)

Figure 5. Metabolic pathway of epinephrine.

that when the nerves to adrenergically innervated tissues are stimulated, the activity of TH, the first and rate-limiting enzyme in the formation of CA, is increased. The activity of the enzyme can increase acutely two- to threefold, thereby allowing for maintenance of NE levels in situations of heavy use of CA. Only under extreme stress are CA levels decreased; under such conditions, even a brisk increase in synthesis can not keep pace with the vigorous utilization. Evidence suggests that normally the levels of CA in the tissue may regulate the activity of TH; when the level of CA begins to decrease, the enzyme activity is increased. This process constitutes feedback inhibition (Spector et al., 1967). Another mechanism may come into play with long-term stimulation in which the actual number of TH molecules increases (Weiner & Rabadjija, 1968).

The second enzyme involved in the synthesis of CA, aromatic L-amino acid decarboxylase, has thus far not shown substantial variation with physiological or psychological states. Little is known about the regulation of dopamine β-hydroxylase, the third enzyme in the formation of CA.

The regulation of the formation of E from NE by the enzyme PNMT in the adrenal gland appears to involve both the adrenal cortex and the adrenal medulla. The adrenal gland with its distinct outer cortex and inner medulla is actually two glands in one. The cortex secretes steroid hormones and plays an essential role in the stress response. Adrenal steroid output is mediated through the pituitary gland and is stimulated by a pituitary hormone,

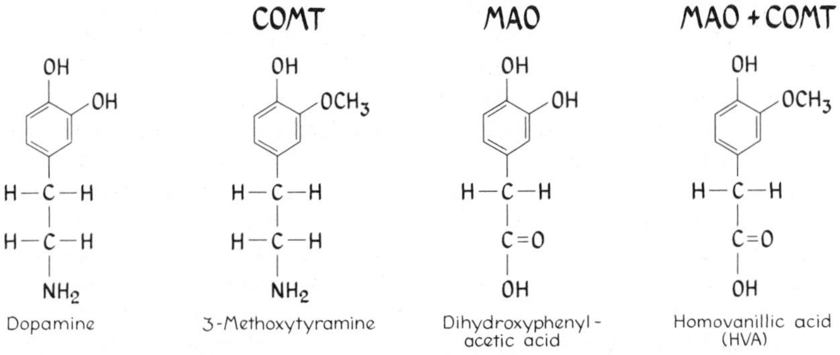

Figure 6. Metabolic pathway of dopamine.

adrenocorticotropic hormone (ACTH). On the other hand, the adrenal medulla also secretes hormones during stress, these being E and NE. Secretion from the adrenal is controlled via peripheral and central nervous system activity. Several avenues of work (Coupland, 1953; Wurtman & Axelrod, 1966) have demonstrated that adrenal steroids are essential in maintaining the levels of PNMT, and, in the absence of adrenal steroids, the level of PNMT is markedly reduced. The extent to which day-to-day stress may affect PNMT and the mechanisms by which severe chronic stress elevates PNMT (Vernikos-Danellis, Ciaranello, & Barchas, 1968; Ciaranello, Barchas, & Vernikos-Danellis, 1969) still remains to be explored. Changes in the capacity to form E by altering PNMT activity with long-term stress could have special significance in terms of the physiological, biochemical, or behavioral aspects of chronic stress.

Selected Aspects of the Pharmacology
of the Adrenergic Nervous System

An understanding of the relationship between the CA or IA and behavior depends, in large measure, upon comprehension of the basic pharmacological actions of various drugs on the nervous system.

Reserpine, a drug used to treat hypertension and occasionally psychosis (Bein, 1953; Kline, 1954), was found to deplete peripheral and CNS stores of endogenous CA, as well as of 5-HT (Carlsson, Rosengren, Bertler, & Nilsson, 1957a). The long-lasting reduction in endogenous CA content was demonstrated as caused by an effect on the storage of the CA in adrenergic nerve granules (Carlsson, Hillarp, & Waldeck, 1963). The resultant biochemical action of reserpine, therefore, is the *intraneuronal* release of stored NE and rapid inactivation by MAO (Glowinski, Iversen, & Axelrod, 1966). The behavioral depression observed after reserpine treatment has been attributed to the reduction in brain CA stores.

Several drugs deplete neuronal CA stores, but do so by mechanisms other than that of reserpine. One of these is a-methyldihydroxyphenylalanine (Aldomet®), which is converted *in vivo* to a-methyl-norepinephrine (a-Me-NE). This drug has been found useful in the treatment of some forms of hypertension and has been used in many psychological studies in animals. By virtue of its structural similarity to NE, a-Me-NE is stored within the neuron in the same manner as endogenous NE (Carlsson, Lundborg, Stitzel, & Waldeck, 1967). Although a-Me-NE has biological activity of its own, it is less potent than NE and results in behavioral depression after protracted administration. It is an example of a class of drugs called "false transmitters."

Amphetamine and related sympathomimetic amines cause physiological effects similar to those seen when the sympathetic nervous system is activated. Certain of these drugs possess prominent central stimulant activity. Amphetamine exerts its activity by several mechanisms, including the release of endogenous CA stores. In contrast to reserpine, amphetamine-like compounds do not usually deplete endogenous CA stores by disrupting intracellular storage processes; rather, amphetamine facilitates the release of a relatively small amount ("pool") of NE from the cell, which then interacts with the normal post-synaptic receptors to cause stimulation (Smith, Trendelenburg, Langer, & Tsai, 1966; Stolk & Rech, 1970).

Another drug that depletes the level of CA is a-methyltyrosine (a-MT). This drug works by a different mechanism in that it inhibits the formation of CA by inhibiting the first enzyme in their formation, TH, which converts tyrosine to DOPA. This compound, therefore, is a potent depletor of the levels of brain CA. The drug a-MT is widely used in basic animal studies involving behavior.

Drugs inhibiting the uptake of CA include the tricyclic antidepressants—imipramine (Tofranil®) and desmethylimipramine (Pertofrane®). These drugs inhibit the neuronal membrane transport system for CA (Figure 3) and prevent released transmitter from being taken up again by the cell and, therefore, they increase the extracellular metabolism of NE (Schanberg, Schildkraut, & Kopin, 1967). Current hypotheses for the antidepressant action of the drugs center upon their reversing a postulated relative deficit of NE at the receptor in depression.

The only class of drugs affecting the enzymes responsible for the degradation of CA that have found extensive use either experimentally or clinically are the MAO inhibitors. As might be expected (Figures 3 and 4), MAO inhibitors cause an increase in CA levels, accompanied by higher levels of COMT-derived catabolites.

The phenothiazines—which include chlorpromazine (Thorazine®), the powerful antipsychotic agent—are thought to have prominent antiadrenergic activity in the brain (Brodie & Costa, 1962). However, the mechanism of the phenothiazines' antipsychotic action is not understood.

SEROTONIN PHYSIOLOGY AND BIOCHEMISTRY

Synthesis and Metabolism of the Indoleamines and Serotonin

The metabolic pathway responsible for the synthesis of the indolealkylamines is diagramed in Figure 7. The initial enzyme in the synthesis of serotonin (5-HT) is tryptophan hydroxylase (TPH). TPH, presumed to be the rate-limiting step in 5-HT biosynthesis, was recently characterized in the elegant

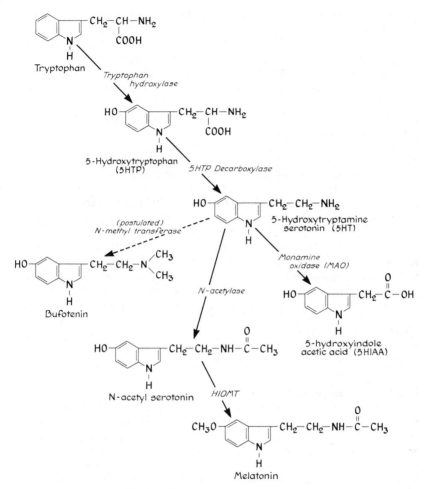

Figure 7. Metabolic pathway of indoleamine formation and metabolism.

studies of Ichiyama, Nakamura, Nishizuka, and Hayaishi (1970). The levels of TPH appear to correlate with the regional distribution of 5-HT in brain.

5-Hydroxytryptophan (5-HTP), the product of tryptophan hydroxylation, is decarboxylated rapidly by the enzyme 5-HTP decarboxylase. The latter enzyme is similar, if not identical, to DOPA decarboxylase, and some investigators propose the use of the name aromatic L-amino acid decarboxylase for the enzyme as a more general name. The product of decarboxylation is 5-HT.

MAO is believed to be the major intracellular catabolic enzyme for 5-HT. The final product of the MAO pathway, 5-hydroxylindoleacetic acid (5-HIAA), is found in the cerebrospinal fluid.

A series of synthetic enzymes is present in the pineal gland for producing the indole, melatonin, from 5-HT. Melatonin may be a pineal hormone but, due to difficulty in its assay, its role is yet to be determined. The body of literature pertinent to melatonin and the pineal has been summarized (Wurtman, Axelrod, & Kelly, 1968; Barchas, DaCosta, & Spector, 1967). Certain derivatives of 5-HT in which the amine is methylated are potent psychotomimetic agents. Active research is currently underway to ascertain whether these compounds are formed endogenously and whether they have any relationship to psychoses. The derivatives include bufotenin (Figure 7) and 5-methoxybufotenin.

Storage of Serotonin

Early work has revealed that most of the 5-HT in brain is particle-bound, as opposed to being "free" in the supernatant of brain homogenates (Giarman & Schanberg, 1958; Schanberg & Giarman, 1962). These results strongly suggested that 5-HT, like NE, is stored in distinct granular structures. Aghajanian and Bloom (1967) studied the localization of radioactive 5-HT after injection of the material into the ventricular spaces of the brain (intraventricular injections). Much less is known about the binding and release of 5-HT from nerve cells than is known about CA. Chase, Breese, and Kopin (1967) and Chase, Katz, and Kopin (1969) have studied these processes in nerve slices and demonstrated the effects of drugs in such preparations. In general, the literature would suggest that 5-HT is probably contained in specific fiber tracts within the brain and released upon nerve stimulation (Aghajanian, Rosecrans, & Sheard, 1967; Fuxe, Hökfelt, & Ungerstedt, 1968; Sheard & Aghajanian, 1968; Eccleston, Ritchie, & Roberts, 1970).

Regulation of Serotonin Synthesis

Surprisingly little is known about the regulation of 5-HT synthesis. The level of tryptophan may be critical in regulating activity of the entire pathway, probably by influencing the TPH step. This is an area under active investigation. It is currently felt that, if 5-HT has important behavioral roles, there must be multiple processes controlling its formation and rate of utilization to allow for the plasticity of emotional behavior. The question is of importance to behavioral neurochemists, but is also important to those attempting to develop improved psychoactive medication for the severe emotional disorders in which IA have been implicated.

Selected Aspects of the Pharmacology of the Serotonergic System

Inhibition of the formation of 5-HT can be accomplished by use of *para*-chlorophenylalanine (PCPA, PCP), which inhibits the first step (TPH) in the formation of 5-HT (Koe & Weissman, 1966). The inhibitor takes several days to achieve depletion of brain 5-HT.

Depletion of brain 5-HT occurs after treatment with reserpine, which decreases the content of 5-HT in storage particles. As described earlier, reserpine has a similar effect on CA and, hence, reserpine is extremely non-specific in terms of the biogenic amine affected by the drug.

The action of several other drugs has been speculatively related to 5-HT with less proof. In particular, the phenothiazine tranquilizers and the tricyclic antidepressants may affect 5-HT in the brain (Schildkraut, Schanberg, Breese, & Kopin, 1969).

An area of intense investigation has been the relation of some of the hallucinogens to 5-HT and its metabolism. Several studies have indicated that LSD (lysergic acid diethylamide) may interfere with the utilization of 5-HT and inhibit the normal functioning of 5-HT-containing nerve cells (Rosecrans, Lovell, & Freedman, 1967; Aghajanian & Freedman, 1968). Since the LSD molecule is related structurally to 5-HT, this type of speculation takes on particular interest (Snyder & Richelson, 1968). A number of other compounds thought to be hallucinogens also resemble 5-HT, raising the question of whether this class of drugs may act in part through inhibiting the utilization of 5-HT in selected areas of the brain (Freedman, Gottlieb, & Lovell, 1970).

ADRENAL MEDULLARY HORMONES

Behavioral Effects of Infused Catecholamines: Human Studies

One approach to studying the behavioral effects of biogenic amines in humans is by infusing the amines in the cardiovascular system and observing the resultant behavior. Infusion studies have presented such difficulties as (1) lack of double blind controls, so that the experimenter, and in most cases the subject, was aware of the drug being administered and what to "expect," (2) drugs were given to an individual already anxious about the experiment so that the range of response was limited, and (3) the pharmacological dose of the drug might have been outside that normally secreted physiologically in physiological and behavioral states.

One of the earliest studies of the psychological effects of E was performed by Wearn and Sturgis (1919). Their paper begins: "With the mobilization of our troops, and especially the drafted troops, at the entrance of this country into the war, the problem of sorting the fit from the unfit was one of the first to come up [p. 248]." Essentially, their question is one of psychological assessment. The investigators gave E and noted that there was a difference between normal individuals and individuals with "anxiety," sometimes called "irritable heart syndrome" or "neuroasthenia." The normals had no reaction while the anxiety subjects had pronounced effects from the E injections but had no response to the control injections. The authors concluded that the subjects with "irritable heart" had a hypersensitivity to E, and that these patients, classed as neurotic and neuroasthenic, are ". . . not good material from which to make a soldier. . . . They are not fit to fight . . . [p. 268]."

The paper of Wearn and Sturgis raises several basic issues, yet to be resolved, concerning the relation of peripheral CA to behavior. First, what is the relationship of E to behavior and what emotional tone is produced by E? Does it have a variety of roles in activation of emotional responses? Further, are there individuals who are more sensitive than others to the psychological effects of CA?

Marañon (1924), and also Cantril and Hunt (1932), described the phenomenon of an "as if" or "cold emotion" in most persons given E. Subjects have physiological changes of emotion but do not have the psychological component of emotion.

Lindemann and Finesinger (1940) performed a thorough study on a population of neurotic individuals, all of whom had symptoms of anxiety attacks. After E injections, the subjects gradually became uncommunicative—they spoke hesitantly, used few words, and seemed to have difficulty in describing their feelings. Remarks tended to be concerned with the internal world of the individual rather than the external world. Thirty percent of the subjects reported feelings of depression after the E injections. A number of questions arise from the report and deserve further investigation: e.g., is there a subpopulation of persons with emotional disorders, such as depression or anxiety, that are more susceptible to the effects of peripheral E?

Of exceptional theoretical and experimental interest have been the studies of Schachter and Singer (1962) and Schachter and Wheeler (1962), who applied the tools of social psychology to investigate the effects of E injections. In one of their experiments, subjects were given E and exposed to various emotional environments. There was a great tendency for the subject to follow the emotional lead of the experimenter's agent (responding with euphoria or anger) unless the subject had been informed in advance of the physiological responses he would experience. In the latter event, the subjects tended to respond in accordance with the advance information. Thus, the specific emotional response may not be determined by E. Rather, E seems to elicit emotional activation, and the cognitive accompaniments of the activation, then, strongly influence the specific form of the response. Subjects attempt to fix a cognition to explain the physiological activation. If they have an explanation available from advance information, they are less likely to "catch" the emotion of the experimenter's agent.

In an extension of the studies on the effect of E on emotional responses, Schachter and Wheeler performed an experiment in which subjects viewed a comedy movie after having been given E or saline. The group treated with E clearly experienced the film as more humorous than did the saline group. The results are interpreted as consistent with the notion that emotional state is "a function of a state of physiological arousal and an appropriate cognition [p. 127]."

There have been a number of attempts to relate E to behavioral states in psychiatric populations with affective illnesses, such as anxiety. The experiments of Schachter, as powerful as they are, do not directly rule out the possibility of such a relationship. For a specific individual, there may be a psychological or biochemical process that predisposes him to experience the arousal caused by E as a signal of anxiety or a situation that leads to anxiety. What would be the results of the Schachter experiments if the same design were used in populations with various types of emotional disorders? Would the social cueing still be as important if the individual did not know what he would be experiencing? Further, even if the subject knew what he was experiencing, would that information be as important a factor, or would the hormone trigger an affective state based on long-term internal cueing? There is a need for further studies that specifically look at these issues.

A study of the effects of E in relation to ego defenses and subjective psychological processes was performed by Basowitz, Korchin, Oken, Goldstein, and Gussack (1956). The most important finding from the study was that general lability of mood and habitual ego defense influence the manner and extent to which E has an effect. Thus, subjects whose behavior typically revealed an openness for new experience and expression of affect, readily perceived both physical and psychological effects of E. On the other hand, subjects who were independently evaluated as having personalities that typically constrict emotional experience and suppress their insight showed less appreciable subjective and objective signs. For some of the subjects, E was capable of precipitating a full-blown anxiety attack; these same doses of E had limited or no physical effects on the cardiovascular system. In terms of physical tests, E caused a decrease in the performance of the motor tasks, such as hand steadiness, but had no effect on sensory threshold or intellectual tasks.

An unusual study to investigate the subjective psychological effects of E and NE was undertaken by Hawkins, Monroe, Sandifer, and Vernon (1960), who used four psychiatrists as their subjects. Higher doses of E produced a difficulty in speech, which was felt to have a CNS component with some disordering of thoughts and difficulty remembering. The subjects were all aware that they were receiving E, and the affect of anxiety was not prominent. The psychological effects diminished with repeated doses although the subjects continued to have a strong physical reaction.

NE was also studied by the Hawkins group, allowing a comparison of the effect of the two amines. NE caused clearcut physiological changes, but there were no changes in affect. The subjects were aware of generalized cooling and very mild restlessness. There was no indication of an increase in the affect of anger. Hawkins and his co-workers conclude by suggesting that the usual assumption that E is associated with anxiety and NE with outward directed anger is incorrect.

A great deal of our knowledge of CA has come from the group led by Kety who had a major influence in establishing a program of research, including metabolic and psychological studies in that area. Included in the investigations were studies of the effects of E in a group of schizophrenic patients. The patients were compared to normals in an attempt to validate or invalidate the hypothesis that E is involved in the symptoms of schizophrenia. As a part of the broad scale observations, which also included metabolic and physiological studies, Pollin and Goldin (1961) investigated the psychological aspects of E. All subjects demonstrated a narrowing of their field of awareness and a shift of attention from the environment to themselves with the onset of the E infusion. Subjects varied as to whether they felt more or less alert and awake after the start of the infusion. Normal behavior in a number of the subjects was exaggerated. Several subjects, both normals and schizophrenics, showed a decreased ability to cope in the situation, although this was most pronounced among the schizophrenic group. The schizophrenic patients did display changes in their behavior, but not to such an extent that it would be considered an increase in psychotic behavior. The schizophrenic patients responded adversely to the stress of the experiment. An untoward response to stress is a characteristic of schizophrenic patients, and could be in response to: (1) the psychological aspects of stress; (2) altered hormonal output; (3) changes in central neuroregulators in response to stress; or (4) a combination of these factors interrelating with one another.

There are several ways in which the varying patterns of personal response to E might be of importance, both theoretically and clinically. Further work has to be done to determine the extent of variations in patterns of response, and whether some individuals are "more sensitive" to the effects of the drug and may have a "true" as opposed to a "cold" emotion. If there are subpopulations who respond in a fixed way regardless of social context, it could be due to a number of causes, including: (1) increased likelihood of associating the drug with a behavior normally experienced, such as anxiety, because the compound is usually excreted by the individual when experiencing such an emotional state—in this explanation, the effect would be the result of conditioning; (2) a difference in susceptibility of the CNS to be affected by E due to such changes as an altered permeability of the BBB or to alteration in the pattern of uptake, utilization, or metabolism of the compound by the brain; (3) altered sensitivity to the arousal aspects of the compound; and (4) varying subjective responses to the peripheral physiological changes secondary to the amine. Drugs that influence any of these processes might alter affective states.

Adrenal Medullary Secretion: Human Studies

This has been the most extensively researched area involving biogenic amines. There have been a great number of studies in which investigators have determined the relative amounts of E and NE in the urine in response to stress and other behavioral conditions. This area has been extensively reviewed (Euler, 1956, 1964; Breggin, 1964; Malmejac, 1964; Levi, 1966; Melmon, 1968; Mason, 1968), and we will provide only a few examples of the wealth of data.

The adrenal medulla response to stress is characterized by a rapid secretion of E and NE into the circulation; the materials are picked up by various organs—including the brain—metabolized, and excreted, primarily in the urine. Measurement of the small amount of CA present in the blood or plasma is very difficult (Udenfriend, 1962, 1969; Anton & Sayre, 1962; Welch & Welch, 1969; O'Hanlon, Campuzano, & Horvath, 1970). Studies on blood CA require as much as 25 to 50 ml of blood, a volume unsuitable for many types of psychological assessment studies. The problem is further complicated by the presence of substances in the blood that interfere with the CA assays. Many of the early studies did not resolve adequately the compounds of interest from these unwanted materials. While it is easier to measure CA in the urine, collection of adequate urine volumes limits the time points at which one may obtain measurements, and affords only a gross measure of CA in relation to the behavioral event under analysis. Ideally, one would hope to sample small amounts of blood plasma at close intervals to obtain a picture of the response to varying behavioral situations and the differing patterns of response.

In evaluating changes in urinary CA, it should be borne in mind that E, NE, and DA are all secreted into the urine. However, only E is primarily derived from the adrenal gland. The remaining amines are primarily a reflection of CA formed in adrenergic neurons throughout the body. The amount of NE secreted is affected by muscular exertion and other processes (Hollister & Moore, 1970). There is essentially no information on DA secreted in the urine and what influences it.

Over 90 percent of the CA secreted into the blood is metabolized before it reaches the urine. Despite this fact, most investigators measure only the unchanged (non-metabolized) urinary CA, thus ignoring by far the largest component of the total urinary amine pool. In some studies, VMA, one of the several CA metabolites, has been measured. Since VMA represents a final common pathway in the metabolism of both E and NE (Figures 4 and 5), measurement of this compound provides no information as to the relative contribution of either amine to the VMA pool.

The normal excretion values of E at rest are about 2 to 3 nanograms per minute, while the NE secretion is about 10 nanograms per minute (a nanogram is 10^{-9} grams).

The studies of Elmadjian, Hope, and Lamson (1957) represent classical investigations of the secretion of these compounds. The investigators studied the secretion of compounds in a variety of situations and found that, in situations involving tense, anxious, but passive emotional displays, there is an increase in E secretion with a normal secretion of NE. In contrast, active, aggressive, emotional displays are related to an increased secretion of NE without any change in E. The studies were performed on persons involved in a variety of athletic competitions, as well as on psychiatric patients.

There have been a number of studies that emphasized psychological assessment. For example, an increased secretion of E has been noted during sensory deprivation and the increase related to a change in time sense (Mendelson, Kubzansky, Leiderman, Wexler, DuToit, & Solomon, 1960). The study of Tolson, Mason, Sachar, Hamburg, Handlon, and Fishman (1965) demonstrated that the levels of CA were increased on first admission to a psychiatric hospital and subsequently decreased. Their data also suggest some of the hazards in conducting endocrine studies in a new environment and point out the "first day" effect. A variety of other stresses have also been investigated. Silverman and Cohen (1960) and Goodall (1962) demonstrated that individuals who were subject to blackout in relation to centrifugation stress produced more E and had more anxiety, while those with high tolerance to centrifugation stress secreted relatively more NE and demonstrated more aggressive affect.

Euler, who discovered NE, has performed investigations ranging from biochemical to psychological. He has studied the effects of a variety of stresses, including aviation stress and movies of various types. The conclusions of his group fit with those of the studies of Elmadjian et al. referred to earlier, and have represented an effort of the greatest importance (Euler & Lundberg, 1954; Levi, 1965, 1969).

A variety of studies has correlated the amounts of hormones secreted to performance in psychologically stressful situations. For example, Franken-haeuser, Mellis, Rissler, Björkvall, and Pátkai (1968) found that subjects with high CA excretion rates performed better under specified conditions.

The work on adrenal medullary secretion represents one area involving hormones and behavior in which there is increasing emphasis on subtle measurements of behavior. Hopefully, with better assay procedures, this will result in extensive detailing of the kinetic processes involving these hormones and their relation to behavior.

METHODS OF STUDYING NEUROREGULATORY AGENTS

Measurement of Metabolites in Spinal Fluid: Human Studies

There are several ways in which knowledge of neuroregulatory agents can be used for psychological assessment. Many of these have already been applied to human studies. The most important to date has been the measurement of metabolites of the neuroregulators in the spinal fluid, although the neuroregulators themselves are not present in spinal fluid.

Two of the major neuroregulators, 5-HT and DA, have metabolites that can be measured in the spinal fluid, 5-HIAA and HVA, respectively. References and values obtained are presented in Table 2. Procedures are now being established for measuring the levels of methoxyhydroxyphenylglycol (MHPG), a metabolite of NE found in spinal fluid.

Two general approaches have been used to study the amine metabolites. The first has been to measure levels of the compounds to determine whether they are altered. Such a strategy has a number of drawbacks, the most formidable being interpretation of the data that deals solely with the level of a compound. The levels of the compound do not provide information on fluctuations in the synthesis, degradation, or utilization rate of the compound. An analogy can be drawn to measuring the levels of water in a dam: the levels can shift somewhat, but we learn little of the rate of the inflow and outflow from a single static measure of the level of the water. Measures of the dynamic state are referred to as *kinetics*.

Obtaining information about the kinetics of processes supplies data about the rates of synthesis and destruction, utilization, release, uptake, and so on. In essence, information is obtained about the effects over time of a particular parameter. It is expected that in the coming years studies correlating behavior with biogenic amines will be concerned increasingly with the measurement of dynamic states. Presently, techniques for studying kinetic processes involving neuroregulatory agents in animals, in relation to behavioral states, are just beginning; there have been very few studies in humans.

Despite the disadvantages, there are certain types of information to be gained from static measurement studies, if the information deviates sufficiently from the norm. For instance, in Parkinson's disease, levels of DA in the brain and levels of HVA, the main metabolite of DA, in the spinal fluid are markedly reduced. For reasons that are not yet clear, the levels of 5-HIAA, the 5-HT metabolite, are also reduced (Gottfries, Gottfries, & Roos, 1969; Olsson & Roos, 1968). The major psychiatric illness in which measurement of

Table 2
Level of Serotonin and Dopamine Metabolites in Spinal Fluid

Neuroregulator	Metabolite	Level of Metabolite	Reference
Serotonin	5-hydroxyindoleacetic acid (5-HIAA)	.030 μg/ml	Gerbode & Bowers, 1968
		.056 μg/ml	Dubowitz & Rogers, 1969
		.040 μg/ml	Gottfries, Gottfries, & Roos, 1969
		.040 μg/ml	Olsson & Roos, 1968
Dopamine	Homovanillic Acid (HVA)	.060 μg/ml	Gottfries et al., 1969
		.050 μg/ml	Olsson & Roos, 1968
		< .010 μg/ml	Curzon, Godwin-Austen, Tomlinson, & Kantamaneni, 1970
		.150 μg/ml	Weiner, Harrison, & Klawans, 1969

amine metabolites has been studied is depression. There is now evidence that suggests that the levels of 5-HT in the brain and its major metabolite, 5-HIAA, may be decreased in some patients with depression.

A technique, using the drug probenecid, is now being developed to study the kinetics of 5-HT metabolism. Probenecid blocks the exit from the spinal fluid of the acid metabolites of the biogenic amines (such as 5-HIAA derived from 5-HT, or HVA derived from DA), presumably by blocking the active transport system that is involved in removing the metabolites from the spinal fluid to the blood. Probenecid has been used extensively in studies in animals, where high doses of the drug can be used (Tozer, Neff, & Brodie, 1966). Under such conditions, there is a rapid rise in the cerebrospinal fluid (CSF) level of 5-HIAA, since the material is not being removed from the spinal fluid. As 5-HT metabolism proceeds, the levels of 5-HIAA continue to increase. From the rate of rise, it is possible to gain information about the rate of metabolism of 5-HT. Such studies are not as easily done in humans, since the doses of probenecid that would cause complete blockage of 5-HIAA transport have untoward side effects. To circumvent this, the drug is given in multiple doses over a 24-hour period and the increase in metabolite levels is monitored. Using this technique, varying conditions may be employed or individuals with different illnesses may be studied. The procedure does not allow an exact calculation of the rate of utilization of 5-HT but does give a relative value. With this technique, it has been found that at least some depressed individuals utilize less 5-HT per unit of time (Praag, Korf, & Puite, 1970). Among the questions to be investigated are: Is 5-HT being metabolized by a different route in such patients? Is probenecid, for some reason, less effective in blocking transport in such individuals? If the findings and interpretation of decreased 5-HT utilization are valid, some important questions arise: Why does decreased utilization occur? What does such a finding tell us of the etiology of depression and of potential therapy?

We have dealt with the use of these measures for brain 5-HT metabolism using spinal fluid in considerable length, because of their potential use in psychological assessment in the future and because they represent one of the few ways of studying neuroregulators in the human brain. Studies that focus on metabolism in the brain have a great advantage over those that measure compounds in the urine. Studies emphasizing the latter are difficult to interpret because the amounts of various materials in the urine are a reflection of both brain and peripheral metabolism of the compounds.

Measurement of Neuroregulatory Agents in Brain: Animal Studies

In animals, there are a number of procedures that can be used to study neuroregulatory agents; the methods are not suitable for humans, although there may be some possibilities for adaptation of some techniques. The levels of compounds in specific regions of the brain can be studied in autopsy material, however many of the compounds are destroyed during the time it takes to obtain the brain tissue. As described earlier, measurement of levels does not enable investigation of the kinetics of metabolic processes. There is now evidence that there may be either a marked increase or decrease in the rate of utilization of the compound, although the levels of the particular compound may be normal.

One approach to an analysis of dynamic states is inhibiting the synthesis of a particular neuroregulatory agent and monitoring the rate of change in the level of the compound. In terms of inhibitors of synthesis, one can stop the formation of CA almost immediately by giving a dose of a-MT. Animals are sacrificed at different times after administering the drug and the levels of the CA determined. The rate of decrease in the levels provides information about the rate of utilization of the compounds and can be changed by varying conditions, including behavioral states (Brodie, Costa, Dlabic, Neff, & Smookler, 1966). This procedure has made it possible to study the rate of utilization of CA in rat brain in various behavioral states.

Inhibitors that stop the destruction of a neuroregulatory agent can be given and the rate of rise in the levels of the compounds determined. Such techniques allow estimation of utilization rates. An example of this technique is the use of MAO inhibitors, such as pargyline, to inhibit the main pathway of 5-HT metabolism, thereby permitting estimation of the rate of 5-HT utilization. The rate of utilization of 5-HT has been shown to increase rapidly with almost any type of novelty stress or more severe stress as shown by Aghajanian and Schwartz (1969). However, such techniques are not without drawbacks. For example, the use of MAO inhibitors appears to be valid for 5-HT but not for CA, even though MAO represents an important metabolic pathway for CA. Included among the reasons for the lack of validity with CA is the presence of alternate pathways for CA metabolism involving COMT. Naturally, none of the procedures just described is applicable to human studies, since the studies with synthesis inhibitors or metabolic blockers require removal of tissues and large numbers of samples. Techniques using blockade of synthesis or destruction of neuroregulatory agents give information about the rate of utilization, but they do not provide information about the metabolic pathways, a vital factor in the assessment of biochemical processes.

Measurement of Patterns of Metabolism of Neuroregulatory Agents in Brain: Animal Studies and Potential Human Application

Many procedures involving the determination of biochemical pathways include the use of radiolabeled compounds. The basis for some of these techniques has been described previously in a review for psychologists (Barchas, Ciaranello, & Levine, 1969). Several procedures are available for assay of CA and IA (Erdelyi, Angwin, & Barchas, 1970; Barchas, Erdelyi, & Angwin, submitted for publication). Amines can be studied biochemically using two procedures: (1) intravenous or intraperitoneal injection of the precursor of the amine, such as tyrosine or tryptophan, and determination of the formation of the resultant CA or IA, or (2) injection of the amine directly into the CSF, via the intraventricular route (Glowinski, Kopin, & Axelrod, 1965; Noble, Wurtman, & Axelrod, 1967) or intracisternal route (Schanberg et al., 1967; Maas & Landis, 1968), and following the rate of disappearance of the amine or the pattern of its metabolites. In the case of NE, some of the compound is taken up by the nerve endings in a pattern similar to the endogenous distribution of the amine. Immediately after intraventricular or intracisternal injection, a considerable amount of the amine is transferred from the cerebrospinal fluid to the blood, but, within a few minutes, the majority of the amine destined to be retained is taken up by the tissues. Some of the amine in CSF is taken up by glial elements or by nerve cells that do not normally contain NE; nevertheless, most of the compound is taken up by the appropriate brain regions. By sacrificing animals at varying time points, the pattern of metabolites and rate of utilization of the compounds can be determined. Techniques are used that allow separation of the various metabolites. For studying NE, Stolk and Barchas (in preparation) have administered radiolabeled DA and studied the NE formed. NE is formed only in neurons containing DβO, thus minimizing the difficulties of uptake by glia or neurons that do not normally contain NE.

Use of intraventricular and intracisternal injection techniques has been of considerable importance in recent studies in which psychological states have been compared, and the effects on rate of utilization and metabolic pathway of CA determined. These procedures have been particularly valuable in studying and theorizing the actions of drugs. These techniques are beginning to be used in the study of behavioral states in animals.

Maas and Landis (1968) have suggested a technique that appears to circumvent the problem of removal of tissues for assay. Radiolabeled NE is administered intracisternally, the goal being to measure the metabolites formed by the brain and excreted in the urine. The NE is metabolized in the brain; the metabolites are transported via the spinal fluid to the blood and ultimately appear in the urine. The investigators faced the problem that immediately after the intracisternal injection, some of the administered NE is transported unchanged into the blood, metabolized peripherally, and excreted in the urine. This raised the dilemma of differentiating the material metabolized by the brain from that metabolized peripherally. The investigators took advantage of the fact that there is no BBB for the material *from* the brain, but there is a BBB from the body *to* the brain. At the same time that tritiated NE (^{3}H) is injected into the cisterna magna, radioactive carbon (^{14}C) labeled NE is injected into one of the peripheral veins. The BBB precludes passage of the ^{14}C material into brain; however, the ^{3}H material can pass from the brain into the body compartments. Thus, the ^{3}H metabolites appearing in the urine originate from both central and peripheral metabolic reactions, while the ^{14}C metabolites are only formed peripherally. By means of a set of equations, the contribution of the body to the metabolism of the tritiated material can be determined and an estimate of the metabolism of the CA by the brain obtained. Such a technique could prove to be extremely effective for it would enable experiments to be performed using the individual subject as his own control and would allow for repeated testing over time without sacrificing the individual subject. Neurologists have expressed the opinion that this technique could be feasible in humans. With more basic research, it could enable a direct test of the hypothesis that there is a deficiency in metabolism of NE in depression or could allow investigation of the biochemical aspects of conditions such as paranoid states.

BRAIN CATECHOLAMINES AND BEHAVIOR

Our goal in this section is to give a sense of the directions of psychological research involving brain CA. We will present the types of questions being asked in the new field of behavioral neurochemistry. The sections are not completely discrete; some material related to 5-HT will appear in the CA sections and vice versa.

Effects of "Stress" and Varied Housing Conditions on Brain Amines

Various experimental procedures falling under the broad category of "stress" have been shown to cause significant alterations in brain biogenic amine levels. Among these procedures are forced swimming, cold exposure, electric foot shock, and immobilization (Barchas & Freedman, 1963; Maynert & Levi, 1964; Bliss & Zwanziger, 1966). Brain biogenic amine levels would be expected to change if (1) formation (anabolism) of the amines was increased or decreased, (2) destruction (catabolism) of the amines was enhanced or suppressed, or (3) a combination of the two processes occurred. The development of procedures for measuring dynamic changes in brain biogenic amine metabolism, described in the previous section, revealed that most of the above stressors affecting endogenous amine levels did so by increasing the turnover and metabolism of NE, DA, and 5-HT (Kety, Javoy, Thierry, Julou, & Glowinski, 1967; Bliss, Ailion, & Zwanziger, 1968; Simmonds, 1969). Interestingly, very few instances of a stress-induced *decrease* in CA or 5-HT turnover are known, these being due to hypothermia (Stone, 1970), shock-induced aggression in rats (see final section of this chapter), and social isolation in mice.

The ability of the social environment to alter brain biogenic amine metabolism has been studied in some detail. The effect of prolonged (i.e., ten weeks) isolation has but a small effect, if any, on brain and adrenal gland CA content or on brain 5-HT levels (Welch & Welch, 1968a; Garattini, Giacalone, & Valzelli, 1969). Dynamic measurements of metabolism, however, reveal that the turnover of endogenous CA and 5-HT stores is slower in isolated mice than in grouped subjects. Additionally, brain 5-HT utilization is directly proportional to the size of the social group. The above changes were observed only in male mice that became aggressive as the result of isolation. Female mice do not show these biochemical changes, regardless of the group size or the duration of differential housing, nor do they become aggressive. Further, males of species that do not become aggressive following isolation also do not demonstrate biochemical differences related to differing social environment.

Welch (1967) presented an hypothesis regarding adrenal and brain stem NE metabolism and what he termed the "mean level of environmental stimulation." By this he means that a given change in the rate of release of NE due to stimulation causes a proportionally greater effect in isolated mice (Welch & Welch, 1968b).

More recently, a report by Axelrod, Mueller, Henry, and Stephens (1970) showed that adrenal medullary activity of CA-metabolizing enzymes can be altered by social grouping. Stimulus enrichment increased enzyme levels, whereas isolation was associated with low enzyme activity. The study by Axelrod and his co-workers represents an important extension of the previously discussed research by showing discrete evidence of psychosocial control of biochemical function.

The presence of similar adaptive mechanisms in biogenic amine metabolism, in species other than the mouse, remains to be determined. Preliminary data collected by Stolk, Conner, and Barchas (in preparation), directed at the relationship between amines and social environment in rats, reveals some prominent differences from similar measurements in mice. Turnover of brain stem NE was significantly greater in the isolated rats than in the grouped subjects. No prominent differences were apparent in 5-HT metabolism between the two groups. The data from the different species reveal differences between the mice and rats; thus, we must be cautious in generalizing the results of social environment studies.

There are no data whatsoever on the crucial question of the effects of stress on brain amines in humans. Thus, for example, we do not know whether various types of stress alter the rate of synthesis or utilization of brain amines and whether there are times when synthesis cannot keep up with the need for these compounds. Clearly, such an issue is of great importance since there are many forms of psychiatric illness in which an inability to respond to stress is a prominent symptom. Genetically determined biochemical abnormalities in brain amine metabolism may well turn out to have clinical significance.

Brain Catecholamines and Behavior: Animal Studies

This area has undergone rapid expansion during the last decade. Numerous studies employing various approaches to the study of behavior and brain CA metabolism attest to the degree of importance of this area. For our purposes here, research from but a few areas will be mentioned to give some idea as to the methodology currently used.

Several lines of evidence point to the importance of brain CA metabolism in the maintenance of normal motor patterns. The clinical application of experimental findings in this area will be discussed in the subsequent section of this chapter. Changes in motor activity of animals following pharmacological reduction of brain CA (Dominic & Moore, 1969; Stolk & Rech, 1970), as well as changes in NE metabolism in animals of different activity levels (Stone & DiCara, 1969), support the postulated relationship between motor behavior and brain CA content.

Another type of motor behavior, characterized by intense grooming, compulsive gnawing, backpeddling, tremor, and circling movements, appears to be related specifically to DA in the basal ganglia. Although initially observed after injection of amphetamine (Ehrich & Krumbhaar, 1937; Quinton & Halliwell, 1963), other compounds, such as DOPA, have been found to elicit this behavior. Pharmacological studies demonstrated that DA metabolism was involved in this syndrome (Randrup & Munkvad, 1970; Taylor & Snyder, 1970).

Most studies investigating the interactions between conditioned behavioral responses and brain CA have been pharmacological in nature. Almost uniformly, such studies have indicated that chemicals that deplete CA in the brain, or that antagonize the effects of the purported neurotransmitters on appropriate brain receptors, tend to disrupt the behavior under investigation. Subsequent pharmacological manipulations of the behaviorally depressed experimental subject are then used to dissect the possible roles of the CA in that particular behavior. Alternatively, several operant techniques allow for the manipulation of stimulated as well as depressed responding. Using both the depressed and the base-line performing operant subject, considerable evidence has been gathered that demonstrates the relative importance of the biogenic amines in modifying or controlling these behaviors.

Various investigators using a discriminated two-way shuttle-box avoidance procedure have depressed responding of previously trained subjects with reserpine. Avoidance behavior depressed by reserpine can be reinstated transiently by drugs that facilitate the release of brain CA, such as amphetamine (Rech, 1964; Hanson, 1966), or by drugs that restore brain CA content, such as DOPA (Seiden & Hanson, 1964; Corrodi & Hanson, 1966; Seiden & Peterson, 1968).

At least one instance in which a discriminated avoidance response, not previously depressed pharmacologically, has been related to CA biosynthesis is presented by Rech (1966) and by Rech and Moore (1971). Using "poor-performers" in a two-way shuttle-box (i.e., rats that did not learn the avoidance response), Rech showed that low doses of d-amphetamine caused a transitory acquisition of the conditioned avoidance response that could be antagonized completely by inhibiting CA synthesis. Similar results have been described in non-discriminated avoidance procedures (Weissman, Koe, & Tenen, 1966; Rech & Stolk, 1970), indicating a relation between CA biosynthesis and amphetamine's behavioral effects.

One behavior studied in great detail has afforded some insight into the specificity of brain amines and behavior. Self-stimulation, as developed by Olds and Milner (1954), has been shown by Stein and his associates to be specifically related to the release of NE, not DA, from a discrete neuroanatomical tract, the median forebrain bundle (MFB). The exhaustive work by Olds (1962) showed that the MFB almost certainly is the principal neural pathway of the reward system in the brain. Histochemical studies revealed that the MFB is a primary pathway of NE-containing neurons (Hillarp, Fuxe, & Dahlström, 1966) as well as having the greatest NE content of any brain area. The pharmacology of the reward system, as studied using the self-stimulation procedure, is summarized well by Stein (1964). Briefly, drugs that release CA from stores in the brain facilitate self-stimulation (i.e., amphetamine). The same is true for drugs that increase the amount of NE released by nerve stimulation. Conversely, drugs that deplete brain CA (i.e., reserpine and a-MT) or antagonize their action (i.e., chlorpromazine) depress self-stimulation and antagonize the facilitatory effects of amphetamine.

Using a series of laborious but ingenious techniques, Stein and his associates have shown that: (1) NE specifically mediates self-stimulation responding in the MFB; (2) NE is released at specific sites in the hypothalamus and limbic system in conjunction with rewarding stimulation, but not with non-rewarding stimulation; and (3) amphetamine is able to facilitate rewarding stimulation in the MFB by causing a similar set of biochemical changes, as self-stimulation itself. Stein and Wise (1969) used a permanent indwelling push-pull cannula to perfuse specific sites in the brain of self-stimulating subjects and collect compounds released from neurons in a localized area of brain tissue. The cannulation studies were very effectively combined with the use of radio-labeled precursors or radiolabeled amines. As a result of these studies, it is now believed that the amygdala, with cells using NE as a transmitter, normally functions in reward to suppress a punishment system, whose fibers run from the amygdala to the lower brain stem (Stein, 1968). This fiber system, called the periventricular punishment system, is cholinergic (i.e., acetylcholine is the purported neurotransmitter) and has a suppressant action on behavior (Domino & Olds, 1968; Olds & Domino, 1969; Margules & Stein, 1969).

Catecholamines and Human Psychological Disorders
There are two major approaches in this area. One of the approaches has as its basis the hypothesis that under some conditions an endogenous psychotogen is formed that influences behavior. A second approach has suggested that an exaggeration of normal processes, rather than an abnormal compound, may be involved in behavioral disorders. This model is usually presented in terms of excess or deficiency of a neuroregulatory agent, but there are a number of steps that could be altered and lead to changes in behavior, e.g., the rate of formation, release, reuptake, or metabolism. Our knowledge of each of these processes is still quite limited. It is not yet clear what the range of normal variation would be or under what conditions an alteration could lead to abnormal mental processes.

The psychoses, particularly schizophrenia, received intense investigation in an attempt to link biogenic amines with this disorder. In the late 1950s, it was postulated that some forms of schizophrenia might be associated with an abnormal metabolite of CA such as adrenochrome, a derivative of adrenaline. These and other hypotheses served as the stimulus for investigation of the metabolism of CA, pioneered by Axelrod and his collaborators in their brilliant series of studies. They were unable to detect adrenochrome as a major product of CA metabolism. Today, the theory involving adrenochrome is no longer held. However, other compounds have been described, such as dimethoxyphenylethylamine and the question remains as to whether this is a normal or abnormal metabolite, and what its role might be in psychological processes. Some of the most appealing hypotheses focus on hypothetical abnormal methylated products. A number of hallucinogens can be considered methylated analogs of CA, while others can be viewed as methylated derivates of IA. The biochemical aspects of some of the psychotomimetics and related topics have been reviewed by Giarman and Freedman in a series of reviews (Giarman & Freedman, 1965; Bloom & Giarman, 1968a; Bloom & Giarman, 1968b). To date, there is no convincing data to prove that these compounds are formed or, if formed, are relevant. This is an area of active research interest, the current status of which has been summarized by Hamburg (1970).

In Parkinson's disease, it has been found that there is a deficiency of DA in the basal ganglia of the brain. These patients can now be treated with dramatic effectiveness by DOPA, the precursor of DA; this is the first biochemical treatment of a neurological disorder that provides replacement of a presumed neurotransmitter, a very important finding (Cotzias, Papavasiliou, & Gellene, 1969). Such replacement is viewed as a model that may be applicable in the future to some psychiatric disorders.

Currently, the major interest in the relationship of CA to disturbed behavior is in the depressions. These formulations were based on the work of numerous individuals and have been compiled and reviewed in the writings of Schildkraut (1970). They are referred to as the catecholamine hypothesis of affective disorders. Briefly, the hypothesis relates depression to a relative deficiency of NE at certain central synapses, and relates the manic states to a relative excess of NE. The data supporting the hypothesis include the following: reserpine (a drug that lowers CA levels) causes depression in about 20 percent of people taking moderate doses; the tricyclic drugs, which are effective in treating depression, all block reuptake of CA after they are released by the neuron and thus functionally increase the relative amounts of NE at the synapse; the MAO inhibitors tend to relieve depression and increase transneuronal metabolism of CA. Each of these phenomena has multiple explanations, and the evidence is far from compelling; nevertheless, the hypothesis has proved stimulating and has given further impetus to determining the role of CA in depression. An example of ways in which such findings can be reinterpreted is provided by research in which the levels of plasma CA in patients with depression were investigated (Wyatt, Portnoy, Kupfer, Snyder, & Engelman, 1971); it was found that levels of both E and NE were increased. The authors raise the issue of whether there is a relative increase, rather than a relative decrease, in CA in brain. In the future, it is likely that hypotheses relating neuroregulators to behavior will become much more specific, involving certain areas of brain and changes in particular processes, such as release, reuptake, or receptors.

A very elegant series of studies, relevant to the relationship of CA to depression, has been conducted by a group of investigators at the NIMH (Bunney, Brodie, Murphy, & Goodwin, in press). They tested the effects of DOPA in depression and found very little effect on depression per se, but this may be because very little of the DOPA actually goes to form NE. On the other hand, in several manic-depressive patients, there was evidence that the drug could elicit manic behavior. They suggest the possibility that manic episodes may be due to a relative excess in the DA system. Brodie, Murphy, Goodwin, and Bunney (in press) also made the important finding that a-MT, the inhibitor of CA synthesis, inhibits manic episodes. This is the best evidence to date suggesting a role of these compounds in manic-depressive illness.

BRAIN SEROTONIN AND BEHAVIOR

Serotonin and Behavior: Animal Studies

There are currently four approaches to the study of the relation between 5-HT and behavior: (1) administer PCPA, which, as described earlier, inhibits the synthesis of 5-HT; (2) increase the levels of 5-HT by administering its precursor, 5-HTP, which passes the BBB and is converted to the amine; (3) study the rate of formation of 5-HT after administering radiolabeled tryptophan; (4) study the rate of utilization of 5-HT by use of inhibitors of its destruction or inhibitors of the exit of 5-HT metabolites from the spinal fluid.

Considerable interest has been focused recently on the effects of PCPA. Various, seemingly disparate, effects of this drug have been reported. Tenen (1967) and Schlesinger, Schreiber, and Pryor (1968) report that PCPA facilitates acquisition of an active avoidance procedure in rats. One possible corollary to its effects on active avoidance is the reports of enhanced sensitivity to shock in rats with low brain 5-HT content (Tenen, 1967; Lints & Harvey, 1969), a finding in accord with other indices of altered sensory modalities (Stevens, Resnick, & Krus, 1967; Conner, Stolk, Barchas, & Levine, 1970). However, increased sensitivity to foot shock cannot explain reports of impaired passive avoidance (Stevens, Fechter, & Resnick, 1969) and response suppression behaviors (Robichaud & Sledge, 1969; Wise, Berger, & Stein, 1970) following PCPA treatment. One would expect that the latter behaviors would be *easier* to acquire if shock sensitivity were enhanced.

Another line of experimentation has revealed changes in sexual behavior after PCPA. For example, treatment with this drug may occasionally alter "sexual" activity in male-male behavior in nonspecific testing situations (Tagliamonte, Tagliamonte, Gessa, & Brodie, 1969; Sheard, 1969; Shillito, 1970; Ferguson, Henriksen, Cohen, Mitchell, Barchas, & Dement, 1970). However, in studying heterosexual behavior, several reports indicate no changes attributable to PCPA (Zitrin, Beach, Barchas, & Dement, 1970; Whalen & Luttge, 1970). Whalen concludes that 5-HT depletion may cause confusion relating to stimulus objects, resulting in the mounting of a previously unacceptable (or inappropriate) object.

A trend noted in the above studies with PCPA has been summarized by both Conner et al. (1970) and Wise et al. (1970). Their basic argument states that 5-HT is involved in behaviors requiring the suppression of responses. After PCPA, when brain 5-HT content is decreased, animals have an impaired ability to suppress "inappropriate" responding in many stimulus conditions (i.e., passive avoidance, punishment paradigms, habituation, homosexual contact). Conversely, suppression is enhanced when 5-HT levels are increased (cf. Wise et al., 1970). Thus, if changes in brain 5-HT levels alter the organism's ability to "evaluate" the contextual cues of its environment, or if 5-HT "sets" this ability at a critical level, then many behaviors, whether they be acquired or innate, would be altered.

Serotonin and Sleep

During the past five years, considerable effort has been directed toward understanding the relationship of neurotransmitters, particularly 5-HT, to sleep. Sleep has been investigated because it is clearly defined compared to many other behaviors and has seemed to be a behavior that would be particularly amenable to biochemical investigation. Four fundamental approaches have been used: (1) administering drugs that inhibit or augment the effects of a particular neuroregulatory agent and studying the effects on sleep and on amines; (2) measuring neuroregulator levels in various states of sleep; (3) making lesions in areas of brain and determining the effects on sleep and on amines; (4) depriving animals of one of the stages of sleep and determining the effect on neuroregulators.

Sleep states can be divided into slow-wave sleep, which constitutes about 80 percent of sleep time, and rapid-eye-movement sleep (REM sleep, dream sleep, D-sleep, paradoxical sleep), which constitutes about 20 percent of sleep time. These various states have been reviewed (Dement, 1966; Hartman, 1967; Hobson, 1969). Among the characteristics of REM sleep are rapid eye movements observable through the closed eyelids and an activated electroencephalogram (EEG). REM sleep has been found in all mammals studied. Deprivation of REM sleep can be accomplished by monitoring the EEG and awaking the subject when he begins to go into the state. REM sleep must be made up when it is lost through deprivation.

The evidence that 5-HT might be involved in states of sleep has largely arisen from the brilliant work of Jouvet (1969). The evidence implicating 5-HT includes the facts that: (1) intracarotid injection of 5-HT induces EEG recordings consistent with sleep (Koella, 1968); (2) injection of PCPA that decreases 5-HT causes insomnia in the cat; and (3) lesions of the midline raphe system, thought to be the cells of origin of part of the serotonergic system, may induce insomnia.

Although this evidence has been widely accepted as demonstrating a close relationship of 5-HT to sleep, there have been a number of other experiments that suggest that the relationship, if it exists, is a more complicated one, and that there may be marked species differences in the transmitters involved in sleep. There are major problems of interpretation of the studies involving lesions or injection of 5-HT.

The most challenging data to reconcile with the serotonergic hypothesis are in regard to the effects of PCPA on sleep. The problem is complicated by marked species differences. Rechtschaffen, Lovell, Freedman, Whitehead, and Aldrich (1969) have found that in the rat the PCPA-induced insomnia is much less than in the cat, while Wyatt (1970), performing studies in man at much lower doses of PCPA, has found that the drug may decrease REM sleep without altering regular slow-wave sleep.

The Stanford group (Dement, Zarcone, Ferguson, Cohen, Pivak, & Barchas, 1969) has found that chronic PCPA treatment results in transitory insomnia lasting several days. During this period there is slow-wave sleep and REM sleep suppression and reduced brain 5-HT. Continuation of drug administration, however, results in return of sleep and REM sleep to about 75 percent of normal, despite continued low levels of 5-HT. When REM sleep returns, there is no REM rebound following deprivation. Of particular interest is the finding that in the 5-HT−depleted cat some of the physiological manifestations of REM sleep occur in wakefulness as long as the 5-HT depletion is maintained.

Another approach to the study of sleep and its underlying biochemistry has been produced by deprivation of REM sleep. Several laboratories (Weiss, Bordwell, Seeger, Lee, Dement, & Barchas, 1968; Pujol, Mouret, Jouvet, & Glowinski, 1968) have evidence that rats deprived of REM sleep have an increased turnover of 5-HT. However, such a change may be quite nonspecific and related to a stress effect. Even so, such a change could be involved in the psychological changes associated with REM sleep deprivation.

Measurement of the levels of neuroregulators in stages of sleep and wakefulness (Sinha, Henriksen, Dement, & Barchas, in preparation) has provided a different approach to the problems of neuroregulators and the control of sleep. The investigations of a number of laboratories (Quay, 1963; Reis, Weinbren, & Corvelli, 1968; Friedman & Walker, 1968; Scheving, Harrison, Gordon, & Pauley, 1968; Manschardt & Wurtman, 1968), demonstrated circadian changes in the levels of neuroregulators and differences at varying times of day, and even multiple rhythms within the 24-hour period. Studies looking at the changes in several transmitters in different stages of sleep will have to be conducted to answer questions such as, what are the levels of the neuroregulators just as an animal enters or exits a stage of sleep.

The data so far suggest a relationship between the neurotransmitters and sleep. Two major questions, as perceived by investigators in the field, are: (1) which transmitter is involved in various aspects of the behavioral repertoire, and (2) to what extent can various manipulations that alter neuroregulators influence the stages of sleep. Such questions have basic relevance to psychiatric illness since, in a number of severe illnesses (depression, schizophrenia), profound disturbances in sleep patterns have been demonstrated by a number of investigators.

Serotonin and Human Psychological Disorders

One of the major research approaches has been an assay for the main metabolite of 5-HT, 5-HIAA, in the spinal fluid. Some of these studies have used the technique of probenecid blockade of the exit of 5-HIAA from the spinal fluid and measurement of the rate of increase of 5-HIAA as a measure of 5-HT utilization rate (Tamarkin, Goodwin, & Axelrod, 1970).

One primary area of investigation has been the role of 5-HT or IA in depressive illness. The results (Roos & Sjöström, 1969; Praag, Korf, & Puite, 1970; Praag & Korf, in press) indicate that in at least some depressed patients, there may be a decrease in the resting levels of 5-HIAA; after probenecid treatment the rate of increase may be decreased.

Another approach has been the direct assay of 5-HT in the brains of individuals who have committed suicide. These studies have suggested a decreased level of brain 5-HT, although there are tremendous problems in such studies: the delay in obtaining the brain tissue, difficulty in matching subjects, and the issue of the type of depression or thought disorder represented in the particular suicidal group. A controversial area has been studies involving administration of the IA precursors (tryptophan or 5-hydroxytryptophan) in treatment of depression. These areas have been reviewed by Glassman (1969). Preliminary data indicate there may be some subpopulations that might benefit from these compounds although further investigation is needed.

Other studies have been concerned with the suggestion that other metabolic pathways involving tryptophan may be altered (Curzon & Bridges, 1970). Of considerable importance are integrative studies in which factors, such as the pituitary-adrenal response, are investigated. Some studies, as exemplified in the careful investigations in Australia of Davies and Carroll (1970), suggest that there may be subpopulations of depressed persons with marked differences in biochemical parameters.

Another area in which 5-HT and its derivatives have been implicated is schizophrenia and the related psychoses. There have been several investigations suggesting that metabolism of 5-HT may be involved in such illness. Many hypotheses involve the possible effects of abnormally-formed methylated derivatives of 5-HT as described earlier (Morgan & Mandell, 1969). Bufotenin, for example, is a dimethylated 5-HT derivative that has been found in urine (Himwich, in press). There is no evidence, however, that these compounds are formed to any greater extent in schizophrenics than in normals or that such compounds are involved in either the etiology or maintenance of any of the subgroups that make up the psychotic disorders (Sankar, 1969).

Of particular interest are studies that have demonstrated that certain drugs (e.g., LSD) that cause model psychoses may alter the utilization of brain 5-HT and may be structurally related to 5-HT. Major impetus to such a conclusion is derived from the work of Freedman (1961) demonstrating that LSD could elevate the levels of brain 5-HT. Such studies have been extended to other drugs, and it has been demonstrated that LSD may inhibit 5-HT-containing neurons (Rosecrans, Lovell, & Freedman, 1967; Foote, Sheard, & Aghajanian, 1969; Holtzman, Lovell, Jaffe, & Freedman, 1969). Wooley (1962) pointed out that some hallucinogens may act through structural similarities to 5-HT and that such relations could be described in terms of metabolite-antimetabolite interrelationships. Other approaches to the action of hallucinogens in relation to 5-HT have included structural similarities, effects on glial cells in the brain, and effects on nucleic acids (Smythies, 1970). Hollister (1968) has reviewed a wide variety of materials related to chemical psychoses, including the comparisons between the chemical psychoses and natural psychotic states.

In relation to serotonin and psychotic states, the laboratories of Dement and Barchas (Dement et al., 1969) have described neurophysiological changes in cats treated with PCPA, which leads them to suggest that some psychotic illness may represent a relative deficiency of 5-HT.

Very few studies have been performed using PCPA to inhibit 5-HT synthesis in humans. The major investigations have been performed at the National Institutes of Health by Sjoerdsma and his group (Sjoerdsma, 1970; Engelman, Lovenberg, & Sjoerdsma, 1967). The psychological changes in those patients have been further studied and reviewed by Carpenter (1970). Persons with the carcinoid syndrome resulting from a 5-HT-secreting tumor were given the drug. Most, but not all, patients with the tumor have no psychological effects, which might be expected since 5-HT has only a limited ability to cross the BBB. When patients were treated with PCPA to relieve some of the peripheral symptoms of the excess 5-HT secretion, emotional changes were noted in a number of the patients, but the changes did not fit any particular psychiatric entity. The degree of change in brain 5-HT levels in the patients is unclear. Emotional changes included anxiety, irritability, depression, social withdrawal, and lack of interest. The results would indicate the need for further studies of the role of serotonin in emotional behavior. PCPA is a drug with complicated biochemical effects and may alter brain NE utilization (Stolk, Barchas, Dement, & Schanberg, 1969). Further studies will have to be undertaken with other compounds that may inhibit 5-HT formation (McGeer & Peters, 1969).

In models of abnormal behavior, which suppose a relative deficiency of 5-HT in an area of the brain, thus predisposing to behavioral disorder, such a relative deficiency could be due to (1) an actual decrease in amount of the transmitter at synapses in some area in brain; (2) an alteration in some process involving the transmitter, such as release, receptor interactions, or reuptake, that would cause the same relative deficiency; or (3) the formation of an abnormal metabolite of 5-HT that would act as a false transmitter and, thus, create a relative deficiency of the natural transmitter.

It is clear that further studies will be necessary to investigate the effect of precursors, analogs, and inhibitors of 5-HT in the treatment of various forms of emotional disorders. More adequate ways of studying 5-HT in man need to be developed, for it is clear that there are several ways in which more information regarding 5-HT may eventually be of aid in psychological assessment.

MUTABILITY AND GENETIC FACTORS RELATING NEUROREGULATORS AND BEHAVIOR

In the preceding sections of this chapter, changes in the rate of synthesis or rate of utilization of various neuroregulators have been described in relation to stress, behavioral, and environmental changes. Within that framework, a number of questions still remain to be investigated to relate neuroregulatory agents to long-term emotional changes in behavior. To date, there have been no adequate studies, for example, of the effects of chronic stress on turnover or utilization of brain amines. Under these conditions, are there changes in the levels of the various enzymes or changes in the receptor that would alter the basic neurochemical response to a stressful situation or an altered environment? If one visualizes a relationship between biochemical and psychological events and assumes synaptic changes in response to a psychological event, then such changes become very important in relation to the length of time that they persist. To account for long-term emotional behaviors and alterability of behaviors, one would have to assume mutability in the processes underlying neurochemical events at the synapses. In the simplest model, we would assume that psychological events affect the neural chemistry and that the chemical change in turn affects the future psychological events. Thus, chemical changes that are permanent in nature could, in effect, "lock" a certain psychological set. One might postulate such processes to be involved in very generalized anxiety states, for example.

It has been found that acute stresses will generally increase the rate of amine turnover, and after certain types of stress, there may even be a decrease (Stolk, Conner, Levine, & Barchas, in preparation) in turnover of amines. Such mutability, both short-term and long-term, is essential if these compounds are indeed involved in emotional behavior. It should be emphasized that this view does not negate a crucial role for psychological processes in behavior but rather suggests that these may have a very close interaction with biochemical processes. At some point in the future, analysis of either one by itself may prove inadequate for conceptualization.

The mutability of processes dealing with neuroregulatory agents involves investigation of genetic processes related to these compounds. There has been surprisingly little investigation to date at this level.

Beginning with the investigations of Maas and his group (Sudak & Maas, 1964), it has been recognized that there may be different levels of 5-HT and NE in brain in different inbred strains of mice. These findings have been extended to rat brain (Miller, Cox, & Maickel, 1968). Schlesinger, Boggan, and Freedman (1965) demonstrated that inbred mouse strains susceptible to audiogenic seizures had lower levels of brain 5-HT and NE at 21 days of age (when they are most susceptible to seizures). To date there has been limited investigation of whether there are differences in enzyme activities, metabolic pathways, utilization rates, or responses to stress in different strains and of the genetic controls on those processes. Metabolic pathways varying in different genetic strains have already been demonstrated to have a considerable importance in terms of the steroid hormones produced by the adrenal cortex (Hamburg, 1967; Hamburg & Kessler, 1967; Hamburg & Lunde, 1967). A number of illnesses have been demonstrated in which there is a genetic difference in formation of adrenal cortical hormones; several of these illnesses lead to marked behavioral change. Interestingly, compounds have been detected in the adrenal medulla, such as 6-hydroxydopamine, which have not been adequately studied from a physiological standpoint. We do not know the extent to which there can be minor or abnormal pathways in adrenal catechols or how controls on these pathways might be regulated genetically or be altered by stress.

The review of Hamburg and Kessler (1967) describes a variety of ways in which genetic defects might change behavior. An extensive listing could be made of possible defects that could occur in relation to CA, either those secreted by the adrenal or those formed and utilized in the brain, and we will discuss only a few of these possibilities.

In terms of E or NE from the adrenal medulla, genetic processes might well control formation, release, passage across the BBB, or metabolism of the hormones. It has been shown in the adrenal cortex that steroids are released in differing amounts in different genetic strains. Applying the same possibility to the adrenal medullary response to stress, two individuals might send the same number of nerve impulses to the adrenal medulla and yet, due to a genetic difference, one might secrete much more E than the other. If this were the case, clearly, there could be behavioral changes when the E reached various target organs, including the brain. Recent work (Ciaranello, Barchas, Kessler, & Barchas, submitted for publication) has demonstrated that there can be twofold differences in the levels of the enzymes involved in the formation of CA in various strains of mice, indicating that we need to know more about genetic factors in the human. Investigation of biogenic amines in the framework of human biochemical genetics presents opportunities for deeper understanding of stress responses.

Similar altered patterns could also be present in terms of 5-HT or CA in the brain. Mechanisms that could be affected could include the regulatory mechanisms, such as the degree to which the rate-limiting enzymes are activated to cause formation of transmitter, the rate of utilization, and metabolic pathways including the formation of abnormal metabolites.

It is difficult at this early point in the development of behavioral neurochemistry to give an adequate general formulation of the relations between biochemistry and behavior. At this stage, it seems reasonable to assume that biochemical and psychological processes are intimately related. Biochemical processes may well affect, for example, activity levels, emotional tones, and susceptibility to stress. Psychological processes may influence biochemical processes, for example, by producing shifts between pathways, altering utilization of transmitters, and inducing enzymatic changes. Such biochemical events might lead to further psychological changes. While we do not assume that emotional distress is primarily caused by biochemical abnormalities, it is also true that biochemical events may profoundly alter the ability of the organism to respond to its environment. We consider it likely that some severe emotional disorders may be based upon genetically determined alterations in normal biochemical processes. These biochemical predispositions may interact in complex ways with environmental factors such as severe psychological stresses.

In terms of psychological assessment, it is as yet too early to say what the role of these compounds and of the various means of measurement of them will be in assessing behavior of individuals. Nevertheless, it has become increasingly clear that these neuroregulatory agents are involved in basic forms of behavior and that investigation of their role in behavior is highly pertinent to a deeper understanding of severe mental illnesses. Over the coming years, one can expect that tests for these compounds and their metabolic products will be of potential importance in diagnosis and differentiation of severe mental illnesses. Hopefully, there will be increasing collaboration between investigators, biochemical and psychological, concerned with psychological assessment.

CHAPTER XIV

A historical survey of
personality scales and inventories

Lewis R. Goldberg

One of the most salient developments in psychological assessment has been
the recent proliferation of multi-scale personality inventories. Yet, historical
accounts of the testing movement (e.g., Du Bois, 1970) have given short shrift
to this important development. The present chapter, which represents an attempt to fill this historical lacuna, will consider the precursors of today's personality inventories. The contents of this chapter should provide the historical
material for later interpretive analyses of the particular traits focused upon by
previous investigators (e.g., Goldberg, 1970) and for analyses of the strategies
used to measure these traits (see Hase & Goldberg, 1967). The chapter is
focused exclusively on structured personality measures; no consideration is
given to significant milestones in aptitude or achievement testing, or to such
less structured measures as projective techniques (e.g., Downey's Will Profile)
and rating procedures (e.g., the Vineland Social Maturity Scales).

A capsule summary of this historical material is presented in Table 1. The
dates listed in Table 1 are only approximate, as the work on a scale or inventory from conception to the first published account may take five years, and
to the first published manual up to ten years. Consequently, the dates—which
are based upon published reports—are systematically biased, the initial work
having been carried out prior to the date listed. Moreover, the entries in
Table 1 may not represent a complete collection of historical milestones. First
of all, they are overwhelmingly of American origin. Second, with only a few
exceptions, all of the milestones either have been published commercially or
have been reported in the general psychological literature; consequently,
many scales developed for industrial and military organizations have not
been included. Third, many of the scales and inventories have been revised
over the years, and most of these revisions have not been included in the
table. Finally, the entries listed in Table 1 do not include any of the purely
methodological books or papers which have profoundly influenced personality scale construction.

The scales and inventories listed in Table 1 have been classified by the type

Financial support during the preparation of this paper was provided by Grant No.
MH 12972 from the National Institute of Mental Health, U.S. Public Health Service.

of individual differences they purport to measure. The first three columns in the table include those measures which have been developed as a response to applied societal pressures, namely to forecast (*a*) personal or social adjustment, (*b*) satisfaction and success in vocational choice, and (*c*) academic achievement (above and beyond that predictable from scholastic aptitude tests). The remaining columns in the table list measures which were less directly stimulated by applied demands, including those scales and inventories directed at two extraordinarily popular targets for structured measurement, namely introversion-extroversion and masculinity-femininity, and at two influential theories of individual differences, namely Spranger's (1928)[1] schema for classifying "personal values" and Murray et al.'s (1938) classification of "manifest needs."

While these distinctions are extremely useful for understanding the development of the early scales, the proliferation of more comprehensive inventories after World War II has made the categorization of these recent measures a difficult undertaking. For example, the majority of modern personality inventories include scales designed to assess aspects of adjustment, introversion, masculinity, scholastic potential, and personal values and needs, and many of these inventories could therefore have been included in each of the major categories. Consequently, one must consider the above distinctions with some caution, since they inevitably reflect the idiosyncrasies of one individual's efforts to reconstruct history on the basis of often-incomplete published accounts. Nonetheless, this chapter may represent the first reasonably systematic effort to link together a number of convergent developments in the history of structured measurement techniques, and a careful perusal of Table 1 should lead to some insights regarding the most salient individual differences included for measurement and the strategies employed to assess them.

PSYCHOPATHOLOGY VERSUS ADJUSTMENT

By far the most significant class of individual differences addressed by developers of personality scales and inventories includes those traits of temperament or character which purportedly distinguish the better "adjusted" members of our society from their "neurotic," "psychotic," or "criminal" neighbors. The measurement of aspects of emotional or social adjustment (or, not necessarily the converse, aspects of neuroticism, psychoticism, or psychopathy) has a relatively long history in psychology, stemming in large part from societal pressures on psychologists to devise indicators of potential emotional breakdown in military and industrial settings. While many early scholars had discussed aspects of personal and social adjustment, it remained for Freud to popularize the topic through the wide currency given his theories in medical,

---

[1]Throughout this chapter, the names of test developers and the dates of publication of a scale or inventory do not necessarily correspond to the references in the Bibliography at the end of this volume. Rather, where possible, these names and dates are based on the citations in Buros (1970). On the other hand, all dates cited in parentheses—e.g., Buros (1970)—refer to published articles or books, and all of these publications *are* included in the Bibliography.

psychological, and lay publications. Freud's own assessment technique of free association led directly to the development of various association tests and later to a host of other projective techniques (e.g., Blum's Blacky Pictures). On the other hand, while his theoretical constructs have influenced the development of a few personality scales (most notably the California F Scale, Krout's Personal Preference Scale, and Grygier's Dynamic Personality Inventory) and the labeling of a few others (e.g., Barron's Ego Strength and Byrne's Repression-Sensitization scales from the MMPI;[2] and Cattell's Ego Strength and Superego Strength scales from the 16PF), Freudian constructs have not been widely employed in structured measures of adjustment.

Rather, most of our present adjustment scales and inventories grew out of the nonpsychoanalytic climate in psychiatry at the turn of the century. Heymans and Wiersma (1906) attempted to catalog those behaviors then considered to be associated with emotional malaise; this schema, expanded and revised by Hoch and Amsden (1913) and Wells (1914), influenced Woodworth's seminal Personal Data Sheet (PDS), the forerunner of all personality and adjustment scales. While diverse sorts of questionnaires had been devised earlier, Woodworth's major contribution lay in popularizing a technique for combining the responses to questionnaire items so as to end up with a single score. The resulting scale of Psychoneurotic Tendencies, which was developed in 1917 in response to a military request for an instrument to weed out emotionally unstable soldiers from the American Expeditionary Forces in World War I, consisted of 116 questions (e.g., "Do you usually feel well and strong?"), to each of which the subject responded "yes" or "no." From an initial set of some 200 items, Woodworth eliminated those to which over a quarter of either college students or draftees gave the "psychoneurotic" response; the resulting 116 items, which are listed in Ferguson (1952), were modified over the years to construct a number of adjustment scales, including revisions of the PDS for children by Johnson (1920) and Mathews (1923), a revision by Cady (1923) for juvenile delinquents, and adult revisions by Laird (1925a, b), House (1927), and Thurstone and Thurstone (1930). The latter was used as the basis for constructing the Neurotic Tendencies scale in Bernreuter's (1933b) extraordinarily popular four-scale Personality Inventory.

One of the few psychologists to eschew this tradition was Pressey, who published preliminary reports of his Cross-Out (X-O) technique for "investigating individual differences in interests and emotional make-up" (Pressey & Pressey, 1919; Pressey & Chambers, 1920; Pressey, 1921). The items in one of the X-O forms consisted of sets of words (e.g., disgust–fear–sex–suspicion–aunt) with directions for the subject to cross out those words which were unpleasant to him and to circle the most unpleasant word. In a second form (e.g., BLOSSOM: flame–flower–paralyzed–red–sew) the subjects were instructed to cross out all words "associated in their minds" with the first word and to circle the most highly associated word. A third form (e.g., begging–swearing–smoking–flirting–spitting) contained directions to cross out

---

[2] For the reader's convenience, a list of the abbreviations used in this chapter is included in Table 1.

Table 1
Some Milestones in the History of Personality Scales and Inventories
(See page 303 for key to abbreviations.)

Approx. Date	Psychopathology-Adjustment	Vocational Interests	Scholastic Predictors	Introversion-Extroversion	Masculinity-Femininity	Personal Values & Manifest Needs	Other Traits
1906	Heymans & Wiersma (Developed symptom list)						
1913	Hoch & Amsden (Revised list)						
1914	Wells (Revised list)	Kelley (Early interest questionnaire)					
1916				Jung (Proposed theory)			
1917	Woodworth—Personal Data Sheet						
1919		Yoakum et al. (Developed item pool)					
1920	Johnson (Revised PDS for children)						
1921	Pressey—X-O Tests for Investigating the Emotions	Moore—Sales vs. Design Engineering Score	Pressey—X-O Tests	McDougall (Extended theory)			Allport & Allport (Theoretical paper)
1922		Freyd—Two interest scales for engineers; Miner—Interest scales for high school students			Terman (Began studies of male vs. female reactions and preferences)		
1923	Mathews (Revised PDS for children); Cady (Revised PDS for juvenile delinquents)			Conklin (Reviewed I-E theories)			

Year				
1924		Ream–Interests of successful vs. unsuccessful life insurance salesmen	Freyd (Developed list of 54 I-E traits)	Travis–Diagnostic Character Test
1925	Laird–Colgate Mental Hygiene Inventory–Form B	Cowdery–Interests of physicians, lawyers, and engineers	Laird–Colgate Mental Hygiene Inventory–Form C	
1926		Strong–Interest scale for personnel managers	Heidbreder–I-E Scale	
1927	House–Mental Hygiene Inventory	Strong–Vocational Interest Blank	Conklin–E-I Interest Ratio	
1928			Allport & Allport–Ascendance-Submission Reaction Study	Spranger (Theory translated into English)
1929			Neymann & Kohlstedt–New Diagnostic Test for I-E; Whitman–Short I-E scale	
1930	Thurstone & Thurstone–Personality Schedule; Jasper–Depression-Elation Scale; Symonds & Jackson–Adjustment Survey	Garretson & Symonds–Interest Questionnaire for High School Students		
1931			Root–I-E Inventory; Gilliland & Morgan–Northwestern University I-E Test	Vernon & Allport–Study of Values

Table 1 (Continued)

Approx. Date	Psychopathology-Adjustment	Vocational Interests	Scholastic Predictors	Introversion-Extroversion	Masculinity-Femininity	Personal Values & Manifest Needs	Other Traits
1932	Willoughby—Emotional maturity scale Bernreuter—Personality Inventory	Brainard & Stewart—Specific Interest Inventory		Bernreuter—Self-sufficiency scale Bernreuter—Personality Inventory	Carter—*M-F* scale from SVIB		Wang—Persistence Scale
1934	Guilford—NPI Bell—Adjustment Inventory	Kuder—Preference Record—Vocational	Wrenn—Study Habits Inventory	Guilford—Nebraska Personality Inventory	Guilford—NPI		
1935	Humm & Wadsworth—Temperament Schedule Washburne—Social Adjustment Inventory	Thurstone—Vocational Interest Schedule		Flanigan (Factor scales from Bernreuter's Personality Inventory)			Lentz et al.—Conservatism-Radicalism Opinionnaire
1936	Rundquist & Sletto—Minnesota Scale for the Survey of Opinions				Terman & Miles-Attitude-Interest Analysis Test		
1937		Cleeton—Vocational Interest Inventory Le Suer—Occupational Interest Blank	Dunlap—Academic Preference Blank	Williamson & Darley—Minnesota Inventory of Social Attitudes			
1938	McFarland & Seitz—*P-S* Experience Blank	Strong—Vocational Interest Blank (Revised)			Strong—SVIB (Revised)	Murray et al. (Developed list of needs, and initial item pools)	
1939	Tiegs, Clark, & Thorpe—California Test of Personality					Maller & Gleser—Interest-Values Inventory	

Year					
1940		Gentry–Vocational Inventory	Guilford & Guilford–Inventory of Factors STDCR		Watson & Fisher–Inventory of Affective Potency
1941	Adams & Lepley–Personal Audit Darley & McNamara–Minnesota Personality Scale Fisher & Watson–Inventory of Affective Tolerance Johnson–Temperament Analysis				
1942		Cardall–Primary Business Interests Test	Evans & McConnell–Minnesota T-S-E Inventory		
1943	Hathaway & McKinley–Minnesota Multiphasic Personality Inventory	Kobal et al.–Inventory of Vocational Interests Lee & Thorpe–Occupational Interest Inventory	Guilford & Martin–GAMIN Myers & Briggs–Type Indicator	Hathaway & McKinley–MMPI (Mf) Guilford & Martin–GAMIN	Guilford & Martin–Inventory of Factors GAMIN & Personnel Inventory
1944	Weider et al.–Cornell Index	Traxler–Survey of Study Habits			
1945	Maslow et al.–Security-Insecurity Inventory	Van Allyn–Job Qualification Inventory			
1946	Thorpe & Clark–Mental Health Analysis	Gregory–Academic Interest Inventory	Drake–MMPI (Si) Gray & Wheelwright–Psychological Type Questionnaire	Kuder–PR-V (Revised)	

Table 1 (Continued)

Approx. Date	Psychopathology-Adjustment	Vocational Interests	Scholastic Predictors	Introversion-Extroversion	Masculinity-Femininity	Personal Values & Manifest Needs	Other Traits
1947		Baldwin—Motivation Indicator			Bell—Personal Preference Inventory		
1948		Guilford, Schneidman, & Zimmerman—Interest Survey; Kuder—Preference Record—Personal					
1949	Heston—Personal Adjustment Inventory		Borow—College Inventory of Academic Adjustment				Cattell & Stice—Sixteen Personality Factor Questionnaire; Guilford & Zimmerman—Temperament Survey; Thurstone—Temperament Schedule
1950							Adorno et al.—California F Scale
1951						Allport-Vernon-Lindzey—Study of Values (Revised)	
1952			Mandler & Sarason—Test Anxiety Questionnaire; Brown & Holtzman—Survey of Study Habits and Attitudes				
1953	Berdie & Layton—Minnesota Counseling Inventory					Edwards—Personal Preference Schedule	Gordon—Personal Profile

Year				
1954	Guilford et al.—DF Opinion Survey			
1955	Rotter (Developed Theory); Phares—Internal vs. External Control Scale			
1956	Gordon—Personal Inventory; Gough—California Psychological Inventory	LaForge & Suczek—Interpersonal Check List	Gough—CPI (Ac, Ai, Ie)	Kuder—Preference Record—Occupational
1957	Heist & Williams—Omnibus Personality Inventory	Gough—CPI (Fe); Jenkins—How Well Do You Know Your Interests?; Heist & Williams—OPI	I. G. Sarason—Test Anxiety Scale; Carter—California Study Methods Survey	Jenkins—How Well Do You Know Your Interests?; Weingarten—Picture Interest Inventory; Curtis—Interest Scale
1958	Holland—Vocational Preference Inventory			Geist—Picture Interest Inventory
1959	Welsh—Figure Preference Test	Welsh—WFPT; Holland—VPI; Eysenck—MPI (Extroversion)		Eysenck—Maudsley Personality Inventory (Neuroticism)
1960	Gordon—Survey of Interpersonal Values; Grygier—Dynamic Personality Inventory; Rokeach—Dogmatism Scale		Alpert & Haber—Achievement Anxiety Test	

Table 1 (Continued)

Approx. Date	Psychopathology-Adjustment	Vocational Interests	Scholastic Predictors	Introversion-Extroversion	Masculinity-Femininity	Personal Values & Manifest Needs	Other Traits
1961	Scheier & Cattell—Neuroticism Scale Questionnaire & IPAT Anxiety Scale	Gordon—Occupational Check List					Cattell et al.—Motivation Analysis Test
1962	Heist & Yonge—OPI (*PI*)	Guilford & Zimmerman—Interest Inventory		Heist & Yonge—OPI (*TI & SE*)	Heist & Yonge—OPI		Heist & Yonge—Omnibus Personality Inventory—Form F
1963	Fricke—OAIS (*Soc A and Emo A*)	Fricke—OAIS (*Bus, Hum., Soc., Phy., Bio.*)	Fricke—Opinion, Attitude, & Interest Survey (*Ach P, Int Q, Cre P*)		Fricke—OAIS (*Mas O*)	Stern—Activities Index	Thorndike—Dimensions of Temperament
1964	Eysenck & Eysenck—Personality Inventory (Neuroticism)			Eysenck & Eysenck—Personality Inventory (Extroversion)			
1965		Clark—Minnesota Vocational Interest Inventory	Siegel & Siegel—Educational Set Scale			Gough & Heilbrun—Adjective Check List	
1966		Campbell et al.—Strong Vocational Interest Blank (Revised)					Edwards—Personality Inventory
1967						Jackson—Personality Research Form	
1970	Comrey—Personality Scales			Comrey—CPS	Comrey—CPS		Comrey—CPS
in press	Jackson & Messick—Differential Personality Inventory	Giddan, King, & Lovell—Academic Behavior Inventory			Giddan, King, & Lovell—ABI		

Key to abbreviations

ABI: Academic Behavior Inventory
ACL: Adjective Check List (Gough)
AI: Activities Index
AIAT: Attitude-Interest Analysis Test
A-S: Ascendance-Submission (scale)
CIAA: College Inventory of Academic Adjustment
CPI: California Psychological Inventory
CPS: Comrey Personality Scales
CSMS: California Study Methods Survey
DFOS: DF Opinion Survey
DOT: Dimensions of Temperament
DPI: Differential Personality Inventory
EPPS: Edwards Personal Preference Schedule
ESS: Educational Set Scale
GAMIN: Inventory of Factors *GAMIN* (Guilford)
GZTS: Guilford-Zimmerman Temperament Survey
IAT: Inventory of Affective Tolerance
ICL: Interpersonal Check List

I-E: Introversion-Extroversion (scale)
IPAR: Institute of Personality Assessment and Research (Berkeley, Calif.)
IPAT: Institute for Personality and Ability Testing (Champaign, Ill.)
IVI: Interest-Values Inventory
MAT: Motivation Analysis Test
M-F: Masculinity-Femininity (scale)
MMPI: Minnesota Multiphasic Personality Inventory
MPI: Maudsley Personality Inventory
MPS: Minnesota Personality Scale
NPI: Nebraska Personality Inventory
OAIS: Opinion, Attitude, and Interest Survey
OPI: Omnibus Personality Inventory
PBIT: Primary Business Interests Test
PDS: Personal Data Sheet
PII: Picture Interest Inventory
PPI: Personal Preference Inventory

PRF: Personality Research Form
PR-O: Preference Record—Occupational (Kuder)
PR-P: Preference Record—Personal (Kuder)
PR-V: Preference Record—Vocational (Kuder)
P-S: Psycho-Somatic (Experience Blank)
PTQ: Psychological Type Questionnaire
SE: Social Extroversion (scale)
SIV: Survey of Interpersonal Values
16PF: Sixteen Personality Factor Questionnaire
SSHA: Survey of Study Habits and Attitudes
SVIB: Strong Vocational Interest Blanks
STDCR: Inventory of Factors STDCR (Guilford)
TI: Thinking Introversion (scale)
T-S-E: Minnesota T-S-E Inventory
VCAI: Vassar College Attitude Inventory
VIS: Vocational Interest Survey
VPI: Vocational Preference Inventory
WFPT: Welsh Figure Preference Test
X-O: Cross-Out Tests for Investigating the Emotions

all words associated with behaviors the subject considered "wrong," and to circle the worst of these. A fourth form (e.g., injustice–noise–self-consciousness–discouragement–germs) contained instructions for the subjects to cross out all the things in each list about which they have ever been worried and to circle the most worrisome. Pressey's adjustment scales, like those from Travis's (1925) Diagnostic Character Test, were constructed by keying statistically infrequent responses; the implicit assumption of both Pressey and Travis that social and emotional maladjustment is related to unconventional test response patterns was later explicitly propounded by Berg (1955) as the "Deviation Hypothesis."

More conventional early attempts to measure aspects of psychopathology included Symonds and Jackson's (1930) Adjustment Survey, Jasper's (1930) Depression-Elation Scale, Willoughby's (1932) Emotional Maturity Scale, and Washburne's (1935) Social Adjustment Inventory. During the same period, however, these global (i.e., single-scale) measures of adjustment began to be supplemented by multi-scale inventories, each scale designed to measure some different facet of psychopathology or adjustment. The forerunner of these inventories was one developed in 1925 by Travis, who attempted to measure 50 "traits" (e.g., stability, inferiority, narcissism, hypochondria, melancholia, sadism, paranoia), each by means of two-item "scales." While inventories composed of much longer scales were soon used to measure vocational interests (e.g., the first version of Strong's Vocational Interest Blank, published in 1927), it remained for Vernon and Allport (1931) and Bernreuter (1933b) to popularize the construction of more comprehensive personality inventories.

Bernreuter combined the items from Thurstone and Thurstone's Personality Schedule, Laird's Colgate Mental Hygiene Inventory (Form C), Allport and Allport's Ascendance-Submission Reaction Study, and his own Self-Sufficiency Scale into one large pool, which he then administered to some 400 college students. For each of the four scales in turn, Bernreuter selected the 50 subjects with the highest scores and the 50 subjects with the lowest scores to be used as criterion groups for an empirical analysis of each item in the combined pool; the resulting four overlapping sets of differentiating items comprised his Personality Inventory. Bernreuter's four scales proved to be at least moderately reliable and to correlate highly with each of the original scales they were meant to replace. Unfortunately, they also turned out to be intercorrelated so highly (e.g., the Neurotic Tendencies and Introversion-Extroversion scales correlated .96) that Flanagan (1935) could later reproduce virtually all of their variance with two orthogonal factor scales. By this time, however, the popular demand for multi-scale inventories was so great that Bernreuter elected to include all six scales (the four original scales plus the two factor scales) in the 1938 revision of his inventory.

Meanwhile, Bell attempted to measure four separate aspects of adjustment with his Adjustment Inventory, which was published in 1934; this popular inventory yielded scores on Home, Health, Social, and Emotional Adjustment, plus a total (composite) score (see Bell, 1935). A similar inventory, Rundquist and Sletto's (1936) Minnesota Scale for the Survey of Opinions, included scales for General Adjustment, Morale vs. Insecurity, Inferiority vs.

Social Ease, Family Intimacy vs. Discord, Respect vs. Disrespect for the Law, Economic Conservatism vs. Radicalism, and Respect vs. Contempt for Education.

An analogous inventory for children, the California Test of Personality, was published by Tiegs, Clark, and Thorpe in 1939; its scales purportedly assessed such aspects of self-adjustment as Self-Reliance, Sense of Personal Worth, Sense of Personal Freedom, Feeling of Belonging, Withdrawal Tendencies, and Nervous Symptoms; plus such aspects of social adjustment as Social Standards, Social Skills, Antisocial Tendencies, and Family, School, and Community Relations. A revision of this inventory was published by Thorpe and Clark in 1946; called the Mental Health Analysis, this later inventory was designed to measure five categories of mental health "assets" (Personal Relationships, Interpersonal Skills, Social Participation, Satisfaction with Work and Recreation, and Adequacy of Outlook and Goals), plus five categories of "liabilities" (Immaturity, Instability, Feelings of Inadequacy, Physical Defects, and Nervous Manifestations), as well as to furnish two part-scores (Assets and Liabilities) and a total Adjustment Index.

By the mid-1930s some inventory developers began turning to diagnosed psychiatric patients as criterion groups for the development of adjustment scales and inventories. This external strategy of scale construction had been used as early as 1921 by Pressey to develop a scale of scholastic potential and by Moore to differentiate sales vs. design engineers. In the 1920s a number of vocational interest scales and inventories utilized the same strategy, the most famous being Strong's Vocational Interest Blank in 1927. However, it was not until the middle 1930s and the development of Humm and Wadsworth's (1934, 1935) Temperament Schedule that this strategy was used to construct adjustment scales. The Temperament Schedule, published in 1935, originally yielded scores on seven of the components of adjustment vs. psychopathology defined by the psychiatrist Rosanoff (1920): Normal, Hysteroid, Manic, Depressive, Autistic, Paranoid, and Epileptoid. The seven scales were developed by item analysis against criterion groups of psychiatric patients and normal subjects who had been judged as being extreme on the component. Interestingly, while the Temperament Schedule was developed from the responses of psychiatric patients, the inventory appears to have enjoyed far more popularity in industrial than in clinical settings.

The publication of the Temperament Schedule was soon followed by the development of another adjustment inventory by the same strategy, namely the P-S Experience Blank (Psycho-Somatic Inventory) reported by McFarland and Seitz (1938). The two highly correlated scales in this inventory, designed to measure physiological dysfunction and psychological maladjustment, were constructed by contrasting the response of "neurotic" and "normal" subjects.

This same external strategy was used to construct what was to become the most popular of all adjustment inventories, Hathaway and McKinley's Minnesota Multiphasic Personality Inventory (MMPI), which was developed in the late 1930s and published in 1943. Each of the original MMPI clinical scales (Hypochondriasis, Depression, Hysteria, Psychopathic Deviancy, Paranoia, Psychasthenia, Schizophrenia, and Hypomania) included items whose responses differentiated psychiatrically diagnosed patient groups from "normal" hospital visitors. While these initial MMPI scales were targeted on the nosological typology originally developed by Kraepelin, later MMPI scales became more catholic; the 550 items in the MMPI proved to be such an extraordinarily fecund source for scale development that within fifteen years after the publication of the inventory, more than two hundred MMPI scales were already available (Dahlstrom & Welsh, 1960), and the next ten years saw the birth of hundreds more.

However, while the enormous popularity of the MMPI led such inventory developers as Berdie and Layton (Minnesota Counseling Inventory), Gough (California Psychological Inventory), and Heist and Williams (Omnibus Personality Inventory) to borrow generously from the MMPI item pool, only two of the many post-MMPI inventories (Gough's CPI and Fricke's OAIS) borrowed its external scale construction strategy. Instead, most of the adjustment inventories published in the 1940s and 1950s were similar to inventories designed in the 1930s.

Adams and Lepley's Personal Audit, published in 1941, fractionated adjustment into the traits of Seriousness-Impulsiveness, Firmness-Indecision, Tranquillity-Irritability, Frankness-Evasion, Stability-Instability, Tolerance-Intolerance, Steadiness-Emotionality, Persistence-Fluctuation, and Contentment-Worry (see Adams, 1941). Another inventory published in the same year, Johnson's Temperament Analysis, reflected a similarly bipolar viewpoint towards aspects of psychopathology, with scales labeled Nervous-Composed, Depressive-Gayhearted, Active-Quiet, Cordial-Cold, Sympathetic-Hard-boiled, Subjective-Objective, Aggressive-Submissive, Critical-Appreciative, and Self-Mastery-Impulsive.

The mass of adjustment scales on the market by the late 1930s led some psychologists to consider merging old inventories to form a new composite, a procedure pioneered by Bernreuter in 1932 and given some impetus by the enormous commercial success of his Personality Inventory. Darley and McNamara (1940) factor-analyzed the scores from Bell's (1935) Adjustment Inventory, Rundquist and Sletto's (1936) Minnesota Scale for the Survey of Opinions, and Williamson and Darley's (1937a, b) Minnesota Inventory of Social Attitudes (an extroversion-introversion inventory) and extracted five factors; their resulting five new scales (Morale, Social Adjustment, Family Relations, Emotionality, and Economic Conservatism) were published in 1941 as the Minnesota Personality Scale (MPS). As sauce for the gander, Berdie and Layton later combined three scales from the MPS (which they relabeled Family Relationships, Social Relationships, and Emotional Stability) with four scales from the MMPI (which they called Conformity [Pd], Adjustment to Reality [Sc], Mood [D], and Leadership [Si], and in 1952 published the combined item pool (the language adapted slightly for high school students) as the Minnesota Counseling Inventory.

Inventory "merging" reached its zenith, however, in the continued efforts of a group of Berkeley psychologists to construct the Omnibus Personality Inventory (OPI). Their conglomerate had its origins in the Vassar College Attitude Inventory (VCAI), assembled early in the 1950s from items developed by Sanford, Barron, and Gough at Berkeley's Institute of Personality Assessment and Research (IPAR) and then revised at Vassar by Sanford, Webster, and Freedman. Darley and McConnell later merged items from the VCAI with those from other inventories, and Heist and Williams prepared Forms A and B of the OPI in 1957; 733 items borrowed from at least four inventories (MMPI, CPI, Minnesota T-S-E-Inventory, and the VCAI) yielded scores on 18 scales. Form O, a popular 1959 abridgment, yielded scores on five scales (Thinking Introversion, Theoretical Orientation, Conformity, Originality, and Estheticism). Forms C and D, two 1963 revisions, included 16 and 12 scales respectively. Form F, published by Heist and Yonge in 1958, contained 385 items and 14 scales (Thinking Introversion, Theoretical Orientation, Estheticism, Complexity, Autonomy, Religious Orientation, Social Extroversion, Impulse Expression, Personal Integration, Anxiety Level, Altruism, Practical Outlook, Masculinity-Femininity, and Response Bias). Interestingly, after all these revisions, approximately 25 percent of the 385 OPI items are essentially the same as items from the MMPI or CPI.

As early as the mid-1930s, when Flanagan (1935) was demonstrating that the four Bernreuter scales could be factored by two, Guilford began a series of factor-analytic investigations of personality scales. His 1934 Nebraska Personality Inventory included one adjustment scale (Emotionality), plus a Social Introversion and a Masculinity scale. Factor analyses of previous introversion-extroversion scales led to Guilford and Guilford's Inventory of Factors STDCR in 1940, with scales (see Guilford & Guilford, 1934, 1936, 1939a, b) called Social Introversion, Thinking Introversion, Depression, Cycloid (mood fluctuation), and Rhathymia (carefree liveliness and impulsivity). By 1943 Guilford and Martin had constructed a number of factorially-based personality measures, which they published as the Inventory of Factors GAMIN and the Personnel Inventory. The former included two more adjustment scales (Inferiority Feelings and Nervous Tenseness), along with scales to measure Pressure for Overt Activity, Social Ascendancy, and Masculinity (Martin, 1945). The latter, aimed at detecting the potential "troublemaker" in industrial settings, included scales for Objectivity, Agreeableness, and Cooperation. A condensation and revision of all three Guilford inventories, Guilford and Zimmerman's Temperament Survey, was published in 1949.

During the same period, Cattell was undertaking a factorial investigation of the "total personality sphere," an endeavor which culminated in the 1949 publication of the Sixteen Personality Factor Questionnaire (16PF). Of the six scales in the 16PF which had been shown to differentiate between neurotic and normal groups, three had high loadings on the braod second-order "Anxiety" factor of the 16PF (see Cattell, Eber, & Tatsuoka, 1970). Scheier and Cattell combined these three scales into one Anxiety score, which was supplemented by the other three differentiating scales (Tender-Mindedness, Depression, and Submissiveness) and published in 1961 as the Neuroticism Scale Questionnaire. A second inventory by Cattell and Scheier, the IPAT Anxiety Scale Questionnaire, measured only components of the second-order anxiety factor and provided five scales (Self-Sentiment Development, Ego Strength, Paranoid Trend, Guilt

Proneness, and Ergic Tension), as well as scores for Covert and Overt anxiety, plus a total anxiety score.

While Guilford and Cattell had been developing factor scales on normal subjects and then testing whether the resulting scales differentiated psychiatric patients from other groups, Eysenck had been constructing factor scales aimed at doing this job from the start. Eysenck and his associates constructed two broad factor scales (Neuroticism and Psychoticism), only the first of which has been incorporated into published inventories. The 1959 Maudsley Personality Inventory (MPI) provided scores for Neuroticism and Extroversion-Introversion. While Bernreuter's Neurotic Tendencies and Introversion-Extroversion scales had correlated .96, the two analogous MPI scales correlated no higher than .30. However, even this modest degree of relationship stimulated Eysenck to revise the scales; the resulting Eysenck Personality Inventory, which included the same two scales (now with virtually no correlation between them), was published in 1964.

While the factor-analytic triumvirate (Cattell, Eysenck, and Guilford) attempted to map personality structure more broadly, a number of other inventory developers were using variants of the same internal strategy to construct specific adjustment scales. For example, Heston had used internal consistency analyses (though not factor analysis) to develop his Personal Adjustment Inventory. This inventory, published in 1949, provided homogeneous (and reasonably independent) scales aimed at the measurement of Emotional Stability, Confidence, Personal Relations, Home Satisfaction, and Analytical Thinking. Around the same period, Gordon utilized factor analysis and a forced-choice item format to isolate four scales (Emotional Stability, Responsibility, Ascendancy, and Sociability), which he published in 1953 as the Personal Profile. A parallel inventory of Gordon's, the Personal Inventory, was published in 1956 and provided scales for Personal Relations, Vigor, Cautiousness, and Original Thinking.

Although the internal strategy of scale construction has dominated other approaches of late, two important post-World War II inventories were developed from the external strategy. The most popular of these was Gough's 1956 California Psychological Inventory (CPI), which borrowed about two-fifths of its items from the MMPI. Eleven of the 18 original CPI scales included items which differentiated between groups of subjects who had been rated (or could be logically seen) as being at extreme poles on the particular trait targeted for the scale. While the CPI was explicitly developed to measure important individual differences not tapped by the host of adjustment inventories on the market at that time, a few CPI scales (e.g., Socialization, Self-Control, Self-Acceptance, Flexibility) appear to tap traits within the adjustment domain.

Unfortunately, inventories constructed by the external strategy have tended to provide highly correlated scales; a host of correlational and factor-analytic studies of SVIB, MMPI, and CPI scale scores attest to the relative redundancy within each of these three inventories, a redundancy which is aggravated by the fact that the same items are scored on more than one scale. For example, the SVIB Chemist and Physicist scales correlated .93 (Strong, 1959), the MMPI Hypochondriasis and Hysteria scales correlated .68 among normal subjects (Thumin, 1969) and .81 among psychiatric patients (Goldberg, 1965), and the CPI Dominance and Sociability scales correlated .67 among females and .61 among males (Gough, 1957). Though most of these correlations are close to the maximum possible, given the reliabilities of the scales, only the first approaches that pinnacle reached by two of the four original Bernreuter scales.

The one exception to this general rule was Fricke's Opinion, Attitude, and Interest Survey (OAIS), the manual for which was released in 1963. Fricke included in each of the OAIS scales only those items whose validity had been established against non-test criteria, and whose correlations with other items were such that the resulting scales would be minimally intercorrelated. Only two of the OAIS scales (Social Adjustment and Emotional Adjustment) fall in the adjustment domain, and their intercorrelations within various samples ranged from about .10 to .40 (Fricke, 1963); the other OAIS scales, which measure aspects of vocational interests and scholastic potential, will be discussed later.

The use of some mixed strategy of inventory construction, exemplified by Fricke's use of both external and internal criteria for item inclusion, is not new. While the very first adjustment scales were constructed using a purely intuitive approach, most scale developers began using a mixture of intuitive and internal strategies as early as the 1920s. A typical procedure was to assemble an item pool on purely intuitive grounds, administer the pool to a sample of subjects, and then correlate responses to each item with total (*a priori*) scale scores; items not significantly associated with total scores were then eliminated from the refined measure. Such a procedure is directly analogous to that of selecting items with high loadings on the first unrotated factor when responses to a set of items purportedly tapping some single dimension are subjected to factor analysis.

The epitome of this mixed intuitive-internal strategy of inventory construction can be found in three recent inventories: Edwards' (1966) Personality Inventory, Jackson's (1967) Personality Research Form, and Jackson and Messick's as yet unpublished Differential Personality Inventory (DPI). Of these three new multi-scale inventories, the first two are not oriented toward the adjustment domain, and therefore only the DPI will be discussed at this point. While items were initially assembled for each of the DPI scales on intuitive grounds, only those items which had "high content saturation" on their respective scales and low correlations with "stylistic" and other content scales were retained (internal strategy). Moreover, all scales were composed of equal numbers of true and false keyed items. The resulting inventory includes scales for Cynicism, Depression, Familial Discord, Health Concern, Hostility, Impulsivity, Irritability, Neurotic Disorganization, Psychotic Tendencies, Rebelliousness, Socially Deviant Attitudes, Somatic Complaints, Defensiveness, Insomnia, Broodiness, Desocialization, Thinking Disorganization, Feelings of Unreality, Hypochondriasis, Ideas of Persecution, Mood Fluctuation, Panic Reaction, Perceptual Distortion, Repression, Sadism, Self-Depreciation,

Shallow Affect, and Headache Proneness. It is likely that this carefully constructed new inventory will begin to replace the MMPI in clinical settings as
soon as the DPI research volume begins to approach that generated by its
thirty-year-old predecessor.

While the developers of most early scales considered adjustment as a unitary dimension, virtually all recent workers have fractionated adjustment (or
psychopathology) into a set of components. The major exceptions to this
trend include Fisher and Watson's (1941) Inventory of Affective Tolerance,
Wieder et al.'s Cornell Index (a 1944 revision of a psychiatric screening scale
for the armed forces—the World War II equivalent of Woodworth's World
War I Personal Data Sheet), Maslow, Hirsh, Stein, and Honigmann's (1945)
Security-Insecurity Inventory, and a few anxiety scales which have appeared
over the past twenty years. The most influential of the latter was Taylor's
(1953) Manifest Anxiety Scale, which was based upon MMPI items. Moreover,
even within the domain of anxiety measurement, the same trend has continued. Cattell and Scheier's IPAT Anxiety Scale Questionnaire, published in
1961, included eight anxiety scores, and Endler, Hunt and Rosenstein's
(1962) S-R Inventory of Anxiousness fractionated the concept into separate
scores for each of a number of potentially anxiety-arousing situations.

VOCATIONAL INTERESTS

Whereas military and clinical demands stimulated the search for predictors
of psychopathology, most of the resulting adjustment scales and inventories
found their greatest use in industrial settings. And paradoxically, whereas
industrial demands may have stimulated the search for predictors of vocational
satisfaction and success, the resulting interest inventories found their greatest
use in clinical and educational settings, especially in high school and college
counseling centers. Both types of measures clearly stemmed from important
societal pressures on psychologists to forecast later performance and morale.

As early as 1914, Kelley had designed an interest blank, which from its
description would appear to resemble some more recent models. In contrast
to the latter, however, Kelley's blank furnished no scores; the vocational
counselor simply read the item responses and used them as an interviewing
and counseling guide. A number of similar (nonscored) interest report questionnaires have been published over the years, including Wallar and Pressey's
Occupational Orientation Inquiry in 1939 and the U.S. Employment Service's
Interest Check List in 1946.

It is likely that the scoring technique popularized by Woodworth's Personal
Data Sheet made its way into interest measurement before the 1920s, and
consequently it is probable that some intuitively constructed interest scales
were developed during this period. However, in contrast to adjustment prediction, interest measurement quickly focused on the external strategy of
scale construction, and the early intuitive scales are difficult to locate. For
some accounts of this early history, see Fryer (1931).

Apparently, the first large-scale investigation of vocational interests was
begun in 1918 by Bingham, Miner, and Yoakum at the Carnegie Institute of

Technology in Pittsburgh. Approximately one thousand interest items were developed in a seminar of Yoakum's in 1919, and subsets of these items were used by many investigators over the next fifty years. In 1921 Moore reported a study of the differential interests of sales vs. design engineers, and one year later Freyd developed some preliminary interest scales for engineers. The same year Miner, who apparently originated the idea of comparing the responses of individuals in a specific occupational group with a sample from diverse occupations (Campbell, 1968), published some interest scales based upon the responses of students tested in Pittsburgh high schools beginning in 1918.

By the early 1920s, a number of the younger members of the Carnegie group had been exploring the differential interests of individuals in various occupations. Ream investigated successful vs. unsuccessful life insurance salesmen, and Cowdery compared the interests of physicians, lawyers, and engineers. By far the most illustrious of this group, however, was E. K. Strong, who, after moving from Carnegie to Stanford in 1923, began to develop his Vocational Interest Blank (SVIB), which was published in 1927. The history of Strong's involvement in interest measurement and of the resulting SVIB (including all its forms and revisions) can be found in Campbell (1968). The approach to interest inventory construction popularized by Strong included at least four salient features: (a) the use of occupational, educational, and avocational preference items from the original Yoakum pool, most of these presented as a single stimulus; (b) the use of a "Like-Indifferent-Dislike" (L-I-D) response option with most of the items; (c) the use of an external strategy of scale construction (keying only those items which had been shown empirically to differentiate among occupational groups); and (d) scale development based upon the comparison of a particular occupational group with a sample of "men in general." While all of these four features of the SVIB influenced later interest inventories, most inventory developers dropped one or more features in designing their own products.

One of the early alternatives to the SVIB was Garretson and Symonds' Interest Questionnaire for High School Students; this 234-item inventory (with a L-I-D response format) was first published in 1930 and revised in 1942. In 1932 Brainard and Stewart published their Specific Interest Inventory; 100 work activities were included, each with a 5-point rating scale (from "like it very much" to "dislike it very much"), intuitively grouped to provide 20 "mode of activity" scores (e.g., Physical Work, Mechanical Work, Vocal Expression, Experimenting, Creative Imagination, etc.). The inventory was revised by Brainard and Brainard in 1945 and renamed the Occupational Preference Inventory; 140 items (with a 5-point response format) yielded intuitively constructed scores for 28 occupations, grouped into seven families. The inventory was revised once again in 1956 to yield scores on Commerical, Mechanical, Professional, Esthetic, Scientific, Personal Service (girls), and Agriculture (boys) interest scales.

By far the most important competitor to the SVIB, however, was Kuder's Preference Record—Vocational, published in 1934. Providing measures of Scientific, Computational, Musical, Artistic, Literary, Social Service, and

Persuasive interests, this inventory originally included 330 items, each a paired comparison between two occupational or avocational activities. Items were clustered on the basis of homogeneity analyses, and the resulting seven scales were reasonably independent of each other. In later versions of this inventory, Kuder switched the format to item triads, with instructions to rank order the three items within each triad. A 1946 revision of the inventory added a Mechanical and a Clerical interest scale, plus a measure of Masculinity-Femininity. A 1956 revision added an Outdoor interest scale. In 1964, a parallel inventory for a slightly younger audience was published as Kuder's General Interest Survey.

While Kuder utilized a popular variant of the internal strategy of scale construction, he did not use factor analysis. It remained for Thurstone to apply factor-analytic procedures to interest items; his Vocational Interest Schedule (VIS) was developed during the same period as Kuder's inventory and published in 1935. Thurstone's VIS, which contained as items 72 occupational titles, each presented with a L-I-D response format, provided scales of Commercial, Academic, Scientific, Biological, Legal, Athletic, and Descriptive (humanistic) interests. By 1947, when a revised version of the inventory was published as the Thurstone Interest Schedule, Thurstone himself had shunned factor analysis in favor of a modified internal consistency procedure. The 1947 Thurstone inventory included as items 100 pairs of occupational titles, with instructions to indicate one's preference within each forced-choice pair. Ten scores were provided: Physical Science, Biological Science, Computational, Business, Executive, Persuasive, Linguistic, Humanitarian, Artistic, and Musical.

A somewhat similar interest inventory was published by Le Suer in 1937; his Occupational Interest Blank included 100 occupational titles as items with a L-I-D response format. In contrast to the VIS, however, Le Suer grouped his items on a purely intuitive basis to construct Professional, Technical, Clerical, Sales, Artistic, Skilled Trades, Semi-skilled Trades, and Adventuresome scales.

The original set of interest items spawned by Yoakum's 1919 seminar was used during the early 1930s to develop Cleeton's Vocational Interest Inventory, which was published in 1937. Cleeton's inventory included 630 of these items, presented in a "like-dislike" response format, plus 40 items designed to measure Social Adjustment. The men's form of Cleeton's inventory provided scores for Biological Science, Physical Science, Social Service, Sales, Business Administration, Financial, Legal-Literary, Mechanical, and Creative occupations; the women's form for Natural Science, Social Service, Sales, Office Work, Personal Service, Mechanical, Creative, Teaching, and Household vocations. A 1943 revision of these two inventories added an Agricultural scale to the men's form, and replaced the Teaching and Household scales on the women's form with scales for Grade School Teaching, High School and College Teaching, Housekeeper-Factory Worker, and Homemaking-Child Care. The Social Adjustment scale was dropped from both forms.

Of all the departures from the Yoakum item pool, the most interesting was that of Cardall, who engaged 106 businessmen to keep work diaries reflecting their hour-to-hour activities. From these diaries, Cardall extracted over two thousand descriptions of business activities (e.g., "pay bills and bring back receipts"), which he then reduced on intuitive grounds to a smaller subset. A cluster analysis of these descriptors formed the basis for Cardall's five-scale Primary Business Interests Test (PBIT), which was published in 1942; the PBIT provided interest scores for Accounting, Collections and Adjustments, Sales-Office, Sales-Store, and Stenographic-Filing activities.

A potpourri of over 400 information, preference, biographical, and completion items were included in Gentry's Vocational Inventory, which was published in 1940; the items were grouped into scales for Social Service, Business, Law-Government, Art, Mechanical Designing, Mechanical Construction, Science, and Literary interests—plus an Introversion-Extroversion scale. Moreover, a spate of similar interest inventories was also published during the 1940s, a symptom of the seemingly voracious market for putative measures of vocational satisfaction and success. Most of these are of interest today only insofar as they demonstrate the sort of items utilized during this period and the kinds of individual differences deemed important for forecasting vocational success. One of these, Kobal et al.'s Inventory of Vocational Interests, was published in 1943 and furnished Mechanical, Academic, Artistic, Business, and Agricultural interest scores. The inventory included 25 questions (e.g., "What would you like to do best with an airplane?"), each presented with 10 alternatives (e.g., "work on it as a mechanic, pilot it, study its history, write a poem about it, advertise its uses," etc.), with instructions to check 3 of the 10 alternatives. A revision of this inventory, published in the late 1950s, used the same sort of items and furnished the same five scores.

Another such attempt was Lee and Thorpe's Occupational Interest Inventory, also published in 1943. This inventory included 240 paired-comparisons activity items, 40 in each of six fields; the items within each field were further stratified by three levels of skill and responsibility, and by three broad types of interest modes. The resulting scales generated scores for six interest fields (Social, Natural, Mechanical, Business, Arts, and Sciences) and three interest types (Verbal, Manipulative, and Computational), plus an overall Interest Level. A 1956 revision of this inventory retained these same features. Another type of item stratification was used in Van Allyn's Job Qualification Inventory, first published in 1945. Within each of 35 occupational areas, one item dealt with preferences, another with past performance, a third with education, a fourth with vocational aspiration, a fifth with paid experience, and a sixth with indications of unusual proficiency; the resulting 210 items were presented in a NO-?-YES response format and yielded 35 occupational scores. A revision of this inventory in 1958 was titled the Qualifications Record and yielded 45 occupational scores, grouped into seven broad families. A shorter version of the Qualifications Record with the same 45 scales was published as the Career Finder in 1960.

In contrast to these intuitive scale construction procedures, at least one inventory developer in the 1940s returned to the external strategy pioneered by Strong. Beginning in the late 1930s, Gregory administered about 900 interest items to a number of samples of college students; the responses of juniors and seniors majoring in each of 28 college curriculum areas were contrasted with the responses of a sample of college freshmen, and the most differentiating items were retained to form Gregory's Academic Interest Inventory, which was published in 1946. The 300-item inventory utilized a five-category response format and yielded 28 academic interest scores (Agriculture, Architecture, Biology, . . . Religion, Secondary Education, Sociology, Speech). A somewhat similar inventory, Baldwin's Motivation Indicator, was constructed by the intuitive strategy and aimed at the high school rather than the college curriculum. This inventory, published in 1947, included 81 curricular activity statements (nine in each of nine areas) and 25 social activity statements (five in each of five areas). All items were presented in sets of four, with instructions to select the two most liked; each item was presented four times (and compared with eight other items). The inventory furnished nine curricular scores (Biological Sciences, Physical Sciences, Social Sciences, Literary Arts, Graphic Arts, Industrial Arts, Agricultural Arts, Clerical-Verbal, and Clerical-Numerical) and five motivational scores (Altruistic, Promotional, Administrative, Distributive [sales], and Creative).

In a more recent attempt to predict college curricular goals, Fricke (1963) used a mixture of the external and internal strategies of scale construction to develop five interest scales (Business, Humanities, Social Science, Physical Science, and Biological Science) for his Opinion, Attitude, and Interest Survey (OAIS). In marked contrast to Gregory, however, Fricke elected to eschew college major as a criterion in favor of a one-item ranking of the five curricular areas. Each of the five OAIS interest scales included about 100 items, each of which differentiated between students who ranked a particular area first or second versus those who ranked it fourth or fifth, when asked to rank order their preferences for the five fields. Moreover, although Fricke simultaneously attempted to keep his scales as independent as possible, about half of the correlations among the five OAIS interest scales were above .30.

By the end of World War II, Guilford and his associates had moved into interest measurement. A pool of 540 activity items (with a "Dislike—Like as Hobby—Like as Vocation" response format) was reduced to 360 items by internal consistency analyses and published in 1948 as the Guilford-Schniedman-Zimmerman Interest Survey. Each of nine interest areas was subdivided into two components: Artistic (Appreciative and Expressive), Linguistic (Appreciative and Expressive), Scientific (Investigatory and Theoretical), Mechanical (Manipulative and Designing), Outdoor (Natural and Athletic), Business-Political (Mercantile and Leadership), Social (Persuasive and Gregarious), Personal Assistance (Personal Service and Social Welfare), and Office Work (Clerical and Numerical); each of the resulting 18 scales, in turn, could be scored both for Hobby and for Vocation, for a total of 36 scores in all. The Interest Survey should not be confused with the Guilford-Zimmerman Interest Inventory, a 1962 publication of Joan Guilford and the same Zimmerman. The latter inventory included 150 items (with a four-category response format), 15 for each of 10 scales (Mechanical, Natural, Aesthetic, Service, Clerical, Mercantile, Leadership, Literary, Scientific, and Creative).

A survey of factor-analytic studies of interest and personality inventories convinced Kuder of the need to measure seven additional dimensions beyond those already included in his Preference Record–Vocational (PR–V), and scales for five of these dimensions were included in the numerous revisions of his Preference Record–Personal (PR–P) during the 15 years after its publication in 1948. The scales in the first edition were labeled Sociable, Practical, Theoretical, Agreeable, and Dominant, though these were soon changed to preferences for Group Activity, Stable Situations, Working with Ideas, Avoiding Conflict, and Directing Others. While Kuder used a variant of the internal strategy to construct his PR–V and his PR–P, by the middle 1950s the enormous popularity of the SVIB stimulated him to develop another competing interest inventory using the external strategy of scale construction. Kuder's Preference Record–Occupational (PR–O), which was published in 1956, contained 100 sets of item triads with instructions to rank-order the items in each triad; items whose responses differentiated between a particular occupational group and a sample of men from many occupations were keyed to provide 22 occupational scores. Like the SVIB, the number of occupational scales available from the PR–O has been gradually increasing over the years; by the time the inventory was revised in 1963, 51 occupational scales were available.

In contrast to the careful scale construction procedures employed in the inventories developed by Kuder, a number of other interest inventories published in the 1950s were practically indistinguishable from some much earlier models. For example, Jenkins' How Well Do You Know Your Interests?, which was published in 1957, was at least faintly reminiscent of Travis' Diagnostic Character Test, which was published in 1925. While the former included 54 scales and the latter 50, 46 of the scales in Jenkins' inventory (and all in Travis') were composed of only two items. However, Jenkins used an internal strategy of scale construction, and he selected the two items with the highest factor loadings from a much larger pool; 7 of the 54 interest scales included four items, and 1 longer scale was provided as a measure of masculinity-femininity. All items were presented with a 6-category response format (from "like tremendously" to "dislike tremendously"). Another such inventory from the same period was Curtis' Interest Scale, published in 1959. This throwback employed 5 items, each with 10 alternatives (one from each of 10 interest areas), with instructions to rank-order the 10 alternatives; the inventory provided scales for Business, Mechanics, Applied Arts, Direct Sales, Production, Science, Entertainment, Interpersonal, Computation, and Farming, plus a five-item scale to measure Desire for Responsibility.

The differences among item types included in all these inventories may have served to mask their one common characteristic–namely, their reliance on verbal statements or verbal titles. Consequently, all of these inventories could only be used with individuals who were neither culturally nor educationally disadvantaged. However, as society began to recognize the need to help its more handicapped members, the demand for nonverbal items began to increase. In response to these pressures, two Picture Interest Inventories (PII) were published, the first by Weingarten in 1958 and the second by Geist in 1959. Weingarten's PII was modeled after Lee and Thorpe's Occupational

Interest Inventory and furnished scales relabeled Interpersonal Service, Natural, Mechanical, Business, Esthetic, Scientific, Verbal, and Computational, as well as a scale to measure Time Perspective. Geist's PII was modeled after Kuder's Preference Record—Vocational and included 11 interest scales (Persuasive, Clerical, Mechanical, Dramatic, Musical, Scientific, Outdoor, Literary, Computational, Artistic, and Social Service) and six motivational scales (Family, Prestige, Financial, Intrinsic, Environmental, and Past Experience). The men's form of Geist's inventory included 132 line drawings of various activities arranged in 44 triads; instructions were to choose the most liked drawing in each triad. A 1964 revision of Geist's PII added a Personal Service scale to the women's form, which included 27 pictorial triads.

Societal pressures to provide counseling services for handicapped and deprived individuals also led to the development of a few recent interest inventories aimed at lower-level positions in the work hierarchy. In contrast to the great mass of measures targeted for the college-oriented, Gordon's Occupational Check List was aimed directly at individuals with high school educations or less. This 1961 inventory, modeled after Mooney's Problem Check List, consisted of 240 task descriptions with instructions to underline the tasks one liked and to circle the tasks one liked best. The items were keyed via internal consistency procedures to provide five scales: Business, Outdoor, Arts, Technology, and Service. A second instrument directed at the same audience, Clark's 1965 Minnesota Vocational Interest Inventory, utilized the external strategy of scale construction to provide occupational scales for lower-level jobs than those included in the SVIB.

SCHOLASTIC PREDICTORS

The preceding attempts to predict occupational satisfaction and attainment are closely related to the development of measures aimed at the prediction of success in various vocational training programs and in colleges and universities. As already noted, one of the earliest applications of the external strategy of scale construction was Pressey's (1921) attempt to differentiate students who earned satisfactory grades in college from their less successful peers by means of their responses to items from his X-O tests. However, most research on scholastic prediction has relied heavily upon aptitude measures, and few early attempts to develop personality scales for use in this area can be found. Moreover, the very success of psychologists' attempts to predict grade point average (GPA) by means of scholastic aptitude tests appears to have led investigators to focus research on measures of more specific aptitudes rather than to pursue the search for nonintellective sorts of predictors.

One of the early exceptions to this trend can be found in the work of Wrenn, who administered 69 items relating to study habits, each with a three-category response format (rarely-sometimes-often), to 220 Stanford students, half of whom were in the top 10 percent and half in the lowest 20 percent of the distribution of college grades; the students in the two groups were matched on IQ test scores. The 30 items which significantly differentiated between these groups formed Wrenn's Study Habits Inventory, which was published in 1934. A 28-item revision was published in 1941.

Dunlap used the same external strategy and 435 interest items to construct scales to predict the subscores of the New Stanford Achievement Test, the Metropolitan Achievement Tests, and the Terman Group Test of Mental Ability; the 100 items with the most significant correlations with these test scores were incorporated into Dunlap's Academic Preference Blank, which was published in 1937. The items were presented with a "Like-Indifferent-Dislike-Unknown" response format, and scores could be obtained for History, Geography, Arithmetic, Literature, Language Usage, Paragraph Meaning, and Word Meaning subscores, plus General Achievement, Mental Age, and IQ scores. Later editions of this unique inventory reduced the item pool to 90 items to facilitate machine scoring.

In the 1940s, the major thrust of scholastic prediction research centered on the construction of differential aptitude tests, a development stimulated by the apparent success of aptitude batteries in selecting military personnel in World War II. While a number of investigators began to assess the incremental validity of existing adjustment, interest, and introversion-extroversion scales in predicting college achievement, there were relatively few attempts to develop new personality measures for this specific purpose. Traxler published an 85-item Survey of Study Habits in 1944, which was intended primarily as a means of student self-analysis in academic counseling settings. However, the major development during this decade was the publication in 1949 of Borow's College Inventory of Academic Adjustment (CIAA), which provided six subscores (Curricular Adjustment, Level of Aspiration, Use of Time, Study Skills, Mental Health, and Personal Relations) plus a total score. The 90 items in this inventory, presented with a "Yes-No" response format, included only those items (from a much larger set initially administered) which differentiated academic overachievers from underachievers at Pennsylvania State College; the differentiating items were grouped intuitively into the six subscales, whose median intercorrelation was about .45. Borow's method of inventory construction insured that CIAA scores had quite low correlations with those from aptitude tests, yet correlated between .30 and .40 with college GPA. Consequently, an admissions officer using this inventory along with an aptitude test battery might be able to raise the correlation with GPA from around .50 (tests alone) to around .60 (tests plus CIAA), the latter value being approximately equal to the predictive validity of high school grades.

The 1950s saw an emerging interest in forecasting academic success via structured personality measures. While critics of aptitude testing had long maintained that certain students obtained lower aptitude scores because of intense "test anxiety," it was not until the 1950s that any systematic research was begun to measure this putative personality trait. One of the early attempts was made by Mandler and S. B. Sarason (1952) at Yale University, culminating in their Test Anxiety Questionnaire. A psychometrically more polished instrument, titled the Test Anxiety Scale, was fashioned by I. G. Sarason (1958) at the University of Washington. While both of these measures provided single scores for test anxiety, Alpert (now Baba Ram Dass) and Haber (1960) fractionated the construct into two components—Facilitating Anxiety and Debilitating Anxiety (postulated to affect examination performance in opposite directions)—in their Achievement Anxiety Test, developed at Stanford University. Interestingly, no one has yet demonstrated unambiguously that any of these anxiety scales function as significant suppressor or moderator variables in the prediction of college grades from aptitude tests, or that their inclusion in a college admissions battery significantly improves the level of predictive validity beyond that achievable by high school grades and aptitude tests alone.

The test anxiety scales, which were constructed by the intuitive assembly of items (sometimes refined by internal consistency procedures), furnish the most salient exceptions to the use of the external strategy in constructing academic prediction scales. The early scales developed by Pressey, Wrenn, Dunlap, and Borow were based upon external criteria, as were the later ones developed by Brown and Holtzman, Gough, and Fricke. Brown and Holtzman's Survey of Study Habits and Attitudes (SSHA), published in 1953, included 75 items referring to various study attitudes, culled from a larger set of statements transcribed from student interviews; separate (but overlapping) male and female SSHA prediction scales included those items which differentiated college overachievers from underachievers. Both scales had quite low correlations with scholastic aptitude test scores and correlated about .45 with college grades. The SSHA was revised in 1966 and 25 items were added; the 100 items were intuitively grouped into four highly correlated 25-item scales (Delay Avoidance, Work Methods, Teacher Approval, and Educational Acceptance), the first two of which could be combined to form a scale of Study Habits and the last two a scale of Study Attitudes—both of which, in turn, could be combined to furnish a total score, dubbed Study Orientation.

A somewhat similar fractionation of study attitudes can be found in Carter's California Study Methods Survey (CSMS), which included three highly correlated subscales (School Attitudes, Study Mechanics, and Planning) plus a total score. This 1958 inventory consisted of 150 questions, presented with a "Yes-No" response format. Like other scholastic inventories, its total score correlated about .45 with college grades. The CSMS should not be confused with Gough's California Psychological Inventory (CPI), which was published in 1956. Three CPI scales were specifically constructed as measures of achievement potential and intellectual efficiency: Achievement via Conformance (Ac), composed of items significantly correlated with high school grades; Achievement via Independence (Ai), which included those items significantly correlated with college grades; and Intellectual Efficiency (Ie), composed of items significantly correlated with intelligence test scores. Over the years, the validity of these CPI scales has been assessed, both singly and in combination, in a host of settings ranging from high schools (e.g., Gough, 1964, 1966a) to medical schools (e.g., Gough, 1967; Gough & Hall, 1964).

As already noted, diverse scales constructed by the external strategy often display rather high intercorrelations; in the case of the CPI, the Ac and Ai scales intercorrelated about .40, and they both correlated around .55 with Ie (Gough, 1957). Fricke (1963) attempted to construct three scholastic predictors for his Opinion, Attitude, and Interest Survey (OAIS) which would be independent of each other (and of the other scales in the OAIS). The OAIS Achiever Personality scale (*Ach P*) included 86 items whose responses differentiated college overachievers from underachievers; the Intellectual Quality scale (*Int Q*) included 85 items with significant correlations with aptitude test scores; and the Creative Personality scale (*Cre P*) included 101 items differentiating students nominated as being unusually creative by their college instructors from students nominated as being low in creativity. The intercorrelations among these three OAIS scales were indeed quite low, as were their correlations with the three CPI scholastic scales; while *Int Q* correlated about .55 with *Ai* and about .35 with *Ie,* the other cross-inventory correlations ranged from zero to .30 (Fricke, 1963). While each inventory developer has interpreted this correlational pattern as evidence for the relative utility of his own scales, no independent investigator has yet tested the comparative validity of the CPI and OAIS in forecasting academic promise.

All of the scholastic scales and inventories discussed so far were constructed as *general* predictors of academic promise, each developed in the expectation that it would provide reasonably uniform predictions across various types of courses and diverse curricular areas. In contrast, Siegel and Siegel (1965) have developed a personality scale specifically as a *differential* predictor of scholastic promise. Their Educational Set Scale (ESS) was composed of 31 item triads (e.g., "Assume you are enrolled in an English course and must learn about the following: (*a*) the dates and major works of well-known poets; (*b*) the role of the playwright in contemporary society; (*c*) the structure of sonnets"), with instructions to select the most preferred and the least preferred alternative. Within each triad, one statement described a task requiring the acquisition of factual information, and another described a more conceptual learning task; the resulting ESS score was designed to measure students' preferences for conceptual versus factual knowledge and thus to relate differentially to academic performance under differing instructional procedures. Unfortunately, the evidence for the differential validity of the ESS is far from compelling (e.g., Goldberg, 1969).

By far the most ambitious attempt to develop scholastic prediction scales can be found in the unpublished Academic Behavior Inventory (ABI), constructed by Giddan, King, and Lovell. Over 850 items (at least a quarter of which were borrowed from the MMPI, CPI, SVIB, OPI, EPPS, ACL, OAIS, PRF, and other inventories) were included in various forms of the ABI and administered during the 1960s to diverse student groups. Form E of the ABI included 458 items, presented in a true-false response format. Fifteen ABI scales were constructed by internal consistency analyses and grouped under five rubrics: Subjective Distress (Manifest Anxiety, Alienation, and Test Anxiety); Extrinsic Motivation (Achievement, Persistence, and Extrinsic Reward); Intrinsic Motivation (Affiliation, Class Participation, and Intrinsic Reward); Creativity (Originality, Flexibility, and Orderliness); and Ideology (Liberalism-Conservatism, Social Activism, and Sexual Permissiveness); these 15 constructs were selected to include the most salient traits purportedly tapped by past scholastic prediction scales as well as conceptions characterizing the more recent concerns and complaints of college students. Nine other ABI scales were constructed by the external strategy, including a Masculinity-Femininity measure, plus separate male and female scales developed to predict Academic Performance, Overachievement, Academic Capacity, and Academic Motivation.

INTROVERSION-EXTROVERSION

As already noted, the diverse measures of psychopathology, vocational interests, and scholastic potential which have proliferated over the years can be viewed as responses to societal pressures upon psychologists to forecast significant personal outcomes. The measures included in the remaining columns of Table 1, on the other hand, are not so easily viewed as reactions to applied demands. Moreover, most of these measures appear to have been spawned by a few highly influential conceptions of the structure of individual differences.

Perhaps the most compelling of all such theoretical constructs has been that of introversion-extroversion (*I-E*), popularized in the theoretical writings of the psychoanalytic rebel Carl Jung about the time of World War I and extended in the writings of the psychologist William McDougall in the early 1920s. From this period on, probably more effort has been expended in attempts to construct measures of *I-E* and the related construct dominance-submissiveness than any trait complex other than intelligence and adjustment. Conklin (1923) published an early review of the *I-E* literature, and the next year Freyd (1924) published a list of 54 types of behaviors purportedly related to the *I-E* construct. This list formed the basis for the development of many early *I-E* scales, including those by Heidbreder (1926) and Root (1931).

One of the first *I-E* scales was Laird's Colgate Mental Hygiene Inventory—Form C, which was published in 1925; a shortened version was reported by Whitman (1929). Laird's primary interest lay in developing a reliable index of adjustment, and he conceived of the *I-E* construct as an important determinant of behavioral differences among psychiatric patients. This viewpoint, which enjoyed wide popularity in the 1920s, influenced the development of Travis' (1925) Diagnostic Character Test. In an early unpublished study, Bathhurst showed that schizophrenics could be differentiated from manic-depressive patients on *I-E* scales, the former achieving more introverted and the latter more extroverted scores. In a 1927 master's thesis, Kohlstedt administered 100 putative *I-E* items to 100 schizophrenic and 100 manic-depressive patients; the 50 most highly differentiating items were included in Neymann and Kohlstedt's (1929) New Diagnostic Test for *I-E*. Gilliland and Morgan (1931) then administered these 50 items to new samples of 60 schizophrenic and 65 manic-depressive patients; the 35 most differentiating items were included in their Northwestern University *I-E* Test. As evidence for the validity of their scale, Gilliland and Morgan (1931) reported a bimodal distribution of *I-E* scores among psychiatric patients (most of the schizophrenics falling within the introverted mode and most of the manic-depressives falling within the extroverted mode) and a normal distribution of scores among college students; in the latter sample, the scale correlated about .50 with peer ratings of *I-E*.

One of the first scale developers to object to this criterion for the construction of *I-E* scales was Conklin (1927), who attempted to develop an *I-E* measure within normal samples. Conklin eschewed the Freyd (1924) list in favor of 100 activity items (e.g., playing baseball, hearing lectures, talking with friends, reading essays, etc.), half judged as likely to be preferred by extroverts and half by introverts. About 350 college students responded to each item on a 9-point scale, and those subjects scoring in the top and bottom 10 percent of the distribution of *a priori* scale scores were used as two criterion groups for item analysis. The 40 most differentiating items (20 preferred by introverts and 20 by extroverts) were included in Conklin's (1927) *E-I* Interest Ratio. As one might expect from a scale constructed by this variant of the internal strategy, the reliability (homogeneity) of the *E-I* Interest Ratio was over .90 in new samples. A similarly constructed measure developed during the same period was Bernreuter's (1933a) Self-Sufficiency scale. Bernreuter administered 132 items, each purportedly tapping individual differences in dependency upon other persons, to 127 college students with a "Yes-?-No" response format. An *a priori* key was used to provide two samples with extreme scores, which were used for all item analyses. Sixty items were included in the revised scale, which had reliability (homogeneity) values around .85.

In contrast, Floyd and Gordon Allport used a variant of the external strategy in constructing their Ascendance-Submission Reaction Study, which was first published in 1928 and revised in 1939. The Allports developed a set of items describing hypothetical situations (e.g., "Are you embarrassed if you have greeted a stranger whom you have mistaken for an acquaintance?"), each presented with two or three alternative answers (e.g., "very much, somewhat, not at all"); 41 of these items were administered to 400 college males, and 49 items to 200 college females, all of whom rated themselves and were rated by four friends on an *A-S* rating scale. Scoring weights for each item alternative were constructed on the basis of the self- and peer-rating criteria. Scale validities against peer ratings in new samples averaged about .30, and reliability (homogeneity) coefficients averaged about .75 (Allport, 1928).

As already noted, 1932 saw the publication of Bernreuter's Personality Inventory, which included scales constructed to predict Laird's *I-E* scale, the Allports' Ascendance-Submission scale, the Thurstones' Neurotic Tendencies scale, and Bernreuter's own Self-Sufficiency scale. While an armchair analysis of the scale labels might have clustered the first two in one group (*I-E*) and the second two in another (Adjustment), Flanagan's (1935) factor analysis of the four scores produced a radically different alignment; the *I-E* measure turned out to be virtually indistinguishable from the Neurotic Tendencies scale (the Adjustment factor), while Self-Sufficiency plus Ascendance-Submission clustered as the *I-E* factor.

While Flanagan (1935) was factoring the four Bernreuter scales, Guilford and Guilford (1934) were factoring a set of typical *I-E* items. The Guilfords culled 75 *I-E* descriptive phrases from the writings of Jung, from Freyd's (1924) list and from the previous *I-E* scales of Laird, Neymann, and Kohlstedt (1929), and Gilliland and Morgan (1931). They then administered 35 representative items from this set to 930 college students and from the item correlations tried to ascertain whether there was a general factor of *I-E* akin to that found with intelligence test scores. After rejecting this hypothesis, the Guilfords rotated four factors and named them Social *I-E*, Emotional Sensitiveness, Impulsiveness, and Interest in Self. A 1936 paper reported another factor analysis of the same items and the same sample; five factors were rotated and named *S* (Shyness, Seclusiveness, or Social *I-E*), *E* (Emotionality), *M* (Masculinity), *R* (Rhathymia, the Guilfords' term for carefree impulsiveness), and *T* (Thinking *I-E*)—the first three of which were incorporated into Guilford's Nebraska Personality Inventory, which was published in 1934. In two 1939 papers, the Guilfords reported factorial investigations of additional items in samples of 1,000 and 600 college students. In one of these studies, the Guilfords rotated nine factors, among them *D* (Depression), *R* (Rhathymia), *LT* (Liking for Thinking), *S* (Shyness), and *T* (Thinking *I-E*); in the second study, they rotated seven factors, including *N* (Nervousness), and *GD* (General Drive). These factors were refined (and some were relabeled) in subsequent factor analyses, and they were included in the Guilfords' Inventory of Factors STDCR, which was published in 1940.

In contrast to the factor-analytic procedures utilized by the Guilfords, Williamson and Darley (1937a, b) used other variants of the internal strategy of scale construction to develop their Minnesota Inventory of Social Attitudes. This inventory was composed of two forms, each of which furnished a single score; the first form consisted of 40 items describing various behaviors and feelings in social situations (Social Behavior), and the second consisted of 40 items asking for preferences for various types of social relationships (Social Preferences). The two scores correlated about .45, and each had reliability (homogeneity) coefficients in the .90s.

The Guilfords' demonstration that *I-E* items clustered on at least three to five factors stimulated Evans and McConnell (1941) into constructing an inventory which would measure three *I-E* facets—labeled Thinking, Social, and Emotional *I-E*—as independently as possible. Their three-scale Minnesota T-S-E Inventory was published in 1942 and revised in 1957. After having formulated the characteristics associated with three distinct types of *I-E*, Evans and McConnell (1941) wrote 216 items reflecting behavior in each category and asked ten judges to classify the items; those 197 items which elicited at least moderate judgmental agreement were supplemented by 43 new ones and administered to about 300 college students. All of the 240 items were correlated with three *a priori* scale scores, and the 151 items which correlated highly with their assigned scale scores and manifested low correlations with the other two scales were included in the final version of the inventory. This variant of the internal strategy of scale construction—an early forerunner of the method later used by Jackson (1967) in developing his Personality Research Form—produced scales with intercorrelations ranging from about −.25 (Thinking vs. Social *I-E*) to around +.25 (Social vs. Emotional *I-E*).

The Minnesota T-S-E Inventory spawned Drake's (1946) MMPI Social Introversion (*Si*) scale, as well as the Thinking Introversion (*TI*) and Social Extroversion (*SE*) scales from the various versions of the Omnibus Personality

Inventory. Drake contrasted the MMPI responses of 50 college females scoring above the 65th percentile on the T-S-E's Social Introversion scale with the responses of 50 college females scoring below the 35th percentile; all students were enrolled in a guidance program at the University of Wisconsin. The 70 most discriminating MMPI items were included in the *Si* scale, which correlated around .70 with the original T-S-E scale in new male and female samples—about the same value as its correlation with the MMPI Psychasthenia (*Pt*) scale. However, *Si* correlated around -.80 with the Sociability (*Sy*) and Social Presence (*Sp*) scales from the CPI, and about .90 with Wiggins' Social Maladjustment (SOC) and Tryon's Introversion (*Cl-I*) item clusters from the MMPI (Goldberg, 1969).

By the advent of World War II, a revival of American interest in Jung's theories, especially his conceptions of introversion-extroversion, led to the development of two rather anomalous *I-E* inventories: Myers and Briggs's Type Indicator and Gray and Wheelwright's Psychological Type Questionnaire. Katherine Briggs and her daughter, Isabel Myers, began the development of their inventory around 1942, and they constructed numerous revisions over the next decade. In an attempt to capture more of the flavor of Jung's theoretical notions than had been reflected in previous *I-E* scales, Myers and Briggs designed their instrument to categorize individuals into dichotomous types along four interlocking dimensions: Extroversion vs. Introversion (*E-I*), Judgment vs. Perception (*J-P*), Thinking vs. Feeling (*T-F*), and Sensation vs. Intuition (*S-N*). The various quasi-theoretical, quasi-psychometric procedures used to construct all of the revisions of this inventory are too numerous and too complex to be detailed here; the interested reader is referred to articles by Stricker and Ross (1963, 1964a, 1964b). The 1962 version of the Type Indicator's *E-I* scale correlated about .65 both with *Si* from the MMPI and *Sy* from the CPI.

During the period of the development of the Type Indicator, another Jungian team was constructing the Psychological Type Questionnaire (PTQ), in an analogous attempt to measure three of the four facets in the Jungian typology (*I* vs. *E, S* vs. *N,* and *T* vs. *F*). In the eleventh revision of the PTQ, reported by Gray and Wheelwright (1946), 75 items were presented with a dichotomous response format (e.g., "In giving praise are you [*a*] reserved, [*b*] outspoken"; "Do you [*a*] spend, [*b*] save"; "Which do you prefer [*a*] keeping house, [*b*] cooking"). Correlations between the pairs of identically labeled scales in the two Jungian inventories ranged from .60 for *S-N* and *T-F* to .80 for *E-I* (Stricker & Ross, 1964b).

During the decade following the initial efforts of the two Jungian teams, another group was attempting to quantify the psychoanalytic notion of personality "levels"; the resulting "interpersonal classification system" of Coffey, Freedman, Leary, and Ossorio was later popularized by Leary (1957). As part of this larger effort, LaForge and Suczek (1955) developed an Interpersonal Check List (ICL), which was proposed both as an inventory for self-assessment and a schedule for rating others. The fourth revision of the ICL included 134 items, 128 of which were keyed to score two major dimensions (Dominance-Submission [*Dom*] and Love-Hate [*Lov*]), and/or alternatively eight "octant" scores, and/or 16 "category" scores. Each of the 16 categories contained eight items, distributed 1:3:3:1 over four levels of "intensity" or social desirability (e.g., [a] "able to give orders"; [b] "forceful"; [c] "bossy"; [d] "dictatorial"), which were used to provide an overall intensity score (Ain). This sophisticated variant of the intuitive and the internal strategies of scale construction yielded a set of octant or category scores whose intercorrelations manifested a pattern approximating that of a circumplex.

About this same time, Eysenck published his Maudsley Personality Inventory (MPI), which included 48 items with a "Yes-?-No" response format; half of the items were keyed to yield an Extroversion (E) score and the other half were keyed for Neuroticism (N). While Eysenck was originally stimulated by Jung's I-E conceptualization, it was Hullian learning theory which provided the framework for most of Eysenck's intensive experimental explorations of the E and N constructs; within Eysenck's own theoretical structure, extroversion has been equated with "cortical inhibition." Eysenck's original E scale was constructed by keying those items which differentiated individuals with high scores from those with low scores on the Rhathymia (carefree impulsiveness) scale from the Guilfords' Inventory of Factors STDCR. Eysenck's resulting E scale correlated about .80 both with the Guilfords' R scale and with the Social I-E scale from the Minnesota T-S-E Inventory. As already noted, the slight negative correlation between the two MPI scales was "corrected" in the corresponding two scales in the Eysenck Personality Inventory, which was published in 1963.

It is important to realize that even those inventories which do not include any single scale explicitly labeled as "introversion-extroversion" often contain scales which purport to measure individual differences within the same general behavioral class, and factor analyses of these scales often produce factors which are then labeled as I-E. For example, Cattell's 16PF included measures of Shyness (H), Surgency (F), and Dominance (E), all of which loaded highly on a second-order factor which Cattell explicitly called I-E. And Gough's CPI included measures of Dominance (Do), Sociability (Sy), and Social Presence (Sp), all of which loaded highly on a CPI factor labeled Person Orientation by Nichols and Schnell (1963). The correlation between the factor scores from these two inventories was around .75 (Goldberg, 1969).

MASCULINITY-FEMININITY

While the search for new measures of I-E can be viewed as a response to an unusually compelling theory of individual differences, the quest for new measures of masculinity-femininity (M-F) has had no such persuasive theoretical rationale. Rather, the proliferation of M-F scales over the years can be viewed as a somewhat indolent reaction to the sheer convenience afforded by nature's provision of two clearly differentiated sexes. The external strategy of scale construction demands some non-test criterion against which to validate items; the fact that males and females abound and that their criterion status is typically obvious appears to have provided all the stimulus needed for the repeated construction of diverse measures of "psychological" M-F.

Moreover, while it could be argued that scales differentiating normal males from females might turn out to be the most potent predictors of homosexuality (Gough, 1952, 1966b), the evidence for this hypothesis is far from compelling. In fact, *M-F* scales have only rarely been validated against any criterion of homosexuality.

On the other hand, interest in the psychological differences between males and females has a long history in both anthropology and sociology as well as in psychology. Important early reviews of the psychological literature can be found in Wooley (1910, 1914), Hollingworth (1916, 1918), Allen (1927, 1930), and Miles (1935). While a number of investigations of *M-F* differences were undertaken before World War I, it was the early psychometric work of Terman which provided the most important impetus for the development of later *M-F* scales. In 1922 Terman began his studies of the responses made by males versus females to diverse stimuli, a project which was to engage his attention for the next fifteen years.

By 1932 Carter had developed the first *M-F* scale from the SVIB item pool, composed of those items whose responses differentiated males from females in a sample of 114 pairs (including 38 pairs of mixed-sex twins) from grades 7 to 12 (see Carter & Strong, 1933). Within the next few years Strong developed an *M-F* scale based upon the responses of a college sample (154 pairs of Stanford students, matched on age, college class, aptitude test scores, and college GPA) and another based upon the responses of an adult sample (335 pairs, 277 of which were husband-wife pairs). Strong later constructed three additional *M-F* scales—each with different scoring weights—based upon the total sample of 603 males and 603 females, and one of these was incorporated into the standard SVIB profile. In contrast to Strong's use of the external strategy for *M-F* scale construction, Guilford labeled one of the scales in his 1934 Nebraska Personality Inventory as Masculinity on the grounds that sex had a loading of .84 on that factor; a revised version of the same scale was published in 1943 as factor *M* in Guilford and Martin's Inventory of Factors GAMIN.

In 1936 Terman and Miles published their landmark volume, *Sex and personality,* which reported the results of a series of investigations of sex differences. Diverse types of stimulus content were administered to various male and female samples, including (*a*) word associations (a stimulus word followed by four alternative responses with instructions to select the alternative most highly related to the stimulus word); (*b*) inkblot associations (an inkblot followed by four alternative responses with similar instructions); (*c*) information items (e.g., "The length of a brick is: 6″, 8″, 10″, 12″"); (*d*) emotional or ethical situations, with directions to select one of four alternative emotional reactions; (*e*) interest items including occupational titles, types of people, avocational activities, books, drawing, reporting, and sightseeing preferences— all presented with a "Like-Dislike-Neutral" response format; and (*f*) *I-E* and other personality, attitude, and opinion items presented with a "Yes-No" response format. From those items whose responses differentiated male from female samples, Terman and Miles (1936) selected 456 items for Form A and 454 other items for Form B of their Attitude-Interest Analysis Test (AIAT), grouped to form seven scales (Word Association, Inkblot Association, Information, Emotional-Ethical responses, Interests, Personality and Opinions, and *I-E* responses). The scales varied in length from 18 items (Inkblot Association) to 119 items (Interests), and all of the items were keyed in the masculine direction. Scale reliabilities ranged from about .25 (*I-E* responses) to about .90 (Personality and Opinions), and intercorrelations among the scales ranged from a low of −.15 (Word Association vs. Emotional-Ethical responses) to a high of almost .50 (Information vs. Personality and Opinions), all in single-sex samples. The reliabilities and scale intercorrelations were higher in mixed-sex samples, and the AIAT total score, as well as the Interest subscore, provided excellent discrimination between male and female samples.

One of Terman's students, E. Lowell Kelly, administered the AIAT to 134 male homosexuals, 46 of whom were classified as taking an active sexual role, 77 as taking a passive role, and 11 whose sex role was less clear. The distribution of AIAT scores for the passive homosexuals lay midway between the distributions for the normal male and female samples, while the distribution of scores for the active homosexuals was similar to, though somewhat more *masculine* than, the distribution for normal males. In general, the AIAT turned out to make rather poor discriminations between the normal male and the total homosexual samples. Consequently, Kelly devised an Invert scale composed of those items whose responses differentiated the passive homosexual sample from normal males; the Invert scale had a rather low correlation with the original AIAT score.

Kelly's research, which was reported in the Terman and Miles (1936) volume, may have led Hathaway and McKinley to attempt to construct a predictor of homosexuality for the MMPI. Their *Mf* scale included MMPI items which differentiated a sample of 13 homosexual males from a normal sample, as well as items with high correlations with the Invert scale, plus some items whose responses differentiated normal male from female samples. While the original *Mf* scale was developed solely as an experimental measure, the scale soon got locked into the standard MMPI profile package, and it has never been revised (Hathaway, 1956).

During the decade following the end of World War II, a number of inventory developers—perhaps stimulated by the *M-F* scales from the MMPI and the SVIB—included new *M-F* scales in their own instruments. In the 1946 revision of his Preference Record—Vocational (PR–V), Kuder included an optional *M-F* scale, which was dropped from the 1956 revision. In 1947 Bell published the Personal Preference Inventory (PPI), a supplement to his older Adjustment Inventory; the PPI included 90 items with a "Yes-No" response format, 30 scored on each of three scales (*M-F,* Criticalness, and Perceived Economic Status). By 1952 Gough had developed his Femininity (*Fe*) scale, composed of those 58 items (out of over 500 initially investigated) whose responses differentiated most highly between male and female samples. The scores from a subset of 32 *Fe* items administered to 38 homosexual and 38 heterosexual prison inmates significantly differentiated between the two samples (Gough, 1952). The longer *Fe* scale was included in Gough's California Psychological Inventory, which was published in 1956.

In the past 15 years, *M-F* has become the single most popular construct for inclusion in new personality inventories. *M-F* scales have been constructed for Jenkins' How Well Do You Know Your Interests?, Welsh's Figure Preference Test, Holland's Vocational Preference Inventory, Heist and Yonge's Omnibus Personality Inventory, Fricke's Opinion, Attitude, and Interest Survey, Comrey's Personality Scales, and Giddan, King, and Lovell's Academic Behavior Inventory. As already noted, there is some significant item overlap between these various inventories, with the result that a number of these different *M-F* scales share a substantial proportion of common items.

At least ten investigators have correlated the *M-F* scales from various inventories, including: (*a*) Heston (1948), who correlated *M-F* scales from the SVIB, MMPI, and Kuder's PR—V; (*b*) de Cillis and Orbison (1950), who used the AIAT and the MMPI; (*c*) Shepler (1951), who included the AIAT, SVIB, MMPI, and a projective measure; (*d*) Gough (1957), who correlated CPI scales with those from the MMPI and SVIB; (*e*) Stanek (1959), who returned to the AIAT and MMPI; (*f*) Barrows and Zuckerman (1960), who included the SVIB, MMPI, and the Guilford-Zimmerman Temperament Survey (GZTS); (*g*) Nichols (1962), who correlated *M-F* scales from the MMPI, CPI, and Guilford-Martin GAMIN; (*h*) Engel (1966), who used the AIAT, SVIB, MMPI, CPI, and a projective measure; (*i*) Klopfer (1966), who included only the SVIB and MMPI; and (*j*) Himelstein and Stoup (1967), who used the SVIB, MMPI, and GZTS. A summary of the major results from these studies is presented in Table 2.

As Table 2 indicates, the correlations among *M-F* scales are moderated by a number of different variables. First of all, *M-F* scale intercorrelations are markedly higher in mixed-sex samples than in single-sex samples. Moreover, as Gough (1957) and Strong (1943) have demonstrated, these correlations are also significantly affected by the age of the subjects (e.g., high school vs. college samples). In addition, as Terman and Miles (1936) originally noted, the correlations are higher among *M-F* scales composed of items with similar content than between scales of differing content, and they are clearly highest when the scales share a set of common items (e.g., the CPI and the MMPI). Furthermore, *M-F* scale correlations with biological sex are moderated by the strategy used in scale construction (Nichols, 1962; Goldberg, 1970); scales composed of items which are both "obvious" sex discriminators (e.g., "I like to wear pretty, frilly panties") and which empirically differentiate between the two sexes provide more clear separation between male and female samples than do *M-F* scales composed of either more subtle discriminating items or of "obvious" items not subjected to any empirical test. These results, which are in accord with those from studies by Goldberg and Slovic (1967) and Norman (1963) on the relationship between face and predictive validity, suggest the substitution for past *M-F* scales of the following single item: "I am a male: True or False."

PERSONAL VALUES AND MANIFEST NEEDS

In contrast to the spirit of ruthless empiricism which has characterized the quest for *M-F* measures, quite a few personality inventories have been focused on two theories of individual differences—the first proposed by the philosopher

Table 2
Intercorrelations among Measures of Masculinity-Femininity

I. Correlations Computed within Single-Sex Samples: Male Samples
above the Diagonal and Female Samples below

	MMPI	SVIB	CPI	AIAT	GZTS
MMPI	--	$.33^h$ $.53^i$ $.50^c$	$.43^d$ $.39^i$	$.30^b$ $.66^c$	$.31^h$ $.28^i$
SVIB	$.48^k$ $.55^c$	--	$.41^d$	$.56^c$	$.34^h$ $.20^i$
CPI	$.52^i$		--		
AIAT	$.17^g$ $.53^c$ $.36^b$	$.67^c$		--	

II. Correlations Computed within Mixed-Sex Samples

	MMPI	SVIB	CPI	PR−V
SVIB	$.83^j$ $.69^a$	--		
CPI	$.71^j$	$.59^j$	--	
PR−V	$.68^a$	$.73^a$		--
AIAT	$.65^j$	$.68^j$	$.60^j$	
SEX	$.74^a$	$.63^a$	$.65^e$ $.78^f$	$.61^a$

[a] Heston (1948): N = 79 mixed sex.
[b] de Cillis and Orbison (1950): N = 129 males; N = 50 females.
[c] Shepler (1951): N = 57 males; N = 67 females.
[d] Gough (1957): N = 152 males.
[e] Gough (1957): N = 7,628 mixed sex (high school).
[f] Gough (1957): N = 1,590 mixed sex (college).
[g] Stanek (1959): N = 132 females.
[h] Barrows and Zuckerman (1960): N = 2,296 males.
[i] Nichols (1962): N = 100 males; N = 100 females.
[j] Engel (1966): N = 100 mixed sex.
[k] Klopfer (1966): N = 98 females.
[l] Himelstein and Stoup (1967): N = 60 males.

Edouard Spranger and the second by the psychologist Henry Murray. However, it was probably the popularity of the initial inventories developed under each of these two frameworks rather than the theories themselves which stimulated so many psychometricians to return to these same traits, since there have been few attempts to justify a focus on these particular individual differences beyond those propounded by the original theorists.

The English translation of Spranger's (1928) book, *Types of men,* which posited six major value orientations (represented by the theoretic, economic, aesthetic, social, political, and religious man) led Vernon and Allport (1931) to construct their seminal Study of Values. From Spranger's writings, Vernon and Allport selected a set of statements presumably descriptive of each of the six value types, and they wrote items which contrasted two or more of these values. The 45 items whose alternatives had nearly equal popularity (endorsement frequency) in college samples and whose responses related most highly to an *a priori* keying of the six scales were included in the original version of the *Study*. While the ipsative character of the *Study's* scoring procedures constrained each subject's mean score across all six scales to the same value, the reliability (homogeneity) values for the six scales differed greatly; they ranged from around .50 (Social and Political) to about .85 (Aesthetic and Religious). A revised version of the *Study*, published in 1951 by Allport, Vernon, and Lindzey, also contained 45 items, but the scale reliability values had been raised to the .75 to .90 range. A third edition by the same authors, published in 1960, was virtually identical to the 1951 model.

In contrast to the intuitive-internal strategy of scale construction used by Allport, Vernon, and Lindzey, the Interest-Values Inventory (IVI), which was published by Maller and Glaser in 1939, was constructed by the external strategy (see Glaser & Maller, 1940). Fifty college students in each of four broad curricular fields (mathematics and science, arts and music, social work and nursing, and business and advertising) were used as criterion groups to develop scales purportedly measuring the relative dominance of four of Spranger's six basic values (theoretic, aesthetic, social, and economic). The IVI contained 116 items of diverse types, including 10 sets of 4 stimulus words with instructions to select the most preferred word, 10 association items with instructions to select the most highly related of 4 alternative responses, 48 answers to 12 basic questions each with a Like-Neutral-Dislike response format, and 48 trait-descriptive adjectives with instructions to indicate whether each trait had "Strong-Average-Weak" self-applicability. While the Study of Values has joined the SVIB as one of the two oldest inventories in popular use today, the IVI had a relatively short history and is now out of print.

Spranger's theory, which spawned these two inventories, had only limited progeny in comparison with the theoretical views of Henry Murray, whose offspring already include Edwards' Personal Preference Schedule, Stern's Activities Index, Jackson's Personality Research Form, Heilbrun's need scales for the Adjective Check List, and Hase's need scales for the CPI; moreover, there are enough questions concerning the paternity of Guilford, Christensen, and Bond's DF Opinion Survey to again implicate that same prolific theory. For a framework described as no more than a "rough, preliminary plan [Murray et al., 1938, p. 143]," this is quite a record!

Henry Murray and his colleagues at the Harvard Psychological Clinic were highly influenced by psychoanalytic theory, and the anatomy of personality structure described in their classic 1938 volume, *Explorations in personality*, represented a unique amalgamation of the thinking of Freud and his followers with that of Allport and other academic psychologists. The major individual

Table 3
The Personality Variables Posited by Murray et al. (1938)

Major Manifest Needs (20)	Trait Descriptive Terms	Original Items	EPPS	ACL	CPI (Hase)	AI	PRF
Abasement	Submissive, acquiescent, passive	10[a]	X	X		X	X
Achievement	Ambitious, competitive, aspiring	10[a]	X	X	X	X	X
Affiliation	Friendly, sociable, good-natured	20[a]	X	X	X	X	X
Aggression	Argumentative, critical, severe	15[a]	X	X		X	X
Autonomy	Independent, defiant, stubborn	10[a]	X	X	X	X	X
Counteraction	Resolute, determined, adventurous	20				X	
Deference	Deferent, respectful, compliant	10[a]	X	X	X	X	
Defendance	Self-defensive, self-vindictive	10			X		X
Dominance	Assertive, forceful, decisive	10	X	X	X	X	X
Exhibition	Dramatic, conspicuous	20	X	X	X	X	X
Harmavoidance	Fearful, timid, cautious, careful	10				X	X
Infavoidance	Sensitive, shy, nervous	20			X		
Nurturance	Sympathetic, gentle, protective	20[a]	X	X	X	X	X
Order	Organized, clean, neat, precise		X	X	X	X	X
Play	Playful, easygoing, jolly	10			X	X	X
Rejection	Exclusive, aloof, discriminating	20[a]					
Sentience	Sensuous, sensitive, aesthetic	20				X	X
Sex	Erotic, sensual, seductive	10	X	X		X	
Succorance	Dependent, helpless, forlorn	20	X	X			X
Understanding	Intellectual, curious, logical	20			X	X	X

Other Manifest Needs (7)

Acquisition	Acquisitive, grasping						
Blamavoidance	Inhibited, fearful, conventional	10					
Cognizance	Curious, inquiring						
Construction	Organizing, creative						
Exposition	Demonstrating, explaining						
Recognition	Boastful, prestige-oriented						X
Retention	Stingy, hoarding, frugal						

Composite Manifest Needs (2)
Inviolacy (Infavoidance + Defendance + Counteraction)
Superiority (Achievement + Recognition)

General Traits (12)

Anxiety (Harmavoidance + Infavoidance + Blamavoidance)							
Creativity							
Conjunctivity/Disjunctivity (Coordination of action and thought)		20				X	
Emotionality vs. Placidity		20				X	
Endurance		10	X	X			X
Exocathection/Endocathection (Outwards vs. inwards orientation)		20				X	
Extraception/Intraception (Imaginative vs. practical)		80	X	X		X	
Impulsion/Deliberation (Impulse expression vs. delay)		20				X	X
Intensity		10					
Projectivity/Objectivity (Projection vs. detachment)						X	
Radical/Conservative							
Sameness/Change		20	X	X		X	X

Other Internal Factors (4)

Ego Ideal (Latent achievement and level of aspiration)		10				X	
Narcism (Self-love)		20				X	
Superego Integration (Acceptance of one's conscience)		10[a]					
Superego Conflict (Guilt and remorse)		10					

Latent Needs (8)
Repressed Abasement (Passivity and Masochism)
Repressed Aggression (Hate and Sadism)
Repressed Cognizance (Voyeurism)
Repressed Dominance (Omnipotence)
Repressed Exhibitionism (Exhibitionism)
Repressed Heterosexuality
Repressed Homosexuality
Repressed Succorance (Helplessness)

Miscellaneous Variables (5)
Expansion/Contraction
Superiority/Inferiority
Optimism/Pessimism
Social Solidarity
Neuroticism

[a]Fifteen additional attitude items included in the Sentiment Questionnaire.

differences posited by the Murray team are displayed in Table 3, along with the number of items from the total pool of 545 personality items and 135 attitude (sentiment) items developed by the Harvard group to measure each of these dimensions. These original items, reported in Murray et al. (1938), were modified over the years for use in the various inventories based upon this conceptual scheme. In fact, later inventory developers tended to focus rather exclusively on precisely those constructs included in the original Harvard questionnaires, namely those from the set of 20 "major manifest needs" and 12 "general traits." Only rarely have any new scales been developed to measure those constructs for which the Harvard group provided no initial item pool: "other manifest needs," "composite manifest needs," "latent needs," "other internal factors," and "miscellaneous variables." Moreover, some constructs have been included in all later inventories (achievement, affiliation, autonomy, dominance, exhibition, nurturance, and order), while others have rarely been copied (rejection, intensity, counteraction, blamavoidance, ego ideal, narcism, superego integration, superego conflict, conjunctivity, emotionality, exocathection, and projectivity).

The first major inventory developed to compete with the original Harvard questionnaire was Edwards' Personal Preference Schedule (EPPS), which was introduced in 1953, fifteen years after the publication of *Explorations in personality*. The EPPS included 225 items keyed for 15 scales (see Table 3), each item a forced-choice between two statements which had been roughly matched on social desirability, one from each of two scales from the original Harvard questionnaire. Reliability (homogeneity) coefficients ranged from about .60 (Deference, Exhibition) to around .85 (Heterosexuality, Abasement, Aggression). Since the EPPS scales were ipsatively scored, scale intercorrelations were quite low; the highest correlation, that between Affiliation and Nurturance, was around .45 (Edwards, 1954). By 1958, five years after the publication of the EPPS and the initial development of Gough's 300-item Adjective Check List (ACL), Heilbrun had constructed a set of ACL scales purporting to tap the same 15 traits included in the EPPS. Heilbrun's 15 need scales, plus 2 he constructed as measures of Defensiveness and Counseling Readiness, were added to 7 ACL scales previously developed by Gough and published in Gough and Heilbrun's (1965) manual for the ACL. Correlations among the ACL need scales ranged into the .70s (Order vs. Endurance) in a sample of 800 subjects (Gough & Heilbrun, 1965). About the same time as the ACL manual was published, Hase constructed 11 need scales from the CPI item pool for a larger project investigating the comparative validity of various strategies of scale construction (Hase & Goldberg, 1967). Eight of these recent CPI scales purportedly measure the same traits as those included among the 15 EPPS and ACL scales (see Table 3).

Probably the most ambitious effort to capture the flavor of the entire Murray system can be found in the development of Stern's Activities Index (AI), which was originally constructed during the 1950s, first published in 1958, and revised in 1963 and 1969. Stern incorporated the complete transactional viewpoint of the Murray team into his own research efforts, and he has consistently sought to construct parallel measures of environmental "presses" along with measures of personal "needs" (see Stern, 1970). Stern's various Environmental Indexes included scales directed at the measurement of the "climates" in high schools, colleges, evening colleges, the Peace Corps, and other organizations. The parallel AI, which included 300 items with a like-dislike response format now provides 49 scores, including 30 need scores (see Table 3), 12 factor scores, 4 second-order factor scores, plus validity and academic aptitude indices. Of the eight AI "needs" labeled differently than any included in the Murray list (Practicalness-Impracticalness, Adaptability-Defensiveness, Ego Achievement, Reflectiveness, Energy-Passivity, Fantasied Achievement, Humanities and Social Science, and Science), the first four doubtless correspond to Extroception-Introception, Defendance, Ego Ideal, and Exocathection-Endocathection, while the fifth may be an analogue of Succorance.

Another recent and unusually sophisticated attempt to measure some of these same constructs can be found in Jackson's (1967) Personality Research Form (PRF). Use of the two PRF forms permits the measurement of 19 constructs (plus Cognitive Structure, a measure of thinking rigidity and intolerance of ambiguity)—a few more scales than the 15 from the EPPS and ACL, but less than the 30 provided in the AI. The PRF scales included those items from a much larger set which satisfied both intuitive and internal criteria for scale membership and which manifested relatively low correlations with other scale scores and with a putative measure of social desirability response set. While PRF scale reliability coefficients were generally quite high, some of the scale intercorrelations ranged up to almost .65 (Jackson, 1967).

While the EPPS, ACL, AI, and PRF scales were directly modeled after the Murray system, one other inventory can be viewed as an indirect product of the original Harvard questionnaire. Over the years, Guilford and his associates factor-analyzed a large set of older personality and interest statements and later devised new items as more direct measures of the factors which emerged from the earlier analyses. Guilford, Christensen, and Bond's DF Opinion Survey (DFOS), which was published in 1954, included 300 new and old items, 30 for each of 10 scales (Need for Attention, Liking for Thinking, Adventure, Self-Reliance, Aesthetic Appreciation, Cultural Conformity, Need for Freedom, Realistic Thinking, Need for Precision, and Need for Diversion). The internal strategy of scale construction used to fashion this inventory produced scales with reliability (homogeneity) values ranging from about .65 to .95. Since correlations between the DFOS scales and those from the EPPS, ACL, AI, and PRF have not been reported, it is difficult to assess the extent to which the concepts of the Guilford group have diverged from those originally devised by the Harvard team.

OTHER TRAITS

The constructs classified in the first six columns of Table 1 certainly do not exhaust the domain of individual differences targeted by personality scales and inventories, and only space limitations prevent the inclusion of other salient assessment foci.[3] For example, attempts to measure aspects of liberal vs. conservative ideology date back to the 1920s (see Shaw & Wright, 1967), culminating in such significant measurement milestones as Lentz's (1930) *C-R* (Conservatism-Radicalism) Opinionnaire, developed in the late 1920s and published in 1935; Rundquist and Sletto's (1936) Economic Conservatism Scale; Levinson's (1949) *E* (Ethnocentrism) Scale and the California *F* (Fascism) Scale, both given wide currency via the classic work on the authoritarian personality (Adorno, Frenkel-Brunswik, Levinson, & Sanford, 1950); and Rokeach's (1960) Dogmatism Scale. More recently, a flurry of research activity has centered on Rotter's (1954) distinction between internal vs. external locus of control (internals perceiving events as manipulable by oneself, externals perceiving events as determined by fate, chance, or the manipulation of others). The instrumentation for measuring this construct was developed in doctoral dissertations at Ohio State by Phares in 1955 and by James in 1957; for reviews of the research stimulated by these measures, see Lefcourt (1966) and Rotter (1966). For details of an inventory developed to assess other aspects of Rotter's (1954) social learning theory, see Liverant (1958).

During the 1940s, Thurstone redirected his attention from attitude scaling to personality structure. After factoring items from Guilford's various batteries, Thurstone (1951) concluded that seven factors were worth developing further, and he tried out a host of items from previous scales and inventories as measures of each factor. His resulting Temperament Schedule, which was published in 1949 and revised in 1953, included seven scales labeled Active, Vigorous, Impulsive, Dominant, Stable, Sociable, and Reflective. A new inventory, Comrey's Personality Scales, has been constructed via the same general strategy. Over the years, Comrey and his collaborators have been clustering sets of new and old personality items to form "factored homogeneous item dimensions," which they have used in a series of factor-analytic investigations (e.g., Comrey, 1961, 1962, 1964; Comrey & Jamison, 1966). Eight of the resulting factor scales (Trust, Orderliness, Conformity, Activity, Neuroticism, Empathy, *I-E,* and *M-F*) were included in the new Comrey inventory, which was published in 1970.

While both Thurstone and Comrey relied upon traditional verbal items, two other inventory developers have avoided these standard types of questions completely. Welsh devised a figure preference test for his doctoral dissertation at Minnesota in 1949; 400 line-drawings were used as items with a "like-dislike" response format. A number of scales were constructed by the external strategy with such criterion groups as males vs. females, psychiatric patients vs. normal subjects, children vs. adults, and artists vs. non-artists— the latter used to construct the popular Barron-Welsh Art Scale. These scales were supplemented by others focused upon preferences for specific kinds of designs (e.g., freehand vs. ruled lines) and published in 1959 as Welsh's Figure

---

[3]A few of these traits, including Persistence (Wang, 1932) and Affective Potency (Watson & Fisher, 1941), seem to have been cast aside in the press to develop measures of other, more popular, constructs.

Preference Test (WFPT). In contrast, Holland used a set of 300 occupational titles (with the same like-dislike response format) to construct his Vocational Preference Inventory (VPI), which was first published in 1953. Holland used the intuitive strategy to select and group items, though he later eliminated some scales and refined others by means of internal consistency analyses (see Holland, 1958). Nine original content scales (Intellectuality, Social Responsibility, Conformity, Verbal Activity, Emotionality, Control, Aggressiveness, Status, and *M-F*) were revised and relabeled in the 1965 revision of the VPI to furnish new scales called Realistic, Intellectual, Social, Conventional, Enterprising, Artistic, Self-control, Status, and Masculinity.

While responses to the items on the WFPT and the VPI are not easily construed as being more or less desirable, most other personality scales and inventories have contained verbal items whose responses were rather obviously related to their overall favorability. Over the years, inventory developers have been concerned about potential individual differences in impression management, and as early as 1931 Vernon and Allport attempted to control for such a possibility by using a forced-choice item format in their Study of Values. More recently, Allen Edwards (1957) redirected psychometric attention to this problem, which he relabeled "social desirability response set," and his EPPS employed a forced-choice format—two statements of approximately equal desirability administered with instructions to select that member of the pair which is most self-descriptive. Soon, a number of other inventory constructors adopted the same general tactic. Gordon used an item format popular in the vocational interest domain—item triads (roughly equated on desirability) with instructions to rank order the three items—to construct his Survey of Interpersonal Values (SIV), which was published in 1960. Thirty item triads were included in the SIV, keyed for each of six scales (Support, Conformity, Recognition, Independence, Benevolence, and Leadership). In a similar vein, Thorndike arranged items of approximately equal desirability in sets of ten, administered with instructions to select the three most characteristic and the three least characteristic items within each set. Thorndike's resulting inventory, the Dimensions of Temperament (DOT), was published in 1963. The DOT contained ten scales labeled Sociable, Ascendant, Cheerful, Placid, Accepting, Tough-minded, Reflective, Impulsive, Active, and Responsible. Both the SIV and the DOT—like the Study of Values and the EPPS—provided ipsative scores.

Not all recent inventories, however, have employed forced-choice and/or ipsative procedures, and a number of these have provided far more scales than those included in most earlier inventories. Grygier attempted to measure 33 psychoanalytic constructs (e.g., orality, hoarding, narcissism) by modifying Krout and Tabin's (1954) Personal Preference Scale, one of the first psychoanalytically-oriented personality inventories. Grygier's 325-item Dynamic Personality Inventory was published in 1961. Even more scores were provided in Cattell and Horn's Motivation Analysis Test (MAT), which was first published in 1959 and revised in 1969. While both inventories share a quasi-dynamic flavor, the MAT was not directly modeled after psychoanalytic theory; instead, the constructs were derived from a series of factor-analytic studies of motivation items. The MAT provided four types of scores (Integrated, Unintegrated, Total, and Conflict) for each of five "ergs" (Mating, Assertiveness, Fear, Narcism, and Pugnacity) and for each of five "sentiments" (Superego, Self, Career, Home, and Sweetheart), plus five total scores (Integration, Interest, Conflict, Autism, and Information). For further details of this unusual inventory, see Cattell, Radcliffe, and Sweney (1963).

The proliferation of scales within one inventory may have reached its apex, however, with the publication of Edwards' (1966) Personality Inventory (EPI), which included 53 scales. Edwards developed an initial pool of over five thousand personality descriptive statements, gleaned from informal conversations with individuals who were asked to describe others they knew. Elimination of duplicated statements left a pool of 2,824 items which were grouped intuitively, administered to a college sample, and then subjected to a series of factor analyses (Edwards, 1966). About 1,200 of the items were finally used to measure the 53 EPI scales, while another 300 items provided parallel measures of 14 scales. While the EPI is administered with instructions to "predict how people who know you best would mark each statement if they were asked to describe you," Edwards (1969) has shown that there is essentially no difference between EPI scores based upon these novel instructions and scores based upon traditional self-descriptions. On the other hand, most of the EPI items—like those included in Jackson's (1967) PRF—are less obviously related to overall response desirability than were many of the items from previous inventories.

SOME CONCLUDING REMARKS

If the future is anything like the past, new personality scales and inventories are at least as likely to be focused upon constructs arising out of applied societal pressures as upon any theories of personality. In fact, the most potent source of variance in the determination of the constructs for past scales and inventories has been sheer historical accident. For better or for worse, psychologists have tended to measure those constructs already identified by their predecessors, and in addition they have tended to borrow heavily from past item pools. Items devised around the turn of the century may have worked their way via Woodworth's Personal Data Sheet, to Thurstone and Thurstone's Personality Schedule, hence to Bernreuter's Personality Inventory, and later to the Minnesota Multiphasic Personality Inventory, where they were borrowed for the California Personality Inventory and then injected into the Omnibus Personality Inventory—only to serve as a source of items for the new Academic Behavior Inventory. As a result of the widespread practice of item borrowing, there is substantial item overlap between a number of present inventories (one result of which is that convergent validity coefficients computed between scales from two inventories—generally lamented as being too low—may, in fact, be spuriously high).

Moreover, among those inventory developers who have avoided past constructs or past item pools, another trend is equally clear. Each original trait has been gradually bifurcated into smaller and smaller constructs. As an example, Introversion-Extroversion was later divided into three components, one of which was social extroversion; the latter, in turn, has been fractionated into at least five components, one of which was dominance; and recently, dominance has shattered into 30 to 40 "facets" (Butt & Fiske, 1968). Analogously, anxiety (Taylor, 1953) has been dichotomized into test anxiety and general anxiety, and the latter, which was construed as five independent factors in the 16PF, has more recently exploded into myriads of "anxiety-by-situation interactions" (Endler, Hunt, & Rosenstein, 1962). Adjustment was once just that—a single global construct; over the years, the construct has been shredded so finely that Jackson and Messick's new Differential Personality Inventory purports to measure some 28 varieties of maladjustment.

In some sense, scientists invariably proceed in the dark, and only their past activities are illuminated. However, historians have long held that the reflected glow from a carefully lighted past may help to outline at least some parts of the near future. Hopefully, this brief history of personality scales and inventories may provide enough light to keep future psychometric investigators from stumbling over the same obstacles that seem to have blocked their progress in the past.

Bibliography

Acheson, G. H. (Ed.) Second symposium on catecholamines. Reprinted from *Pharmacolog. Rev.*, 1966, *18*, No. 1. Published for the American Society for Pharmacology and Experimental Therapeutics. Baltimore, Md.: Williams and Wilkins Co., 1966.

Acker, M., & McReynolds, P. The obscure figures test: An instrument for measuring "cognitive innovation." *Percept. mot. Skills*, 1965, *21*, 815-821.

Acker, M., & McReynolds, P. The "need for novelty": A comparison of six instruments. *Psychol. Rec.*, 1967, *17*, 177-182.

Adams, C. R. A new measure of personality. *J. appl. Psychol.*, 1941, *25*, 141-151.

Adorno, T. W., Frenkel-Brunswik, E., Levinson, D. J., & Sanford, R. N. *The authoritarian personality*. New York: Harper, 1950.

Aghajanian, G. K., & Bloom, F. E. Localization of tritiated serotonin in rat brain by electronmicroscopic autoradiography. *J. pharmacol. exp. Ther.*, 1967, *156*, 23-30.

Aghajanian, G. K., & Freedman, D. X. Biochemical and morphological aspects of LSD pharmacology. In D. Efron (Ed.), *Psychopharmacology*. Washington, D.C.: U.S. Government Printing Office, 1968. Pp. 1185-1193.

Aghajanian, G. K., Rosecrans, J. A., & Sheard, M. H. Serotonin: release in the forebrain by stimulation of midbrain raphe. *Sci.*, 1967, *156*, 402-403.

Aghajanian, G. K., & Schwartz, A. Environmental influences on brain serotonin metabolism. *Comm. Behav. Biol.*, 1969, *4*, 97-103.

Albrecht, P. A., Glaser, E. M., & Marks, J. Validation of a multiple assessment procedure for managerial personnel. *J. appl. Psychol.*, 1964, *48*, 351-360.

Allen, C. Studies in sex difference. *Psychol. Bull.*, 1927, *24*, 294-304.

Allen, C. Recent studies in sex differences. *Psychol. Bull.*, 1930, *27*, 394-407.

Allison, J., Blatt, S., & Zimet, C. *The interpretation of psychological tests*. New York: Harper & Row, 1968.

Allport, F. H. *Theories of perception and the concept of structure*. New York: John Wiley, 1955.

Allport, G. W. A test for ascendance-submission. *J. abnorm. soc. Psychol.*, 1928, *23*, 118-136.

Allport, G. W. *Personality: A psychological interpretation*. New York: Henry Holt, 1937.

Allport, G. W. *Becoming: Basic considerations for a psychology of personality*. New Haven: Yale University Press, 1955.

Allport, G. W. *Pattern and growth in personality*. New York: Holt, Rinehart & Winston, 1961.

Allport, G. W., Vernon, P. E., & Lindzey, G. *Study of values*. (3rd ed.) Boston: Houghton-Mifflin, 1960.

Alousi, A., & Weiner, N. The regulation of norepinephrine synthesis in sympathetic nerves: Effect of nerve stimulation, cocaine, and catecholamine-releasing agents. *Proc. nat. acad. Sci.*, 1966, *56*, 1491-1496.

Alpert, R., & Haber, R. N. Anxiety in academic achievement situations. *J. abnorm. soc. Psychol.*, 1960, *61*, 207-215.

Altmann, S. A., & Wagner, S. S. Estimating rates of behavior from Hansen frequencies. Unpublished manuscript, Yerkes Regional Primate Research Center, Atlanta, Georgia, 1970.

American Psychological Association. Technical recommendations for psychological tests and diagnostic techniques. *Psychol. Bull.*, 1954, *51*, 1-38.

Ammons, R. B., and Ammons, C. H. *Full-range picture vocabulary test.* Missoula, Montana: Psychological Test Specialists, 1954.
Anastasi, A. *Psychological testing.* (3rd ed.) New York: Macmillan Co., 1968.
Anastasi, A. (Ed.) *Testing problems in perspective.* Washington, D.C.: American Council on Education, 1966.
Anton, A. H., & Sayre, D. F. A study of the factors affecting the aluminum oxide-trihydroxyindole procedure for the analysis of catecholamines. *J. pharmacol. exp. Ther.,* 1962, *138,* 360-375.
Apfelbaum, E. Études expérimentales de conflit: Les jeux expérimentaux. *L'Annee Psychologique,* 1966, *66,* 599-621. English translation available as order No. 68-14980 from National Translations Center, John Crerar Library, 35 West 33rd Street, Chicago, Illinois, 60616.
Apfelbaum, E. *Interdependence, renforcement social, et réactivité: Analyse de la dynamique des interactions dans le cadre des 'jeux expérimentaux.'* Doctoral dissertation, Sorbonne, Paris, 1969. (English translation to be published by Academic Press.)
Appleyard, D. Why buildings are known: A predictive tool for architects and planners. *Environ. Behav.,* 1969, *1,* 131-156.
Arnold, M. B. *Story sequence analysis.* New York: Columbia University Press, 1962.
Arthur, A. Z. A decision-making approach to psychological assessment in the clinic. *J. consult. Psychol.,* 1966, *30,* 435-438.
Arthur, A. Z. Diagnostic testing and the new alternatives. *Psychol. Bull.,* 1969, *72,* 183-192.
Atkinson, J. W. (Ed.) *Motives in fantasy, action, and society.* Princeton, N.J.: D. Van Nostrand, 1958.
Atkinson, J. W. *An introduction to motivation.* Princeton, N. J.: D. Van Nostrand, 1964.
Atkinson, J. W., Bastian, J. R., Earl, R. W., & Litwin, G. H. The achievement motive goal setting and probability preferences. *J. abnorm. soc. Psychol.,* 1960, *60,* 27-36.
Atkinson, J. W., & Feather, N. T. (Eds.) *A theory of achievement motivation.* New York: John Wiley, 1966.
Atkinson, J. W., & Litwin, G. H. Achievement motive and test anxiety conceived as motive to approach success and motive to avoid failure. *J. abnorm. soc. Psychol.,* 1960, *60,* 52-63.
Attneave, F., & Arnoult, M. D. Methodological considerations in the quantitative study of shape and pattern perception. *Psychol. Bull.,* 1956, *53,* 452-471.
Ax, A. F. The physiological differentiation between fear and anger in humans. *Psychosom. Med.,* 1953, *15,* 433-442.
Axelrod, J. Metabolism of epinephrine and other sympathomimetic amines. *Physiol. Rev.,* 1959, *39,* 751-776.
Axelrod, J., Mueller, R. A., Henry, J. P., & Stephens, P. M. Changes in enzymes involved in the biosynthesis and metabolism of noradrenaline and adrenaline after psychosocial stimulation. *Nature,* 1970, *225,* 1059-1060.
Ayllon, T., & Azrin, N. *The token economy: A motivational system for therapy and rehabilitation.* New York: Appleton-Century-Crofts, 1968.
Azrin, N. H., & Powell, J. Behavioral engineering: The reduction of smoking by a conditioning apparatus and procedure. *J. appl. behav. Anal.,* 1968, *1,* 193-200.
Bandura, A. *Principles of behavior modification.* New York: Holt, Rinehart & Winston, 1969.
Bandura, A., & Huston, A. C. Identification as a process of incidental learning. *J. abnorm. soc. Psychol.,* 1961, *63,* 311-318.
Bandura, A., Ross, D., & Ross, S. A. Transmission of aggression through imitation of aggressive models. *J. abnorm. soc. Psychol.,* 1961, *63,* 575-582.
Bandura, A., Ross, D., & Ross, S. A. Imitation of film-mediated aggression models. *J. abnorm. soc. Psychol.,* 1963, *66,* 3-11.
Bandura, A., & Walters, R. H. Aggression. In H. W. Stephenson (Ed.), *Child psychology: The sixty-second yearbook of the National Society for the Study of Education.* Chicago: University of Chicago Press, 1963. Pp. 364-415.
Barchas, J. D., Ciaranello, R. D., & Levine, S. Instrumentation for study of neuroregulatory agents and behavior. *Amer. Psychologist,* 1969, *24,* 271-275.
Barchas, J. D., Ciaranello, R. D., & Steinman, A. M. Epinephrine formation and metabolism in mammalian brain. *Biol. Psychiat.,* 1969, *1,* 31-48.
Barchas, J. D., DaCosta, F., & Spector, S. Acute pharmacology of melatonin. *Nature,* 1967, *214,* 919-920.
Barchas, J. D., Erdelyi, E., & Angwin, P. Simultaneous determination of 5-hydroxytryptamine and catecholamines in tissues using a weak cation exchange resin (submitted for publication).

Barchas, J. D., & Freedman, D. X. Brain amines: Response to physiologic stress. *Biochem. Pharmacol.,* 1963, *12,* 1232-1235.

Barclay, A. M. The effect of hostility on physiological and fantasy responses. *J. of Pers.,* 1969, *37,* 651-667.

Barclay, A. M. The effect of female aggressiveness on aggressive and sexual fantasies. *J. proj. Tech. pers. Assmt.,* 1970, *34,* 19-26.

Barker, R. G. On the nature of the environment. *J. soc. Issues,* 1963, *19,* 17-38.

Barker, R. G. Explorations in ecological psychology. *Amer. Psychologist,* 1965, *20,* 1-14.

Barker, R. G. *Ecological psychology: Concepts and methods for studying the environment of human behavior.* Stanford, Calif.: Stanford University Press, 1968.

Barker, R. G., & Wright, H. F. *Midwest and its children.* Evanston, Illinois: Row, Peterson, 1955.

Barlow, D. H., Lietenberg, H., & Agras, W. S. Experimental control of sexual deviation through manipulation of the noxious scene in covert sensitization. *J. abnorm. Psychol.,* 1969, *74,* 596-601.

Barnett, H. G. *Innovation: The basis of cultural change.* New York: McGraw-Hill, 1953.

Barnette, W. L. (Ed.) *Readings in psychological tests and measurements.* (2nd ed.) Homewood, Ill.: Dorsey, 1968.

Barron, F., & Welsh, G. S. Artistic perception as a factor in personality style: Its measurement by a figure-preference test. *J. Psychol.,* 1952, *33,* 199-203.

Barrows, G. A., & Zuckerman, M. Construct validity of three masculinity-femininity tests. *J. consult. Psychol.,* 1960, *24,* 441-445.

Basowitz, H., Korchin, S. J., Oken, D., Goldstein, M. S., & Gussack, H. Anxiety and performance changes with a minimal dose of epinephrine. *A. M. A. Arch. neurol. Psychiat.,* 1956, *76,* 98-105.

Bass, B. M. Development of a structured, disguised personality inventory. *J. appl. Psychol.,* 1956, *40,* 393-397.

Bass, B. M. Validity studies of a proverbs personality test. *J. appl. Psychol.,* 1957, *41,* 158-160.

Battle, C. C., Imber, S. D., Hoehn-Saric, R., Stone, A. R., Nash, C., & Frank, J. D. Target complaints as criteria of improvement. *Amer. J. Psychother.,* 1966, *20,* 184-192.

Beach, H. R., & Graham, M. Notes on use of sentence completion in assessing aggression in normal school children. *Psychol. Rep.,* 1967, *20* (1), 9-10.

Beck, A. T., Ward, C. H., Mendelson, M., & Mock, J. An inventory for measuring depression. *Arch. gen. Psychiat.,* 1961, *4,* 461-471.

Becker, H. S. Notes on the concept of commitment. *Amer. J. Sociol.,* 1960, *64,* 32-40.

Bein, H. J. Zur pharmakologie des reserpin, eines neuen alkaloids aus *Rauwolfia serpentina* benth. *Experientia,* 1953, *9,* 107-110.

Bell, H. M. *The theory and practice of personal counseling with special reference to the adjustment inventory.* Stanford, Calif.: Stanford University Press, 1935.

Bell, H. M. *The adjustment inventory: Revised student form, research edition.* Palo Alto. Calif.: Consulting Psychologists Press, 1962.

Bellak, L. *The Thematic Apperception Test and Children's Apperception Test in clinical use.* New York: Grune & Statton, 1954.

Bendig, A. W. Factor analytic scales of overt and covert hostility. *J. consult. Psychol.,* 1962, *26,* 200.

Benton, A. A., Gelber, E. R., Kelley, H. H., & Liebling, B. A. Reactions to various degrees of deceit in a mixed-motive relationship. *J. pers. soc. Psychol.,* 1969, *12,* 170-180.

Bentz, V. J. The Sears' experience in the investigation, description, and prediction of executive behavior. In F. R. Wickert & D. E. McFarland (Eds.), *Measuring executive effectiveness.* New York: Appleton-Century-Crofts, 1967. Pp. 147-205.

Bentz, V. J. *In-Basket factors, combined years: 1968 and 1969.* Report, Chicago: Sears Roebuck & Co., August, 1969. (Mimeo.)

Berg, I. A. Response bias and personality: The deviation hypothesis. *J. Psychol.,* 1955, *40,* 61-72.

Berkowitz, L. Impulse, aggression, and the gun. *Psychol. Today,* 1968, *2,* 18-22.

Berkowitz, L., & Daniels, L. R. Affecting the salience of the social responsibility norm. *J. abnorm. soc. Psychol.,* 1964, *68,* 275-281.

Berlew, D. E. *Early challenge, performance, and success.* Presented at 36th annual meeting of the Eastern Psychological Association. Atlantic City, 1965.

Berlew, D. E., & Hall, D. T. The socialization of managers: Effects of expectations on performance. *Admin. Sci. Quart.,* 1966, *11,* 207-224.

Berlyne, D. E. Novelty and curiosity as determinants of exploratory behavior. *Brit. J. Psychol.,* 1950, *41,* 68-80.

Berlyne, D. E. An experimental study of curiosity. *Brit. J. Psychol.*, 1954, *45*, 256-265.
Berlyne, D. E. The influence of complexity and novelty in visual figures on orienting responses. *J. exp. Psychol.*, 1958, *55*, 289-296. (a)
Berlyne, D. E. The influence of the albedo and complexity of stimuli on visual fixation in the human infant. *Brit. J. Psychol.*, 1958, *49*, 315-318. (b)
Berlyne, D. E. *Conflict, arousal, and curiosity.* New York: McGraw-Hill, 1960.
Berlyne, D. E. Complexity and incongruity as determinants of exploratory choice and evaluative behavior. *Canad. J. Psychol.*, 1963, *17*, 274-290.
Berlyne, D. E. Curiosity and education. In J. Krumboltz (Ed.), *Learning and the educational process.* Chicago: Rand McNally, 1965.
Berlyne, D. E. Arousal and reinforcement. In D. Levine (Ed.), *Nebraska symposium on motivation.* Lincoln, Nebr.: Univ. Nebr. Press, 1967.
Berlyne, D. E., & Lewis, J. L. Effects of heightened arousal on human exploratory behavior. *Canad. J. Psychol.*, 1963, *17*, 398-411.
Bernberg, R. E. An analysis of the responses of a male prison population to the Edwards Personal Preference Schedule. *J. gen. Psychol.*, 1960, *62*, 319-324.
Bernreuter, R. G. The measurement of self-sufficiency. *J. abnorm. soc. Psychol.*, 1933, *28*, 291-300. (a)
Bernreuter, R. G. The theory and construction of the personality inventory. *J. soc. Psychol.*, 1933, *4*, 387-405. (b)
Bernstein, L. The examiner as an inhibiting factor in clinical testing. *J. consult. Psychol.*, 1956, *20*, 287-290.
Beswick, D. G. *Scoring manual for curiosity in TAT stories.* Unpublished manuscript, 1961.
Beswick, D. G. Theory and measurement of human curiosity. Ph.D. dissertation, Harvard University, 1964.
Beswick, D. G. Studies in curiosity. Paper presented to Australian Psychological Society, 1968.
Beswick, D. G. Cognitive process theory of individual differences in curiosity. Presented at Symposium on Intrinsic Motivation in Education, Ontario Institute for Studies in Education, Toronto, 1970.
Biemiller, A. *On the definition and measurement of curiosity.* B.A. thesis, Harvard University, 1962.
Bijou, S. W. Promoting optimum learning in children. In P. Wolff & R. MacKeith (Eds.), *Planning for better learning.* London: Spastics International Medical Publications, 1969.
Bijou, S. W., Birnbrauer, J. S., Kidder, J. D., & Tague, C. Programmed instruction as an approach to teaching of reading, writing, and arithmetic to retarded children. *Psychol. Rec.*, 1966, *16*, 505-522.
Bijou, S. W., Peterson, R. F., & Ault, M. H. A method to integrate descriptive and experimental field studies at the level of data and empirical concepts. *J. appl. behav. Anal.*, 1968, *1*, 175-191.
Bijou, S. W., Peterson, R. F., Harris, F. R., Allen, K. E., & Johnston, M. S. Methodology for experimental studies of young children in natural settings. *Psychol. Rec.*, 1969, *19*, 177-210.
Birnbrauer, J. S., Wolf, M. N., Kidder, J. D., & Tague, C. Classroom behavior of retarded pupils with token reinforcement. *J. exp. Child Psychol.*, 1965, *2*, 219-235.
Bixenstine, V. E., Chambers, N., & Wilson, K. V. Effect of asymmetry in payoff on behavior in a two-person non-zero sum game. *J. confl. Resol.*, 1964, *8*, 151-159.
Bixenstine, V. E., & O'Reilly, E. F. Money vs. electric shock as payoff in a Prisoner's Dilemma game. *Psychol. Rec.*, 1966, *16*, 251-264.
Bixenstine, V. E., Potash, H. M., & Wilson, K. V. Effects of level of cooperative choice by the other player on choices in a Prisoner's Dilemma game: Part I. *J. abnorm. soc. Psychol.*, 1963, *66*, 308-313.
Bjerstedt, A. Review of the Rosenzweig P-F study. In O. K. Buros (Ed.), *The sixth mental measurements yearbook.* Highland Park, N.J.: The Gryphon Press, 1965.
Blackburn, R. Emotionality, extraversion, and aggression in paranoid and nonparanoid schizophrenic offenders. *Brit. J. Psychiat.*, 1968, *115*, 1301-1302. (a)
Blackburn, R. Personality in relation to extreme aggression in psychiatric offenders. *Brit. J. Psychiat.*, 1968, *114*, 821-828. (b)
Blackburn, R. Dimensions of hostility and aggression in abnormal offenders. Department of Psychology, Broadmore Hospital, Crowthorne, Berkshire, England, 1969. (Mimeo.) (a)
Blackburn, R. Personality patterns in homicide: A typological analysis of abnormal offenders. Paper presented at the Fifth International Meeting of Forensic Sciences, Toronto, Canada, June 1969. (b)

Bliss, E. L., Ailion, J., & Zwanziger, J. Metabolism of norepinephrine, serotonin, and dopamine in rat brain with stress. *J. Pharmacol. exp. Ther.*, 1968, *164*, 122-134.

Bliss, E. L., & Zwanziger, J. Brain amines and emotional stress. *J. psychiat. Res.*, 1966, *4*, 189-198.

Block, J. *The Q-Sort Method in personality assessment and psychiatric research.* Springfield, Ill.: Charles C. Thomas, 1961.

Block, J. Group discussion: Measuring personality change. In H. H. Strupp & L. Luborsky (Eds.), *Research in psychotherapy.* Vol. 2. Washington, D.C.: American Psychological Association, 1962. Pp. 164-177.

Block, J. *The challenge of response sets.* New York: Appleton-Century-Crofts, 1965.

Block, J. Some reasons for the apparent inconsistency of personality. *Psychol. Bull.*, 1968, *70*, 210-212.

Block, J., & Thomas, H. Is satisfaction with self a measure of adjustment? *J. abnorm. soc. Psychol.*, 1955, *51*, 254-259.

Bloom, F. E., & Giarman, N. J. Physiologic and pharmacologic considerations of biogenic amines in the nervous system. *Annu. rev. Pharmacol.*, 1968, *8*, 229-258. (a)

Bloom, F. E., & Giarman, N. J. Current status of neurotransmitters. In C. K. Cain, J. Biel, B. Bloom, L. Cheney, R. Heinzelman, I. Tabachnick, & E. Smissman (Eds.), *Annual reports in medicinal chemistry, 1967.* New York and London: Academic Press, 1968. Pp. 264-274. (b)

Bloom, P. M., & Brady, J. P. An ipsative validation of the multiple affect adjective checklist. *J. clin. Psychol.*, 1968, *24* (1), 45-46.

Bock, R. D., & Jones, L. V. *The measurement and prediction of judgment and choice.* San Francisco: Holden-Day, 1968.

Borah, L. A., Jr. The effects of threat in bargaining: Critical and experimental analysis. *J. abnorm. soc. Psychol.*, 1963, *66*, 37-44.

Bordin, E. S. Simplication as a strategy for research in psychotherapy. *J. consult. Psychol.*, 1965, *29*, 493-503.

Bourne, P. G., Coli, W. M., & Datel, W. E. Affect levels of ten Special Forces soldiers under threat of attack. *Psychol. Rep.*, 1968, *22* (2), 363-366.

Boutourline, S. The concept of environmental management. *Dot Zero*, 1967, *4*, 1-7.

Braun, J. R., & La Faro, D. A further study of the fakability of the Personal Orientation Inventory. *J. clin. Psychol.*, 1969, *25*, 296-299.

Brawley, E. R., Harris, F. R., Allen, J. E., Fleming, R. S., & Peterson, R. F. Behavior modification of an autistic child. *Behav. Sci.*, 1969, *14*, 87-97.

Bray, D. W. The management progress study. *Amer. Psychologist*, 1964, *19*, 419-420. (a)

Bray, D. W. The assessment center method of appraising management potential. In J. W. Blood (Ed.), *The personnel job in a changing world.* New York: American Management Association, 1964. (b)

Bray, D. W. Three global constructs in the study of the growth of managers. Paper presented at the 74th annual meeting of the American Psychological Association, New York, N.Y., 1966.

Bray, D. W., & Grant, D. L. The assessment center in the measurement of potential for business management. *Psychol. Monogr.*, 1966, *80*, No. 17 (Whole No. 625).

Breger, L. Conformity as a function of the ability to express hostility. *J. Pers.*, 1963, *31*, 247-257.

Breger, L. Psychological testing: Treatment and research implications. *J. consult. Psychol.*, 1968, *32*, 176-181.

Breggin, P. R. The psychophysiology of anxiety. *J. nerv. ment. Dis.*, 1964, *139*, 558-568.

Brehm, J. W., & Cohen, A. R. *Explorations in cognitive dissonance.* New York: John Wiley, 1962.

Brender, W. J., & Kramer, E. A comparative need analysis of immediately-recalled dreams and TAT responses. *J. proj. Tech. pers. Assess.*, 1967, *31* (1), 74-77.

Bricklin, B., Piotrowski, Z. A., & Wagner, E. E. *The hand test.* Springfield, Ill.: Charles C. Thomas, 1962.

Brodie, B. B., & Costa, E. Some current views on brain monoamines. *Psychopharmac. serv. cent. Bull.*, 1962, *2*, 1-24.

Brodie, B. B., Costa, E., Dlabac, A., Neff, N. H., & Smookler, H. H. Application of steady state kinetics to the estimation of synthesis rate and turnover time of tissue catecholamines. *J. pharmacol. exp. Ther.*, 1966, *154*, 493-498.

Brodie, H. K. H., Murphy, D. L., Goodwin, F. K., & Bunney, W. E., Jr. Catecholamines and mania: The effect of alpha-methyl-paratyrosine on manic behavior and catecholamine metabolism. *Clin. pharmacol. Ther.*, in press.

Brodsky, S., & Brodsky, A. M. Hand test indicators of antisocial behavior. *J. proj. Tech. pers. Assmt.*, 1967, *31* (5), 36-39.
Broverman, D. M., Jordan, E. J., & Phillips, L. Achievement motivation in fantasy and behavior. *J. abnorm. soc. Psychol.*, 1960, *60*, 374-378.
Brown, F. G. *Principles of educational and psychological testing.* Hinsdale, Ill.: Dryden, 1970.
Bunney, W. E., Jr., Brodie, H. K. H., Murphy, D. L., & Goodwin, F. K. Studies of alpha-methyl-paratyrosine, L-DOPA, and tryptophane in depression and mania. *Amer. J. Psychiat.*, in press.
Buros, O. K. *Personality tests and reviews.* Highland Park, N.J.: Gryphon Press, 1970.
Burton, I., & Kates, R. W. The perception of natural hazards in resource management. *Natural Resources J.*, 1964, *3*, 412-441.
Burton, I., Kates, R. W., & White, G. F. *The human ecology of extreme geophysical events.* Toronto: University of Toronto, Department of Geography, Working Paper No. 1, 1968.
Buss, A. H. *The psychology of aggression.* New York: John Wiley, 1961.
Buss, A. H., & Durkee, A. An inventory for assessing different kinds of hostility. *J. consult. Psychol.*, 1957, *21*, 343-348.
Buss, A. H., Durkee, A., & Baer, M. The measurement of hostility in clinical situations. *J. abnorm. soc. Psychol.*, 1956, *52*, 84-86.
Buss, A. H., Fisher, H., & Simmons, A. J. Aggression and hostility in psychiatric patients. *J. consult. Psychol.*, 1962, *26*, 84-89.
Bussey, S., Marks, R., & Escover, L. The development of cooperation: Child to adult. Tech. rep., Nonr 3897(07), Dartmouth College, 1968.
Butcher, H. J. *Human intelligence: Its nature and assessment.* London: Methuen, 1968.
Butcher, J. N. Manifest aggression: MMPI correlates in normal boys. *J. consult. Psychol.*, 1965, *29*, 446-454.
Butcher, J. N. (Ed.) *MMPI: Research developments and clinical applications.* New York: McGraw-Hill, 1969.
Butler, J. M. Self-ideal congruence in psychotherapy. *Psychother.*, 1968, *5*, 13-17.
Butler, J. M., & Haigh, G. V. Changes in the relation between self-concepts and ideal concepts consequent upon client-centered counseling. In C. R. Rogers and R. F. Dymond (Eds.), *Psychotherapy and personality change.* Chicago: University of Chicago Press, 1954. Pp. 55-75.
Butt, D. S., & Fiske, D. W. Comparison of strategies in developing scales for dominance. *Psychol. Bull.*, 1968, *70*, 505-519.
Byham, W. C. *The uses of assessment centers.* Report, New York: J. C. Penney Co., 1969. (Mimeo.)
Byrne, D. Anxiety and the experimental arousal of affiliation need. *J. abnorm. soc. Psychol.*, 1961, *63*, 660-662.
Byrne, D., McDonald, R. D., & Mikawa, J. Approach and avoidance affiliation motives. *J. Pers.*, 1963, *31*, 1-20.
Cady, V. M. The estimation of juvenile incorrigibility. *Juv. Delinq. Monogr.*, 1923, *2*.
Caine, T. M. The expression of hostility and guilt in melancholic and paranoid women. *J. consult. Psychol.*, 1960, *24*, 18-22.
Campbell, D. P. Achievements of counseled and non-counseled students, twenty-five years after counseling. *J. counsel. Psychol.*, 1965, *12*, 287-293.
Campbell, D. P. The Strong Vocational Interest Blank: 1927-1967. In P. McReynolds (Ed.), *Advances in psychological assessment.* Vol. 1. Palo Alto, Calif.: Science and Behavior Books, 1968. Pp. 105-130.
Campbell, D. P., Borgen, F. H., Eastes, S. H., Johansson, C. B., & Peterson, C. B. A set of basic interest scales for the Strong Vocational Interest Blank for men. *J. appl. psychol. Monogr.*, 1968, *52* (6, Whole Part 2).
Campbell, D. T., & Fiske, D. W. Convergent and discriminant validation by the multitrait-multimethod matrix. *Psychol. Bull.*, 1959, *56*, 81-105.
Campbell, D. T., & Stanley, J. *Experimental and quasi-experimental designs for research.* Chicago: Rand-McNally, 1963.
Campbell, J. P., Dunnette, M. D., Lawler, E. E., & Weick, K. E. *Managerial behavior, performance, and effectiveness.* New York: McGraw-Hill, 1970.
Canter, D. *The measurement of meaning in architecture.* Unpublished report. Strathclyde, Scotland: University of Strathclyde, 1968.
Canter, D. An intergroup comparison of connotative dimensions in architecture. *Environ. Behav.*, 1969, *1*, 37-48.

Cantor, G. N. Responses of infants and children to complex and novel stimulation. In L. P. Lipsitt & C. C. Spiker (Eds.), *Advances in child development and behavior.* New York: Academic Press, 1963.

Cantril, H., & Hunt, W. A. Emotional effects produced by the injection of adrenalin. *Amer. J. Psychol.,* 1932, *44,* 300-307.

Carlsson, A., Hillarp, N. Å., & Waldeck, B. Analysis of the $Mg^{++}-ATP$ dependent storage mechanism in the amine granules of the adrenal medulla. *Acta. Physiol. Scand.,* 1963, *59,* suppl. 215, 1-38.

Carlsson, A., Lundborg, P., Stitzel, R., & Waldeck, B. Uptake, storage, and release of H^3-α-methylnorepinephrine. *J. pharmacol. exp. Ther.,* 1967, *158,* 175-182.

Carlsson, A., Rosengren, E., Bertler, A., & Nilsson, J. Effect of reserpine on the metabolism of catecholamines. In S. Garattini & V. Ghetti (Eds.), *Psychotropic drugs.* Amsterdam: Elsevier Publishing Co., 1957. Pp. 363-372.

Carpenter, W. Serotonin in affective disorders. *Ann. intern. Med.,* 1970, *73,* 613-619.

Carr, J. E., & Whittenbaugh, J. Sources of disagreement in the perception of psychotherapy outcomes. *J. clin. Psychol.,* 1969, *25,* 16-21.

Carr, S., & Schissler, D. The city as a trip: Perceptual selection and memory in the view from the road. *Environ. Behav.,* 1969, *1,* 7-36.

Carrigan, W. C., & Julian, J. W. Sex and birth-order differences in conformity as a function of need affilation arousal. *J. pers. soc. Psychol.,* 1966, *3,* 479-482.

Carter, H. D., & Strong, E. K., Jr. Sex differences in occupational interests of high-school students. *Personnel J.,* 1933, *12,* 166-175.

Cartwright, D. S., Kirtner, W. L., & Fiske, D. W. Method factors in changes associated with psychotherapy. *J. abnorm. soc. Psychol.,* 1963, *66,* 164-175.

Cartwright, D. S., Robertson, R. J., Fiske, D. W., & Kirtner, W. L. Length of therapy in relation to outcome and change in personal integration. *J. consult. Psychol.,* 1961, *25,* 84-99.

Cartwright, R. D., & Lerner, B. Empathy, need to change, and improvement with psychotherapy. *J. consult. Psychol.,* 1963, *27,* 138-144.

Castaneda, A., McCandless, B. R., & Palermo, D. The children's form of the Manifest Anxiety Scale. *Child Develpm.,* 1956, *27,* 317-26.

Cattell, J. McK. Mental tests and measurements. *Mind,* 1890, *15,* 373-381.

Cattell, R. B., & Eber, H. W. *Handbook for the sixteen personality factors questionnaire.* Champaign, Ill.: Institute for Personality and Ability Testing (IPAT), 1957 (1964).

Cattell, R. B., Eber, H. W., & Tatsuoka, M. M. *Handbook for the sixteen personality factors questionnaire (16 P.F.) in clinical, educational, and research psychology.* Champaign, Ill.: Institute for Personality and Ability Testing, 1970.

Cattell, R. B., Radcliffe, J. A., & Sweney, A. B. The nature and measurement of components of motivation. *Gen. psychol. Monogr.,* 1963, *68,* 49-211.

Cattell, R. B., Rickles, K., Weise, C., Gray, B., & Yee, R. The effects of psychotherapy upon measured anxiety and regression. *Amer. J. Psychother.,* 1966, *20,* 261-269.

Cattell, R. B., & Scheier, I. H. *Handbook for the IPAT anxiety scale questionnaire.* Champaign, Ill.: Institute for Personality and Ability Testing, 1963.

Cautela, J. R., & Kostenbaum, R. A reinforcement survey schedule for use in therapy, training, and research. *Psychol. Rep.,* 1967, *20,* 1115-1130.

Chapin, F. S. *Contemporary American institutions.* New York: Harper & Brothers, 1935.

Chapin, F. S., Jr. Activity systems and urban structure: A working schema. *J. Amer. Inst. Planners,* 1968, *34,* 11-18.

Chapin, F. S., Jr., & Hightower, H. C. *Household activity systems—a pilot investigation.* Chapel Hill, N. Carolina: Center for Urban and Regional Studies, 1966.

Chapin, F. S., Jr., & Logan, T. H. Patterns of time and space use. In H. S. Perloff (Ed.), *The quality of the urban environment: Essays on "new resources" in an urban age.* Baltimore: Johns Hopkins Press, 1969. Pp. 305-332.

Charen, S. The awareness of hostile feelings in patients by their nurses. *J. consult. Psychol.,* 1955, *19,* 290.

Chase, T. N., Breese, G. R., & Kopin, I. J. Serotonin release from brain slices by electrical stimulation: Regional differences and effect of LSD. *Sci.,* 1967, *157,* 1461-1463.

Chase, T. N., Katz, R. I., & Kopin, I. J. Release of [^{3}H]serotonin from brain slices. *J. Neurochem.,* 1969, *16,* 607-615.

Christie, R. C., Gergen, K. J., & Marlowe, D. The penny-dollar caper. In R. C. Christie & F. Geis (Eds.), *Studies in Machiavellianism.* New York: Academic Press, in press.

Christie, R. C., & Merton, R. K. Procedures for the sociological study of the values climate of medical schools. *J. med. Educ.,* 1958, *33,* 125-153.

Ciaranello, R. D., Barchas, J. D., & Vernikos-Danellis, J. Compensatory hypertrophy and phenylethanolamine N-methyl transferase (PNMT) activity in the rat adrenal. *Life Sci.*, 1969, *8* (Part 1), 401-407.

Ciaranello, R. D., Barchas, R., Kessler, S., & Barchas, J. D. Catecholamines: Strain differences in biosynthetic enzyme activity in mice. (Submitted for publication.)

Clark, W. G., & Guidice, J. D. *Principles of psychopharmacology.* New York: Academic Press, 1970.

Clarke, W. V. The construction of an industrial selection personality test. *J. Psychol.,* 1956, *41,* 379-384.

Cline, V. B. Interpersonal perception. In B. A. Maher (Ed.), *Progress in experimental personality research:* Vol. 1. New York: Academic Press, 1964. Pp. 221-284.

Clyde, D. J. *Manual for the Clyde mood scale.* Biometric Laboratory, University of Miami, Coral Gables, 1963.

Cogswell, J. F. Computers in student appraisal and education planning. In J. W. Loughary (Ed.), *Man-machine systems in education.* New York: Harper & Row, 1966. Pp. 157-167.

Cogswell, J. F., & Estavan, D. P. *Explorations in computer-assistant counseling.* TM-2582. Santa Monica, Calif.: Systems Development Corporation, 1965.

Cohen, J., Gurel, L., & Stumpf, J. C. Dimensions of psychiatric symptom ratings determined at thirteen time points from hospital admission. *J. consult. Psychol.,* 1966, *30,* 39-44.

Cohn, F. S. Fantasy aggression in children as studied by the Doll Play technique. *Child Developm.,* 1962, *33,* 235-250.

Colby, K. W., Watt, J. B., & Gilbert, J. P. A computer method of psychotherapy: Preliminary communication. *J. nerv. ment. Dis.,* 1966, *142,* 148-152.

Cole, D., Jacobs, S., Zubok, B., Fagot, B., & Hunter, I. The relationship of achievement imagery scores to academic performance. *J. abnorm. soc. Psychol.,* 1962, *65,* 208-211.

Cole, J. K., & Magnussen, M. G. Where the action is. *J. consult. Psychol.,* 1966, *30,* 539-543.

Coleman, J. C. Stimulus factors in the relation between fantasy and behavior. *J. proj. Tech. pers. Assmt.,* 1967, *31* (1), 68-73.

Collins, J. B. Some verbal dimensions of architectural space perception. *Architectural psychol. Newsletter,* 1968, *2,* 4-5.

Collins, J. B. *Perceptual dimensions of architectural space validated against behavioral criteria.* Doctoral dissertation, University of Utah, 1969.

Committee on Nomenclature. *Diagnostic and statistical manual of mental disorders.* Washington, D.C.: American Psychiatric Association, 1968.

Comrey, A. L. Factored homogeneous item dimensions in personality research. *Educ. Psychol. Measmt.,* 1961, *21,* 417-431.

Comrey, A. L. A study of thirty-five personality dimensions. *Educ. Psychol. Measmt.,* 1962, *22,* 543-552.

Comrey, A. L. Personality factors compulsion, dependence, hostility, and neuroticism. *Educ. Psychol. Measmt.,* 1964, *24,* 75-84.

Comrey, A. L., & Jamison, K. Verification of six personality factors. *Educ. Psychol. Measmt.,* 1966, *26,* 945-953.

Condry, J. C., Jr. The effects of situational power and personality upon the decision to negotiate or not in a 2-person bargaining situation. *Dissert. Abstr.,* 1967, *27,* 2612.

Conklin, E. S. The definition of introversion, extroversion, and allied concepts. *J. abnorm. soc. Psychol.,* 1923, *17,* 367-382.

Conklin, E. S. The determination of normal extravert-introvert interest differences. *J. gen. Psychol.,* 1927, *34,* 28-37.

Conner, R., Stolk, J. Barchas, J., & Levine, S. Parachlorophenylalanine and habituation to repetitive auditory startle stimuli in rats. *Physiol. Behav.,* 1970, *5,* 1215-1219.

Cook, W. W., & Medley, D. M. Proposed hostility and pharasaic virtue scales for the MMPI. *J. appl. Psychol.,* 1954, *38,* 414-418.

Cooke, G. The efficacy of two desensitization procedures: An analogue study. *Behav. res. Ther.,* 1966, *4,* 17-24.

Cooke, G. Evaluation of the efficacy of the components of reciprocal inhibition psychotherapy. *J. abnorm. Psychol.,* 1968, *73,* 464-467.

Cooper, J., Bloom, F., & Roth, R. *The biochemical basis of neuropharmacology.* New York: Oxford University Press, 1970.

Corrodi, H., & Hanson, L. C. F. Central effects of an inhibitor of tyrosine hydroxylation. *Psychopharmacologia* (Berl.), 1966, *10,* 116-125.

Cottle, W. C. A factorial study of the Multiphasic, Strong, Kuder, and Bell inventories using a population of adult males. *Psychometrika*, 1950, *15*, 25-47.
Cotzias, G. C., Papavasiliou, P., & Gellene, R. Modification of Parkinsonism: Chronic treatment with L-DOPA. *New Eng. J. Med.*, 1969, *280*, 337-345.
Coughlin, R. E., & Goldstein, K. A. *The extent of agreement among observers on environmental attractiveness.* Philadelphia, Penn.: RSRI Discussion Paper Series, No. 37, Regional Science Research Institute, 1970.
Coupland, R. E. On the morphology and adrenaline-noradrenaline content of chromaffin tissue. *J. Endocrinol.*, 1953, *9*, 194-203.
Cowan, G., & Goldberg, F. J. Need achievement as a function of the race and sex of figure in selected TAT cards. *J. Pers. soc. Psychol.*, 1967, *5*, 245-249.
Craik, K. H. Environmental display Adjective Check List (ED-ACL) (A-K), Berkeley, Calif.: Institute of Personality Assessment and Research, University of California, 1966. (a)
Craik, K. H. *The prospects for an environmental psychology.* IPAR Research Bulletin. Berkeley, Calif.: Institute of Personality Assessment and Research, University of California, 1966. (b)
Craik, K. H. The comprehension of the everyday physical environment. *J. Amer. Inst. Planners*, 1968, *34*, 29-37.
Craik, K. H. *Forest landscape perception.* Final report to U. S. Forest Service, Berkeley, Calif.: Institute of Personality Assessment and Research, University of California, 1969. (a)
Craik, K. H. Human responsiveness to landscape: An environmental psychological perspective. In G. J. Coates & K. H. Moffett (Eds.), *Response to environment.* Student publication of School of Design. Volume 18. Raleigh, N. Carolina: North Carolina State University, 1969. Pp. 168-193. (b)
Craik, K. H. Transportation and the person. *High Speed Ground Transportation J.*, 1969, *3*, 86-91. (c)
Craik, K. H. *A system of landscape dimensions: Appraisal of its objectivity and illustration of its scientific application.* (Report to Resources for the Future, Inc.) Berkeley, California: Institute of Personality Assessment and Research, University of California, 1970. (a)
Craik, K. H. Environmental psychology. In K. H. Craik et al., *New directions in psychology.* Vol. 4. New York: Holt, Rinehart & Winston, 1970. Pp. 1-122. (b)
Craik, K. H. The environmental dispositions of environmental decision-makers. In S. Z. Klausner (Ed.), Society and its physical environment. *Ann. Amer. acad. polit. soc. Sci.* 1970, *389*, 87-94. (c)
Crenshaw, D. A., Bohn, Suzanne, Hoffman, Marlene, Mathews, J. M., & Offenback, S. G. The use of projective methods in research: 1947-1965. *J. proj. Tech. pers. Assmt.*, 1968, *32*, 3-9.
Cronbach, L. J. *Essentials of psychological testing.* (2nd ed.) New York: Harper, 1960.
Cronbach, L. J. *Essentials of psychological testing.* (3rd ed.) New York: Harper, 1970.
Cronbach, L. J., & Gleser, G. C. *Psychological tests and personnel decisions.* (2nd ed.) Urbana, Ill.: University of Illinois Press, 1965.
Crowne, D. P. Family orientation, level of aspiration, and interpersonal bargaining. *J. pers. soc. Psychol.*, 1966, *3*, 641-645.
Crowne, D. P., & Marlowe, D. A new scale of social desirability independent of psychopathology. *J. consult. Psychol.*, 1960, *24*, 349-354.
Culbert, S. A., Clark, J. V., & Bobele, H. K. Measures of change toward self-actualization in two sensitivity training groups. *J. counsel. Psychol.*, 1968, *15*, 53-57.
Curzon, G., & Bridges, P. K. Tryptophan metabolism in depression. *J. neurol. neurosurg. Psychiat.*, 1970, *33*, 698-704.
Curzon, G., Godwin-Austen, R. B., Tomlinson, E. B., & Kantamaneni, B. D. The cerebrospinal fluid homovanillic acid concentration in patients with Parkinsonism treated with L-DOPA. *J. neurol. neurosurg. Psychiat.*, 1970, *33*, 1-6.
Dahlstrom, W. G., & Welsh, G. S. (Eds.) *An MMPI handbook: A guide to use in clinical practice and research.* Minneapolis, Minn.: University of Minnesota Press, 1960.
Dana, R. H. Proposal for objective scoring of the TAT. *Percept. mot. Skills*, 1959, *9*, 27-43.
Dana, R. H. Thematic techniques and clinical practice. *J. proj. Tech. pers. Assmt.*, 1968, *32* (3), 204-214.
Daniels, F. V. Communication, control, and incentive in interpersonal interaction. University Microfilms, Order No. 66-4742, Ann Arbor, Mich., 1966.
Darley, J. G., & Hagenah, T. *Vocational interest measurement.* Minneapolis, Minn.: University of Minnesota Press, 1955.

Darley, J. G., & McNamara, W. J. Factor analysis in the establishment of new personality tests. *J. educ. Psychol.*, 1940, *31*, 321-334.

Darlington, R. B., and Stauffer, G. F. Use of evaluation of discrete test information in decision making. *J. appl. Psychol.*, 1966, *50*, 125-129.

Davies, B. M., & Carroll, B. J. Hypothalamic dysfunction in severe depression. *American Psychiatric Association scientific proceedings*, 1970. P. 232.

Davison, G. C. Systematic desensitization as a counter-conditioning process. *J. abnorm. Psychol.*, 1968, *73*, 91-99.

Day, H. I. Exploratory behavior as a function of individual differences and level of arousal. Ph.D. dissertation, University of Toronto, 1965.

Day, H. I. Evaluations of subjective complexity, pleasingness, and interestingness for a series of random polygons varying in complexity. *Percept. Psychophys.*, 1967, *2*, 281-286.

Day, H. I. The importance of symmetry and complexity in the evaluation of complexity, interest, and pleasingness. *Psychon. Sci.*, 1968, *10*, 339-340.

Day, H. I. A progress report on the development of a test of curiosity. Paper read at National Seminar on Adult Education Research, Toronto, Feb. 10, 1969.

Day, H. I. The measurement of specific curiosity. Presented at Symposium on Intrinsic Motivation in Education, Ontario Institute for Studies in Education, Toronto, 1970.

DeCharms, R. *Personal causation.* New York: Academic Press, 1968.

De Cillis, O. E., & Orbison, W. D. A comparison of the Terman-Miles M-F Test and the Mf Scale of the MMPI. *J. appl. Psychol.*, 1950, *34*, 338-342.

Degan, J. W. Dimensions of functional psychosis. *Psychol. Monogr.*, 1952, No. 6.

Dember, W. N., & Earl, R. W. Analysis of exploratory, manipulation, and curiosity behaviors. *Psychol. Rev.*, 1957, *64*, 91-96.

Dement, W. Psychophysiology of sleep and dreams. In S. Arieti (Ed.), *American Handbook of psychiatry.* Vol. 3. New York: Basic Books, 1966. Pp. 290-332.

Dement, W., Zarcone, V., Ferguson, J., Cohen, H., Pivak, T., & Barchas, J. Some parallel findings in schizophrenic patients and serotonin-depleted cats. In D. V. Siva Sankar, *Schizophrenia—current concepts and research.* Hicksville, N.Y.: PJD Publications Ltd., 1969. Pp. 775-811.

DeRidder, J. C. *The personality of the urban African in South Africa: A Thematic Apperception Test study.* New York: Humanities, 1961.

Deutsch, M. Trust, trustworthiness, and the F scale. *J. abnorm. soc. Psychol.*, 1960, *61*, 138-140.

Deutsch, M., & Krauss, R. M. The effect of threat upon interpersonal bargaining. *J. abnorm. soc. Psychol.*, 1960, *61*, 181-189.

Dicken, C. F., & Black, J. D. Predictive validity of psychometric evaluations of supervisors. *J. appl. Psychol.*, 1965, *49*, 34-37.

Dinwiddie, F. W. An application of the principle of response generalization to the prediction of aggressive responses. Ph.D. dissertation, Catholic University of America, 1954.

Dishman, R. W., Birds, V. G., & Dunlop, E. Validation of a new health-sickness scale: The M.I., Multiphasic Index. Unpublished manuscript. Personal communication, 1969.

Dixon, W. J. *BMD: Biomedical computer programs.* Los Angeles: University of California Press, 1968.

Dolbear, F. J., Lave, L. B., Bowman, G., Lieberman, A., Prescott, E., Rueter, F., & Sherman, R. Collusion in the Prisoner's Dilemma: Number of strategies. *J. confl. Resol.*, 1969, *13*, 252-261.

Dollard, J., Doob, L. W., Miller, N. E., Mowrer, O. H., & Sears, R. R. *Frustration and aggression.* New Haven, Conn.: Yale University Press, 1939. Abridgement reprinted in E. I. Megargee & J. E. Hokanson (Eds.), *Dynamics of aggression.* New York: Harper & Row, 1970.

Dollard, J., & Mowrer, O. H. A method of measuring tension in written documents. *J. abnorm. soc. Psychol.*, 1947, *42*, 3-32.

Dominic, J. A., & Moore, K. E. Acute effects of α-methyltyrosine on brain catecholamine levels and on spontaneous and amphetamine-stimulated motor activity in mice. *Arch. int. Pharmacondyn.*, 1969, *178*, 166-176.

Domino, E. F., & Olds, M. E. Cholinergic inhibition of self-stimulation behavior. *J. pharmacol. exp. Ther.*, 1968, *164*, 202-211.

Domino, G. A validation of Howard's test of change-seeking behavior. *Educ. psychol. Measmt.*, 1965, *25*, 1073-1078.

Donaldson, R. J. *Validation of the internal characteristics of an industrial assessment center using the multitrait-multimethod matrix approach.* Ph.D. dissertation, Case Western Reserve University, 1969.

Drake, L. E. A social I. E. scale for the MMPI. *J. appl. Psychol.*, 1946, *30*, 51-54.
Drummond, F. A failure in the discrimination of aggressive behavior of undifferentiated schizophrenics with the hand test. *J. proj. Tech. pers. Assmt.*, 1966, *30*, 275-279.
DuBois, P. H. (Chairman) *Proceedings of the invitational conference on testing problems.* Princeton, N.J.: Educational Testing Service, 1969.
DuBois, P. H. *A history of psychological testing.* Boston: Allyn & Bacon, 1970.
Dubowitz, V., & Rogers, K. J. 5-Hydrozyindoles in the cerebrospinal fluid of infants with Down's syndrome and muscle hypotonia. *Devel. Med. Child Neurol.*, 1969, *11*, 730-734.
Dunlop. E. *Essentials of the automated MMPI.* Glendale, Calif.: Institute of Clinical Analysis, 1966.
Dunnette, M. D. Predictors of executive success. In F. R. Wickert & D. E. McFarland (Eds.), *Measuring executive effectiveness.* New York: Appleton-Century-Crofts, 1964.
Dymond, R. F. Adjustment changes over therapy from self-sorts. In C. R. Rogers & R. F. Dymond (Eds.), *Psychotherapy and personality change.* Chicago: University of Chicago Press, 1954. Pp. 76-84. (a)
Dymond, R. F. Adjustment changes over therapy from Thematic Apperception Test ratings. In C. R. Rogers and R. F. Dymond (Eds.), *Psychotherapy and personality change.* Chicago: University of Chicago Press, 1954. Pp. 109-120. (b)
Easter, L. V., & Murstein, B. I. Achievement fantasy as a function of probability of success. *J. consult. Psychol.*, 1964, *28* (2), 154-159.
Eber, H. W. Automated personality description with 16-PF data. *Amer. Psychologist*, 1964, *19*, 544.
Eccleston, D., Ritchie, I. M., & Roberts, M. H. T. Long term effects of mid-brain stimulation on 5-hydrozyindole synthesis in rat brain. *Nature*, 1970, *226*, 84-85.
Edwards, A. E. Prophylactic psychopharmacology and age-correlated intellectual changes. *J. Gerontol.*, 1967, *7*, 20-23.
Edwards, A. E. Personal communication, 1969.
Edwards, A. L. *Manual for the Edwards personal preference schedule.* New York: Psychol. Corp., 1954.
Edwards, A. L. *The social desirability variable in personality assessment and research.* New York: Dryden, 1957.
Edwards, A. L. *Edwards personal preference schedule.* New York: Psychol. Corp., 1959.
Edwards, A. L. *Edwards personal preference schedule manual.* New York: Psychol. Corp., 1959.
Edwards, A. L. *Edwards personality inventory.* Chicago: Science Research Associates, 1966.
Edwards, A. L. *Manual for the Edwards personality inventory.* Chicago: Science Research Associates, 1966.
Edwards, A. L. Correlations between scores on personality scales when items are stated in the first and third person form. *Educ. Psychol. Measmt.*, 1969, *29*, 561-563.
Edwards, W., Lindman, H., & Phillips, L. D. Emerging technologies for making decisions. In F. Barron et al. (Eds.), *New directions in psychology.* Vol. 2. New York: Holt, Rinehart & Winston, 1965.
Efron, D. H. (Ed.), *Psychopharmacology—a review of progress 1957-1967.* Washington, D.C.: U.S. Government Printing Office (PHS Publication No. 1836), 1968.
Ehrich, W. E., & Krumbhaar, E. B. The effects of large doses of benzedrine sulfate in the albino rat: functional and tissue changes. *Ann. intern. Med.*, 1937, *10*, 1874-1888.
Eiduson, S., Geller, E., Yuwiler, A., & Eiduson, B. *Biochemistry and behavior.* Princeton, N.J.: D. Van Nostrand, 1964.
Eisenman, R. Birth-order and sex differences in aesthetic preference for complexity-simplicity. *J. gen. Psychol.*, 1967, *77*, 121-126. (a)
Eisenman, R. Complexity-simplicity: I: Preference for symmetry and rejection of complexity. *Psychon. Sci.*, 1967, *8*, 169-170. (b)
Eisenman, R. Complexity-simplicity, II: Birth order and sex differences. *Psychon. Sci.*, 1967, *8*, 171-172. (c)
Eisenman, R. Personality and demography in complexity-simplicity. *J. consult. clin. Psychol.*, 1968, *32*, 140-143.
Eisenman, R., & Rappaport, J. Complexity preference and semantic differential ratings of complexity-simplicity and symmetry-asymmetry. *Psychon. Sci.*, 1967, *7*, 147-148.
Elizur, A. Content analysis of the Rorschach with regard to anxiety and hostility. *J. proj. Tech. pers. Assmt.*, 1949, *13*, 247-284.
Ellsworth, R. B., Foster, L., Childres, B., Arthur, G., & Krocker, D. Hospital and community adjustment as perceived by psychiatric patients, their families, and staff. *J. consult. clin. psychol. Monogr.*, 1968, *32*, 1-41.

Elmadjian, F., Hope, J. M., & Lamson, E. T. Excretion of epinephrine in various emotional states. *J. clin. Endocrinol.*, 1957, *17*, 608-620.

Endicott, N. A., & Jortner, S. Objective measures of depression. *Arch. gen. Psychiat.*, 1966, *15*, 249-255.

Endler, N. S., & Hunt, J. McV. S-R inventories of hostility and comparisons of the proportions of variance from persons, responses, and situations for hostility and anxiousness. *J. pers. soc. Psychol.*, 1968, *9*, 309-325.

Endler, N. S., Hunt, J. McV., & Rosenstein, A. J. An S-R inventory of anxiousness. *Psychol. Monogr.*, 1962, *76* (17) (Whole No. 536).

Engel, I. M. A factor-analytic study of items from five masculinity-femininity tests. *J. consult. Psychol.*, 1966, *30*, 565.

Engelman, K., Lovenberg, W., & Sjoerdsma, A. Inhibition of serotonin synthesis by parachlorophenylalanine in patients with the carcinoid syndromes. *New Eng. J. Med.*, 1967, *277*, 1103-1108.

England, G. W. Personal value systems of American managers. *Acad. Mgt. J.*, 1967, *10*, 53-68.

Epstein, S. Some theoretical considerations on the nature of ambiguity and the use of stimulus dimensions in projective techniques. *J. consult. Psychol.*, 1966, *30*, 183-192.

Erdelyi, E., Angwin, P., & Barchas, J. Simultaneous determination of 5-hydroxytryptamine and catecholamines in tissues using a weak cation exchange resin. *The Pharmacologist*, 1970, *12*, 204.

Erikson, R. B., & Roberts, A. H. An MMPI comparison of two groups of institutionalized delinquents. *J. proj. Tech. pers. Assmt.*, 1966, *30*, 163-166.

Eron, L. D. A normative study of the Thematic Apperception Test. *Psychol. Monogr.*, 1950, *64*, No. 9 (Whole No. 315).

Erspamer, V. (Ed.) 5-Hydroxytryptamine and related indolealkylamines. *Handbook of experimental pharmacology.* Vol. 19. New York: Springer-Verlag, 1966.

Euler, U. S. v. *Noradrenaline.* Springfield, Ill.: Charles C. Thomas, 1956.

Euler, U. S. v. Problems in neurotransmission. In C. F. Cori, V. G. Foglia, L. F. Leloir, & S. Ochoa (Eds.), *Perspectives in biology.* New York: Elsevier, Inc., 1962. Pp. 387-394.

Euler, U. S. v. Quantitation of stress by catecholamine analysis. *Clin. pharmacol. Ther.*, 1964, *5*, 398-404.

Euler, U. S. v. Adrenal medullary secretion and its neural control. In L. Martini & W. F. Ganong (Eds.), *Neuroendocrinology.* Vol. 2. New York: Academic Press, 1967. P. 283.

Euler, U. S. v., & Lundberg, U. Effect of flying on the epinephrine excretion in Air Force personnel. *J. appl. Physiol.*, 1954, *6*, 551-555.

Evans, C., & McConnell, T. R. A new measure of introversion-extroversion. *J. Psychol.*, 1941, *12*, 111-124.

Evans, G. W., & Crumbaugh, C. M. Effects of Prisoner's Dilemma format on cooperative behavior. *J. pers. soc. Psychol.*, 1966, *3*, 486-488. (a)

Evans, G. W., & Crumbaugh, C. M. Payment schedule, sequence of choice, and cooperation in the Prisoner's Dilemma game. *Psychon. Sci.*, 1966, *5*, 87-88. (b)

Ezekiel, R. S. The personal future and Peace Corps competence. *J. pers. soc. Psychol. Monogr. Suppl.* (Part 2), 1968, *8*, 1-26.

Farley, F. H., & Farley, S. V. Extroversion and stimulus-seeking motivation. *J. consult. Psychol.*, 1967, *31*, 215-216.

Farnsworth, K. Application of scaling techniques to the evaluation of counseling outcomes. *Psychol. Bull.*, 1966, *66*, 81-93.

Faucheux, G., & Moscovici, S. Self-esteem and exploitative game behavior in a game against chance and nature. *J. pers. soc. Psychol.*, 1968, *8*, 83-88.

Ferguson, J., Henriksen, S., Cohen, H., Mitchell, G., Barchas, J., & Dement, W. Hypersexuality and changes in aggressive and perceptual behavior caused by chronic administration of parachlorophenylalanine in cats. *Sci.*, 1970, *168*, 499-501.

Ferguson, L. W. *Personality measurement.* New York: McGraw-Hill, 1952.

Ferreira, A. J., & Winter, W. D. Family interaction and decision-making. *Arch. gen. Psychiat.*, 1965, *13*, 214-223.

Ferster, C. B. Classification of behavioral pathology. In L. Krasner & L. P. Ullmann (Eds.), *Research in behavior modification: New developments and implications.* New York: Holt, Rinehart & Winston, 1965.

Feshbach, S. The drive-reducing function of fantasy behavior. *J. abnorm. soc. Psychol.*, 1955, *50*, 3-11.

Feshbach, S. The influence of drive arousal and conflict upon fantasy behavior. In J. Kagan & G. Lesser (Eds.), *Contemporary issues in Thematic Apperception methods.* Springfield, Ill.: Charles C. Thomas, 1961. Pp. 119-138. (a)

Feshbach, S. The stimulating versus cathartic effects of vicarious aggressive activity. *J. abnorm. soc. Psychol.,* 1961, *63,* 381-385. (b)

Festinger, L. *A theory of cognitive dissonance.* Stanford, Calif.: Stanford University Press, 1957.

Festinger, L., Allen, V., Braden, M., Canon, L. K., Davidson, J. R., Jecker, J. D., Kiesler, S. B., & Walster, E. *Conflict, decision, and dissonance.* Stanford, Calif.: Stanford University Press, 1964.

Finney, B. C. Rorschach test correlates of assaultive behavior. *J. proj. Tech. pers. Assmt.,* 1955, *19,* 6-16.

Finney, J. C. Methodological problems in programmed composition of psychological test reports. *Behav. Sci.,* 1967, *12,* 142-152.

Fisher, V. E., & Watson, R. I. An inventory of affective tolerance. *J. Psychol.,* 1941, *12,* 149-157.

Fiske, D. W., & Maddi, S. R. *Functions of varied experience.* Homewood, Ill.: Dorsey, 1961.

Fiske, D. W., & Pearson, P. H. Theory and techniques of personality measurement. *Annu. rev. Psychol.,* 1970, *21,* 49-86.

Flanagan, J. C. *Factor analysis in the study of personality.* Stanford, Calif.: Stanford University Press, 1935.

Flanagan, J. C. Defining the requirements of the executive's job. *Personnel,* 1951, *28,* 28-35.

Flint, R. A., & Harris, R. J. Archetypes: A study of human interaction. Paper presented at Rocky Mountain Psychological Association meetings, Salt Lake City, Utah, May, 1970. (a)

Flint, R. A., & Harris, R. J. Relative importance of structure and individual differences in two-person games. Unpublished manuscript, University of New Mexico, 1970. (b)

Foote, W. E., Sheard, M. H., & Aghajanian, G. K. Comparison of effects of LSD and amphetamine on midbrain raphe units. *Nature,* 1969, *222,* 567-569.

Ford, D. H., & Urban, H. B. Psychotherapy. *Annu. Rev. Psychol.,* 1967, *18,* 333-372.

Ford, L. H., & Sempert, E. L. Relations among some objective measures of hostility, need aggression, and anxiety. *J. consult. Psychol.,* 1962, *26,* 486.

Forehand, G. A., & Gilmer, B. Environmental variation in studies of organizational behavior. *Psychol. Bull.,* 1964, *62,* 361-381.

Forsyth, R., & Fairweather, G. W. Psychotherapeutic and other hospital treatment criteria. *J. abnorm. soc. Psychol.,* 1961, *62,* 598-695.

Fowler, R. D., Jr. The current status of computer interpretation of psychological tests. *Amer. J. Psychiat.,* 1969, *125,* Suppl., 21-27.

Fowler, R. D., Jr., & Miller, M. L. Computer interpretation of the MMPI. *Arch. gen. Psychiat.,* 1969, *21,* 502-508.

Fox, J., Knapp, R. R., & Michael, W. B. Assessment of self-actualization of psychiatric patients. Validity of the Personal Orientation Inventory. *Educ. psychol. Measmt.,* 1968, *28,* 565-569.

Frank, J. D. Problems of controls in psychotherapy as exemplified by the psychotherapy research project of the Phipps Psychiatric Clinic. In E. A. Rubinstein & M. B. Parloff (Eds.), *Research in psychotherapy.* Vol. 1. Washington, D.C.: American Psychological Association, 1959. Pp. 10-26.

Frank, J. D., Gliedman, L. H., Imber, S. D., Stone, A. R., & Nash, E. H. Patients' expectancies and relearning as factors determining improvement in psychotherapy. *Amer. J. Psychiat.,* 1959, *115,* 961-968.

Frank, L. K. Projective methods for the study of personality. *J. Psychol.,* 1939, *8,* 343-389.

Frankenhaeuser, M., Mellis, I., Rissler, A., Björkvall, C., & Pátkai, P. Catecholamine excretion as related to cognitive and emotional reaction patterns. *Psychosom. Med.,* 1968, *30,* 109-120.

Franks, C. M. (Ed.) *Behavior therapy: Appraisal and status.* New York: McGraw-Hill, 1969.

Freedman, D. X. Effects of LSD-25 on brain serotonin. *J. pharmacol. exp. Ther.,* 1961, *134,* 160-166.

Freedman, D. X., Gottlieb, R., & Lovell, R. A. Psychotomimetic drugs and brain 5-hydroxytryptamine metabolism. *Biochem. Pharmacol.,* 1970, *19,* 1181-1188.

French, E. G., & Lesser, G. S. Some characteristics of the achievement motive in women. *J. abnorm. soc. Psychol.,* 1964, *68,* 119-128.

Freud, S. Civilization and its discontents. (Originally published, 1929.) In J. Strachey (Ed.), *The standard edition of the complete psychological works of Sigmund Freud.* Vol. 21. London: Hogarth, 1961. Pp. 64-148.

Freyd, M. Introverts and extroverts. *Psychol. Rev.*, 1924, *31*, 74-87.
Fricke, B. G. *Opinion, attitude, and interest survey handbook.* Ann Arbor, Mich.: OAIS Testing Program, 1963.
Friedell, M. F. A laboratory experiment on retaliation. *J. confl. Resol.*, 1968, *12*, 357-373.
Friedman, A. H., & Walker, C. A. Circadian rhythms in rat midbrain and caudate nucleus biogenic amine levels. *J. Physiol.*, 1968, *197*, 77-85.
Fry, C. L. Personality and acquisition factors in the development of coordination. *J. pers. soc. Psychol.*, 1965, *2*, 403-407.
Fryer, D. *The measurement of interests.* New York: Henry Holt & Co., 1931.
Funkenstein, D. H., King, S. H., & Drolette, M. *Mastery of stress.* Cambridge: Harvard University Press, 1957.
Fuxe, K., Hökfelt, T., & Ungerstedt. U. Localization of indolealkylamines in CNS. *Advan. Pharmacol.*, 1968, *6* (Part A), 235-251.
Gahagan, J. P., Horai, J., Berger, S., & Tedeschi, J. T. Status and authoritarianism in the Prisoner's Dilemma game. Paper presented at Southeastern Psychological Association meetings, Atlanta, April, 1967.
Gallo, P. S., Funk, S. G., & Levine, J. R. Reward size, method of presentation, and number of alternatives in a Prisoner's Dilemma game. *J. pers. soc. Psychol.*, 1969, *13*, 239-244.
Galton, F. *Inquiries into the human faculty and its development.* London: Macmillan & Co., 1883.
Game is set to get collision-bound marriages on track. *New York Times*, Dec. 28, 1968, *118*, 41.
Ganzer, G. J., & Sarason, I. G. Interrelationships among hostility, experimental conditions, and verbal behavior. *J. abnorm. soc. Psychol.*, 1964, *68*, 79-84.
Garattini, S., Giacalone, E., & Valzelli, L. Biochemical changes during isolation-induced aggressiveness in mice. In S. Garattini & E. B. Sigg (Eds.), *Aggressive behavior.* Amsterdam: Excerpta Medica Fdn., 1969. Pp. 179-187.
Garattini, S., & Shore, P. Advances in pharmacology. *Biological role of indolealkylamine derivatives.* In Vol. 6A and 6B. New York: Academic Press, 1968.
Garattini, S., & Valzelli, L. *Serotonin.* New York: Elsevier, 1965.
Garlington, W. K., & Cotler, S. B. Systematic desensitization of test anxiety. *Behav. res. Ther.*, 1968, *6*, 247-256.
Garlington, W. K., & Shimota, H. The change-seeker index: A measure of the need for variable stimulus input. *Psychol. Rep.*, 1964, *14*, 919-924.
Gathercole, C. E. *Assessment in clinical psychology.* Baltimore, Md.: Penguin, 1968.
Geer, J. H. The development of a scale to measure fear. *Behav. res. Ther.*, 1965, *3*, 45-53.
Geffen, L. B., & Livett, B. G. Synaptic vesicles in sympathetic neurons. *Physiol. Rev.*, 1971, *51*, 98-157.
Gekoski, N. *Psychological testing: Theory, interpretation, and practice.* Springfield, Ill.: Charles C. Thomas, 1964.
Gerbode, F., & Bowers, M. Measurement of acid monoamine metabolites in human and animal cerebrospinal fluid. *J. Neurochem.*, 1968, *15*, 1053-1054.
Giarman, N. J., & Freedman, D. X. Biochemical aspects of the actions of psychotomimetic drugs. *Pharmacol. Rev.*, 1965, *17*, 1-25.
Giarman, N. J., & Schanberg, S. M. Intracellular distribution of 5-hydroxytryptamine (5-HT:serotonin) in rat's brain. *Biochem. Pharmacol.*, 1958, *1*, 301-306.
Gilberstadt, H. Comprehensive MMPI code book for males. *VA Information Bull. 1B11-5.* Washington, D.C.: U.S. Government Printing Office, 1970.
Gilbert, J. *Clinical psychological tests in psychiatric and medical practice.* Springfield, Ill.: Charles C. Thomas, 1969.
Gilliland, A. R., & Morgan, J. J. B. An objective measure of introversion-extroversion. *J. abnorm. soc. Psychol.*, 1931, *26*, 296-303.
Glanzer, M. Curiosity, exploratory drive, and stimulus satiation. *Psychol. Bull.*, 1958, *55*, 302-315.
Glaser, E. M., & Maller, J. B. The measurement of interest values. *Charac. Pers.*, 1940, *9*, 67-81.
Glaser, R., Schwarz, P. A., & Flanagan, J. C. The contribution of interview and situational procedures to the selection of supervisory personnel. *J. appl. Psychol.*, 1958, *42*, 69-73.
Glassman, A. Indoleamines and affective disorders. *Psychosom. Med.*, 1969, *31*, 107-114.
Glowinski, J., Iversen, L. L., & Axelrod, J. Storage and synthesis of norepinephrine in the reserpine-treated rat brain. *J. pharmacol. exp. Ther.*, 1966, *151*, 385-399.
Glowinski, J., Kopin, I. J., & Axelrod, J. Metabolism of H^3-norepinephrine in the rat brain. *J. Neurochem.*, 1965, *12*, 25-30.

Goldberg, L. R. Diagnosticians versus diagnostic signs: The diagnosis of psychosis versus neurosis from the MMPI. *Psychol. Monogr.*, 1965, *79*, No. 9 (Whole No. 602).
Goldberg, L. R. Simple models or simple processes? Some research on clinical judgments. *Amer. Psychologist*, 1968, *23*, 483-496.
Goldberg, L. R. Student personality characteristics and optimal college learning conditions. *Ore. res. inst. res. Monogr.*, 1969, *9* (1).
Goldberg, L. R. Why measure *that* trait? An historical analysis of personality scales and inventories. *Ore. res. inst. tech. Rep.*, 1970, *10* (3).
Goldberg, L. R., & Slovic, P. Importance of test item content: An analysis of a corollary of the deviation hypothesis. *J. counsel. Psychol.*, 1967, *14*, 462-472.
Goldberg, S. C. Prediction of response to antipsychotic drugs. In D. H. Efron, J. O. Cole, J. Levine, & J. R. Wittenborn (Eds.), *Psychopharmacology: A review of progress 1957-1967*. Washington, D.C.: U.S. Government Printing Office, 1968.
Goldstein, A. P., Heller, K., & Sechrest, L. B. *Psychotherapy and the psychology of behavior change.* New York: John Wiley, 1966.
Goodall, McC. Sympathoadrenal response to gravitational stress. *J. clin. Invest.*, 1962, *41*, 197-202.
Gordon, R., Reid, J. V. O., Sjoerdsma, A., & Udenfriend, S. Increased synthesis of norepinephrine in the rat heart on electrical stimulation of the stellate ganglia. *Mol. Pharmacol.*, 1966, *2*, 606-613.
Gorham, D. R., Moseley, E. C., & Holtzman, W. W. Norms for the computer-scored Holtzman Inkblot Technique. *Percep. mot. Skills*, 1968, *26*, 1279-1305.
Gorman, B. S. 16 PF correlates of sensation-seeking. *Psychol. Rev.*, 1970, *26*, 741-742.
Gottfries, C. G., Gottfries, I., & Roos, B. E. Homovanillic acid and 5-hydroxyindoleacetic acid in the cerebrospinal fluid of patients with senile dementia, presenile dementia, and Parkinsonism. *J. Neurochem.*, 1969, *16*, 1341-1345.
Gottschalk, L. A., & Gleser, G. C. Three hostility scales applicable to verbal samples. *Arch. gen. Psychiat.*, 1963, *9* (3), 254-279.
Gottschalk, L. A., & Gleser, G. C. *The measurement of psychological states through the content analysis of verbal behavior.* Los Angeles: University of California Press, 1969.
Gottschalk, L. A., Winget, C. N., & Gleser, G. C. *Manual of instructions for using the Gottschalk-Gleser content analysis scales: Anxiety, hostility, and social disorganization—personal disorganization.* Berkeley, Calif.: University of California Press, 1969.
Gough, H. G. A short social status inventory. *J. educ. Psychol.*, 1949, *40*, 52-56.
Gough, H. G. Identifying psychological femininity. *Educ. psychol. Measmt.*, 1952, *12*, 427-439.
Gough, H. G. *Manual for the California Psychological Inventory.* Palo Alto, Calif.: Consulting Psychologists Press, 1957.
Gough, H. G. Academic achievement in high school as predicted from the California Psychological Inventory. *J. educ. Psychol.*, 1964, *55*, 174-180.
Gough, H. G. *Manual for the California Psychological Inventory.* Palo Alto, Calif.: Consulting Psychologists Press, 1964.
Gough, H. G. Cross-cultural validation of a measure of asocial behavior. *Psychol. Rep.*, 1965, *17*, 379-387.
Gough, H. G. Graduation from high school as predicted from the California Psychological Inventory. *Psychol. Sch.*, 1966, *3*, 208-216. (a)
Gough, H. G. A cross-cultural analysis of the CPI femininity scale. *J. consult. Psychol.*, 1966, *30*, 136-141. (b)
Gough, H. G. Nonintellectual factors in the selection and evaluation of medical students. *J. med. Educ.*, 1967, *42*, 642-650.
Gough, H. G., & Hall, W. B. Prediction of performance in medical school from the California Psychological Inventory. *J. appl. Psychol.*, 1964, *48*, 218-226.
Gough, H. G., & Heilbrun, A. B., Jr. *The Adjective Check List manual.* Palo Alto, California: Consulting Psychologists Press, 1965.
Grant, D. L. Situational tests in the assessment of managers. Part II: Contributions to the assessment process. *The executive study conference: Management games in selection and development.* Princeton, N.J.: Educational Testing Service, 1964, 129-134.
Grant, D. L., & Bray, D. W. Contributions of the interview to assessment of management potential. *J. appl. Psychol.*, 1969, *53*, 24-34.
Grant, D. L., Katkovsky, W., & Bray, D. W. Contributions of projective techniques to assessment of management potential. *J. appl. Psychol.*, 1967, *51*, 226-233.
Grant, M. J., & Sermat, V. Status and sex of others as determinants of behavior in a mixed-motive game. *J. pers. soc. Psychol.*, 1969, *12*, 151-157.

Gray, H., & Wheelwright, J. B. Jung's psychological types, their frequency of occurrence. *J. gen. Psychol.,* 1946, *34,* 3-17.

Greenwood, J. M., & McNamara, W. J. Interrater reliability in situational tests. *J. appl. Psychol.,* 1967, *51,* 101-106.

Greiner, L. E., Leitch, D. P., & Barnes, L. B. The simple complexity of organizational climate in a governmental agency. In R. Tagiuri & G. H. Litwin (Eds.), *Organizational climate: Explorations of a concept.* Boston: Graduate School of Business Administration, Harvard University, 1968. Pp. 195-224.

Griffith, A. V., & Lemley, D. W. Teeth and threatening look in Draw a Person as indicating aggression. *J. clin. Psychol.,* 1967, *24* (4), 489-492.

Grinker, R. R., Sr., Miller, J., Sabshin, M., Nunn, R., & Nunnally, J. C. *The phenomena of depressions.* New York: Hoeber, 1961.

Guertin, W. H. A factor-analytic study of schizophrenic symptoms. *J. consult. Psychol.,* 1952, *16,* 308-312.

Guilford, J. P. *Psychometric methods.* New York: McGraw-Hill, 1954.

Guilford, J. P. Structure of intellect. *Psychol. Bull.,* 1956, *53,* 267-293.

Guilford, J. P. *Personality.* New York: McGraw-Hill, 1959.

Guilford, J. P., & Guilford, R. B. An analysis of the factors in a typical test of introversion-extroversion. *J. abnorm. soc. Psychol.,* 1934, *28,* 377-399.

Guilford, J. P., & Guilford, R. B. Personality factors S, E, and M, and their measurement. *J. Psychol.,* 1936, *2,* 109-127.

Guilford, J. P., & Guilford, R. B. Personality factors D, R, T, and A. *J. abnorm. soc. Psychol.,* 1939, *34,* 21-36. (a)

Guilford, J. P., & Guilford, R. B. Personality factors N and GD. *J. abnorm. soc. Psychol.,* 1939, *34,* 239-248. (b)

Gump, P. V., & James, E. V. *Patient behavior in wards of traditional and modern design.* Topeka, Kans.: Environmental Research Foundation, 1970.

Guttman, L. What lies ahead for factor analysis? *Educ. psychol. Measmt.,* 1950, *10,* 3-31.

Haber, R. N., & Alpert, R. The role of situation and picture cues in projective measurement of the achievement motive. In J. W. Atkinson (Ed.), *Motives in fantasy, action, and society.* Princeton, N.J.: D. Van Nostrand, 1958.

Hafner, A. J., & Kaplan, A. M. Hostility content analysis of the Rorschach and TAT. *J. proj. Tech. pers. Assmt.,* 1960, *24,* 127-143.

Halpin, S. M., & Pilisuk, M. Probability matching in the Prisoner's Dilemma. *Psychon. Sci.,* 1967, *7,* 269-270.

Halpin, S. M., & Pilisuk, M. Prediction and choice in the Prisoner's Dilemma. *Behav. Sci.,* 1970, *15,* 141-153.

Hamburg, D. Genetics of adrenocortical hormone metabolism in relation to psychological stress. In J. Hirsch (Ed.), *Behavior-genetic analysis.* New York: McGraw-Hill, 1967. Pp. 154-175.

Hamburg, D. A. (Ed.) *Psychiatry as a behavioral science.* (Behavioral Social Sciences Survey Monograph Series.) Englewood Cliffs, N.J.: Prentice-Hall, 1970.

Hamburg, D., & Kessler, S. A behavioral-endocrine-genetic approach to stress problems. In S. Pickett (Ed.), *Memoirs of the society for endocrinology no. 15: Endocrine genetics.* Cambridge: Cambridge University Press, 1967. Pp. 249-270.

Hamburg, D., & Lunde, D. Relation of behavioral, genetic, and neuroendocrine factors to thyroid function. In J. Spuhler (Ed.), *Genetic diversity and human behavior.* Chicago: Aldine Press, 1967. Pp. 135-170.

Hamburger, H. Separable games. *Behav. Sci.,* 1969, *14,* 121-132.

Hamlin, R. M., & Nemo, R. S. Self-actualization in choice scores of improved schizophrenics. *J. clin. Psychol.,* 1962, *18,* 51-54.

Hammer, E. F. Projective drawings. In A. I. Rabin (Ed.), *Projective techniques in personality assessment.* New York: Springer, 1968.

Haner, C. F., & Brown, P. A. Clarification of the instigation to action concept in the frustration-aggression hypotheses. *J. abnorm. soc. Psychol.,* 1955, *51,* 204-206.

Hanson, L. C. F. Evidence that the central action of amphetamine is medicated via catecholamines. *Psychopharmacologia,* 1966, *9,* 78-80.

Harford, T., & Cutter, H. S. G. Cooperation among Negro and white boys and girls. *Psychol. Rep.,* 1966, *18,* 818.

Harford, T., & Hill, M. Variations in behavioral strategies and interpersonal trust in a two-person game with male alcoholics. *J. clin. Psychol.,* 1967, *23,* 33-35.

Harford, T., & Solomon, L. "Reformed sinner" and "lapsed saint" strategies in the Prisoner's Dilemma game. *J. confl. Resol.,* 1967, *11,* 104-109.

Harford, T., & Solomon, L. Effects of a "reformed sinner" and a "lapsed saint" strategy upon trust formation in paranoid and non-paranoid schizophrenic patients. *J. abnorm. Psychol.,* 1969, *74,* 498-504.

Harlow, H. F. Learning and satiation of response in intrinsically motivated complex puzzle performance by monkeys. *J. comp. physiol. Psychol.,* 1950, *43,* 289-294.

Harlow, H. F. Mice, monkeys, men, and motives. *Psychol. Rev.,* 1953, *60,* 23-32.

Harlow, H. F., Harlow, M. K., & Meyer, D. R. Learning motivated by a manipulation drive. *J. exp. Psychol.,* 1950, *40,* 228-234.

Harris, D. B. A scale for measuring attitudes of social responsibility in children. *J. abnorm. soc. Psychol.,* 1957, *55,* 322-326.

Harris, R. H., & Lingoes, J. C. Subscales for the MMPI: An aid to profile interpretation. San Francisco: University of California School of Medicine, 1955.

Harris, R. J. Comments on Dr. Rapoport's comments. *Psychol. Rep.,* 1969, *25,* 825. (a)

Harris, R. J. A geometric classification system for 2 x 2 interval-symmetric games. *Behav. Sci.,* 1969, *14,* 138-146. (b)

Harris, R. J. Note on Howard's theory of meta-games. *Psychol. Rep.,* 1969, *24,* 849-850. (c)

Harris, R. J. Note on "Optimal policies for the Prisoner's Dilemma." *Psychol. Rev.,* 1969, *76,* 363-375. (d)

Harris, R. J. Cooperativeness of paranoid versus non-paranoid patients in the Prisoner's Dilemma. Unpublished manuscript, University of New Mexico, 1970. (a)

Harris, R. J. An interval-scale classification system for all 2 x 2 games. Unpublished manuscript, University of New Mexico, 1970. (b)

Harris, R. J. Paradox regained. *Psychol. Rep.,* 1970, *26,* 264-266. (c)

Harrison, R. Studies in the use and validity of the Thematic Apperception Test with mentally disordered patients, II: A quantitative validity study. *Charact. Pers.,* 1940, *9,* 122-133. (a)

Harrison, R. Studies in the use and validity of the Thematic Apperception Test with mentally disordered patients, III: Validation by the method of "blind analysis." *Charact. Pers.,* 1940, *9,* 134-138. (b)

Harrison, R. Thematic apperceptive methods. In B. B. Wolman (Ed.), *Handbook of clinical psychology.* New York: McGraw-Hill, 1965. Pp. 562-620.

Harrower, Molly. *Appraising personality: An introduction to the projective techniques.* New York: Simon & Schuster, 1968.

Hartman, E. *The biology of dreaming.* Springfield, Ill.: Charles C. Thomas, 1967. Pp. 1-206.

Hartmann, H., Kris, E., & Loewenstein, R. M. Notes on the theory of aggression. In A. Freud, H. Hartmann, & E. Kris (Eds.), *The psychoanalytic study of the child.* Vol. 3 and 4. New York: International Universities Press, 1949. Pp. 9-36.

Hase, H. D., & Goldberg, L. R. Comparative validity of different strategies of constructing personality inventory scales. *Psychol. Bull.,* 1967, *67,* 231-248.

Hathaway, S. R. Some considerations relative to nondirective counseling as therapy. *J. clin. Psychol.,* 1948, *4,* 226-231.

Hathaway, S. R. Scales 5 (Masculinity-Femininity), 6 (Paranoia), and 8 (Schizophrenia). In G. S. Welsh & W. G. Dahlstrom (Eds.), *Basic readings on the MMPI in psychology and medicine.* Minneapolis, Minn.: University of Minnesota Press, 1956. Pp. 104-111.

Hathaway, S. R., & McKinley, J. C. *The Minnesota Multiphasic Personality Inventory manual.* (Rev. ed.). New York: The Psychol. Corp., 1951.

Hathaway, S. R., & Monachesi, E. D. *Analyzing and predicting juvenile delinquency with the MMPI.* Minneapolis, Minn.: University of Minnesota Press, 1953.

Hawkins, D. R., Monroe, J. T., Sandifer, M. G., & Vernon, C. R. Psychological and physiological responses to continuous epinephrine infusion—an approach to the study of the affect, anxiety. *Psychiat. Res. Rep., Am. Psychiat. Assoc.,* 1960, *12,* 40-52.

Hawkins, R. P., Peterson, R. F., Schweid, E., & Bijou, S. W. Behavior therapy in the home: Amelioration of problem parent-child relations with the parent in a therapeutic role. *J. Exp. Child Psychol.,* 1966, *4,* 99-107.

Haworth, M. R. Responses of children to a group projective film and to the Rorschach, CAT, Despert Fables, and D-A-P. *J. proj. Tech.,* 1962, *26,* 47-60.

Haywood, H. C. Novelty-seeking behavior as a function of manifest anxiety and physiological arousal. *J. Pers.,* 1962, *30,* 63-74.

Haywood, H. C. Individual differences in motivational orientation: A trait approach. Presented at Symposium on Intrinsic Motivation in Education, Ontario Institute for Studies in Education, Toronto, 1970.

Haywood, H. C., & Dobbs, V. H. Motivation and anxiety in high school boys. *J. Pers.,* 1964, *32,* 371-379.

Haywood, H. C., & Weaver, S. J. Differential effects of motivational orientations and in- centive conditions on motor performance in institutionalized retardates. *Amer. J. ment. Def.*, 1967, *72*, 459-467.

Haywood, N. *Occupational Preference Inventory*, unpublished test, 1968.

Hebb, D. O. The organization of behavior. New York: John Wiley, 1949.

Heckhausen, H. *The anatomy of achievement motivation*. New York: Academic Press, 1967.

Heidbreder, E. Measuring introversion and extroversion. *J. abnorm. soc. Psychol.*, 1926, *21*, 120-134.

Heilbrun, A. B. Relationships between the Adjective Check List, Personal Preference- Schedule, and desirability factors under varying defensiveness conditions. *J. clin. Psychol.*, 1958, *14*, 283-287.

Heilbrun, A. B., Jr. Social learning theory, social desirability, and the MMPI. *Psychol. Bull.*, 1964, *61*, 377-387.

Heimstra, N. W., Ellingstad, V. S., & DeKock, A. R. Effects of operator mood on per- formance in a simulated driving task. *Percept. mot. Skills*, 1967, *25* (3), 729-735.

Heist, P., & Yonge, G. *Manual for Omnibus Personality Inventory*. New York: Psychol. Corp., 1968.

Helm, C. E. Simulation models for psychometric theories. *Proceedings of American fed- eration of information processing societies.* Vol. 27 (Part 1). Washington, D.C.: Spar- tan Books, 1965.

Hemphill, J. K. Dimensions of executive positions. Ohio Studies in Personnel. *Res. Monogr.*, No. 98, Columbus, Ohio: Bureau of Business Research, Ohio State Uni- versity, 1960.

Henry, A., & Henry Z. Doll play of Pillga Indian children: An experimental field analysis of the behavior of the Pillga Indian children. *Res. monogr. Amer. orthopsychiat. Assn.*, 1944 (No. 4).

Henry, W. *The analysis of fantasy, the Thematic Apperception technique in the study of personality.* New York: John Wiley, 1956.

Henry, W. E., & Farley, J. Symposium on current aspects of the problems of validity: A study in validation of the Thematic Apperception Test. *J. proj. Tech.*, 1959, *23*, 273-277.

Hershberger, R. G. *A study of meaning and architecture.* Doctoral dissertation, University of Pennsylvania, 1968.

Herzberg, F., & Hamlin, R. M. A motivation-hygiene concept of mental health. *Ment. Hygiene*, 1961, *45*, 394-401.

Herzberg, F., Mausner, B., & Snyderman, B. B. *The motivation to work.* New York: John Wiley, 1959.

Heston, J. C. A comparison of four masculinity-femininity scales. *Educ. Psychol. Measmt.*, 1948, *8*, 375-387.

Heymans, G., & Wiersma, E. Beitrage zur Speziellen Psychologie auf Grund einer Massen- untersuchung. *Zeitschrift für Psychologie*, 1906, *43*, 81-127, 258-301.

Hilgard, E. R., & Russell, D. H. Motivation in school learning. In N. B. Henry (Ed.), *The forty-ninth yearbook, national society for study of education.* Chicago: University of Chicago Press, 1950.

Hill, M. H., & Blane, H. T. Evaluation of psychotherapy with alcoholics. *Quart. J. stud. Alcohol.*, 1967, *28*, 76-104.

Hillarp, N. Å., Fuxe, K., & Dahlstrom, A. Adrenergic mechanisms in the nervous system. C. Demonstration and mapping of central neurons containing dopamine, noradrenaline and 5-hydroxytryptamine and their reactions to Psychopharmaca. *Pharmacol. Rev.*, 1966, *18*, 727-742.

Hiltmann, H. *Kompendium der psychodiagnostischen tests.* Bern: Hans Huber, 1966.

Himelstein, P., & Stoup, D. D. Correlation of three Mf measures for males. *J. clin. Psy- chol.*, 1967, *23*, 189.

Himwich, H. E. *Biochemistry, schizophrenias and the affective illnesses.* Baltimore, Md.: Williams and Wilkins, in press.

Hinrichs, J. R. Comparison of "real life" assessments of management potential with situational exercises, paper-and-pencil ability tests, and personality inventories. *J. appl. Psychol.*, 1969, *53*, 425-433.

Hobson, J. A. Sleep: biochemical aspects. *New England J. Med.*, 1969, *281*, 1468-1470.

Hoch, A., & Amsden, G. S. A guide to the descriptive study of personality. *Rev. neurol. Psychiat.*, 1913, *11*, 577-587.

Hodge, J. R., Wagner, E. E. & Schreiner, F. Hypnotic validation of two hand test scoring categories. *J. proj. Tech. pers. Assmt.*, 1966, *30*, 385-386.

Hoggatt, A. C. Measuring the cooperativeness of behavior in quantity variation duopoly games. *Behav. Sci.*, 1967, *12*, 81-84.

Hokanson, J. E. Psychological evaluation of the catharsis hypothesis. In E. I. Megargee & J. E. Hokanson (Eds.), *The dynamics of aggression: Individual, group, and international analyses.* New York: Harper & Row, 1970.

Holland, J. L. A personality inventory employing occupational titles. *J. appl. Psychol.*, 1958, *42*, 336-342.

Holland, J. L. *The psychology of vocational choice.* Waltham, Mass.: Blaisdell, 1966.

Hollenberg, E., & Sperry, M. Some antecedents of aggression and effects of frustration in doll play. *J. Pers.*, 1951, *1*, 32-43.

Hollingworth, L. S. Sex differences in mental traits. *Psychol. Bull.*, 1916, *13*, 377-383.

Hollingworth, L. S. Comparison of the sexes in mental traits. *Psychol. Bull.*, 1918, *15*, 427-432.

Hollister, L. E. *Chemical psychoses, LSD, and related drugs.* Springfield, Ill.: Charles C. Thomas, 1968.

Hollister, L. E., & Moore, F. Factors affecting excretion of catecholamines in man: Urine flow, urine pH, and creatinine clearance. *Res. com. chem. Path. Pharmacol.*, 1970, *1*, 193-302.

Holt, R. R. Yet another look at clinical and statistical prediction. *Amer. Psychologist*, 1970, *25*, 337-349.

Holtzman, D., Lovell, R. A., Jaffe, J. H., & Freedman, D. X. 1-Δ^9-Tetrahydrocannabinol: Neurochemical and behavioral effects in the mouse. *Sci.*, 1969, *163*, 1464-1467.

Holtzman, W. H., Thorpe, J. S., Swartz, J. D., & Herron, E. W. *Inkblot perception and personality.* Austin, Texas: University of Texas Press, 1961.

Holzberg, J. D. Reliability re-examined. In Richers-Ovsiankina Maria (Ed.), *Rorschach psychology.* New York: John Wiley, 1960. Pp. 161-179.

Homans, G. C. *Social behavior: Its elementary forms.* New York: Harcourt, Brace, & World, 1961.

Homme, L., Csanyi, A. P., Gonzales, M. A., & Rechs, J. R. *How to use contingency contracting in classroom.* Champaign, Ill.: Research Press, 1969.

Horowitz, M. J. A study of clinicians judgments from projective test protocols. *J. consult. Psychol.*, 1962, *26*, 251-256.

Horst, P. *Personality: Measurement of dimensions.* San Francisco: Jossey-Bass, 1968.

House, S. D. A mental hygiene inventory. *Arch. Psychol.*, 1927, *14* (No. 88).

Howard, K. I. A test of stimulus-seeking behavior. *Percept. mot. Skills*, 1961, *13*, 416.

Howard, K. I., & Diesenhaus, H. I. Personality correlates of change-seeking behavior. *Percept. mot. Skills*, 1965, *21*, 655-664.

Howard, N. The theory of meta-games. *Gen. Syst.*, 1966, *11*, 167-186.

Howard, N. Comments on Harris' "Comments on Rapoport's comments." *Psychol. Rep.*, 1969, *25*, 826.

Howard, N. Note on the Harris-Rapoport controversy. *Psychol. Rep.*, 1970, *26*, 316.

Hull, C. L. *Aptitude testing.* Yonkers: World Book, 1928.

Humm, D. G., & Wadsworth, G. W., Jr. The Humm-Wadsworth Temperament Scale: Preliminary report. *Pers. J.*, 1934, *12*, 314-323.

Humm, D. G., & Wadsworth, G. W., Jr. The Humm-Wadsworth Temperament Scale. *Amer. J. Psychiat.*, 1935, *92*, 163-200.

Hunt, J. McV. Motivation inherent in information processing and action. In O. J. Harvey (Ed.), *Motivation and social interaction.* New York: Ronald Press, 1963.

Hyman, R., & Berger, L. The effects of psychotherapy: Discussion. *Inter. J. Psychiat.*, 1965, *1*, 317-322.

Ichiyama, A., Nakamura, S., Nishizuka, Y., & Hayaishi, O. Enzymic studies on the biosynthesis of serotonin in mammalian brain. *J. biol. Chem.*, 1970, *245*, 1699-1709.

Imber, S. D., Frank, J. D., Nash, E. H., Stone, A. R., & Gliedman, L. H. Improvement and amount of therapeutic contact: An alternative to the use of non-treatment contols in psychotherapy. *J. consult. Psychol.*, 1957, *21*, 309-315.

International Business Machines Corporation. *IBM 1401 or 1440 operating system computer assisted instruction.* (Form C24-3253-0.) New York: IBM, 1964.

Isch, M. J. Fantasied mother-child interaction in doll play. *J. genet. Psychol.*, 1952, *81*, 233-258.

Ittleson, W. H. Environmental psychology of the psychiatric ward. In C. W. Taylor, R. Bailey, & C. H. H. Branch (Eds.), *Second national conference on architectural psychology.* Salt Lake City: University of Utah Press, 1967. Pp. 2-1 through 2-21.

Jackson, D. N. *Personality research form manual.* Goshen, N.Y.: Research Psychologists Press, 1967.

Jackson, D. N. Multimethod factor analysis in the evaluation of convergent and discriminant validity. *Psychol. Bull.*, 1969, *72*, 30-49.

Jackson, D. N. A sequential system for personality scale development. In C. D. Spielberger (Ed.), *Current topics in clinical and community psychology*. New York: Academic Press, 1970.

Jackson, D. N., & Guthrie, G. M. Multitrait-multimethod evaluation of the personality research form. *Proc., 76th Ann. Conv., APA*, 1968, *3*, 177-178.

Jackson, D. N., & Messick, S. Response styles on the MMPI: Comparison of clinical and normal samples. *J. abnorm. soc. Psychol.*, 1962, *65*, 285-299.

Jackson, D. N., & Messick, S. (Eds.) *Problems of human assessment*. New York: McGraw-Hill, 1967.

Jacobs, B., Jr. A method for investigating the cue characteristics of pictures. In J. W. Atkinson (Ed.), *Motives in fantasy, action, and society*. Princeton, N.J.: D. Van Nostrand, 1958. Pp. 617-629.

James, Patricia B., & Mosher, D. L. Thematic aggression, hostility-guilt, and aggressive behavior. *J. proj. Tech. pers. Assmt.*, 1967, *31* (1), 61-67.

Jarrett, H. (Ed.) *Environmental quality in a growing economy: Essays from the Sixth RFF Forum*. Baltimore: Johns Hopkins University Press, 1966.

Jasper, H. H. The measurement of depression-elation and its relation to a measure of extraversion-introversion. *J. abnorm. soc. Psychol.*, 1930, *25*, 307-318.

Jenkins, R. L., & Blodgett, E. Prediction of success or failure of delinquent boys from sentence completions. *Amer. J. Orthopsychiat.*, 1960, *30*, 741-756.

Jensen, A. R. Thematic Apperception Test. In O. K. Buros (Ed.), *Fifth mental measurements yearbook*. Highland Park, N.J.: Gryshon Press, 1959. Pp. 310-313.

Johns, E. Symmetry and asymmetry in the urban scene. *Area*, 1969, No. 2, 48-57.

Johnson, B. Emotional instability in children. *Ungraded*, 1920, *5*, 73-79.

Johnson, S. M., & Brown, R. A. Producing behavior change in parents of disturbed children. *J. child psychol. Psychiat.*, 1969, *10*, 107-121.

Johnson, S. M., & Sechrest, L. B. Comparison of desensitization and progressive relaxation in treating test anxiety. *J. consult. clin. Psychol.*, 1968, *32*, 280-286.

Jones, L. W., & Thomas, C. P. Studies on figure drawings: A review of the literature (1949-1959). *Psychometric quart. Suppl.*, 1961, *35*, 212-261.

Jouvet, M. Biogenic amines and the states of sleep. *Sci.*, 1969, *163*, 32-41.

Jurjevich, R. M. Normative data for the clinical and additional MMPI scales for a population of delinquent girls. *J. gen. Psychol.*, 1963, *69*, 143-146. (a)

Jurjevich, R. M. Relationships among the MMPI and HGI hostility scales. *J. gen. Psychol.*, 1963, *69*, 131-133. (b)

Kagan, J. Measurement of overt aggression from fantasy. *J. abnorm. soc. Psychol.*, 1956, *52*, 390-393. Reprinted in E. I. Megargee (Ed.), *Research in clinical assessment*. New York: Harper & Row, 1966.

Kagan, J. The stability of TAT fantasy and stimulus ambiguity. *J. consult. Psychol.*, 1959, *23*, 266-271.

Kagan, J., & Lesser, G. S. (Eds.), *Contemporary issues in thematic apperceptive methods*. Springfield, Ill.: Charles C. Thomas, 1961.

Kagan, J., & Moss, H. A. Stability and validity of achievement fantasy. *J. abnorm. soc. Psychol.*, 1959, *58*, 357-363.

Kahn, M., Baker, B. L., & Weiss, J. M. Treatment of insomnia by relaxation training. *J. abnorm. Psychol.*, 1968, *73*, 556-558.

Kahoe, R. D. A factor-analytic study of motivation-hygiene variables. *Peabody papers in human development*, 1966, *4*, No. 3.

Kanfer, F. H. Self-monitoring: Methodological limitations and clinical applications. *J. consult. clin. Psychol.*, in press.

Kanner, L. *Child psychiatry*. (2nd Ed.) Springfield, Ill.: Charles C. Thomas, 1948.

Kaplan, M. F. The effect of cue relevance, ambiguity, and self-reported hostility on TAT responses. *J. proj. Tech. pers. Assmt.*, 1967, *31*, 45-50.

Kaplan, M. F. The ambiguity of TAT ambiguity. *J. proj. Tech. pers. Assmt.*, 1969, *33*, 25-29. (a)

Kaplan, M. F. Reply to Murstein's "Comment on the ambiguity of the TAT ambiguity." *J. proj. Tech. pers. Assmt.*, 1969, *33*, 486-488. (b)

Kaplan, M. F. A note on the stability of interjudge and intrajudge ambiguity scores. *J. proj. Tech. pers. Assmt.*, 1970, *34*, 201-203.

Kaplan, M. L., Colorelli, N. J., Gross, R. B., Leventhal, D., & Siegel, S. M. *The structural approach in psychological testing*. New York: Pergamon Press, 1970.

Kasmar, J. V., Griffin, W. V., & Mauritzen, J. H. Effect of environmental surroundings on outpatients' mood and perception of psychiatrists. *J. consult. clin. Psychol.,* 1968, *32,* 223-226.

Kasmar, J. V., & Vidulich, R. N. *A factor analytic study of environmental description.* Unpublished report. Los Angeles: Medical Center, University of California, 1968.

Kates, R. W. Perceptual regions and regional perception in flood plain management. *Papers and proceedings of the regional science association,* 1963, *11,* 217-228.

Katz, M. M. A phenomenological typology of schizophrenia. In M. Katz, J. O. Cole & W. E. Barton (Eds.), *The role and methodology of classification in psychiatry and psychopathology.* Washington, D.C.: U.S. Government Printing Office, 1968.

Katz, M. M., Lowery, H. A., & Cole, J. O. Behavior patterns of schizophrenics in the community. In M. Lorr (Ed.), *Explorations in typing psychotics.* Oxford: Pergamon Press, 1966.

Kaufman, H., & Becker, G. M. The empirical determination of game-theoretical strategies. *J. exp. Psychol.,* 1961, *61,* 462-468.

Kay, B. R. Key factors in effective foreman behavior. *Personnel,* 1959, *36,* 25-31.

Kelley, T. L. *Statistical method.* New York: Macmillan Co., 1923.

Kelly, E. L. *Assessment of human characteristics.* Belmont, Calif.: Brooks/Cole, 1967.

Kelly, G. A. *The psychology of personal constructs.* New York: N. W. Norton, 1955.

Kenny, D. T. A theoretical and research reappraisal of stimulus factors in the TAT. In J. Kagan & G. S. Lesser (Eds.), *Contemporary issues in thematic apperceptive methods.* Springfield, Ill.: Charles C. Thomas, 1961. Pp. 288-310.

Kerr, W. A., & Remmers, H. H. *Manual for the American home scale.* Chicago: Science Research Associates, 1942.

Kety, S. S., Javoy, F., Thierry, A. M., Julou, L., & Glowinski, J. A sustained effect of electroconvulsive shock on the turnover of norepinephrine in the central nervous system of the rat. *Proc. Nat. Acad. Sci.,* 1967, *58,* 1249-1254.

Kety, S. S., & Sampson, F. E. Neural properties of the biogenic amines: A report of an NRP work session. *Neurosci. Res. Program Bull.,* 1967, *5,* 1-119.

Keutzer, C. S. Use of therapy time as a reinforcer: Application of operant conditioning techniques within a traditional psychotherapy content. *Behav. res. Ther.,* 1967, *5,* 367-370.

Kiesler, D. J. Some myths of psychotherapy research and the search for a paradigm. *Psychol. Bull.,* 1966, *65,* 110-136.

Kiesler, D. J. Mathieu, P. L., & Klein, M. H. Sampling from the recorded therapy interview: A comparative study of different segment lengths. *J. consult. Psychol.,* 1964, *28,* 349-357.

Kilgard, B. J. A comparison of minimax behavior with observed behavior in a two-person zero-sum game interaction. *Res. Rep.* (Nonr 2794(03)), Tempe, Arizona: Arizona State University, June, 1966.

Kingsley, L. A comparison of the sentence completion responses of psychopaths and prisoners. *J. clin. Psychol.,* 1961, *17* (2), 183-185.

Kinzie, W., & Zimmer, H. On the measurement of hostility, aggression, anxiety, projection, and dependency. *J. proj. Tech. pers. Assmt.,* 1968, *32* (4), 388-391.

Kipnes, D., & Resnick, J. H. Experimental prevention of underachievement among intelligent impulsive college students. *J. consult. clin. Psychol.,* in press.

Kish, G. Cognitive innovation and stimulus-seeking: A study of the correlates of the Obscure Figures Test. *Percept. mot. Skills,* 1970, *30,* 95-101.

Kish, G., & Busse, W. Correlates of stimulus-seeking: Age, education, intelligence, and aptitudes. *J. consult. clin. Psychol.,* 1968, *32,* 633-637.

Kish, G. B., Donnenwerth, G. V. Interests and stimulus-seeking. *J. counsel. Psychol.,* 1969. (a)

Kish, G. B., & Donnenwerth, G. V. The Similes Preference Inventory: The unsuccessful search for construct validity in a clinical setting. *J. clin. Psychol.,* 1969, *25,* 439-442. (b)

Klein, D., & Davis, J. *Diagnosis and drug treatment of psychiatric disorders.* Baltimore, Md.: Williams and Wilkins, 1969.

Klein, E. B., & Solomon, L. Agreement response tendency and behavioral submission in schizophrenia. *Psychol. Rep.,* 1966, *18,* 499-509.

Kleinmuntz, B. *Personality measurement: An introduction.* Homewood, Ill.: Dorsey, 1967.

Kleinmuntz, B. *Clinical information processing by computer.* New York: Holt, Rinehart & Winston, 1969. (a)

Kleinmuntz, B. Personality assessment by computer. *Sci. J.,* 1969, *5,* 59-64. (b)

Klett, C. J. Assessing change in hospitalized psychiatric patients. In P. McReynolds (Ed.), *Advances in psychological assessment.* Vol. 1. Palo Alto, Calif.: Science and Behavior Books, 1968.

Klett, C. J., & Moseley, E. C. The right drug for the right patient. *J. consult. Psychol.,* 1965, *29,* 546-551.

Kline, N. S. Use of *Rauwolfia serpentina* in neuropsychiatric conditions. *Ann. N. Y. Acad. Sci.,* 1954, *59,* 107-132.

Klopfer, W. Correlation of women's Mf scores on the MMPI and Strong VIB. *J. clin. Psychol.,* 1966, *22,* 216.

Knapp, R. R. Relationship of a measure of self-actualization to neuroticism and extraversion. *J. consult. Psychol.,* 1965, *29,* 168-172.

Knapp, R. R., Zimmerman, W. S., Roscoe, D. L., & Michael, W. B. The suggested effects of experience with a college entrance examination on measurable effects of anxiety, depression, and hostility. *Educ. psychol. Measmt.,* 1967, *27* (4, Part 2), 1121-1126.

Knapp, W. M., & Podell, J. E. Mental patients, prisoners, and students with simulated partners in a mixed-motive game. *J. confl. Resol.,* 1968, *12,* 235-241.

Knight, R. P. Evaluation of the results of psychoanalytic therapy. *Amer. J. Psychiat.,* 1941, *98,* 434-446.

Koch, S. Behavior as "intrinsically" regulated: Work notes towards a pre-theory of phenomena called motivational. In M. R. Jones (Ed.), *Nebraska symposium on motivation.* Lincoln, Nebr.: University of Nebraska Press, 1956.

Koe, B. K., & Weissman, A. *P*-Chlorophenylalanine: A specific depletor of brain serotonin. *J. pharmacol. exp. Ther.,* 1966, *154,* 449-516.

Koella, W. What is the functional role of central nervous serotonin? *Neurosci. Res.,* 1968, *2,* 229-251.

Kogan, N., & Wallach, M. *Risk taking: A study in cognition and personality.* New York: Henry Holt, 1964.

Komorita, S. S., & Mechling, J. Betrayal and reconciliation in a two-person game. *J. pers. soc. Psychol.,* 1967, *6,* 349-353.

Koppitz, E. M. Emotional indicators on human figure drawings of shy and aggressive children. *J. clin. Psychol.,* 1966, *22* (4), 466-469.

Kranz, P. What do people do all day? *Behav. Sci.,* 1970, *15,* 286-291.

Krasner, L. Studies of the conditioning of verbal behavior. *Psychol. Bull.,* 1958, *55,* 148-170.

Krivohlavy. J. Experimentalni hry I. (Experimental games: I.) *Ceskoslovenska Psychologie,* 1967, *11,* 209-221. English translation available as MR No. 1042, National Translations Center, The John Crerar Library, 35 West 33rd St., Chicago, Illinois, 60616. (a)

Krivohlavy, J. Experimentalni hry II. (Experimental games: II.). *Ceskoslovenska Psychologie,* 1967, *11,* 301-317. English translation available as MR No. 1033, National Translations Center, The John Crerar Library, 35 West 33rd St., Chicago, Illinois, 60616. (b)

Krout, M. H., & Tabin, J. K. Measuring personality in developmental terms: The personal preference scale. *Gen. psychol. Monogr.,* 1954, *50,* 289-335.

Krumboltz, J. D. Behavioral goals for counseling. *J. counsel. Psychol.,* 1966, *13,* 153-159.

Krumboltz, J. D., & Thoresen, C. E. The effect of behavioral counseling in group and individual settings on information-seeking behavior. *J. counsel. Psychol.,* 1964, *11,* 324-333.

Kuder, G. F. *Kuder preference record—vocational.* Chicago: Science Research Associates, 1953.

Kunca, D. F., & Haywood, N. P. The measurement of motivational orientation in low mental age subjects. *Peabody papers in human development,* 1969, *7,* No. 2.

Lacey, J. I. Psychophysiological approaches to the evaluation of psychotherapeutic process and outcome. In E. A. Rubinstein & M. B. Parloff (Eds.), *Research in psychotherapy.* Vol. 1. Washington, D.C.: American Psychological Association, 1959. Pp. 160-208.

Ladd, C. E. Record-keeping and research in psychiatric and psychological clinics. *J. counsel. Psychol.,* 1967, *14,* 361-367.

LaForge, R., & Suczek, R. F. The interpersonal dimension of personality: III. An interpersonal check list. *J. Pers.,* 1955, *24,* 94-112.

Laird, D. A. Detecting abnormal behavior. *J. abnorm. soc. Psychol.,* 1925, *20,* 128-141. (a)

Laird, D. A. A mental hygiene and vocational test. *J. Educ. Psychol.,* 1925, *16,* 419-422. (b)

Lang, P. J. Fear reduction and fear behavior: Problems in treating a construct. In J. S. Shlien (Ed.), *Research in psychotherapy*. Vol. 3. Washington, D.C.: American Psychological Association, 1968.

Lang, P. J. The mechanics of desensitization and the laboratory study of human fear. In C. M. Franks (Ed.), *Behavior therapy: Appraisal and status*. New York: McGraw-Hill, 1969. Pp. 160-191.

Laska, E. M., Weinstein, A., Logemann, G., Bank, R., & Breuer, F. The use of computers at a state psychiatric hospital. *Comprehensive Psychiat.*, 1967, *8*, 476-490.

Laumann, E. O., & House, J. S. Living room styles and social attributes: The patterning of material artifacts in a modern urban community. *Sociol. soc. Res.*, 1970, *54*, 321-342.

Lave, L. B. Factors affecting co-operation in the Prisoner's Dilemma. *Behav. Sci.*, 1965, *10*, 26-38.

Lazarus, A. A. Group therapy of phobic disorders by systematic desensitization. *J. abnorm. soc. Psychol.*, 1961, *63*, 504-510.

Lazarus, A. A. The results of behavior therapy in one hundred and twenty-six cases of severe neurosis. *Behav. res. Ther.*, 1963, *1*, 69-79.

Lazarus, R. S. A substitutive-defensive conception of apperceptive fantasy. In J. Kagan & G. Lesser (Eds.), *Contemporary issues in thematic apperceptive methods*. Springfield, Ill.: Charles C. Thomas, 1961. Pp. 51-69.

Lazarus, R. S. Storytelling and the measurement of motivation: The direct versus substitutive controversy. *J. consult. Psychol.*, 1966, *30* (6), 483-487.

Leary, T. *Interpersonal diagnosis of personality*. New York: Ronald Press, 1957.

LeBar, F. M. A household survey of economic goods on Romonum Island, Truk. In W. H. Goodenough (Ed.), *Explorations in cultural anthropology: Essays in honor of George P. Murdock*. New York: McGraw-Hill, 1964. Pp. 335-350.

Lefcourt, H. M. Internal versus external control of reinforcement: A review. *Psychol. Bull.*, 1966, *65*, 206-220.

Leibowitz, G. Comparisons of self-report and behavioral techniques of assessing aggression. *J. consult. clin. Psychol.*, 1968, *32*, 21-25.

Lent, J. Personal communication, 1970.

Lentz, T. F. Utilizing opinion for character measurement. *J. soc. Psychol.*, 1930, *1*, 536-542.

Lesser, G. S. The relationship between overt and fantasy aggression as a function of maternal response to aggression. *J. abnorm. soc. Psychol.*, 1957, *55*, 218-221. Reprinted in E. I. Megargee (Ed.), *Research in clinical assessment*. New York: Harper & Row, 1966.

Lesser, G. S., Krawitz, R. N., & Packard, R. Experimental arousal of achievement motivation in adolescent girls. *J. abnorm. soc. Psychol.*, 1963, *66*, 59-66.

Leuba, C. Toward some integration of learning theories: The concept of optimal stimulation. *Psychol. Rep.*, 1955, *1*, 27-33.

Levi, L. The urinary output of adrenalin and noradrenalin during pleasant and unpleasant emotional states. *Psychosom. Med.*, 1965, *27*, 80-85.

Levi, L. Sympatho-adrenomedullary responses to emotional stimuli: Methodologic, physiologic, and pathologic considerations. In E. Bajusz (Ed.), *An Introduction to clinical neuroendocrinology*. Basel, N. Y.: S. Karger, 1966.

Levi, L. Sympatho-adrenomedullary activity, diuresis, and emotional reactions during visual sexual stimulation in human females and males. *Psychosom. Med.*, 1969, *31*, 251-268.

Levin, H., & Wardwell, E. The research uses of doll play. *Psychol. Bull.*, 1962, *89*, 27-56.

Levinson, D. J. An approach to the theory and measurement of ethnocentric ideology. *J. Psychol.*, 1949, *28*, 19-39.

Levis, D. J. The phobic test apparatus: An objective measure of human avoidance behavior to small objects. *Behav. res. Ther.*, 1969, *7*, 309-316.

Levis, D. J., & Carrera, R. Effects of ten hours of implosive therapy in the treatment of outpatients: A preliminary report. *J. abnorm. Psychol.*, 1967, *72*, 504-508.

Levy, L. H. The meaning and generality of perceived actual-ideal discrepancies. *J. consult. Psychol.*, 1956, *20*, 396-398.

Lewin, K. *Field theory in social science*. New York: Harper & Row, 1951.

Lewin, K. Behavior and development as a function of the total situation. In L. Carmichael (Ed.), *Manual of child psychology*. (Rev. ed.). New York: John Wiley, 1954.

Lewin, K., Lippitt, R., & White, R. K. Patterns of aggressive behavior in experimentally created "social climates." *J. soc. Psychol.*, 1939, *10*, 271-299.

Lewinsohn, P. M. Manual of instructions for the behavior ratings used for the observation of interpersonal behavior. Unpublished manuscript, University of Oregon, 1968.

Lewinsohn, P. M., & Atwood, G. E. Depression, a clinical research approach: The case of Mrs. G. *Psychother.*, 1969, *6*, 166-171.

Lewinsohn, P. M., & Shaffer, M. The use of home observation as an integral part of the treatment of depression: Case reports and preliminary findings. *J. consult. clin. Psychol.*, in press.

Lewis, O. The possession of the poor. *Scientif. Amer.*, 1969, *221*, 114-124.

Lichtenstein, E., & Bryan, J. H. Acquiescence and the MMPI: An item reversal approach. *J. abnorm. Psychol.*, 1965, *70*, 290-293.

Lindemann, E., & Finesinger, J. E. The subjective response of psychoneurotic patients to adrenaline and mecholyl (acetyl-B-methyl-choline). *Psychosom. Med.*, 1940, *2*, 231-248.

Lindzey, G. *Projective techniques and cross-cultural research.* New York: Appleton-Century-Crofts, 1961.

Lindzey, G. Seer versus sign. *J. exp. res. Pers.*, 1965, *1* (1), 17-26.

Lingoes, J. C. An IBM-7090 program for Guttman-Lingoes Smallest Space Analysis: I. *Behav. Sci.*, 1965, *10*, 183-184. (a)

Lingoes, J. C. An IBM-7090 program for Guttman-Lingoes Smallest Space Analysis: II. *Behav. Sci.*, 1965, *10*, 487. (b)

Lingoes, J. C. An IBM-7090 program for Guttman-Lingoes Smallest Space Analysis: III. *Behav. Sci.*, 1966, *11*, 75-76. (a)

Lingoes, J. C. An IBM-7090 program for Guttman-Lingoes Multidimensional Scalogram Analysis: I. *Behav. Sci.*, 1966, *11*, 76-78. (b)

Lints, C. E., & Harvey, J. A. Altered sensitivity to footshock and decreased brain content of serotonin following brain lesions in the rat. *J. comp. physiol. Psychol.*, 1969, *67*, 23-31.

Little, K. B., & Shneidman, E. S. Congruencies among interpretations of psychological test and anamnestic data. *Psychol. Monogr.*, 1959, *73*, No. 6 (Whole No. 476).

Litton, R. B., Jr. *Forest landscape description and inventories: A basis for land planning and design.* USDA Forest Service Research Paper PSW-49. Berkeley, Calif.: Pacific Southwest Forest and Range Experiment Station, 1968.

Litton, R. B., Jr., & Twiss, R. H. The forest landscape: Some elements of visual analysis. *Proc. of the Soc. of Amer. Foresters, 1966.* Washington, D.C.: Society of American Foresters, 1967. Pp. 212-214.

Liverant, S. The use of Rotter's social learning theory in developing a personality inventory. *Psychol. Monogr.*, 1958, *72*, No. 2 (Whole No. 455).

Loevinger, J. Objective tests as instruments of psychological theory. *Psychol. Rep.*, 1957, *3*, 635-694. Reprinted in D. N. Jackson & S. Messick (Eds.), *Problems in human assessment.* New York: McGraw-Hill, 1967. Pp. 78-123.

Longstreth, L. E. The relationship between expectations and frustration in children. *Child Develpm.*, 1960, *31*, 667-671.

Loomis, J. L. Communication, the development of trust, and cooperative behavior. *Hum. Relns.*, 1959, *12*, 305-316.

Lopez, F. M. Jr., Evaluating executive decision-making: The in-basket technique. *AMA Research Study 75.* New York: American Management Association, 1966.

LoPiccolo, J. Effective components of systematic desensitization. Doctoral dissertation, Yale University, 1969.

Lord, F. M., & Novick, M. R. *Statistical theories of mental test scores.* Reading, Mass.: Addison-Wesley, 1968.

Lorenz, K. *On aggression.* New York: Bantam, 1966. Abridgement reprinted in E. I. Megargee & J. E. Hokanson (Eds.), *The dynamics of aggression.* New York: Harper & Row, 1970.

Lorr, M. Rating scales and check lists for the evaluation of psychopathology. *Psychol. Bull.*, 1954, *51*, 119-127.

Lorr, M. (Ed.) *Explorations in typing psychotics.* Oxford: Pergamon Press, 1966.

Lorr, M. & Cave, R. L. The equivalence of psychotic syndromes across two media. *Multivariate behav. Res.*, 1966, *1*, 189-195.

Lorr, M., Daston, P., & Smith, J. R. An analysis of mood states. *Educ. psychol. Measmt.*, 1967, *27*, 89-96.

Lorr, M., & Hamlin, R. M. A multimethod factor analysis of behavioral and objective measures of psychopathology. *J. consult. clin. Psychol.*, 1971, *36*, 136-141.

Lorr, M., Jenkins, R. L., & O'Connor, J. P. Factors descriptive of psychopathology and behavior of hospitalized psychotics. *J. abnorm. soc. Psychol.*, 1955, *50*, 78-86.

Lorr, M., & Klett, C. J. Constancy of psychotic syndromes in men and women. *J. consult. Psychol.,* 1965, *29,* 309-313.

Lorr, M., & Klett, C. J. Major psychotic disorders. A cross-cultural study. *Arch. gen. Psychiat.,* 1968, *19,* 652-658.

Lorr, M., & Klett, C. J. Psychotic behavioral types. *Arch. gen. Psychiat.,* 1969, *20,* 592-597. (a)

Lorr, M., & Klett, C. J. Cross-cultural comparison of psychotic syndromes. *J. abnorm. Psychol.,* 1969, *74,* 531-543. (b)

Lorr, M., Klett, C. J., & Cave, R. L. Higher level psychotic syndromes. *J. abnorm. Psychol.,* 1967, *72,* 74-77.

Lorr, M. Klett, C. J., & McNair, D. M. *Syndromes of psychosis.* Oxford: Pergamon Press, 1963.

Lorr, M., Klett, C. J., McNair, D. M., & Lasky, J. J. *Inpatient multidimensional psychiatric scale: Manual.* Palo Alto, Calif.: Consulting Psychologists Press, 1962.

Lorr, M., & McNair, D. M. Methods relating to evaluation of therapeutic outcome. In L. A. Gottschalk & A. H. Auerbach (Eds.), *Methods of research in psychotherapy.* New York: Appleton-Century-Crofts, 1966. Pp. 573-594.

Lorr, M., McNair, D. M., Klett, C. J., & Lasky, J. J. Evidence of ten psychotic syndromes. *J. consult. Psychol.,* 1962, *26,* 185-189.

Lorr, M., McNair, D. M., Michaux, W. M., & Raskin, A. Frequency of treatment and change in psychotherapy. *J. abnorm. soc. Psychol.,* 1962, *64,* 281-292.

Lorr, M., O'Connor, J. P., & Stafford, J. W. Confirmation of nine psychotic symptom patterns. *J. clin. Psychol.,* 1957, *13,* 252-257.

Lorr, M., & Radhakrishnan, B. K. A comparison of two methods of cluster analysis. *Educ. psychol. Measmt.,* 1967, *27,* 47-53.

Lorr, M., Sonn, T. M., & Katz, M. M. Toward a definition of depression. *Arch. gen. Psychiat.,* 1967, *17,* 183-186.

Lorr, M., & Vestre, N. D. The psychotic inpatient profile: A nurse's observation scale. *J. clin. Psychol.,* 1969, *25,* No. 2, 137-140.

Loussef, Z. J. The role of race, sex, hostility, and verbal stimulus in inflicting punishment. *Psychon. Sci.,* 1968, *12* (6), 285-286.

Lövass, O. L. Effect of exposure to symbolic aggression on aggressive behavior. *Child Developm.,* 1961, *32,* 37-44.

Lowenthal, D. *An analysis of environmental perception.* Interim Report. Washington, D.C.: Resources for the Future, Inc., 1967.

Lubin, B. Adjective check lists for the measurement of depression. *Arch. gen. Psychiat.,* 1965, *12,* 57-62.

Luborsky, L., & Strupp, H. H. Research problems in psychotherapy: A three year follow-up. In H. H. Strupp & L. Luborsky (Eds.), *Research in psychotherapy.* Washington, D.C.: American Psychological Association, 1962.

Luce, R. D., & Raiffa, H. *Games and decisions.* New York: John Wiley, 1957.

Lutzker, D. R. Internationalism as a predictor of cooperative game behavior. *J. confl. Resol.,* 1960, *4,* 426-430.

Lutzker, D. R. Sex role, cooperation, and competition in a two-person, non-zero sum-game. *J. confl. Resol.,* 1961, *5,* 366-368.

Lyerly, S. B., & Abbott, P. S. *Handbook of psychiatric rating scales (1950-1964).* Washington, D.C.: U.S. Government Printing Office, 1966.

Maas, J. W., & Landis, D. H. *In vivo* studies of the metabolism of norepinephrine in the central nervous system. *J. pharmacol. exp. Ther.,* 1968, *163,* 147-162.

Machover, K. *Personality projection in the drawing of the human figure.* Springfield, Ill.: Charles C. Thomas, 1949.

Mackay, C. *Extraordinary popular delusions and the madness of crowds.* Wells, Vt.: Fraser, 1932.

MacKinnon, D. W. Assessing creative persons. *J. creat. Behav.,* 1967, *1,* 291-304.

Maddi, S. R., & Berne, N. Novelty of productions and desire for novelty as active and passive forms of the need for variety. *J. Pers.,* 1964, *32,* 270-277.

Maddi, S. R., Charlens, A. M., Maddi, D., & Smith, A. J. Effects of monotony and novelty on imaginative productions. *J. Pers.,* 1962, *30,* 513-527.

Maddi, S. R., Propst, B. S., & Feldinger, I. Three expressions of the need for variety. *J. Pers.,* 1965, *33,* 82-98.

Madsen, C. H., Jr., Becker, W. C., & Thomas, D. R. Rules, phrase and ignoring: Elements of elementary classroom control. *J. appl. behav. Anal.,* 1968, *1,* 139-150.

Mahrer, A. R. *New approaches to personality classification.* New York: Columbia University Press, 1969.

Malmejac, J. Activity of the adrenal medulla and its regulation. *Physiol. Rev.*, 1964, *44*, 186-218.

Mandell, A. J., & Mandell, M. P. *Psychochemical research in man—methods, strategy, and theory.* New York: Academic Press, 1969.

Mandell, A. J., & Spooner, C. E. Psychochemical research studies in man. *Sci.*, 1968, *162*, 1442-1453.

Mandler, G., & Sarason, S. B. A study of anxiety and learning. *J. abnorm. soc. Psychol.*, 1952, *47*, 166-173.

Manshardt, J., & Wurtman, R. J. Daily rhythm in the noradrenaline content of rat hypothalamus. *Nature*, 1968, *217*, 574-575.

Marañon, G. A contribution to the study of the action of adrenalin on the emotions. *Revue Française D'Endocrinologie*, 1924, *2*, 301-325.

Margules, D. L., & Stein, L. Cholinergic synapses in the ventromedial hypothalamus for the suppression of operant behavior by punishment and satiety. *J. comp. physiol. Psychol.*, 1969, *67*, 327-335.

Marks, P. A., & Seeman, W. *The actuarial description of abnormal behavior.* Baltimore, Md.: Williams & Wilkins, 1963.

Marlowe, D. Some personality and behavioral correlates of conformity. Ph.D. dissertation, Ohio State University. Ann Arbor, Mich.: University Microfilms, 1959. Order No. UM 59-5919.

Marlowe, D. Psychological needs and cooperation-competition in a two-person game. *Psychol. Rep.*, 1963, *13*, 364.

Marlowe, D., & Kalin, R. The effects of inter-group competition, personal drinking habits, and frustration on intra-group cooperation. Paper presented at Western Psychological Association meetings, March, 1968.

Martin, B. Expression and inhibition of sex motive arousal in college males. *J. abnorm. soc. Psychol.*, 1964, *68*, 307-312.

Martin, H. G. The construction of the Guilford-Martin inventory of factors G-A-M-I-N. *J. appl. Psychol.*, 1945, *29*, 298-300.

Martin, M. L., Weinstein, M. S., & Lewinsohn, P. M. The use of home observations as an integral part of the treatment of depression: The case of Mrs. B. Unpublished manuscript, University of Oregon, 1968.

Marwell, G., Ratcliff, K., & Schmitt, D. R. Minimizing differences in a maximizing differences game. *J. pers. soc. Psychol.*, 1969, *12*, 158-163.

Marwell, G., & Schmitt, D. R. Are trivial games most interesting psychologically? *Behav. Sci.*, 1968, *13*, 125-128.

Masling, J. The influence of situational and interpersonal variables in projective testing. *Psychol. Bull.*, 1960, *57*, 65-85.

Maslow, A. H. *Motivation and personality.* New York: Harper, 1954.

Maslow, A. H. Deficiency motivation and growth motivation. In M. R. Jones (Ed.), *Nebraska symposium on motivation.* Lincoln, Nebr.: University of Nebraska Press, 1955.

Maslow, A. H., Hirsh, E., Stein, M., & Honigmann, I. A clinically derived test for measuring psychological security-insecurity. *J. gen. Psychol.*, 1945, *33*, 21-41.

Mason, J. W. A review of psychoendocrine research on the sympathetic—adrenal medullary system. *Psychosom. Med.*, 1968, *30*, 631-653.

Masterson, S. The sensation-seeking scale: a review and critique. Unpublished manuscript, 1970. (a)

Masterson, S. Cognitive innovation, rigidity, and sensation-seeking among college students. Unpublished manuscript, 1970. (b)

Masterson, S. Cognitive innovation in children. M.A. thesis, University of Nevada, Reno, 1970. (c)

Mathews, E. A study of emotional stability in children. *J. Delin.*, 1923, *8*, 1-40.

Matsushima, J. An instrument for classifying impulse control in boys. *J. consult. Psychol.*, 1964, *28*, 87-90.

Maw, W. H. *A definition of curiosity: A factor analysis study.* Cooperative Research Project (No. S-109), U.S. Office of Educ., 1967.

Maw, W. H. Differences in the personalities of children differing in curiosity. Presented at Symposium on Intrinsic Motivation in Education, Ontario Institute for Studies in Education, Toronto, 1970.

Maw, W. H., & Maw, E. W. Nonhomeostatic experiences as stimuli of children with high curiosity. *Calif. J. educ. Res.*, 1961, *12*, 57-61.

Maw, W. H., & Maw, E. W. Selection of unbalanced and unusual designs by children high and low in curiosity. *Child Develpm.*, 1962, *33*, 917-922.

Maw, W. H., & Maw, E. W. The differences between the scores of children with high curiosity and children with low curiosity on a test of general information. *J. educ. Res.*, 1963, *57*, 76-79.

Maw, W. H., & Maw, E. W. *An exploratory investigation into the measurement of curiosity in elementary school children.* Cooperative Research Project (No. 801), U.S. Office of Educ., 1964.

Maw, W. H., & Maw, E. W. *Personal and social variables differentiating children with high and low curiosity.* Cooperative Research Project (No. 1511), U.S. Office of Educ., 1965.

Maynert, E. W., & Levy, R. Stress-induced release of brain norepinephrine and its inhibition by drugs. *J. pharmacol. exp. Ther.*, 1964, *143*, 90-95.

McCarroll, J. E., Mitchell, K. M., Carpenter, R. J., & Anderson, J. P. Analysis of three stimulation-seeking scales. *Psychol. Rep.*, 1967, *21*, 853-856.

McClelland, D. C. Longitudinal trends in the relation of thought to action. *J. consult. Psychol.*, 1966, *30* (6), 479-483.

McClelland, D., Atkinson, J. W., Clark, R. A., & Lowell, E. L. *The achievement motive.* New York: Appleton-Century-Crofts, 1953.

McClelland, D. C., Clark, R. A., Roby, T., & Atkinson, J. W. The projective expression of needs, IV: The effect of the need for achievement on thematic apperception. *J. exp. Psychol.*, 1949, *39*, 242-255.

McClintock, C. G., Gallo, P. S., & Harrison, A. A. Some effects of variations in other's strategy upon game behavior. *J. pers. soc. Psychol.*, 1965, *1*, 319-325.

McClintock, C. G., & McNeel, S. P. Cross cultural comparisons of interpersonal motives. *Sociometry*, 1966, *29*, 406-427. (a)

McClintock, C. G., & McNeel, S. P. Reward and score feedback as determinants of cooperative and competitive game behavior. *J. pers. soc. Psychol.*, 1966, *4*, 606-613. (b)

McClintock, C. G., & McNeel, S. P. Prior dyadic experience and monetary reward as determinants of cooperative and competitive game behavior. *J. pers. soc. Psychol.*, 1967, *5*, 282-294.

McCully, R. S. Current attitudes about projective techniques in APA approved internship centers. *J. proj. Tech. pers. Assmt.*, 1965, *27*, 271-280.

McFall, R. M. The effects of self-monitoring on normal smoking behavior. *J. consult. clin. Psychol.*, in press.

McFarland, R. A., & Seitz, C. P. A psychosomatic inventory. *J. appl. Psychol.*, 1938, *22*, 327-339.

McGee, S. Measurement of hostility: A pilot study. *J. clin. Psychol.*, 1954, *10*, 280-282.

McGeer, E. G., & Peters, D. A. V. *In vitro* screen of inhibitions of rat brain serotonin synthesis. *Canad. J. Biochem.*, 1969, *47*, 501-506.

McKee, J. P., & Turner, W. S. The relationship of "drive" ratings in adolescence to CPI and EPPS scores in adulthood. *Vita Humana*, 1961, *4* (1-2), 1-14.

McKeown, D. C., Gahagan, J. P., & Tedeschi, J. T. The effect of prior power strategy on behavior after a shift of power. *J. exp. res. in Pers.*, 1967, *2*, 226-233.

McNair, D. M., Callahan, D. M., & Lorr, M. Therapist "type" and patient response to psychotherapy. *J. consult. Psychol.*, 1962, *26*, 425-429.

McNair, D. M., & Lorr, M. An analysis of mood in neurotics. *J. abnorm. soc. Psychol.*, 1964, *69*, 620-627.

McReynolds, P. Perceptualization: a restricted theory of human motivation. Paper presented at Annual Meeting, Amer. Assoc. for Advan. of Sci., Berkeley, Calif., 1954.

McReynolds, P. A restricted conceptualization of human anxiety and motivation. *Psychol. Rep.*, 1956, *2*, 293-312.

McReynolds, P. Anxiety, perception, and schizophrenics. In D. Jackson (Ed.), *The etiology of schizophrenics.* New York: Basic Books, 1960. Pp. 248-292.

McReynolds, P. Exploratory behavior: a theoretical interpretation. *Psychol. Rep.*, 1962, *11*, 311-318.

McReynolds, P. Reactions to novel and familiar stimuli as a function of schizophrenic withdrawal. *Percept. mot. Skills*, 1963, *16*, 847-850.

McReynolds, P. Toward a theory of fun. *Amer. Psychologist*, 1964, *19*, 551-552.

McReynolds, P. The concept evaluation technique: A survey of research. *J. gen. Psychol.*, 1966, *74*, 217-230.

McReynolds, P. An introduction to psychological assessment. In P. McReynolds (Ed.), *Advances in psychological assessment.* Vol. 1. Palo Alto, Calif.: Science and Behavior Books, 1968. Pp. 1-13.

McReynolds, P. The Assessment of anxiety: A survey of available techniques. In P. McReynolds (Ed.), *Advances in psychological assessment.* Vol. 1. Palo Alto, Calif.: Science and Behavior Books, 1968. Pp. 244-264.

McReynolds, P. The three faces of cognitive motivation. Presented at Symposium on Intrinsic Motivation in Education, Ontario Institute for Studies in Education, Toronto, 1970. (a)

McReynolds, P. Motivational characteristics of newly admitted schizophrenics. Unpublisted manuscript, 1970. (b)

McReynolds, P. Behavioral choice as a function of novelty-seeking and anxiety-avoiding motivations. *Psychol. Rep.,* in press.

McReynolds, P., & Acker, M. The obscure figures test, Form I: Manual for administration and scoring. Unpublished manuscript, 1968.

McReynolds, P., & Pietla, C. Relation of object curiosity to psychological adjustment in children. *Child. Develpm.,* 1961, *32,* 393-400.

McReynolds, P., & Bryan, J. Tendency to obtain new percepts as a function of the level of unassimilated percepts. *Percept. mot. Skills,* 1956, *6,* 183-186.

McReynolds, P., & Guevara, C. Attitudes of schizophrenics and normals toward success and failure. *J. abnorm. soc. Psychol.,* 1967, *72,* 303-310.

Megargee, E. I. The utility of the Rosenzweig picture-frustration study in detecting assaultiveness among juvenile delinquents. Paper presented at the meeting of the Southwestern Psychological Association, San Antonio, Texas, April, 1964.

Megargee, E. I. Assault with intent to kill. *Trans-Action,* 1965, *2* (6), 27-31. (a)

Megargee, E. I. The relation between Barrier scores and aggressive behavior. *J. abnorm. Psychol.,* 1965, *70,* 307-311. (b)

Megargee, E. I. (Ed.) *Research in clinical assessment.* New York: Harper & Row, 1966. (a)

Megargee, E. I. Undercontrolled and overcontrolled personality types in extreme antisocial aggression. *Psychol. Monogr.,* 1966, *80,* No. 3 (Whole No. 611). (b)

Megargee, E. I. Hostility on the TAT as a function of defensive inhibition and stimulus situation. *J. proj. Tech. pers. Assmt.,* 1967, *31,* 73-79.

Megargee, E. I. Conscientious objectors' scores on the MMPI *O-H* (over-controlled hostility) scale. *Proc. 77 Ann. Conv. Amer. Psychol. Assoc.,* Washington, D.C.: American Psychological Association, 1969. Pp. 507-508. (a)

Megargee, E. I. The psychology of violence: A critical review of theories of violence. In D. J. Mulvihill & M. M. Tumin (Eds.), *Crimes of violence: A staff report to the National Commission on the Causes and Prevention of Violence.* N.C.C.P.V. Staff Report Series, Vol. 13. Washington, D.C.: U.S. Government Printing Office, 1969. Pp. 1037-1115. (b)

Megargee, E. I. The prediction of violence from psychological tests. In C. D. Spielberger (Ed.), *Current topics in clinical and community psychology.* Vol. 2. New York: Academic Press, 1971. (a)

Megargee, E. I. Role of inhibition in the assessment and understanding of violence. In J. E. Singer (Ed.), *Cognitive and psychological factors in aggression.* New York: Little, Brown, in press. (b)

Megargee, E. I., & Cook, P. E. The relation of TAT and inkblot aggressive content scales with each other and with criteria or overt aggression in juvenile delinquents. *J. proj. Tech. pers. Assmt.,* 1967, *31* (1), 48-60.

Megargee, E. I., Cook, P. E., & Mendelsohn, G. A. Development and validation of an MMPI scale of assaultiveness in overcontrolled individuals. *J. abnorm. Psychol.,* 1967, *72,* 519-528.

Megargee, E. I., & Hokanson, J. E. (Eds.) *The dynamics of aggression: Individual, group, and international analyses.* New York: Harper & Row, 1970.

Megargee, E. I., & Mendelsohn, G. A. A cross validation of 12 MMPI indices of hostility and control. *J. abnorm. soc. Psychol.,* 1962, *65,* 431-438. Reprinted in E. I. Megargee (Ed.), *Research in clinical assessment.* New York: Harper & Row, 1966.

Megargee, E. I., & Parker, G. V. C. An exploration of Murrayan needs as assessed by the adjective check list, the TAT, and the Edwards Personal Preference Schedule. *J. clin. Psychol.,* 1968, *24,* 47-51.

Melloan, G. Young men move into executive suite faster at many companies. *The Wall Street Journal,* August 26, 1966.

Melmon, K. L. Catecholamines and the adrenal medulla. In R. Williams (Ed.), *Textbook of Endocrinology.* Philadelphia, Penn.: Saunders, 1968. Pp. 379-403.

Mendelson, J., Kubzansky, P., Leiderman, P. H., Wexler, D., DuToit, C., & Solomon, P. Catecholamine excretion and behavior during sensory deprivation. *A. M. A. arch. gen. Psychiat.,* 1960, *2,* 147-155.

Merenda, P. F., & Clark, W. V. Relationships among AVA and ACL scales as measured on a sample of college students. *J. clin. Psychol.,* 1968, *24* (1), 52-60.

Messe, L. A., & Sawyer, J. Unexpected cooperation: The Prisoner's Dilemma resolved? Paper presented at Midwestern Psychological Association, Chicago, May, 1966.

Messick, D. M., & McClintock, C. G. Motivational bases of choice in experimental games. *J. exp. soc. Psychol.*, 1968, *4*, 1-25.

Messick, D. M., & Thorngate, W. B. Relative gain maximization in experimental games. *J. exp. soc. Psychol.*, 1967, *3*, 85-101.

Messick, S., & Jackson, D. N. Acquiescence and the factorial interpretation of the MMPI. *Psychol. Bull.*, 1961, *58*, 299-304.

Meyer, H. H., Walker, W. B., & Litwin, G. H. Motive patterns and risk preferences associated with entrepreneurship. *J. abnorm. soc. Psychol.*, 1961, *63*, 570-574.

Meyerson, L., Kerr, N., & Michael, J. L. Behavior modification in rehabilitation. In S. W. Bijou & D. M. Baer (Eds.), *Child development: Readings in experimental analysis.* New York: Appleton-Century-Crofts, 1967. Pp. 214-239.

Miles, C. C. Sex in social psychology. In C. Murchison (Ed.), *Handbook of social psychology.* Worcester, Mass.: Clark University Press, 1935. Pp. 683-797.

Miller, F. P., Cox, R. H., Jr., & Maickel, R. P. Intrastrain differences in serotonin and norepinephrine in discrete areas of rat brain. *Sci.*, 1968, *162*, 463-464.

Miller, G. A. Assessment of psychotechnology. *Amer. Psychologist*, 1970, *25*, 991-1001.

Miller, H., & Baruch, D. W. A study of hostility in allergic children. *Amer. J. Orthopsychiat.*, 1950, *20*, 506-519.

Miller, L., Spilka, B., & Pratt, S. Manifest anxiety and hostility in "criminally insane" patients. *J. clin. exp. Psychopath.*, 1960, *21*, 41-48.

Miller, N. E. Theory and experiment relating psychoanalytic displacement to stimulus-response generalization. *J. abnorm. Psychol.*, 1948, *43*, 155-178.

Miller, R. R. No play: A means of conflict resolution. *J. pers. soc. Psychol.*, 1967, *6*, 150-156.

Mills, H. D. The research use of projective techniques: A seventeen year survey. *J. proj. Tech. pers. Assmt.*, 1965, *29*, 513-515.

Minas, J. S., Scodel, A., Marlowe, D., & Rawson, H. Some descriptive aspects of two-person non-zero-sum games: II. *J. confl. Resol.*, 1960, *4*, 193-197.

Mischel, W. *Personality and assessment.* New York: John Wiley, 1968.

Mizushima, K., & DeVos, G. An application of the California Psychological Inventory in a study of Japanese delinquency. *J. soc. Psychol.*, 1967, *71*, 45-51.

Model-railroad marriage therapy. *Life*, Oct. 6, 1967, *63*, 93-95.

Moldawsky, P. A study of personality variables in patients with skin disorders. Doctoral dissertation, State University of Iowa, 1953. (Reported in Buss, 1961).

Molof, M. J. Differences between assaultive and non-assaultive juvenile offenders in the California Youth Authority. Research report no. 51, Division of Research, State of California, Department of the Youth Authority, Feb.., 1967.

Montgomery, K. C. "Spontaneous alteration" as a function of time between trials and amount of work. *J. exp. Psychol.*, 1951, *42*, 82-93.

Moore, N. I. Cognitive styles and the schizophrenics. Ph.D. dissertation, University of California, Berkeley, Calif., 1970.

Moore, T. V. The essential psychoses and their fundamental syndromes. *Stud. psychol. Psychiat.*, 1933, *3*, 1-28.

Moos, R. H. Behavioral effects of being observed: Reactions to a wireless radio transmitter. *J. consult. clin. Psychol.*, 1968, *32*, 383-388.

Moos, R. H., Harris, R., & Schonborn, K. Psychiatric patients and staff reaction to their physical environments. *J. clin. Psychol.*, 1969, *25*, 322-324.

Moos, R. H., & Houts, P. S. Assessment of the social atmospheres of psychiatric wards. *J. abnorm. Psychol.*, 1968, *73*, 595-604.

Moran, L. J., Kimble, J. P., Jr., & Mefferd, R. B., Jr. Repetitive psychometric measures: Memory-for-faces. *Psychol. Rep.*, 1960, *7*, 407-413.

Morgan, C., & Murray, H. A. A method for investigating phantasies: The Thematic Apperception Test. *Arch. neurol. Psychiat.*, 1935, *34*, 289-306.

Morgan, M., & Mandell, A. J. Indole(ethyl)amine N-methyltransferase in the brain. *Sci.*, 1969, *165*, 492-493.

Morris, D. *The naked ape.* New York: McGraw-Hill, 1967.

Mosher, D. L., Mortimer, R. L., & Grebel, M. Verbal aggressive behavior in delinquent boys. *J. abnorm. soc. Psychol.*, 1968, *73* (5), 454-460.

Moss, H. A., & Kagan, J. Stability of achievement- and recognition-seeking behavior from early childhood through adulthood. *J. abnorm. soc. Psychol.*, 1961, *62*, 504-513.

Muench, G. A. The assessment of counseling and psychotherapy: Some problems and trends. In P. McReynolds (Ed.), *Advances in psychological assessment*. Vol. 1. Palo Alto, Calif.: Science and Behavior Books, 1968. Pp. 205-222.

Munsinger, H., & Kessen, W. Uncertainty, structure, and preference. *Psychol. Monogr.*, 1964, *78*, No. 9.

Murdoch, P. Exploitation-accommodation and social responsibility in a bargaining game. *J. Pers.*, 1968, *36*, 440-453.

Murphy, G. *Personality: a biosocial approach to origins and structure*. New York: Harper, 1947.

Murray, E. J. *Motivation and emotion*. Englewood Cliffs, N.J.: Prentice-Hall, 1964.

Murray, H. A. *Explorations in personality*. New York: Oxford University Press, 1938.

Murray, H. A., & Kluckhohn, C. Outline of a conception of personality. In C. Kluckhohn & H. A. Murray (Eds.), *Personality in nature, society, and culture*. (2nd ed.) New York: Knopf, 1953.

Murray, H. A., & McKinnon, D. W. Assessment of OSS personnel. *J. consult. Psychol.*, 1946, *10*, 76-80.

Murstein, B. I. The projection of hostility on the Rorschach and as a result of ego threat. *J. proj. Tech. pers. Assmt.*, 1956, *20*, 418-428.

Murstein, B. I. *Theory and research in projective techniques (emphasizing the TAT)*. New York: John Wiley, 1963.

Murstein, B. I. A normative study of TAT ambiguity. *J. proj. Tech. pers. Assmt.*, 1964, *28*, 210-218.

Murstein, B. I. (Ed.) *Handbook of projective techniques*. New York: Basic Books, 1965. (a)

Murstein, B. I. New thought about ambiguity and the TAT. *J. proj. Tech. pers. Assmt.*, 1965, *28*, 219-225. (b)

Murstein, B. I. Projection of hostility on the TAT as a function of stimulus, background, and personality variables. *J. consult. Psychol.*, 1965, *29*, 43-48. (c)

Murstein, B. I. Assumptions, adaptation level, and projective techniques. *Percept. mot. Skills*, 1961, *12*, 107-125. Reprinted in E. I. Megargee (Ed.), *Research in clinical assessment*. New York: Harper & Row, 1966.

Murstein, B. I. Discussion for current status of some projective techniques. *J. proj. Tech. pers. Assmt.*, 1968, *32* (3), 229-232. (a)

Murstein, B. I. Effect of stimulus, background, personality, and scoring system on the manifestation of hostility on the TAT. *J. consult. clin. Psychol.*, 1968, *32*, 355-365. (b)

Murstein, B. I. Comment on "the ambiguity of the TAT ambiguity." *J. proj. Tech. pers. Assmt.*, 1969, *33*, 483-485.

Murstein, B. I., & Collier, H. L. The role of the TAT in the measurement of achievement as a function of expectancy. *J. proj. Tech.*, 1962, *26* (1), 96-101.

Murstein, B. I., David, C., Fisher, D., & Furth, H. G. The scaling of the TAT for hostility by a variety of scaling methods. *J. consult. Psychol.*, 1961, *25*, 497-504.

Mussen, P. H., & Naylor, H. K. The relationships between overt and fantasy aggression. *J. abnorm. soc. Psychol.*, 1954, *49*, 235-240.

Mussen, P. H., & Rutherford, E. Effects of aggressive cartoons on children's aggressive play. *J. abnorm. soc. Psychol.*, 1961, *62*, 461-464.

Naar, R. An attempt to differentiate delinquents from non-delinquents on the basis of projective drawings. *J. crim. Law, criminol. & Police Sci.*, 1964, *55* (1), 107-110.

Neill, J. A., & Jackson, D. N. An evaluation of item selection strategies in personality scale construction. *Educ. psychol. Measmt.*, 1970, in press.

Nelson, C. H. *Measurement and evaluation in the classroom*. New York: Macmillan Co., 1970.

Nelson, J. T., & Epstein, S. Relationships among three measures of conflict over hostility. *J. consult. Psychol.*, 1962, *26*, 345-350.

Neuringer, C. A variety of thematic methods. In A. I. Rabin (Ed.), *Projective techniques in personality assessment*. New York: Springer, 1968.

Newell, A., Shaw, J. C., & Simon, H. A. Elements of a theory of problem-solving. *Psychol. Rev.*, 1958, *65*, 151-166.

Neymann, C. A., & Kohlstedt, K. D. A new diagnostic test for introversion-extroversion, *J. abnorm. soc. Psychol.*, 1929, *23*, 482-487.

Nichols, R. C. Subtle, obvious, and stereotype measures of masculinity-femininity. *Educ. Psychol. Measmt.*, 1962, *22*, 449-461.

Nichols, R. C., & Schnell, R. R. Factor scales for the California psychological inventory. *J. consult. Psychol.*, 1963, *27*, 228-235.

Noble, E. P., Wurtman, R. J., & Axelrod, J. A simple and rapid method for injecting H³-norepinephrine into the lateral ventricle of the rat brain. *Life Sci.,* 1967, *6* (Part 1) 281-293.

Norman, W. T. Relative importance of test item content. *J. consult. Psychol.,* 1963, *27,* 166-174.

Nowlis, V. The development and modification of motivational systems in personality. In *Current theory and research in motivation.* Lincoln, Nebr.: University of Nebraska Press, 1953. Pp. 114-138.

Nowlis, V., & Nowlis, H. H. The description and analysis of mood. *Ann. New York Acad. Sci.,* 1956, *55,* 345-355.

Nunnally, J. C. *Introduction to psychological measurement.* New York: McGraw-Hill, 1970.

Nuttall, R. L. Some correlates of high need for achievement among urban northern Negroes. *J. abnorm. soc. Psychol.,* 1964, *68,* 593-600.

Ober, D. C. Modification of smoking behavior. *J. consult. clin. Psychol.,* 1968, *32,* 543-549.

Office of Strategic Services (OSS) Assessment Staff. *Assessment of men.* New York: Holt, Rinehart, & Winston, 1948.

O'Hanlon, J., Campuzano, H., & Horvath, S. A fluorometric assay for subnanogram concentrations of adrenaline and noradrenaline in plasma. *Anal. Biochem.,* 1970, *34,* 568-581.

Okel, E., & Mosher, D. L. Changes in affective states as a function of guilt over aggressive behavior. *J. consult. clin. Psychol.,* 1968, *32* (3), 265-270.

Olds, J. The influence of practice on the strength of secondary approach drives. *J. exp. Psychol.,* 1953, *46,* 232-236.

Olds, J. *The growth and structure of motives.* New York: Free Press, 1956.

Olds, J. Hypothalamic substrates of reward. *Physiol. Rev.,* 1962, *42,* 554-604.

Olds, J., & Milner, P. Positive reinforcement produced by electrical stimulation of septal area and other regions of rat brain. *J. comp. physiol. Psychol.,* 1954, *47,* 419-427.

Olds, M. E., & Domino, E. F. Comparison of muscarinic and nicotinic cholinergic agonists on self-stimulation behavior. *J. pharmacol. exp. Ther.,* 1969, *166,* 189-204.

O'Leary, K. D. Diagnosis of children's behavior problems. In H. C. Quay & J. S. Werry (Eds.), *Behavior disorders of children.* New York: John Wiley, in press.

O'Leary, K. D., O'Leary, S. G., & Becker, W. C. Modification of a deviant sibling inter-action pattern in the home. *Behav. res. Ther.,* 1967, *5,* 113-120.

Olsson, R., & Roos, B. E. Concentrations of 5-hydroxyindoleacetic acid and homovanillic acid in the cerebrospinal fluid after treatment with probenecid in patients with Parkinson's disease. *Nature,* 1968, *219,* 502-503.

Orne, M. T. On the social psychology of the psychological experiment: With particular reference to demand characteristics and their implications. *Amer. Psychologist,* 1962, *17,* 776-783.

Orso, D. P. Comparison of achievement and affiliation arousal on n ach. *J. proj. Tech. pers. Assmt.,* 1969, *33,* 230-233.

Osgood, C. E., Suci, G., & Tannenbaum, P. H. *The measurement of meaning.* Urbana, Ill.: University of Illinois Press, 1957.

Overall, J. E. Configural analysis of psychiatric diagnostic stereotypes. *Behav. Sci.,* 1963, *8,* 211-219. (a)

Overall, J. E. Dimensions of manifest depression. *J. psychiat. Res.,* 1963, *1,* 239-245. (b)

Overall, J. E., Bailly, R., & Pichot, P. Stereotypes of psychiatric diagnosis of psychoses by French psychiatrists: A comparison with American stereotypes. In Proceedings Fifth International Congress: Collegium Internationale Neuro-Psychopharmacologium, 1968.

Overall, J. E., & Hollister, L. E. Computer procedures for psychiatric classification. *J. Amer. med. Assoc.,* 1964, *187,* 583-588.

Overall, J. E., & Hollister, L. E. Nosology of depression and differential response to drugs. *Multidiscipline Res. Forum,* JAMA, 1966, *195,* March, 1966.

Overall, J. E., & Hollister, L. E. Studies of quantitative approaches to psychiatric classi-fication. In M. M. Katz, J. O. Cole, & W. E. Burton (Eds.), *The role and methodology of classification in psychiatry and psychopathology.* Washington, D.C.: U.S. Govern-ment Printing Office, 1968.

Overall, J. E., Hollister, L. E., & Pichot, P. Major psychiatric disorders. *Arch. gen. Psychiat.,* 1967, *16,* 146-151.

Pace, C. R. The measurement of college environments. In R. Tagiuri & G. H. Litwin (Eds.), *Organizational climate: Explorations of a concept.* Boston, Mass.: Graduate School of Business Administration, Harvard University, 1968. Pp. 129-150.

Page, I. H. *Serotonin.* Chicago: New York Book Medical Publishers, 1968.
Palmer, J. O. *The psychological assessment of children.* New York: John Wiley, 1970.
Panton, J. H. Predicting prison adjustment with the MMPI. *J. clin. Psychol.,* 1958, *14,* 308-312.
Pascal, G. R., & Zax, M. Psychotherapeutics: Success or failure. *J. consult. Psychol.,* 1956, *20,* 325-331.
Patterson, G. R. Behavioral intervention procedures in the classroom and in the home. In A. E. Bergin & S. L. Garfield (Eds.), *Handbook of psychotherapy and behavior change.* New York: John Wiley, in press.
Patterson, G. R., & Harris, A. Some methodological considerations for observation procedures. Paper presented at the meeting of the American Psychological Association. San Francisco, September 1968.
Patterson, G. R., Ray, R. S., & Shaw, D. A. Direct intervention in families of deviant children. Unpublished manuscript, Oregon Res. Inst., 1969.
Paul, G. L. *Insight versus desensitization in psychotherapy.* Stanford, Calif.: Stanford University Press, 1966.
Paul, G. L. Strategy of outcome research in psychotherapy. *J. consult. Psychol.,* 1967, *31,* 104-118.
Paul, G. L. Behavior modification research: design and tactics. In C. M. Franks (Ed.), *Behavior therapy: Appraisal and status.* New York: McGraw-Hill, 1969. Pp. 29-62. (a)
Paul, G. L. Outcome of systematic desensitization, I: Background procedures and uncontrolled reports of individual treatment. In C. M. Franks (Ed.), *Behavior therapy: Appraisal and status.* New York: McGraw-Hill, 1969. Pp. 63-104. (b)
Paul, G. L. Outcome of systematic desensitization, II: Controlled investigations of individual treatment, technique variations, and current status. In C. M. Franks (Ed.), *Behavior therapy: Appraisal and status.* New York: McGraw-Hill, 1969. Pp. 105-199. (c)
Payne, D. A., & McMorris, R. F. *Educational and psychological measurement.* Waltham, Mass.: Blaisdell, 1967.
Pearson, J. S., and Swenson, W. M. *A user's guide to the Mayo Clinic automated MMPI program.* New York: Psychol. Corp., 1967.
Pearson, P. H. Relationships between global and specified measures of novelty seeking. *J. consult. clin. Psychol.,* 1970, *34,* 199-204.
Pearson, P. H., & Maddi, S. R. The Similes Preference Inventory. *J. consult. Psychol.,* 1966, *30,* 301-308.
Penney, R. K. Reactive curiosity and manifest anxiety in children. *Child Develpm.,* 1965, *36,* 697-702.
Penney, R. K., & McCann, B. The children's reactive curiosity scale. *Psychol. Rep.,* 1964, *15,* 323-334.
Penney, R. K., & Reinehr, R. C. Development of a stimulus-variation seeking scale for adults. *Psychol. Rep.,* 1966, *18,* 631-638.
Pepitone, A. *Attraction and hostility.* New York: Atherton Press, 1964.
Pepitone, A., Faucheux, C., Moscovici, S., Cesa-Branchi, M., Magistretti, G., Iaconoa, G., Asprea, A. M., & Villoni, G. The role of self-esteem in competitive choice behavior. *Inter. J. Psychol.,* 1967, *2,* 147-159.
Personnel Research Staff. *Personnel assessment program: follow-up study.* New York: American Telephone and Telegraph Co., 1965.
Peters, R. D., & Penney, R. K. Spontaneous alteration of high and low reactively curious children. *Psychon. Sci.,* 1966, *4,* 139-140.
Peterson, D. R. Behavior problems of middle childhood. *J. consult. Psychol.,* 1961, *25,* 205-209.
Peterson, R. F. Expanding the behavioral laboratory: From clinic to home. Paper presented at the meeting of the American Psychological Association, Washington, D.C., 1967.
Peterson, R. F., Cox, M. A., & Bijou, S. W. Training children to work productively in classroom groups. *Except. Child.,* in press.
Phillips, E. L., Raiford, A., & El-Batrawi, S. The Q-sort re-evaluated. *J. consult. Psychol.,* 1965, *29,* 622-625.
Pilisuk, M., Potter, P., Rapoport, A., & Winter, J. A. War hawks and peace doves: Alternate resolutions of experimental conflicts. *J. confl. Resol.,* 1965, *9,* 491-508.
Pilisuk, M., Skolnick, P., & Overstreet, E. Predicting cooperation from the two sexes in a conflict simulation. *J. pers. soc. Psychol.,* 1968, *10,* 35-43.
Pine, F. A manual for rating drive content in the TAT. *J. proj. Tech.,* 1960, *24,* 32-45.

Piotrowski, Z. A. A new evaluation of the Thematic Apperception Test. *Psychoanal. Rev.*, 1950, *37*, 101-127.

Piotrowski, Z. A. Digital-computer interpretation of inkblot test data. *Psychiat. Quart.*, 1964, *38*, 1-26.

Piotrowski, Z. A., & Abrahamsen, D. Sexual crime, alcohol, and the Rorschach test. *Psychiat. quart. Suppl.*, 1952, *26* (Part 2), 248-260.

Pollin, W., & Goldin, S. The physiological and psychological effects of intravenously administered/epinephrine and its metabolism in normal and schizophrenic men—II: Psychiatric observations. *J. psychiat. Res.*, 1961, *1*, 50-67.

Pope, B., & Scott, W. H. *Psychological diagnosis in clinical practice.* New York: Oxford, 1967.

Powell, J., & Azrin, N. The effects of shock as a punisher for cigarette smoking. *J. appl. behav. Anal.*, 1968, *1*, 63-71.

Praag, H. M. v., & Korf, J. A pilot study of some kinetic aspects of the metabolism of 5-hydrozytryptamine in depressive patients. *J. biol. Psychiat.*, in press.

Praag, H. M. v., Korf, J., & Puite, J. 5-hydroxyindoleacetic acid levels in the cerebrospinal fluid of depressive patients treated with probenecid. *Nature*, 1970, *225*, 1259-1260.

Pressey, S. L. A group scale for investigating the emotions. *J. abnorm. soc. Psychol.*, 1921, *16*, 55-64.

Pressey, S. L., & Chambers, O. R. First revision of a group scale designed for investigating the emotions, with tentative norms. *J. appl. Psychol.*, 1920, *4*, 97-104.

Pressey, S. L., & Pressey, L. W. "Cross-Out" tests with suggestions as to a group scale of the emotions. *J. appl. Psychol.*, 1919, *3*, 138-150.

Proshansky, H. M., Ittelson, W. H., & Rivlin, L. (Eds.) *Environmental psychology.* New York: Holt, Rinehart, & Winston, 1970, in press.

Pruitt, D. G. Reward structure and cooperation: The decomposed Prisoner's Dilemma game. *J. pers. soc. Psychol.*, 1967, *7*, 21-27.

Pujol, J. F., Mouret, J., Jouvet, M., & Glowinski, J. Increased turnover of cerebral norepinephrine during rebound of paradoxical sleep in the rat. *Sci.*, 1968, *159*, 112-114.

Purcell, K., & Brady, K. Adaptation to the invasion of privacy: Monitoring behavior with a miniature radio transmitter. *Merrill-Palmer Quart.*, 1966, *12*, 242-254.

Pytkowicz, A. R., Wagner, N., & Sarason, G. An experimental study of the reduction of hostility through fantasy. *J. pers. soc. Psychol.*, 1967, *5* (3), 295-303.

Quay, H. C. Personality patterns in pre-adolescent delinquent boys. *Educ. Psychol. Measmt.*, 1966, *26*, 99-110.

Quay, W. B. Circadian rhythm in rat pineal serotonin and its modifications by estrous cycle and photoperiod. *Gen. comp. Endocrinol.*, 1963, *3*, 473-479.

Quinton, R. M., & Halliwell, G. Effects of α-methyl DOPA and DOPA on the amphetamine excitatory response in reserpinized rats. *Nature*, 1963, *200*, 178-179.

Rabin, A. I. (Ed.) *Projective techniques in personality assessment.* New York: Springer, 1968.

Rabinowitz, C. B., & Coughlin, R. E. *Analysis of landscape characteristics relevant to preference.* Philadelphia, Pa.: RSRI Discussion Paper Series, No. 38, Regional Science Research Institute, 1970.

Rachman, S. Systematic desensitization. *Psychol. Bull.*, 1967, *67*, 93-103.

Radcliffe, J. R. Review of the Edwards personal preference schedule. In O. K. Buros (Ed.), *The sixth mental measurements yearbook.* Highland Park, N.J.: The Gryphon Press, 1965. Pp. 195-200.

Raimy, V. C. Self-reference in counseling interviews. *J. consult. Psychol.*, 1948, *12*, 153-163.

Randrup, A., & Munkvad, I. Biochemical, anatomical, and psychological investigations of stereotyped behavior induced by amphetamines. In E. Costa & S. Garattini (Eds.), *International symposium on amphetamines and related compounds.* New York: Raven Press, 1970. Pp. 695-714.

Rapoport, Amnon. Optimal policies for the Prisoner's Dilemma. *Psychol. Rev.*, 1967, *74*, 136-148.

Rapoport, Anatol. *Fights, games, and debates.* Ann Arbor, Mich.: University of Michigan Press, 1956.

Rapoport, A. *Two-person game theory: The essential ideas.* Ann Arbor, Mich.: University of Michigan Press, 1966.

Rapoport, A. Escape from paradox. *Scient. Amer.*, 1967, *217*, 50-56. (a)

Rapoport, A. Exploiter, leader, hero, and martyr: The four archetypes of the 2 x 2 game. *Behav. Sci.*, 1967, *12*, 81-84. (b)

Rapoport, A. Comments on Dr. Harris' "note on Howard's theory of metagames." *Psychol. Rep.*, 1969, *25*, 765-766. (a)

Rapoport, A. Reply to Dr. Harris' comments on my comments. *Psychol. Rep.*, 1969, *25*, 857-858. (b)

Rapoport, A., & Chammah, A. M. *Prisoner's Dilemma.* Ann Arbor, Mich.: University of Michigan Press, 1965. (a)

Rapoport, A., & Chammah, A. M. Sex differences in factors contributing to the level of cooperation in the Prisoner's Dilemma game. *J. pers. soc. Psychol.*, 1965, *2*, 831-838. (b)

Rapoport, A., & Dale, P. S. Models for Prisoner's Dilemma. *J. math. Psychol.*, 1966, *3*, 269-286.

Rapoport, A., & Guyer, M. A taxonomy of 2 x 2 games. *Gen. Systs.*, 1966, *11*, 203-214.

Raven, J. C. *Guide to using progressive matrices (1938).* London: Lewis, 1956. (U.S. Distributor: Psychol. Corp., New York.)

Ravich, R. A. Short-term, intensive treatment of marital discord. *Voices*, 1966, *2*, 42-48.

Ravich, R. A. The interpersonal behavior game-test (IBGT). Paper presented at Conference on Systematic Research on Family Interaction, Eastern Pennsylvania Psychiatric Institute, Philadelphia, Pa., 1967.

Ravich, R. A. The use of an interpersonal game-test in conjoint marital psychotherapy. *Amer. J. Psychother.*, 1969, *23*, 217-229.

Ravich, R. A., Deutsch, M., & Brown, D. An experimental study of marital discord and decision-making. *Psychiat. res. Rep.*, 1966, *20*, 91-94.

Raynor, J. O. Future orientation and motivation of immediate activity: An elaboration of the theory of achievement motivation. *Psychol. Rev.*, 1969, *76*, 606-610.

Raynor, J. O. Relationships between achievement-related motives, future orientation, and academic performance. *J. pers. soc. Psychol.*, 1970, *15* (1), 28-33.

Rech, R. H. Antagonism of reserpine behavioral depression by *d*-amphetamine. *J. pharmacol. exp. Ther.*, 1964, *146*, 369-376.

Rech, R. H. Amphetamine effects on poor performance of rats in a shuttle box. *Psychopharmacologia*, 1966, *9*, 110-117.

Rech, R. H., & Moore, K. *An introduction to psychopharmacology.* New York: Raven Press, 1971. Pp. 1-353.

Rech, R. H., & Stolk, J. M. Amphetamine-drug interactions that relate brain catecholamines to behavior. In E. Costa & S. Garattini (Eds.), *Proceedings of the Mario Negri Institute for pharmacological research, Milan, Italy.* New York: Raven Press, 1970. Pp. 385-413.

Rechtschaffen, A., Lovell, R., Freedman, D., Whitehead, P., & Aldrich, M. Effect of parachlorophenalanine on sleep in rats. *Psychophysiol.*, 1969, *6*, 223.

Redd, W. H., & Birnbrauer, J. S. Adults as discriminative stimulative for different reinforcement contingencies with retarded children. *J. exp. Psychol.*, 1969, *7*, 440-447.

Rehfisch, J. M. A scale for personality rigidity. *J. consult. Psychol.*, 1958, *22*, 11-15.

Rehm, L. P., & Marston, A. R. Reduction of social anxiety through modification of self-reinforcement: An investigation therapy technique. *J. consult. clin. Psychol.*, 1968, *32*, 565-574.

Reis, D. J., Weinbren, M., & Corvelli, A. A circadian rhythm of norepinephrine regionally in cat brain: Its relationship to environmental lighting and to regional diurnal variations in brain serotonin. *J. pharmacol. exp. Ther.*, 1968, *164*, 135-145.

Rickard, H. G. Tailored criteria of change in psychotherapy. *J. gen. Psychol.*, 1965, *72*, 63-68.

Risley, T. R., & Hart, B. Developing correspondence between non-verbal and verbal behavior of preschool children. *J. appl. Behav. Anal.*, 1968, *1*, 267-281.

Ritter, B. The use of contact desensitization, demonstration—plus participation and demonstration—alone in the treatment of acrophobia. *Behav. res. Ther.*, 1969, *7*, 157-164.

Robbins, L. L., & Wallerstein, R. S. The research strategy and tactics of the psychotherapy research project of the Menninger Foundation and the problem of control. In E. A. Rubinstein & M. B. Parloff (Eds.), *Research in psychotherapy.* Vol. 1. Washington, D.C.: American Psychological Association, 1959. Pp. 27-43.

Robichaud, R. C., & Sledge, K. L. The effects of *p*-chlorophenylalanine on experimentally induced conflict in the rat. *Life Sci.*, 1969, *8* (Part 1), 965-969.

Roe, A. *The psychology of occupations.* New York: John Wiley, 1956.

Rogers, C. R. Changes in the maturity of behavior as related to therapy. In C. R. Rogers & R. F. Dymond (Eds.), *Psychotherapy and personality change.* Chicago: University of Chicago Press, 1954. Pp. 215-237.

Rogers, C. R. A tentative scale for the measurement of process in psychotherapy. In E. A. Rubinstein & M. B. Parloff (Eds.), *Research in psychotherapy.* Vol. 1. Washington, D.C.: American Psychological Association, 1959. Pp. 96-107.

Rogers, C. R., & Dymond, R. F. *Psychotherapy and personality change.* Chicago: University of Chicago Press, 1954.

Rogers, C. R., Gendlin, E. T., Kiesler, D. J., & Truax, C. B. *The therapeutic relationship and its impact.* Madison, Wis.: University of Wisconsin Press, 1967.

Rohde, A. R. Explorations in personality by the sentence completions method. *J. appl. Psychol.,* 1946, *30,* 169-180.

Rokeach, M. *The open and closed mind.* New York: Basic Books, 1960.

Roos, B. E., & Sjöström, R. 5-hydroxyindoleacetic acid (and homovanillic acid) levels in patients with manic-depressive psychosis. *Pharmacologia Clinica,* 1969, *1,* 153-155.

Root, A. I. A short test of introversion-extroversion. *Pers. J.,* 1931, *10,* 250-253.

Rorer, L. G. The great response-style myth. *Psychol. Bull.,* 1965, *63,* 129-150.

Rorer, L. G., & Goldberg, L. R. Acquiescence in the MMPI? *Educ. psychol. Bull.,* 1965, *63,* 233-243.

Rosanoff, A. J. A theory of personality based mainly on psychiatric experience. *Psychol. Bull.,* 1920, *17,* 281-299.

Rosecrans, J. A., Lovell, R. A., & Freedman, D. X. Effects of lysergic acid diethylamide on the metabolism of brain 5-hydroxytryptamine. *Biochem. Pharmacol.,* 1967, *16,* 2011-2021.

Rosen, A. Stability of new MMPI scales and statistical procedures for evaluating changes and differences in psychiatric patients. *J. consult. Psychol.,* 1966, *30,* 142-145.

Rosen, B. C. Family structure and achievement motivation. *Amer. soc. Rev.,* 1961, *26,* 574-585.

Rosenbaum, M. E., & Stanners, R. F. Self-esteem, manifest hostility, and an expression of hostility. *J. abnorm. soc. Psychol.,* 1961, *63,* 646-649.

Rosenfeld, H. M., & Franklin, S. S. Arousal need for affiliation in women. *J. pers. soc. Psychol.,* 1966, 245-248.

Rosenquist, C. M., & Megargee, E. I. *Delinquency in three cultures.* Austin, Texas: University of Texas Press, 1969.

Rosenthal, R. *Experimenter effects in research.* New York: Appleton-Century-Crofts, 1966.

Rosenthal, R. Covert communication in the psychological experiment. *Psychol. Bull.,* 1967, *67,* 356-367.

Rosenwald, G. C. The Thematic Apperception Test. In A. E. Rabin (Ed.), *Projective techniques in personality assessment.* New York: Springer, 1968. Pp. 172-221.

Rosenzweig, S. Levels of behavior in psychodiagnosis with special reference to the picture-frustration study. *Amer. J. Orthopsychiat.,* 1950, *20,* 63-72. Reprinted in E. I. Megargee (Ed.), *Research in clinical assessment.* New York: Harper & Row, 1966.

Roth, R. H., Stjärne, L., & Euler, U. S. v. Acceleration of noradrenaline biosynthesis by nerve stimulation. *Life Sci.,* 1966, *5,* 1071-1075.

Rothballer, A. The effects of catecholamines on the CNS. *Pharmacol. Rev.,* 1959, *11,* 494-547.

Rotter, J. B. Levels of aspiration as a method of studying personality, II: Development and evaluation of a controlled method. *J. exp. Psychol.,* 1942, *31,* 410-422.

Rotter, J. B. *Social learning and clinical psychology.* Englewood Cliffs, N.J.: Prentice-Hall, 1954.

Rotter, J. B. Generalized expectancies for internal versus external control of reinforcement. *Psychol. Monogr.,* 1966, *80,* No. 1 (Whole No. 609).

Rubin, B. M., Katkin, E. S., & Weiss, B. W. Factor analysis of a fear survey schedule. *Behav. res. Ther.,* 1968, *6,* 65-75.

Rundquist, E. A., & Sletto, R. F. *Personality in the depression.* Minneapolis, Minn.: University of Minnesota Press, 1936.

Ryder, J. M. Aggression with balloons, blocking, and doll play. In L. M. Stultz and collaborators (Eds.), *Father relations of war-born children.* Stanford, Calif.: Stanford University Press, 1954. Pp. 212-243.

Saarinen, T. F. *Perceptions of the drought hazard on the Great Plains.* Chicago: University of Chicago, Department of Geography, Research Paper No. 106, 1966.

Saltz, G., & Epstein, S. Thematic hostility and guilt responses as related to self-reported hostility, guilt, and conflict. *J. abnorm. soc. Psychol.,* 1963, *67,* 469-479.

Sampson, E. E. Achievement in conflict. *J. Pers.,* 1963, *31,* 510-516.

Sampson, E., & Kardush, M. Age, sex, class, and race differences in response to a two-person non-zero-sum game. *J. confl. Resol.,* 1965, *9,* 212-220.

Sanders, R. M., Hopkins, B. L., & Walker, M. B. An inexpensive method for making data records of complex behaviors. *J. appl. behav. Anal.*, 1969, *3*, 221-222.

Sankar, D. V. S. *Schizophrenia: Current concepts and research*. Hicksville, N.Y.: PJD Publications Ltd., 1969.

Sanoff, H. Visual attributes of the physical environment. In G. J. Coates & K. H. Moffett (Eds.), *Response to environment*. (Student Publication of the School of Design, Volume 18.) Raleigh, N.C.: North Carolina State University, 1969. Pp. 37-62.

Santostefano, S., & Wilson, G. Construct validity of the minature situations test, II: The performance of institutionalized delinquents and public school adolescents. *J. clin. Psychol.*, 1968, *24* (3), 355-358.

Sarason, I. G. Interrelationships among individual difference variables, behavior in psychotherapy, and verbal conditioning. *J. abnorm. soc. Psychol.*, 1958, *56*, 339-344.

Sarason, I. G. Interrelationships among measures of hostility. *J. clin. Psychol.*, 1961, *17*, 192-195.

Sarason, I. G., & Minard, J. Interrelationships among subject, experimenter, and situational variables. *J. abnorm. soc. Psychol.*, 1963, *67*, 87-91.

Sargent, H. D. Intrapsychic change: Methodological problems in psychotherapy research. *Psychiat.*, 1961, *24*, 93-108.

Savage, R. D. *Psychometric assessment of the individual child*. Baltimore, Md.: Penguin, 1968.

Sawyer, J. The Altruism scale: A measure of cooperative, individualistic, and competitive interpersonal orientation. *Amer. J. Sociol.*, 1966, *71*, 407-416. (a)

Sawyer, J. Measurement *and* prediction, clinical *and* statistical. *Psychol. Bull.*, 1966, *66*, 178-200. (b)

Sawyer, J., & Friedell, M. F. The interaction screen: An operational model for experimentation on interpersonal behavior. *Behav. Sci.*, 1965, *10*, 446-460.

Schachter, J. Pain, fear, and anger in hypertensives and normotensives. *Psychom. Med.*, 1957, *19*, 17-29.

Schachter, S., & Singer, J. E. Cognitive, social, and physiological determinants of emotional state. *Psychol. Rev.*, 1962, *69*, 379-399.

Schachter, S., & Wheeler, L. Epinephrine, chlorpromazine, and amusement. *J. abnorm. soc. Psychol.*, 1962, *65*, 121-128.

Schaefer, J. B., & Norman, M. Punishment and aggression in fantasy responses of boys with antisocial character traits. *J. pers. soc. Psychol.*, 1967, *4*, 237-240.

Schanberg, S. M., & Giarman, N. J. Drug-induced alterations in sub-cellular distribution of 5-hydroxytryptamine in rat's brain. *Biochem. Pharmacol.*, 1962, *11*, 187-194.

Schanberg, S. M., Schildkraut, J. J., & Kopin, I. J. The effects of psychoactive drugs on norepinephrine-^{3}H metabolism in brain. *Biochem. Pharmacol.*, 1967, *16*, 393-399.

Schenthal, J. E., Sweeney, J. W., Nettleton, W. J., Jr., & Yoder, R. D. Clinical application of electronic data processing apparatus. *J. Amer. med. Assoc.*, Oct., 1963, *186*, 101-105.

Scheving, L. E., Harrison, W. H., Gordon, P., & Pauly, J. E. Daily fluctuation (circadian and ultradian) in biogenic amines of the rat brain. *Amer. J. Physiol.*, 1968, *214*, 166-173.

Schildkraut, J. J. *Neuropsychopharmacology and the affective disorders*. Boston: Little, Brown, 1970. Pp. 1-111.

Schildkraut, J. J., & Kety, S. S. Biogenic amines and emotion. *Sci.*, 1967, *156*, 21-30.

Schildkraut, J. J., Schanberg, S. M., Breese, G. R., & Kopin, I. J. Effects of psychoactive drugs on the metabolism of intracisternally administered serotonin in rat brain. *Biochem. Pharmacol.*, 1969, *18*, 1971-1978.

Schlesinger, K., Boggan, W., & Freedman, D. X. Genetics of audiogenic seizures, I: Relation to brain serotonin and norepinephrine in mice. *Life Sci.*, 1965, *4*, 2345-2351.

Schlesinger, K., Schrieber, R. A., & Pryor, G. T. Effects of *p*-chlorophenylalanine on conditioned avoidance learning. *Psychon. Sci.*, 1968, *11*, 225-226.

Schloss, Stephen S. A bibliography of publications in the theory of games. Scientific rep. No. 1, Contr. AF19(604)-4573, Electronics Research Laboratory, Northeastern University, Boston, Mass., October, 1959.

Schmahl, D. P., Lichtenstein, E., & Harris, D. E. Successful treatment of habitual smoking with warm, smoky air and rapid smoking. *J. consult. clin. Psychol.*, in press.

Schofield, W. The structured personality inventory in measurement of effects of psychotherapy. In L. A. Gottschalk & A. H. Auerback (Eds.), *Methods of research in psychotherapy*. New York: Appleton-Century-Crofts, 1966. Pp. 536-550.

Schultz, S. D. A differentiation of several forms of hostility by scales empirically constructed from significant items on the MMPI. *Penn. St. Univ. Absts. Doct. Diss.*, 1954, *17*, 717-720.

Schultz, W. C. *FIRO: A three-dimensional theory of interpersonal behavior.* New York: Holt, Rinehart, & Winston, 1958.

Schwitzgebel, R., & Kolb, D. A. Inducing behavior change in adolescent delinquents. *Behav. res. Ther.*, 1964, *1*, 297-304.

Screven, C. G. The effects of interference on response strength. *J. comp. physiol. Psychol.*, 1954, *47*, 140-144.

Sears, P. S. Doll-play aggression in normal young children: Influence of sex, age, sibling status, father's absence. *Psychol. Monogr.*, 1951, *65*, No. 6 (Whole No. 323).

Sears, P. S., & Pintler, M. H. Sex differences in doll-play aggression. *Amer. Psychologist*, 1947, *2*, 420. (Abstract)

Sears, R. R. Influence of methodological factors on doll-play performance. *Child Develpm.*, 1947, *18*, 190-197.

Seashore, C. E., Lewis, D., & Saetveit, J. G. *Seashore measures of musical talents.* New York: Psychol. Corp., 1939.

Sedvall, G. C., & Kopin, I. J. Acceleration of norepinephrine synthesis in the rat submaxillary gland *In vivo* during sympathetic nerve stimulation. *Life Sci.*, 1967, *6*, 45-51.

Segal, S. J. A psychoanalytic analysis of personality factors in vocational choice. *J. counsel. Psychol.*, 1961, *8*, 202-210.

Seiden, L. S., & Hanson, L. C. F. Reversal of the reserpine-induced suppression of the conditioned response in the cat by L-DOPA. *Psychopharmacologia*, 1964, *6*, 239-244.

Seiden, L. S., & Peterson, D. D. Reversal of the reserpine-induced suppression of the conditioned avoidance response by L-DOPA: Correlation of behavioral and biochemical differences in two strains of mice. *J. pharmacol. exp. Ther.*, 1968, *159*, 422-428.

Sells, S. B. An approach to the nature of organizational climate. In R. Tagiuri & G. H. Litwin (Eds.), *Organizational climate: Explorations of a concept.* Boston, Mass.: Graduate School of Business Administration, Harvard University, 1968. Pp. 85-106.

Sells, S. B. Ecology and the science of psychology. In E. P. Willems & H. L. Raush (Eds.), *Naturalistic viewpoints in psychological research.* New York: Holt, Rinehart, & Winston, 1969. Pp. 15-30.

Shafer, E. L., Jr., Hamilton, J. F., Jr., & Schmidt, E. A. Natural landscape preferences: A predictive model. *J. Leisure Res.*, 1969, *1*, 1-19.

Shafer, E. L., Jr., & Thompson, R. C. Models that describe use of Adirondack campgrounds. *For. Sci.*, 1968, *14*, 383-391.

Shalit, B. Environmental hostility and hostility in fantasy. *J. pers. soc. Psychol.*, 1970, *15* (2), 171-174.

Shaw, M. E., & Wright, J. M. *Scales for the measurement of attitudes.* New York: McGraw-Hill, 1967.

Sheard, M. H. The effect of *p*-chlorophenylalanine on behavior in rats: Relation to brain serotonin and 5-hydrozyindoleacetic acid. *Brain Res.*, 1969, *15*, 524-528.

Sheard, M. H., & Aghajanian, G. K. Stimulation of the midbrain raphe: Effect on serotonin metabolism. *J. pharmacol. exp. Ther.*, 1968, *163*, 425-430.

Shelby, E. L. V., & Toch, H. H. The perception of violence as an indicator of adjustment in institutionalized offenders. *J. crim. Law, criminol. Police Sci.*, 1962, *53* (4), 463-469.

Shemberg, K. M., Levanthal, D. B., & Allman, L. Aggression machine performance and rate aggression. *J. exp. res. Pers.*, 1968, *3* (2), 117-119.

Shepler, B. F. A comparison of masculinity-femininity measures. *J. consult. Psychol.*, 1951, *15*, 484-486.

Shernberg, K., & Keeley, S. Psychodiagnostic training in the academic setting. *J. consult. clin. Psychol.*, 1970, *34*, 205-211.

Shillito, E. E. The effect of *para*-chlorophenylalanine on social interaction of male rats. *Brit. J. Pharmacol.*, 1970, *38*, 305-315.

Shipley, W. C. A self-administering scale for measuring intellectual impairment and deterioration. *J. Psychol.*, 1940, *9*, 371-377.

Shipman, W. G. The validity of MMPI hostility scales. *J. clin. Psychol.*, 1965, *21*, 186-190.

Shipman, W. G., & Marquette, C. H. The manifest hostility scale: A validation study. *J. clin. Psychol.*, 1963, *19*, 104-106.

Shlien, J. M. Toward what level of abstraction in criteria? In H. H. Strupp & L. Luborsky (Eds.), *Research in psychotherapy.* Vol. 2. Washington, D.C.: American Psychological Association, 1962. Pp. 142-154.

Shlien, J. M. Cross theoretical criteria for the evaluation of psychotherapy. *Amer. J. Psychother.*, 1966, *20*, 125-134.

Shlien, J. M., Mosak, H. H., & Dreikurs, R. Effect of time limits: A comparison of two psychotherapies. *J. counsel. Psychol.*, 1962, *9*, 31-34.

Shore, M. F., Massimo, J. L., & Mack, R. The relationship between levels of guilt in thematic stories and unsocialized behavior. *J. proj. Tech. pers. Assmt.*, 1964, *28*, 346-349.

Shostrom, E. L. A test for the measurement of self-actualization. *Educ. psychol. Measmt.*, 1964, *24*, 207-218.

Shostrom, E. L., & Knapp, R. R. The relationship of a measure of self-actualization (POI) to a measure of pathology (MMPI) and to therapeutic growth. *Amer. J. Psychother.*, 1966, *20*, 193-202.

Sidle, A., Acker, M., & McReynolds, P. "Stimulus-seeking" behavior in schizophrenics and nonschizophrenics. *Percept. mot. Skills*, 1963, *17*, 811-816.

Sidle, A., Moos, R., Adams, J., & Cady, P. Development of a coping scale. *Arch. gen. Psychiat.*, 1969, *20*, 226-232.

Siegel, A. E. Film-mediated fantasy aggression and strength of aggressive drive. *Child Develpm.*, 1956, *27*, 385-378.

Siegel, L., & Siegel, L. C. Educational set: A determinant of acquisition. *J. Educ. Psychol.*, 1965, *56*, 1-12.

Siegel, R. S., & Rosen, I. C. Character style and anxiety tolerance: A study in intrapsychic change. In H. H. Strupp & L. Luborsky (Eds.), *Research in psychotherapy.* Vol. 2. Washington, D.C.: American Psychological Association, 1962. Pp. 206-217.

Siegel, S. M. The relationship of hostility to authoritarianism. *J. abnorm. soc. Psychol.*, 1956, *52*, 368-372.

Siegel, S. M., Spilka, B., & Miller, L. The direction of manifest hostility: Its measurement and meaning. Paper presented at the meeting of the American Psychological Association, New York, September, 1957.

Siegelman, M., & Peck, R. F. Personality patterns related to occupational roles. *Gen. psychol. Monogr.*, 1960, *61*, 291-349.

Siess, T. F. Personal history factors and their relation to vocational preferences. Doctoral dissertation, University of Minnesota, 1964.

Siess, T. F., & Jackson, D. N. Vocational interests and personality: An empirical integration. *J. counsel. Psychol.*, 1970, *17*, 27-35.

Silverman, A. J., & Cohen, S. I. Affect and vascular correlates to catecholamines. *Psychiat. Res. Rep. Amer. Psychiat. Assoc.*, 1960, *12*, 16-30.

Simmonds, M. A. Effect of environmental temperature on the turnover of noradrenaline in hypothalamus and other areas of rat brain. *J. Physiol.*, 1969, *203*, 199-210.

Simmons, R. F. Answering English questions by computer: A survey. *Comm. assoc. comp. Mach.*, 1965, *8*, 53-69.

Sims, V. M. Sims score card for socio-economic status. Bloomington, Ill.: Public School Publishing Co., 1927.

Sjoerdsma, A. Serotonin now: Clinical implications of inhibiting its synthesis with parachlorophenylalanine. *Ann. int. Med.*, 1970, *73*, 607-629.

Skinner, B. F. *The technology of teaching.* New York: Appleton-Century-Crofts, 1968.

Skolnik, A. Motivational imagery and behavior over twenty years. *J. consult. Psychol.*, 1966, *30* (6), 463-478.

Skrzypek, G. J. Effect of perceptual isolation and arousal on anxiety, complexity preference, and novelty preference in psychopathic and neurotic delinquents. *J. abnorm. Psychol.*, 1969, *74*, 321-329.

Sloane, H. N., Johnston, M. G., & Bijou, S. W. Successive modification of aggressive behavior and aggressive fantasy play by management of contingencies. *J. Child Psychol. Psychiat.*, 1967, *8*, 217-226.

Smith, C. B., Trendelenburg, U., Langer, S. Z., & Tsai, T. H. The relation of retention of norepinephrine-H^3 to the norepinephrine content of the nictitating membrane of the spinal cat during development of denervation supersensitivity. *J. pharmacol. exp. Ther.*, 1966, *151*, 87-94.

Smith, M. S. The computer and the TAT. *J. sch. Psychol.*, 1968, *6*, 206-214.

Smith, W. G. A model for psychiatric diagnosis. *Arch. gen. Psychiat.*, 1966, *14*, 521-529.

Smith, W. L., & Philippus, M. J. (Eds.) *Neuropsychological testing in organic brain dysfunction.* Springfield, Ill.: Charles C. Thomas, 1969.

Smock, C. D., & Holt, B. G. Children's reactions to novelty: An experimental study of "curiosity motivation." *Child Develpm.*, 1962, *33*, 631-642.

Smythies, J. (Ed.) The mode of action of psychotomimetic drugs. *Neurosci. res. program Bull.*, 1970, *8*, 1-152.

Snider, J. G., & Osgood, C. E. *The semantic differential technique.* Chicago: Aldine, 1969.

Snoke, M. L. A study in the behavior of men students of high and low measured hostility under two conditions of goal clarity. Ph.D. dissertation, University of Minnesota, 1955.

Snyder, S., & Richelson, E. Relationships between the conformation of psychedelic drugs and their psychotropic potency. In D. Efron (Ed.), *Psychopharmacology.* Washington, D.C.: U.S. Government Printing Office, 1968. Pp. 1199-1210.

Snyder, W. U. An investigation of the nature of non-directive psychotherapy. *J. gen. Psychol.*, 1945, *33*, 193-223.

Sommer, R., & Sommer, D. T. Assaultiveness and two types of Rorschach color responses. *J. consult. Psychol.*, 1958, *22*, 57-62. Reprinted in E. I. Megargee (Ed.), *Research in clinical assessment.* New York: Harper & Row, 1966.

Sonnenfeld, J. Equivalence and distortion of the perceptual environment. *Environ. Behav.*, 1969, *1*, 83-100.

Sorokin, P. A., & Berger, C. Q. *Time-budgets of human behavior.* Cambridge, Mass.: Harvard University Press, 1939.

Spector, S., Gordon, R., Sjoerdsma, A., & Udenfriend, S. End-product inhibition of tyrosine hydroxylase as a possible mechanism for regulation of norepinephrine synthesis. *Mol. Pharmacol.*, 1967, *3*, 549-555.

Spielberger, C. D., Lushene, R. E., & McAdoo, W. G. Theory and measurement of anxiety states. In R. B. Cattell (Ed.), *Handbook of modern personality.* Chicago: Aldine, in press.

Spitzer, R. L. Mental status schedule: Potential use as a criterion measure of change in psychotherapy research. *Amer. J. Psychother.*, 1966, *20*, 156-167.

Spitzer, R. L., Endicott, J., & Cohen, G. *The psychiatric status schedule: Technique for evaluating social and role functioning and mental status.* New York: State Psychiatric Institute and Biometrics Research, 1967.

Spitzer, R. L., Fleiss, J. L., Endicott, J., & Cohen, J. Mental status schedule. *Arch. gen. Psychiat.*, 1967, *16*, 479-493.

Spranger, E. *Types of men (lebensformen).* Halle: Niemeyer, 1928.

Srivastava, R. K., & Good, L. R. *Patterns of group interaction in three architecturally different psychiatric treatment environments.* Topeka, Kans.: Environmental Research Foundation, 1968.

Stanek, R. J. A note on the presumed measures of masculinity-femininity. *Pers. guid. J.*, 1959, *37*, 439-440.

Starkweather, J. A. Computest: A computer language for individual testing, instruction, and interviewing. *Psychol. Rep.*, 1965, *17*, 227-237.

Steele, M. W., & Tedeschi, J. T. Matrix indices and strategy choices in mixed-motive games. *J. confl. Resol.*, 1967, *11*, 198-205.

Stein, L. Self-stimulation of the brain and the central stimulant action of amphetamine. *Fed. Proc.*, 1964, *23*, 836-850.

Stein, L. Chemistry of reward and punishment. In D. H. Efron (Ed.), *Psychopharmacology, a review of progress, 1957-1967.* Washington, D.C.: U.S. Government Printing Office, 1968. Pp. 105-123.

Stein, L., & Wise, C. D. Release of norepinephrine from hypothalamus and amygdala by rewarding medical forebrain bundle stimulation and amphetamine. *J. comp. physiol. Psychol.*, 1969, *67*, 189-198.

Stern, G. G. *Activities index, preliminary manual.* Syracuse, N.Y.: Syracuse University Research Institute, 1958.

Stern, G. G. Environments for learning. In R. N. Sanford (Ed.), *The American college: A psychological and social interpretation of higher learning.* New York: John Wiley, 1962. Pp. 690-730. (a)

Stern, G. G. The measurement of psychological characteristics of students and learning environments. In S. Messick & J. Ross (Eds.), *Measurement in personality and cognition.* New York: John Wiley, 1962. (b)

Stern, G. G. *Manual: Activities index—college characteristics index.* Syracuse, N.Y.: Syracuse University Psychological Research Center, 1963.

Stern, G. G. *People in context: The measurement of environmental interaction in school and society.* New York: John Wiley, 1970.

Stern, J. A., & Plapp, J. M. Psychophysiology and clinical psychology. In C. D. Spielberger (Ed.), *Current topics in clinical and community psychology.* Vol. 1. New York: Academic Press, 1969.

Sternbach, R. A. *Principals of psycho-physiology.* New York: Academic Press, 1966.

Stevens, D. A., Fechter, L. D., & Resnick, O. The effects of *p*-chlorophenylalanine, a depletor of brain serotonin, on behavior, II: Retardation of passive avoidance learning. *Life Sci.,* 1969, *8* (Part II), 379-385.

Stevens, D. A., Resnick, O., & Krus, D. M. The effects of *p*-chlorophenylalanine, a depletor of brain serotonin, on behavior, I: Facilitation of discrimination learning. *Life Sci.,* 1967, *6,* 2215-2220.

Stewart, R. *Managers and their jobs.* London: Macmillan Co., 1967.

Stock, W. A., & Looft, W. R. Relationships among several demographic variables and the change seeker index. *Percept. mot. Skills,* 1969, *29,* 1011-1014.

Stodola, Q., & Stordahl, K. *Basic educational tests and measurements.* Chicago: Science Research Associates, 1967.

Stolk, J. M., Barchas, J., Dement, W., & Schanberg, S. Brain catecholamine metabolism following *para*-chlorophenylalanine (pCP) treatment. *The Pharmacologist,* 1969, *11,* 258.

Stolk, J. M., & Rech, R. H. Antagonism of *d*-amphetamine by alpha-methyl-L-tyrosine: Behavioral evidence for the participation of catecholamine stores and synthesis in the amphetamine stimulant response. *Neuropharmacology,* 1970, *9,* 249-263.

Stone, E. A. Behavioral and neurochemical effects of acute swim stress are due to hypothermia. *Life Sci.,* 1970, *9* (Part I), 877-888.

Stone, E. A., & DiCara, L. V. Activity level and accumulation of tritiated norepinephrine in rat brain. *Life Sci.,* 1969, *8* (Part I), 433-439.

Stone, P. J., Dunphy, D. C., Smith, M. S., & Ogilvie, D. M. *The general inquirer, a computer approach to content analysis.* Cambridge, Mass.: MIT Press, 1967.

Straus, M. A. *Family measurement techniques: Abstracts of published instruments, 1935-1965.* Minneapolis, Minn.: University of Minnesota Press, 1969.

Stricker, L. J. Review of the Edwards personal preference schedule. In O. K. Buros (Ed.), *The sixth mental measurements yearbook.* Highland Park, N.J.: The Gryphon Press, 1965. Pp. 200-207.

Stricker, L. J., & Ross, J. Intercorrelations and reliability of the Myers-Briggs type indicator scales. *Psychol. Rep.,* 1963, *12,* 287-293.

Stricker, L. J., & Ross, J. An assessment of some structural properties of the Jungian personality typology. *J. abnorm. soc. Psychol.,* 1964, *68,* 62-71. (a)

Stricker, L. J., & Ross, J. Some correlates of a Jungian personality inventory. *Psychol. Rep.,* 1964, *14,* 623-643. (b)

Strivzer, G. L. *Thematic sexual and guilt responses as related to stimulus-relevance and experimentally induced drive and inhibition.* Doctoral dissertation, University of Massachusetts, 1961.

Strong, E. K., Jr. *Manual for the Strong vocational interest blanks for men and women: Revised blanks (Forms M & W).* Palo Alto, Calif.: Consulting Psychologists Press, 1959.

Strupp, H. H. The outcome problem in psychotherapy revisited. *Psychother.,* 1963, *1,* 1-13.

Strupp, H. H., & Bergin, A. E. Some empirical and conceptual bases for coordinated research in psychotherapy. *Inter. J. Psychiat.,* 1969, *7,* 18-90.

Strupp, H. H., & Bergin, A. E. Research in individual psychotherapy: A bibliography. *Public Health Service Publication No. 1944.* Washington, D.C.: U.S. Government Printing Office, undated.

Stuart, R. B. Operant-interpersonal treatment for marital discord. *J. consult. clin. Psychol.,* 1969, *33,* 675-682.

Sudak, H. S., & Maas, J. W. Central nervous system serotonin and norepinephrine localization in emotional and non-emotional strains in mice. *Nature,* 1964, *203,* 1254-1256.

Suinn, R. M. The STABS, a measure of test anxiety for behavior therapy: Normative data. *Behav. res. Ther.,* 1969, *7,* 335-340.

Suinn, R. M., & Oskamp, S. *The predictive validity of projective measures.* Springfield, Ill.: Charles C. Thomas, 1969.

Sundberg, N. D. The practice of psychological testing in clinical services in the United States. *Amer. Psychologist,* 1961, *16,* 79-83.

Sundberg, N. D., & Tyler, L. E. *Clinical psychology.* New York: Appleton-Century-Crofts, 1962.

Super, D. E. A theory of vocational development. *Amer. Psychologist,* 1953, *8,* 185-190.

Suppes, P., & Atkinson, R. C. *Markov learning models for multiperson interaction.* Stanford, Calif.: Stanford University Press, 1960.

Swensen, C. H., Jr. Empirical evaluation of human figure drawings. *Psychol. Bull.*, 1957, *54*, 431-466. Reprinted in E. I. Megargee (Ed.), *Research in clinical assessment.* New York: Harper & Row, 1966.

Swensen, C. H., Jr. Empirical evaluations of human figure drawings: 1957-1966. *Psychol. Bull.*, 1968, *70*, 20-44.

Symonds, P. M., & Jackson, C. E. An adjustment survey. *J. educ. Res.*, 1930, *21*, 321-330.

Taft, R. Multiple methods of personality assessment. *Psychol. Bull.*, 1959, *56*, 333-352.

Tagiuri, R. Person perception. In G. Lindsey & E. Aronson (Eds.), *Handbook of social psychology.* (2nd ed.) Reading, Mass.: Addison-Wesley, 1969. Pp. 395-449.

Tagiuri, R., & Litwin, G. H. (Eds.) *Organizational climate: Explorations of a concept.* Boston, Mass.: Graduate School of Business Administration, Harvard University, 1968.

Tagliamonte, A., Tagliamonte, P., Gessa, G. L., & Brodie, B. B. Compulsive sexual activity induced by *p*-chlorophenylalanine in normal and pinealectomized male rats. *Sci.*, 1969, *166*, 1433-1435.

Tamarkin, N., Goodwin, F., & Axelrod, J. Rapid elevation of biogenic amine metabolites in human CSF following probenecid. *Life Sci.*, 1970, *9*, 1397-1408.

Taylor, C. W., Bailey, R., & Branch, C. H. H. (Eds.) *Second national conference on architectural psychology.* Salt Lake City, Utah: University of Utah, 1967.

Taylor, J. A. A personality scale of manifest anxiety. *J. abnorm. soc. Psychol.*, 1953, *48*, 285-290.

Taylor, K. M., & Snyder, S. H. Amphetamine: Differentiation by *d* and *i* isomers of behavior involving brain norepinephrine or dopamine. *Sci.*, 1970, *168*, 1487-1489.

Taylor, R. L., & Levitt, E. E. Category breadth and the search for variety of experience. *Psychol. Rec.*, 1967, *17*, 349-352.

Tedeschi, J. T., Bonoma, T., & Lindskold, S. Threateners' reactions to prior announcement of behavioral compliance or defiance. *Behav. Sci.*, 1970, *15*, 171-179.

Tedeschi, J. T., Lesnick, S., & Gahagan, J. Feedback and "washout" effects in the Prisoner's Dilemma game. *J. pers. soc. Psychol.*, 1968, *10*, 31-34.

Tenen, S. S. The effects of *p*-chlorophenylalanine, a serotonin depletor, on avoidance acquisition, pain sensitivity, and related behavior in the rat. *Psychopharmacologia (Berl.)*, 1967, *10*, 204-219.

Terhune, K. W. A note on thematic apperception scoring of needs for achievement, affiliation, and power. *J. proj. Tech. pers. Assmt.*, 1969, *33*, 364-370.

Terman, L. M., & Miles, C. C. *Sex and personality: Studies in masculinity and femininity.* New York: McGraw-Hill, 1936.

Teuber, H. L., & Powers, E. Evaluating therapy in a delinquency prevention program. *Psychiat. Treatment*, 1953, *21*, 138-147.

Thelen, M. H., Varble, D. L., & Johnson, J. Attitudes of academic clinical psychologists toward projective techniques. *Amer. Psychologist*, 1968, *23*, 517-521.

Thibaut, J., & Coules, J. The role of communication in the reduction of interpersonal hostility. *J. abnorm. soc. Psychol.*, 1952, *47*, 770-777.

Thibaut, J. W., & Kelley, H. H. *The social psychology of groups.* New York: John Wiley, 1959.

Thomas, C. B., Ross, D. C., & Freed, E. S. *An index of responses to the group Rorschach test.* Baltimore, Md.: Johns Hopkins Press, 1965.

Thomas, D. R., Becker, W. C., & Armstrong, M. Production and elimination of disruptive classroom behavior by systematically varying teacher's behavior. *J. appl. beh. Anal.*, 1968, *1*, 35-45.

Thomson, H. A. *Internal and external validation of an industrial assessment center program.* Ph.D. dissertation, Case Western Reserve University, 1969.

Thoresen, C. E., & Krumboltz, J. D. Relationship of counselor reinforcement of selected responses to external behavior. *J. counsel. Psychol.*, 1967, *14*, 140-144.

Thoresen, C. E., & Krumboltz, J. D. Similarity of social models and clients in behavioral counseling: Two experimental studies. *J. counsel. Psychol.*, 1968, *15*, 393-401.

Thumin, F. J. A correlational study of the MMPI. *Measmt. Eval. Guid.*, 1969, *2*, 41-46.

Thurstone, L. L. The dimensions of temperament. *Psychometrika*, 1951, *16*, 11-20.

Thurstone, L. L., & Thurstone, T. G. A neurotic inventory. *J. soc. Psychol.*, 1930, *1*, 3-30.

Tinbergen, N. *Social behavior in animals.* London: Methuen, 1953.

Tinbergen, N. On war and peace in animals and man. *Sci.*, 1968, *160*, 1411-1418.

Tolson, W. W., Mason, J. W., Sachar, E. J., Hamburg, D. A., Handlon, J. H., & Fishman, J. R. Urinary catecholamine responses associated with hospital admission in normal human subjects. *J. psychosom. Res.*, 1965, *8*, 365-372.

Tomlinson, T. M., & Hart, J. T. A validation study of the process scale. *J. consult. Psychol.*, 1962, *26*, 74-78.

Touchstone, F. V. A. A comparative study of Negro and White college students' aggressiveness by means of sentence completion. *Dissert. Abst.*, 1957, *17*, 1588-1589.

Tozer, T. N., Neff, N. H., & Brodie, B. B. Application of steady state kinetics to the synthesis rate and turnover time of serotonin in the brain of normal and reserpine-treated rats. *J. pharmacol. exp. Ther.*, 1966, *153*, 177-182.

Travis, R. C. The measurement of fundamental character traits by a new diagnostic test. *J. abnorm. soc. Psychol.*, 1925, *19*, 400-420.

Troland, L. T. *The fundamentals of human motivation.* Princeton, N.J.: D. Van Nostrand, 1928.

Truax, C. B., Carkhuff, R. R., & Kodman, F., Jr. Relationships between therapist-offered conditions and patient change in group psychotherapy. *J. clin. Psychol.*, 1965, *21*, 327-329.

Truax, C. B., Schuldt, W. J., & Wargo, D. G. Self-ideal concept congruence and improvement in group psychotherapy. *J. consult. clin. Psychol.*, 1968, *32*, 47-53.

Truax, C. B., Wargo, D. G., Frank, J. D., Imber, S. D., Battle, C. C., Hoehn-Saric, R., Nash, E. H., & Stone, A. R. Therapist empathy, genuineness, and warmth and patient outcome. *J. consult. Psychol.*, 1966, *30*, 395-401.

Tryk, H. E. Assessment in the study of creativity. In P. McReynolds (Ed.), *Advances in psychological assessment.* Vol. 1. Palo Alto, Calif.: Science and Behavior Books, 1968.

Tryon, R. C. Cumulative communality cluster analysis. *Educ. Psychol. Measmt.*, 1958, *18*, 3-36. (a)

Tryon, R. C. General dimensions of individual differences: Cluster analysis versus multiple factor analysis. *Educ. Psychol. Measmt.*, 1958, *18*, 477-495. (b)

Tryon, R. C. Predicting group differences in cluster analysis: The social area problem. *Multivariate behav. Res.*, 1967, *2*, 453-475.

Turner, G. C., & Coleman, J. C. Examiner influences on Thematic Apperception Test responses. *J. proj. Tech.*, 1962, *26*, 478-486.

Tyler, L. T. *The psychology of human differences.* New York: Appleton-Century-Crofts, 1965.

Tyler, L. *Intelligence: Some recurring issues.* Princeton, N.J.: D. Van Nostrand, 1969.

Udenfriend, S. *Fluorescence assay in biology and medicine, molecular biology series.* New York: Academic Press, Vol. I 1962, Vol. II 1969.

Uejio, C. K., & Wrightsman, L. S. Ethnic-group differences in the relationship of trusting attitudes to cooperative behavior. *Psychol. Rep.*, 1967, *20*, 563-571.

Ullmann, L. P., & Krasner, L. *Case studies in behavior modification.* New York: Holt, Rinehart & Winston, 1965.

Uribe, B., & McReynolds, P. Comparison of two measures of innovative performance. *Percept. mot. Skills*, 1967, *25*, 777-780.

Van de Castle, R. L. Perceptual defense in a binocular rivalry situation. *J. Pers.*, 1960, *28*, 448-462.

Vanderplas, J. M., & Garvin, E. A. The association value of random shapes. *J. exp. Psychol.*, 1959, *57*, 147-154.

Van der Ryn, S. *Dorms at Berkeley: An environmental analysis.* Berkeley, Calif.: Center for Planning and Development Research, 1967.

van der Veen, F., & Stoler, N. Therapist judgments, interview behavior, and case outcome. *Psychother.*, 1965, *2*, 158-163.

Veldman, D. J. Computer-based sentence-completion interviews. *J. counsel. Psychol.*, 1967, *14*, 153-157.

Veldman, D. J., & Jennings, E. Computer applications in psychology. In A. Wolman (Ed.), *Handbook of psychology.* Engelwood Cliffs, N.J.: Prentice Hall, in press.

Veldman, D. J., Menaker, S. L., & Peck, R. F. Computer scoring of sentence completion data. *Behav. Sci.*, 1969, *14*, 501-507.

Vernikos-Danellis, J., Ciaranello, R. D., & Barchas, J. D. Adrenal epinephrine and PNMT activity in the rat bearing a transplantable pituitary tumor. *J. Endocrinol.*, 1968, *83*, 1357-1358.

Vernon, P. E. *Intelligence and cultural environment.* London: Methuen, 1969.

Vernon, P. E., & Allport, G. W. A test for personal values. *J. abnorm. soc. Psychol.*, 1931, *26*, 231-248.

Veroff, J. Thematic apperception in a nationwide sample survey. In J. Kogan & G. Lesser (Eds.), *Contemporary issues in thematic apperceptive methods.* Springfield, Ill.: Charles C Thomas, 1961. Pp. 83-110.

Veroff, J., Atkinson, J. W., Feld, S. C., & Gurin, G. The use of thematic apperceptions to assess motivation in a nationwide interview study. *Psychol. Monogr.*, 1960, *74*, No. 12 (Whole No. 499).

Veroff, J., Feld, S. C., & Crockett, H. Explorations into the effects of picture cues on thematic apperceptive expression of achievement motivation. *J. pers. soc. Psychol.*, 1966, *3*, 171-181.

Veroff, J., Feld, S. C., & Gurin, G. Achievement motivation and religious background. *Amer. sociol. Rev.*, 1962, *27*, 205-217.

Vielhauer, J. *The development of a semantic scale for the description of the physical environment.* Ph.D. dissertation, Louisiana State University, Baton Rouge, La., 1965.

Vinacke, W. E., & Ragusa, D. Two tests to measure exploitative and accommodative strategy. Tech. Rep. No. 7, Nonr 4374(00), State University of New York at Buffalo, 1964.

Vitz, P. C. Preference for different amounts of visual complexity. *Behav. Sci.*, 1966, *11*, 105-114.

Vogt, M. The concentration of sympathin in different parts of the central nervous system under normal conditions and after the administration of drugs. *J. physiol., London,* 1954, *123*, 451-481.

Volsky, T., Jr., Magoon, T. M., Norman, W. T., & Hoyt, D. P. *The outcomes of counseling and psychotherapy: Theory and research.* Minneapolis, Minn.: University of Minnesota Press, 1965.

Von Neumann, J., & Morgenstern, O. *The theory of games and economic behavior.* Princeton, N.J.: Princeton University Press, 1944.

Wagner, E. E., & Hawkins, R. Differentiation of assaultive delinquents with the hand test. *J. proj. Tech. pers. Assmt.*, 1964, *28*, 363-365.

Wagner, E. E., & Medredeff, E. Differentiation of aggressive behavior of institutionalized schizophrenics with the hand test. *J. proj. Tech. pers. Assmt.*, 1963, *27*, 110-112.

Wahler, R. G. Setting generality: Some specific general effects of child behavior therapy. *J. appl. behav. Anal.*, 1969, *2*, 239-246.

Wahler, R. G., Winkel, G. H., Peterson, R. F., & Morrison, D. C. Mothers as behavior therapists for their own children. *Behav. res. Ther.*, 1965, *3*, 113-124.

Walk, R. D. Self-ratings of fear in a fear-invoking situation. *J. abnorm. soc. Psychol.,* 1956, *52*, 171-178.

Walker, A. M., Rablen, R. A., & Rogers, C. R. Development of a scale to measure process changes in psychotherapy. *J. clin. Psychol.*, 1960, *16*, 79-85.

Walker, E. L. Psychological complexity as a basis for a theory of motivation and choice. In D. Levine (Ed.), *Nebraska symposium on motivation.* Lincoln, Nebr.: Univ. Nebraska Press, 1964.

Wallace, D., & Rothaus, P. Communication, group loyalty, and trust in the Prisoner's Dilemma game. *J. confl. Resol.*, 1969, *13*, 370-380.

Walters, R. H., & Zaks, M. S. Validation studies of an aggression scale. *J. Psychol.*, 1959, *47*, 209-218.

Wang, C. K. A. A scale for measuring persistence. *J. soc. Psychol.*, 1932, *3*, 79-90.

Washburne, J. N. A test of social adjustment. *J. appl. Psychol.*, 1935, *19*, 125-144.

Waterhouse, I. K., & Child, I. L. Frustration and the quality of performance, III: An experimental study. *J. Pers.*, 1953, *22*, 298-311.

Watson, R. I., & Fisher, V. E. An inventory of affective potency. *J. Psychol.*, 1941, *12*, 139-148.

Watts. R. T. The athlete and the nonathlete in the Prisoner's Dilemma. Ph.D. dissertation, University of New Mexico, 1970.

Wearn, J. T., & Sturgis, C. C. Studies on epinephrine, I: Effects of the injection of epinephrine in soldiers with "irritable heart." *Arch. int. Med.*, 1919, *24*, 248-268.

Webb, E. J., Campbell, D. T., Schwartz, R. D., & Sechrest, L. *Unobtrusive measures: nonreactive research in the social sciences.* Chicago: Rand-McNally, 1966.

Weber, D. S. A time perception task. *Percep. mot. Skills,* 1965, *21*, 863-866.

Weiner, I. B. *Psychodiagnosis in schizophrenia.* New York: John Wiley, 1966.

Weiner, N., & Rabadjija, M. The regulation of norepinephrine synthesis. Effect of puromycin on the accelerated synthesis of norepinephrine associated with nerve stimulation. *J. pharmacol. exp. Ther.*, 1968, *164*, 103-114.

Weiner, W., Harrison, W., & Klawans, H. L-dopa and cerebrospinal fluid homevanillic acid in Parkinsonism. *Life Sci.*, 1969, *8* (Part I), 971-976.

Weiskrantz, L. *Analysis of behavioral change.* New York: Harper and Row, 1968.

Weiss, E., Bordwell, B., Seeger, M., Lee, J., Dement, W., & Barchas, J. Changes in brain 5-HT and 5-HIAA in REM sleep deprived rats. *Psychophysiol.*, 1968, *5*, 209.

Weissman, A., Koe, B. K., & Tenen, S. S. Antiamphetamine effects following inhibition of tyrosine hydroxylase. *J. pharmacol. exp. Ther.*, 1966, *151*, 339-352.

Weizenbaum, J. Eliza: A computer program for the study of natural language communication between man and machine. *Comm. assoc. comp. Mach.*, 1966, *9*, 36-45.

Welch, A. S., & Welch, B. L. Solvent extraction method for simultaneous determination of norepinephrine, dopamine, serotonin, and 5-hydroxyindoleacetic acid in a single mouse brain. *Anal. Biochem.*, 1969, *30*, 161-179.

Welch, B. L. Discussion of the paper "Aggression, defense, and neurohumors" by A. B. Rothballer. In C. D. Clemente & D. B. Lindsley (Eds.), *Aggression and defense: Neural mechanisms and social patterns, brain function, vol. 7, UCLA forum in medical sciences no. 7.* Los Angeles: University of California Press, 1967. Pp. 150-170.

Welch, B. L., & Welch, A. S. Greater lowering of brain and adrenal catecholamines in group-housed than in individually-housed mice administered DL-α-methyltyrosine. *J. pharm. Pharmac.*, 1968, *20*, 244-246. (a)

Welch, B. L., & Welch, A. S. Differential activation by restraint stress of a mechanism to conserve brain catecholamines and serotonin in mice differing in excitability. *Nature, London*, 1968, *218*, 575-577. (b)

Wells, F. L. The systematic observation of the personality—in its relation to the hygiene of mind. *Psychol. Rev.*, 1914, *21*, 295-333.

Welsh, G. S. A projective figure-preference test for diagnosis of psychopathology, I: A preliminary investigation. Ph.D. dissertation, University of Minnesota, 1949.

Wetsel, H., Shapiro, R. J., & Wagner, E. E. Prediction of recidivism among juvenile delinquents with the hand test. *J. proj. Tech. pers. Assmt.*, 1967, *31* (4), 69-72.

Whalen, R. E., & Luttge, W. G. P-Chlorophenylalanine methyl ester: An aphrodisiac? *Sci.*, 1970, *169*, 1000-1001.

Wherry, R. J. Hierarchical factor solutions without rotation. *Psychometrika*, 1959, *24*, 45-51.

Whitman, R. H. A short scale for measuring introversion-extroversion. *J. appl. Psychol.*, 1929, *13*, 499-504.

Williams, C. B., & Vantrees, F. E. Relations between internal-external control and aggression. *J. Psychol.*, 1969, *71*, 59-61.

Williams, M. *Mental testing in clinical practice.* New York: Pergamon, 1965.

Williams, R. E. *A description of some executive abilities by means of the critical incident technique.* Ph.D. dissertation, Columbia University, 1964.

Williams, R. Metabolism and Mentation. *J. clin. endocrinol. Metab.*, 1970, *31*, 461-479.

Williamson, E. G., & Darley, J. G. The measurement of social attitudes of college students, I: Standardization of tests and results of a survey. *J. soc. Psychol.*, 1937, *8*, 219-229. (a)

Williamson, E. G., & Darley, J. G. The measurement of social attitudes of college students, II: Validation of two attitude tests. *J. soc. Psychol.*, 1937, *8*, 231-242. (b)

Willis, R. H., & Joseph, M. L. Bargaining behavior, I: "Prominence" as a predictor of the outcome of games of agreement. *J. confl. Resol.*, 1959, *3*, 102-113.

Willoughby, R. R. A scale of emotional maturity. *J. soc. Psychol.*, 1932, *3*, 3-36.

Wilson, W., Chun, N., & Kayatani, M. Projection, attraction, and strategy choices in intergroup competition. *J. pers. soc. Psychol.*, 1965, *2*, 432-435.

Wilson, W., & Kayatani, M. Intergroup attitudes and strategies in games between opponents of the same or of a different race. *J. pers. soc. Psychol.*, 1968, *9*, 24-30.

Wilson, W., & Wong, J. Intergroup attitudes and strategies in non-zero-sum dilemma games, I: Differential response to cooperative and competitive opponents. Unpublished paper, University of Hawaii, 1965.

Winget, C. N., Gleser, G. C., & Clements, W. H. A method for quantifying human relations, hostility, and anxiety applied to TAT productions. *J. proj. Tech. pers. Assmt.*, 1969, *33*, 433-437.

Winkel, G. H., Thiel, P., & Malek, R. *Response to the roadside environment.* San Francisco, Calif.: Arthur D. Little, Inc., 1968.

Winter, W. D., & Ferreira, A. J. *Research in family interaction: Readings and commentary.* Palo Alto, Calif.: Science and Behavior Books, 1969.

Winter, W. D., & Ferreira, A. J. A factor analysis of family interaction measures. *J. proj. Tech. pers. Assmt.*, 1970, *34*, 55-63.

Winter, W. D., Ferreira, A. J., & Olson, J. L. Story sequence analysis of a family TAT. *J. proj. Tech. pers. Assmt.*, 1965, *29* (3), 392-397.

Winter, W. D., Ferreira, A. J., & Olson, J. L. Hostility themes in the family TAT. *J. proj. Tech. pers. Assmt.*, 1966, *30* (3), 270-274.

Wirt, R. D., & Briggs, P. F. Personality and environmental factors in the development of delinquency. *Psychol. Monogr.*, 1959, *73* (Whole No. 485).

Wise, C. D., Berger, B. D., & Stein, L. Brain serotonin and conditioned fear. *Proc., 78th Ann. Conv.* American Psychological Association, 1970. Pp. 821-822.

Wittenborn, J. R., & Holzberg, J. D. The generality of psychiatric syndromes. *J. consult. Psychol.*, 1951, *15*, 372-380.

Wohlford, P. Extension of personal time in TAT and story completion stories. *J. proj. Tech. pers. Assmt.*, 1968, *32* (3), 267-280.

Wohlford, P., & Herrera, J. H. TAT stimulus-cues and extension of personal time. *J. proj. Tech. pers. Assmt.*, 1970, *34*, 31-37.

Wohlwill, J. F. Amount of stimulus exploration and preference as differential functions of stimulus complexity. *Percept. Psychophys.*, 1968, *4*, 307-312.

Wohlwill, J. F. The emerging discipline of environmental psychology. *Amer. Psychologist*, 1970, *25*, 303-312.

Wolf, M. N., Risley, T., & Mees, H. Application of operant conditioning procedures to the behavior problems of an autistic child. *Behav. res. Ther.*, 1964, *1*, 305-312.

Wolf, R. The measurement of environments. In A. Anastasi (Ed.), *Testing problems in perspective.* Princeton, N.J.: Educational Testing Service, 1966. Pp. 491-503.

Wolf, S., Cardon, P. V., Shephard, E. M., & Wolff, H. G. *Life stress and essential hypertension.* Baltimore, Md.: Williams and Wilkins, 1955.

Wollowick, H. B., & McNamara, W. J. Relationship of the components of an assessment center to management success. *J. appl. Psychol.*, 1969, *53*, 348-352.

Wolpe, J. *Psychotherapy by reciprocal inhibition.* Stanford, Calif.: Stanford University Press, 1958.

Wong, J. Variables influencing intragroup and intergroup responses in a modified Prisoner's Dilemma game, I: The effect of cooperative, competitive, and accommodating intergroup strategies. Unpublished manuscript, University of Hawaii, 1964.

Woodworth, R. S. *Dynamic psychology.* University of California Press, 1918.

Woodworth, R. S. Reinforcement of perception. *Amer. J. Psychol.*, 1947, *60*, 119-124.

Woodworth, R. S. *Dynamics of behavior.* New York: Henry Holt, 1958.

Wooley, D. W. *The biochemical bases of psychoses.* New York: John Wiley, 1962.

Wooley, H. T. A review of the recent literature on the psychology of sex. *Psychol. Bull.*, 1910, *7*, 335-342.

Wooley, H. T. The psychology of sex. *Psychol. Bull.*, 1914, *11*, 353-379.

Wright, H. F., & Barker, R. G. *Methods in psychological ecology: A progress report.* Topeka, Kans.: Ray's Printing Service, 1950.

Wrightsman, L. S. Measurement of philosophies of human nature. *Psychol. Rep.*, 1964,*14*, 743-751.

Wrightsman, L. S. Personality and attitudinal correlates of trusting and trustworthy behaviors in a two-person game. *J. pers. soc. Psychol.*, 1966, *4*, 328-332.

Wrightsman, L. S., Davis, D. W., Lucker, W. G., Bruininks, R. H., Evans, J. R., Wilde, R. E., Paulson, D. C., & Clark, G. M. Effects of other person's race and strategy upon cooperative behavior in a Prisoner's Dilemma game. Unpublished manuscript, George Peabody College, 1967.

Wurtman, R. *Catecholamines.* Boston: Little, Brown, 1966.

Wurtman, R., & Axelrod, J. Control of enzymatic synthesis of adrenaline in the adrenal medulla by adrenal cortical steroids. *J. biol. Chem.*, 1966, *241*, 2301-2305.

Wurtman, R., Axelrod, J., & Kelly, D. *The pineal gland.* New York: Academic Press, 1968.

Wyatt, R. Role of serotonin in human sleep. *Ann. intern. Med.*, 1970, *73*, 619-622.

Wyatt, R., Portnoy, B., Kupfer, D., Snyder, F., & Engelman, K. Resting plasma catecholamine concentrations in patients with depression and anxiety. *Arch. gen. Psychiat.*, 1971, *24*, 65-70.

Wyer, R. S. Prediction of behavior in two-person games. *J. Pers. soc. Psychol.*, 1969, *13*, 222-238.

Zaks, M. S., & Walters, R. H. First steps in the construction of a scale for the measurement of aggression. *J. Psychol.*, 1959, *47*, 199-208.

Zax, M., & Klein, A. Measurement of personality and behavior changes following psychotherapy. *Psychol. Bull.*, 1960, *57*, 435-448.

Zitrin, A., Beach, F. A., Barchas, J. D., & Dement, W. C. Sexual behavior of male cats after administration of parachlorophenylalanine. *Sci.*, 1970, *170*, 868-870.

Zlotowski, M. Behavioral differences between process and reactive schizophrenics in a monotonous repetitive task. *J. pers. soc. Psychol.*, 1965, *1*, 240-244.

Zlotowski, M., & Bakan, P. Behavioral variability of process and reactive schizophrenics in a binary guessing task. *J. abnorm. soc. Psychol.*, 1963,·66, 185-187.
Zubin, J. E., Eron, L. O., & Schumer, F. *An experimental approach to projective techniques.* New York: John Wiley, 1965.
Zucker, K. B., & Jordan, D. C. The paired hands test: A technique for measuring friendliness. *J. proj. Tech. pers. Assmt.*, 1968, *32*, 522-529.
Zuckerman, M. The validity of the Edwards personal preference schedule in the measurement of the tendency-rebelliousness. *J. clin. Psychol.*, 1958, *14*, 379-382.
Zuckerman, M., Kolin, E. A., Price, L., & Zoob, I. Development of a sensation-seeking scale. *J. consult. Psychol.*, 1964, *28*, 477-482.
Zuckerman, M., & Link, K. Construct validity for the sensation-seeking scale. *J. consult. clin. Psychol.*, 1968, *32*, 420-426.
Zuckerman, M., & Lubin, B. *Manual for multiple affect adjective check list.* San Diego, Calif.: Educational and Industrial Testing Service, 1965.
Zuckerman, M., Persky, H., Eckman, K. M., & Hopkins, T. R. A multitrait-multimethod measurement approach to the traits (or states) of anxiety, depression, and hostility. *J. proj. Tech. pers. Assmt.*, 1967, *31* (2), 39-48.
Zuckerman, M., Persky, H., Hopkins, T. R., Murtaugh, T., Basu, G. K., & Schilling, M. Comparisons of stress effects of perceptual and social isolation. *Arch. gen. Psychiat.*, 1966, *14*, 356-365.

Name Index

Abbott, P. S., 193
Abrahamsen, D., 152
Acheson, G. H., 262
Acker, M., 163, 166, 167, 174, 175
Adams, C. R., 306
Adams, J., 9
Adorno, T. W., 333
Aghajanian, G. K., 270, 271, 278, 288
Agras, W. S., 188
Ailion, J., 280
Albrecht, P. A., 99
Aldrich, M., 287
Allen, C., 325
Allen, K. E., 71, 72, 75, 77
Allen, V., 237
Allison, J., 3-4
Allman, L., 139
Alousi, A., 265
Allport, F. H., 321
Allport, G. W., 109, 155, 158, 160, 167, 304, 321, 329, 334
Alpert, R., 185, 228, 230, 317-18
Altmann, S. A., 74
Ammons, C. H., 18
Ammons, R. B., 18
Amsden, G. S., 295
Anastasi, A., 3, 40
Anderson, J. P., 167
Angwin, P., 279
Anton, A. H., 274
Apfelbaum, E., 236, 238, 259
Appleyard, D., 57
Armstrong, M., 74
Arnold, M. B., 217, 219
Arnoult, M. D., 171
Arthur, A. Z., 4, 7, 10
Arthur, G., 194
Asprea, A. M., 255
Atkinson, J. W., 169, 216, 217, 220-21, 225, 230
Atkinson, R. C., 237
Attneave, F., 171
Atwood, G. E., 187, 193, 195
Ault, M. H., 75
Ax, A., 154
Axelrod, J., 262, 267, 270, 279, 281, 287
Ayllon, T., 194
Azrin, N. H., 188, 194

Baer, M., 142
Bailey, R., 40
Bailly, R., 205
Bakan, P., 173
Baker, B. L., 188
Bandura, A., 135, 139, 140, 179, 182
Bank, R., 34
Barchas, J. D., 263, 267, 270, 279, 280, 281, 285-86, 287, 289, 290, 291
Barclay, A. M., 231, 232
Barker, R. G., 9, 40, 59, 61, 165

Barlow, D. H., 188
Barnes, L. B., 60
Barnett, H. G., 161
Barnette, W. L., 3
Barron, F., 171, 306-7
Barrows, G. A., 327
Baruch, D. W., 154
Basowitz, H., 273
Bass, B. M., 147
Bastian, J. R., 225
Basu, G. K., 165
Battle, C. C., 193, 196
Beach, F. A., 285
Beach, H. R., 149
Beck, A. T., 187
Becker, G. M., 237
Becker, H. S., 111
Becker, W. C., 71, 74
Berger, B. D., 285-86
Berger, C. Q., 59
Berger, L., 178
Berger, S., 255
Bergin, A. E., 179, 181, 183, 186, 187, 191, 196, 197
Bein, H. J., 267
Bell, H. M., 143, 304, 306, 326
Bellak, L., 217
Bendig, A. W., 147
Benton, A. A., 250, 251
Bentz, V. J., 86, 88
Berg, I. A., 304
Berkowitz, L., 139, 257
Berlew, D. E., 102, 103
Berlyne, D. E., 160, 161, 162, 164, 170, 171, 175
Bernberg, R. E., 144
Berne, N., 164, 169
Bernreuter, R. G., 295, 304, 306, 321
Bernstein, L., 230
Bertler, A., 267
Beswick, D. G., 169
Biemiller, A., 164, 170
Bijou, S. W., 66, 71, 72, 73, 74, 75, 77
Birks, V. G., 27
Birnbrauer, J. S., 72, 73, 74
Bixenstine, V. E., 249, 251, 256
Bjerstedt, A., 149
Björkvall, C., 276
Black, J. D., 99
Blackburn, R., 146
Blane, H. T., 194
Blatt, S., 3-4
Bliss, E. L., 280
Block, J., 4, 50, 183, 186
Blodgett, E., 149
Bloom, F. E., 262, 270, 284
Bloom, P. M., 141
Bobele, H. K., 186
Bock, R. D., 4
Boggan, W., 290

Bohn, S., 234
Bonoma, T., 250
Borah, L. A., Jr., 251
Bordin, E. S., 179
Bordwell, B., 287
Borgen, F. H., 111
Bourne, P. G., 141
Bouterline, S., 60
Bowers, M., 277
Bowman, G., 251
Braden, M., 237
Brady, J. P., 141
Brady, K., 195
Branch, C. H. H., 40
Braun, J. R., 186
Brawley, E. R., 71, 77
Bray, D. W., 80, 86, 89, 96, 103, 104-5
Breese, G. R., 270, 271
Breger, L., 4, 228, 232
Breggin, P. R., 274
Brehm, J. W., 237
Brender, W. J., 228
Breuer, F., 34
Bricklin, B., 151
Bridges, P. K., 288
Briggs, P. F., 145, 323
Brodie, B. B., 268, 277, 278, 285
Brodie, H. K. H., 285
Brodsky, A. M., 151
Brodsky, S., 151
Broverman, D. M., 225
Brown, D., 258
Brown, F. G., 3
Brown, P. A., 155
Brown, R. A., 189
Bruininks, R. H., 253, 257
Bryan, J. H., 170, 183
Bunney, W. E., Jr., 285
Buros, O. K., 3, 294n
Burton, I., 40, 41
Buss, A. H., 133, 134, 139, 142, 147, 152, 155, 223, 258
Busse, W., 165
Bussey, S., 253
Butcher, H. J., 4
Butcher, J. N., 145, 146
Butler, J. M., 185, 186
Butt, D. S., 336
Byham, W. C., 81n
Byrne, D., 230, 232

Cady, P., 9
Cady, V. M., 295
Caine, T. M., 155
Callahan, D. M., 184, 190, 191
Cameron, N., 212-13
Campbell, D. P., 111, 190, 311
Campbell, D. T., 99, 113, 180, 181, 189, 190, 195, 197
Campbell, J. P., 79, 80, 82n, 103

383

Subject Index